# THE BATTLE FOR THE AMERICAN CHURCH

THE BASIS FOR THE GALILEO QUINCH

*MSGR. GEORGE A. KELLY*

# The Battle for the American Church

DOUBLEDAY & COMPANY, INC.  Garden City, New York, 1979

Grateful acknowledgments are made to the following sources:

Excerpts from *Vatican II The Conciliar and Post Conciliar Documents*. Copyright © 1975 by Costello Publishing Company, Inc., and Reverend Austin Flannery, O.P. Reprinted by permission.

Excerpts from *The Documents of Vatican II*, Walter M. Abbott, S.J., General Editor, Very Rev. Msgr. Joseph Gallagher, Translation Editor. Copyright © 1966 by The America Press. Reprinted by permission.

Excerpts from *Journeys* by Gregory Baum, Paulist Press. Reprinted by permission.

Excerpts from *Church Ministries in New Testament Times* by Manuel Miguens. Christian Classics. Reprinted by permission.

Excerpts from "Catholicism Midwest Style: A Symposium." *America* magazine. February 12, 1966. Reprinted by permission.

Excerpt from *The Word* by Irving Wallace. Copyright © 1972 by Irving Wallace. Reprinted by permission of Simon & Schuster, a division of Gulf & Western Corporation.

ISBN: 0-385-13266-2
Library of Congress Catalog Card Number 77-12858

# CONTENTS

# Who's in Charge?

A guerrilla-type warfare is going on inside the Church and its outcome is clearly doubtful. The Pope and Roman Curia are fending off with mixed success the attacks of their own theologians who, in the name of scholarship, demand more radical accommodation with Protestant and secular thought. The issues at stake are the correctness of Catholic doctrine and the survival of the Catholic Church as a significant influence in the life of her own communicants.

Social institutions are, after all, more than the lengthened shadows of the men and women who make them up. They are at base root the incarnation of ideas—good and bad. A society, for example, based on the presumption of man's natural goodness is likely to be different from one that organizes around man's defective nature. The primacy of character development over personality development makes for a different kind of school, as free enterprise creates an economy distinguishable from socialism. Society gets whatever kinds of people prevailing doctrines fashion, which is why the fiercest contests are usually philosophical or theological.

The Catholic Church gives the clearest example of what happens to a public institution when someone tampers with its basic tenets. The Catholic Church also has never made any bones about its doctrines. Many people do not like their pretensions, but Catholic propositions have been clearly stated with the expectation that those who enter or remain in membership agree to their binding force. Bishops and religious superiors have been eager entrepreneurs at having their personnel knowledgeable about what the Church taught about the Catholic way to God. In thousands of American Catholic catechetical centers specialists have been trained to explain what Catholic doctrine means and why people should embrace its message. What makes post-Vatican II Catholicism different is that Church authorities no longer can assume that this is being done. Teaching priests and diocesan officials recently seem doubtful about any academic arrangement that confines itself to Catholic doctrine. Catholic universities, Catholic theologians, Catholic canon lawyers weekly declare independence of bishops and the Pope. A large segment of the Church's middle management—teachers, editors, administrators—has come to have suspicion of teaching effort that appears to be narrowly Catholic. Indeed, concentration on Catholic doctrine is no longer greeted in some Catholic circles, *even as a pluralistic option.*

The patent decline and the alleged fall of the Catholic Church have evoked so many explanations that the Vatican library may need one section dealing with that subject alone. These books differ in style and scholarly content, but differ also by reason of the value system they seek to protect—that is, by ideology. One category of books lays stress on the ecclesiastical situation, giving primacy to the Church institution and pastors; others accent the world's salvation, unbelievers and separated brethren, enlarging the role of prophets and academicians.

One thesis worth examining, however, is the manner in which the Second Vatican Council and its implementation has been mismanaged for such unsatisfactory effects to follow. Ordinarily, change to new programs and structure follows orderly procedures in well-managed institutions. Corporations that diversify, for example, maintain strict control of their basic markets, which supply the money to finance new experiments. In the Church's case, however, change became a feast for those who would redefine the basic postulates of Catholic Christianity itself. When Rome began to restrict meaning or application of conciliar doctrines, controversy over the legitimacy of Vatican decisions was under way. Contemporary bishops with little experience in public conflict, or psychologically unprepared for it, seemed helpless in the face of blatant deviance. Doctrines were denied or undermined before in history, but dissenters were not permitted in recent centuries to exercise power from high positions within Catholic infrastructures. Once honorable status was achieved in the post-Vatican II era by rivals of episcopacy, institutional division and subsequent demoralization were inevitable.

Leaders usually embody what an institution is about. If bishops are the ones appointed to say what the Church is, then all other opinions eventually must be reconciled with their definitions or at least be tolerated by them. Since their place at Christ's altar symbolizes not only unifying but also ruling power, bishops are empowered to oversee change, determine what those changes may be, and stage the course of adjustment. Since change also brings conflict, bishops are called upon to organize support and develop friends for those policies. In the face of threats bishops must decide which are serious, when "common law" arrangements can be permitted, and when short-range discomfort must be endured for long-range value. The timing of change and defense of unity are critically related to institutional effectiveness and durability.

The Catholic Church was once such a marvel of good management that outsiders began to search for its secrets. The American Institute of Management, for example, was so fascinated by the Church (which it called "the world's largest society") that "unrequested, unbiased, and uncensored" it undertook in 1948 a study to determine "what administrative lessons might be learned from the Church's nineteen centuries of varied problems and remedies." Any Church that had baptized five billion Christians and ordained fifty million priests from the date of St. Peter's martyrdom had something to teach besides a catechism lesson.

Eight years of collating data led the AIM to conclude that the Catholic Church was one of the two most efficient management enterprises in the Western World. (The other paradigm of efficiency was Detroit's General Motors Corporation.) The *Management Audit*, as the report was called, pointed the finger at major ecclesial weaknesses, among which the following are worth noting:

- Overconcentration of line and staff responsibility in the Pope.
- Decision-making by intuition as much as from research data.
- Dissipation of resources through a proliferation of overlapping agencies.
- Poor public-information and public-relations programs.
- A tendency to unnecessary sectarianism.

On the other hand, the *Management Audit* told fifteen thousand members of AIM the lessons they might learn from the Catholic Church, which in its judgment was entering a new and ascendant stage of growth, expected (in AIM's judgment) to last for several centuries. In view of occurrences two years after the last rosy report was issued (1960), some of the recommended lessons make for interesting reading.

- The importance of doctrine and indoctrination in assuring unity of thought and action.
- The need of instilling all employees with a sense of their social contribution.

• The absolute value of integrity, ability, and industry before au-
thority is granted; promotion from the ranks.
• Once chosen, chief executives are to have full authority.
• The atmosphere must be one of struggle, humility, and strict dis-
cipline.
• Praise should come slowly, condemnations even slower, a modest
exercise of zeal once in power.
• All dealings should be characterized by diplomacy with deviations
from fixed rules when advisable.
• Whenever authority is imperiled, the need of defensive action.

Many of these norms of good management, which were elements of
the Church's accumulated wisdom, became inoperative during the Second Vatican Council. It is departure from these norms that contributed
to subsequent Catholic decline. The Second Vatican Council did not
bring the Church in the United States from old strengths to new. Instead, Catholic resources were depleted without assurance that the
goals of Pope John XXIII would be realized. The present "guerrilla
warfare" within the Church is no mere battle over ownership and control of Church machinery. What is involved is the credibility and via-
bility of the Christian message itself. Popes and bishops are capable of
political errors, but they are guarantors of the Christian message.
How they will cope finally with the contemporary challenge to their legitimacy awaits events still unfolding. The choices facing Catholics
were delineated by the National Conference of Catholic Bishops on
July 4, 1974, as it prepared to send delegates to the Third Roman
Synod:

> The emerging question for the Catholic community may well
> be whether it will in the future, as in the past, derive its fun-
> damental beliefs and attitudes from the traditional value sys-
> tem of Catholic Christianity or whether its beliefs and atti-
> tudes will be drawn more and more from the secularistic,
> humanistic value system around it [*Origins*, July 4, 1974].

This writer has no question about the ultimate triumph of Catholic
Christianity's value system, as it is authenticated by Pope and bishops.
But the struggle during this dark night of the Church's soul calls for a
close look at what is going on now. This book is one man's view of that
struggle. To take sides in any conflict means, of course, that the cast of
characters is divided into knights and errants, and so this book does, in
the knowledge that on a given issue knights can be errants and vice

versa. But this is a risk any writer takes if he stays with his point of view, although by so doing he is not implying that the side with which he disagrees is any less virtuous or competent, that the "knights" have any special halo or possess the Spirit in any special degree. One ought to be able to choose sides on the preferred issues without regard to personalities, even though persons must be used to represent the agreeable and disagreeable sides.

John Courtney Murray once suggested, "Let us lay down our arms and take up our arguments." Hopefully, this book will help sharpen the arguments and ultimately lead to correct choices by the Church and its Catholic adherents.

A word of thanks to Mr. Joel Well of *The Critic* for publishing an article "The Uncertain Church" (Fall 1976) on which this book is based, and to Mr. John Delaney, retired editor of Doubleday and Company, Inc., who thought that *The Critic* thesis might be developed into a full-length book. Special appreciation must be expressed to the commentators, more than one hundred in number, who criticized various parts of this manuscript throughout its development. These commentators represent many competencies or constituencies—the episcopacy, the priesthood, religious life, the pastoral ministry, the laity, family life, and the world of the academe. They gave a great deal of time to refine the various chapters. Finally, as in the case of all book writing, Mrs. Gloria Lombardo, with the typing, and Miss Carol Hand, with both her research ability and her secretarial skills, were invaluable partners in the final product. Only the author is responsible for the thrust and details of the presentation.

# THE BATTLE FOR THE AMERICAN CHURCH

PART ONE

# OF MODERNISM AND MODERNIZATION

CHAPTER I

Vatican II: Aftershocks of an Ecclesiastical Earthquake

The first one to ask the question: Can the Council fail? was Hans Küng. He raised that doubt even before the bishops convened in Rome. Six years later, John Cogley would be asking: Was Vatican II a failure? And on the tenth anniversary of the Council's opening (1972), Malachi Martin publicly confessed that his friend Pope John XXIII's grand design had been a failure. While the "prophets of gloom" here mentioned are identified with the Catholic left, it was the schismatic of the right, Archbishop Marcel Lefebvre, who declared Vatican II to be a non-Council—that is, nonbinding on him or his followers.

What happened to cause disillusion over such a wide area of Catholic thought, when the early hopes everywhere were so high?

Those who wanted no change in the Church and those who sought radical change might have anticipated disappointment from the start. The first group, thinking that all was rosy in the Church, was doomed to regret contamination by intimate contact with alleged unbelievers and sinners. Radicals, on the other hand, not sharing Pope John's confidence in Catholic *vitality* (the Pope's word), would look for the Church's future in close links with the world. Martin thought the Catholic system of 1962 was in bad shape:

> Things simply do not work. The school system does not work. Marriage laws, anti-abortion laws, anticontraception laws, do not work. Celibacy does not work. The traditional relationships of bishop to parish priest and of parish priest to his assistants do not work. The traditional system of nuns and

women's religious orders (way of life, clothes, occupation, rules, housing, etc.) does not work nor does the traditional system of men's religious orders: Monastic poverty does not work; obedience to the religious superior does not work; community life does not work; clerical clothes do not work. Local Church finances do not work. The hierarchic system does not work. Church rituals do not work. Church "holidays" do not work. The Vatican way of ruling the Church does not work. The Pope's office and function do not work. His infallibility does not work. Traditional beliefs do not work. The lists could be multiplied [*Three Popes and the Cardinal*, p. 62].

However one saw *The Event* in foresight, the Ecumenical Council proved to be a bomb falling from a great height with percussion cap intact. Explosions did not occur immediately but in a series. The fallout came in stages. First there came an innocent clash of ideas, which is what councils are about. Theologians and academic persons, who like to be innovative, meet *in camera* with pastors whose daily lives are rooted in Catholic tradition. No one in the beginning anticipated irreconcilable differences, nor disagreement about who makes the final decisions. Changes were agreed upon and few anticipated organizational chaos. Then again, at the Council's opening the preparatory schemas varied in their possible effect on Church policy. Liturgical reformers, for example, had been at work for the better part of the previous century, and their thinking was already accepted in Rome. Indeed, practical liturgical change had been approved by the Holy See prior to the Council with the revision of the Easter Vigil rite (1951), Holy Week services (1952), simplified rubrics (1955), and the widespread use of the missal and dialogue Masses. The hierarchy of the Church was ready for liturgical reform. The Church was well prepared also for a renewed social apostolate to the world. The Council's document *The Church and the Modern World* (*Gaudium et Spes*) merely placed the weight of twenty-five hundred bishops behind what Popes had been teaching for seventy years. Liturgical reform and social involvement of Catholics, although based on theological considerations, were practical issues, with which Catholic bishops could come to grips.

Other issues would prove to be more troublesome to Council Fathers and their faithful, especially if they were theologically undeveloped or unfamiliar to Catholic churchgoers. When official documents are controversial or ambiguous it is inevitable that ideological forces in the Church, as elsewhere, line up in opposition to each other. Concepts such as "collegiality," "religious liberty," and "ecumenism" were natural subject areas for controversy. Ideological fights are always value fights. Program fights, which deal with means to ends, never beget the same passions that disturb institutional calm. When the bishops first assembled in Rome on October 11, 1962, there was serenity. But by December 7, 1965, when Pope Paul VI formally brought Council deliberations to an end, the fallout of Vatican II was obvious to everyone.

*The first fallout of Vatican II was the rise of Catholic masochism.* This might have been an expected by-product, although the volume and intensity of abuse against the Catholic body by its own surprised everyone. Changemakers suddenly became rebels with a cause. Lacking political power, their weapons were the pen, the dialogue, the microphone, the picket line. During the decade after 1960 these forms of dissent were the order of the American day. The hippie movement, the civil-rights movement, and the peace movements were the active protest movements against wrongdoing, whether real or imagined. The generals of these protesting armies frequently were denizens of academe. In hindsight, therefore, it should not be surprising that Catholic academics, given the opportunity, would approach the Church problems of 1962 in similar fashion.

Pope John's invitation for Catholics to turn to the world became an opportunity for some literary Catholics to turn on the Church. The papal call to officer-bishops to leave their Tridentine castles for an open Council ended up with many bishops, and John's successor, shot at by their own soldiers. Though no bloody Reign of Terror *à la* France, it was the beginning of a guerrilla war within the Church that began in and around St. Peter's Square and has continued to the present day. Ordinary Catholics did not realize what was going on during the first session of the Council, and since no document was issued, Catholic life went on as usual. But the debate about contraception was just beginning. This was to stir up home-based Catholics, although other debates did not. How often St. John the Evangelist used *agape* instead of *eros* would excite very few. By the opening of the third session (September 15, 1964), however, politicking in the public press—by a few bishops, but mostly by *periti* (experts)—was so noticeable that the Council president, Eugene Cardinal Tisserant, regretting "certain incidents" that occurred during the second session, urged the duty of secrecy concerning Council discussions. The Council's Secretary General, Archbishop Pericle Felici, also directed fire at the "experts." He enjoined them from lobbying for any point of view, from organizing factions, from publicity campaigns to spread a particular opinion, and from the unauthorized distribution of documents in or near the council hall. Although the bishops generally took this *monitum* in stride as part of the rules of the game, the periti resented Felici's threat to strip them of their status in the Council if they continued a political course. The secretary general's effort to limit the public-relations efforts of the "experts," however, did not succeed. The periti continued to resist restriction on their public use of media representatives, whom Robert Kaiser confesses were mostly on the side of the "progressives," as he called them. Using highly successful tactics of political activists in the United States, the periti sought to develop public opinion outside the Council hall, in order to establish the climate within the Council that would fashion the way Council Fathers would do their thinking. The presumed political clout of the "conservatives" was offset by making their positions appear reactionary or ridiculous. Stories like this, for example, were passed from mouth to mouth: "Cardinal Ottaviani came out of his apartment one day looking for a taxi. 'To the Council,' he commanded the driver. And without turning his head the cabbie took Ottaviani to Trent." For all his Roman experience, Ottaviani never recovered from this sort of treatment.

Many years later a key staff assistant to the President of the United States would cause public stir with the aspersion that "the Catholic Church does a better job of screwing people up than any other institution." But beginning with the Council years and thereafter this sort of thing became common occurrence among Catholic media figures. If the Church was not being humiliated before the world, her prelates were. Philip Berrigan announced "the Church is a whore" (NCR, January 19, 1973). Cardinal Spellman may have been a respected churchman to the rank and file of his diocesans, but to Ken Woodward of Newsweek he was a "shameless ecclesiastical Sammy Glick" (NCR, July 2, 1971). Speaking of bishops, scripturist John McKenzie likened some of them to "a drunken father" whom "we try to hide when company comes, and we worry about what half-wit blunders he will make next" (The Critic, July–August, 1971). Priests, elsewhere described as nothing more than "mass produced eunuchs for the Church's bureaucracy" were called by Gary Wills "bishop ridden pastors" and products of the "dogma factory centered in Rome" (Bare Ruined Choirs, p. 47). As for religious orders they are "already dead" according to Brother Gabriel Moran, onetime provincial of the Long Island-New England Province of the Christian Brothers. As for structural renewal, "I stand for destruction," Moran declared. "I am against both the existence of the religious order and the parish." He suggested that future religious communities may resemble hippie communes where men and women live together and raise children (NCR, February 2, 1973). Even lay leaders in official position felt the need to demonstrate truculent independence. Don Zirkel, editor of the *Brooklyn Tablet*, conducted what was called the "first lectors' strike in history," refusing at a parish Mass to read First Corinthians 7:32–35 because he did not like the comparison St. Paul made between virgins and the married (*BT*, February 8, 1973).

The slaughter of reputations did not exempt even hitherto approved "liberal" ecclesiastics if they "broke" their stride as changemakers. During the Council, for example, Bishop John Wright of Pittsburgh was the darling of "liberals" because he favored all of the "right" things—liturgical reform, religious liberty, ecumenism. When gentleman John Heenan, archbishop of Westminster, criticized *periti*, Wright rose to defend "the scholarly humility, the admirable patience, the loving faith and forbearance with which the overwhelming majority of the *periti* work." After Wright gave up his Pittsburgh see to become an official in the Pope's Chancery, the Council's wish for pastors in the Roman Curia, not bureaucrats, seemed to be realized. Moves like the promotion of Wright were widely approved. But once Wright began to do his job, which was implementing Council decrees and papal laws concerning Catholic clergy and catechetics, he felt the sting hitherto reserved for Italian curialists. Suddenly he was editorialized as a man "whose beliefs are dangerous to the Church." This was the judgment of the *National Catholic Reporter*.

> Had the Cardinal lived in an earlier more inquisitorial age, we might speculate that, as he turned the thumb screw for the faith, he would genuinely be pained at your pain—but he would nevertheless still turn the screw [August 4, 1972].

Caustic comments about bishops and Catholic loyalists are as old as Peter and Paul. In the nineteenth century, converts like Henry Edward Manning, England's most distinguished archbishop since pre-Reformation days, and Orestes Brownson were badly treated by the literati. Manning suffered partially because in his role as pastor-archbishop he placed higher value on protecting the Catholic faith of Irish peasant immigrants to London than catering to the Catholic intellectuals of his time, even though he was something of an intellectual himself. On this side of the Atlantic, Brownson had similar difficulties. His conversion to Catholicism in 1844 has been called by Donna Merwick "one of the great disasters to befall Boston Catholicism." This Catholic apologist is frequently dismissed as too Catholic and ungentlemanly in his confrontations. The difference between then and now is that earlier abuse or counterabuse had little practical effect on the religious life of the Catholic masses, who rarely were aware of what was being said in the journals or remained unaffected by the diatribes of angry Catholic journalists. But television gave Catholic criticism wide coverage and currency.

The message passed on to the faithful, especially in classrooms, was that bishops and Rome were standing against Catholic peoples' needs. Critics of bishops achieved a high level of visibility. Few bishops were as well known as Michael Novak, Daniel Callahan, John Leo, John Cogley, and Xavier Rynne, unless it was Leo Cardinal Suenens whose image became that of a friendly dissenter in the papal household. Departures from the priesthood of men as intellectually different as James Kavanaugh, Charles Davis, or Richard Ginder would in an earlier day have been little-noticed items in the daily life of the Church. But television cameras carried these men's complaints to the average family parlor. Those who had a natural aptitude for this medium frequently made the case of dissidents seem persausive. The newsmen, operating on the principle of "news for news' sake," detached themselves from the impact of these presentations on public life or the Church, although it is commonly understood that their ideology affected selection of the newsworthy. Investigative reporting customarily was also a one-way process—against the establishment. During the years when Los Angeles priest William Dubay was dividing the Church on the West Coast, he came across as an oppressed underdog, and his bishop, J. Francis A. McIntyre, as a bully. Hardly anyone then examined either Dubay's character or credentials or the objective validity of conduct. When several years later Dubay made several public confessions, they held no interest for headlinemakers or television producers.

"Maria Monk" confessions certainly hurt the Church. So does the public denigration of bishops, stories of repressive childhoods or of unhappy nunneries and rectories. When these became customary fare at the American breakfast table, the young, whose ties to the Church were not yet solid, were adversely affected. Remorse set in later among "renewalists" when they discovered they lost the battle for the minds of bishops. In the early postconciliar period abuse of the establishment seemed a powerful technique for putting new life in the Church body. Even though only the hierarchy could effectuate the institutional reforms renewalists wanted, bishops were equivalently asked to proclaim publicly their *mea culpa* for poor leadership, for treating priests and laity badly, for toleration of institutional corruption. If this strategy did not alienate bishops, it succeeded in fracturing the loyalty of many Catholics to their bishops.

The affront to the Church by Catholics themselves led directly to what might be called *the second fallout of Vatican II: Catholic acceptance of stereotypes about the Church that were first invented by the Church's enemies.*

A stereotype is a two- or three-word summary of what people think about other people whom they do not like. "The absent-minded professor," "the sex-starved Victorian lady," or the "hard-drinking Irishman" are not meant to be compliments. Even though they do not tell the good side of the story, they usually have some basis in fact. Normally resented as put-downs, stereotypes become the basis of what is called ethnic humor. Stereotypes are also "private" jokes that remain offensive if used by the wrong person in the wrong place, or when they lower the public image of a minority.

Throughout the nineteenth century, nativists, usually Protestants, ridiculed the Catholic Church, its leaders, doctrines, and the behavior of the Catholic people. Ray Allen Billington's *Protestant Crusade* documents the story. Bishop John England of Charleston in the early 1830s credited the misuse of history and science and "the abusive spirit of American writers" for the raging anti-Catholicism. Writing against the Church was profitable to authors, and books on the subject became a regular industry. Every practice of the Church was scrutinized for its harmful effects. Not only was it important that the West be saved from the Pope, but also the arguments used by papal defenders must always be bested in the press. Historical studies were undertaken to prove how the papacy had corrupted Christianity.

Billington lists the objectives of Protestant propagandists as threefold: (1) Show that Catholicism was not early Christianity. (2) Show that Catholicism was irreconcilable with democratic institutions. (3) Show that Catholic moral standards would be ruinous to the nation (in the nineteenth century for being too loose, in the twentieth for their strictness). Doctrines concerning the divine origin of the Church, the primacy and infallibility of the Pope, veneration of Mary, transubstantiation, confession, purgatory, extreme unction—all distinctive features of Catholicism—were branded as pure legend, without a scriptural basis, or invented to build up the power of priests and the institutional Church. Early Church Fathers were poor defenders of these doctrines because they too were unfamiliar with the scriptures. The despotic control of "the most humble worshipers," the persecution of dissidents, and convents as "slave factories" were *prima facie* evidence of later corruption. Priestly celibacy was a particular horror. A book proposed in 1836—with a fifty-dollar reward for the successful author—was to be called *The Happiness and Horrors of a Roman Catholic Priest in Never*

*Being Allowed to Marry a Beautiful Young and Virtuous Wife.* Catholic bishops who stood up for the rights of the Church were called arrogant.

Catholics always resented these stereotypes when used against them either by Protestants or by the upper-class Catholics. The latter, however circumspectly they behaved in public toward the Church, often agreed in secret with many of the charges leveled against Catholicism.

During the post-Vatican II period Catholic circumspection was thrown to the winds. Greeley and Rossi in *The Education of Catholic Americans* prior to the Council reported on the religious effects of Catholic schools:

> Sunday Mass, monthly communion, confession several times a year, Catholic education of children, financial contribution to the Church, acceptance of the Church as an authoritative teacher, acknowledgment of papal and hierarchical authority, informality with the clergy, strict sexual morality, more detailed knowledge about one's religion . . .

> These are not only the apparent effects of Catholic education, they comprise as well a reasonable description of what the American Church has expected from its laity during the years when it was still concentrating on the preservation of the faith of the immigrant and his children and grandchildren [p. 230].

Later descriptions of Catholic life would not be so reportorial. Earlier Catholic pride in high levels of religious observance was replaced by frequent deflation of the significance of external religious behavior. Though the list of deflations is long, a few examples illustrate the new response of literary Catholics.

Gary Wills, for example, whose rise to fame began in 1961 when he joined William F. Buckley in saying Mater Sí, Magistra, No to Pope John's social doctrine, was by 1972 part of a larger chorus singing aloud the sad tale of his Catholic boyhood, in his memory hardly more than the sum of

> prayers offered, heads ducked in unison, crossings, chants, christenings, grace at meals; beads, incense, candles, nuns in the classroom alternately too sweet and too severe, priests garbed black on the street and brilliant at the altar; churches lit and darkened, clothed and stripped, to the rhythm of liturgical recurrences; the crib in the winter, purple February and

lilies in the spring; confession as intimidation and comfort and so forth [*Bare Ruined Choirs*, pp. 15–16].

Ex-bishops justified their own misconduct with a similar unflattering stereotype. Bernard Kelly, once the auxiliary bishop of the Providence diocese, justified his resignation from the priesthood in 1971 by downgrading the Church in which he grew up.

David J. O'Brien, who was employed in 1972 by the bishops to help write the history of the American priesthood and later in 1976 to help organize their Detroit Call to Action, told the National Federation of Priest Councils in 1974 of the Catholic need

> to find liberation from the heavy-handed ecclesiastical bureaucracy, the cultural sterility and moral hypocrisy which seemed to us the dominant elements of our Catholic heritage [*Origins*, April 4, 1974].

What began as a trickle of adversary opinion poured into the media, including the Catholic press, as a flood of discontent. There was no stereotype that did not make its way approvingly into many Catholic homes. Columnists would inform readers that it was no longer possible to equate the Catholic system with the one true Church. Child-centered Catholicism and parochial schools would be called elements of a discredited ghetto mentality. Nineteenth- and early twentieth-century priests were written off as brick-and-mortar men, as system builders without any interest in human relationships. Catholic schools would be accused of filling children with the sex problems of Henry VIII and Martin Luther, not with their legitimate arguments against the Church.

Some years earlier a non-Catholic psychologist, Gordon Allport, had decided that nine tenths of all Church members were "extrinsically religious." This meant they used religion as a security blanket for the way in which they already lived, but harboring more prejudice against blacks or Jews than unbelievers. Such reasoning was picked up by psychologist Eugene Kennedy, whose book *In the Spirit, in the Flesh* applauds the movement of Catholics away from "extrinsic religion"—based on ritual, rules, and dogmas—and toward an "intrinsic religion" based on the gospel's invitation to a life of risk-taking. The pre-Vatican II Church, according to Kennedy, was extrinsic religion, one that sought to impose answers to all questions that the faithful would face, resulting in Catholic conformism. Vatican II, on the other hand, offered instead intrinsic religion, calling believers to search deeper into their own humanity. Their questions would still be numerous, but now they would have to find their own answers. Catholics were also told that they believed too much in the Church. According to Joseph Cunneen (*Commonweal*, November 17, 1972), Catholicism was a religion performed and believed—by priests, bishops, and pope—in people's name. Outward acts were the rule for Catholics without a proper understanding of their interior significance.

The deflation of the Church as a sacred protective ark in favor of Church as a pilgrim people searching for answers brought on some interesting experiences for the young attending Catholic schools during the 1960–69 period. Externals were out—the rosary, novenas, benedictions, and weekly confession. By virtue of Vatican II, it was said, Sunday Mass no longer was to be the criterion of Catholic identity. The orientation then offered to the young was described by Beverly Swaren in *America* (September 21, 1974):

> Commitment to Catholicism in any specific form [was made] next to impossible by replacing true belief with an overriding skepticism. In college we were forever being admonished not to tie our faith to any particular dogma or precept—advice that may be indisputable in theory but proves destructive in practice because it encourages (in fact, demands, in the face of social pressures today) a disbelief in every doctrine that becomes burdensome, irrelevant or otherwise socially unacceptable.

A similar re-education was going on at the parish level. Some priests, especially visiting lecturers from local Catholic campuses, moved by *Gaudium et Spes*, were telling hard-core Catholics that they were selfish and materialistic, did not love the poor, and if they favored American involvement in Vietnam loved war, that their motivation for giving to charitable causes was wrong. They were also told that ritualism, legalism, and clericalism had filled the Catholic Church with baptized pagans, that what goes on within the Church is not where the action in life really is, that "dogma factories centered in Rome" have isolated the Church from the intellectual currents of the world.

The *third fallout of Vatican II* followed almost automatically: *Around these stereotypes political parties formed within the Church— for or against the values favored or ridiculed by the stereotypes.* Dissent in the Church is not new. Neither is factional strife. Diversity and strife did not end with Trent, although fifteen hundred years of varying disorder had brought on better ground rules and reasonable discipline.

It was possible after Trent to know what the ideal Catholic Church should look like at the local level. The young American Church, beset by early differences, profited from early Tridentine and papal guidelines. By 1962 this Church had put public brawling among its own behind, and a large measure of public scandals also. No heresies had developed on the American scene. This serenity may not have been esteemed at all levels, but was the fruit of a conscious effort by American bishops.

Vatican II put an end to Catholic serenity. Organized factionalism came quickly, customarily identified by the usual political labels—"left" or "right." These categories are somewhat unfair to all parties, if only because on any given issue convictions and loyalties shift. However, those who placed high value on the security of the Church were distinguishable from those who wanted all possible accommodation with the secular world if you will. For want of a better terminology, *ecclesialists* and *modernizers* marshaled troops according to their cherished priorities.

The *National Catholic Reporter* and the *Wanderer* probably are the obvious meeting places for the extreme competing forces that the Council unleashed. The ideology of most other journals fell on one side or the other without the same extremism: the *National Catholic Register*, *Our Sunday Visitor*, the *Homiletic and Pastoral Review*, *Alba House*, and the *Daughters of St. Paul* providing different and at times contradictory fare from what readers of *America*, *Commonweal*, *Chicago Studies*, or the *Paulist Press* and the *Ave Maria Press* were offered. While all shades of gray prevailed in the practical order, there is little question that the core differences between the *ecclesialists* and the *modernizers* are somewhat black and white.

*Ecclesialists* tend to accept established Church positions, a nature of things ordained by God, the necessity of formulas to embody for men what God has revealed, the unique position of the Church as the Body of Christ, the authoritative role of bishops and Pope in defining Catholic faith and morals, and the obligation of obedience to the Church's major directives, which bind all who profess the Catholic faith.

*Modernizers*, on the other hand, believe that God is as much moving through the world (immanence) as he is in his heaven (transcendence). Divine revelation, therefore, is ongoing, not merely "a deposit of faith," a revelation about a Person, not so much a body of ideas. The modernizer stresses the evolving nature of man's understanding of God's purposes, the importance of personal human experience to that understanding, the voice of believers as important as the voice of hierarchy. In this view, pilgrim people need flexibility in choosing their answers to religious questions, and no prefixed solutions to human problems.

Because the modernizing position certainly reflects the sentiments of contemporary cultural leadership, it is unquestionable that the Council made a real effort to subsume some of its postulates into conciliar documents. The modernizers after Vatican II would make telling points on doctrinal development with the educated elite of the Church, sometimes at the expense of solidly held traditional positions also reiterated by the Council Fathers. A few examples will illustrate the difficulties.

Modernizers alleged that the older Judeo-Christian and Catholic tradition had a tendency, now to be uprooted, of elevating religious myth to the level of historical fact and literal reality—for example, the stories in Genesis, perhaps the infancy narratives. As a result, pure Christianity became encrusted with man-made barnacles. Christianity was originally "good news" about salvation through Jesus, but went on to become a body defending "truths" about the world. Modernizers prefer to look at man and his human problems first, then look back to see if the gospel has anything meaningful to say about the human situation. God is still with us, as the Church always taught, but we no longer can be sure of what he is saying. We can be sure now, however, that, given man's importance to God, war, inflation, racial discrimination are better religious issues than infancy narratives, theological formulas, the incantation of litanies, or communion in the hand, all of which do not relate to pressing contemporary problems. We must, therefore, return Catholicism to what it was on the Mount of the Transfiguration—a private experience with God—a faith to be encouraged and supported, more than taught as such. Monica Hellwig's *Tradition: The Catholic Story Today*, speaking of catechesis for children, insists that the experience is handed on to newcomers by including them in an event, not so much by telling them about it.

Since Holland was the only country where the Catholic hierarchy identified with this radical turnaround in theological and catechetical emphasis (Gabriel Moran once praised the Dutch Catechism more for what it did not say), it was not surprising that reaction to this modernizing would come not only from other hierarchies, but from lay people too. Catholics United for the Faith—a lay organization—was established as early as 1968 without visible support from bishops, precisely to resist the modernizing trend. Some self-styled pre-Vatican II liberals, welfare statists but orthodox dogmatists, began to change sides. James Hitchcock's *Decline and Fall of Radical Catholicism*, published in 1971, was written as a challenge to changemakers. He argued that the central issue now in contest among Catholics was supernatural faith itself, that the doubts raised among the faithful were not moot questions, but struck at the heart of Catholicism.

Did Christ establish the Catholic Church to perform a unique function? Did he give its management over to Peter and the Twelve? Are Pope and bishops his legitimate successors? Do Catholics have to attend Sunday Mass, marry in accordance with Church law, confess sins to the priest? What moral prescriptions of the Church bind seriously in conscience? Did Christ offer us heaven if we are good and hell as the final resting place of the seriously unreconstructed sinners? Is prayer of any value—especially if it is directed to Mary and to saints? These are fundamental questions for which reasonable answers must be provided by a certain Church. An ecclesiastical climate where one answer is as good as another, in which pastors can preach and people receive without reproach different doctrines, in the ecclesiasts' view destroys Catholic credibility.

Since official documents emanating from Rome after Vatican II began to reject one by one most of the modernizing positions on faith and morals, the political forces in opposition inevitably lined up for or against the institutional Church, for or against the papacy. The Gregory Baums sought a "protestantization" of hierarchy's role—"in the light of Vatican II." The Rosemary Reuthers went more directly to the heart of the Catholic matter: The hierarchical-monarchical Church was not Christ's invention at all, but Roman imperialism transplanted to the gospel setting; the believing community must not act as if God had put himself under the control of any institution.

Deflation of Pope and hierarchy came in this analysis of the Church by Michael Novak in *All the Catholic People*:

I find the sacralizing and immobilizing tendencies among the Roman people destructive on human grounds and inadequate on Catholic grounds. They are in this epoch a perversion of the Roman Catholic principle, a perversion all the more deleterious when they are championed, as they often are, by Popes, curial officials, bishops, and official documents. It is no surprise to me that those in authority should wish to sacralize the authority and immobilize any efforts to humanize and to Christianize it. Their self-interest encourages the ideology they so strictly (and ably) defend. Nonetheless, they and their ideology must be displaced from the center of Catholic life. Their usual tactic is to excommunicate reformers. But after four centuries of experiment, reformers have learned a variety of countertactics. One of these is neither to fear or to honor excommunication [pp. 39–40].

This political infighting within the Church undermined what sociologist Peter Berger calls Catholic "plausibility structures." Faith of any kind is always interiorized through a particular tradition. Judgments about Christ, loyalty among believers, and common religious practices are colored by inherited associations. Bible Christians and Catholic Christians alike maintain their particular faith but in different ways and by different mechanisms. For Catholics the basic "plausibility structure" is the Church. If its doctrines are debunked or its leadership is debased, the faithful are drawn in many directions, much as sheep without a shepherd.

From the standpoint of later management disarray, *the fourth and perhaps most radical fallout of Vatican II* was the *legitimacy it gave to public debate about the meaning and finality of Catholic doctrine.*

Challenges to traditional Church statements of Catholic doctrine occurred on the floor of St. Peter's Basilica itself, which were reported all over the world, even in the classrooms of children of tender years. Although the Council Fathers did not endorse any view that contradicted the customarily defined faith, the impression was given that change could be expected. The fact that the Council Fathers or the Pope, to avoid future misunderstanding, went out of their way to insert footnotes or textual changes that reasserted the Catholic doctrine on marriage, the nature of the Church, and the limits of collegiality, did not seem to count. Succeeding Vatican documents have had no better success.

But challenges to doctrine, quite customary in democratic societies, are not easily withdrawn if they are effectively made. Democratic debate in secular society has a dynamism of its own. No position can be final, no statement is so sacred that it cannot be reversed, no principle is ever admitted to be absolute. The possibility of a change of mind or a change of vote always remains—if the political pressure is sufficiently fierce. What this understanding of the appropriate political procedure does to a theocratic Church that purports to "speak for God" requires little imagination. For God's mind and will to arrive not from prophets or Popes but through consensus-building among people is an entirely new development in the history of revealed religion.

The situation has been summarized neatly by sociologist Daniel Bell:

> The paradox of the postconciliar Church—a paradox which Tocqueville pointed out about the nature of revolution—is that as the authority grows progressively weaker, the protest against it intensifies. Persons who were acquiescent under the rigid preconciliar regime now declare authority repressive even though the new system is more liberal.

The rebellion against authority in the Church is of two kinds. The one, with deepest implications for the nature of belief, is the denial of mystical authority. . . . The second rebellion is against bureaucratic authority, the arbitrary power of bishops and chancery officials to rule the parishes and direct the priests.

But if the old structure of authority is shaken, whose voice is authentic? For some persons in the Church, the answer is periti. . . . [In] the more radical view . . . authority will derive from the communion, the people of God [in Patrick H. McNamara's *Religion American Style*, pp. 171–72].

However one views the theological significance of this development, Bell's description is sufficiently accurate to make the present difficulties of the Church understandable. Catholic sociologist Thomas O'Dea had no illusions about the scope of the problem. He credited Protestant rethinking of the Christian message to be "one of the great achievements of the modern mind," but concluded that the experience only succeeded in "transforming the wine of Christian faith into the price of scholarly opinion." Why Catholic bishops did not examine this Protestant experience as a guide to their own conduct of Vatican II remains a serious management question. Little consolation can be derived from the admission that churchmen were unable to control at home the forces they unleashed in Rome, nor from John Cogley's surmise that "the Fathers of the Council did not realize the full implications of the doctrines they were proclaiming, due above all to some failure of the clerical imagination."

*Ecclesialists* of the extreme persuasion consider conciliar proceedings "a manual on how to tear an institution apart without really trying." Equally convinced *modernizers* see Vatican II as a complete reversal of the theology that dominated Catholic thought for four hundred years. Obviously extremist positions do not adequately reflect the Council nor the customary fallouts. The Catholic Church has never considered impossible the admission that its system of belief or its structural arrangements were perfect. Nor does the Church consider it unseeming to borrow from Protestantism or secularism, as once she did from Judaeists, Stoics, and Greeks.

The postconciliar problems of the Church may derive from the misuse by the media of Pope John XXIII. He never set himself up as a revolutionary.

John Cardinal Heenan of Westminster saw harm to the Church in the "myths" circulated about Pope John. Opportunities he afforded were not intended to mean radical change in the Church. Heenan claimed that John had little concrete idea of the Pandora's box he had opened. Recalling how at the end of the first session the aging Pontiff called a few cardinals together, Heenan remembered the papal question: "How can we call this thing off gracefully without this thing going into more sessions?" Heenan cited as an example of the ambivalence John's opening address to the Council Fathers (October 11, 1962) in which—with Protestant observers not fifty feet away—the Pope speaks of the "ardent desires with which those Christians separated from this Apostolic See desire to be united with us."

The myth that Pope John XXIII was forcing the Church to revolt against its past—a myth that haunted Paul VI—was common gossip. When John was alleged to answer a question whether the new Council would clarify his infallibility, his cute answer was said to be: "No, I am infallible enough." There is also the story of how a newly appointed bishop came to Pope John confessing his difficulty in following someone who was an overwhelming personality, to which John by legend responded: "Do the same thing I do. I try to imagine what my predecessor would have done and then I do just the opposite." And the rumor was rife too that because John set up a papal commission to study the morality of "the pill," he, unlike Paul, was prepared to endorse contraception.

Gregory Baum, who was at the Council, once thought that Pope John smiled in two directions. Critics of Pope Paul suggest that he prayed the same way. The problems of the postconciliar Church reflect this predicament. The documents of the Council contain enough basic ambiguities to make the postconciliar difficulties understandable. Political forces within the Church have drawn their own segments of those documents to bolster particular causes.

The Council taught that the Church is the institution of salvation, managed by hierarchy but also that it is the People of God, who by God's mysterious design freely move toward their destiny as his sons.

The Church leads men to that other world; yet, if they neglect their responsibilities to this world, their salvation is endangered.

God's word can be found in the Bible, but that word must be understood in the light of what the Church says it is intended to mean.

The Catholic Church is Christ's Church, but believers in other churches belong to the Church of Christ too.

These are old Catholic tensions that now have led to open conflict within the Church, impelling competing political forces to absolutize one side of the doctrinal pole. The fights about God, Christ, redemption, revelation, Church, about the final things in life, are substantive.

## CHAPTER II

Reading and Misreading the Council Documents

The problems of Church management that followed the Council are partly traceable to the disparity between the folklore about what was expected from Vatican II and the reality of Pope John's intentions. Sifting one from the other requires more documents than are currently available. The papal decision to convoke an ecumenical gathering seemed impetuous, to be sure. Pius XII considered calling an ecumenical council but rejected the idea because of his declining years. John XXIII, however, was no inexperienced youngster in Church affairs. He may have been an old man in a hurry, but he was also a successful ecclesiastical bureaucrat. The fact that he spent almost three years planning the Council meant that he was hardly naïve about the problems associated with having 2,540 bishops from every nook and cranny of the world meet for an indeterminate number of years.

Which raises the question: What were the objectives sought by the Pope in convoking Vatican II?

From a management standpoint it is important to search out these objectives and to measure the success of the Council against their realization or lack. When objectives are unclear, misstated, or misunderstood, organizational ennui results. When more goals are sought than can be realized in a given time period, or when leadership loses control of their implementation, the institution—any institution—is in trouble.

There are only three currently available sources for determining what the Council was intended to accomplish: (1) the official declarations of Pope John, (2) the official decrees of the Council itself; and (3) the implementing decisions of the Vatican and the National Conferences of Bishops. The validity of anyone's opinion as to what Pope John had in mind must be measured against the bottom lines of those documents.

What, then, did Pope John put on the record concerning his plans for the Council?

An examination of all that Pope John had to say on this subject from his announcement (Jan. 25, 1959) to his address at the opening session (Oct. 11, 1962) makes it possible to list various purposes in the order of their presentation by the Pope. These purposes as stated were:

1. Reform of Canon Law
2. Growth of the Catholic faith
3. Renewal of Catholic habits
4. An adapted ecclesiastical discipline
5. Consolidation of agencies
6. Diffusion of revealed truth
7. Outreach to separated brethren and all men of good will
8. Doctrinal clarity
9. Concern for the temporal order
10. Championship of human rights
11. Enlarged missionary work of the Church
12. Enhanced influence of the Holy See
13. Solutions for society, the family, irreligious men, the poor, sinners
14. Succor of the poor
15. Vindication of the Church's liberty
16. Resisting war, seeking peace
17. Exaltation of fellowship among men

These objectives fell into two categories: *internal*, directed toward the greater efficiency and spirituality of the Church, and *external*, directed toward unifying Christendom and toward penetrating, if only modestly, the unbelieving segment of the world's population and institutions. This latter purpose would be accomplished, it was thought, by supporting man's legitimate quests in this world. The effectiveness of the Council, therefore, will ultimately be judged on how several questions are answered: Are the Catholic people holier? Is the Church doing its work better? Is Christian unity actually realized? Is the unbelieving segment of the world and secular institutions influenced by conciliar teaching? Many more decades must pass before a fair answer to any of these questions can be expected.

But in view of the unsettling effect of the Council on the internal affairs of the Church itself, it is evident that the dysfunctional aspects of the Council were related in part to the planned objectives. It may suffice at this point to suggest briefly what may have been sources of unanticipated difficulty:

1. The objectives were too numerous and frequently conflicting—for example, growth in Catholic faith as against new definitions that would appeal to non-Catholics.
2. Attempting more than one council could possibly accomplish—for example, consolidating agencies while enlarging the scope of Church activity.
3. Seeking to dismantle ancient structures before adequate substitutes were developed. Liturgical changes are the clearest example of this.
4. Reaching out to non-Catholics without making provision for solidifying the ongoing commitment of faithful Catholics. While debates were going on in Rome, children were being taught (and through them, parents) that missing Sunday Mass was no longer a mortal sin.
5. Adopting broad conciliar policies without evaluation of their possible dysfunctional aspects. Two suggestions of Pope John in his opening statement to the Council were to haunt not only the bishops' deliberations between 1962 and 1965 but also the subsequent pontificate of Paul VI. These were:

   A. Changes in doctrinal formulas are desirable if Catholic doctrine could thereby be made more attractive to unbelievers.
   B. Condemnations of error are not to be contemplated.

These principles enunciated by Pope John were later used to justify serious doctrinal dissent within the Church and to insulate dissenters against its chief doctrinal authorities. The Pope was no longer sovereign once he authorized 2,540 bishops to air their views. Controversies within the Council among bishops merely set the stage for more radical and unauthorized differences of opinion about what the Council actually said or meant to say.

Yet, as in any exercise of constituted authority, it is the final approved documents and their authentic meaning that alone set policy for the institution, including the Church. The conciliar debates, what was said in the antechambers of St. Peter's Basilica or in the coffee houses of Rome have no post-Vatican II standing except in conjunction with the official texts, which are in Latin. Not even vernacular translations count. Differing translations of the Latin texts can be "confusing to one seeking to learn exactly what the Council *said* than what someone outside the Council *thought* about the matter," as John Cardinal Wright pointed out in his Preface to Austin Flannery's *Vatican Council II: The Conciliar and Post-Conciliar Documents*. Not only must one seek the authentic meaning of the Council in the Latin texts themselves but also in their implementing decrees, which bring the Council meaning down to particular cases and into real-life situations. For example, the Council's *Constitution on the Sacred Liturgy*, a document about whose interpretation there is little disagreement, has been implemented so far by 120 Vatican decrees!

It is not possible here to recapture in words all that the sixteen documents of the Council—approximately two hundred thousand words— said. However, the controversies of the past thirteen years relate only to specific documents. There is some advantage in singling out each important controversy and the document with which it is associated.

### I. The Controversy over the Nature of the Church

Using the *Dogmatic Constitution on the Church (Lumen Gentium)* as justification, various authors allege one or more of the following propositions.

1. *The Catholic Church no longer equates itself with the Church of Christ.*
   Section 8 of *Lumen Gentium* reads:

This is the sole Church of Christ, which in the creed we profess to be one, holy, Catholic, and apostolic, which our Savior, after his resurrection, entrusted to Peter's pastoral care, commissioning him and the other apostles to extend and rule it. . . . This Church, constituted and organized as a society in the present world, subsists in the Catholic Church, which is governed by the successor of Peter and by the bishops in communion with him. Nevertheless, many elements of sanctification and of truth are found outside its visible confines. Since these are gifts belonging to the Church of Christ, they are forces impelling toward Catholic unity [No. 8].

The deliberate use by the Council Fathers of the words "the sole Church of Christ . . . *subsists in* [not *is*] the Catholic Church" is interpreted as willingness to accept a more modest role for the Catholic Church in the community of diverse Christian bodies.

2. *The most important description of the Church in Vatican II is that of "People of God."*

Since the stress here is on the priesthood of all Christians, the "People of God" concept is alleged to be ample evidence that the Council intended to declericalize the Church, to give nonordained ministers a vital role in decision-making and in determining the sense of what Catholic faith and morals actually mean in our day.

As frequently used, the "People of God" is translated as "laity," to distinguish them from the hierarchy.

3. *The Catholic Church is a pilgrim Church, sinful like all creatures, and in need of purification.*

This imagery is frequently used to justify public criticism of and public dissent within the Church. Intended first as a reminder to Catholics to recognize their personal and institutional shortcomings, that much remains to be done if the Church would fulfill its ultimate vocation, the concept of "pilgrim Church" (that is, struggling, unsettled, uncertain, weak Church) has been set against the notion of the "triumphal Church," which in its majestic pretensions to speak for Christ hardly represents (it is said) Christ at all.

These three propositions are in a real sense distortions of Vatican II, which in its totality retains the common sense of Catholics that the "Catholic Church is the Church of Christ." Recognizing (through the use of "subsists in") that there are Christian elements outside the visible confines of the Catholic body was an ecumenical gesture of no mean significance. But it was not intended to suggest that the Catholic Church has abandoned its unique claim as the Church that Christ founded. As a matter of fact, in the *Decree on the Catholic Eastern Churches* (No. 2), the Council Fathers explicitly state: "The holy Catholic Church, which *is* the Mystical Body of Christ."

Nor was the "People of God" concept the most important Vatican description of the Church. The Council used seven symbols to describe the Church, of which this image was only one. As a matter of fact, the longest section of *Lumen Gentium* deals with the role and function of the hierarchy. To make it perfectly clear that the People of God include hierarchy with their special role, *Lumen Gentium* (No. 18) says: "The bishops under Peter are the shepherds of the Church until the end of the world, as the First Vatican Council defined. They "take the place of Christ himself, teacher, shepherd, and priest, and act as his representative (that is, in his name and person)." There is a "collegiate character and structure of the episcopal order" as the holding of ecumenical councils in the course of centuries unmistakably indicates. The college has no authority unless united with the Roman Pontiff, whose primatial authority extends over all, whether pastors or faithful. The Pope has "full, supreme, and universal power over the whole Church," a power that he can always exercise unhindered. The college of bishops, however, "cannot be exercised without the agreement of the Roman Pontiff."

Then, as if to make it clearer that bishops participate in infallibility, No. 25 states: "Although the bishops, taken individually, do not enjoy the privilege of infallibility, they do, however, proclaim infallibly the doctrine of Christ on the following conditions: namely when, even though dispersed throughout the world but preserving for all that among themselves and with Peter's successor the bond of communion, in their authoritative teaching concerning matters of faith and morals, they are in agreement that a particular teaching is to be held definitively and absolutely. This is still more clearly the case when, assembled in an ecumenical council, they are for the universal Church teachers and judges of faith and morals, whose decisions must be adhered to with loyal and obedient assent of faith."

Apart from invalidating a "sense of the faithful" against bishops, *Lumen Gentium* in an explanatory note further says that a college of bishops cannot exist against the Pope. The note concludes: "The Pope alone, in fact, being head of the college, is qualified to perform certain actions in which the bishops have no competence whatsoever—for example, the convocation and direction of the college, approval of the norms of its activities, and so on. It is for the Pope, to whom the care of the whole flock of Christ has been entrusted, to decide the best manner of implementing this case. . . . The Roman Pontiff undertakes the regulation, encouragement, and approval of the exercise of collegiality as he sees fit."

## II. The Controversy over the Renewal of Religious Life

Since the most bitter controversies still exist over the renewal of religious life, it is important to see what the Council decree (*Perfectae Caritatis*) said on this subject:

1. The patrimony of each institute, especially "the spirit and aims of each founder, should be faithfully accepted and re-

tained"; when adapted, spiritual renewal must be assigned primary importance.

2. Lifestyles and mode of government should be in harmony with the present-day physical and psychological condition of the members and the needs of the apostolate.

3. "Effective renewal and right adaptation cannot be achieved save with the co-operation of all the members of an institute." However, only competent authorities can legislate and provide for sufficient prudent experimentation. The approval of the Holy See and local ordinaries must be sought when the law requires this.

4. Members of each institute must be recalled to their special consecration, which is to love God above all else, some through contemplation, some through apostolic and charitable activity, some through monastic observances.

5. Chastity must be "esteemed as an exceptional gift of grace [because] it uniquely frees the heart of man so that he becomes more fervent in love for God and for all men."

6. Poverty should be cultivated. It is not enough to be subject to superiors in the use of property. Religious should be poor. The institute itself should bear a quasicollective witness to poverty by avoiding any semblance of luxury.

7. The religious profession of obedience means the sacrifice of their own wills. Religious should be humbly submissive to their superiors. Superiors should exercise authority in a spirit of service, foster a spirit of voluntary subjection, allowing due liberty with regard to the sacrament of penance and the direction of conscience. Superiors should listen to their subjects.

8. Common life should be constant in prayer and spirit, in liturgy, etc.

9. Religious habits must be simple and modest, poor and becoming; they should be so changed as to conform to these norms.

10. Conferences of major superiors are to be welcomed.

Six instructions on religious life have been issued by the Holy See since 1966, three of which reflect various stages of the relations of Rome with religious congregations.

Pope Paul himself issued his own *motu proprio* called *Ecclesiae Sanctae* on August 6, 1966, nine months after he ratified the Council's decree on religious life. He encouraged "experiments that run counter to common law" as long as they are "embarked upon with prudence," and expected the revised constitutions to be submitted "for approval to the Holy See or to the competent hierarchy." Out-of-date rules and obsolete elements that have lost meaning and impact are to be eliminated. Renewal in religious life, however, in the first instance means the deepening of interior life through public prayer, mortification, the practice of poverty, and life in common. After "a due measure of experimentation," the Pope expected each institute to draw up proper rules for training its subjects. He also expressed the hope that conferences of major superiors would relate to and co-operate with episcopal bodies and the Sacred Congregation of Religious.

Five months later, on January 6, 1969, the Congregation for Religious issued *Renovationis Causam*, which equated renewal with strengthened spirituality. Major superiors are counseled "no adaptation to modern requirements should be put into effect that is not inspired by a spiritual renewal." Speaking of religious profession, the Congregation advised: "By the very nature of this consecration, the vows of obedience, whereby a religious consummates the complete renunciation of himself and, along with the vows of religious chastity and poverty, offers to God as it were a perfect sacrifice, belongs to the essence of religious profession. . . . It cannot be asserted that the very nature of religious profession must be changed or that there should be a lessening of the demands proper to it." Religious communities are clearly distinguished from "other" institutes "whose members, whether bound or not by sacred commitments, undertake to live in common and to practice the evangelical counsels in order to devote themselves to various apostolic or charitable activities."

Two and a half years went by before the Congregation for Religious, now caught up in conflict with "experimenters," issued what was called an "apostolic exhortation on the renewal of religious life." This document, dated June 29, 1971, is called *Evangelica Testificatio*, and its second paragraph tells the story:

> We wish to respond to the anxiety, uncertainty, and instability shown by some; at the same time we wish to encourage those who are seeking the true renewal of the religious life. The boldness of certain arbitrary transformations, an exaggerated distrust of the past—even when it witnesses to the wisdom and vigor of ecclesial traditions—and a mentality excessively preoccupied with hostility conforming to the profound changes which disturb our times, have succeeded in leading some to consider as outmoded the specific forms of

religious life. Has not appeal even unjustly made to the Council to cast doubt on the very principle of religious life?

### III. *The Controversy over Divine Revelation*

This may be the most fundamental controversy in the post-Vatican II Church, although it has captured the fewest headlines. Questions have been raised about whether and how much God has revealed to man even through Jesus Christ, whether or not God is revealing as much through contemporary events, if not more, as he is alleged to have made known through prophets or in gospels. Questions in this area, if seriously entertained without answers, undercut all supernatural claims from Christian churches, including the Catholic Church. This probably explains why the Vatican document is called *Dei Verbum* (The Word of God) and why it was written as a *dogmatic* constitution, since it deals with "*true* doctrine on divine revelation and its transmission." It is a critical document because all Christian faith depends on what people understand about the things God is said to have revealed. Critical, too, because there can be as much argument over the meaning of this constitution called *Dei Verbum* as there is over Scripture itself.

What is the *Dei Verbum* according to the Fathers of the Second Vatican Council (No. 7)?

1. Divine revelation is God addressing men as his friends, moving among men, and receiving men into his own company. God manifested himself to our first parents, to Abraham, to Moses and the prophets and finally through Christ, who is "the sum total of revelation."
   Christ completed and perfected revelation, confirmed it with divine guarantees—that is, his words and works, signs and miracles, and above all by his death and resurrection.
   No new public revelation is to be expected before Christ's final manifestation.
   Man commits himself to this revealing God by faith. But his faith too is a result of God's grace and the help of the Holy Spirit.
   The sacred synod also professes that God can be known with certainty from the created world.
   Revelation makes that knowledge firmer and easier.
2. The revelation of God was transmitted to man through Christ

and at his command through the apostles by their spoken word, then by them and by others associated with apostles who committed the message of salvation through writing. The bishops now stand in the apostles' place, the guarantors of apostolic preaching in a continuous line of succession until the end of time.

"The tradition that comes from the apostles makes progress in the Church, with the help of the Holy Spirit. There is growth in insight into the realities and words that are being passed on. This comes about in various ways. It comes through the contemplation and study of believers who ponder these things in their hearts. It comes from the intimate sense of spiritual realities that they experience. And it comes from the preaching of those who have received, along with their right of succession in the episcopate, the sure charism of truth." . . .

"The task of giving an authentic interpretation of the Word of God, whether in its written form or in the form of tradition, has been entrusted to the living teaching office of the Church alone." Its authority in this matter is exercised in the name of Jesus Christ. Yet this Magisterium is not superior to the Word of God, but is its servant. It teaches only what has been handed on to it."

## IV. The Controversy over Religious Freedom in the Church

The Vatican II decree on religious liberty—called *Dignitatis Humanae* (known also as the "American contribution to Vatican II")— was designed to endorse the principle of religious freedom in civil society. Pope Paul VI considered it "one of the major texts of the Council." Essentially as a matter of human dignity, the document asserts man's right to worship God free "from coercion in civil society." While admitting that civil society has the right to protect itself against possible abuses committed in the name of religion, "the Vatican Council declares that the human person has the right to religious freedom. Freedom of this kind means that all men should be immune from coercion on the part of individuals, social groups, and every human power."

It was not long, however, before some authors extended the right of religious freedom from coercion to members of the Church against Church authorities. *Dignitatis Humanae* (No. 1) professes, "We believe this one true religion continues to exist in the Catholic and Apostolic Church" and "in forming their consciences the faithful must pay careful attention to the sacred and certain teaching of the

Church" (No. 18). Even so, there are not wanting recent authors arguing for a Catholic right to determine for themselves the sacredness and certitude of Catholic truth in faith and morals.

Fr. John Courtney Murray, S.J., in many ways the "Father" of this decree, interprets the Council mind as follows:

> The Council directs a word of pastoral exhortation to the Christian faithful. They are urged to form their consciences under the guidance of the authority of the Church. It might be noted here that the Council intended to make a clear distinction between religious freedom as a principle in the civil order and the Christian freedom that obtains even inside the Church. These two freedoms are distinct in kind and it would be perilous to confuse them. Nowhere does the declaration touch the issue of freedom within the Church. Undoubtedly, however, it will be a stimulus for the articulation of a full theology of Christian freedom in its relationship to the doctrinal and disciplinary authority of the Church [Abbott and Gallagher, *Documents of Vatican II*, pp. 694–95].

It is precisely the "doctrinal and disciplinary authority of the Church" that since Vatican II has been challenged.

## V. *The Controversy over Catholic Doctrine on Contraception*

It is frequently alleged that the Council itself left the choice of means of family limitation to married couples. In point of fact, the Council in its *Pastoral Constitution on the Church in the Modern World* (*Gaudium et Spes*) (Nos. 50–51), after warning Catholics of the contemporary state of marital affairs (polygamy, divorce, free love, selfishness, hedonism, unlawful contraceptive practices), went on to describe marriage as a holy thing, founded on love and ordained to the fruitfulness of progeny. Children are called the supreme gift of marriage, and although judgments about family size are the responsibility of couples themselves before God, the Council concluded:

"When it is a question of harmonizing married love with the responsible transmission of life it is not enough to take only the good intention and the evaluation of motives into account: The objective criteria must be used, criteria drawn from the nature of the human person and the human action, criteria which respect the total meaning of mutual self-giving and human procreation in the context of true love; all this is possible only if the virtue of married chastity is seriously practiced. In questions of birth regulation the sons of the Church, faithful to these principles, are forbidden to use methods disapproved of by the teaching authority of the Church in its interpretation of the divine law."

(The Council did not go further on this subject because Pope Paul VI had reserved the question to himself.)

## VI. The Controversy over the Extent of Church Involvement in Worldly Affairs

There is no question that building upon papal teaching over three-score and ten years, the Second Vatican Council in Gaudium et Spes (No. 30) unequivocally asserts: "No one can allow himself to close his eyes to the course of events or indifferently ignore them and wallow in the luxury of a merely individualistic morality. . . . Let everyone consider it his sacred duty to count social obligations among man's chief duties today and observe them as such."

Internal problems began to appear in the Church, however, when sections of Gaudium et Spes were extrapolated from the whole to suggest (1) that the salvation of the world was the Church's primary concern, (2) that religious and laity without distinction were called to the active social ministry above all other faith demands, (3) that it was possible for Catholics to be truly Christian and truly Marxist at one and the same time, and (4) that violence was a legitimate defense against injustice. Sections of Gaudium et Spes widely used to defend various kinds of social involvement include those declaring the need to control power (No. 4), the value of social change (No. 26), the autonomy of earthly affairs (No. 36), and the importance of freedom of inquiry (No. 62). Less attention was given in these controversies to warnings of the Council against overconfidence in man's inventiveness (No. 57), or the monitum (No. 43): "No one is permitted to identify the authority of the Church exclusively with his own opinions."

Practically all the recent controversies in the Church can be reduced to these six categories.

## CHAPTER III

Of Modernism and Modernization: Alfred Loisy and
Hans Küng

There are many ways of describing the struggle going on within the contemporary Church. One way to summarize its cause and direction is to call it a "battle of ideas." The expected prize is control of the lives of the faithful accomplished through control of Church machinery itself. Although scholars are pitted against scholars, and scholars against hierarchy in what looks like a power struggle, it is "ideas" that ultimately will prevail in the Church. Whose ideas? That is the undecided question at the moment. Unquestionably, dissenting scholars are hawking their ideological wares with more effectiveness than bishops and their supporters, who look very much like men on the run.

Ideas start with idea men and eventually find favor with power brokers of one kind or another. At that point they become pawns in a game as old as the one that began with Adam and Eve over wearing clothes. Emperors, prelates, poets, playwrights, and parents organize their lives and those of their dependents around ideas—partly their own, but mostly someone else's.

The Catholic way of life is built around the claims of Christ and his Church to reveal and represent the mind and will of God about what human beings should do in this life in order to be happy with him forever. Through two thousand years the Christian world-view has developed to a point where "beliefs" (the doctrines, dogmas, or creeds) are numerous and precise, and directives about Catholic Christian behavior (the precepts and the counsels) are just as numerous and not always so precise. To keep these ideas moving in the lives of men, an elaborate Church machinery has unfolded that is based on an intricate code of concepts about status and office, educational techniques, enforcement, and reconciliation procedures. Tinker with one idea and you tinker with many others—a kind of an ecclesiastical domino game—with the institution designed to protect and promote ideas changed accordingly. For example:

If Jesus Christ is not the Son of God made man, or

If his basic revelation was not fully given in his short lifespan or

If he founded a Church only in the loose sense of a community of friendly believers, and

If all believers are relatively equal in office before the Father

If they must search in their own way for the mind and will of God—with the counsel from priests perhaps but without being subject to them

If institutional structures such as papacy, priesthood, minute laws, or confessionals are considered a human invention, not the divine will

Then, we are dealing with a different understanding of Christianity than that found in the definitions of the Catholic Church.

"Incomplete" or even "alien" ideas have worked their way into Catholicism before, but not without tension of varying kinds. Trouble ensued when these "ideas" could not find a home in the Church. Some contemporary fighting—about the baptism of infants or general absolution for the forgiveness of sin—are really battles over whether the concepts "original sin" (as "absence of God's presence within"), or "power of the keys" (as implying the need for absolution of sins) are valid.

The battle of ideas is as old as the Church. Arianism denied that Christ was really God. Manicheism affirmed that man is basically bad. Pelagianism affirmed that man could earn his own salvation without God's help. Calvinism denied the real presence of Christ in the Eucharist. These personal conceptions were considered important enough for men to argue that their life here and hereafter depended on the exactness of their formulation. This especially was common once Christianity became a social force as much as a religious faith.

### I. *The Battle Outside the Church*

What makes this battle of ideas in the post-Vatican II era different? Because Church authorities themselves in Council decided to experiment with applying some of these "alien" ideas to Catholic thought structures. The secularized Western world, for example, had become so dominated by unbelief that the Church began to look like a tiny island in a sea of capitalistic materialism, democratic socialism, Soviet imperialism, Chinese communism, and Third World revolutionism. The world of the future hardly seemed a friendly place for an other-world-minded religion.

What did the Council propose the contemporary Church do about this? Simply go into the marketplace of modern ideas and fight the battle of Christ in terms that modern man understands and accepts. Since it was expected that the Church could make appropriate accommodations to modern man's view of religion, it is important to take a look at the "modern ideas" with which the Church is expected to come to terms. The following items are high on the list of many contemporary authors:

1. Nothing must be demanded by religion that offends scientific rationality—miracles, for example.
2. "Truth" and "right" must be sought more from what people say and do than from abstract reasoning or ancient documents.
3. Relativism and pluralism in theology and philosophy (somewhat as in astronomy and physics) are natural products of the scientific method.
4. Formalism and legalism must give way to religious experience as the ultimate test of any Church's relevance to contemporary man.
5. New knowledge concerning the force of man's unconscious drives calls for an end to repressive measures of social control.
6. Both individuals and society are perfectible (that is, they evolve). Change rather than structured life is natural to man. Religion and theology must stress both change and evolution, unhampered by frayed doctrines and mythologies.
7. The action of God in the world and earthly existence are the vital concerns of modern man and must preoccupy any religious group that expects a modern hearing.
8. The path of human progress comes through conflict. Men must

be educated for conflict, expect conflict, accept the benefits of conflict—as consistent with the Christian gospel.

9. An overarching socialized society, which institutionalizes secular values and legislates those values through the consensus of free citizens, will enhance the unity proper to civilized men.

## II. The Modern Mind and Protestantism

These ideas—individually and in concert—had a profound impact first on Protestant thinkers. Protestantism by definition was geared to almost any idea that accentuated individual religious experience. Lacking magisterium, by which all new Catholic interpretations must be measured, Protestantism (except its fundamentalists) was forced by its inner logic to make faith concepts and moral precepts almost a matter of scientific determination. Ernest Troeltsch (1865–1923), though not the first important Protestant authority to recognize the challenge of "modern" ideas, was an important contributor to Protestant accommodation. He wanted a vital Christianity, and thought its survival depended on a restructured modern dress. "Absolutes" had to go and "personal satisfaction" had to rise as a norm of religious relevance. Troeltsch does not ask: "How can I find God?" but "How can I find my soul?" He did not even think that Jesus was necessary to Christianity, since Christ was more a symbol of a community than a spokesman of God's revelation. Though a Protestant, Troeltsch thought the reformed churches retained too many features of Catholic Christianity. The modern age to him meant the religious autonomy of man—against both Protestant and Catholic world-views, if need be.

## III. Early Catholic Accommodation

The Catholic Church has not remained beyond influence from these pressures. During the nineteenth century a Catholic movement called Modernism sought an end to the religious postures characteristic of Catholicism since the Council of Trent. Critical minds, the modernists alleged, could no longer submit to a Church that denied most of what was affirmed as necessary facts of life by modern science. Essential to the future progress of religious truth was intellectual freedom. Answers to questions raised by scientific biblical studies, for example, called for educated intelligence, not tradition, a theology no longer bound by Scholastic categories.

The Modernist approach to Catholicism is typified in Alfred Firmin Loisy (1857–1940). His difficulty in reconciling the Catholic doctrines of his boyhood with the theological reflections of mature manhood made him a crusader for the renewal of Catholic theology from top to bottom, "to substitute the religious for the dogmatic spirit." In his judgment, renewal began first by the scrutiny of all Catholic documents, including the Scriptures, according to the historical method. Once historically conditioned elements of Christianity were understood and set aside, the doctrines of the Church could then be adapted to the exigencies of contemporary thought. Loisy's idea of Catholicism differed radically from what the Church regularly taught the faithful, but he was convinced that continued acceptance of Catholicism among the educated depended upon the Church's acceptance of his revised "model."

Loisy attacked as scientifically untenable three Catholic "postulates": (1) Old Testament teaching on God and Creation, (2) Old Testament foreshadowing of Christ and the Church, and (3) Christ's direct institution of the Catholic Church with its doctrines and hierarchy. The revised concept of revelation would eliminate any notion that God hurled absolutes at the world from his heavenly throne. A scientific look at Scripture offered opposite evidence that divine revelation was "progressive education" of men, rational, proportioned to the human condition of peoples to whom it was addressed. Revelation as a body of thought cannot be discussed apart from the human experience from which it derived.

Furthermore, the original gospel of Jesus was smothered by the large overlays of dogmas and rituals of Catholicism. The authoritarian claims and posture of the Church themselves were unacceptable to the modern world. The business of Catholicism is to stimulate religious faith in people, so he argued, not to ossify itself by substituting formulas for faith. Unlike liberal Protestant scholars (for example, Adolf Harnack), Loisy did consider the Church necessary for Jesus' work to be done, but his Church adapted to the needs of each age as a child does on his way to maturity. Loisy would argue, also, that Christianity had no fixed "core" of beliefs or doctrines that stood outside of time and culture. In *Roman Catholic Modernism* Bernard Reardon summarizes Loisy's mind:

> Once the ship of faith had cut loose from her moorings in history the exact course followed would have to be determined by the winds and tides of circumstance. Catholicism would be justified, if at all, not by dubious claims deriving from documents or traditions incapable of verification or precise interpretation, but on actual experience [pp. 32–33].

Other specifics of Loisy's thought included the following: Jesus was not conscious of himself as a divine being; the Church was founded more as a community of faith than as a historical institution; the sacraments gain their effectiveness from faith in the resurrected Christ.

In the latter years of his life Loisy, now in oblivion, wrote a book entitled *My Duel with the Vatican* (published in 1924, republished in 1968), which capsulated the reasons for his condemnation and final excommunication. His views then were more bitterly expressed, but they had not changed.

About Christ's divinity he continued to say: "Who can guarantee to us that Christ was God if he never gave himself out as such, if even he displayed no consciousness whatever of being divine?" (p. 239).

On the question of revelation, the older Loisy had this to say: "What has been called revelation cannot be anything else than the consciousness acquired by man of his relationship with God [p. 243] . . . For a long while I have not found it possible to pray to God as one beseeches an individual from whom some favor is anticipated. My prayers consist in retiring into the depths of my own consciousness. . . . There is an infantile aspect to the ordinary notion of future life that is not highly moral, and is even immoral" [pp. 275–76].

About the Virgin birth and resurrection: "I cannot very well conceive of myself as reconciled *in extremis* by an explicit profession of faith in the Virgin birth and the bodily resurrection of Christ" [p.275].

Concerning the Church: "The Church was not instituted by Jesus during his lifetime but was born of faith in the glorified Christ" [pp.241–42].

His judgment about the sacraments, including the Eucharist, was tersely stated: "The two rites practiced by the earliest Christian communities—baptism and the Last Supper—were not instituted by Christ himself. The general idea of the institution of the sacraments, as it is announced in the decrees of the Council of Trent, is not a historical representation of what Jesus did or of what the apostolic Church thought, but an authentic interpretation—I mean one authorized by faith—of the traditional fact" [pp. 244–45]. In his little book *Autour d'un Petit Livre* (1903), Loisy even ridiculed the idea of divine institution of the Eucharist with a series of questions: "Do you think," he asked, "that the apostles during the Last Supper had any idea of transubstantiation, of the permanence of Christ whole and entire under the species of bread and wine, that they were conscious of being priests?" [p. 236]. For Loisy those who presided over the early Eucharists became priests only when the Christian community made the Eucharist into a liturgical act.

"Ambiguity" is the word frequently used to describe Loisy's Catholicism. He once said: "I did not accept any article of the Catholic creed, except that Jesus had been crucified under Pontius Pilate." In his *Memoirs* he confessed: "Christ has less importance in my religion than he has in that of the liberal Protestants; for I attach little importance to the revelation of God the Father for which they honor Jesus. If I am anything in religion, it is more pantheist-positivist-humanitarian than Christian." He spoke this as a priest still saying daily Mass (in which he no longer believed) but struggling nonetheless to renew Catholicism on his terms. Until the very end he regularly submitted to ecclesiastical authority but always with graceful "ambiguity." Reardon concludes: "His most sincere belief is that science is autonomous and cannot allow its rights to be inhibited by external authority, even in the name of divine revelation" [p. 36]. He regarded himself as a Catholic as long as Church authorities tolerated him, but when on March 7, 1908, he was excommunicated by name, he left behind not only his Catholicism but Christianity as well.

## IV. The Roman Response to Modernism

Much has been made since 1908 in and out of the Church of St. Pius X's reaction to Modernism—the so-called "synthesis of all heresies." Volumes have been written on the "witch-hunt" against Modernists carried on by the Pope and Cardinal Merry del Val during their respective lifetimes. At one point the papal assault on Modernism was taken by some as indication of Pius' lack of sanctity. Nonetheless, a brief summary of the essential elements of the papal condemnations in *Pascendi Dominici Gregis* (September 8, 1907) and *Lamentabili Sane Exitu* (July 3, 1907) makes interesting reading seven decades later.

*Pascendi* made these points among others:

1. The Pope "may no longer keep silence, lest we should seem to fail in our most sacred duty."
2. Partisans of error are to be sought not only among the Church's open enemies, but also in her very bosom, even among priests. The less they are out in the open, the more mischief they cause.
3. These "partisans of error" have lost all sense of modesty. They "put themselves forward as reformers of the Church but assail all that is most sacred in the work of Christ."
4. As *philosophers* Modernists are agnostics. They confine reason entirely within the field of *phenomena* (the appearances of

things) and so deny man's natural capacity to know God from reason or revelation.

5. As *believers* Modernists come to faith in a strange way. Man may not know God by reason. Still religion is a universal human phenomenon. How does this come about? The explanation must be found within man himself (immanence). God originates in man's need of the divine. As an external being God is unknowable. Man just believes, but that faith has no rational basis.

6. As *theologians,* Modernists similarly find revelation in human experience. Revelation is man's consciousness of God. Even the Church must submit to the test of the collective consciousness of men, which evolves and continues to evolve through history. ["Venerable brethren, these are not merely the foolish babblings of unbelievers. There are Catholics, yea, and priests too, who say these things openly; and they boast that they are going to reform the Church by these ravings!"]

7. As *historians,* Modernists distinguish exegesis that is scientific from that which is theological or pastoral. So as scientists they "are wont to display a manifold contempt for Catholic doctrines, for the Holy Fathers, for the ecumenical councils, for the ecclesiastical Magisterium; and should they be taken to task for this, they complain that they are being deprived of their liberty."

The *Lamentabili* document condemned sixty-five propositions which the Pope insisted represented not progress but corruption of dogmas. Only a few citations will be made, merely to manifest the flavor of the issues at stake in the Church at the turn of the twentieth century.

The proposition is to be proscribed that says:

No. 6 "The *Church learning* and the *Church teaching* collaborate in such a way in defining truths that it only remains for the *Church teaching* to sanction the opinions of the *Church learning.*

No. 16 "The narrations of John are not properly history, but a mystical contemplation of the gospel."

No. 21 "Revelation, constituting the object of the Catholic faith, was not completed with the Apostles."

No. 27 "The divinity of Jesus Christ is not proved from the gospels. It is a dogma that the Christian conscience has derived from the notion of Messiah."

No. 35 "Christ did not always possess the consciousness of his
Messianic dignity."

No. 42 "The Christian community imposed the necessity of
Baptism, adopted it as a necessary rite, and added to it the
obligation of Christian profession."

No. 47 "The words of the Lord in John 20:22–23 in no way
refer to the sacrament of Penance, in spite of what is pleased
the Fathers of Trent to say."

No. 55 "Simon Peter never even suspected that Christ entrusted the primacy in the Church to him."

No. 59 "Christ did not teach a determined body of doctrine
applicable to all times and all men, but rather inaugurated a
religious movement adapted or to be adapted to different
times and places."

These and similar opinions were to be resurrected three generations
later in the Church. For rejecting Modernism so completely St. Pius X
would be criticized, if not vilified. But on the occasion of his death the
editorial writer for the London *Times* (August 21, 1914), then representing an Anglican view of the dead Pope's accomplishments, had
this to say:

. . . The sweeping condemnation of "Modernism" was the
most conspicuous act of his pontificate within the domain of
dogma. It was a consequence of his position and of his character as inevitable as his repudiation of compromise with the
secularism of M. Combe or M. Briand. Few persons familiar
with the elementary doctrines of the Roman Church would
suppose that the tendencies of the new school were compatible with them. To the downright plain sense of the Pope the
desperate efforts of men who had explained away the content
of historical Christianity to present themselves as orthodox
Roman Catholics were simply disingenuous. . . .

## V. *The Church Battle Revisited*

The Catholic Church enjoyed a remarkable tranquillity for the next
fifty years in a world wracked by a major economic depression and two
major wars. The suppression of Modernist ideas at least in rectories,
seminaries, and chancery offices seemed to work. Pastors and seminary
professors took the oath against Modernism even when few knew what
the old fight was about. In some places before Vatican II, bishops for-

got to ask officials to make this routine gesture of support for Catholicism. But in scholarly circles, especially in Germany and France, new stirrings were noticed. World War II had a devastating effect on middle Europe. The savagery of Nazism in its annihilation of Jews and other religious dissenters, notably Catholic priests, the acquiescence of so many Christians to the German political juggernaut organized by Hitler, the mutual sufferings of Protestants, Catholics, and Jews sharing the same bread lines and the same churches, the rigidities and separateness of Catholic life in places like prewar Holland, the threats from Communist Russia, brought about serious re-evaluation of external religion, the power of the clergy (in Holland pastors at one point told political officials how to vote), the needless isolation of the churches from each other, the problems of poverty, homelessness, and child-bearing, all had a cumulative effect. European thinkers went back to their sources for better answers to human problems than prewar predecessors provided. If European Catholic intellectuals were in advance of their American Catholic counterparts in bitterness at what had been and in daring to try novelty, this is explainable in view of the severe social misery in postwar Europe. Also, European Catholicism had endemic problems unknown to the American Church. It is not surprising, therefore, that problem solvers in postwar Catholic Europe looked to change, almost any change, as the solution to pressing human problems. Catholic scholars took a new look at European Protestant scholarship searching for new Catholic insights to Scripture, theology, ecumenism, and social reform. Borrowed positions from older Protestant scholars, rather than creative Catholic innovation, was the immediate result (only in liturgy—because liturgy was a special Catholic preserve—did an independent and advanced indigenous Catholic viewpoint exist). The Holy See followed cautiously the romance of Catholic scholarly circles of France and Germany with the Modernist ideas of an earlier generation. At the turn of the century Rome was restrictive about how much Protestant scriptural research would be allowed to enter Catholic teaching (for example, reconciliation of Genesis I, II, and III with evolutionary theories, the relation of Moses to the Pentateuch, etc.). Catholic "dogmas" would accept "development," but only if the "given faith" would not be undermined by "scientific" judgments in areas where science by itself had little competence. However, during the postwar years Catholic academicians in Europe began to pass around in underground fashion off-the-record lectures and unpublished notes containing hitherto proscribed ideas, which were looked upon as exciting discoveries in some seminaries and Catholic universities. In 1950, one month after he issued his infallible declaration on Mary's assumption—

a most unscientific declaration by modern standards—Pius XII also issued his encyclical *Humani Generis*. Eugenio Pacelli, at that moment probably the Church's outstanding papal intellectual of recent memory, had personally encouraged biblical and liturgical studies, established a high tone for theological discourse by his allocutions and encyclical, relaxed ancient liturgical and canonical norms, initiated dialogue with nuclear scientists, geneticists, astronomers, political scientists, demographers—and then issued one of his bluntest documents. On this occasion he sounded more like his predecessor than his diplomatic self. Pius XI's teachings on marriage, labor, communism, nazism, and fascism were quite definite. In *Humani Generis* Pius XII found fifty-six errors against the faith moving through the corridors of Catholic seminaries and universities—doubts about transubstantiation, inspiration and inerrancy of Scripture, original sin, the relevance of the Church and its authority to define faith and morals too. Reformers bent on "modernizing" the Church resented *Humani Generis*, and considered it Pius XII's most reactionary document. But until he died Catholic scholars trod a careful course.

The Second Vatican Council a dozen years later was to become a safe forum for giving public airing to "ideas" that bothered Pius XII, as they once bothered Pius XI and St. Pius X. This has led to the confrontation going on within the Church today—a battle of ideas about Christ and the Church. The major idea in contest is: *The concept of God (or Christ) as a supernatural reality, apart from or against the world of space and time, and of his supernatural interventions in the world.* Teilhard de Chardin was reported once as saying of St. Augustine: "Don't mention that unfortunate man; he has spoiled everything by introducing the supernatural." (Dietrich Hildebrand, *The Trojan Horse in the City of God*, p. 227.) But the important questions for the Church are: Has God intervened in the world at all? Does he now? Are such alleged interventions credible to scientific-minded men?

An examination of the manner in which Hans Küng approaches these questions sheds light on the contemporary problem. Every age of crisis has a symbolic antagonist, and Küng is the best-known symbol of confrontation with the Church. He may not have been as important during Vatican II as Karl Rahner, but today Küng is a leading and popular publicist. He speaks as if the fresh air let into the Church by Pope John should be the German *Geist* he is spreading. Hardly a major place in the world exists to which he has not brought his vision of Christianity—to the Catholic University of America, Notre Dame, Georgetown, and the "Today" show. If his books are best sellers it is because he is their best seller. He is more widely read than any other "scientific" theologian. Purists in theological science sometimes scoff at the partiality of his scholarship (or ask why American scholars lionize him when German scholars no longer value his scholarship highly), but Küng says precisely and frankly what he thinks. Others use his arguments without stating their implications as clearly. He is the only major theologian in recent years publicly admonished by the Holy See for his views on Catholic doctrine and the Church (February 15, 1975). His new book *On Being a Christian* is a source of his views about theology or the Christian life. Küng himself considers the book a "small Summa of the Christian faith," while his friend Andrew Greeley calls it "a masterpiece" and "the best defense of Catholic Christianity to appear in this century."

## VI. *Hans Küng*

What is Hans Küng's Catholic Christianity? It is a religion that must be made meaningful for present-day society, must be ecumenical, must dialogue with other great religions, and must be built on Jesus Christ. Küng sets out to capture for himself and the Church the essence of Christianity and the real Christ so frequently hidden under "the dust and debris of two thousand years" (p. 20) and under sectarianism.

What are the sources of Hans Küng's essence of belief? He is remarkable in his selectivity. He starts with the New Testament and the teaching of the first ecumenical councils (between the fourth and eighth centuries). But before long he criticizes what he alleges those councils added to the Christian essence. He ignores the Magisterium of the Church thereafter, including subsequent ecumenical councils and Vatican II. He minimizes the New Testament content. St. John's Gospel, St. Luke's, the Acts of the Apostles, and most of St. Paul's epistles are not considered valid sources for a genuine image of Christ, because already in the first century they reflect accommodations toward making a Jewish rabbi into a Son of God whom Greeks could accept. As for the Synoptics, Küng downgrades Matthew and Luke because they betray later influences too, and is left depending for his conclusions on Mark and the hypothetical Q Document (invented by scholars as hypothesis because the gospels contain data that cannot be explained by intrinsic evidence alone). Küng, therefore, begins with a small amount of "revealed data," on which he bases his own image of Jesus.

Most Catholic Scripture scholars would not accept Küng's scriptural base. St. Paul, for example, was converted around A.D. 36 and he was already talking of handing down only what was handed on to him: Even the Anglican bishop John A. T. Robinson recently asked in his latest book *Can We Trust the New Testament?* and his answer is a categorical yes.

What does Hans Küng have to say about the divinity of Christ, God's Revelation, miracles, the resurrection, the Church, and the Eucharist? These are fundamental issues not only for Catholics but also for all Christian believers. Küng's treatment of all these subject areas follows the plan of his purpose and his postulates.

### Küng on Christ's Divinity

Christ is not simply God (p. 130). The later decree of Ephesus in 431 concerning the two natures of Christ is not what we read in the New Testament (pp. 131ff). The account of the Evangelist John was developed out of the need to satisfy pagan concepts (pp. 437–39). The title "Son of God" was not intended to describe an ontological reality. Christ was God's special friend and advocate but nothing more (p. 317). Everything that was later said about divine sonship, pre-existence, creation, and incarnation were postpaschal developments, intended to substantiate the claims made known in Jesus (p. 449). The transference of the title "Son of God," therefore, with its divine attributes, happened because Hellenistic readers would not understand that title in any other sense. The idea of incarnation is nothing more than a theological "theory" (pp. 440–41).

The tragedy of Catholic distortions is that they tend to depress the humanity of Jesus, which modern man can understand (pp. 131ff). Jesus the man has been overshadowed by the suggestion that revelation came from above. The process began from the opposite direction. Jesus is the embodiment of God's word and will. Jesus pre-existed because he was always in God's thoughts, not that he had prior personal existence (p. 445). Modern man cannot accept a pre-existent divine element that became human.

### Küng on God's Revelation

Jesus does not see "the law" as positively revealed by God or as permitting no dispensation (p. 240). Jesus never gave moral or ritual instructions on how people should pray, fast, or make times or places holy. His statements are expansive and helpful directives about the human condition, frequently overstatements (pp. 242ff).

What is the basic will of God? Man's well-being. God cannot be

seen apart from man. Nor man from God. Service to man takes precedence over law and even over service to God (p. 253). If love of God is
said to come first, it is because this too is in man's interest (pp. 251ff).
Humanity replaces legalism, institutionalism, juridicism, dogmatism.
Man is the measure of his own law (pp. 207ff). God left man to decide whether to keep the Sabbath.

Küng makes no distinction between law and legalism, between law as
the expression of God's will as distinct from Christ as the complete expression, between Christ legislating "I say to you" for the apostles and
against Jewish interpretations of God's law (on divorce, for example).

### Küng on Miracles

He dismisses all miracles that cannot be given a natural explanation.
The "onus of proof is on anyone who would accept miracles in the
strict sense. And miracles in the strictly modern sense of breaking
through the laws of nature cannot be historically proved" (p. 233).
Many alleged miracles have a perfectly natural explanation. Postresur-
rection enthusiasm made up the others. He presumes that the existing
laws of nature cannot be tampered with, while never asking why God
cannot intervene in nature or why open-minded scientific man denies
possibilities because he cannot provide explanations.

### Küng on Christ's Resurrection

The resurrection is a "real event" for the faithful but is not historically verifiable (p. 350). The empty tomb leads us nowhere (all it
means is "He is not here," p. 365), and the reported apparitions
before the women and the disciples were spiritual experiences about
which science knows very little. The glorified body is a 'new corporality"
(p. 366). Küng nowhere explains why a "new corporality" is less
offensive to scientific man than a changed old body; or why modern
man cannot be open to a real world that transcends the scientific.

### Küng on the Church

Jesus did not found an institutional Church in his lifetime (p. 199).
His thoughts on the Kingdom of God were highly unorganized, still
less identified with a Church (p. 220). He did not think of a mission
among pagan nations (pp. 285ff, 478ff). As distinct from Israel, the
Church was the result of an eschatological collective movement (p.
478) that began after the resurrection. Since Christ was antihierarchical

(p. 199), whatever community developed in his name had no need of priests (p. 481).

### Küng on the Eucharist

We cannot ascribe to Jesus ideas that came later. In Jesus' time communal meals were ordinary among Jews as a celebration. The Last Supper was just that. It was the last of a series of meals Jesus had with his apostles. They continued that tradition with no understanding that Jesus had found a new liturgy (p. 323). The Eucharist then is a commemoration of thanksgiving, not a repetition of the sacrifice of the cross.

(Küng's explanation ignores the early and different understanding of St. Paul [1 Co. 10:16–22], who looked upon the Eucharistic celebration as a proclamation of Christ's death—not just common membership or commemoration.)

### Küng's Approach to Modern Man

Scripturist Manuel Miguens describes the methodological problem of Hans Küng this way:

> The fundamental question is Küng's commitment to the demythologizing process. His purpose and intentions fall beyond any scholarly evaluation. But the risks involved in any demythologizing are obvious, and cannot be minimized. Not the least of the dangers is the inevitable relativization of Christ and his significance. No one denies today that the message of the New Testament has to be carefully analyzed and grasped in its own environment and then made understandable to men of each epoch. But it is neither realistic nor wise to contend that Christian truth must be any less challenging and startling and even shocking to modern man than it has been in every age, not the least shocking to Paul and his contemporaries. A radical demythologizing makes Christ meaningless and irrelevant to any man, ancient or modern. In any case, Jesus Christ aside, the greatest myth of all for modern man remains God himself. [In *The Teaching Church in Our Day*, edited by George A. Kelly, St. Paul Editions, pp. 201–2.]

Moreover, there is the underlying postulate of Hans Küng's approach to Catholic doctrine—namely, that modern man will only accept

Küng's concept of Jesus Christ and the gospel. In view of the fact that evangelical Christianity is the only growing segment of Christianity, while the "accommodating" churches, including Roman Catholic, continue to decline, does the Küng postulate represent the demands of the people? Or just an elite? In Catholic terms the revealed message surpasses man's ability to comprehend what he believes. Is the message for that reason less true?

There is also the use of the Küng methodology by other Catholic scholars or their attitude toward his conclusions. Avery Dulles points up one side of the difficulty, even as he expresses some sympathy (*America*, November 20, 1976):

> My difficulties with certain of Küng's doctrinal positions are not peculiarly my own. They have already been voiced by other Catholic theologians in Europe. But let the prospective reader not be deterred. Küng has every right to a fair hearing. His positions are consistent, forcefully argued, and merit serious consideration. Perhaps in the course of time these positions will win an acknowledged right of existence within the Catholic community. If so, Küng himself will deserve a large share of the credit.

If Küng by presupposition is a prophet whose reinterpretation of Christ is likely to become acceptable for many—whether they are true or not—where does that leave the credibility of the teaching Church? Or even that of Christ? If Christ is not really God or dubiously God, a large part of the Catholic controversy is irrelevant.

This poses the question of the Church's relevance. What "Catholic community" is likely to give sanction to Küng's redefinitions? The whole Catholic community in union with Pope and bishops? Or a segment against Pope and bishops? The differences of opinion here transcend matters of opinion or the technicalities of Canon Law. The substance of divine revelation is the issue. The Catholic Church can afford to shift its position on usury or on religious freedom in civil society without compromising its essential nature. But the Catholic Church cannot survive where any large following from its onetime faithful adherents adopt Küng's views on Christ's divinity, Mary's virginity, the Eucharist, the papal primacy, and the moral law.

Hans Küng himself poses the dilemma: "It is not a question for me of being ultimately proven right against Rome and the bishops. The question is not who is right but where does the truth lie. The truth will assert itself where it is found."

But who will decide the truth? Should Hans Küng be judged wrong and a misleader of the Church, on what grounds will people follow the Church, rather than Küng or his sympathizers? Küng recently expressed the view (after additional solicitous inquiries from German bishops) that he be left alone to do his work in peace. Raymond Brown (*America*, November 20, 1976) thought Church authorities, especially Roman ones, should leave "his [Küng's] errors to be pointed out voluntarily by competent theologians."

Richard N. Ostling—a reviewer for *Time* magazine (January 3, 1977), sees the problem as a confrontation of social forces struggling for dominance in the Church.

> Küng's compendium of doctrine, innovative and stimulating, has one problem at its core. No theologian has been more impatient than Küng with the Catholic Church's old Magisterium (teaching office). Yet throughout the book urges his readers, in effect, to trust the authority of a new Magisterium of university scholars on what should be believed about Jesus and what should be discarded. In doing so, Küng has become the leading theologian of what could be called the liberal Protestant party within the Catholic Church.

A common thread of understanding runs through the thinking of Hans Küng, as it did in earlier days for Alfred Loisy: Christianity is a human invention, the "revelation" on which it is based really no revelation at all. Scripture, far from being inspired of God, is formed into something divine. Even Christ as Son of God is the creature of his followers. It was they who made him equal to God as surely as they made the Church, which is nothing more than the community of those who became involved with the cause Christ represented. God may be moving through history, to be sure, and Jesus can be considered central to God's dynamic relationship with men, but no believer need understand (and no scientist would) that God "spoke" to man, spoke "once and for all," or speaks now in a special way through a Church. The "experience" of twentieth-century men of faith may in this view be as prophetic as that handed down by Christ's first followers, most of whom were not educated men.

While both Loisy and Küng explain that their scholarly effort is intended to provide an acceptable rational base for faith, the net effect of these reinterpretations is real doubt about anything supernatural or transcendental. Their methodology cuts the ground from under all forms of Christianity that claim divine content. While some Christian thinkers reject the Loisy-Küng conclusions, at least in their cruder form, they are convinced that modernity requires the historic-critical approach to religious subjects, thus inclining them to minimal acceptance of religious propositions. Many of the controversies over ongoing revelation, process theology, existential morality, and experiential catechesis have their beginning with this acceptance.

PART TWO

# THE BATTLE FOR THE
# AMERICAN CHURCH

## CHAPTER IV

The Battle for the Catholic Campus

## I. The Background

Church confrontation with the forces of Modernism was a facing up
to scholars who wanted to emancipate their scientific research from
Catholic dogma. Modernism—as distinct from liberalizing Catholic
views—was seen as the Church's mortal enemy and was dealt with vigorously. While the whole story of the anti-Modernist campaign against
scholars is yet to be written (most of the commentaries come from the
pens of those who suffered or thought they suffered, from their
defenders and sympathizers), there is little question that Catholic
scholarship suffered and in the outside intellectual world the Church
was held up to ridicule. Following Pius X's effective control of the
Church's internal enemies, Benedict XV was able to adopt a more
relaxed policy toward scholarship. Not long after the termination of
World War I hostilities, a Catholic intellectual revival was much in ev-
idence. Literary names—not all scholars in the strict sense—achieved or
were on their way to achieving international prominence. The English
Catholic firmament was studded with stars like Wilfrid and Bernard
Ward, Ronald Knox, Maurice Baring, Robert Hugh Benson, Philip
Hughes, Gervase and David Matthew, Evelyn Waugh, Sheila Kaye
Smith, G. G. Wyndham Lewis, Christopher Dawson, Abbot Vonier,
Abbot Butler, Martin D'Arcy, C. C. Martindale, Alfred Noyes, Barbara
Ward, Eric Gill, Shane Leslie, Stephen Dessain, G. K. Chesterton,
Hilaire Belloc, E. I. Watkin, Frank Sheed, and Maisie Ward. Most of
these prominent writers were not academic persons, although a great
deal of research went into their creative works. Practically all of them

were rabid defenders of Catholic intelligence and the rationality of Catholic claims. It would be hard to point to any one of them having any ultimate trouble squaring their intellectual work with the claims of the Magisterium, whatever trouble any one of them may have had with a particular Pope or bishop.

On the European continent literateurs like François Mauriac, Leon Bloy, Peguy, and Henri Gheon were joined by philosophers of the stature of Jacques Maritain and Étienne Gilson, scripturists like Garrigou-La Grange, rising theological stars like Jean Danielou, Henri de Lubac, and Yves Conger (Karl Rahner in Germany), and liturgical explorers such as Dom Gueranger and Louis Bouyer, to provide the Church with some respectability in secular intellectual circles. The theologians—and scientists like Teilhard de Chardin when he moved out of his field— were chided at times by Rome, but all of them, perhaps only with Teilhard excepted, eventually became important Church figures.

The American Church was somewhat slower in "producing" intellectual scholars or prominent literary figures. Those who surfaced were better known in their own country and frequently more eminent within Catholic circles than outside. Prior to World War II American Catholic thinkers were less likely to be invited to European intellectual centers or to Yale and Harvard either. The intellectual movement at that time was toward America, not in the other direction. Also, many truly Catholic scholars never achieved the proper public reputation they deserved, unless, like John Courtney Murray, they struck a responsive American chord. There are those within the Church who think that the dark authoritarian conspiracy that is Catholicism itself explains the lack of solid and creative scholarship among American Catholics. The more basic fact, which Andrew Greeley lays out with some authority, is that it takes time to develop an intellectual, literary, or theological tradition. American Catholics only now in this generation have arrived at the moment with the resources and leisure that are absolutely necessary for this laborious work.

Even so, American Catholics at the time of World War II and well in advance of Vatican II were not without a fair share of reasonably good thinkers, scholars, and writers. Forgotten today may be the names like Carleton J. H. Hayes, pioneer in the historical study of nationalism; the Dante scholar, Jesuit Gerald G. Walsh; Anton C. Pegis, an outstanding student of St. Thomas Aquinas; or even Robert Howard Lord, who achieved eminence as a Harvard professor before he became a well-known Boston priest.

But there were others, too. Many Catholics could hold their own in the academic or literary world, especially in fields that became attractive to Catholics. Rudolph Allers, Thomas Vernon Moore, Robert Odenwald, and Francis Braceland were prominent in the psychology-psychiatry professions. Social science was a particular area of interest for Catholics. Paul Hanley Furfey, Jerome Kerwin, Waldemar Gurian, Goetz Briefs, Yves Simon, Heinrich Rommen, Regina Herzelf, and John L. Thomas were the equal of their secular peers. Martin McGuire and Ray Deferrari in classics, Stephen Kuttner or Porter Chandler in legal research, Ignatius Cox in ethical studies, John Quasten in patristics, John A. Ryan in theology, Gerald Ellard in liturgy, Karl Herzfeld in physics, Peter Guilday, John Tracy Ellis, Ross Hoffman, Oscar Halecki, Raymond Sontag, and Helen White in various aspects of historical research were not without deserved stature. And although American Catholic writers did not always identify with the Church or carry a "Catholic" message, as their English counterparts did, there were some distinguished literary personages on the American scene, including Agnes Repplier, Edwin O'Connor, John Farrow, Eugene Fowler, Anne Fremantle, Helen Iswolsky, Emmet Lavery, and Henry Morton Robinson.

This Catholic intellectual revival was not fully appreciated at all levels of the Church. In 1945 John M. Cooper, professor of anthropology at the Catholic University of America, set a new tone and developed the methodology for a new public discussion in which for two decades Catholic intellectual life and Catholic universities in particular would be chastised by in-house critics. Cooper's argument (*Commonweal*, May 25, 1945) was that "Catholic" contributions to scientific research were conspicuously rare. The issue raised by him later became a great debate over the question: Why was there so little Catholic contribution to the intellectual life of the nation? John Tracy Ellis, Thomas O'Dea, Gustav Wiegel, and Walter Ong were to become protagonists in this debate, each insisting that without recognized intellectual stature, Catholics would continue to be denied entry into the American mainstream.

Perhaps the larger question may be why this argument reached heated proportions at a time when Catholic education in the United States, including colleges and universities, was entering a golden age of development, both in quality as well as quantity. Success was everywhere visible, growth in students, staff, and facilities, a new sense of satisfaction with achievement. Catholics were appearing in the upper echelons of the business, labor, and governmental bureaucracies, were leading the way out of city slums into the unchartered bliss of the suburbs, taking their places in medicine and law, on the staffs of medical and law schools, on court benches, in the Wall Street Stock Exchanges, in Washington power centers. This was neither minimal nor insignificant progress—at least to observers at the grass-roots level—and progress directly related to the improved educational achievement of Catholics. As if to symbolize the extent of acceptance, a Catholic President appeared on the horizon as early as 1956, who would take the oath of office five years later.

But the multiplication of cultivated minds throughout the Church left the real issue in debate unresolved. That issue was scholarship. Scholarship means research and published findings. Creative scholarship means new research and new findings. These findings have to pass muster with competent intellectual peers. If Catholics wish to be taken seriously as scholars, they have to undertake this research, publish the results, and compete in the scholarly world for acceptance of their contributions. And if they want to be identified as Catholics also, they must take their places in a recognized Catholic intellectual tradition that goes back to Justin Martyr through the Church Fathers and the medieval Scholastics. That tradition continued to be visible in the later works of Mirandola, More, Descartes, Moeller, Newman, Pastor, Lingard, and the Bollandists. That there was a discernible lessening in creative intellectual pursuits after Trent and for reasons of introspective Catholic concern with survival, few would deny. Roman universities were not recognized as great centers of learning, even in theology. Seminaries, especially the prominent ones, did their work of training competent parish priests, but their faculties generally failed to establish scholarly credentials or to leave behind a scholarly record. In their turn bishops, who in spite of malingerers rarely can be accused of stifling creativity when creativity really wished to be heard, just as rarely failed to encourage, recognize, or reward the scholars they knew or could be found not far from the cathedral. This is the trend critics would like to reverse. They continue to raise serious doubts about Catholic scholarship ability, either because there is a genetic anti-intellectualism within Catholicism that precludes the desire for open scientific inquiry or because, improve as they may, Catholics still turn out an inferior scholarly product. At some point the shortcomings of Catholic scholars were blamed on the unnecessarily close ties that were allowed to develop between Church and academe, especially at the university level. In the post-Vatican II rush to gain scholarly respectability, a strenuous effort would be made to break these ties.

## II. Declaration of Independence

Independence Day for the American Catholic revolution in Catholic higher education was July 23, 1967, when twenty-six Catholic educators representing ten institutions signed the "Land O' Lakes Document," declaring independence of Church authority to be a desirable quality in those Catholic universities and colleges that intended to compete on equal footing with their secular counterparts. Catholic presence, henceforth, was to be maintained through the personal Christian witness of faculty and a campus ministry organized to serve religious needs. In other respects, the Catholic institution would follow the acceptable American model—ownership by lay trustees, not a religious order; scholars hired without regard to status in the Church; academic freedom in research and teaching as the rule. Catholic theology would be only one of many disciplines on campus dealing with religious thought. In essence, schools of Catholic theology were to become departments of religious studies.

The authors of this document were not turning their back on Catholic identity and service to the Church. They were merely making the modern institution more relevant to the contemporary scene, more acceptable to professional associations, to government and private funding agencies, and more capable of achieving academic excellence. Since traditional Church-related schools seemed condemned to live on the fringe of American society in much the same fashion as Amish schools, Orthodox Jewish yeshivas, and southern Baptist colleges, the time had come for the Catholic university to search for a modern identity. "Land O' Lakes" was presented as the "ideal type" of a new and highly desired form of Catholic higher education.

That 1967 meeting in Wisconsin was to have profound impact on the thinking, teaching, and spirit of all the 260 Catholic colleges in the United States, although in the judgment of a few, only about 6 had Harvard possibilities. "Land O' Lakes" became a manifesto for all Catholic educators, even though it was drafted without consultation with the institutions conducted by religious brothers and religious sisters, who probably were educating two thirds of the 340,000 American Catholic college students. This agreement came to dominate the thinking of the National Catholic Education Association's college and university department, which generally speaks for Catholic higher education. (Actually, the "Land O' Lakes" meeting did not intend to speak for everyone. Only seven large American institutions were represented— Boston College, Catholic University, Fordham, Georgetown, Notre Dame, St. Louis, and Seton Hall—and the guest participants selected included John Cogley, George Schuster, Archbishop Paul Hallinan of Atlanta, and Bishop John Dougherty of Seton Hall.)

Later, one of the cosigners denied that "Land O' Lakes" represented "a full philosophy or description of the Catholic university" and did not pose to be "holy writ" for the average Catholic college. Nonetheless, it was widely circulated through the machinery of Catholic higher education and into the houses of religious orders. *America* reprinted its text in entirety. Within a short space of time "Land O' Lakes" became the "right" position for leading spokesmen of Catholic higher education. While the diocesan press had some criticism of it, the document did not raise many eyebrows among American bishops.

What does this document of less than two thousand words say that makes it so important? The first paragraph sets the tone:

> The Catholic university today must be a university in the full modern sense of the word, with a strong commitment to and concern for academic excellence. To perform its teaching and research function effectively the Catholic university must have a true autonomy and academic freedom in the face of authority of whatever kind, lay or clerical, external to the academic community itself. To say this is simply to assert that institutional autonomy and academic freedom are essential conditions for life and growth and indeed of survival for Catholic universities as for all universities.

The Catholic distinctiveness is said to mean that:

> The Catholic university must be an institution, a community of learners or a community of scholars, in which Catholicism is perceptively present and effectively operative.

Included in the document are expressions concerning the importance and needed excellence of the theological faculty, of interdisciplinary dialogue covering a wide range of subjects. The Catholic university also must be the "critical reflective intelligence" for the Church, which will benefit from its counsel. (This, the document avers, "may well be one of the most important functions of the Catholic university of the future.") Additionally, the Catholic university does research, performs public service, operates quality collegiate schools, and is concerned about the pressing problems of our time.

Finally, the university organization will encourage student involvement, good student-faculty relationships, shared decision-making, experimentation, and to be Catholic in its ways.

While the word "Church" appears twice in the document—each time as the recipient of criticism *from the university*—at no other place in the document does the word "Church" appear again, not even to indicate what the Catholic university might be expected to receive *from the Church.*

## III. The "Jamaica Tea Party"

If "Land O' Lakes" in 1967 was the "Declaration of Independence" by a few Catholic universities from Church authority, the first shot toward independence was made two years earlier by faculty members at St. John's University in New York. The decision by St. John's Board of Trustees (on December 7, 1965) not to renew the contracts of thirty-three professors for 1966–67 was heard through the nation. Twenty-two faculty were suspended immediately (though with full pay) from all class activity for the duration of that academic year. This action, unprecedented in the recent annals of American higher education, was symbolic of that troubled decade of uproar on many fronts. Confrontation was the order of the day, with the media prone to dramatize charges of iniquity and inequity whenever they were made. The St. John's University case was no exception.

Five years later (in 1970), after St. John's University became the first private university in the United States to sign a labor agreement with the American Association of University Professors, the Vincentian fathers, who sponsored the university one century earlier, were still in charge. Their contract ultimately became a model in the university field. But 1965–66 was a year of conflict. Enrollment at the university had almost doubled in a decade—from 7,000 to 13,000. Faculty size alone grew from 250 to 650. What once was a family-type institution in Brooklyn now became big business in Jamaica. Most of the new faculty were "outsiders," young men affected by the turmoil around them, and in the university rush to hire teachers for bulging classrooms they were not always carefully screened. In turn, few Vincentians realized that bigness of its nature called for new administrative procedures and a new approach to faculty, many of whom were unfamiliar with the Vincentian tradition. In the early days of their relationship the Vincentians and AAUP leadership were more like stalking animals around a bird of prey than friends sitting down at a pleasant banquet. Activists, impatient with the progress of negotiations over conditions of employment, introduced the United Federation of College Teachers—AFL-CIO into the picture and a new issue was created. Negotiations became more heated, demands turned into threats, and for an entire semester beginning in September 1965 the classrooms of several schools became debating rather than teaching centers.

On October 25, 1965, President Joseph T. Cahill, C.M., reported to the university Board (composed of laymen and priests) the problem as he saw it:

> A deeper and more basic question is at issue: Does a Catholic university have the right to defend and protect its trust and identity? . . . Our answer is an unqualified yes. . . . St. John's University regards it as a solemn duty at this time to reaffirm its position as a Roman Catholic institution of higher learning. . . . This trust means that St. John's University must adhere not only to the highest standards of excellence, but also to the teaching, legislation, and spirit of the Roman Catholic Church. Nothing whatsoever shall be allowed to compromise this resolve.

From that moment on the controversy swung into high gear. But, as fully reported in Barbara Morris's research project for Columbia University (*St. John's: An Analytical Study of a Catholic University*), many of the problems, conflicts, and issues later associated with modern Catholic higher education were foreshadowed in this local dispute.

The burning issue for the faculty was union recognition. An AAUP chapter, organized in 1963, recognized by the administration in 1964, did not yet have a contract in 1965. The UFCT, invited to enter the picture by Rosemary Lauer, soon fell under the direction of a Chicago priest named Peter O'Reilly. Though hired only a few months earlier, he appeared as the UFCT's chief spokesman. The UFCT never had support of more than 10 per cent of the six hundred faculty members, but its leadership was very vocal and very anti-Vincentian. The year 1965 was also the time when direct and radical confrontations were profitable to protestors. Protestors managed to obtain direct access to media coverage, which tended to highlight the complaints and the alleged injustices. O'Reilly and Lauer argued forcefully that the faculty would not gain justice unless the Vincentians were forced out of St. John's, unless the traditional commitment to the Catholic Church was terminated.

The majority of St. John's faculty was already on record that academic freedom in classroom activity, in teaching or choice of textbooks, was not the issue. No internal complaints against St. John's were leveled on that score. The national AAUP, the Middle States accrediting agency, and the New York Department of Education up to this moment were favorable to the steps so far taken to turn a small family-type college into a large university. The UFCT, once upon the scene, branded the local AAUP as a company union and undertook a barrage of hostile publicity against the university. Then, sensing that the Vincentians might enter an agreement with the AAUP, the UFCT established an off-campus office to help relocate their members (none of whom had tenure) at other universities for the next academic year, 1966–67.

With a growing realization that the second semester was likely to be more turbulent for students than the first, the Board of Trustees met on December 7, 1965, and decided to declare thirty-three faculty contracts nonrenewable for the following year. Twenty-two were immediately suspended with pay but removed from classes during the spring term.

The strike at St. John's University began. How many of the faculty went on strike? Figures vary, but at no point were there more than seventy-nine on the picket line, of whom fifty-eight merely refused to cross a picket line. The bottom line of solid UFCT membership has been placed at twenty-one. Eighty-five per cent of the faculty worked every day and 90 per cent of the student body attended class daily. George Meany refused to intervene, and the Teamsters Union, many of whose sons attended St. John's, made their deliveries at night. St. John's University remained open for the duration of the semester.

But the public view of the controversy was quite different. The UFCT used interviews, press releases, and television to good effect. TV cameras came on Sunday to televise the campus, when no school was held, and the pictures, shown nationally during the week, suggested that the university had been closed down by popular support of the strike. The UFCT also put its professional contacts to good use. Shortly after the strike was called, the national AAUP, the New York State Education Department, and the Middle States accrediting agency, hitherto sympathetic, called for new investigations and new hearings, demanding the university to show cause why it should not be reprimanded.

The administration was vulnerable on one score. Although the decision to let thirty-three faculty go was legally correct, the suspension of twenty-two without a hearing had not been done to professors in a long time. Had the key leaders of UFCT alone been suspended—approximately eight in number—St. John's case would have been stronger. Professional associations, tending to side with professionals, inevitably would decide that the university had cut too wide a swath with its sword of suspension without hearing. The Board of Trustees, however, judged that public hearings would only be used to defame not only St. John's University but also relatively innocent faculty. Unprofessional conduct was already going on among some strikers. Spurious telegrams had been sent in the name of the university to other faculty members, appearing to cancel their contracts. The United Federation of Teachers asked its teacher members throughout the country to discourage young people from coming to St. John's, and even made an effort to inhibit other schools from accepting St. John's undergraduates into their graduate schools or to hire their graduates. The Board of Trustees decided to make no compromise, saying it was prepared to close St. John's rather than tolerate in the classroom nontenured

> persons who were academically, temperamentally, or otherwise unsuited for consideration as permanent members of the faculty, who were planning to leave without notices, or who were determined to obtain their will, regardless of the effect on the academic program of the university [Morris, *St. John's* . . .].

The strike had some unanticipated side effects.

1. The administration of St. John's received more sympathy from secular educators than from Catholic educators. The seculars had long experience with the bruising that goes with controversies like this. Several who in private communication expressed admiration for St. John's determination to fight for its principles excused themselves from making that support public.

The other surprise was the number of Catholics ready not only to disassociate themselves from the struggle but also to denounce St. John's. Well-known Catholic educators from New York to Chicago to San Francisco are on record with public criticism, making an effort to have the university condemned by Catholic bodies, devoting sections of articles or books to the "scandal"—without the critics having firsthand knowledge of the situation.

2. The surfacing of the "secularization issue" before the Second Vatican Council had completed its work came as a surprise.

Rosemary Lauer thought it perfectly proper for serious scholars to teach heresy on the Catholic campus (*America*, February 12, 1966). In 1976, during an interview with Barbara Morris, she still thinks that churches and universities don't mix:

> Faithfulness to the teaching Magisterium of the Catholic Church precluded the existence of a true university since the assent to a body of truth which comes from a source external to the academic community eliminates the freedom which is the essential characteristic of a university.

That was an important issue in the Jamaica controversy, which was to be raised in many places later.

## IV. The Disagreements in Between

The creation by Pius XII in 1949 of the International Federation of Catholic Universities, as an organ of the Sacred Congregation for Seminaries and Universities, was motivated by a desire to bring the growing academic world of the Church under the purview of Church authority. From its listening post at the center of Christendom, Rome was aware of intellectual stirrings in Europe, which had begun to create problems for the Church. At first Rome authorities acted toward college officials as if they were seminary rectors. The Second Vatican Council (1962–65) also created a situation that would put some distance (as part of collegiality) between a university federation and Rome. But it was difficult to anticipate that distance might lead to separation.

To understand the present state of affairs it may be advisable to begin at the end of a decade (1977) rather than at the beginning (1967), when the "Land O' Lakes" statement was issued. ("Land O' Lakes" as used here symbolizes the common positions of Fr. Theodore Hesburgh, C.S.C. and Fr. Robert J. Henle, S.J., the National Catholic Education Association, and the International Federation of Catholic Universities, whose presidency after Hesburgh went to Fr. Herve Carrier, S.J., of the Gregorian University, Rome.) There are minor differences among them, but their fundamental thesis is the same. Fr. Robert J. Henle, S.J.—who correctly defines the issue as "Catholic universities and the Vatican" (*America*, April 9, 1977)—capsulates the position of the Land O' Lakes group well and in clear language.

Fr. Henle is dedicated to an institution whose charter should state its Catholicity, whose commitment must be recognized and accepted as such by directors, administrators, faculty, staff, and students, whose faculty must be selected with this in mind, whose program must establish Catholicism and permeate society with its forms, attitudes, and ideas. He completes his presentation with a statement of those convictions. The practical question, however, is: How does a Catholic university attain these goals in contemporary society? Fr. Henle answers: By the efforts of the people within the institution. In support of his position he points out correctly the situations where institutions under juridical control of the Church have lost their substantive Catholicism, and then he adds, "while institutions with no juridical dependence are *vital centers of Catholic culture*" (emphasis added). This may touch the raw edge of the questions: Is a Catholic university to find its justification in the transmission of *Catholic culture?* What is the place of *Catholic faith* in this university? Fr. Henle says, "University cannot simply be designated as a pastoral arm of the Church." But if not, what is the significance of the word "Catholic"? Culture can be inspired by a faith view, but the term "Catholic" essentially refers to a divinely revealed faith.

Even if this apparent perplexity of definitions can be clarified as nothing more than a semantic problem, a practical difficulty remains. The "Catholics within" the present university command—who are the guarantors of ongoing Catholicity—are the products of what Fr. Henle calls "a typical ghetto-type Catholic college." They are still large in numbers and their commitment was forged in a university system shaped under precise Catholic terms. One president of a large and prominent women's college stated the future problem this way: "I worry about continued Catholic commitment here. It probably will last a little longer at the university uptown where at least fifty priests still exercise some influence. But I have lost most of my nuns and the few I have wear no identity, so I wonder just how long we can hold on. The newer faculty or the visitors would hardly know this place was Catholic, if the name did not indicate that it was." There is one other problem to maintaining Catholicity indefinitely. Since Catholic faculty members now contest Church positions in their classrooms, since the defections of priests and religious are numerous, some of whom maintain key positions at Catholic universities, how is the future Catholic commitment to be protected by the Catholics trained under such conditions?

Drawing on the Roman document of 1972, Fr. Henle goes to the heart of his argument:

> Most important of all—and a point not fully accepted—is the recognition that a genuinely and substantively Catholic university need have no juridical dependence on or relationship to the Vatican or to any ecclesiastical superior. This is a truly historical breakthrough and one which will solve many practical and political problems in Catholic higher education in a variety of countries. *It can also serve as a precedent for other types of Catholic institutions in post-Vatican II society.* [emphasis added] . . .
>
> Acceptance of the principle that juridical control by an ecclesiastical authority is not the essence of a Catholic university is, in my opinion, essential for the future development, in some cases for the very existence of Catholic universities. . . .

The [1972] report clearly recognizes the academic freedom of the Catholic university, not as privileges granted by the Vatican but as inherent in the nature and function of any university.

To justify this detached position Fr. Henle speaks of "great social pressures." He points to the social pressures on Catholic universities in Communist and Muslim countries and in Japan, but also to the inspiration of Vatican II. Two translations of Fr. Henle's Council citation— the Abbot version used by him, and the more recent Flannery retranslation of the same paragraph (cf. *Pastoral Constitution on the Church in the Modern World*, No. 36), read as follows:

| *Abbot Translation* | *Flannery Translation* |
|---|---|
| If by autonomy of earthly affairs we mean that created things and societies themselves enjoy their own laws and values, which must gradually be deciphered, put to use and regulated by men, then it is right to demand that autonomy. | If by the autonomy of earthly affairs is meant the gradual discovery, exploitation and ordering of the laws and values of matter and society, then the demand for the autonomy is perfectly in order. |

What point is Fr. Henle trying to make? Simply that the Council Fathers' statement on the autonomy of secular organizations (for example, labor unions) applies univocally to the Catholic university. This certainly is the position of Land O' Lakes. Whether this position can be vindicated by the documents from the Second World Congress of Catholic Universities in November 1972 remains to be seen.

What are *not* areas of disagreement?

• Not excellence, because Catholic universities and colleges can be as excellent as any others.

• Not the importance of superior faculties or the penetration of the secular world through research.

• Not the convictions of those who maintain they can guarantee Catholicity, at least for a time, without juridical ties to the Church.

• Not Catholic presence through good liturgy or good campus ministers.

• Not the money pressures that threaten to drive much Catholic higher education out of business.

• Not the importance of academic prestige denied to Church-related schools as a matter of secular principle.

• Not the attractiveness of government money, which almost everywhere is available to Catholic colleges, excellent or not, if they are prepared to mute their relationship to the Church.

What are areas of disagreement?

• Whether autonomy from the Church represents a philosophy of Catholic education at any level.

• Whether Catholic universities should compete for government money on secular terms.

• Whether the final product of Land O' Lakes will be Catholic at all.

In Fr. Henle's view two propositions are basic to his concept of the future Catholic university:

1. No juridical relationship with the Church.
2. Complete academic freedom within the university—and this means the same freedom for the theology scholar as for the economist, biologist, or geopolitician.

In controversy the problem is never the documents but their meaning. Fr. Henle uses Vatican II to justify autonomy for the Catholic university because the Council Fathers approve autonomy for human societies in their management of "earthly affairs." The document he cites deals with the problems of the world, about the AFL-CIO, the United Nations, the University of Chicago. It is not dealing with the Catholic Interracial Council, the Catholic Association for International Peace, or Georgetown University, all of which by definition are concerned with more than earthly affairs. Even if Georgetown University were engaged only in "earthly affairs," for which Fr. Henle demands special autonomy, the same section of *Gaudium et Spes* (No. 36) that he quotes contains a sentence that he does not quote.

| *Abbot Translation* | *Flannery Translation* |
|---|---|
| But if the expression, the independence of temporal affairs is taken to mean that created things do not depend on God, | However, if by the term "the autonomy of earthly affairs" is meant that material being does not depend on God and that |

and that man can use them without the Creator, anyone who
acknowledges God will see how
false such a meaning is.

man can use it as if it had no
relation to its Creator, then the
falsity of such a claim will be
obvious to anyone who believes
in God.

If the term "Catholic" is used, it is clear that the Council does not
grant autonomy that frees members of the Church, individually or
collectively, from dependence on the Church.

There are certain ancillary aspects to this discussion of the principles
that underlie (or ought not to underlie) the modern Catholic university, aspects which may be as important as the subject matter. These
are the attitudes of the participants. Fr. Henle credits Gabriel Cardinal
Garrone, prefect of the Congregation for Catholic Education, for having "cordial relations" with the university world, but when Garrone's
positions are distasteful, he reminds the reader that Christ founded the
papacy, not the Vatican bureaucracy. Henle admits threatening Garrone in 1972 with responsibility for forcing "a number of Catholic institutions [to] immediately renounce their *official* status" [emphasis
his] if the Holy See published norms for Catholic universities"
(*America*, April 9, 1977). In the face of the possibility that Rome
might move unilaterally against Catholic universities, Henle says "the
1972 Roman document should be regarded as a finalization of basic positions, at least for the foreseeable future." Later, addressing himself to
university activity, he advises his peers: "We should freely and crea-
tively move beyond it [the 1972 Roman document]. We certainly do
not need or want a new rigidity."

## V. The Various Documents

Between 1967 and 1977 meetings were held by the Land O' Lakes
group among themselves, within the Councils of NCEA, with the International Federation of Catholic Universities, and with officers of the
Congregation for Catholic Education in Rome. Many of these documents are frequently at odds with each other on the key questions.
Even more subtle are the omissions from one document to another, the
byplay among conflicting parties, and sometimes the not so subtle open
confrontations. Rome is criticized publicly more than once or told what
answers will not be accepted from the Congregation for Catholic Education. Gabriel Cardinal Garrone and Archbishop (now Cardinal)
Joseph Schoeffer are prefect and secretary, respectively, of the Roman
Congregation, to which Fr. Henle refers. Both were involved in the Sec-

ond Vatican Council, one as archbishop of Toulouse (France), the other as bishop of Eisenstadt (Germany). Each gave up his see as part of Pope Paul's internationalization of his Curia by bringing to Rome officers who had pastoral experience in other places. Garrone and Schoeffer were considered "progressives" at the Council. While Americans once complained that Romans did not understand the "American situation" in higher education, these two prelates were good learners. Both had pastoral backgrounds and were considered "open" to new ideas and proposals. They were patient during dialogue, never losing their tempers even if critics did. They also recognized their role as the Pope's chief officers for Catholic education throughout the world.

The two curial cardinals recognized the potential for danger in certain definitions or postures, but instead of argument, tended to suggest a variation in language, new terminology, or the elimination of controverted phraseology, so that the edited text permitted an interpretation satisfactory to the Holy See.

The very diplomacy created difficulties later on for Cardinal Garrone. He found himself misunderstood or quoted in ways that did not represent his thinking or his understanding of the documents that he, as the Pope's agent, had endorsed. For example, shortly after the 1972 meeting, Fr. Henle, then president of Georgetown University, held a press conference (January 1973) in which he announced his pleasure that the recent Congress "endorse the principles of academic freedom and autonomy for Catholic colleges and universities." This unqualified statement did not meet with Cardinal Garrone's approval.

Cardinal Garrone and Archbishop Schoeffer entered the world of Catholic Higher Education after the 1968 meeting of IFCU in Kinshasa, Congo (now Zaire), where the majority of IFCU delegates rejected two basic Land O' Lakes propositions: (1) Catholic universities could exist without a juridical relationship to Church authority. (2) Institutional commitment could be left to self-determination of the universities themselves. After this impasse between divergent forces, the Congregation for Catholic Education in Rome decided to take an active role in reconciling the groups.

1. *Cardinal Garrone's (1969) Survey of Catholic Universities*

Garrone decided first to survey world university opinion to test thinking about the role of the Catholic university, the place of laity, of non-Catholics, and of bishops in the establishment and government of academic institutions. Rome also had in mind an international congress of universities, where the survey answers would be discussed.

The different approaches to Cardinal Garrone's questions are found in the answers of Fr. Henle and those of Fr. Joseph T. Cahill, C.M., president of St. John's University, New York. The answers were distributed to university presidents, with the permission of Fr. Hesburgh, on February 15, 1969, and were sent to Rome on February 28, 1969.

| *Fr. Robert J. Henle, S.J.* | *Fr. Joseph T. Cahill, C.M.* |
|---|---|
| It is very important that the atmosphere on a Catholic campus be ecumenical and open, that it not be burdened with legalisms and juridical limitations. | The Catholic university should be established and operate within a given diocese with the consent of the local ordinary and according to the provisions of Canon Law (although the bishop should respect academic autonomy). |
| Magisterium is effectively present in the Catholic universities primarily through the conscience of the individual Catholics. | The Magisterium is concretely present in the Catholic universities as the most important guideline in the teaching of Catholic theology and, where the sciences touch, of Catholic philosophy. |
| It is vitally important that the Catholic university have at least the same autonomy as any other private university and more autonomy than the state university. This means that there must not be any completely external authority, whether a bishop, a religious superior, a government official, or anyone else who makes final decisions on university matters. | The obvious tension which arises through the recognition of both axioms (that is, autonomy and Catholicity) must be regulated by norms laid down by the Sacred Congregation after study and consultation with all Catholic institutions. We respectfully stress the word *all* because certain outspoken Catholic educators and educational groups, even of a quasi-official status, do not necessarily reflect the thinking of the rest of Catholic-educational America. |
| In the future it will no longer be possible to say of any real university that it is owned and operated by any given group. | [Without] religious institutes these Catholic universities would not have existed or been preserved. This fundamental relationship between the university and the religious institute gives the institute a moral right. In American law, it is called equity. |

Primarily the catholicity [small "c" in text] of the institution depends upon the presence in the institution of Catholics who are concerned about the faith and about the catholicity of the institution.

It is most important that, without inhibiting the autonomy and freedom of the university, the rights of the sponsoring religious institute, the diocese, and the Church be preserved.

The American Catholic university must have "academic freedom" or "scientific liberty" that is every bit as genuine and real as that which exists in non-Catholic institutions.

No Catholic university need worry about the granting of true academic freedom, which is a necessary part of a true university. Academic freedom obviously implies and expects concomitant academic responsibility. Our university, for example, can and has endorsed without difficulty the 1940 Statement on Academic Freedom of the AAUP. [This permitted the religious college to obtain at the time of hiring prior commitment of faculty to respect the religious commitment of the college or university.]

2. *First Congress of Catholic Universities in Rome* (April 25–May 1, 1969)

Thirty-nine delegates from twenty-two nations assembled for this week-long Congress. Most of the intense discussions centered on the nature of the Catholic university and its relationship to Church authority. The conclusions of the Congress were written as follows:

The essential characteristics of a Catholic university are:

A. A Christian Inspiration not only of individuals but of the community as well;
B. A continuing reflection in the light of the Christian faith upon the growing treasury of human knowledge;
C. Fidelity to the Christian message as it comes to us through the Church;
D. An institutional commitment to the service of Christian thought and education.

All universities that realize these conditions are Catholic universities, whether canonically erected or not. The purposes of the Catholic university can be pursued by different means and modalities according to diverse situations of time and place, and taking seriously into account the different natures of the disciplines taught in the university.

The Land O' Lakes group succeeded in obtaining approval for language with which it could live. Delegates who one year earlier at Kinshasa voted against identifying the word "Catholic" with a university that lacked a bond with the Church, approved this language because it admitted a traditional meaning. The "Land O' Lakes" group was pleased, also, not only because "Vatican officials had begun to listen," but mainly because their American interpretations of the language made alternative understandings possible.

3. *Response of Rome to the First Congress* (*November 30, 1969*)

The forty-three cardinals and eight bishops who comprise the Sacred Congregation for Catholic Education met in plenary session October 3–4, 1969, to discuss the "position paper" presented by the May Congress. The responses given by the Congregation to the Congress, while described as "friendly and sincere, tactful and intelligent, pastoral and paternal," took positions directly opposite to what the University Congress proposed, especially as the latter was being interpreted by the Land O' Lakes.

The cardinals and bishops went to the heart of the autonomy-academic freedom issue:

A Catholic university must be seen as existing not only in the world, but also in the Catholic community, and therefore it is related to those who preside over the Catholic community: the Catholic hierarchy. Obviously, this specific purpose of the Catholic university cannot be realized if those whose proper function it is to be the authentic guardians of the deposit of faith are relegated to a marginal place in its life and activity (*Response of the Sacred Congregation*).

The underlying assumption of the Land O' Lakes position is that the state and the secular world now establish the rules governing the university world; the Catholic Church and the Catholic university must accept those rules, especially concerning autonomy and academic freedom. The bishops responded: Not so; Catholic universities have their root in the Catholic world, too; however much they must obey secular rules, they must obey Church rules also.

The bishops also rejected the principle that Church-owned institutions and state-chartered Catholic institutions relate to the teaching office (Magisterium) in different ways. To admit a difference would mean that Church authority could deal effectively with heretics in a seminary, but not in a Catholic university. The Congregation insisted that institutional commitment to the Magisterium is the same for all Catholic institutions of higher learning.

The cardinals and bishops had other fine points of objection to the university declaration (telling the academicians that they do not distinguish accurately "the university properly so called and other institutions concerned with higher studies"), but their chief answers represent the central concerns of the Holy See. The Congregation's response made one thing clear: The issue in controversy was not bishops' domination of the university, but bishops' pre-eminence in the formulations of Catholic truth with which the Catholic university advertises itself to be concerned.

The Congregation asked the universities to restudy the matter once more and report their findings to Rome by March 1970.

4. *Response of Universities to Rome* (1970)

The Land O' Lakes group sent their reply to the Cardinal on February 27, 1970, in which they made the following points:

A. The cardinals and bishops base their responses "on assumptions and principles which are no longer operative, tenable, or even relevant to American higher education."

B. "Even well-intentioned efforts by Rome to formulate universal norms or guidelines based upon such assumptions and principles would seriously jeopardize the future of important Catholic institutions of higher learning in the United States."

C. "It is a sheer impossibility to state more specifically and more completely the elements comprising the image of the Catholic university."

D. After stressing the importance of federal and state aid, the response adds:

"Moreover, in the American academic community freedom to research and freedom to teach are limited only by the scholarly community. Our leading Catholic institutions would find it well nigh impossible to attract and hold outstanding scholars and professors if there were any semblance of control or establishment of policy from Rome."

E. "Finally, any attempt 'to lay down the principles and suitable norms which should regulate Catholic university structure and life today' by an outside agency would violate the primary canons of the academic and professional crediting groups whose approval is a necessary fact of life in the American academic community.

The signers closed respectfully with a request "that the Sacred Congregation refrain from promulgating 'the principles and suitable norms which would regulate Catholic university structure and life today.'"

The meaning of the American message was clear: In order to satisfy the requirements of secular society, it was imperative that there be no directives to Catholic universities from the Church.

5. *"The Grottaferrata Document"* (February 3–5, 1972)

This document, named after the religious house outside Rome in which it was composed, was drafted in preparation for the Second International Congress of Catholic Universities, planned for late 1972. The Grottaferrata Document was also criticized by the Congregation. The continued anxieties of the Holy See about the Catholic identity of universities are expressed in these statements.

A. "Fidelity to the message of Christ as it is passed on by the Church"—as an essential characteristic of a Catholic university —must not be stated once at the beginning of the text, but must inspire the whole document.

B. The responsibility of the research theologian is not stressed as much as his freedom.

C. The relationship of hierarchy is not merely with the theology department but also with the whole university.

D. Episcopal conferences should take a more "lively interest in their responsibilities regarding Catholic universities."

E. Since theology departments also have candidates for the priesthood among their students, bishops have vital interest in the courses.

F. "One cannot exclude the possibility that ecclesiastical authority in carrying out its duty, should its [nonjuridical] intervention prove ineffective, can declare that this institution no longer offers sufficient guarantees to be recognized as Catholic. . . .

The university on its part shares in the responsibility for the common good of the Church."

These last lines represent as close as Rome ever came to scolding the representatives of the International Federation of Catholic Universities.

6. *The Catholic University in the Modern World* (November 20–29, 1972)

This is the famous document approved at the Second Congress of Catholic Universities in November 1972 by delegates representing institutions all over the world.

The text of the document contains some refinement of earlier university positions:

A. Against the position that universities without canonical ties are somewhat related to Church authority differently than those who have such ties, the document makes clear:

"Every Catholic university's fidelity to the Christian message as it comes to us through the Church involves a recognition of the teaching of the Church in doctrinal matters" [No. 15].

B. Against the position that the Catholic university can stand outside the Catholic community, the document states:

"When we affirm the autonomy of the university we do not mean that it stands outside the law: We are speaking rather of the *internal autonomy* [emphasis added] and integrity which flow from its very nature and purpose" [No. 20].

[The autonomy of which the document speaks means a selection of academic staff, student-admission policy, curriculum planning, research projects, and apportionment of budget. It also includes granting academic degrees. Nothing is said of autonomy for theology or pastoral ministry [No. 21].

C. Against those who consider academic freedom an absolute, the document says:

"The statutes of each institution should safeguard such freedom, taking due account of the religious inspiration which characterizes a university precisely as Catholic" [No. 28].

D. Against those who assert the right to keep the hierarchy at arm's length, the document, while giving university officials the primary responsibility for Catholic character and requesting that interventions by bishops respect the academic and administrative procedures of the university, nonetheless states that when the truth of the Christian message is at stake the bishop has the right and the duty to intervene (1) by advising the person or persons involved, (2) by advising the administration, (3) in an extreme case by a public declaration. The voice of the bishops may also be heard when the pastoral work of the Church is adversely affected by the work of a university "committed to fidelity to the Christian message" [Nos. 58–60].

7. *Cardinal Garrone's Covering Letter* (April 25, 1973)

Rome issued its second "scolding" five months later, when Cardinal Garrone, reporting on the review of the 1972 document by thirty-seven cardinals and bishops belonging to his congregation, issued a covering letter. In this he requested "that whenever this document is presented to anyone the full contents of this letter are also presented *at the same time* [emphasis added]." The reasons for this demand were the misuses of the 1972 document, especially in the United States.

The Garrone letter is interesting for what it enjoins.

A. The French text is authentic, not the English or Spanish version. The reason for this is that French has precise technical terminology which cannot easily be misunderstood. Vague English terms were used at times to suggest varying meaning.
B. While the 1972 document represents "a considerable improvement on that of 1969" and is "valid," it "needs improvement" because it is not explicit on two points:
  (1) "On the necessity for each Catholic university to set out formally and without equivocation either in statutes or in some other internal document, its character and commitment as 'Catholic.'
  (2) "On the necessity for every Catholic university to create within itself appropriate and efficacious instruments so as to be able to put into effect proper self-regulation in the sectors of faith, morality, and discipline."
  [This point is at least as important as juridical ties to Rome or bishops, because it is self-discipline in important Catholic areas that many Catholic institutions of higher learning have given up.]

C. "The document must be considered 'as a whole,' so that no single element can be extrapolated from its entirety and used out of context, especially regarding the treatment given to autonomy of teaching and research."

D. "Although the document envisages the existence of university institutions without statutory bonds linking them to ecclesiastical authority, it is to be noted that this *in no way* [emphasis added] means that institutions are removed from those relationships with the ecclesiastical hierarchy which must characterize all Catholic institutions."

## VI. Fr. Theodore Hesburgh and Notre Dame

If the Land O' Lakes group has a leader, it is Fr. Hesburgh. If Notre Dame ever becomes a multiversity it will be his determination that did it. His accomplishments in the public forum, in government, in representing the Church give him a social influence unexcelled in our time, more than was ever exercised by John A. Ryan, Francis J. Haas, or John Courtney Murray. The older men's essential thinking on sociopolitical matters gained the endorsement of Church authority. At this time Fr. Hesburgh is in the vanguard of those Catholics who wish to redefine the Catholic university and perhaps to redefine the Catholic Church, too. Since the issues are important and Fr. Hesburgh is a well-known exponent of dialogue, his personal views and administration call for the same analysis he applies to the Church and its leadership.

Catholic concern over "the Hesburgh position" is best directed at his acceptance of the Alexander Meiklejohn Award (the first to a Catholic) from the American Association of University Professors in June 1970. The award for "outstanding contribution to the cause of academic freedom" was itself inoffensive. But the terms under which the award was given and accepted are of a different order and quality. In justifying the presentation, the AAUP went out of its way to highlight the fact that Fr. Hesburgh not only believed a "Catholic university must have a true autonomy and academic freedom in the face of authority of whatever kind, lay or clerical, external to the academic community itself," but also, as evidence of his serious intent, the AAUP mentioned the fact that Notre Dame scholars were in the center of the confrontation with Pope Paul VI over *Humanae Vitae*. The citation praised him finally because "external ecclesiastical controls at some other Catholic universities have not been permitted at the University of Notre Dame" (*AAUP Bulletin*, June 1970).

The University of Notre Dame refers to its "Catholic character" as follows: "Even if all other Christian universities were to forfeit their religious character (as many formerly Christian universities have done) we affirm that Notre Dame must continue to be a Catholic university." But in view of the Meiklejohn award, the pressing question must be asked: Is a public challenge to the Pope when he makes a solemn pronouncement on a serious moral matter a praiseworthy feature for an important segment of a Catholic university? Or consistent with its nature? The award as given and received is at least symbolic of the willingness to separate a Catholic university from the teaching of the Church.

In common with many large Catholic universities in recent years, Notre Dame has experienced its share of "horror stories"; illicit liturgical experiments and practices; ex-priests hired without regard to the sensitivity of Rome, the local ordinary, or alumni; people like Ti Grace Atkinson on campus with vulgarities; a motion picture, banned by the police department, screened nonetheless for willing undergraduates. These may be "peccadillos" that reflect the turbulence of our times, more than administrative laxity, with which the best-intentioned university found it difficult to deal. Or, since they would not have been tolerated formerly, they symbolize a shift in a university's sense of responsibility.

"Peccadillos" resulting from the exuberance of youthful miscreants take on a different significance if their repeated occurrence creates the impression that such activities are reconcilable with a Catholic university's purpose. It is fashionable in books like Hesburgh's Notre Dame: Triumph in Transition (by two ex-campus journalists, Joel R. Connolly and Howard J. Dooley) to ridicule the old Notre Dame for watching students "more closely than the average galley slave" and to praise Fr. Hesburgh for unleashing scholars from bed checks, daily Mass, and Communion counts. But, as one Notre Dame alumnus had reason in 1974 to remind the administration, no Catholic university can forswear its "responsibility as a governing community." He called the abandonment of discipline "one of the great intellectual failures of our time." Among the high priorities of a Catholic university, in his view, was loyalty to the teaching authority of the Church. He also raised questions as to how an "independent Catholic university" can exist without reference to Church authority, about what "Catholic character" means if the university does not speak in the name of the Church. While American courts invented the phrase in loco parentis (with hundreds of judicial decisions to prove it) to justify the right of colleges and universities to regulate campus life (parent substitution being as good as any other justification), the Catholic university, standing in loco communitatis Christianae, offered no such rationale. Its differentiating characteristics,

its special curriculum, its unique pastoral life did not depend on a delegation of authority or permission from parents, but belonged to it by
virtue of the unique Church community the Catholic university was.

The meeting of the Planned Parenthood Federation of America on
the Notre Dame campus in June 1973 also indicated the directional
drift of Notre Dame. Planned Parenthood is not a simple community
group, nor an association of birth-control clinics. This federation is an
integral part of a well-financed international organization of population
controllers (1) whose philosophy of sexuality, marriage, and the purposes of life itself are violently opposed to what the Catholic Church
stands for, (2) that places as much stress on re-education of the world's
population to its views as it does on dispensing prophylactics, and (3)
is in the forefront and the backfront of the pro-abortion crusade, engag-
ing in these efforts with an unusual amount of determination. Planned
Parenthood uses these meetings as opportunities to organize new units
of influence.

Bishop Leo Pursley of the Fort Wayne-South Bend diocese publicly
protested the meeting when pro-abortion positions taken on campus
went unchallenged by the university administration. The university's
defense of its decision to permit Planned Parenthood on campus was
twofold: Approval had been given at a lower level without the knowledge of top administration; second, it was a proper function of a university. Few really believed the first explanation. This event had too much
significance for the Catholic community to be the result of anything
but a top-management decision.

Fr. Hesburgh's personal explanation, when it appeared (*Origins*
October 25, 1973), can be summarized as follows: Neither the Church
nor the university can be harmed by the public disagreement of sincere
men; universities often discuss ideas like communism, with which administration officers disagree; a certain type of Catholic seems to revel
in publicizing such university discussions; we must discuss; if intelligent
Catholics had held such discussions in the past, instead of mainly talking to themselves, we might not now be in the present deplorable situation.

Under the most extenuating circumstances, Fr. Hesburgh's explanation would reflect a naïve understanding of the history and functioning
of the Planned Parenthood Federation. Catholics had been dialoguing
with Planned Parenthood prior to 1963, when it sponsored Dr. John
Rock's book *The Time Has Come*. Cass Canfield, chairman, and
Donald Strauss, president, were able and adept expositors of their cause
to major Catholic family-life leaders, not only in the United States but
also in Europe. During the Vatican Council their representatives

visited Catholic intellectuals in places like Louvain, even in Rome itself. While these gentlemanly officers sincerely found abortion repugnant, assuring Catholics that "contraceptions now will forestall widespread abortion later," their executive director, Dr. Alan B. Guttmacher, openly insisted that abortion was part of Planned Parenthood's medical and population policy. After ten years of private and public dialogue between Catholic leaders and Planned Parenthood officers, only ignorance of the record or naïveté could incline anyone in 1973 to believe that Planned Parenthood was open to any dialogue that would alter its basic positions. Planned Parenthood was interested only in dialogue that would enhance its prestige among audiences where its following was weak. Notre Dame provided that opportunity.

Fr. James Burtchaell, Notre Dame's provost at the time, later advanced the Hesburgh argument one step further. After deploring the homicidal abortion program of Planned Parenthood, Fr. Burtchaell asked (*Notre Dame* magazine, August 1973): "Is it not appropriate that on the campus of a great Catholic university we invite Planned Parenthood to enlarge their discussion and that the people earnestly dialogue about what family and child-bearing and infant life are meant to be?" This question might have come better from someone who had not bitterly attacked Pope Paul's *Humanae Vitae* within weeks of its issuance (*Commonweal*, November 15, 1968). Even so, this question can be answered in a sense other than the one intended by Burtchaell. First, the issue in controversy is not the discussion of an idea—for example, the advisability or inadvisability of abortion. Nor might there be objection to an open debate of conflicting and equal sides on the contraception issue. The propriety of a pro-abortion organization regrouping or reshaping its forces on a Catholic campus is the issue. The Catholic university, like any well-managed society, usually excludes whatever threatens or is likely to threaten its basic values. A meeting of this kind could be justified if the ideology of the Church and Planned Parenthood about marriage and sexuality no longer were in conflict. In the same connection there is also to be considered the counsel given by Fr. Hesburgh to weak Catholic leadership to imitate the vigor demonstrated by Jewish leadership in the pursuit of Jewish goals. According to Fr. Hesburgh, Jewish leadership knows how to get what it wants (aid to Israel) and how to frustrate what Jewish leadership does not want (deny trade favors to the Soviet Union for its treatment of Jews). It is not likely, in the presence of this determination, that the American Nazi Party could organize a convention on the campus of Yeshiva University? Possibly not even on the Harvard campus.

The core of the difficulty may be philosophical. If Catholic academic leaders become as uncertain of their values as their secular counterparts, they may develop a similar inaptitude to take authoritative stands. Or they may be satisfied to be critics of authoritative positions. The Catholic university leadership recently has expressed resentment at Church authority looking over its shoulder. It seeks freedom to do as well for the future Church what older educators did in the past.

But if that is the program, what may be expected of the future graduates? What more is promised beyond scholars qualified to render unique service to state and Church? Fr. Hesburgh himself provides certain answers to questions like "Where is the Church going? What will it be like when my children are my age?" (put to him by an alumnus). His response in *Notre Dame* magazine (June 1974) explains what the new education is getting away from and where it will likely lead.

First, his attitude to the *old* Church:

> When I grew up, the Church had all the answers to every conceivable question and the answers were always black and white. We were right and everyone else was wrong. There was no partial truth, no tentative searching, no intellectual modesty. The leadership simply said yes or no, right or wrong, and that was that. . . . I am, of course, speaking somewhat in caricature but certainly not altogether so.

Very few Catholics at the local level—parish priests or parishioners—would recognize this description of the Church they knew, nor about their pastors or confessors having all the answers or being autocrats. There was a great deal of tentativeness in the pre-Vatican Church and freedom for Catholics, including priests, to do far more than bishops are credited with permitting, tolerating, or ignoring.

But even if things were as bad as Fr. Hesburgh says they were, what does he suggest for the future?

First, he suggests Catholics rid themselves of the old frames of reference, the old modes of thought and leadership trained in that mold. These elements he considers disastrous to the "open Church," one that has no more safety, security, peace, or orderliness than the world itself. Openness to him means finding others more than having others finding us, more collegiality, more "moral weight placed upon the informed individual conscience of the lay Christian." Openness means leaders who establish credibility before they expect followership. Unlike olden days, deep involvement in political action is a must. ("In the past Catholic laymen and laywomen in the Church were said to be those who prayed and paid.") This new Church will have unity, but uniformity will not prevail. "More progress will be made unofficially than in the context of the ecclesiastical establishments," concludes Fr. Hesburgh.

Fr. Hesburgh's inquiring alumnus has reason to believe that new Church Catholics will be liberated from controls, that the individual conscience will have options in the face of uncertain or nondirective guidance, that the chief moral imperative will be political-action post-Vatican II goals. These newer forms will be institutionalized not by bishops, but by unofficial forces within the Church. The question might enter the alumnus' mind: Are these the main elements of Roman Catholicism?

Fr. Hesburgh seems to be leading Notre Dame in the direction of his answers. Intellectual gatherings in recent years on the Notre Dame campus incline toward the kind of Church he envisages. Dialogue at Notre Dame involves customarily the same single ideological party within the Church. In January 1976, for example, Notre Dame conducted a symposium for almost a hundred leading Catholics (including sixteen bishops) on the subject "evangelization." Archbishop Joseph L. Bernardin, the president of NCCB, led the conference off with the compelling need to provide the right prelude to the next two days' discussion. He talked on the Magisterium of the bishops and the Pope, reminding his audience, in the words of Vatican II, that "Bishops, teaching in communion with the Roman pontiff, are to be respected by all as witnesses to divine and Catholic truth. In matters of faith and morals, the bishops speak in the name of Christ, and the faithful are to accept their teaching and adhere to it with a religious assent of soul (*Lumen Gentium* 25)." All reports of the symposium indicated that the Bernardin presentation encountered a chilly response. This should not be surprising when the invitees were largely composed of those who in recent years have contested Church authorities—John Egan, David O'Brien, Michael Novak, John Murphy, John Padberg, Agnes Cunningham, Joseph Cuneen, David Tracy, Michael Gannon, etc.

Eighteen months later (June 1977), Notre Dame sponsored a colloquium entitled "Vatican III—The Work to Be Done," designed to draw up the "new agenda" for the Church. Led by writers for *Consilium* (a theological publication that regularly dissents from Church teaching) and selected members of the Catholic Theological Society, the colloquium covered the favorite topics of theological change-makers: the Roman Curia, the election of bishops, intercommunion with Protestants, deviation from traditional sexual norms, remarriage after divorce, optional celibacy, validity of Protestant ministries (all Hans Küng's favorite themes), about which the bishops have spoken not once but many times and in ways directly contrary to what

*Concilium* and the Catholic Theological Society characteristically promote. In scrutinizing the list of invitees for these sessions, many names of philosophers and theologians, who support Magisterium on all these subjects, seem to be absent.

In 1967 John Cogley, one of the original Land O' Lakers, already convinced that the concept "Catholic university" was an illusion, said this about Notre Dame (*Commonweal*, June 2, 1967):

> Today Notre Dame is the best Catholic university in the nation. But this is so precisely because in a certain sense Notre Dame is the least "Catholic" university.

## VII. *The National Catholic Education Association*

NCEA, almost three quarters of a century old (it was established in 1904), was founded to improve Catholic education at all levels. A national organization since 1927, NCEA boasts an affiliation with approximately 15,000 Catholic institutions. About four out of five of the 250 Catholic colleges and universities are associated with NCEA's College and University Department.

For most of its history the priest in charge of NCEA (the professionals) was also the head of the Department of Education of the National Catholic Welfare Conference (renamed in 1978 the Association of Catholic Colleges and Universities). Up until 1966 there was little to distinguish the policies of NCEA from those of NCWC. When Msgr. George Johnson suddenly dropped dead at Trinity College's graduation (1944), Archbishop John T. McNicholas, O.P., of Cincinnati, then presiding bishop at NCWC, brought in his own priest, Msgr. Frederick G. Hochwalt, to manage both the education world of the professionals (NCEA) and the bishops (NCWC). Hochwalt held both posts until his death in 1966.

Following Vatican II and the reorganization of the American bishops into the United States Catholic Conference, Msgr. Hochwalt's double role was terminated. USCC continued to have a director of education, whereas NCEA obtained its own executive secretary (Fr. Albert Koob, O. Praem.) and an associated secretary for college affairs in the person of Fr. Clarence W. Friedman, S.J. The detachment of NCEA from the bishop-controlled USCC took on more than symbolic importance, since it occurred at the very moment Fr. Hesburgh was president of the International Federation of Catholic Universities. The social turbulence of the 1960s had begun to reach Catholic campuses and the religious orders that managed the Church's higher-education enterprise. When

Fr. Friedman ended his tour of duty at NCEA (1974), he summed up the changes to occur in Catholic higher education during the previous decade:

> . . . establishment of independent self-perpetuating boards of trustees in Catholic colleges and universities; the development of a concept of campus ministries and greater strength and diversities in religious studies; and a notable increase in involvement in the community [*Momentum*, May 1974].

Not all of these developments took place peacefully, nor did they equally represent the entire reality of most Catholic campuses.

Certainly the years 1966–68 were to become troubled ones for important Catholic universities. The strike against St. John's University in 1966 received the widest press coverage. While St. John's University managed to survive the brouhaha, and in many ways strengthened its internal machinery and local appeal, NCEA officialdom at the time sought to have the Vincentians terminate the strike on terms totally unsuitable to the university. The local ordinaries, Bishop Bryan J. McEntegart of Brooklyn and Francis Cardinal Spellman of New York, when asked by the Vincentians about this possibility, made no such request. The two bishops refrained from public support to St. John's University during the strike, but they were sympathetic regarding the issues in controversy. A review of the press clippings for those months, however, reveals many names associated with NCEA entering the public forum to disavow or disown St. John's University. The general source of embarrassment seemed to be the disfavor St. John's, and allegedly all Catholic higher education, was receiving from the secular university world. There was no criticism of the professors for unprofessional conduct, nor serious research into the origins of the conflict.

Fr. Clarence W. Friedman, S.J., NCEA secretary for university affairs, came to Philadelphia personally to request Fr. Sylvester Taggert, C.M., the provincial of the Vincentians, to terminate the strike so as to eliminate the embarrassment. On February 9, 1966, Fr. Friedman wrote Fr. Taggert, asking how anyone could look at us Christians when we publicly quarrel and tenaciously cling to our so-called principles. He also thought crude indifference to the rights of the students to an education was a scandal to the educational world. The strike apparently was more effective on the front pages of the country's metropolitan newspapers than in the classrooms of Jamaica, where classes went on according to schedule. In earlier years NCEA would have been less concerned about outside opinion and more about the well-being of one of

its constituent members. The change of interest was one of the signs of
the times.

More relevant to the contemporary university situation is NCEA's
dealings with Catholic colleges in the United States and with the Sacred Congregation for Catholic Education. Following Vatican II, the
Congregation was asked to draft a more suitable academic law for
Catholic educational institutions than the constitution *Deus Scien-
tiarum Dominus,* presently in effect for almost fifty years. In August
1975, when the International Federation of Catholic Universities convened in New Delhi, India, with American institutions represented by
Fr. Theodore Hesburgh, Fr. John Padberg, S.J., Msgr. Terence Murphy,
Fr. Edmund Ryan, S.J., and Msgr. John Murphy (now executive secretary for the College and University Department of NCEA), the "academic law" became an issue. At New Delhi the American delegates expressed "surprise and anxiety" to Cardinal Garrone, who was also in
attendance, about the Congress planned for Rome in November 1976
as a step toward writing a new academic law for the Church. Since the
1976 meeting was strictly to be the Second International Congress of
Pontifical Universities and Faculties of Ecclesiastical Studies, the Americans were anxious that any legislation not be understood to apply to
American universities and their theology departments. Cardinal Garrone assured them that in writing to the presidents of Catholic universities he was merely seeking input from everyone, not only seminary rectors. When NCEA offered to reply on behalf of American higher
education, Garrone agreed.

Msgr. John Murphy of NCEA, after returning home, wrote to all
member college presidents (on September 10, 1975) asserting the following:

1. "Cardinal Garrone was apologetic for the 'tone' of the June 20
   letter and wanted it clearly understood that its juridical character was not intended by him. He regretted the wrong impression
   this created."
2. He informed the presidents that Cardinal Garrone was willing
   to accept a "national response" to the June 20 letter, "so long as
   it was made known to the institutions that they could make an
   individual response if they chose." Msgr. Murphy added: "Let
   me point out that no one need respond separately to the June
   20, 1975, letter from the Congregation. If any president does respond, we would be happy to have him share the contents of
   the response with us."
3. "It was readily apparent (as it has been in the past) that some

of the tensions that are noted arise from inadequate communications and the difficulty the Roman congregation has in understanding American Catholic higher education."

This letter irritated the very urbane and usually unflappable Cardinal Garrone, because it suggested that Garrone had made a mistake in writing to college presidents in the first place. Because Garrone knew that not every American college official agreed with NCEA policy, the Cardinal decided to send his own personal interpretation of New Delhi to the presidents, which he did on January 10, 1976. Garrone countered Murphy with the following points:

1. Without questioning the good faith of anyone, I feel I would like to stand by only my public remarks made officially at New Delhi. . . . Private conversations should not be used without agreement with me concerning their tone.
2. The NCEA offered its services to receive and synthesize the replies. I, thinking this might simplify the work and please some people, happily accepted this proposal, with the reservation that the thoughts of all be respected perfectly. However, in no way did I suppose that there could be any imposition on all to deal through NCEA.
3. I would strenuously object if it could be believed that I could be divided in some way from my staff whose confidence and good faith, in my eyes, are beyond discussion. . . . I am personally responsible for everything I sign.

Cardinal Garrone clearly is expressing displeasure at anyone's thought that he regretted the "tone" of his letter, that the NCEA response precluded other responses, or that he or his staff were at fault for bad communications or misunderstanding the American scene. The problem was not "inadequate communications" between Rome and NCEA but basic disagreement.

NCEA delivered in March 1976 its "national response" to Cardinal Garrone and the "American" concept of the relations of Catholic colleges and universities to the Church. The Congregation for Catholic Education is accused of violating the spirit of Vatican II, if not its "vocabulary and substance," by continuing to look upon the university as an "area of the Church" rather than (as NCEA sees it) "the locus for interplay between Church and the world." No problem would exist with faulty teaching of Catholic doctrine if only "bishops and theologians maintain dialogue about theological teachings." NCEA advocates

a relationship of service to the Church rather than a juridical relationship. In a warning to Cardinal Garrone, NCEA reveals its special
anxiety:

> If the integrity and freedom of the academy is attacked, un-
> dermined by "an academic law of the Church," the Church
> will be the first to suffer. Its enemies will contend derisively
> that truth cannot be upheld and defended without resort to
> penalties and outside sanctions. Catholic colleges and univer-
> sities in the United States cannot deprive members of their
> civil rights as defined by American law, or limit their academic
> rights which are supported by accrediting any other profes-
> sional associations, without severe penalty to the institutions,
> not least of which would be the loss of prestige and influence
> in American society and particularly in the American intel-
> lectual community.

One American university official responded to the NCEA position
echoing the concerns of Cardinal Garrone. Writing to Msgr. John
Murphy (March 3, 1976), he made five points:

1. The focus of the American response seems to have lost. NCEA
   was asked to collate replies to the congregation's questions, not
   draft another comprehensive overview. The NCEA compilation
   should be anything but unanimous; agreements and disagreements will of necessity be of interest to Cardinal Garrone.
2. Cardinal Garrone should be told of the "darker side of contemporary Catholic college life." "Aberrant patterns of belief and
   practice are not totally unrelated to contemporary teaching and
   formation procedures." "Campus ministry is a valid apostolate;
   but hitherto the entire college operation was Catholic ministry."
3. Too much stress is placed for survival on government aid.
   While the statement "acknowledges the rights of secular society
   over higher education it does not support sufficiently the rights
   of Church and hierarchy, who represent the common good of
   the Church." There are alternatives to government aid.
4. The Sacred Congregation ought to know that accrediting agencies judge any institution on what it of itself professed itself to
   be in its own statutes. Government, accrediting agencies, and
   faculty unions recognize Catholic commitment, which accompa-
   nies hiring. Accrediting agencies recognize "state overview" of

competence. The Church has no less vested interest in "Catholic" competencies, especially in theology.

5. Cardinal Garrone ought to know how many, if any, colleges consider his April 1973 requests reasonable. At that time he insisted that (A) Catholicity be expressed in college statutes. (B) Machinery for self-discipline in doctrinal matters be spelled out in those statutes. (NCEA in its 1976 response completely ignored these stipulations.)

NCEA did not take kindly to these opposing views, going to the Congress of seminaries in November 1976 determined to keep American Catholic colleges out of control by the Holy See. Msgr. John F. Murphy in Rome formally requested that civilly erected faculties of theology not be mentioned in the new Apostolic Constitution governing pontifical faculties. A French delegate suggested contrariwise that, despite the mentioned American problems, the Congress of Universities and Faculties of Ecclesiastical Studies respect and recognize the work of colleagues in civilly erected theological faculties all over the world. The Congress finally approved affirmative answers to four questions. Should there be a body of academic laws? Yes. Should the Church recognize ecclesiastical faculties that only have civil erection? Yes. Should the academic law require a special *nihil obstat* (an ecclesiastical security clearance) for those teaching in canonically erected faculties? Yes. Should the *nihil obstat* be reserved to the Holy See or left to local or regional authorities? Answered: Reserved to the Holy See. (Here the majority indicated distrust of local mishaps in this area of judgment.)

One of the real problems, which transcends NCEA, is the tendency of Americans to transmit to Rome a glowing view of the condition of American Catholic higher education. Many questionnaires returned in response to Roman inquiries were filled with optimism. Catholic schools of theology alleged themselves to have large influence on American theological education and to have prospered from freedom in curriculum formation and student training. Assertions of loyalty to magisterium, that nonco-operation with professional associations destroys academic credibility, that ecumenical co-operation demands flexibility in teaching were made without condition. Hardly any mention was made that some Catholic schools of theology have been badly influenced by the ecumenical collaboration, that their theologians are at variance with magisterium, that pressure, including psychological coercion, is used to force co-operation with new approaches, that civil authorities are used as excuses to prevent bishops from interfering with what goes on; that the American Association of Theological Schools (a non-

Catholic group) exercises more influence on the teachings of theology in some places than Rome, bishops, or religious superiors, that many theologians in ecumenical work are not respected because they do not pretend to speak for the Church, and non-Catholic scholars have come to recognize that they are not hearing the sound Catholic thought they came to expect.

Until these disagreeable facts reach the upper consciousness of both academicians and hierarchy, a two-level Church in the academe will continue.

## VIII. *The Price of State Subsidy*

Molloy College in the Rockville Centre Diocese is only one of four in New York State that can legally call itself Catholic (the others are Lemoyne in Syracuse, Niagara in Buffalo, and St. John's in New York City). In order to receive state subsidy under the so-called Bundy Law (named after McGeorge Bundy, who headed the commission that proposed such aid) twenty other Catholic colleges had to declare themselves "private independent" (that is, unaffiliated with a Church). Under the formula $940 is granted for each undergraduate degree, $1,500 for each graduate degree.

Sr. Janet Fitzgerald, president of Molloy College, in a report made for the *Long Island Catholic* (October 21, 1976), thinks the price for conformity to state law is too high: "Once a college is secularized any corporate commitment to the Church is gone." Not only must the link with the bishop of the diocese be severed, but so also must the connection with the founding religious community. Neither bishop nor superior general of the order may serve ex-officio (though they can be elected) on the Board of Trustees, and the majority of the Board must be laypersons.

According to Henry Lucey of the New York State Department of Education:

> If we feel a college may be eligible we send a (non-Catholic) theologian to the campus to evaluate the content of the theology and philosophy course offerings. He looks at curricula, exams, library holdings, talks to students, faculty, and administrators.

The written questions asked deal with control of college and religious teaching. Faith or creed must be irrelevant for board members, faculty, and students.

A sample question is the following: "Is any denominational tenet or doctrine taught in its institution?" Mr. Lucey answers: "You can teach courses in religion but you cannot indoctrinate. The most important thing is whether or not there's any denomination or doctrine being taught as superior to others."

The college can keep its name as representing a tradition, but no mention of Catholicity or Church affiliation can appear in the philosophy, objectives, goals, or statutes of the institution. Religious symbols may remain as *objets d'art*. No student may be required to attend chapel or participate in religious observance or take any specific theology course. If religious studies and philosophy are required in the core curriculum, the number may not be disproportionate to other courses. (While the administration of this law is relatively lenient in New York, civil suits that would result in courts outlawing all religiosity still have to be faced. A recent U. S. Supreme Court decision upheld a Maryland law giving direct aid to three Catholic institutions, which may open the way for federal aid, but the guidelines on open Catholicity are still murky.)

Molloy College, on the other hand, has a faculty contract that demands that a professor respect the Catholic faith. Even a tenured professor can be dismissed for teaching heresy. Organizations that are anti-Catholic are forbidden. But as Sr. Janet Fitzgerald concluded her appraisal of the situation: "The intangible element of commitment is the pervasiveness of Catholicity." This latter element, of course, could be managed without juridical ties to the Church by those who wanted Catholicity to be pervasive on campus.

## IX. Where Are the Catholic Bishops?

When Msgr. Murphy's September 10, 1975, letter (seeking to reinterpret Cardinal Garrone's mind) reached Rome, two questions were asked: Where are the American bishops? Is there no voice for higher education in America other than Fr. Hesburgh and NCEA? The questions were not irrelevant. The Holy See faced the secularization of Catholic colleges as a philosophical issue as early as the 1965 meeting of IFUC in Tokyo. Pragmatic-minded American bishops faced the same issue since then as *faits accomplis* in their own dioceses without confronting the philosophy that underlay the practical decisions of their Catholic-education leaders. Many Catholic colleges were secularized in a short space of time without reference to the bishop or a public complaint from him. Some bishops sat by while the Church's large college machinery was cut from its roots. When Sister Jacqueline

Grennan told the faculty and students of Webster College (January 11, 1967): "It is my personal conviction that the very nature of higher education is opposed to juridical control by the Church," Webster College in St. Louis ceased to be Catholic, and Miss Grennan ceased to be a nun (*America*, January 28, 1967).

The NCEA, on the other hand, speaks highly on the performance of American bishops. College presidents were told (February 13, 1976) how the "Borders Committee" (named after the archbishop of Baltimore and composed of bishops and college presidents) was a "new forum" for airing opinions, concerns, and hopes about Catholic higher education in the United States. Msgr. Murphy of NCEA also told Cardinal Cooke (March 2, 1976) that he saw "a quickening in the movement of bishops and educational leaders toward one another." Yet the Roman question still sought an answer: Was there no other voice for higher education in America other than Fr. Hesburgh and NCEA? A delegation representing "another voice," also concerned about the implications of Msgr. Murphy's (September 10, 1975) letter, did arrange to take their point of view to Archbishop Bernardin on November 14, 1975. The president of the American hierarchy knew the problems of American universities firsthand, including the presence of heretics on Catholic campuses. Among the issues discussed with Bernardin were the large number of students who come to Catholic colleges woefully ignorant of Catholic teaching, the large number who do not practice their faith, whose moral values are clearly in doubt. The archbishop was also told that priests, religious, and laity willing to maintain standards set by the Holy See experience little support even from bishops. The interview ended on the note that institutions of Catholic higher education willing to obey the Roman rules needed support from the American bishops if they were to survive as Catholic. Archbishop Bernardin, acknowledging the seriousness of the situation, agreed to bring the presentation to the attention of the NCCB through the Bishop's Committee on Education (whose new chairman was Bishop William McManus, then auxiliary bishop of Chicago) and then get back to the delegation in question. The formal request to Bernardin for response was buried in the NCCB machinery. No acknowledgment of the meeting was ever made.

Five months later, at their spring meeting (1976), the Administrative Committee of NCCB invited Fr. Theodore Hesburgh to address its forty-seven bishops on the subject of Catholic higher education. The bishops were told that as far back as the Middle Ages hierarchy had problems with Catholic universities, but that the universities could be trusted. The meeting was significant (within the context of the problems Rome was having) because not only was "an anti-NCEA" voice not invited to make a presentation to the NCCB but also no bishop raised a serious question to confront Hesburgh's views.

Thus far, three years later, the American bishops have taken no steps, even within their own dioceses, to bring pressure on self-proclaimed autonomous colleges and universities to bring their operations closer to conformity to Roman norms.

## CHAPTER V

The Battle of the Theologians

## I. The Signs of Revolution

Catholic theologians in the United States have been at war with Church authority from the day Fr. Charles Curran celebrated his victory over the American bishops in April 1967 to the announcement of Sr. Agnes Cunningham last year that the Catholic Theological Society of America, of which she is president, has through the good offices of the Paulist Press published a study called *Human Sexuality*, a book that the New York *Times* (April 7, 1977) editorialized as "a profound note of dissent [from Catholic teaching] among those entrusted with teaching the young."

This is not the only war of the moment going on in the Catholic Church. Archbishop Lefebvre is leading an assault of his own on behalf of Latin and tradition. Catholic socialists are seeking to make the Church the left arm of Karl Marx's doctrine of government ownership and control of the means of production. One war, confined to pockets of old-line Catholicism, will have little effect on the Church in the United States; the other will achieve a peak of power only in Latin America, possibly Africa, where the problems of poverty are acute. Church authority in time will effectively contain the traditionalists because these Catholics venerate Church authority; the Catholic social gospel has a good chance to triumph over Marxism, once Catholic leadership learns to organize its troops as well as the Marxist do theirs.

But the revolt of the theologians against bishops and Pope (which began in Germany and France) is a different matter. This revolt now

firmly in the hands of American theologians, is real and more dangerous than the other two. It is a guerrilla war in which the opposition
comes out of hiding at times of its own choosing, retreating after making a tactical gain. The war is expected to take a long time. If the new
Catholic university wishes to be liberated from "juridical control," the
Catholic theologians want no "juridical control," either. Fr. Richard
McBrien, in his 1974 presidential address, told the Catholic Theological Society of America that Catholic theologians were not in the first
instance defenders of Catholic doctrine (that is, "magisterial-episcopal
pronouncements"): "Our first allegiance is to the truth." And then he
added: "We are not the Church's Ron Zieglers; we are her Tom
Wickers." Control by theologians over Catholic meaning and function
is to come through Church democracy. Although the people had nothing to do with the changes scholars persuaded Council Fathers to make
during Vatican II, power to the people of God is the instrument of
hinder reforming Catholic theologians from succeeding in their objec-
final renewal. Decrees from bishops or Pope must not be permitted to
tives. Contemporary reformers will not make the mistake Martin Luther
made by pushing Rome too hard, too soon. Head-on collision of large
confronting forces of theologians against bishops must be avoided, if
possible; sorties like a symposium, a book, or an article can make haste
slowly; if bishops react, seek a peace conference; allow no single center
of opposition to bishops develop; instead, this or that scholar, one or
the other learned society can contest an established position; keep the
controversies centered on the nonessentials of Catholicity, clerical celibacy, or liturgical accommodations to ecumenical needs; do not say
directly that the Catholic Church is not the Church of Christ, nor that
Christ did not know he was a pre-existing Son of God, nor that his
words may not have been recorded accurately by the Evangelist, etc.

This, of course, is Catholic revolution and a different creature than
the normal family type of war that goes on in every organization. No
one knows how or where a revolution begins. It certainly does not begin
with the people. Revolutions look as if they begin on the streets or in
the pews, and sometimes they end there. But as one scans the recent
and more successful examples, it is fair to say that revolutions (as distinguished from *coup d'états*) begin in the drawing rooms of well-paid
leisurely intellectuals, who, even when they win, rarely settle down to
the prosaic business of running anything. Sociologist Karl Mannheim
thought that the peculiar characteristic of modern society was the existence of whole classes devoted to its disintegration. Thomas Molnar
caught the sense of this when he wrote that revolution began with the
"République des Lettres,"

> The loose yet solid network of writers and philosophers with-
> out institutional or organizational ties, but ever-present; elu-
> sive but self-assertive; fearful of persecution but full of te-
> merity [*The Counter Revolution*, p. 6].

Revolutionary *littérateurs* not only wish to change laws; they also wish to topple an existing political structure. Like crusaders with enormous will, they neither measure their motives nor their deeds by the standards of those whom they would overthrow. They expect always to be jailed or suffer martyrdom, and sometimes do, but as often they fill a vacuum present in the power centers of their own household. Capable of rewriting history if only to make it, they have learned one thing well: *A successful revolution needs the support of the people in the respectable middle of society.* Rousseau and Voltaire foisted a revolution on France because they first seduced the patrons of the salons who gorged themselves (they thought safely) on wild conversation. Modern Marxists tend to concentrate their energies on universities and their upwardly mobile clientele.

Intellectuals make good revolutionary leaders because they are smart and because they are good at manipulating the communications media. That is a lesson they learned from the French Revolution. In the long run they may improve the institution they would overthrow very little. But at a given moment, by demanding action now, a remedy for a complaint now, the enlargement of freedom for an oppressed minority now, they create a bandwagon mood for change. Common sense, the wisdom of the ages, God's law means nothing to revolutionaries. They open as many sore wounds in the body politic as they can by hammering away at institutional defects. They may not even have answers, only the promise of a better world. If their proposed remedies do not work, or bring on a catastrophe they did not foresee, revolutionaries do not lose following immediately, because disaster usually occurs after they have departed the arena. Their genius remains in their ability to excite people and in their "flair for events."

How does officialdom counter a well-packaged revolutionary force without becoming oppressive? This is no easy task because being the "ins," they already have been made to look like reactionaries, opposed to people's welfare. In Church matters, for example, "the outs" present themselves as God-centered people with trust in human goodness, tolerant of man's defects, flexible about the answers to man's problems. They depict "the ins" as rigid, legalistic institutionalists clustered around hierarchy with an overconcern for hidebound and unprovable principles.

Once revolution gains momentum, defenders of the establishment have a hard time making God's revelation or the wisdom of the ages count for much. Raising the specter of long-range evil effects that might result from change never seems to temper change at revolution time. That is another generation's problem. The presumption of the moment is that change itself is good. The institutional leader, even if he be charismatic, has difficulty persuading his constituency of the old order's substantial virtue. Occasionally, a General DeGaulle arises out of dire necessity. But DeGaulles, or Franklin Roosevelts, are few. Furthermore, revolutionaries stay close to the machinery they are tearing apart. Official leadership finds it difficult to believe that revolutionaries are really revolutionaries. Dissenters cannot mean what they say, so establishment thinks. It is this hesitancy in officialdom in the face of emerging revolution that gives advantage to rebels. The power of revolutionary argument or the size of the following tempts hesitant institutional leaders to seek accommodation. Indeed, the leaders themselves may join the revolution. When royalty went out of fashion after the French Revolution, Napoleon III was alleged to exclaim: "We are all socialists now."

Successful revolutionaries, once in power, are not so accommodating or tolerant of dissent. In the secular world "revolutionary tribunals" and "political prisoners" are commonplace. Successful revolutionaries demand the obedience they once denied to legitimate government.

As the story unfolds of what has been going on within the Catholic Church in the past ten years, the elements of the Catholic revolution will become clear. The question of legitimate vs. illegitimate authority over "Catholic truth" is crucial to that history.

## II. The Point of Attack: Human Sexuality

The Catholic revolutionaries needed three things on their side if they were to make headway against the strongholds of bishops and Pope: (1) a popular issue; (2) the right kind of scholarly support; and (3) an approach or methodology that provided solid underpinning for conclusions and proposals. The popular issue proved to be sex.

The last citadel in the Western world of God-given moral prescriptions concerning man's use of his sexual faculties is the Catholic Church. The Catholic Theological Society recently has decided that the Church has been wrong. Its commissioned work *Human Sexuality* is the most outspoken contradiction of the Catholic moral code by Catholic theologians in the recent history of the American Church. *Human Sex-*

*uality* is the climax of an orchestrated volley of shots against the Church's sexual ethics that began during Vatican II, when European theologians, notably Bernard Häring, gave lectures quietly disseminating contraception. That was a large Catholic issue after 1963, but in the fifteen ensuing years theologians have traveled farther away from Catholic doctrine than contraception. The consultors for this particular book may be more important than the co-authors, who are generally unknown. But consultors Gregory Baum, Charles E. Curran, and Richard A. McCormick, S.J., are widely known, and each of them in his own way has pioneered in the effort to reshape the authentic moral doctrine of the Church. *Human Sexuality* puts their moral theologies together and offers pastoral guidelines to the Catholic faithful, some of which are the following:

- "Concerning revelation we [so the authors say] cannot guarantee the exact words of Jesus" (p. 19) and "Scripture is not even concerned with sexuality as such" (p. 30).

- "The question of artificial contraception has not yet found a definitive resolution in the Church" (p. 126). Therefore, the use of contraception can be a morally sound decision.

- "Sterilization, like that of contraception, is still far from a universally acceptable and definitive resolution in the Church" (p. 134). Therefore the options of sterilization are with the interested parties.

- Artificial insemination with semen from a man other than the husband cannot be prohibited (p. 139).

- While "mate swapping" is not ideal from a scriptural standpoint, the final word on this subject has not been said (p. 149).

- Adulterous relationships generally offend against the quality of fidelity, "but there may occasionally arise exceptions" (p. 151).

- Premarital intercourse may be justified if it represents "a loving relationship and some measure of mutual commitment before sexual involvement" (p. 166).

• Christian "homosexuals have the same rights to love, intimacy, and relationships as heterosexuals" (p. 214) "and to receive Holy Communion too" (p. 215).

• Masturbation is not objectively and seriously wrong (p. 228).

• Bestiality is pathological "when heterosexual outlets are available" (p. 230).

• Therapists and patients may enjoy sexual intercourse, if in fact it "results in making the patient whole."

It is important to indicate (1) the selective nature of the treatment (nowhere is the Decalogue mentioned), (2) the authors' failure to consider the explicit teaching of the Church, even that of Vatican II, as binding as anyone, (3) their distortions of Vatican II on marriage, when the authors say that the Council "recognizes that there are times when the decision to use artificial methods of contraception is both morally responsible and justified" (p. 116). This claim is false. *Gaudium et Spes* (No. 51) says just the opposite.

*Human Sexuality*, as an explicit effort to overturn the two-thousand-year tradition of the Church in the name of Christianity, has much in common with the teaching of the American Humanist Movement and The Ethical Culture Society. The New York *Times* saw this connection (July 7, 1977) when its editor praised the book precisely because "the values for which it speaks owes much to humanist psychology." The January 1976 issue of the *Humanist* unveiled a "New Bill of Sexual Rights and Responsibilities." To celebrate sexual freedom after centuries of bondage to Church and state, the humanist marriage is still "a cherished human relationship" but other sexual relationships "are also significant." The thirty-four sexologists who signed the Bill of Rights predicted a growing acceptance of premarital, homosexual, and bisexual relationships, looked upon prostitution and sadomasochism as "limiting" but . . . ," called children's learning experiences helpful for integrating a healthy sexuality into the personality; and masturbation to be "fully accepted" as "a viable mode of satisfaction for many individuals, young and old." The co-authors of *Human Sexuality* reflect this thinking.

Perhaps the manner in which this study was commissioned by CTSA is more significant than its content. The scholarly community consistently claims among its rights, the objective search for truth, openness to all data and all viewpoints, and severe peer criticism as essential mechanisms for reaching scientific conclusions. The manner in which this study was conceived, organized, evaluated, and published during the presidency of five CTSA theologians (John Wright, S.J., of Berkeley; Richard McBrien of Boston College; Luke Salm, F.S.C., of Manhattan College; Avery Dulles, S.J., of Catholic University; and Agnes Cunningham, S.S.H.M., of Mundelein Seminary) suggests that anything but the rigorous canons of scientific scholarship was followed.

Fr. Henry Sattler, C.S.R., of the University of Scranton and author of the best-selling book *Parents and the Sex Education of Children*, has noted a number of complaints that summarize the dissatisfaction of many members of CTSA. (It is worth reporting that all the above-mentioned CTSA officers were elected to the presidency by a mere majority of 150–170 voters present at the convention and voting out of a membership of approximately 1,500.) Fr. Sattler notes some faulty procedures of CTSA as follows:

1. The method by which the study committee was established preordained its conclusions. The chairman, Fr. Anthony Kosnik, a Detroit priest teaching at the Orchard Lake Seminary, seemed committed in advance to the points of view later published.

2. Some CTSA members who volunteered their assistance and sent materials did not receive acknowledgment or response to their suggestions. (Fr. Joseph Farraher, S.J., of Santa Clara University, reports that at the 1974 CTSA convention his offer to assist was denied because he lacked an open mind on moral issues. He had supported *Humanae Vitae*.)

3. Input was sought only by routing letters to the membership. Letters of inquiry to the committee were ignored.

4. Although the committee met fifteen times in two years, no progress reports were available to the general membership.

5. At the 1975 convention in New Orleans, consultants numbering at least twelve were reported as having been approached to evaluate the report. During this preliminary progress report to the membership, the names of the consultants were not divulged. Fr. Sattler raised his hand to obtain the floor. He thought some serious questions should be answered. Fr. Anthony Kosnik, the presiding officer and chairman of the committee writing *Human Sexuality*, did not recognize him during the entire discussion period.

6. No prepublication of the manuscript was available for scrutiny for CTSA members in general, or at individual request.

7. The text was not examined and evaluated by any competent
Church authority. It carries neither the *imprimatur* (let it be
published), which would indicate its general orthodoxy, nor
even the *imprimi potest* (it can be published), which permits
publication but withholds endorsement of content.

Comments made by responsible participants in the study at the time
of publication also reflect the underlying attitudes of CTSA officialdom:

• *About the importance of the book*

Sr. Agnes Cunningham asserted: "This is not the work simply
of five theologians." and "We need to provoke discussion"
[*National Catholic Reporter*, July 1, 1977].

Frs. Charles Curran and Avery Dulles found nothing in the
book that some theologians have not already been saying [*National Catholic Reporter*, May 27, 1977].

John Giles Milhaven considers important the respectability
given to these views by CTSA. Speaking of what has been
going on in the Church, he says:

"But almost all of this has been done in private or in restricted professional circles. Scarcely a theologian or pastor of
the Church has brought it out in a clear public account" [*National Catholic Reporter*, June 17, 1977].

• *About Church and sex*

Sr. Agnes Cunningham spoke of "individuals' rights to take
charge of their own sex lives." She asserted that "the ban on
artificial contraception isn't working," but does not explore the
contribution of CTSA to that situation [New York *Daily
News*, June 27, 1977].

• *About bishops*

Fr. Richard A. McCormick hoped the discussion of the report
"doesn't become an authority matter," as if the authority of

bishops in this area is irrelevant [*National Catholic Reporter*, June 3, 1977].

Calling the study a "responsible development" of Roman Catholic teaching on sexuality rather than dissent, Sr. Agnes Cunningham did not expect reaction by the body of bishops: "I do not know on what grounds they could intervene" (*National Catholic Reporter*, July 1, 1977).

The Catholic bishops did condemn *Human Sexuality*, although their own publication *Origins* (June 9, 1977) in one brief notice made the strange comment that the book "is likely to elicit a strong reaction in the Church from *some who believe* [italics added] it contradicts official Church teaching." Other comments ranged from Catholic columnist Fr. John Reedy, C.S.C., who in his syndicated column in *Long Island Catholic* looked upon the study as "a sincere effort to serve the Church by making theological thought available to Catholics who do not ordinarily have it" to secular columnist William Reel, who told his readers, "The 1977 Award for Pious Poppycock is herewith tendered to the Catholic Theological Society for its just-released study of human sexuality. The study espouses a sugary, *Cosmopolitan* woman magazine morality" (New York *Daily News*, June 8, 1977).

### III. Not the First Rebellion

The decision by CTSA in 1977 to go most of the way with Fr. Anthony Kosnik's treatise on human sexuality represented another triumph for Fr. Charles Curran of the Catholic University of America. Kosnik merely walked in the footsteps of a master confronter who confronted the hierarchy on several occasions. Curran lost only once—to Rochester Bishop James Kearney, who removed him from a teaching post at St. Bernard's Seminary. In post-Vatican II this removal qualified him for an assistant professorship at Catholic University. When the rector of CUA, while waiting for Pope Paul VI's arrival at Yankee Stadium (October 4, 1965), was asked how a man whose theological views offended his own ordinary could end up in Washington, Bishop William McDonald could only claim he was badly advised. Even then, McDonald sensed that CUA would be troubled by Curran. Two years later (April 10, 1967), the university Board (mostly bishops) decided to rid itself of trouble before Curran acquired tenure, and by a 28–1 vote in Chicago decided not to renew Curran's contract. (Every university has the right to terminate the service of a nontenured professor without explanation and with adequate notice to afford opportunity to gain new employment.) Since this occurred during the turbulent 1960s, the personable Curran demanded that charges be brought against him and that judgment of his case be made by peers, not by bishops. He was entitled to neither of these legal or professional courtesies. But when it appeared that the Board of Trustees might stand firm, Curran closed CUA down with a strike.

CUA was vulnerable to the pressures Curran exerted because the Bishops' Hall of Learning was not exactly a happy place. Conversations at Curley Hall complained about the pay scale, budgets, and promotion policies. Conservatives were just as critical as liberals, although many complaints on both sides, characteristic of that academic world, were petty. When Charles Curran decided to revolt he was supported even by those who could not abide his ideology or his classroom attacks on the teaching authority of the Church. Later Curran remarked that the birth-control controversy "was paradigmatic of the dissent in all specific moral questions" (*National Catholic Reporter*, October 24, 1975). When a faculty resolution by a vote of 460–18 favored his cause, it was clear that the American bishops had lost control of their own university. Bishop-trustees tried first to compromise by offering to renew Curran's contract for a year. Curran would have none of this. Sensing total victory, the young assistant professor demanded tenure immediately (after only two years' service) and was given it. Permitting Curran to bluster his way into tenure proved to be a costly mistake.

The "tenure fight" of 1967 was merely a warmup for the big event, which took place on July 29, 1968, when Curran decided to take on the Pope. The day on which Pope Paul VI issued *Humanae Vitae* was made to order for Charles Curran. During the previous four years he had faithfully followed the lead of his mentor, Fr. Bernard Häring, in questioning the Church's position on contraception. The leak of the majority report of the Papal Birth Control Commission to the press in April 1967 gave Curran courage. But when rumors began to spread that the Pope was ready to reject this report, Curran was ready. Before July 29 had ended, ten priests in the Washington area, led by Curran, met in Caldwell Hall of Catholic University to draft the rebuttal to the encyclical (which most had not read). Shortly, the dissenters made contact with seventy-seven others around the country, and at a press conference the following day in the Mayflower Hotel issued their statement. The following key sections of the dissent read as follows:

> No. 8 "It is common teaching in the Church that Catholics may dissent from authoritative, noninfallible teaching of the Magisterium when sufficient reasons for doing so exist."

No. 9 "Therefore, as Roman Catholic theologians conscious of our
duty and our limitations, we conclude that spouses may
responsibly decide according to their conscience that artificial contraception in some circumstances is permissible
and indeed necessary to preserve and foster the values and
sacredness of marriage."

No. 10 "It is our conviction also that true commitment to the mystery of Christ and the Church requires a candid statement
of mind at this time by all Catholic theologians."

Later, the rebels asserted that the statement of dissent was not a rebellion or revolution, but a loyal act of theological interpretation by loyal
Roman Catholics who accept the Petrine office of the Church.

However valid or invalid the line of argumentation, however carefully
nuanced were the phrases chosen to explain the theologians' conduct
before the world, "The Statement of Dissent" was planned to forestall
any general acceptance of *Humanae Vitae* by other theologians and to
offset in advance any vigorous defense of the encyclical by the American hierarchy. Bishop Alexander Zaleski, chairman of the Bishops Committee on Doctrine, was told to his face two weeks later that this was
the purpose: to beat the bishops to the punch by neutralizing the effect
of any statement the bishops might make. The immediate response of
the bishops was mild, asking *Humanae Vitae* to be received with sincerity and for people "to study it carefully and to form their consciences in
its light." Commenting on that episcopal reaction, the dissenters a year
later suggested that their strategy had paid dividends: "Would they
have adopted a 'harder' line if the theologians had not reacted?" (Curran et al., *Dissent in and for the Church*, Sheed and Ward, 1969, p. 8.)

As for the dissent itself, Bishop Zaleski's paper on the subject,
prepared for his committee, contains the following stipulations:

Dissent can be expressed but it must be done in a manner
becoming to a docile believer and loyal son of the Church.

Such a dissent must show that it is an expression from a believing person—a man of faith.

Such dissent can only be expressed in a manner that does not
disturb the conscience of other believing people.

Dissent must be accompanied by an open mind and a willingness to alter one's view in the light of new evidence.

Such dissent must be brought to the proper authorities in the proper manner and quietly.

This understanding of dissent is not what Curran and company had in mind. Over the centuries—and as a result of public brawling not only among theologians but also among bishops—some gentlemen's rules had been developed to permit withholding assent to doctrinal statements (as a necessary element in the development of doctrine) as long as pastoral chaos did not result. The Zaleski report reflected those refinements. The Curran response, on the other hand, tried to equate the right to withhold assent with the right to dissent in public about the meaning of Christianity and its obligations.

The bishop-trustees of Catholic University knew they were not dealing this time with scholars searching the frontiers of knowledge, and for a moment threatened to suspend from the classroom anyone who repeated public defiance of the Pope. But in the end the trustees settled on a Board of Inquiry to make judgments and recommendations about the professional and Catholic conduct of the dissenters during the July 29 crisis.

Revolutions are won or lost mostly because one side has greater determination than the other. In the seven months that followed, the dissenters made very clear that they would exercise every right and use every piece of armor the American Association of University Professors could give them. The trustees in their stead hesitated to use the full power of the bishops to protect Catholic doctrine. It is difficult in hindsight to understand why the Catholic University Board would accept any inquiry into a major Catholic doctrinal matter by a five-man board consisting of an engineer, an English teacher, a psychologist, and two priests who were predisposed to view dissent leniently. But they did. Then, too, they chose Bishop James Shannon (who later married a divorcee) to be their representative to the Board of Inquiry. This also was a strange decision. Shannon, as a college president, was sympathetic to dissenters. When called upon as bishop to clarify for the Inquiry Board what the trustees' intentions were, he did not offer a vigorous defense of the bishops' expectations. Later, his September 23, 1968, letter to the Pope, which found its way to the *National Catholic Reporter* (June 4, 1969), was an expression of his own dissent.

The dissenters in their turn were not bashful. They identified themselves as professors, not as priests. They prepared a massive documentation justifying their actions—published (in 1969) in two volumes entitled *Dissent in and for the Church* and *The Responsibility of Dissent: The Church and Academic Freedom*. (As in other issues, the bishops

lost the public-relations battle by confining their defense to press statements, leaving history to defend their position.) The dissenters were
anxious to establish an adversary hearing—to confront charges with
witnesses and argument. The threat of suspension by bishops was
angrily dismissed as "bringing a huge piece of artillery to bear on a
quite irrelevant point."

When the Board of Inquiry completed its hearings and presented its
conclusions to the Board of Trustees, the results were a complete white-
wash of the dissenting professors. The report concluded that the conduct of the professors

- Does not conflict with their profession of faith.
- They are entitled to interpret the Magisterium.
- They may communicate their interpretations to others.
- There are historical parallels to their behavior.
- Noninfallible pronouncements are reversible.
- Bishops themselves acknowledge the right of dissent.
- The distinction between public and private dissent is "objec-
tively invalid and a disservice to truth."
- People have a right to know.
- The manner of dissent is a matter of opinion.

In summary, the dissenters were said to have the right to act as they
did and in doing so they acted responsibly. As for the effect of their action on the faithful, the greater scandal would have been (so the report
said) to pretend to the press that they agreed with the encyclical or had
nothing to say. (This latter conclusion suggests that, unlike other
officials of society in sensitive positions, university professors are freed
of responsibility for saying to the press "no comment" when comment
would betray a trust or cause disunity.)

The dissenters considered the Inquiry Board's report to be a vindication. Still, the dissenters had more to do. When the bishop released a
summary of the results, they called the summary "inaccurate." They
called for the release of the whole report, regardless of what the trustees
wished to do with it. When the chairman of the trustees asked them
privately not to flaunt the findings to the embarrassment of Patrick
Cardinal O'Boyle, they refused the request as an infringement on academic freedom. When the bishops set up a review committee they
requested participation even at that level, determined to accept no conditions from the Board of Trustees.

The trustees at the end "received" the inquiry report without expressing approval or disapproval. Some trustees wanted to reject the report;

others endorsed its findings. However, a vote to accept the report never came to a vote. In "receiving" the report the trustees expressed confidence that teachers at Catholic University will

> Carry out their teaching function and conduct their scholarly research consonant with their Roman Catholic faith commitment.

> [The] faculty in its teaching of doctrine continues to be subject to the teaching authority of the Church with specific recognition of the supreme teaching authority of the Holy See [Hunt et. al. *The Responsibility of Dissent*, p. 166].

Thus was completed the rout of the American bishops by a group of their own young theologians, a defeat whose impact has been felt in the Catholic Church until this day.

Could the bishops have acted differently? As the governing body—and final authority—of a university the Board of Trustees at Catholic University had the power to conduct its own inquiry (simultaneously with the faculty), make its own public record and proposals, discover how far the dissenters were "open" to the Pope, and to take whatever action was needed to defend the Catholicity of the university against those who would not respect Magisterium. A Board of Trustees must fill its contracts, but it does not have to assign hostile professors to a classroom. The Board also has the power to fire disobedient tenured professors. AAUP will protest and censure the university in question, but each year threescore institutions of higher learning appear on the AAUP displeasure list. Some of these are prestigious who decide that the AAUP value system does not promote the best interests of their schools. Catholic bishops had the opportunity to make a displeasure list of their own meaningful to Catholics and did not take it.

The lesson was not lost on Catholic theologians, but Catholic universities thereby have not gained additional secular respect for the defiance.

### IV. Certainly Not the Last

That minirevolutions have been going on in the Church for ten years is not news. It may be news that a Vatican III council is seen as possibly the way to institutionalize the "revolution" begun by Vatican II. German theologian Johann B. Metz does not want a future council "to reproduce or confirm the present misery of the Church." Theodore

Hesburgh, on the other hand, has long been convinced that "we can best justify the efforts of the theologians today by seeing them as the vanguard of Vatican Council III" (NCEA Bulletin, August 1969). Unsurprisingly, eight years later (May 19–June 1, 1977) Hesburgh convoked a symposium on Vatican III.

What may be more important than the meeting at Notre Dame is Fr. Hesburgh's concept of who the architects of the Vatican III Church should be. Msgr. John Egan of Chicago, designated by Fr. Hesburgh to host this event, assembled the "architects" of the future Church as follows: Edward Schillebeeckx of Belgium; Johann Metz of Germany; Hans Küng of Switzerland; and Avery Dulles, Charles Curran, and William C. McCready of the United States, among others. All these scholars entertain some difficulty with the Magisterium. The dialoguers (who totaled a body of threescore and ten theologian-scientists) from the North American scene included William Bassett (San Francisco), Gregory Baum (Toronto), David Tracy, Eugene Kennedy, Agnes Cunningham, Andrew Greeley (Chicago), Luke Salm (New York), David Burrell (Notre Dame), Richard McCormick and Charles Curran (Washington, D.C.), and three officials of the Seabury Press. All these, too, are only one segment of the Church's ideological spectrum.

John A. Coleman, S.J., of Berkeley, a participant, summed up the event as follows: "The new paradigm for theology is the American equivalent of liberation theology's model of theology as a reflection of a living experience" (National Catholic Reporter, June 17, 1977). Coleman was surprised that so little attention was given to the growing gap between bishops and theologians. He reports that few participants cited the documents of Vatican II at all.

The two most interesting papers at the symposium were those prepared by Hans Küng and Avery Dulles. (Even Charles Curran was by comparison hardly controversial, confined by the host to the murky waters of social ethics—although Curran managed to make his customary pitch for dissent, which he now calls pluralism, in matters "such as contraception, sterilization, divorce, and even abortion and euthanasia.") Johann Metz's call to change the Church to "a Church of class conflict" was not so radical as his implication that the present leadership of the Church lacked "religious competency." Both Küng and Dulles agreed that the Church has backed away from Vatican II principles. What these two theologians envisage for the Church of Vatican III requires explanation.

Küng talked on "Problems and Opportunities for the Future." The ecumenical movement in his view has been brought to a halt by "the inflexibility of many Church leaderships, especially that of Rome." But he hopes that Rome can be forced to move, providing pressure on her remains intense. Certain things are settled for him: Scripture has primacy over tradition; Luther's views of justification by faith no longer is a problem, nor are issues concerning Church office and the Eucharist (except maybe "the practical attitudes of Church authorities"). But the time has come, Küng says, to attack the problem of Church authority "directly," especially the "concrete (juridical) form assumed by the papacy." What Küng counts on to achieve his redesign of the Church is the "compromise character of so many conciliar documents" and "the intentional unclarity of many an overcautiously or diplomatically formulated passage." These ambiguities provide leeway for creative theologians. If polarization occurs, the blame lies not with the theologians but can be attributed to "the lack of convincing leadership on the part of the papacy and the episcopate."

Against the trend toward "specialized provincial theology out of touch with contemporary reality," Küng tells the audience: "We must consciously take our stand." Since problems among Christians arose because "the Catholic Church acted on the supposition that it alone was the true Church of Christ," this concept must be disestablished. All excommunications must be withdrawn, the "premature decisions of Trent" and doctrinal formulas about Mary and the papacy must be reconsidered. The Church must be democratized so that Catholicism can "seek a place between the churches of the Reformation and the churches of the East." Plans for the new Church must be drawn up by theological commissions devised by professionals of all denominations, "not left to the arbitrary will of particular ecclesiastical authorities." If theological proposals find root "in the lower levels of the Church" an eventual "conciliar union" of churches is possible. But nothing is possible until the Catholic Church divests itself of certain historical prerogatives, especially an exclusively Catholic notion of apostolic succession, the jurisdictional primacy of Popes, and the verbal infallibility of Popes and councils. How can the Catholic Church be moved to adopt these reforms? Hans Küng offers three conceivable ways:

1. *Open protest* by bishops, theologians, pastors, "and all those who are in a position to exercise public pressure on the Church."
2. Leaders in ecumenical affairs should co-ordinate *public signs* of unity (presumably even if these signs violate existing Church law).
3. Unflagging argument by pastors and theologians who "have the

duty to protect those on the front lines of ecumenism from defamation and eventual sanctions when, in obedience to their own consciences and to their faith in the one Jesus Christ, these front-line fighters push into new ecumenical territory beyond the lines of official policy."

Avery Dulles is important not so much for the added support he gave to Küng's agenda for the new Church, but for his underlying assumptions about the meaning of Vatican II and his attitude toward Church authority. His greatest concern is "to protect the clear teachings of Vatican II against the obfuscation and retrenchment by which they are threatened 'by Roman authorities.'" The Vatican II principles that he wants reasserted by Vatican III ("so that they can no longer be ignored or interpreted out of existence") include the following: The Church of Jesus Christ is not exclusively identical with the Roman Catholic Church; several Christian communities already have with one another a real but imperfect communion; communion demands common witness, common worship, common service; each group must be careful to maintain its integrity; the goal of the ecumenical movement is not the reabsorption of all into the Roman Catholic Church, as the latter presently exists; dialogue is necessary.

Dulles admits that his understanding of Vatican II is "not widely understood or accepted by Catholic clergy and faithful." The job to be done, therefore, is to reaffirm "so as to make it unmistakably clear that the Catholic Church is firmly and publicly committed to these principles," as Dulles interprets their meaning. But to obtain proper reaffirmation, it may be necessary to move around obstacles placed by the Holy See in favor of the reformulations either by the International Synod of Bishops, the National Conferences of Bishops, or by teams of "theologians in dialogue" who could be expected "to move ahead of their respective churches and to reach agreements that are not presently within the reach of their parent bodies."

Dulles sees the ecumenical Church growing out of any one of three models:

1. *The Roman Model*—one faith, one rule, one sacramental system. Vatican II, he alleges, outdated this model by insisting on Church reform of its structures and admitting that Christ is at work in other communities.

2. *The Uniate Model*—groupings of local Catholic, Anglican, and Orthodox churches who share common doctrines, ministry, and

Eucharist, although they have different worshiping traditions and different formulations for the one faith. Dulles thinks this model is a "very pessimistic hypothesis" because it really is the Roman model in modified form. As such it leaves little hope for strictly Protestant churches.

3. *The Plural Model*—in which unity in Christ does not demand that "churches cling perpetually to some *supposed apostolic patrimony* [italics added] or to normative doctrines, ministries, or sacramental rites, for all such forms may be changed as the spirit may inspire." The World Council of Churches would be the closest realization of this model.

Dulles concludes: "Reflecting on the three models of ecumenism here proposed, I see no necessity to choose among them." Neither does he think one model superior to the other (Tracy et. al. *Toward Vatican III*, p. 99).

Richard McBrien, who usually reflects at the popular level what Dulles says to scholars, reviewing the deliberations at Notre Dame, concluded that symposium on Vatican III "highlighted once again the wariness of Catholic scholars toward the hierarchy of their own Church" (Brooklyn *Tablet*, July 14, 1977). The actual documents of the symposium did more than that: They set theologians on a collision course with bishops. No one at the Notre Dame symposium radically contested the Küng-Dulles view of Vatican II and the Catholic Church.

This state of affairs may be, as *Commonweal* editors think (December 28, 1973), the price of dragging "a doddering Church into the twentieth century and a too-late acceptance of the discoveries of modern science, the results of advanced Scripture scholarship, and those principles of individual liberty that most of the world has held for generations." The Catholic situation may be more serious than that. Betterment of the world by accommodation is not the only thing modern theologians have in mind. The world does not need theologians to improve its secular condition. Rigid application of the scientific method can do this, even if it includes the ruthless enforcement of government decrees. The struggle within the Church is about the word of God. Catholic theologians wish to control the meaning of God's words. Seven years ago the *Concilium* directorate held its first major symposium (in Brussels) on the future of the Church. That congress of theologians was described by Richard A. McCormick, George W.

McRae, and Ladislas Orsy as having "a definite and laudable political purpose: the identification and institutionalization of the theological voice in a way that simply cannot be ignored in the contemporary Church" (*America*, October 3, 1970). The theologians' word of God at that meeting was identified with women's rights, election of pastors by people, bishops, and Pope, and social action on behalf of the poor. The Catholic Church is interested in some of these things, though not necessarily in the order the Brussels or Notre Dame theologians decree. The Catholic Church's primary interest is in personal holiness and sanctification.

## V. The Scope of Revolution

Is this "war of the theologians" being won by the theologians? Küng and Dulles do not think so. They have not yet won over the bishops and the Pope to their positions. Hard-core resistance from older priests and laity annoy the scholars. Nonetheless, the victories of theologians and their supporters are not inconsiderable.

Twice within the past decade the *National Catholic Reporter* has celebrated those victories—once when the editor toasted the "victory for the renewalist program of the liberal wing of the Roman Catholic Church" (December 11, 1970) and for ridding the Catholic body of that "religious infantilism" that "allowed Churchmen in high places to determine the conduct of their private lives." Sixteen months later (March 24, 1972), NCR again rejoiced, this time in the claim of Joseph O'Donoghue, executive director of the National Association of Laity (now defunct), that liberals have "gained control of the Roman Catholic Church in America." How did O'Donoghue know that? "Liberal Catholics have a lock-tight grip on the publications of catechisms and religious-formation texts, and a similarly tight grip on the university religious education departments, which train religious teachers at all levels. Liberal Catholics have mastered the techniques of designing structures and liaison patterns to multiply total impact. Pity the poor establishment, which sees the once docile Catholic populace of its area now constantly infused by liberal itinerants whose words endure in small but solid local liberal movements."

While the self-declared "liberal Catholicism" may not have enlarged Church adherence and may have created the fundamentalist backlash it disdains, reformers continue to push their designs where they think the hope of their future Church lies—in the machinery of Catholic education itself, including that segment owned and operated by the Church's bishops and pastors.

The list of "horror stories" is now quite long:

> • In every major academic center there are professors teaching orthodox doctrine or defending authentic Catholic positions who feel isolated. They do not experience support from local superiors or local bishops or from their ideological peers.
> • Young parish priests find themselves resisted by teaching nuns in parochial schools, and undefended by diocesan education offices—if they follow instructions of the Holy See on teaching doctrine. Some priests no longer teach in parochial schools precisely because Catholic doctrine is not taught there.
> • In seminaries where dissenters dominate the intellectual and moral formation of future priests. One seminarian was told by his rector that he was sexually immature if he did not dance with girls.
> • Parents who are denied a voice in the education of their children if they insist on orthodox presentations. Some cannot get first confession for their children and, if they insist, are often told by teachers to train them yourself.

But if, as Joseph O'Donoghue has indicated, the reforming scholars have developed the facility of supporting their friends, of obtaining teaching assignments and friendly reviews for their writings, they also have developed the skill of freezing out their "enemies." The Catholic University of America is an interesting case in point. CUA from its inception always contained an interesting mishmash of contending professors, some political liberals, some conservatives, most of the faculty unconcerned about the politics of state or Church. At the present moment that is probably still true—except in its School of Religious Studies. As one watches the drift of young men from seminaries and religious-education offices across the country to CUA teaching positions, one observes an interesting bias in the selection. Ordinarily this should not call for comment because, as sociologist Peter Berger observes, "Birds of a feather flock together not as a luxury but out of necessity." Samuel Gompers believed that rewarding friends and punishing enemies was the name of the game. Democrats and Republicans do it all the time. Bishops used to do it. The academic community now does this best. Such selectivity or the sanctions acquire pressing social or ecclesial significance only when a state of war exists.

President Clarence Walton's "Reflections on the Catholic University of America" (September 1972) contained this paragraph:

The Catholic scholar in a Catholic university does not receive a pastoral mandate from the university and, most assuredly, not one to espouse what the Church formally condemns or to deny what the Church formally asserts. He acknowledges the deposit of faith which relates to Church teachings regarding the death and resurrection of the Son of God, the meanings of Mary as the Mother of God, the primacy of Peter and his successors as teachers of faith and morals.

In view of what goes on under the aegis of some CUA professorships, Walton's statement remains an unrealized ideal. Indeed, there are those who have been denied tenure at CUA (they claim) because they stood solidly behind Catholic Magisterium.

The case of Manuel Miguens, O.F.M., S.T.D., S.S.D. may be a good example of how reformers use power. Charles Curran, who was denied tenure, led a successful strike against the rector, who gave him no reasons for not renewing his contract after two years' apprenticeship. Miguens is a different kind of scholar—Spanish, religious priest, gentle, solitary—but scholar. His graduate work was done in Rome, Jerusalem, and Louvain. One of few people with doctorates in theology and Scripture, he has taught in Jerusalem and Salamanca before coming to CUA in 1968 as a full professor. His language skills include English, French, German, Italian, Portuguese, Spanish, Latin, and four biblical languages (Hebrew, Aramaic, Greek, and Syriac). His publications are found in Spanish, Italian, Latin, and English. His best-known scriptural works are entitled The Virgin Birth and Church Ministry in New Testament Times.

In February 1973—after five probationary years at CUA—Miguens applied for tenure. The promotion committee in the School of Theology unanimously endorsed his request. The vote of the entire theological faculty was also favorable, with one negative vote and one abstention. The results were forwarded to the Academic Senate of the university. Miguens was turned down at that level. He appealed. In the meantime he requested reasons for the denial. C. J. Nuesse informed Miguens (September 18, 1973) that reasons are not disclosed to candidates for continuous tenure. As the appeal process unfolded, numerous petitions were filed in his behalf by students and others.

One of the "others" in Miguens' corner was Fr. James A. Corriden, chairman of the Theology Department. In a letter to Dr. Nuesse (December 6, 1973), Fr. Corriden made the following points:

1. Fr. Miguens is a credit to our faculty and we need his services.
2. Fr. Miguens' scholarly background and academic achievements are beyond question, being the only person on our campus who possesses a doctorate in Sacred Scripture.
3. Fr. Miguens is successful in teaching our seminarians. The response to his classes has been favorable and manifests a reverent appreciation for God's Revealed Word.
4. He is extremely competent, and he fits in with our needs and our students.

All this to the contrary, Fr. Miguens' appeal was denied at the same meeting of the academic senate at which a dissenter from *Humanae Vitae* received tenure, wherein too the voice of another dissenter from the papal encyclical carried overwhelming weight against Fr. Miguens.

Why was Fr. Miguens denied tenure? Fr. Corriden's letter to Nuesse anticipated the result: an allegation going around that the reason for denying Fr. Miguens' tenure was his espousal of conservative theological views. Fr. Corriden could not believe that this was the case against Fr. Miguens.

But it was the case. Fr. Miguens was denied tenure and (indisposed by Franciscan temperament) left CUA without conducting the public fight his friends wanted him to undertake.

What were the conservative views that brought Fr. Miguens into disrepute with the controlling forces in the CUA Academic Senate?

He severely criticized in a scholarly review Fr. Raymond Brown's booklet *Priest and Bishop*.

Brown's booklet had raised biblical questions about the Catholic view of apostolic succession, arguing that the Twelve were not bishops in the sense of local church leaders, but instead a council convoking sessions to deal with major problems (p. 58). They did not govern Christian communities (p. 52). "Sacramental powers were given *to the Christian community* [Brown's italics] in the persons of the Twelve" (p. 54). The theological conclusion follows for Brown that sacramental power, therefore, can be given to whomever the Church designates—without a lineal connection to the twelve (p. 55). St. Paul is responsible for missionary presbyter-bishops, according to Brown, and it is these who are prototypes of the modern episcopacy. In the New Testament, therefore, presbyter-bishops are not in any way traceable through succession to the Twelve Apostles, and possibly only traceable to some of St. Paul's (pp. 72–73). Possibly, too, says Brown, some churches with no bishops lived in fellowship with churches that had bishops, suggesting the possibility of two such churches living in union today (p. 83). (The significance of Brown's biblical conclusions for Dulles' view of what the new Church might be should not be overlooked.)

Miguens' review (which appeared April 1972 in the "wrong" magazine, *Triumph*) was not unkind to Brown, but severe in its judgment of his approach to the problem of apostolic succession. Scripturist Miguens says to scripturist Brown: "Brown's argument is affected (and infected) by constructions like likelihood, probability, almost certainly, plausibly, it would seem, seemingly, etc. This precaution and uncertainty in argumentation is in sharp contrast to the certainty with which he states his conclusions. Brown appears to be not nearly so certain of his arguments as he is about what he wants them to prove."

The details of Miguens' rebuttal of Brown need not be of concern here except in its general thrust. Miguens maintains that the New Testament is not a document separate from the community that gave it birth and (alluding to Brown) "it looks distinctly suspicious to discover in the New Testament novelties which are not in accordance with this living tradition of the Christian faith." Miguens, then, examines St. Paul's writings, the letter of Pope St. Clement I to the Corinthians (he was the third Pope after Peter and wrote only thirty years after Paul's death), and the letters of St. Ignatius of Antioch (A.D. 110) to conclude: "The authority of the Church is the authority of God, who delegated it to Christ, and Christ in turn to his Apostles, and the Apostles to the bishops and deacons. This order is a dogmatic question for the primitive Church." Miguens' final advice to anyone who reads Brown's book: "My hope is that the result will lead him to read the New Testament for himself in the light of the teaching of the Church."

"The Miguens case" may be more important for what it symbolizes than for the mere fact of denying him tenure. It may suggest that those academic persons who successfully war on the Magisterium do not like to be warred on by those of their peers who support the Magisterium.

The treatment accorded Fr. Miguens' next scholarly contribution, *The Virgin Birth*, follows a familiar pattern. Fr. Raymond Brown, S.S., and Fr. Joseph Fitzmyer, S.J., had explored earlier the question whether Catholic belief in Jesus' virginal conception rested on a sound historical basis. They were concerned about the *scriptural evidence* for the virgin birth. Each of these authors in turn concluded that the scriptural basis for the belief is dubious if not negative. Miguens' book, re-examining the same evidence, concludes quite oppositely that the scriptural evidence as to the historicity of the virgin birth is affirmative.

Miguens' book on the virgin birth was welcomed in many quarters. A Lutheran review calls it "a devastating defeat for the critical methodology employed by Brown and Fitzmyer," adding: "It is always a delight to read a superior defense of divine revelation." A Greek Orthodox priest called it "a ringing affirmation of the historical credibility of the virgin birth of Jesus."

From the point of view of thorough favorable analysis, John Redford (*Clergy Review*, February 1977) in England, taking account of European Catholic doubts on the subject, calls Miguens' book a "fascinating study for the virgin birth" by an author who "is scrupulous to avoid rancour and the language of polemic." He quotes Miguens to the effect that Brown and Fitzmyer will accept criticism in the forum of scholarly analysis, and then Redford adds: "and then (Miguens) proceeds to give it to my mind most effectively."

Redford's final paragraph reads:

> Fr. Miguens has done an invaluable service with this little book, doing what he set out to do in demonstrating that the Christian faith in the virginal conception of Jesus is indeed well founded in the New Testament, based as it is upon a firm and primitive tradition.

The American evaluation of Miguens' book as found in *The Catholic Biblical Quarterly* (Vol. 38, 1976, pp. 576–77) and *Theological Studies* (Vol. 37, No. 1, 1977, pp. 160–62), two journals closely associated with the views of Fr. Brown and Fr. Fitzmyer, was of a different kind. The first journal provides this view of Miguens' book: "The literary genre of this monography can best be described as polemical exegesis. But to the present reviewer, the exegesis is faulty and the polemic wide of the mark." The second journal, after chastising Miguens for "repeated forcing of texts to fit into [his] theological presumptions," ends with the following monitum to readers:

> Because of this book's great potential misuse by the nonspecialist, it is dangerous. The Church surely has a right to expect that its trained scriptural theologians will provide it with sound, critical, balanced, and cautious exegetical fruits. Miguens has not provided this, and therefore the book's greatest flaw is its irresponsibility to the Church.

Because liberal Protestant scholars have long since argued that the virgin birth story is really a second-century legend created to enhance Christ's role as Son of God, Miguens' last word on the subject deserves repetition (*The Virgin Birth*, p. 162), if only to confront the nagging doubt that a virginal conception of anyone, including Christ, is unthinkable:

> The inference is that God's real interest in Christ's birth, and coming in general, is by far more aptly and efficaciously signified by a genuine and factual intervention than through a narrative which has to fabricate an imaginary event where, after all, the message remains highly conceptual and dialectic. Obviously, there is no conflict between the doctrine of God's interest in Christ and God's factual intervention—virginal conception—to make his interest clear. Even more: The only convincing and unequivocal manner is a personal and factual intervention. This is the way God has acted throughout the ages in Salvation History: Committing His power to His interest.

The cavalier treatment of Fr. Miguens by the power structure in Catholic academic circles is not an isolated case. A tide once with bishops and Pope is now running against them. Bishops have been talked out of using certain scholars or using certain texts because they are "too orthodox." One young bishop was heard to say: "Doctrine is passé and the social realm is the only valuable realm for the thinking Christian." Criticism of bishops, which formerly was low-key, sometimes subtle, is now strident on the right as it is among the revolutionaries on the left. Bishops themselves are complaining: "Rome speaks with two voices." Or as one remarked: "Rome cries while the Church dies."

And the "revolt of theologians" continues to run its course.

## CHAPTER VI

The Birth-Control Battle

## I. The Background

How the Catholic Church lost the support of its people over birth control is a story still to be told with finality. But lose many of its people to contraception the Church did, and in a very few years.

Fr. Andrew Greeley (1976) has announced with ferocious certainty that the deterioration in American Catholicism is due to the encyclical *Humanae Vitae*, which in 1968 upheld the Church's ban on contraception. Greeley has a chapter in his *Catholic Schools in a Declining Church* that "proves" by mathematical formula that what he has been saying since 1968 is true: A continued ban on contraception was a disaster for the American Church (p. 316).

That book itself deserves comment later, but for the purposes of this chapter it is sufficient to say that the Greeley thesis can be maintained as a working hypothesis only if "the contraceptive issue" is seen not as a single item but as a "mixed bag" of many Catholic issues that were the subjects of fierce attack before, during, and after Vatican II. Although the direct confrontations seemed at first to center on steroid pills such as Enovid and Ortho-Novum, later on condoms and diaphragms, the basic controversy was always over more basic questions: What is the law of God? What is the will of Christ? Who says so and with what authority?

Those priests and married couples who after World War II organized what was the most successful family-life apostolate in the history of the American Church saw their work crumble within the space of a few years. The Cana and Pre-Cana conferences, the Christian Family Movement, the Cana clubs and Holy Family guilds, the marriage-preparation courses, family-consultation centers, marriage counseling training of priests, regular attention to Catholic family life by all Catholic magazines, especially *Sign* and *America*, under the respective editorships of Fr. Ralph Gorman, C.P., and Fr. Thurston Davis, S.J., were the crests of rocklike Catholic family formations that supported the Catholic family value system, by then a lonely isle in an all-embracing, surrounding sea of broken homes, one-or-two-child families, and rising rates of illegitimacy, divorce, and abortion. Sociologist John L. Thomas, S.J., wrote a pioneer book, *The Catholic Family*, which laid out the ingredients necessary to protect the identity and future of the Catholic family system as a viable subculture when the power of secularized culture was overwhelming. Continuing education, mechanisms of motivation, and regular support systems were the instruments by which the Church kept Catholic family life intact and guaranteed its future.

Looking backward from the time when the American bishops created the Family Life Bureau in the National Catholic Welfare Conference (1931) to the eve of the Second Vatican Council (1961), the rise and rapid growth of the family-life apostolate was phenomenal. In fact, this apostolate seemed to take off all by itself (sometimes without bishops knowing what was going on), as if parish priests (most of the early organizers were priests) and married couples were driven by a compulsive need to survive as a Catholic body. In view of the bitterness later demonstrated by Catholic contraceptionists, a flashback to those days only reveals enthusiasm, love of the Church, and outpourings of energy on behalf of *The Word*.

And *The Word* was what the Church said it was (including the rejection of contraception). Not only were the private discussions and the nationwide network of Cana, Pre-Cana, and CFM meetings positive in their exploration and appreciation of Catholic Family values, but the literature was also formative and enthusiastic. John J. Delaney, editor for Doubleday, published a book in 1958 designed to show that Catholic family values were not "the imposition of the will of a few cranky clerics on the Catholic populace" and to show further that "there is nothing arbitrary about the Church's stand" on marriage matters. The book was John L. Thomas' *The Catholic Viewpoint on Marriage and the Family*. Rereading Fr. Thomas' exposition of the "Catholic problem" offers *prima facie* evidence of how secure Catholic scholars were then interpreting not only the mind of the Church but also the mood and needs of Catholic people. What was the source of the Catholic problem in 1958? Fr. Thomas listed a few: (1) the sixteenth-century denial of the sacramental bond of marriage; (2) the gradual rejection of the influence of religious doctrine on the formation of marriage and family values; (3) the tendency of social scientists to look upon the human person as nothing more than a complex combination of basic urges, conditioned reflexes, and acquired habits; and (4) the American habit of being "practical" in judgment without necessary reference to principle or doctrine (pp. 25–27).

In the face of the practical options being offered at that time to marrieds and about-to-be marrieds in America, on what did the special Catholic family system depend? According to Thomas: on its clearly defined but distinctive set of ideals, standards, and patterns of conduct related to sex and marriage. Said Thomas in 1958: "If you want to know why people judge certain family practices to be right or wrong you must find out how they define the nature and purpose of marriage. If you want to understand why they define marriage as they do, you must discover their view of human nature. In the final analysis, therefore, all definitions of human values are ultimately derived from some view of man, the human agent. If people hold different views concerning the origin, nature, and destiny of man they will logically define the purposes of marriage differently and will develop different patterns of conduct in relationship to marriage" (p. 23). For almost two hundred pages Fr. Thomas proceeds to explain why Catholics do not agree with other Americans on the essential purposes of marriage, the moral laws regulating marital relations, and the use of sex outside of marriage.

In those halcyon days it was clear that the marital issue separating Catholics from non-Catholics was not the condom or the diaphragm but a cluster of issues having to do with the sacred elements of human nature and the Church's understanding of God's revelation. Popes Pius XI and Pius XII frequently used terms like "divine institution," "divine design," and "divinely established order" when speaking of many subject areas of religious thought. Contraception was only one of them. As seculars first, then more and more Protestants and Jews moved away from these notions, behavioral patterns changed with the changed concepts. The Catholic world view, on the other hand, retained the "wholeness" that underpinned its family life. However, when tampering began either with a practice (contraception) or with an idea (divine design), it was inevitable that changed behavior would call for changed ideas, and vice versa also. Even if the average Catholic did not always understand the connection between mind and conduct, Fr. Thomas saw this quite clearly.

However, assertions about the coherence of the Catholic family value system or the Church's struggle to make it operative in the lives of people led to the following practical questions: Did the Church's labors succeed? Did Catholics actually live by the Church's book?

Almost all priests who heard confessions or were effective parochial pastors of souls in the past half century would agree that the answers to both questions were yes. Family-life directors of any major diocese, also, where sexual aberrations among the faithful were always higher, can bear witness that the best Catholic family apostolates in the nation were precisely in the large metropolitan centers where the pressures on couples, old and young, were most severe.

But there is still a better witness to what was going on in American Catholic family life prior to 1962.

He is Andrew Greeley.

In the spring of 1963 Fr. Greeley wrote an article for *Chicago Studies* entitled "Family Planning Among American Catholics." He was not yet ten years a priest and still a curate at Christ the King parish in Chicago. The *Chicago Studies* article based its conclusions on two secular studies—one a 1959 Michigan study, the other a 1961 Princeton study—through which Greeley hoped to demolish "some favorite myths about Catholic family planning." He reported as follows:

1. Concerning the myth that most Catholic families really do not accept the Church's teaching on birth control, Greeley says: "The Michigan study shows the contrary to be true: *Catholics accept the Church's teaching with a vengeance*" [italics added].

   Only 32 per cent of Catholics gave unqualified approval to birth control, compared to 72 per cent of Protestants and 88 per cent of Jews.

   Greeley concludes that on the subject of family limitation "Some Catholic respondents were more Catholic than the Church."

2. Concerning the myth that family-limiting Catholics use methods condemned by the Church, Greeley reports that only 30 per cent used contraceptives.

   Only 22 per cent of regular Massgoers used contraception.

3. Greeley concludes: "Religious affiliation is a very powerful determinant of behavior in this area—the success of Church

efforts to induce the younger generation of Catholic couples to adopt approved methods [contradicts] assertions occasionally made that Catholics are increasingly adopting appliance methods."

4. Concerning the myth that upper-class Catholics more likely adopt contraception, Greeley concludes: "The more education, the more income, the higher the occupational category, the more likely Catholics are to keep the Church's law and the more likely they are to have or to want larger families."

5. Concerning the myth that periodic continence is an inefficient method of family limitation, Greeley estimates: "The rhythm method is not drastically less efficient than the others."

Greeley also warns the reader that "such studies do not merit the same kind of acceptance as would, let us say, mathematical demonstrations or experiments in the physical or biological sciences." In defending the professional integrity of sociologists, he chides those who think "that demographers do not understand the consistency of the Church's teaching on sex and procreation, that they do not have a respect for the Catholic conscience, that they expect the Church to change its position, or that they expect Catholics to violate their moral principles." Greeley's article may have demolished myths but it also underlined the existence of Catholic moral principles on contraception, a Catholic conscience on the subject, and a Church firmly committed to its principles.

From this high plateau of adherence and practical observance there followed a precipitous decline among Catholics within the ten-year period following 1963. Obviously, something more was at work than a new Catholic desire to use a condom, a diaphragm, or a pill. The Catholic people earlier under equally adverse social pressures—the Great Depression and the great wars—continued to recognize contraception as a sinful use of marriage. Something else must have happened after 1961.

## II. The Catholic People Are Indoctrinated

Many things were going on in the Catholic community relative to contraception since the postwar baby boom began to alarm population experts. In 1944 government statistician Oliver E. Baker was declaring demography to be the most exact of the social sciences. He also predicted (on the basis of statistical computations) the leveling off of population growth in the United States. But people changed the numbers by placing high value on parenthood. Whereas in 1936 1,000 women aged 15–44 bore 76 children, a similar cohort of women bore 121 children in 1956. Later demographers coined phrases such as "population explosion," "the population bomb," and "standing room only" to make their point that planned parenthood (soon to be euphemistically retitled "responsible parenthood") was now as much a requirement for Americas as it was for Third World peasants.

The tools of persuasion would become more sophisticated, but the motivation was similar to that made into a crusade years earlier by Margaret Sanger. During the depth of the Depression, when almost one quarter of all women of child-bearing age had no children at all, the founder of the birth-control movement wrote an article for *The American Weekly* (May 27, 1934) in which she proposed an "American Baby Code." The essential ingredients of her philosophy are found in the following articles:

> Article 3. A marriage shall in itself give husband and wife only the rights to a common household and not the right to parenthood.

> Article 4. No woman shall have the legal right to bear a child and no man shall have the right to become a father without a permit for parenthood. . . .

> Article 6. No permit shall be valid for more than one birth.

These embarrassing statements are now buried in library stacks, but Mrs. Sanger's haunting fears of unwanted and unneeded babies have worked their way into the psyche of American intellectuals and through them into the souls of mothers and prospective mothers. But technical advances, which provided the power by which unmarried and married adults alike could separate sexual activity from parenthood, did not automatically mean social approval of contraception or wide-spread dissemination of devices, as long as there was popular consensus that contraception was evil. In fact, the "Protestant ethic" about contraception was frequently enforced by written and unwritten laws. Contraceptives could not be sent through the mails, they could not be advertised (although obtainable at the back of drugstores), they could not be sold to minors or the unmarried, nor could birth-control advice be given in public hospitals. Those restrictions lasted as long as the religious consensus lasted—that is, up until the late 1950s.

The birth-control crusaders, however, were not without determination. They had begun as early as 1908 working to persuade the Church of England to give at least limited endorsement of the use of contraception by Christians. Successively they were turned down by the Lambeth conferences of 1908 and 1920, but gained sympathetic hearing from some Anglican bishops for exceptional use of contraception in "abnormal cases." This was the view that prevailed at Lambeth in 1930 when for the first time a prominent Christian body, while still insisting that "the primary and obvious method is complete abstinence (as far as may be necessary) in a life of discipline and self-control lived in the power of the Holy Spirit," gave permission for contraceptive use in abnormal cases. Contraception hereafter for Anglicans was a tolerated practice, though still without approval. Once this breakthrough was accomplished, further dispensations from standard Anglican behavior were readily granted. The Lambeth Conference of 1958 favored "a positive acceptance of the use of contraceptives within Christian marriage and family life." This is the first time that contraception is seen as enriching married life, that the term "responsible parenthood" is introduced to the ecclesial vocabulary, that family planning is raised to the status of noble duty. The revolution within Protestantism was complete. (Five years later a booklet entitled *Toward a Quaker View of Sex* would reject almost completely the traditional approach of the organized Christian Church to sexual morality, specifically its *a priori* judgments about fornication, adultery, and homosexuality.)

It is not without significance that in the late fifties an organized effort was made—successfully, as it turned out—to put the medical profession in the forefront of a birth-control campaign to break down all written or unwritten resistance to contraceptive advice or clinical assistance for clients. The effort was first made in New York in 1956, then in Denver, Maryland, and Chicago. By 1959 the American Public Health Association was on record in favor of birth-control services. The White House Conference on Children and Youth followed this lead in 1960. By 1961 John D. Rockefeller III was in favor of government-supported birth-control programs. Simultaneously, but less spectacularly, was the success in making the social workers employed by the network of bureaus of public-assistance agents of contraceptive advice. The public-relations stress was on freedom for the client, but the welfare recipient was not unmindful of the social worker's position.

These political efforts were accompanied by widespread public-relations programs and intensive lobbying. Planned Parenthood still encountered some resistance in high places. One of its setbacks came when William H. Draper, an investment banker and Planned Parenthood activist, heading up a government committee, released a report (July 24, 1959) calling for government-financed and -managed population programs. Draper avoided the term "birth control" and stressed the word "request," but it was clear that the International Planned Parenthood Federation wanted the United States Government to endorse and underwrite its worldwide efforts to "sell" contraception. While Catholic politicans such as John Kennedy and Edmund Brown walked a tightrope on the subject, President Dwight D. Eisenhower buried the Draper Report and banned all government family-planning assistance for the duration of his term, with the comment that nothing was more improper for government than activity of this type.

But if Eisenhower was firmer on the subject of contraception than other politicians, Planned Parenthood came to recognize the vulnerability of public officeholders on this issue, particularly Catholics. Though the U.S. Catholic bishops immediately (1959) warned the public that Catholics would not support assistance programs that promote artificial birth prevention, Planned Parenthood stepped up their campaign to change public opinion. They held a World Population Emergency Conference in 1960, took out full-page ads soliciting $1,120,000 to promote the plans of the Draper Committee, brought Margaret Sanger out of retirement (June 14, 1960) as a fund-raiser, and induced the National Council of Churches in the U.S.A. to take positions favorable not only to contraception but to sterilization as well. (New York *Times*, February 24, 1961, p. 16). The NCC statement justified its endorsements on the basis of "the general Protestant conviction that the motives rather than the methods form the primary moral issue." The editorial comment of *America* (March 11, 1961) on the NCC statement reads: "At stake in these matters is not merely the integrity of marriage but the very nature of morality. Christian morality is increasingly penetrated by a tendency to scuttle all objective norms of conduct and rationalize the flight from the absolute by appeals to the spirit of the gospel."

Planned Parenthood also realized the importance of enlisting for their campaign important public figures. By 1962 they had former Secretary of State Christian Herter taking up their cause. As an Episcopalian gentleman of some standing, he came to Planned Parenthood's annual conference in New York to be a bridge to the Catholic community. Herter told his audience that it was no longer correct to think that discussion of the population crisis was offensive to Catholics. He counted on the new ecumenical atmosphere, which Pope John XXIII encouraged, to help because the Vatican is well aware that the issue of birth control is one of the most important bars to a reunion of Catholics and Protestants (New York *Herald Tribune*, October 28, 1962).

The Planned Parenthood leadership had made a significant gesture toward its only formidable opponent—the Catholic Church. The key through the door of the Church was to be "dialogue." At first, Planned Parenthood's leaders did not expect to have any radical effect on the Catholic doctrinal positions, hoping merely to debilitate whatever political force was left in the anticontraception movement. They took advantage of the fact that Catholic jurisprudence allowed greater leeway in public law for moral evil than Comstock legislators did. The distinction between the propriety of public policy in a plural society from the moral positions of its citizens was well known. Catholic experts like John Courtney Murray and Gustave Weigel, professors from Woodstock, and bishops like Cardinal Suenens were quoted liberally, as if they blessed the political aspirations of Planned Parenthood. Another Catholic distinction also came into play, namely between responsible parenthood and contraception. Catholics were comfortable with the differences. Stress came to be laid on research to develop morally acceptable methods of family limitation. This was a soothing proposal in 1962, even though comparatively little money or results have since been realized.

In the dialogues between Planned Parenthood and Catholic family-life leaders after 1958 the following subjects were *never* discussed: the virtues of the unplanned family, the positive values of motherhood, and the rejection of contraceptive use by teen-agers. (Ten years later the Planned Parenthood Federation launched a $4,000,000, two-year program to have available in New York City contraceptive counseling and service to every teen-ager.) In the early stages of dialogue subjects like sterilization and abortion were soft-pedaled. Planned Parenthood officials did not say publicly what some would admit privately, namely that there was then (even more now) greater reliability for family limitation through natural family planning than for at least half the contraceptives on the market. Probably the most troubling part of the one-sided dialogue in 1962 was Planned Parenthood's downgrading of the risks of "the pill." Most doctors, when asked, rejected the notion of giving "the pill" to their wives or daughters. The British Medical Society was already facing up to its harmful effects on women who took them. But Dr. Alan F. Guttmacher was dismissing this evidence, arguing that potential risks (like heart attacks, embolisms, and cancer) had to be balanced against the risks of child-bearing. Twenty years later, as "the pill" diminished in popularity (for its proven dangers to women's health and longevity), Planned Parenthood came under criticism for this neglect.

Yet at one point of dialogue the "the pill" was the putative "savior" of interfaith co-operation on birth control. The "pill" might provide the natural planning acceptable to Catholics. Not a few Catholics swallowed this pill.

Planned Parenthood had quietly been working on selected Catholics for some time prior to 1962. "Leading Catholic members" of the American Public Health Association were credited with helping draft a pro-birth-control resolution as early as 1959. During 1960 the association polled 166 Catholic educators, lawyers, editors, and public officials seeking a sense of Catholic lay opinion. They found more than half of their interviewers (while asserting Catholic orthodoxy on the subject) ready to accept a tolerant public policy, if that is what non-Catholics wanted. The news media, naturally, made much of this release, as they did earlier of the Draper Report. Panel discussions and interviews with disgruntled welfare clients who (allegedly) could not obtain birth-control information became quite common, with the Catholic Church always pictured as the ogre interfering with freedom.

By 1962 Planned Parenthood extended their forays deeply into Catholic territory. Rev. William Genne of the National Council of Churches and Naomi Gray of the Planned Parenthood staff appeared at the National Catholic Family Life Convention in St. Louis. Other representatives sought meetings with leading Catholic family-life directors throughout the country or made trips to Europe seeking dialogue and understanding from leading Catholics in the ancient citadels of Christendom. One internal memorandum (of Planned Parenthood), not intended for public consumption, recapped each visit with a paragraph or two on how "Father X" or "Monsignor Y" looked at the problem. It was obvious that Planned Parenthood expected support for its objectives from people inside the Catholic University of Louvain (Belgium) and within the Vatican itself. In the cited memorandum one described visit to (a poorly concealed) Msgr. Luigi Ligutti in Rome (Ligutti then being a leading American rural-life expert) is interpreted as indicating how sympathetic prelates could be in the Holy City itself. Cass Canfield, chairman of the Editorial Board of Harper & Brothers, and the most sophisticated promoter of Planned Parenthood's cause, was so encouraged by his own "illuminating conversations with officials at the Vatican" that in a letter dated July 5, 1962, he extended an invitation to Msgr. John C. Knott, the American bishops' national director of family life, to become one of four Catholics who would dialogue with eight non-Catholics, in part to show that the area of differences between Catholics and non-Catholics is smaller than is popularly supposed.

Canfield's procedures, designed to attract leading Catholics, met with modest success, at first with Catholic journalists in the East, and later with some Catholic family-life leaders in the Midwest. But Catholic resistance to contraception had not yet in 1962 crumbled. Practically all Catholic spokesmen, including scholars, were still calling contraception a moral evil.

Cass Canfield was not revealing all his approaches to the Catholic community. In production (1962) was a volume that would be a Planned Parenthood *coup de grâce*. Dr. John Rock became the author and Christian Herter the endorser of a book (released in 1963) that would stir up real controversy *within the Catholic Church*. The book was skillfully conceived. Its title: *The Time Has Come: A Catholic Doctor's Proposal to End the Battle over Birth Control*. Herter called Rock's contribution to religious discussion on birth control only slightly less important than his scientific contribution to the discovery of the pill. The publisher Alfred A. Knopf praised the special qualifications of John Rock for this role, proposing him "as a dedicated Roman Catholic." Although his publishing house never offered evidence of his Catholic qualifications. Rock was (by virtue of thirty years' direct service) a dedicated Planned Parenthood Federationist and a distinguished Harvard professor of gynecology, but his Catholic qualifications are not recognized in any edition of the American Catholic Who's Who for any of the ten years prior to the publication of *The Time Has Come*. Rock's familiarity with things Catholic became evident, too, when asked at a press conference why the book, if it was Catholic, lacked an *imprimatur*, Rock replied that he was unaware of this requirement. Dr. Herbert Rattner, commissioner of public health at Oak Park, Illinois, raised serious questions at that late date in Rock's life about the propriety of appending the word "Catholic" to the author's qualifications. Rock's statements justifying abortion (for example, "embryos have the same responsibility to the preservation of the human race as soldiers") and predictions about the ultimate acceptability of abortion, also, according to Rattner, made the use of the word "Catholic" a misleading promotional aspect for the sale of this book (*Commonweal*, July 5, 1963). When Rock co-authored *Voluntary Parenthood* in 1947 with the public-information director of Planned Parenthood, there was no reference to his Catholicity. The reasons for introducing the religious identification in 1963 were compelling from the Federation's public-relations perspective.

But Catholic complaints to the contrary, Planned Parenthood's ploy proved to be successful. Rock's book was widely discussed in Catholic circles. While some Catholic critics looked upon it as a piece of Planned Parenthood propaganda, a careful compilation of half truths about Catholic doctrine, a literary pill to lull unsuspecting Catholics into the reasonableness of the contraceptive cause, Catholics read the book and discussed it. The editors of *Commonweal* (May 17, 1963), though admitting Rock distorted important facts of Catholic life (most Catholic theologians opposed Rock's view on the morality of the pill and opposed his effort to downgrade the papal doctrine as an "authoritative position binding on Catholics"), thought that the time had come for Catholic theologians to confront the issues Rock raised.

This was precisely what Planned Parenthood hoped would happen. And the new affluent, well-educated middle-class Catholics apparently were ready.

## III. The Issues Facing the Catholic Church

The issues that by 1960 began to surface for the Catholic Church were the same issues that faced the Church of England in 1930.

The question uppermost in the minds of many was: Is contraception really intrinsically immoral?

All other matters in the discussion about contraception were side issues.

The debate frequently raged on those side issues, but the core questions about contraception always remained: Was there something in the very nature of the marriage act—a "given" from God—that precluded the moral right of human beings directly and effectively to exclude his purposes while pursuing their own? Was there by divine intent a necessary connection between sexual loving in marriage and God-loving, too, at least to the extent that every sexual union must be open to a child, if so be God's will?

The Catholic Church had always said yes.

But in 1960 old questions were raised anew. Catholics who wanted the condemnation lifted would be required to demonstrate that contraception was not intrinsically immoral, that contraceptive use of marriage can be positively virtuous.

This moral-theological controversy over contraception factually was only a small argument within a much larger debate exploring more radical ground: Has God commanded anything absolutely? Is there really a divinely established moral order? Are we talking about a real God or man's own primitive myths about "God"? Has God revealed himself in nature as in Jesus Christ? Who says he has, and who decides what he revealed, if he did?

For purposes of separating the later arguments, it is well to understand what the issues were not:

• Condemnation of contraception did not necessarily imply a denigration of sex itself or sexual loving by husband and wife. Loving is an integral part of married life, even when childbearing is unlikely or impossible.

• Hardship in childbearing or social difficulties in raising a family have nothing to do with the morality or the immorality of a contraceptive marital act.

• The intrinsic morality or immorality of any human act is not decided by popular vote. (Obviously the Catholic vote in 1950 was different from what is reported for 1970.)

• The conscience of the individual person does not decide the goodness or badness of contraception. At best a person's conscience—if it is a good conscience—declares him sinless or guiltless. He does not judge rightness or wrongness except for himself.

• The "pill" is not the issue. Standard Catholic moral doctrine permits therapy, even chemical therapy, for all kinds of disorders. Steroids were discovered as therapy for disorders before it was realized that they also sterilized fertile women while they were being taken. The morality of chemical contraceptives must be decided on the same basis as mechanical devices.

• The formal note "infallibility" used or not used in connection with pronouncements of the Church in moral matters is not a central issue to the evaluation of contraception as immoral. The Church teaches many things without fear of error —that is, with certainty—without explicitly calling the doctrine "infallible," a technical term rarely used, and used for special reasons to make clear to the faithful the special solemnity of a particular pronouncement. In other words, if a doctrine is not pronounced "infallible," this does not mean (in English terminology) that it is "fallible"—that is, likely to be wrong.

• The right of dissent is not an issue in determining the morality of contraception, if by that is meant dissenters represent another rule of faith apart from the teaching Church. Catholics may as individuals disagree, deny, disobey (and in that sense "dissent") a Church teaching or ruling, but the fact that dissenting voices exist does not mean that they exist by right, especially if dissenting views have been condemned by the teaching Church.

The subsequent encyclical *Humanae Vitae* addressed itself to all the side issues but centered attention first on the central issue of contraception's intrinsic immorality and in a way many Catholics did not like.

## IV. Catholic Contraception Prior to 1965

Almost until 1963 no one conceived that the Catholic Church would ever accept artificial contraception as an approved method of birth control.

From the early days of Christian history the bishops of the Catholic Church all over the world from different cultural settings, together with many Popes, had taught consistently that contraception was wrong, had insisted that Catholic people take that rejection as part of God's law. It is also true that Catholic people understood and accepted the Church's doctrine, even when they departed from its norm, as many frequently did.

But contraception was said to be wrong, was taught to be wrong everywhere in the Church, and the issue appeared closed forever. John T. Noonan's review of the doctrine's history concluded:

> The teachers of the Church have taught without hesitation or variation that certain acts preventing procreation are gravely sinful. No Catholic theologian has ever taught, "contraception is a good act." The teaching on contraception is clear and apparently fixed forever. [*Contraception*, p. 6]

Though at the end of his volume Noonan goes on to question this fixity, the former Notre Dame law professor was able to make that positive judgment in 1965.

A report prepared for the American bishops in the same year in response to a query from the Holy See concerning the birth-control tendencies among American Catholics summarized the state of the questions as follows:

American theologians and moralists have not defended in published articles a departure from traditional teaching on birth control. They have unanimously condemned contraception, whether by means of interference with the marriage act or by means of sterilizing operations. Even with regard to the "pill" American theologians have disapproved its use to prevent conception, apparently, *with practical unanimity* [italics added]. Nor is there any tendency in their published writings to defend the idea that the Church will or can change her substantial teaching on birth control.

This paragraph was written during the period in which the professional theologian assigned himself an active but modest role in the teaching Church. In 1962 the retiring president, Fr. Aloysius McDonough, C.P., reminded the seventeenth annual convention of CTSA that while the professional theologian made influential and invaluable contributions to the Church, "in relation to the hierarchy, the position of the theologian in the economy of the teaching Church is auxiliary, subsidiary." Even Catholic journalist John Cogley admitted to a New York *Times Magazine* audience that those in the Church who rejected the Catholic doctrine were, as of June 20, 1965, only a small group.

All American Catholic scholars upheld Catholic doctrine with remarkable unity, so that the faithful experienced no deviance between abstract teaching and Catholic practice, either in the pulpit or the confessional—at least until the latter months of 1964.

In 1960, John L. Thomas, S.J. (*Theological Studies*, Vol. 20), specified contraception's particular evil to be the prevention of the marital act from fulfilling its "primary natural purpose." In the December 1961 issue of *Theological Studies*, Joseph J. Farraher, S.J., clearly taught the same. In 1962 Fr. Enda McDonagh of Maynooth says "the two ends (of marriage) are not separable. They are not even completely distinct" (*Irish Theological Quarterly*, 1962, p. 283). In 1963, Gerald Kelly, S.J., explained to the eighteenth annual convention of the Catholic Theological Society of America why contraception was evil. With colleague John C. Ford in the same year he told why the Church's teaching on birth control will not change (*Catholic World*, November 1963), a conclusion their colleague D. O'Callaghan would reassert with conviction a year later in *The Irish Ecclesiastical Record* (November 1964). Felix F. Cardegna, S.J., in 1964, while expressing the hope that "the Church will again and more strongly condemn all forms of contraception," predicted, too, that "all Catholics are ready to accept the judgment of the Holy See in this matter" (*Theological*

*Studies,* December 1964). On June 15, 1965, Fr. Richard A. McCormick, S.J., informed the Catholic Physicians' Guild of Chicago that the Catholic norms on contraception, even for using the pill, were still in force.

One statement of the Catholic case was made in 1963 by Jesuit moralist Joseph Fuchs, in his little book on the relationship of chastity to sexuality (*De Castitatate et Ordine Sexual,* p. 45).

> The Creator so arranged the sexual act that it is simultaneously both per se generative and per se expressive of intimate oblative love. He has so arranged it that procreation would take place from an act intimately expressive of conjugal love and that this act expressive of conjugal love would tend toward procreation. Therefore, an act which *of itself* does not appear to be apt for procreation is by this very fact shown to be one which does not conform to the intentions of the Creator. The same thing should be said about an act which *of itself* is not apt for the expression of oblative love. Indeed, an act which is not apt for procreation is by this very fact shown to be one which is of itself not apt for the expression of conjugal love; for the sexual act is one.

Fuchs says here that within Christian understanding what God has joined together (the procreative and loving elements of sexual relations in marriage), no man may put asunder. Anything that destroys the essential God-given purpose of life-giving or spouse-loving is wrong. Contraception offends the procreative meaning, but other practices— such as artificial insemination, condemned by Pius XII—are also intrinsically evil, although conducive to procreation, because such behavior radically denies the essential love element required for natural, morally good sexual relations between husband and wife.

Pope Paul VI five years later will say the same thing in other words, but by then Fr. Fuchs was himself ready to accept contraception.

## V. What Went Wrong?

Although family-life movements in the United States were flourishing (and even in 1960 Europe an obscure auxiliary bishop in Belgium named Leon Joseph Suenens began a book, *Love and Control,* with the assumption that contraception was taboo for Catholics), pressures were being brought to bear on the Church authorities and Catholic faithful designed to soften the Catholic climate considerably.

First, there was the subtle shift within Catholic circles in the stress from having children to responsible parenthood, to restricting family size.

Second, the deliberations of the Second Vatican Council itself contributed to a new mood.

The pressure for smaller and smaller Catholic families was considerable. A book like *The Catholic Marriage Manual* sold 250,000 copies from 1958 onward in part because of its positive approach to multichild families. When a sequel followed in 1963, entitled *Birth Control and Catholics*, reviewer Fr. John A. O'Brien of Notre Dame observed: "A serious defect [of the latter book] is the overemphasis placed upon the large family" (*Ave Maria*, November 30, 1963). O'Brien also objected to tying family planning to contraception and sterilization.

Fr. O'Brien became an early advocate of "responsible parenthood" among Catholics. While not yet endorsing contraception, the erstwhile Catholic apologetician's calls for responsible parenthood were avidly greeted, not only by Notre Dame's *Ave Maria*, but also by such Protestant publications as *Christian Century* and the slick weekly *Look*. On November 21, 1961, Fr. O'Brien joined such Planned Parenthood advocates as Philip Hauser, William Vogt, and William Draper in a symposium of opinion for *Look* entitled "America's Population Crisis." Hauser was concerned about what population growth was doing to parking and driving in New York City. Vogt asked (in 1961): "Do you think your children have a right to offspring beyond perhaps the second one?" Draper praised postwar Japan for radically cutting its birth rate "by drastic measures such as legalized abortion," which, Draper said, "we would not approve."

This was the rising climate in the immediate pre-Vatican II period for those Catholics discussing birth control publicly. Panelists on TV—usually three or four to one in favor of contraception, sterilization, and abortion—always made it appear that the orthodox Catholic was an oddity in American society. In the *Look* piece Fr. O'Brien followed the Planned Parenthood agenda. His article, entitled "A Priest's View: Let's Take Birth Control out of Politics," suggested to Catholics that they cease fighting public policy on contraceptive measures. In spite of many state laws (said O'Brien), "the Roman Catholic Church sanctions a much more liberal policy on family planning." Since the Catholic Church had nothing to do with birth-control laws on state books, Catholics who fight to retain them are compared by O'Brien to prohibitionists. His final suggestion, that Catholics carry their fight about contraception into theological circles but not into the political arena, seems naïve in hindsight. The politics of contraception in 1961 became its theology in 1965. Later, permissive politics on abortion would lead to a theological shift on that subject also.

Two years later, Fr. O'Brien simultaneously published in *Ave Maria* and in *Christian Century* an article entitled "Family Planning in an Exploding Population." A development in O'Brien's thinking has occurred. There is now something intrinsically good about a regulated family. While Winfield Best, executive vice president of Planned Parenthood, praised the article, Msgr. John C. Knott of the Family Life Bureau—NCWC chided O'Brien for the things he did not say about Catholic family planning:

> I am afraid he leaves in the minds of both Catholic and Protestant readers that these things (about the legitimacy of regulation births) are all that the Church says. And this is not so. The very authorities he cites go on to insist in the next breath that the Church does not and will not accept the contraceptive view of married life, which the birth-control ideology takes for granted [*America*, September 7, 1963].

If one Catholic mood countenanced political silence about the spread of contraception, a different temper of popular writing and television appearances dictated attacks by Catholics on the Church doctrine. In *Jubilee* (December 1963), a man and a woman express doubts about the Catholic position. Later on, in the *Saturday Evening Post* (April 10, 1964), the same woman pleads more explicitly for a reversal of traditional doctrine, claiming that the Church "places married Catholics in an impossible position." The crescendo of dissenting Catholics wending their way to television studios became so intense that when the American Broadcasting Company wished to balance a series of one-sided procontraceptive presentations by televising a panel of religious leaders who opposed contraception, one distinguished Orthodox Jewish scholar refused to participate because he doubted the determination of the Catholic Church to defend the essentials of the Judaeo-Christian tradition on contraception.

What made ABC concerned about having an "Orthodox" presentation of the issue is symptomatic of how the Church was treated in general by the media. During a dispute in New York City over whether social workers should have authority to dispense birth-control counsel to the poor, a Catholic leader was kinescoped in the afternoon saying that no one in New York over sixteen was unknowledgeable about where to purchase a contraceptive. When the presentation was made on the evening news, the ABC reporter had in the meantime found a

Spanish lady (provided by Planned Parenthood) to say that *she* did not know and her priest would not tell her. The reporter later was discharged, but anti-Catholic bias of the new stories remained a factor in motioning the Catholic community toward contraception.

Other ancillary factors also helped loosen Catholic loyalties to traditional doctrine. Books like *Contraception and Holiness, Contraception and Catholics, Catholics and Birth Control, Population: Moral and Theological Considerations, The Experience of Marriage,* and *Contraception vs. Tradition* began to receive favorable comment in Catholic magazines. The *National Catholic Reporter,* freed of its Kansas City foundation, became, under the editorship of Robert Hoyt, a widely read newspaper for priests and religious. NCR devoted featured views favorable to contraception. Even a bishop-financed "Catholic Hour" was programmed for four nationally televised panel discussions on birth control written by *Commonweal* editor John Leo and narrated by former *Commonweal* editor Philip Sharper, both contraceptionists. *Time* (January 18, 1968) indicated surprise at the program's recall, but the real wonder is that these programs reached the point of production and distribution with money supplied by Catholic bishops.

The educational machinery of the federal government was another element in popularizing family planning, or at least muting opposition to government involvement in such activity. Catholic bishops in 1959 said they would not support publicly financed programs of this kind, but four years later 53 per cent of American Catholics were reported by Gallup as favoring governmental dispensation of information on birth control. By 1965, when 78 per cent of Catholics had moved to the affirmative side of the question, federal involvement in birth-control programs was on the upswing. The first grant of federal funds had already been made by the Office of Economic Opportunity to Corpus Christi, Texas, for a community birth-control program. Through the Public Health Service, many projects related to birth control were already under way.

On January 4, 1965, in a carefully worded sentence, the newly reelected President Lyndon B. Johnson told Congress in his State of the Union message: "I will seek new ways to use our knowledge to help deal with the explosion in world population and the growing scarcity in world resources." This was the first time in the nation's history that a President gave official sanction to government efforts in this area.

Congress was not idle either. Senator Ernest F. Gruening of Alaska, a longtime advocate of the goals of Planned Parenthood, introduced a family-planning bill into the Senate. Feeling that his greatest contribution to the cause was to turn Senate hearings into a public platform,

Gruening first called those witnesses who could glamorize the principles of his bill. When Gruening questioned John Rock, he raised possible changes in Catholic teaching and about the "immorality" of the social conditions that grew out of the absence of birth control. The New York *Times* and the Washington *Post* gave extensive coverage to these hearings, as did the Huntley-Brinkley report on TV. In the meantime, National Educational Television, financed in part by government money, prepared a series of six films on the population crises of Brazil, Europe, Japan, India, and the United States. Filming took place in every part of the world, and a panel of demographers contributed to their production. The last film dealt with the medical aspects of family planning.

The full impact on Catholics of this contraceptive promotion during 1963–65 was not yet measureable. Catholic partisans of contraception usually shied away from endorsing the wrong methods publicly. But they talked repeatedly about liberal public policy, about civil freedom for the non-Catholic conscience, for responsible parenthood by Catholics. Later, the effect of this quiet approach was noticeable. Fr. John A. O'Brien, for example, who never previously endorsed contraception, published almost simultaneously with *Humanae Vitae* a new book, *Family Planning in an Exploding Population*, with three distinctive features: (1) The book was dedicated to President Lyndon B. Johnson, John D. Rockefeller III, and Senator Ernest F. Gruening. (2) It contained an insert citing Catholic university professors who publicly dissented from *Humanae Vitae*. (3) The last two paragraphs pleaded with the Pope to let Catholics use contraceptives.

## VI. *The Second Vatican Council*

Many people blame the Council itself for the ultimate confusion of the Catholic faithful. Others trace dissent from Catholic doctrine to false allegations about what the Council said about marriage and family life.

Before recalling the dynamic confrontations between Catholic Fathers over Vatican II's final document (*Pastoral Constitution on the Church in the Modern World—Gaudium et Spes*), it is important to summarize the Council's final decisions on this controverted subject:

1. God himself is the author of marriage and has endowed it with various benefits and with various ends in view. [No. 48].
2. By its very nature the institution of marriage and married love is

ordered to the procreation and education of the offspring. [No. 48].

3. It is imperative to give suitable and timely instruction to young people—about the dignity of married love. [No. 49].

4. Without intending to underestimate the other ends of marriage, it must be said that the true married love and the whole structure of family life which results from it is directed to disposing the spouses to co-operate valiantly with the Love of the Creator and Savior, who through them will increase and enrich his family from day to day. [No. 50].

5. It is the married couples themselves who must in the last analysis arrive at these judgments before God. [No. 50].

6. Among the married couples who thus fulfill their God-given message, special mention should be made of those who after prudent reflection and common decision courageously undertake the proper upbringing of a large number of children. [No. 50].

7. When it is a question of harmonizing married love with the responsible transmission of life, it is not enough to take only the good intention and the evaluation of motives into account; the objective criteria must be used, criteria drawn from the nature of the human person, criteria which respect the total meaning of mutual self-giving and human procreation in the context of true love. [No. 51].

8. In questions of birth regulation the sons of the Church, faithful to those principles, are forbidden to use methods disapproved of by the teaching authority of the Church in its interpretation of the Divine law. [No. 51]. [Here follows famous footnote 14, which refers to the statements of Pius XI, Pius XII, and Paul VI upholding the ban on contraception and a reminder also that Paul VI had reserved certain birth-control questions to himself. The last line of the footnote has been used to "prove" the Council's intended ambiguity. It reads: "With the doctrine of the Magisterium in this state, this Holy Synod does not intend to propose immediately concrete solutions."]

*Gaudium et Spes* attempted to reconcile the personalist values symbolized in the expression "married love" without downgrading its relationship to child-bearing, even the bearing of many children. The positive endorsement of private judgment in matters of birth regulation is balanced by the reminder that objective as well as subjective norms of morality govern decision-making, with the special reminder that "methods disapproved of by the teaching authority of the Church were forbidden." All this seems clear in the final texts.

But all was not so crystal clear in the conciliar debates and the jockeying over the terminology to be used, especially as the disagreements were related to the general public by media representatives already committed to the proposition that the Catholic Church must change, will change.

First, the jockeying over terminology. The preliminary text of the section on marriage (May 16, 1965) was vague on contraception, and a second schema (November 16, 1965) was drafted to include a reference to objective moral criteria and contraception. Omitted at that time, however, was any reference to previous papal statements on the subject. Some parties to the drafting preferred that the document remain as it was; others sought to limit the possibility of loose interpretation of the Council's meaning *after* the bishops went home by having contraception specifically mentioned. The fear that silence in the text would be taken to suggest a Church backing away from its historic condemnation of contraception was not small. Prior to submission for final approval, the Council Fathers tightened the proposed schema.

On November 23, 1965, the Pope instructed the Secretary of State to inform the Council's Theological Commission that he wanted the final text to contain clear and open references to Pius XI's *Casti Conubii* (1930) and Pius XII's *Allocution to Midwives* (1951), both of which condemned contraception. The Commission added these references and also Pope Paul's own statement of June 23, 1964, ("They [the norms given by Pius XII] should, therefore, be regarded as valid, at least as long as we do not consider ourselves obliged in conscience to modify them."), with its advisory that the Pope was reserving certain questions to himself. This turned out to be one of the strongest interventions of Pope Paul during the Council but proved to be only partially effective.

The intervention was looked upon by contraception-minded periti as a blow to their efforts to place the Church behind a doctrinal statement that effectively granted couples the right to choose conjugal love over children (without regard to the means of birth control). The Pope's intervention, though private, made front page-news in next morning's Roman papers implying in its text that a showdown of conciliar forces was in the making. The move to strengthen the text against contraception was interpreted as a strike at the independence of the Council. Bishops were quoted as resenting being "bulldozed" by the Pope. But the Pope responded that while not choosy about *how* the Council took up his demands (with his permission some accommodations on the actual formulations were reached), he wanted no tampering with Catholic doctrine in the Council text (Rynne, *The Fourth Session*, pp. 211–24). Whether the Pope was as firm as he has been reported is a matter of dispute.

Prior to the vote, the Council Fathers heard explained that the submitted text was intended in No. 47 to condemn "illicit practices against generation" (called "unlawful contraceptive practices" in the Flannery translation). Some use this explanation to suggest that the Council was implying that there were "lawful" contraceptive practices. It was amid this confusion that the schema was brought to a vote on December 4, 1965, and passed. (A strange thing occurred two days before the vote: The printed text given to the bishops lacked the exact page reference to *Casti Conubii*'s specific condemnation. The Holy Father himself had this omission called to public attention and the page reference reinserted in the promulgated document.)

Footnote 14 later was to be used to "prove" that all questions on contraception were still open, that the Pope allowed the footnote to say so. (See John L. Thomas, S.J., *America*, February 2, 1966, and the response of John C. Ford, S.J., *America*, April 16, 1966.) However, the publication of *Humanae Vitae* illegitimizes such an interpretation. The only open question on June 23, 1964, was the relation of the "pill" to Catholic doctrine, not the doctrine itself. Those who read otherwise tried to establish a linguistic case, but clearly they did not read Pope Paul's mind correctly. (They claim, however, the correctness of their reading of the Council's mind. But there was no single conciliar mind to which anyone can refer on this matter—because the accepted formulas are ambiguous.)

During the same pre-*Humanae Vitae* period another justification of contraception appeared in Catholic journals—namely, single married acts need not be procreative if the entire marriage was. This defense of contraception was based on the allegation that the Council equated marital love with intercourse, that married love without intercourse is not a love of husband and wife in the conciliar sense, that contraceptive intercourse can be a real marital act. The Council did not say so, but Catholic readers were told it did. (See Fr. Theodore Mackin's article "Vatican II, Contraception, and Christian Marriage," *America*, July 15, 1967.) Following 1965 the procontraceptive Catholic literature became voluminous.

Regarding the conciliar debates themselves, certain bishops were clearly counted among the procontraceptionists. Bernard Cardinal Alfrink, representing the Dutch hierarchy, made the method of choice a matter of conflict of duties, in which private conscience reigns supreme. Cardinal Leger of Canada and Cardinal Suenens of Belgium were quoted at length on the need of doctrinal re-examination and re-formulation. Bishop Reuss of Mainz without equivocation was a contraceptionist (and a member of the Birth Control Commission). All these prelates were quoted at length in the press and in articles, while outside of official documents there was little extended or sympathetic treatment of traditional views held by Cardinal Ottaviani, Ruffini, and Browne. John Cardinal Heenan for the British bishops tried to end the debate in England (as he said) "once and for all" by declaring that for the Council Fathers "contraception is not an open question." Heenan was contradicted by Fr. Bernard Häring, C.S.s.R., who thought that "the British bishops erred." (*Newsweek*, May 25, 1964). Häring, a member of the Birth Control Commission, in advance of any decision by Pope or Council, was pushing the "pill." During lulls in Council deliberations, he conducted workshops in the United States, mostly in the Midwest, where with the help of Fr. John A. O'Brien of Notre Dame and Fr. Walter Imbiorski, director of Chicago's Cana Conference activity, he insinuated the advisability of married couples making up their own minds on the matter. The year was 1964 and Pope Paul had already said Catholic norms are still in force, but in such a gentle way that insinuating future change did not seem unreasonable. Häring, in an interview with Fr. O'Brien first passed around in mimeographed form and later published in the *Homiletic and Pastoral Review* (July 1964), stressed this possibility of doctrinal reformulation, thought the Church could change on parenthood as it had on usury (this was not true even in 1964), belabored the catastrophe of four children in four years, categorized as rigorism any position "which forbids almost all tenderness to those couples who do not wish a new pregnancy [and which] is responsible for many broken homes and broken hearts," leaving the final impression that sexual sins need not be looked upon as mortal—that is, serious.

While Häring was more discreet in his 1964 formulations than later, his "message" of tolerance of methods of birth regulation other than periodic continence encouraged partisans of contraception in South Bend and Chicago. At the twenty-ninth National Catholic Family Life convention in Washington, D.C. (June 25, 1964)—whose theme was "The Rights of Children"—the pressure was strong on delegates to open up the convention to a discussion of contraception, though this effort did not succeed.

Following the close of the Council the pressures increased. Pope Paul tried to stem the tide by repudiating the idea that the Church was in doubt about contraception (October 29, 1966). But a publicly noticed shift came (*Theological Studies*, December 1966) when Richard McCormick concluded his treatment of contraception indicating how easy it was to sympathize with the view that "one might still be tempted to wonder, notwithstanding contrary opinions, whether the existing laws on contraception are the object of a purely theoretical doubt, which is admitted by all, or whether a practical doubt—ultimately freeing conscience—may legitimately be posited." In June 1967 his confrere Robert H. Springer, S.J., writing in the same journal, said the traditional Catholic teaching already had been modified by Vatican II, thus making future realignment necessary. The *Dutch Catechism* (published also in 1967), representing the Dutch hierarchy, declared (p. 403) that in spite of Vatican II's cautionary against immoral methods, "the last word lies with conscience," not with doctor or confessor. *America* magazine, which under the editorship of Thurston Davis valiantly fought contraceptionists, on September 30, 1967, under the direction of sociologist Donald Campion, S.J., called upon the first synod of bishops meeting in Rome to sanction "the use of contraception for the achievement of a truly Christian marriage." When Richard McCormick decided (*Theological Studies*, June 1967, pp. 799–800) that Pope Paul's earlier repudiation of doubt (October 29, 1966) was not enough ("Only an authentic teaching statement is capable of dissipating genuine doctrinal doubt."), the tide had turned. The authentic teaching statement was to come a year later, but by then the doubters were not inclined to listen.

## VII. *The Papal Birth-control Commission*

The Papal Birth-control Commission, if it was planned only as a "pill commission," certainly ended accomplishing little good for the Church. The Commission began a study of steroids that in view of *Humanae Vitae* served the practical purpose of sowing division within the Church over issues other than contraception. In hindsight, it would have been better to let the bishops argue about contraception on the Council floor, thus finishing the matter once and for all, than to allow an ever-expanding group of experts to feed doubts into local arenas throughout the Catholic world and insulting statements about the rectitude of the traditional Catholic position. *Humanae Vitae* has ratified the Catholic teaching on contraception as a matter of God-given moral law. A century from now—when natural family planning may be commonly used as the means of regulating family size—intellectuals, presently enamored of chemical and surgical warfare on the human body, may take note of the Church's courage in sticking to its principles under heavy fire. But in 1964–65 Pope Paul, who through the National Catholic Welfare Conference canvassed the bishops of the world on contraception (as Pius XII did prior to declaring Mary's Assumption), knew precisely where bishops stood on this doctrine. (Of the American bishops responding to the questionnaire distributed through the National Catholic Welfare Conference, only one or two favored modification of the doctrine.) Characteristically, Pope Paul VI, cautious administrator of the Church that he was, inclined to the belief that public discussion of this emotionally packed issue by bishops might prove scandalous and upsetting to the Catholic faithful, so reserved this matter to himself. Critics still downgrade *Humanae Vitae* because it was not the collegial decision of the Council rather than of the Pope *solo cum solo*. The truth is, however (short of an outright public vote), that the birth-control encyclical followed more discussion with bishops (and their private vote locally) than any other similar papal decision in the history of the Church. The trouble for the Church originated with the four-year delay between consultation and decision. The Pope took a powder keg off the floor of the Aula and stored it in the basement of the Vatican with a long fuse, then seemingly forgot that fuses can be ignited unintentionally. During the period of study, the Pope afforded contraceptionists the time they needed to raise questions about artificial devices, and questions, too, about whether the Church's understanding of marriage was correct, whether God had anything much to say about marriage at all, especially about having or not having babies, whether it was within the province of the Church to bind consciences on such personal matters, whether the Church could give more than advice, and whether the papacy itself had not become an outdated autocracy that should be tailored to proper, if not primitive, size.

The creation and management of the Papal Birth-control Commission was an example of how not to organize a scientific study group. The questions to be studied were never defined. The members were not instructed in the procedures to be used in doing their work. Had the questions been precise and the members required to submit briefs in support of specific answers, votes would have been as unimportant as the number of lawyers pleading before a court. Only arguments would count. The meetings of the Commission did not provide for genuine debate and cross-examination, so that preponderance of people, rather than argument, became a major factor in determining "rightness." High Church authorities were interested in answers to questions, but the method they chose to get them was hardly rigorous. They did not even appreciate the role the media would play, or how the media would be used by Commission members in disseminating procontraceptive

views to the faithful. As well-known priests (and bishops) began to disagree with each other, laity followed priests of their choice. As months
of study passed into years, the opinion was circulated that the Pope was
looking for a face-saving device before altering the Catholic position.
Expectancy of change became practical doubt for many Catholics.

The historical record shows, of course, that the guessers were wrong
and the conservative minority, which said that the Church would not
change its doctrinal position, were right. Both in the record of the
Council and thereafter there was evidence that the Pope's only uncertainty concerned the morality of the pill. Was it capable really of
regulating women's monthly cycles so that natural family planning
would become more secure? Were Enovid and Ortho-Novum sterilizing
agents or abortofacients rather than contraceptives? What were the
long-range medical effects of fooling with a woman's pituitary gland?
Dr. John Rock and Planned Parenthood had huckstered the pill as a
soporific to Catholic family planners. Indeed, advertisements suggested
that pill-taking was just another form of natural family planning. European theologians like Fr. Louis Janssens and Fr. Bernard Häring
swallowed the pill as an antidote to the Catholic birth-control problem.
The first birth-control commission did not agree on the pill, and the
second quickly began to understand (what was even clearer in 1978
than in 1965) that the pill was medically dangerous for long-term use.
Theologians continued to argue about the conditions under which the
pill could be morally acceptable, as the Pope's medical advisers wrote it
off as the universal answer to the birth-control problem.

About the time this conclusion was reached, the focus of attention
turned to any and all kinds of contraception and to the Church's basic
and historic position. This change was also unanticipated by Church
authority. While morning vision is always clearer, a commission composed of sociologists, economists, biologists, theologians, parish priests,
married couples, and statisticians—fifty-seven in all—would tend to be
empirical rather than doctrinal and divided in their opinions. A social
scientist could only say that contraception works or does not, that people want this method or that, or none. Once the world of doctrine was
left behind, no scientist, no married couple, no individual priest could
demonstrate with certitude a moral position on any subject. Apart from
doctrine, a private reading, a common reading, or an official Church
reading would prevail at the same time for different audiences. Using
the tools of science or sophisticated logic cannot guarantee conviction
that contraception (or abortion or divorce, etc.) is right or wrong always or sometimes. A private reading satisfies many religionists and
humanists; a common reading is helpful to the determination of public

policy in a democratic society; but a Catholic Church reading was bound to be based on the two-thousand-year teaching as an interpretation of God's law.

There are other questions that can be raised about the Commission. Granted that it represented an honest effort to explore new scientific developments, why was not membership confined to scientists who knew about such things and theologians who were professionally qualified to evaluate new discoveries against the Church's insistence that their use be governed by the *objective* requirements of the moral law? The Commission then would have been "scientific," less moved by subjective feelings, factual states, or political forces. Subjective feelings and factual states were worth knowing, and population statistics and the extent of resistance to Church doctrine also needing knowing (even though the reported resistance was found mostly in the better economically situated Catholics of the West). But these data contributed nothing to determining the morality of contraception. Rome knew this from the time the secretary of the second Commission began to propose members and to determine the Commission's agenda. Fr. Henri de Riedmatten, O.P., the son of a diplomatic European family, has been variously criticized since for the makeup of the Commission and the agenda, yet he was Rome's choice for secretary. If, at the final session of the Pope's Commission, Riedmatten was observed standing, clapping, and cheering the vote that put the majority on the side of contraception, the question earlier might have been asked: Will he balance the interests of the Holy See against his own preferences and/or political pressure? On March 9, 1965, immediately prior to the first Roman meeting, Riedmatten was forwarding to commission members the work of John Noonan (American) and Canon de Locht (Belgian), both of whom were procontraceptionists. The first formal session of the theological section of the Commission began with an exposition by Noonan, whose chief thrust suggested that the Church's condemnation of contraception was a historically conditioned response to protect the value of infant life itself. If that value could be protected nowadays in other ways, the continued condemnation of contraception might not be necessary. De Locht, while no fan of contraception, had argued a year earlier that for many people contraception was better than nothing.

Almost from the start, therefore, the trend of the commission's labor was toward opening up the entire issue. Noonan, for example, set one framework for the debate by asserting that the Church's ancient doctrine on contraception was merely an ancient response to attacks on sexuality, marriage, and childbearing from stoics, Gnostics, Manicheans, and the like. The onetime Notre Dame scholar gave little emphasis to the fact that early Christian thinkers more likely reflected their Jewish ethical background (which in orthodox circles was always critical of most circumstances surrounding contraception) rather than the need to answer pagans or heretics. The Christian heritage of anticontraceptionism was not, therefore, an accident of time and place, but derived from a common understanding of the relationship of marriage to parenthood that went back to the Jewish patriarchs and was consistently restated by Church Fathers. Even the repeated use of Onan's sin (Gn. 38:9–10) as a scriptural base for the Catholic doctrine (in spite of modern research, which makes his sin merely the refusal to have children by his brother's wife, not spilling his seed) tells what the Church was teaching about contraceptive intercourse. The fact that Orthodox Jews and Protestant Christians factually held to this interpretation until recent times only confirms the traditional reading of Genesis 38, regardless of its acceptance by modern scholars. (No one, however, should concede infallibility to the newer interpretation, which possibly may have grown out of a modern scholarly attempt to undercut the anticontraceptive interpretation of Onan's sin.)

Another dubious device of Noonan (which has been used by procontraceptive debaters, notably Fr. Häring) is the argument that since the Church after consistently and solemnly condemning usury for centuries, later found ways to justify interest-taking, so the Church can find ways to justify contraception. But factually, the teaching of the Church on usury (taking money on a loan without some extrinsic title) has not changed. Usury in that sense is still condemned. Furthermore, the Church's teaching on usury was never proclaimed as long, as consistently, as universally, or as solemnly as the Church's teaching on contraception reflected in *Casti Conubii*. The proper comparison to the usury case would be the development of approval for "periodic continence," once science discovered the existence of fertile and infertile periods in women.

Once, however, relativism entered the Commission's deliberations, it should have been seen as a foregone conclusion that absolute principles could not be maintained. Without an absolute anchor moral judgments necessarily follow subjective determinations. As early as December 1962, the Hugh Moore Foundation (a Planned Parenthood-sponsored organization) distributed "An Appeal to the Vatican" by Dr. Suzanne Le-Soeur Chapelle, a French mother of five and a gynecologist, which spoke of "the immense cry of distress from innumerable homes, torn between their faith and parental duties." She considered "it impossible that the paternal goodness of the Holy Father will not be able to bring a solution to this destructive problem." Not only did an official of the

Holy Office (M. Leclerq) assure her that "the decision of the (forth-coming) Council will certainly be sought," but also, after her visit to Archbishop Jean Levillain, he expressed his sincere "wishes that the problem [birth regulation] may be reconsidered from top to bottom."

Soliciting these opinions became a function of the birth-control commission. Riedmatten (prior to the 1965 Roman meeting) sent questionnaires around the world seeking to discover, among other things, the acceptability among Catholics of the various methods of regulation and the methods also that ran "the greatest risk of hindering the couple's emotional maturity." In the United States the Christian Family Movement became the instrument of distribution. As might be expected, the "horror stories" justifying contraception were many. One of the better and early accounts of what went on in the Papal Birth-control Commission was published in the *Ladies' Home Journal* (March 1966). The opening paragraphs contain the following poignant lines:

> Emotionally and psychologically the rhythm method has been harmful to our marriage. Our love, which is continually deepening in Christ and in each other, must, of its nature, seek union. This union is almost continually denied, and the frustration is great. . . .

> Ten children in twelve years—it hardly seems as if it works. After a complete nervous breakdown and an attempted suicide, we have nothing left to do but abstain.

Quoting the summary of responses to the Holy See, the article continues:

> They represent so much anguish and suffering. When there is this much widespread unhappiness, this much that is destructive of the very ideals of marriage the Church wants to preserve, something is wrong.

Drawing on what could only be inside information intended to depre-cate the traditional Catholic view of marriage, Lois R. Chevalier, the author, made this reference to what only could have been the presentation to the Commission by Dr. and Mme. Rendu, France's equivalent of America's CFM: "The French are wild. They have a full-blown mystique about sex and love. Their expositions were poetry and prose: absolutely incomprehensible to an Anglo-Saxon." The Rendus talked with Commission members about sex within the context of Christian married love and the beauty of marital chastity for perfecting true married love.

John and Eileen Farrell, formerly of Chicago's Cana Conference, were dubious from the beginning about what the Commission's questionnaire might elicit beyond the pressing urgency of contraception for aggrieved couples. Questionnaires, like prophesies, often contribute to their fulfillment. The Farrells raised the central question that the questionnaire raised in their minds.

It is hoped that the questionnaire does not represent the mentality of the [birth control] Commission but is somehow intended to stimulate discussion leading to a clearer understanding of the Church's consistent teaching. There seems to be no other explanation for initiating an inquiry about contraceptive methods with no mention of the basic issue, which is the natural and supernatural value of children.

On reading the questionnaire from Rome closely, the Farrells found it also inconceivable that in the Papal Birth-control Commission's list of subject matters "no mention is made of continence or mortification." Neither did they like the questionnaire's assumption of an ongoing high rate of "fertility which does not exist," nor "the tone of many questions [which] suggests that family planning is a foregone conclusion." In providing their view of the world to come, the Farrells prophesied (January 1965) that "sterilization is the family-planning method of tomorrow" and suggested at the same time (what would later be a concern of Pope Paul) that a close look at the correlation of contraception and sexual promiscuity among the young should be taken.

These views, however, did not compete on equal terms with the humanist concerns of the growing majority, nor with the natural sympathy for the burdens sometimes placed on fertile married couples advancing in age and already fruitful. The Holland Dutch representatives offered existentialist arguments, and several German spokesmen also leaned in that direction. World War II cruelties had radically touched both Dutch and German intellectuals. Dutch Catholicism in particular, which once was rigid and separatist (bishops there frequently told politicians how to vote, Catholics and Protestants were highly ghettoized), developed in the postwar era a passionate desire to break down barriers with other religionists. One professor from the Catholic University of Nijmegen explained: "When you share bunkers and churches with fellow countrymen of all persuasions under a cascade of bombs sent by an unbelieving madman, religious differences do not seem to count for much."

African and Indian Commission members viewed birth control differently. Africans respected large families. One of the best defenders of natural family planning came from India. For those who were interested, a highly successful government plan of natural family planning on the Indian Ocean island of Mauritius (mostly non-Catholic) was brought to the attention of the delegates.

In the end, however, the influence of the mid-European intellectuals prevailed, with some solid help from the American delegation, whose majority had gone contraceptionist. The Americans were encouraged also by what was going on at home, such as the statement prepared by thirty-seven Catholic academicians meeting in conference at Notre Dame. The Notre Dame group concluded that old Catholic norms are no longer operative because they do not reflect "the complexity and the inherent value of sexuality in human life."

Sharp division among commission members was taken by some to mean that the "Church's mind" was not settled on the subject. Michael Novak thought the obstacle to Catholic acceptance of contraception was "emotional, not theological" (*Newsweek* April 12, 1965). Charles Davis, writing later in the *Clergy Review* (December 1966), asserted "the Church is in danger of losing its soul to save its face." All the while the Pope kept studying the question. John Noonan sympathized with the Pope: "In a matter of such great importance to millions of persons, born and to be born, he believes he cannot discharge his office by accepting the report of experts. He, himself, must know and judge personally. This is the decision not of a callous but a conscientious man. Its honesty requires respect" (*Commonweal*, February 17, 1967).

But someone soon decided that the Pope's conscientiousness and honesty needed nudging, so they leaked the drafts of both majority and minority conclusions of the Papal Birth-control Commission to the *National Catholic Reporter*. The story made front-page news everywhere on April 17, 1967. The squeeze on the Pope was real.

*Commonweal* editorialists told its readership (April 28, 1967) what the commission drafts meant to them:

> For better or worse, the debate over birth control in the Church has served as a focal point for all manner of issues far more basic than the morality of contraception. Among these have been the nature of marriage, the man-woman relationship, the role and value of the Church's teaching author-

ity, the place of the free conscience in the Church, the validity of natural law, the nature of morality, and the Church's witness to the world.

These certainly were the fundamental issues, which would continue to be argued in the press, in classrooms, and in parish halls of the Church throughout the ensuing fifteen months. While changemakers had the Catholic faithful primed for the Church's acceptance of contraception, apparently no one at the highest level of the Church gave consideration to counterefforts of education to prepare Massgoers for *Humanae Vitae*. This proved to be a disastrous error in judgment.

## VIII. Humanae Vitae

On July 25, 1968, Pope Paul issued his now much-abused encyclical *Humanae Vitae*. Though dealing with the transmission of human life, as its title indicated, the United States Catholic Conference published its contents under the title *The Regulation of Birth*. This is what interested the Western world, even if that was not what the encyclical was *all* about.

No papal pronouncement was ever greeted with such hostility from its own. Up to the moment of publication the Catholic converts to contraception thought their fight was ended. A special eleven-page report for *U.S. Catholic* on the status of the birth-control question, issued one month before (June 1968), concluded that the traditional Catholic law was in doubt and no longer applied. On the secular front *Time* magazine began on June 21 to publish what would be the first of six articles in three months on Catholic birth control. One week before July 25, family-life pioneer John L. Thomas, S.J., predicted for an Omaha audience Catholic Church approval of medically acceptable birth-control methods other than sterilization (*NCR*, July 24, 1968).

And then the Pope dropped a population bomb of his own. Important sentences (Nos. 11–12) of *Humanae Vitae* read as follows:

> The Church calling men back to the observance of the norms of the natural law, as interpreted by their constant doctrine, teaches that each and every marriage act must remain open to the transmission of life.

> That teaching, often set forth by the Magisterium, is founded upon the inseparable connection, willed by God and unable to

be broken by man on his own initiative, between the two meanings of the conjugal act: the unitive meaning and the procreative meaning.

In Section 14 the Pope goes on to outline the Catholic doctrine on "illicit ways of regulating birth," saying: "We must once again declare that the direct interruption of the generative process already begun and, above all, directly willed and procured abortion, even if for therapeutic reasons, are to be absolutely excluded as licit means of regulating birth." The Pope warned (No. 17) about the grave consequences of desacralizing marriage in this manner and the social consequences of contraception.

These specific references to contraception and its rejection by the Pope do not stand alone. They must be seen within the context of his entire teaching, which can be summarized as follows:

1. *On Human Life*

The encyclical *Humanae Vitae* is a sharp reminder that human life is unique. Every human being who comes into existence is a person the exact life of whom the world has never seen before and will never see again, someone whom God himself wants to exist with him for all eternity, an individual with a capacity to reach out beyond himself and help build new worlds and transform this one. Because of this, the act that brings him into existence involves co-operation by two human beings with the creative power of God, who alone can bring this immortal person into existence—and this act of procreation acquires a sacredness that may never be denied.

This is why the Church has always been so concerned with human life, why she has opposed abortion and euthanasia, why she has taken care even of infants born so malformed that they will never reach full mental maturity in this life. It is why her social doctrine has been so concerned, over the past century, to help men live in the conditions that are worthy of their human dignity. It is why she is concerned with peace at a time when modern weapons of war can wipe out human lives on a scale undreamed of in the past.

*Humanae Vitae* recalls men to a deeper recognition of the importance of human life and ways that God has provided for human beings to share in bestowing it on others.

2. *On Sex*

The encyclical *Humanae Vitae* is a sharp reminder that sex is sacred in God's eyes—something that may not be cut off from its proper relationship to the origin of human life. This does not mean that sex has no other important roles to play—as a concrete experience of the marrfage bond's unity, as something joyful and enjoyable, as a celebration of human life itself. But it does mean that sex loses its truest and most profound meaning in God's plan if it is separated from its necessary relationship to the origins of life. The evidence of where this kind of separation leads is all around: a flood of pornography that would have been inconceivable fifteen years ago, a commercialization of sex in stage and film productions that leave nothing sacred, a casual acceptance of promiscuity in varying degrees, a so-called sexual revolution in the matter of premarital relationships, a tendency to disregard any moral implication in homosexuality.

*Humanae Vitae* recalls a deeper acknowledgment of the sacredness and the beauty of sex, because God created sex to enable men to cooperate with him in the greatest of all natural acts and powers—bringing a new person into the world.

### 3. On Absolute Principles

The encyclical *Humanae Vitae* is a sharp reminder that, in a world of shifting values, there are still principles that hold now as in the past —in all places and circumstances—and that will still hold true on the day when God calls the whole of the human race to be happy with him forever. Many things that were once worthwhile no longer are so. The modern world encourages use and comfort and enjoyment of the good life, holds out promise of greater goods to come—and in this sense has positive values. But good values can be dismissed with worn-out customs. Ease and comfort can lead men to give up what they believe in. The promise of a better life can lead us to forget moral responsibilities in the present.

*Humanae Vitae* reminds men that God wants the law of the Lord obeyed, that what seems to be easiest is not always best, that God's grace enables us to live up to his norms even when it requires great effort.

### 4. On the Supernatural

The encyclical *Humanae Vitae* is also a reminder that the Holy Spirit is real in the life of a Christian and at work in our own day. In asking for acceptance of what the Church had always taught in this matter, the Holy Father appeals to the promise of assistance from the Holy Spirit made to Peter and the Apostles and through them to Pope and bishops. Pope Paul knew that if the arguments were so clear in either direction as to exclude all doubt, there would never have been a wait of four years for a final answer. But he also knew that the Holy Spirit, who had been with the Church in harder days than these, would not fail to provide the direction that was needed.

Also, the Pontiff knew that Catholics, whose lives are built on faith in things that are not fully seen, would realize that God's plan was at work even in those cases where contraception would seem from a human point of view to offer a simpler solution. Someone looking at a consecrated host without the eyes of faith misses the true reality that is there; someone speaking to Jesus as he walked the street of Nazareth would never, on his own, recognize that this man was God; someone beholding an infant fresh from the baptismal font doesn't see the life of God within him; those who looked at a man suffering on a Cross two thousand years ago did not see redemption. But the eyes of faith, and the virtues of trust, and our love of God, who loves us more than we love him, even when he asks hard things of us, assure us that God's ways are the best ways, in this as in all other things.

*Humanae Vitae* reminds men to look beyond the surface view of things to the divine truth beneath.

5. *On Involvement with Others.*

The encyclical *Humanae Vitae* is a sharp reminder that every Christian must be concerned with the problems of every other human being. The teaching of the encyclical makes hard demands on some people. It is not enough for bishops, priests, or laity to consider this someone else's problem. If there is something that Catholics can do—to solve problems or relieve them, with better medical information, or economic aid, with spiritual guidance and support of the sacraments—with sympathy and concern in cases where there is no simple answer, this must be done.

*Humanae Vitae* reminds men of the obligation imposed by Christian love.

## IX. *Immediate Response to* Humanae Vitae

Probably the most harmful response to *Humanae Vitae* came in Rome itself from the man entrusted by the Holy See to release the encyclical to the world's press, Msgr. Fernando Lambruschini, a professor at Lateran University and a member of the Birth-control Commission who in the end voted with the majority. The rationale for selecting this particular man to be press secretary for the Pope on this subject defies understanding. Lambruschini in the press conference literally undercut any possibility that *Humanae Vitae* would tip the scale back toward Catholic doctrine, by telling the press not once, but twice that the encyclical was *not an infallible pronouncement* (*Catholic Mind*, September 1968).

Not only was this an invitation for continuing debate on an issue the

Pope thought he was closing, it also was to suggest to Richard McCormick seven years later the very ongoing debate about contraception, not the Pope's words, constituted the clear sign of God's will (*The Tablet* [London], February 7, 1975). That was precisely the assumption procontraceptionists wished to use as justification for their vigorous dissent.

That public acceptance of the encyclical did not follow should surprise no one. Charles Curran and fifty-one Washington priests gained notoriety over their rejection. But all over the United States priests and theologians followed Lambruschini's lead. Five days after issuance (July 30, 1968), Fordham University sponsored a panel discussion for two thousand ready listeners and reporters for the New York *Times*, *Newsweek*, *Time*, and the *Religious News Service* too. The panel was staffed against the Pope. The one priest of five cast in the role of "Pope's man" is quoted as giving only a "qualified defense" of the encyclical (*America*, August 17, 1968). *America* itself, in the same issue, justified continued dissent in the Church and the use of contraceptives by Catholics, noting that Lambruschini, "as official spokesman in Rome for the encyclical," hinted a possible future and radical change. James T. Burtchaell, at that time chairman of Notre Dame's Theology Department, called for "conscientious resistance," in part on the principle that the Pope's responsibility must be recalled "to more conscionable limits," in part because "practically the only spokesmen to support the encyclical vocally are men whose careers depend on ecclesiastical preferment" (*Commonweal*, November 15, 1968). John Cogley asked: "Why not say that the Anglican and Protestant churches were more correct in their ecclesiology, their moral teachings, and their faithfulness to the spirit of the gospel than the Church of Rome, which for so long made the kind of claim its own best theologians are now rejecting? If, for example, the Anglicans were right about contraception all along and the Romans were wrong, who are the surer moral teachers? (*Commonweal*, October 11, 1968). Bishop James Shannon of St. Paul told the Holy Father (September 23, 1968) that his "rigid teaching is simply impossible of observance" (*NCR*, June 6, 1969).

And so the dissent continued down to the low levels of the Church, prompting the *Christian Science Monitor* to editorialize (October 11, 1968): "Birth Control Wins." The Protestant newspaper, citing a Notre Dame study showing that 95 per cent of assistant pastors under thirty favored contraception, predicted that "nothing on the face of the earth can stem or reverse" the rejection.

The Pope appeared very much like a defeated man.

### X. *Catholic War on the Potomac*

While dissenters worldwide began to follow identical patterns of resistance, the Pope, facing this opposition, built a few defenses of his own. Within a month of his pronouncement on birth control Paul VI was on his way to Bogotá, Colombia, for the Latin American Bishops' Assembly. He decided once more to confront his critics with the reminder of who they were and who he is.

Among the Pope's remarks that received scant attention in the United States were the following:

> Unfortunately among us some theologians are not on the right path. . . .

> Some have recourse to ambiguous doctrinal expression and others arrogate to themselves the permission to proclaim their own personal opinions on which they confer that authority which they more or less covertly question him who by divine right possesses such a protected and awesome charism. And they even consent that each one in the Church may think and believe what he wants. . . .

> [*Humanae Vitae*] is, ultimately, a defense of life, the gift of God, the glory of the family, the strength of the people. God, grant also that the lively discussion which our encyclical has aroused may lead to a better knowledge of the will of God [NC (Foreign) *News*, August 24, 1968].

When this visit was ended the Pope had his Secretary of State, Amleto Cardinal Acognani, tell papal representatives all over the world that, in view of the "bitterness" that *Humanae Vitae* has caused, "all priests, secular and religious, and especially those with responsibility as general and provincial superiors of religious orders" . . . [are] to put forward to Christians this delicate point of Church doctrine, to explain it, and to vindicate the profound reasons behind it. The Pope counts on them and on their devotion to the Chair of Peter, their love for the Church, and their care for the true good of souls" (*NC News*, September 6, 1968).

As far as fifty-one priests in the archdiocese of Washington were concerned, the Pope could count on nothing of the kind. These priests were ready for public battle over contraception, even before the encyclical was in the offing.

The international notoriety of these fifty-one priests (later to be scaled down to the "Washington Nineteen") in their contest with Patrick Cardinal O'Boyle had its beginning in Baltimore, not Washington. Lawrence Cardinal Shehan of Baltimore saw a need in 1967 for the publication of *Guidelines for the Teaching of Religion*. Because part of the Washington archdiocese overlapped the state of Maryland, he persuaded Cardinal O'Boyle to make the project a common enterprise. Such collaboration made sense. The early draft of these *Guidelines* caught the attention of diocesan education officers in faraway places, because two years after the Council's close, strange things were going on in the religion classrooms of the nation. On the advice of some priests a section was added to the *Guidelines* on contraception, which instructed the teacher that "he may not permit or condone contraceptive practices." A year later, when the *Guidelines* were to be ratified by the two cardinals for use in both dioceses (*Catholic Standard* [Baltimore], June 27, 1968), the Washington Archdiocesan Council of High School Teachers called the guidelines "triumphal as well as negative in content," objectionable too because they were drafted without prior consultation with the Council. Though no one knew at the time, *Humanae Vitae* was only four weeks away.

At this moment Fr. John E. Corrigan, chairman of the executive committee of the Association of Washington Priests, intervened. The Association, which began as a Vatican II study club, followed the pattern set by Msgr. John Egan of Chicago, who developed there a priest's association distinct from the Priests' Senate. (The Senate is the only organization recommended by Vatican II.) Priests' associations, because they are voluntary, usually represent only a minority of priests, whereas the Priests' Senate collaborates with the bishop of each diocese representing the interests of all priests. The Washington Association sounded the second protest against the *Guidelines*, releasing a "statement of conscience" for 142 of the 1,200 priests in Washington, D.C. Calling some magisterial and doctrinal tenets "mere theological tenets," Corrigan stated that "the bishops issuing the guidelines" in and of themselves do not constitute the authentic Magisterium." Because Corrigan's group favored the approach of the *Dutch Catechism*, the *Guidelines* of Cardinals Shehan and O'Boyle were accused of adding to confusion in the Church.

On July 29, 1968 (as if anticipating the momentary release of the

Pope's long-awaited decision—the press had advance copies), Charles Curran was quoted in the Washington *Star:*

> I believe the majority of contemporary theologians and Catholics today believe Catholic couples are free in conscience to use contraception in the responsible exercise of their marital relationship. I believe the bishops as well as all the people of the Church should speak out to prevent the Pope from making a statement that would merely reaffirm the former teaching of the hierarchical Magisterium. . . . It seems incredible that the Pope should be thinking of such a statement. . . . It would be disastrous.

Diocesan Corrigan had arranged a press conference for July 30, 1968, in the Mayflower Hotel to protest the *Guidelines.* Curran took over that room for his own protest against *Humanae Vitae,* leading some to conclude that Corrigan, who participated in Curran's July 28 meeting, was an active participator in Curran's well-planned strategy to mount an all-out campaign against any encyclical forthcoming from Rome. In return, Corrigan received support from Curran's group in his confrontation with Cardinal O'Boyle. (Without the tactical assistance of professors at the Catholic University of America, the celebrated "War on the Potomac" might have failed quickly.)

On July 31, 1968, the American bishops called upon "priests and people to receive with sincerity what he [the Pope] has taught, to study it carefully, and to form their consciences in its light" (*NC News*).

On August 1, 1968, Cardinal O'Boyle told his priests that they must follow *Humanae Vitae.* He issued a pastoral letter (August 2, 1968), which said in part:

> The Church can do without the dissent of those gentlemen who forget that in the Catholic Church even the most expert theologian must accept the teaching authority of the Church —that authority which resides in the bishops, and especially in the successor of Peter. Pope Paul listened to the theologians and to the rest of the Church, in fact to the whole world—for five long years, now it is our turn to listen to him.

For the fifty-one dissenters the conscience was the independent judge of moral doctrine and the opinion of dissenting theologians an alternative to the Church's authentic teaching.

On August 4, 1968, Fr. T. Joseph O'Donoghue, the priest who after his defection headed up the short-lived National Council of the Laity, was suspended.

The confrontation was on.

O'Donoghue later told a rally, which included Protestants:

> You are saying what our brethren of other faiths have long been waiting for you to say, something we have not clearly said since the Reformation. Namely, that Catholics are men and women of faith who in conscience listen to the word and in conscience decide (Washington *Post*, September 16, 1968).

On August 10, 1968, Cardinal O'Boyle wrote to each of the dissenters a ten-page letter explaining the historical background of the problem and the present status of doctrine and dissent, concluding with the following official policy for his priests:

> Since I am the bishop of Washington, you recognize me as a successor of the Apostles sent by Christ. I have commissioned you to teach and preach Catholic doctrine, and to exercise your pastoral ministry both in confession and out of it in strict accordance with the authentic teaching of the Catholic Church. To present this teaching merely as one alternative is not in accordance with it. I cannot allow you to diverge from this teaching, because I can only authorize you to do what I am authorized to do myself.

Not only was this a customary statement from a Catholic bishop, but a standard response from a chief executive of any enterprise which expects discipline among officials.

The New York *Times* editorialized (October 1, 1968) that O'Boyle's mistake was refusing to accept dissent, in view of the Catholic trend to use contraceptives anyway. The Washington *Evening Star* lamented (October 3, 1968) the "tragic escalation" as a result of O'Boyle's stand: "Despite Pope Paul's refusal to move the Church off its present stand on birth control, such a move will come soon. No organization, spiritual or temporal, can long disregard the overwhelming sentiments of its members."

Some Catholic statements were more unsympathetic. John B. Mannion, former executive secretary of the Liturgical Conference, thought Cardinal O'Boyle had "blown his cool." Defending the dissenters,

Mannion said their most deeply felt fear was "the prospect of not being a priest." (At least twenty-five of the fifty-one ultimately left the priesthood.) Mannion concluded:

> We see at work in the birth-control issue the celibacy debate, the germinal drive for divorce and remarriage, the frequency of intercommunion, and a number of more doctrines such as purgatory, hell, transubstantiation, Mary as coredemptrix, and so on. What a decade it is going to be for the O'Boyles of this world.

In his delineation of the issues Mannion was perfectly correct (*Commonweal*, October 18, 1968).

On the other side of the dispute, few people at the time took notice that two days after *Humanae Vitae* (August 1, 1968), the Washington *Star* polled 315 priests to discover that 203 supported the Pope. Notice had been given to the 13 Jesuits at Georgetown University who opposed O'Boyle, but not much attention to the 17 Jesuits there who supported him. No significance at all was seen in Catholic University's Fr. Robert L. Faricy's immediate withdrawal from dissent when it was clear that Curran and company were turning the difference into an authority fight. Less public comment was made later when Jesuit Faricy's contract at Catholic University was not renewed. During the weeks following the publication of *Humanae Vitae*, O'Boyle was a busy man. Forced to discipline a minority of his diocesan priests, he found more testy opponents among the priests at the Catholic University of America, of which he was chancellor. (In any pontifical Catholic university established under a papal charter the chancellor is the man assigned by the Holy See as the guarantor of orthodoxy.) After listening to what CUA dissenters had to say, O'Boyle was prompted to make a poignant observation: "I wonder whether theology is not being perverted from its high office in the service of the Catholic faith into an instrument for destroying the faith we have received and replacing it with a new set of man-made ideas" (*NC News*, August 22, 1968).

O'Boyle, of course, was not without resources—and supports of his own. A flight to Rome on August 10, 1968, brought assurance from Pope Paul VI that the Pope intended *Humanae Vitae* to be taken as a full affirmation of the Catholic teaching. Returning to his see, the cardinal insisted (August 31, 1968) that dissenters accept the authentic teaching of the Church, especially in their classroom activity, confessional practice, and counseling, at the same time terminating public dissent. The dissenting priests' answer was continued insistence on the superiority of conscience. When O'Boyle announced his decision in the pulpit of St. Matthew's Cathedral, the Mass-attenders cheered. All during this protracted dispute his personal mail ran heavily in his favor.

For enforcing the encyclical at a time when the entire American culture was going through its worst anti-authority days, the cardinal of Washington paid a price. He was picketed at the Shrine of the Sacred Heart on the occasion of the Labor Day Mass, September 2, 1968. The following day at the Cathedral Latin School he was greeted with obvious hostility by the media representatives. That night on national television the edited version of the press conference made the hearty and friendly cardinal look unbending and grimacing.

On October 9, 1968, Cardinal O'Boyle instructed his priests further:

> I do not accept an opinion concerning conscience that reduces the Church of Christ to the role of just one more adviser among many.

This was and still is the key issue in the dispute.

The contest with his priests continued for two years, until September 1, 1970. Thirty-eight priests still remained under discipline. During this period Cardinal O'Boyle expended from diocesan monies more than one hundred thousand dollars toward the maintenance of these priests —over and above what they received from their pastors or former pastors.

Pope Paul VI encouraged Cardinal O'Boyle (May 15, 1969) with this assurance: "Not only did you give immediate acceptance of the teaching of the Magisterium, but you also strove, with exemplary and apostolic concern, that all priests and laity should give the same acceptance." By this time O'Boyle had initiated scores of interviews, individually and in groups, with the priests who were giving him trouble. With encouragement from the Pope, the archbishop of Washington returned to these men (June 27, 1969, on the occasion of the first anniversary of *Humanae Vitae*) seeking agreement with the following statement:

> Having considered the message addressed to us by the Holy Father, I responded by declaring that I accept the teaching of *Humanae Vitae* as the authentic teaching of the Church with regard to contraception and shall follow it without reservation in my teaching, preaching, counseling, and hearing confessions.

A few of the dissenting priests accepted O'Boyle's offer at this juncture. Fr. Corrigan celebrated the anniversary of *Humanae Vitae* (August 3, 1968) with an irregular liturgical ceremony in a Protestant church.

The "Washington Nineteen" took their case to Rome in 1970, although by this time no one knew for sure the exact number of priests still under discipline. On April 26, 1971, the Congregation for the Clergy issued the verdict that prompted the New York *Times* (April 30, 1971) headline: "Vatican Rules Against Priests Who Disagreed on an Encyclical." Not only did the Vatican find that Cardinal O'Boyle followed canonical procedures, but also that his theology was soundly Catholic. The document read:

> The ordinary Magisterium—that is, the Pope and the bishops in their local churches—has the duty and responsibility to teach on matters pertaining to faith and morals. . . .

> Those who receive canonical faculties of a diocese are assumed to communicate this teaching, according to the traditional norms of the Church, to those under their care.

However, the priests who were still functioning were not required to withdraw their public rejection of *Humanae Vitae*.

Ten years earlier, priests would not publicly contest their bishop on a matter of doctrine, agitate the Catholic faithful, or divide their loyalties. The ongoing dialogue over three years did not seem to solve anything, since the confrontation was politically motivated.

Cardinal O'Boyle stood up for the Catholic principle of Church organization and was vindicated in the end. But he did seem to stand alone.

## XI. What About the Other Bishops?

Cardinal Shehan criticized the Washington dissenters several months after *Humanae Vitae* (Washington *Post*, November 13, 1968), but earlier, when seventy-two of his Baltimore priests signed a statement similar to Washington's, he made no effort to force a change in their position (Washington *Post*, September 16, 1968). Twenty-six Newark priests, led by CUA's Robert Hunt, seventy-six others in Minneapolis, and sixty-four in Oklahoma City, following the lead of Bernard Cooke also challenged the Pope without penalty. Some Canadian bishops are cited expressing "horror" at the sanctions Cardinal O'Boyle imposed (*Commonweal*, October 18, 1968).

The pastoral problems—after as well as before the encyclical—were many. The bishops as a body may not have been as permissive as they appeared because the dissident priests were comparatively few, and these few in most cases issued only one press release and were heard from no more in public. Had CUA clubs existed in other dioceses with the same determination to establish ongoing dissidence against local bishops as the Curran-Corrigan group did, there probably would have been more suspended priests. There is a limit to the insubordination the most indulgent bishop will tolerate if he exercises the responsibility of his office.

Even without Washington-type confrontations, bishops were required to deal with pastoral confusion. During the length of the controversy contraceptives had been blessed in some confessionals, but not in others. The use of contraceptives by married couples was a grave matter and serious sin, if all other conditions for serious sin were present. What would Church authority do about dissent in the bedroom? Historically, the Church has been strict with its people only when the people themselves are disciplined in the practices of Catholic life, stricter in the early Church than later, in Ireland and Poland more than in France or Italy, in small towns more than in cities. Whatever the reason, the "power of loosing" rather than the "power of binding" was to be a matter of silent policy during the post-*Humanae Vitae* turbulence. Some looked upon this as retreat from the high standards of observance to which the American Church had become accustomed. In a sense it was. But most American priests, even after *Casti Conubii* (1930), preached a firm Gospel in the pulpit while practicing mercy in the confessional. Absolution was rarely denied to Catholics practicing "birth control" unless arrogance or defiance appeared in the penitent. Customarily, the promise "to try" to cure contraceptive habits, as would be sought for other sexual sins, was sufficient to gain penitents absolution.

The difference in recent pastoral practice is the new phenomenon of priests sanctioning contraception and sexual sins of all kinds. The new approach is alleged to be a reaction to the puritanical attitudes of the nineteenth-century Church. Factually, however, sexual sins were always major objects of the Church's penitential discipline precisely because their privacy and their power made self-control by the individual or social control by the Church (or society) rather difficult. The Church intervened in these matters where few others dared—in the consciences of her faithful.

The pastoral problem now—after as before the encyclical—would be to raise the sights of Catholic people so that they understood where virtue lay, to move (even prod) them to make themselves virtuous as the Church understood that term.

It is in this area of the formation of conscience that Church authorities recently have created some of their own problems. Rome prompted national hierarchies to respond to the encyclical and they did, most of them reaffirming the papal ban without equivocation. The Holy See apparently did not expect that some hierarchies might blur the teaching. Pastoral practice (binding or loosing) always varies from nation to nation. African bishops had no problem with *Humanae Vitae* because Africans—an unsophisticated people—were not contraceptionists. Nor did the Philippine bishops. These statements were ignored by the American press because they were strict (*NC News*, November 7, 1968). The Australian bishops told their people: "Every member of the Church must be considered bound to accept the decision given by the Pope. To refuse to do so would be a grave act of disobedience" (*NC News*, August 10, 1968). (The Australian bishops recently felt compelled to restate that the Church ban on contraception binds all "without ambiguity" *Tablet* [Brooklyn], February 17, 1977). The Mexican bishops: "It is never licit to accept the opinions of theologians against the constant teaching of the Church" (*NC News*, August 13, 1968). The bishops of England and Wales took note of conscience but stressed the necessity of a conscience formed by doctrine (*NC News*, October 4, 1968).

The secular press and the dissenting theologians, however, were not interested in affirmation and reaffirmation. They wanted confirmation of the right to have two contrary doctrinal positions and still be "loyally Catholic." Here the French, Dutch, Canadian, German, Austrian, and Scandinavian hierarchies provided statements that gave the press the seeming loopholes they sought. They have been exploiting these loopholes ever since.

The Dutch statements were the most damaging chiefly because the secular press had come to realize how newsworthy Holland's hierarchy was from the moment in March 1963 when Bishop W. Bekkers made it clear on television that people must make up their own minds on contraception (*Herder Correspondence*, October 1963). *Humanae Vitae* was no sooner made public than the Dutch hierarchy was being cited as leaving the matter to conscience, regardless of what the Pope said. The first Sunday after publication (August 4), sermons throughout Holland told churchgoers that the final decision must be made by them (*NC* [Foreign] *News*, August 9, 1968). Msgr. H. J. Roygers, vicar general of the Breda diocese, declared: "A papal encyclical has no other authority than the force of the arguments used. The Pope is not infallible, only the Church is infallible—that is, the Pope together with his bishops and priests" (*NC* [Foreign] *News*, July 30, 1968). The American-born bishop of Stockholm, John E. Taylor, O.M.I., pointed out that the encyclical "does not have to be regarded as infallible" and "no one should act against the conscience" (*NC* [Foreign] *News*, August 5, 1968). The French bishops took a different tack but ended up going in the same direction. Conceding that "contraception can never be a good," they leave the decision with couples if they face a conflict of duties between their service to each other and to Church teaching.

Closer to home, the Canadian bishops made a statement that some now regret. But in 1968 these bishops, while asserting solidarity with the Pope, refrained from endorsing this reaffirmation of the immorality of contraception. They did not encourage dissenters but consoled the faithful and talked about a conflict of duties. Their remarks were interpreted by Canadian reporter Douglas J. Roche as (1) upholding the prohibition of contraception as an ideal; (2) permitting those in good conscience to receive Holy Communion without going to confession first (*Commonweal*, October 18, 1968). Bishop Alexander Carter, president of the Canadian Catholic Conference, was quoted (*Washington Post*, September, 25, 1968) as saying:

> We know there are going to be days and times when they are not going to know how to live up to this ideal. . . . If the time comes for them to make a decision on contraception and if they are convinced they are doing their best, they should not feel they are violating God's word.

The American bishops, on the other hand, were more consistent in their response to Paul VI but found difficulty anyway. Part of their problem originated with their soft first response, which merely asked people "to receive it [the encyclical] with sincerity, to study it carefully, and to form consciences in its light." Several dissenting theologians leaped on that sentence to argue that this is what they had been saying. Bishop Joseph Bernardin, then general secretary of the National Conference of Bishops, immediately denied this, insisting (what dissenting theologians do not insist) that the consciences were to be formed correctly.

Their collective pastoral *Human Life in Our Day* (November 15, 1968) repeated standard Catholic theology:

1. Contraception is objectively evil.
2. Circumstances reduce guilt.

3. Sinners should use the sacraments of Penance and the Eucharist.
4. Disagreeing theologians have to follow the Church's rules on such matters.

However, because words and phrases like "conscience," "reduced moral guilt," and "licit theological dissent," all technical theological concepts, appeared in a statement intended to be read in lay language, the media were able to distort the tenor of its content. One New York radio station on Friday night said, "The American bishops have approved a limited use of contraceptives for Catholic couples." The New York *Times* headlined the story for Saturday (November 16): "Bishops Temper Curbs on Birth Control." The Washington *Evening Star* on the same day had this lead-in: "Bishops Back Birth Edict: Note Roles of Conscience: Prelates Assert Church Shouldn't Deny Sacraments." The New York *Times* on Sunday in its "Review of the Week" reported that no matter what the thrust of the pastoral, a "loophole" had been provided for a Catholic to practice contraception.

Loopholes were sought or invented. Fr. John B. Sheerin, C.S.P., in a Foreword to the Paulist Press edition of the pastoral, himself invented a loophole that is not in the text. Quoting the bishops who asked those "who have resorted to artificial contraception never to lose heart but to continue to take advantage of the strength which comes from the sacrament of Penance," then (p. 7) Sheerin added his own *obiter dicta* "without saying they must go to confession." The bishops could not mean this because the sacrament of Penance involves confession. Unquestionably, some priests and couples found the same loophole—the bishops not seeming to anticipate how the sentence would be interpreted. Sheerin also raises in his Foreword (p. 11) what he calls "unanswered questions" about the encyclical: Why was it not the decision of the Council rather than the Pope alone? Why did the Pope keep the matter off the bishops' 1967 synod agenda in Rome? Will papal authority be irretrievably damaged by dissent? Questions raised about the encyclical in a publication of the bishops' own pastoral did not help the literal credence of the pastoral itself.

On the other hand, Kenneth Woodward, religious editor of *Newsweek*, an active proponent of contraception himself, saw the exact meaning of what the American bishops had said. *Newsweek* (November 25, 1968) reported: "Unlike the liberal Dutch and French bishops, the Americans showed scant respect for the supremacy of conscience—particularly in the face of debatable teaching. They were chiefly concerned with defending the teaching authority of the Church."

This review of bishops' reactions to *Humanae Vitae* prompts the question first raised by St. Paul in the early Church: "If the bugle call is uncertain, who will get ready for battle?" (1 Co. 14, 18). Pope Paul's bugle call was clear enough. But some generals in the field sounded a different tune. Bishop John Wright of Pittsburgh placed a finger on the problem (*NC News*, August 2, 1968) when, after denying that the Pope had consigned to Gehenna Catholics trapped in contraception, gave stern warning to those who foster, counsel, or impose what is especially wrong, especially if they are spiritual directors. Fr. John C. Ford, S.J., also took *America* magazine to task for seeming to suggest that Cardinal O'Boyle restore his dissenting priests in a spirit of reconciliation (April 25, 1970), accusing O'Boyle of being unfair, inequitable, and unjust.

Fr. Ford made two important rejoinders to this editorial (May 30, 1970):

1. No group of priests has the right of public, scandalous dissidence from their own bishop on a point of doctrine that he is teaching with the explicit support of the Holy Father.

2. When priests publicly and persistently refuse to do so, their bishop is bound in conscience to withdraw their authorization.

Editor Donald Campion, S.J.'s, view of reconciliation was rejected by the Holy See in 1971, but his reply to Fr. Ford in 1970 rejected the Ford reading. He denies Ford's "talent for interpreting papal letters that is not granted to the hierarchies of several nations" (*America*, May 30, 1970).

Pope Paul VI never expressed a word of approval for the hierarchical statements of Holland, France, Sweden, or Canada, as he praised Cardinal O'Boyle's stand on *Humanae Vitae* many times, but as long as bishops themselves were counted as dissidents, and remained unreproved, the suspicion circulated that Rome might settle this problem fraudulently by holding to its anticontraceptive terminology while countenancing "exceptions." This would make the encyclical in time a dead letter. Some scholars say this now.

## XII. The Alleged Right to Dissent

Probably there is no more serious question to be faced by the officers of the Catholic Church than the alleged right to dissent claimed by contemporary theologians. It makes no difference what the Church says about anything if theologians, eminent or pedestrian, can set themselves up as rival teachers of the Gospel. It makes little difference whether the questioned teaching is infallible, because dissenters, who once resisted noninfallible statements (the Mosaic authorship of the Pentateuch, religious freedom in civil society, the primary and secondary purposes of marriage), now argue over admittedly infallible positions of the Church (on Christ's nature, Mary's role in redemption, the primacy and infallibility of the Pope).

Other Christian churches do not have this difficulty. They define themselves differently, usually as congregations or assemblies of believing Christians with a common fellowship in their faith, who celebrate this faith through common prayer and share a common understanding of what Christ wants. But evangelical churches never claim to *stand as mediators between* Christ and the believer.

The Catholic Church makes this claim. The Catholic Church claims to speak with the authority Christ gave, asserts its right to bind and loose not only conduct but also minds. The assumption of Catholic faith is that the believer is willing to make that submission. If he does not, he cannot remain a Catholic, at least not for long.

Therefore, in the Catholic Church two voices of Christ, if it means that the Church formally teaches two different things as Christ's mind, cannot coexist. Two voices saying that Christ did, did not rise from the dead; Mary is, is not a virgin; the Church is, is not divinely established; bishops are, are not the successors of the Apostles, cannot be simultaneously true. A great deal of speculation can go into explaining how these "mysteries" of Catholic faith are true, but not that they might be false. That is speculation reserved for unbelievers. Dissent as defined by contemporary theologians means two rival teaching voices in theory, and two different churches in practice.

The fact that the Jewish and Protestant religious traditions provide living space within the same body for contradictory Orthodox, Conservative, and Reform styles of believing and behaving is not reason for the Catholic Church to consider these as acceptable models. Factually, the genius of the Church is its ability to tolerate high, middle, and low behavior patterns in her people *while insisting on one creed, one code, one cult*. Decisions about Catholic truth are made authoritatively, not as the result of consensus among theologians. *Church authority permits theologians, as special experts in God's word, to counsel the faithful authoritatively*. When the Church clearly states doctrine it denies permission—explicitly or equivalently—to anyone to teach or preach other than what was authentically pronounced as coming from Christ. The modern dissenting theologian denies the Church this authority, placing himself between pastors of souls and the faithful as an alternate voice of Christ, considering it his right and duty over the heads of those pastors to oppose what they authentically teach.

In two millennia ground rules have developed for expressing theological opinions, which permitted development while preventing wild speculation or irresponsible behavior from weakening the faith of Catholic people or compromising high Church standards. Five basic rules have come to govern theological speculation that contravened existing Catholic formulas:

1. Believing Catholics may not openly dissent from their faith.

2. Pastors of souls may not accept dissenting views as norms of parochial ministry.

3. The faithful may not follow the opinions of dissenting theologians in practice.

4. Theologians may research Church questions freely, but if they doubt the validity of any teaching they must bring their doubts and evidence discreetly and privately to the attention of Church authority.

5. Catholics in doubt about a noninfallible teaching may suspend or withhold their assent, while they take every opportunity to resolve their difficulty through study, consultation, or prayer.

The mature understanding of theologians who developed these principles are many. A few typical citations reveal the flavor of their thinking:

[The Pope] must not be publicly contradicted, nor may an opposing doctrine be publicly defended, unless that he himself permits the matter to be debated by Catholics so that truth more clearly be revealed or to provide a period of study leading to solemn definition, or for some other reason [D. Palmieri, *Tractatus De Romano Pontifice*, 1931, p. 551].

Noninfallible doctrinal pronouncements from the Pope or from the Roman Congregation are universally obligatory—

[this] does not prevent anyone from raising questions and respectfully proposing to legitimate authority arguments—[then] it is permissible for him to suspend internal assent—[but] he must maintain external respect for the decree as long as it remains in force [J. M. Herve, *Manuale Theologicae Dogmaticae*, Vol. I, 1935, pp. 551ff].

G. Van Noort (*Dogmatic Theology*, 1961, p. 275) calls Magisterium "a practically certain expert" so that when assent may legitimately be suspended, the posture is still one of reverence.

The only author cited by Charles Curran (*Dissent in and for the Church*, p. 12) who can be said to offer him a handle for his own dissidence is Otto Karrer in *Handbuch Theologischer Grundegriffe*, Vol. 2, 1967, p. 274, which reads: "These personal (that is, of the pope) and curial pronouncements demand reverential assent *salva conscientia*—that is, with the right of conscience respected."

In summary, dissidence within the Church came to be exercised according to these norms:

• Noninfallible teaching required assent from all Catholics.
• Outward disobedience is always excluded.
• Noninfallible teaching can be refined by further study.
• The presumption of truth is on the side of Magisterium.
• Magisterial officers are in control of the findings from research.

Traditional doctrine did not really sanction dissent at all; it permitted withholding assent during private research. A rival teaching office to Magisterium was excluded by the nature of things. This policy resulted in the adoption of Canon 2317 of the *Code of Canon Law* (1918), which, referring specifically to noninfallible teachings, reads:

All who obstinately teach or either publicly or in private defend a doctrine that has been condemned by the Apostolic See or by an ecumenical council, but not as a formal heresy, are to be excluded from the ministry of preaching the Word of God or hearing confessions, and from the Office of teaching. This in addition to the penalties which the sentence of condemnation decrees against them and the penalty which the Ordinary, after a due warning, may consider necessary to repair the scandal given."

After the Council's close, the First Synod of Bishops took up the relationship of theologians to the authentic Magisterium, and while bishops were encouraged to seek the advice of theologians and encourage their investigations, they—the bishops—were to protect the Magisterium by repeated proclamation of its content (*NC News*, September 5, 1968). This position favors the rights of Church authority. The burden of proof always remained on changemakers. Bishops and Rome did not invoke traditional sanctions against dissenters. But neither did they accept the rationale justifying dissent.

A variety of arguments has been assembled to bolster the case against what was called an uncreative hierarchy. One argument alleges that bishops and Pope have erred in the past because theologians were not consulted. Another argument alleges that doctrinal development is due to inventive theologians working outside teaching formulas. However, the function of the Catholic theologians to propose new propositions does not imply that their function to invent incorporates the right to determine the orthodoxy of the inventions.

The more fundamental and substantial arguments for dissent can be summarized under four headings:

1. The effort of dissenters to reinterpret the decrees of the Second Vatican Council.
2. The effort to redefine Catholic theology.
3. The effort to create a second Magisterium in the Church.
4. The effort to redefine the Catholic Church.

While many theologians can be cited to defend one or all of these arguments, this presentation will confine itself to the writings of moralists Charles Curran and Richard McCormick.

1. *Reinterpretation of Vatican II*

Charles Curran and his co-authors in *Dissent in and for the Church* (pp. 100–1) speak as follows:

> With all reverence, theologians recognize that the documents of Vatican II were "dated" on the first day after solemn promulgation. . . .

> The spirit of Vatican II might be ignored in favor of the letter and limitations of officially promulgated formulations. Reference in the future to the letter of the pronouncements of Vatican II as the final norm for evaluating data would bring Roman Catholic ecclesiological progress to a halt. This is not

because Vatican II formulations are unsuitable; rather, it is because they are intrinsically limited to what the Council Fathers intended them to be—formulations which express, for the most part, the maximum capacity of that time but which do not preclude future, ongoing developments beyond the categories of Vatican II itself.

If that statement were made in 1998, thirty-three years after Vatican II, when the Church had evaluated the practical effect of 1965 decrees, the pluses and minuses, and the new needs of the Church seen by Magisterium, the previous paragraphs might be reasonable statements for reforming an aging status quo. But these lines were penned in 1965 before the Pope's signature on documents was hardly written, before anyone knew what Vatican II meant, before the Holy See itself had organized implementing decrees!

The practical import of the Curran thesis is that documents—any documents, including the most sacred—have no real binding power in what they say. For dissenters, they are at best useful tools for subjectively interpreting what they really mean. If, for example, the Council rejected, as it did, the move of periti to separate the *unitive* from the *procreative* purposes of marriage, or the *collegiality* of bishops from the *primatial* power of the Pope, then, argues Curran, those restrictive documents must not be allowed to inhibit immediate moves to complete the job he thinks should have been done. Within this ideology it is impossible to have dissent because it is impossible to have orthodoxy.

2. *Redefinition of Catholic Theology*

Process theology is an invitation to religious skepticism. As the argument is developed: Revelation comes from study, not from God; it is a process, never an offer of final truth; statements by the Church as to what revelation is, says, teaches, and requires must always be subject to personal reinterpretation; if at any given time statements of the Church are taken simply as truth itself, without scrutiny, re-examination or retesting "new truths" will never be discovered and the Church stands still. Presumably, the best interpreters of Church statements are theologians, the suppliers of "new truths."

There is enough plausibility in this position to gain it a superficial hearing. Development of doctrine comes because the Church gains new insights into unchangeable truths when it applies the Gospel principles to situations that are different from one century to the next. The challenges of atomic war or genetic engineering were not the things Peter and Paul faced. However, there are also constants in Christianity—Jesus is God, Mary is a virgin, there is a heaven, adultery (even contraception) is wrong. All the ratiocination does not alter the basic reality of their simple meaning given by Christ himself.

Even the simple truth that the Magisterium decides when "the process" comes to a halt, when the presumed man of faith accepts or does not accept (assents to or dissents from) the "truth" of faith, when "the faithful" are called to say "*credo*" is a *constant*. The reason why so many theologians did not like Pope Paul's *Credo of the People of God* is because it laid stress on the constants of Christianity.

A theology that is "in process" indefinitely is not Catholic theology. A theology that no longer finds certitude in what the Church defines as absolutely certain is not Catholic theology. A theology that does not recognize that it is at the service of Magisterium, not Magisterium itself, is not Catholic theology.

Once Charles Curran led his eighty-seven dissenters in public revolt against *Humanae Vitae*, the Committee on Doctrine for the Catholic Bishops was forced to say that contemporary theologians were insensitive to the pastoral care of the faithful and minimized the importance of Magisterium. To correct and alleviate the scandal caused, Bishop Bernardin arranged a meeting in the Statler Hotel, New York City, August 18–19, 1968, among four American bishops, six dissenters, and four auditors. These included Bishops Joseph Bernardin, Philip Hannon, John Wright, and Alexander Zaleski, dissenters Charles Curran, John F. Hunt, Daniel Maguire, Walter Burghardt, Bernard Häring, and James McGivern, acting rector of Catholic University John P. Whelan, and three nondissenters—Carl Peter, Paul McKeever, and Austin Vaughan. Bernardin at the outset had hopes the dissenters would move toward a position more acceptable to the bishops. But that never materialized. Some of the dissenters admitted they wanted to create a crisis. Besides elevating their own role in the Church, they reduced the Pope's role radically. Some even wanted the bishops to disagree with the Pope. The capstone of the entire meeting was the threat by one scientific theologian that, if the Bishops used penalties against them, as many as twenty thousand, including nuns, would leave the Church!

3. *A New Status for Theologians*

The claim that there is a second Magisterium in the Church—staffed by theologians—has brought this response from Jesuit Joseph F. Costanzo, who, while at Fordham University, evaluated this claim:

The insistence [of dissenters] that theologians are intrinsic to the ecclesial Magisterium is the most rootless of all protestations. There is no warrant for it in the mandate of Christ, neither explicitly, implicitly, or by any manner of prolonged inferential ratiocinations. There is no evidence of such a role for theologians in the writings of the Fathers of the Church nor in any of the official documents of the Church, papal or conciliar. And for all the dissidents' facile rhetorical references to Vatican II, the Council Fathers never graced them with a distinct classification or separate consideration as they did with the Roman Pontiff, the Bishops, the Religious, laity and priests. Indeed, the word itself "theologians" appears *only once* among the 103,014 words of the sixteen official texts promulgated by the Ecumenical Council. Considering the centrality of the dissidents' concept of the role of theologians as "an intrinsic element in the total magisterial function of the Church" to their ecclesiology, it seems that they have been slighted by a Council celebrated for its formulation of the collegiality of bishops and by those very bishops who were accompanied by periti" [*Thomist*, October 1970].

### 4. *The Redefinition of the Catholic Church*
Richard McCormick rightly concludes that concepts about the binding force of Church teaching and the right to dissent are closely tied into what one thinks about the Catholic Church. He writes:

If a heavily juridical notion of the Church prevails, is it not inevitable that a heavily juridical notion of the Magisterium will accompany this? This means that the teaching office of the Church could easily be confused, to some extent or other, with the administrative (or disciplinary) office. . . .

The Second Vatican Council enlarged our notion of the Church by moving away somewhat from the juridical model. The dominant description of the Church became the People of God. If this notion of the Church is weighed carefully, would it not affect the notion of the Church as teacher? Just one of the effects would be a clearer separation of teaching and administration (discipline). In the light of this separation magisterial teachings would not be viewed as "imposed," commanded, demanding submission and obedience, for these terms suggest disciplinary jurisdiction, not teaching authority. Rather, noninfallible Church teachings would be seen as offered to the faithful. Obviously, such teaching must still be viewed as authoritative, but the term "authoritative" would shed many of its juridical, and sometimes almost military connotations. The proportionate response to authoritative teaching might nor immediately be religious assent, even though such acceptance would generally follow" [*Theological Studies*, December 1968, pp. 714–15].

Apart from the fact that general acceptance of Church teaching does not seem to follow after dissenting teachers have done their work, these two paragraphs lay the groundwork for McCormick's own reversal on contraception and for other theologians' dissent on more fundamental Catholic issues. Their underlying assumptions call for some scrutiny.

First, the dominant description of the Church in Vatican II is not "the People of God." That concept is merely one of seven used. It is an additional emphasis provided, but not an entirely new one. The "People of God" described in *Lumen Gentium* are not a mass of flattened bodies and souls scattered across the plains of the Church, but a community of believers varying in their faith needs, faith responses, and faith roles, all shepherded by leaders called priests, bishops, and Pope. Priests, bishops, and Pope are very much part of the People of God and are the divinely instituted leaders of those people.

However, if dissenting scholars succeed in flattening the Church into an amorphous mass, then it is easier to make a case for a leadership other than hierarchy.

Second, the notion of the Church as a lawmaking body is central to the teaching of *Lumen Gentium*. Teaching with authority is teaching within the context of discipline. A teacher with knowledge is not on the same footing as the learner. The Church does not merely give friendly advice to believers about Christ and the requirements of salvation. The classroom teacher does not place the formula "2 plus 2 equal 4" on that basis either. The authoritative teacher insists on his teaching —if he knows it to be true. He gives failing grades to the student who insists on writing "2 plus 2 equal 5," or to the alleged believer who says Jesus Christ is not God.

If proposed as a pedagogical device for reaching unbelievers, McCormick's approach is useful. John Dewey was not the first teacher to decide that indirect discourse or the parable may be more effective tools for educating the retarded, the culturally deprived, and skeptics. But this is not the way Christ dealt with his believing disciples, nor the way the catechisms of the Church, from Augustine to Trent, taught the faithful. In these source books authoritative teachings of the Church did not merely enjoy a presumption of truth waiting for endorsement by theologians prior to intellectual commitment. The obligation of acceptance was stated unambiguously by the Church, and became incumbent on the believer, and the theologian as well, to give assent. Any other principle of operation would have rendered the Church superfluous.

One thing worth noting is that although McCormick and others reject the juridical conception of Magisterium, they keep a juridical or legalistic conception of obedience. They say that authority is not legalistic but then proceed to give legalistic reasons why one is at liberty to think or do as one wishes.

But a faithful person does not look at a magisterial document and ask: "Do I *have* to accept this?" Or, "how much of this may I deny before I run afoul of some legal-moral obligation?" The faithful person instead regards the Magisterium within its sphere with confidence and trust, and takes its judgments as *inherently* authoritative very much as —though for different reasons—the average person trusts a judge or a surgeon within their respective competencies.

McCormick and the other theologians do not reject this concept of authoritative competency as if they thought it had *no* application in the domain of religious truth. Rather, *they displace this sort of authority to themselves—to scholars. They do this because they think of religious truth as if it were to be gained primarily by scholarly inquiry, not as a personal truth about man's relation to God received from him by personal communication.*

Cardinal O'Boyle met the McCormick position head on (August 21, 1968) when he confronted CUA's theologians:

> What they are saying is either that human judgment stands above the law of God or that the Catholic Church is lying when it claims divine authority for its moral teaching [NC News, September 5, 1968].

Historic Church limitations on public dissent by theologians were acknowledged by the U.S. bishops in Human Life in Our Day (November 15, 1968). One sentence, however, written under the title "Norms of Licit Dissent," leaves the bishops open to the charge of conceding what the Holy See might not concede: "The expression of theological dissent from the Magisterium is in order only if the reasons are serious and well-founded, if the manner of the dissent does not question or impugn the teaching authority of the Church and is such as not to give scandal." It should have been clear by November 15, 1968, when this was written, that the dissent going on, however serious the intent, was not well founded in Church tradition, did impugn the teaching authority of the Church, and gave scandal, if by that is meant that obstacles were deliberately placed in the way of observance by the people for whom *Humanae Vitae* was intended.

Why did the American bishops make the above concession?

There are those who say that the bishops were intimidated by the sheer volume of the opposing voices, amplified no doubt by sympathetic mass media. Then, the U.S. bishops were aware of what other hierarchies, notably the Canadians, had said. Some of them also believed (mistakenly) that this was a tempest that quickly would pass over so that the ship of the Church would move readily into the peaceful waters to which it was accustomed.

What is not fully documented at this time is the extent to which a few bishop advocates of contraception kept the document from taking a stronger line. The American pastoral does support *Humanae Vitae* and says nothing erroneous in doctrinal aspects of the question. But dissenters were saying and advertising widely that spouses could responsibly make birth-control decisions for themselves (ignoring *Humanae Vitae*, if need be). The bishops had an opportunity to condemn that opinion and did not. By withdrawing from that particular contest, they provided the basis for the theologians to reaffirm their counsel to Catholic married couples.

Another unresearched aspect of the bishops' retreat was their failure to harness scholarly and popular support of the Church's position. At that point (November 15, 1968) Catholics had not been alienated as they would be later. There was also a large body of Catholic scholarship, perhaps a majority, still faithful to Magisterium. Solid Catholic scholars with very few exceptions remained silent in public. The general feeling among some was that their academic reputations or careers might be hurt by vigorously confronting dissenting peers; or they felt the problem was so acute that only the hierarchy can or should handle it. In any event, the bishops did not attempt to harness the scholarly opinion that supported *Humanae Vitae*.

## XIII. The Aftermath of Humanae Vitae

In the ten years since Pope Paul VI ended the period of ambiguity and speculation about the Church's position on birth control, five different trends are observable in and out of the Church:

1. The dramatic rise in the use of contraceptives by Catholics.
2. Growing concern about contraception in non-Catholic circles.
3. Grand silence about contraception by Church authorities.

4. The continuance of contradictory counsel to the Catholic faithful.

5. The rise of new support for the papal position.

### 1. Catholic Contraception

Charles F. Westoff and Larry Bumpass, both reputable demographers, drew the contemporary Catholic picture in one short article (*Science*, January 5, 1973). Their conclusions can be summarized as follows:

1. The use of contraceptives by Catholic women increased as follows:
   1955: 30 per cent
   1965: 51 per cent
   1970: 68 per cent
2. In 1970 the use according to age was:
   20–24: 78 per cent
   25–29: 74 per cent
   30–34: 68 per cent
   35–39: 50 per cent
3. Whereas formerly the less-educated Catholics practiced birth control against Church norms, by 1970 this trend was reversed. Educated Catholic women more frequently resorted now to contraception.
4. Whereas formerly the less pious Catholics used contraception, now the committed Catholics who go to Communion at least monthly violate Catholic norms.

In 1965 only 33 per cent of monthly Communiongoers, compared to 53 per cent in 1970, used contraceptives. More remarkably, 67 per cent of this group under age 30 now use contraceptives.

The Westoff-Bumpass study takes note of two trends going on among Catholics—attrition from the Church and rejection of Catholic teaching on contraception. The authors do not relate one to the other.

These data certainly lend basis to the opinion that the Catholic Church in America has lost the battle for contraception among its own faithful. The losses certainly are serious. But considering what has gone on in the Church, the remarkable datum may be the percentage under 30 who *do not* use contraceptives. Andrew Greeley makes much of the argument that *Humanae Vitae* caused the leakage. The situation is more complex. As the review of the years 1961–68 has made clear, the dissenting scholars (often merely to justify their views on contraception) felt compelled to undermine confidence in the Church itself. Once people were placed into "the conscience box" for this major issue, there was only one exit permitted if they wanted escape—rejection of the Church on many fronts, perhaps rejection of the Church itself. If one considers that the under-30 group of Catholics likely reject many doctrines—and so are nominally Catholic only—then the per cent *not* using contraceptives can be called impressive. Many of them are the Catholics associated both with the prolife and natural-family-planning movements.

2. *Non-Catholic Contraception*

Those who once were called Catholic alarmists about contraception are now being vindicated by the growing concerns about what is happening to women, children, men, and the family because of contraception. Demographer Charles F. Westoff believes that the United States is coming closer and closer to the perfect contraceptive population—that is, a nation with no unwanted births. In one recent study he discovered that only 14 per cent of all births were unwanted (*Science*, January 9, 1977). As body counts go this statistic is impressive. The birth-no birth calculus, beyond demonstrating a victory for scientific sex, also has raised once more the long since sidetracked matter of human values, to say nothing of religious values, in sexual activity, natural (God-given) processes, marital stability, human health, family health, and social well-being. As Americans become more technological about sex (sterilization is rapidly replacing the pill as the preferred method of child prevention), the serious questions once raised by Catholics alone are now to the front and center of public discussion. The one million annual abortions in the United States say something about American value on life. (Planned Parenthood used this figure in 1957 about the alleged "alley" abortions, but this was a figure used for propaganda purposes, without basis in fact.)

Dr. Robert Kistner of the Harvard Medical School, who helped develop the pill (with Pincus and Rock), recently remarked (Cincinnati *Inquirer*, April 14, 1977): "For years I felt the pill would not lead to promiscuity. But I have changed my mind. I think it probably has—as so has the IUD." In 1976 there were one million teen-age pregnancies.

The use of the pill, which Dr. Herbert Ratner calls "chemical warfare on women," is no longer the panacea it once was thought to be. While statisticians have various correlations between the pill and its perils—its relation to cancer, thrombosis, gallbladder disease, erosion of cells of the cervix, heart disease, blood-vessel disease, and death itself—it is still important in birth-control procedures, because its use is fostered by drug companies with assistance from government domestic and foreign-aid agencies. In 1970 the Food and Drug Administration published a booklet called *What You Should Know About the Pill* for distribution in every packet of oral contraceptives. The booklet ended up not in pharmacies but in doctors' offices, where most pill users never see it. Another FDA warning of IUD dangers (forty-three deaths in recent years) also has not found its way to the users.

Contraception has always been big American business. Profits in pills are larger than ever. Vested interests protect those profits. Dr. Gordon Duncan, associate director of a population study center, says: "There is also very little fundamental biologic research being done that would support innovative developments." The perfection of a natural-family method does not attract large grants because successful research in this area has no profitable return. More money is earned in condoms than in continence. Dr. Allan Barnes, a vice president at the Rockefeller Foundation, adds a further indictment: "It is entirely possible that if the ideal contraceptive were developed today, it would never be introduced in the United States" (New York *Times*, March 5, 1975). There is not enough profit in a creative discovery of this kind.

Meanwhile, another zero point has been reached—what Kenneth Keniston of the Massachusetts Institute of Technology calls "the emptying family." The "latchkey" child and possibly his one other sibling grow with no care at all, awash in skateboards and stereos, while emancipated mothers work to fulfill themselves. Not only have parents disappeared from many children's lives (two out of five now live in a single-parent family), but grandparents, aunts, and uncles have gone as well. Since over one million children are propelled by divorce into single-parent families annually, the problem will get worse before it gets better.

3. *The Grand Catholic Silence*

Fr. Richard McCormick coined the expression "The Silence Since *Humanae Vitae*" when he surveyed the Catholic scene on the fifth anniversary of the encyclical (*America*, July 7 and October 20, 1973). The "silence" he infers is, of course, the seeming willingness of hierarchy to let the matter of contraception in the Church rest without further confrontation. McCormick suggests that a new commission be established, this time to discover what God's will on this subject really is.

Silence certainly represents a vacuum within the Church permitted to grow in Catholic catechesis on matrimony. McCormick himself claims that contraception is not necessarily evil and may occasionally be used. The Magisterium, on the other hand, says contraception is always evil, a grave evil, and may never be used by a Catholic. Furthermore, a "little contraception" exists nowhere in the world. Contraception, once accepted, becomes a way of life. It logically follows, therefore, that Catholic leadership would normally follow through with counter-measures.

But the articulation of the Church's position has all but disappeared from Cana and Pre-Cana conferences, and never really became an essential part of the marriage-encounter program. Catechetical magazines, seminars, and worships for religious educators, and continuing-education courses for priests and religious almost never deal with the subject. Sex education courses continue to increase in Catholic schools, aimed at training the young to become persons rather than to form them to use sexuality within a Catholic context. During 1974, the United Nations-designated "Population Year" (initiating a series of international conferences on the subject), *Theological Studies* (March issue) assembled an accumulated rejection of Catholic doctrine. The Catholic archbishop of Durban, South Africa, Denis E. Hurley, O.M.D., on behalf of the Church, made the following contribution to the population question:

> To keep the Catholic conscience bound to the official view on birth control would, in the circumstances today, require superhuman insistence on the part of Magisterium. This insistence is not manifest. Rather there is a tendency to avoid the topic or to treat it with tolerance or benign interpretation. So by default a major change is occurring in the moral teaching of the Church—which hardly enhances the image of the Magisterium [p. 163].

Since the credibility of Magisterium is clearly at stake, the question has been raised by more than Archbishop Hurley why Catholic leadership has not been boldly effective in helping people live Catholic married life in conformity with the principles of *Humanae Vitae*. In small countries like New Zealand, bishops have natural-family-planning centers in almost every parish and/or town. In the United States, no nationally successful effort by the Church has yet proved its effectiveness in forming the attitudes, supplying the knowledge and training, or providing the support necessary to make *natural family planning* work, especially among the poor. Motivating Catholics to accept the unwanted baby (the essential meaning of being "open" to life), which the contraceptionist customarily destroys, has not been dramatically noticeable in Catholic circles in recent years.

In 1969 Cardinal O'Boyle secured an initial grant of $800,000 from the American bishops to establish the Human Life Foundation which was to organize research in natural family life procedures and educational programs. The United States has invested $1.5 million in research since then, and WHO has research projects going in twenty countries. Up until 1975 no serious effort was made to bring natural-family programs into the dioceses of the country. John Kippley's Couple to Couple League in Cincinnati and Fr. Paul Marx's Human Life Center in Collegeville, Minnesota, were localized efforts to effectuate *Humanae Vitae* principles in Catholic lives. The Human Life Foundation (recently changed to Human Life and Natural Family Planning Foundation) now promises to nationalize the effort, although it has a long way to go with only single training centers in most dioceses. The trend is changing. At the present time $4.00 is being invested in Foundation programs by government for every $1.00 contributed by the American bishops. As *natural family planning* takes its place with contraception as a technique of birth regulation endorsed by government, the programs of the Human Life Foundation, which transcend technique, continue to grow. But the Church has yet to bring natural family planning to the parish level, where it will do the most good.

Leo Cardinal Suenens' *Love and Control* in 1964 provided an educational blueprint necessary to make Catholic principles of marital chastity work. As the International Planned Parenthood Federation organizes multiple fortunes and worldwide programs to influence citizens of the world toward contraception and abortion, the Catholic Church is only beginning to marshal its forces for a belated effort to back *Humanae Vitae* with programs of comparable proportions and public acceptability.

4. *Contradictory Catholic Counsel*

Catholic priests, nuns, magazines, and even diocesan newspapers frequently do not reinforce Catholic doctrine proclaimed by bishops and Pope, which encouraged the secular press to continue its habit of reporting imminent official Catholic change. *Newsweek* (July 30, 1973, pp. 40–41), never reconciled to *Humanae Vitae*, celebrated the encyclical's fifth anniversary by "uncovering" an alleged statement being secretly edited for Colombian bishops that would support all forms of contraception, except sterilization and abortion. The story also placed those bishops in support of government family-planning centers at which birth-control pills are dispensed. A year later, the New York *Times* (January 23, 1974) published another report of a confidential Vatican circular to bishops, allegedly easing Catholic opposition to birth control.

If the secular organs continue to make repeated references to Catholic contraception, so do Church spokesmen. Parishioners have become accustomed to parish discussions where competing priests argue for and against the Pope (*Tablet* [Brooklyn], February 24, 1972). The clearest example of what the current pastoral picture is was given by the issues of the Brooklyn *Tablet*, following a presentation made (January 9, 1975), when Msgr. Francis B. Donnelly, Brooklyn pastor and former chief judge of the diocese, wrote an article calling for Catholic obedience to the Pope's encyclical, asserting that "the teaching of theologians or of individual priests, however intelligent or persuasive, may not be preferred to the Church's official teaching." For nine months following, the readers were treated to a newspaper debate among editor, priests, subscribers, and other columnists over how much attention must be paid to the Pope. Msgr. Donnelly was not lacking in supporters, but the *Tablet* editor thought the Brooklyn pastor was interfering with Vatican II-guaranteed freedom of conscience, and *Tablet* columnist Mary Carson accused Donnelly (January 9, 1975) of not understanding Church teaching on parenthood. A young Brooklyn College seminary professor later (September 23, 1976) told *Tablet* readers that "in reality most Catholics don't come to a moral judgment to practice birth control by plowing through statements from Magisterium. . . . Being good, conscientious people, they know in their heart what they must do; what Catholics who decide to practice birth control usually say is: 'I believe in my heart what I'm doing is right.'" And then the young seminary professor added, as an afterthought: "Understand here is not that birth control is right. It can never be a good."

On the other hand, in the neighboring diocese of Rockville Centre, the editor of the Long Island *Catholic* provided this counsel (October 7, 1976):

> Are we obligated then to accept the constant teaching of the Church on artificial contraception—as affirmed by the Pope and the bishops prior to *Humanae Vitae*, as affirmed by the Pope in *Humanae Vitae*, as affirmed by the Pope and the bishops today? Yes.

### 5. New Support for the Pope
The Church supported lost causes at other times in history, even when its defense of those causes was timid. A moral position, to be moral, need not have effective technological guarantees. A moral view may be correct and, if adopted, involve personal or social risk. This is evident in issues of social justice, of war and peace. The Church, for ex-

ample, may state a principle on race relations without necessarily committing itself to a particular affirmative-action program of government. Or it may receive abuse for proposing a specific program for enforcement. Similarly, the Church can be correct on contraception without having the ability to make practical decisions of the faithful easy or palatable. Government has that same problem. Obliteration bombing can effectively terminate a war, may be the only way to win a war, and still receive condemnation on moral grounds. Gaining a good can be highly immoral if achieved wrongly. Contrariwise, a saint like St. Francis of Assisi can be holy and, by human standards, inefficient too.

Pope Paul VI waited so long to speak that in 1968 he appeared like a lonely defender of the Church's position. Ten years later, few perceived as clearly as he that sexual activity may not be separated from its procreative purpose without dire consequences for individuals, for society, for sex, and for the moral order itself. The American bishops, however, in issuing their *Catholic Hospital Directives* in their condemnation of contraceptive or sterilizing practices in Catholic hospitals (1971), reaffirmed the necessity of these links.

Lawrence Cardinal Shehan, who in 1966 approved the majority report of the Papal Birth-control Commission, said the following five years later (*Homiletic and Pastoral Review*, November 1973):

> The dissenters will insist it has not been proved that contraception is intrinsically evil. That may be true if one disallows the norms drawn from human nature by Paul VI, and the norms drawn from the nature and dignity of the human person as presented by Vatican II; and if one rules out the light shed by divine revelation, particularly by Paul's Epistle to the Romans, taken in conjunction with the constant tradition of the Church—that is, if one approaches the problem of contraception from the purely rationalistic and not from the Christian point of view. But the whole point is that we are Christians and we have to approach the problem of contraception and family limitation and birth regulation from the Christian point of view.

Peter Riga, who was an early dissenter, changed his mind when in October 1973 he wrote for *Triumph* ("I wrote it for *Triumph*—no one else would take it."):

> Acts which seek directly to separate sexuality from procreation have no future, and therefore are doubly sterile. They enter into no transcendent endeavor, which is precisely what the

family is about. Marriage and its necessary consequence, the family, is a transcendent relationship in which two persons engage themselves and seek to perfect themselves in a common endeavor that reaches outside of the relationship, to new life, to the future of the human race, to God's glory. There is no more important or vital work than this.

Dr. Hanna Klaus, otherwise known as Sr. Miriam Paul, S.C.M.M., is a gynecologist. After seven years as a medical missioner among the Pakistani, she returned by way of Europe convinced that *Humanae Vitae* was more of an ideal than a norm. Theologians whom she had met on her way home through Europe impressed her with this. Once face to face with abortion in the affluent contraceptive culture of her own country, she was forced to rethink the relationship between womanhood and contraception. Her final conclusion was that for the "feminine woman" every coitus contains within it the psychic germs of a child, that *Human Vitae* speaks of "the integral vision of humanity beyond partial perspectives: What it proposes is not optional for human nature but completes it" (*Homiletic and Pastoral Review*, October 1973).

The work of Dr. John Billings of Melbourne, Australia, promoter of natural family planning, is perhaps a harbinger of Pope Paul's ultimate vindication. In the nineteenth century the Church, by taking a strong stand against craniotomy, helped encourage the perfection of the Caesarian section. The hand of science, again as a result of the Church's condemnation of direct interference with life and the process of giving life, may contribute toward new developments in the science of reproduction.

## XIV. *The Ford-Grisez Thesis*

Fr. John C. Ford, S.J. and Dr. Germain Grisez focus on the common teaching of the Church on contraception, of which *Human Vitae* is only the latest handing on of authentic teaching. On the tenth anniversary of *Humanae Vitae*, in a lengthy article for *Theological Studies* (June 1978), they take up the ancient origin of the teaching, the universal scope of the teaching, and the certainty with which it has been proposed as an imperative determinant in the behavior of married Catholics.

From 1963 on, however, theologians seeking to justify contraception, after observing (correctly) that the teaching had not been formally defined, proceeded to infer (erroneously) that the doctrine had not been infallibly taught. This "dethroning" of the Church teaching enabled them (so they argued) to attack more forcibly the certainty and truth of the traditional position.

Ford-Grisez believe, in the light of the way the teaching on contraception has been proposed through the centuries, that the "infallibility" claim of the teaching is very much alive, that the received Catholic teaching is still being proposed infallibly by the ordinary and universal Magisterium. The conditions under which the ordinary Magisterium of the bishops dispersed throughout the world can proclaim the teaching of Christ infallibly have been articulated by the Second Vatican Council. Ford-Grisez argue that *Humanae Vitae* meets those criteria, thus making the Church doctrine a divinely guaranteed teaching.

They make an important point. Frequently, dissenters start with the assumption that teachings not formally defined are not infallible. This is not true. Many Catholic teachings are *de facto* infallibly taught, even though not formally defined. *Lumen Gentium* (No. 25) reads:

> Although the bishops individually do not enjoy the prerogative of infallibility, they nevertheless proclaim the teaching of Christ infallibly, even when they are dispersed throughout the world, provided that they remain in communion with each other and with the Successor of Peter and that in authoritatively teaching on a matter of faith and morals they agree in one judgment as that to be held definitively.

The declaration, as Council debates indicated, extends ordinary infallibility in the Church not only to matters formally revealed (for example, the divinity of Christ) but also to things virtually revealed (for example, Mary's Immaculate Conception), to what is necessarily connected with revelation (for example, the existence of a natural moral law), to things that are to be believed, *and* to things that are to be done.

The four conditions of *Lumen Gentium* under which bishops, dispersed throughout the world, proclaim the doctrine of Christ infallibly are summarized by Ford-Grisez as follows:

1. The bishops who remain in communion with one another and teach with the Pope.
2. They teach authoritatively too in a matter of faith and morals.
3. They agree on one judgment.
4. They propose this judgment as one to be held definitively.

Just as the divinity of Christ was taught by the ordinary and universal Magisterium of the Church prior to its definition by the Council of Nicea in 325, so the teaching on contraception has been proposed by the Church as a teaching to be held definitively by believers. Factually, while many Arian bishops denied the doctrine of Christ's divinity before and after definition, no more than a handful of Catholic bishops during or after Vatican II denied the teaching on contraception as *the taught and believed Catholic doctrine.*

Indeed, as John Noonan abundantly documents, no Catholic theologian up until 1963 ever taught that contraception was good. What is clear also is that in spite of internal opposition, Catholic teaching was and still is proposed as the *constant doctrine of the Church.* Even when scholars—outside the Church, later within—questioned the doctrine's scriptural base or the validity of some rational arguments in its favor, the Pope and bishops continued to reaffirm the Catholic norm.

Pope Paul, while not using the term "infallible" (Pius XII did not use the term in proclaiming Mary's Assumption), does speak in solemn language. He is not speaking as another theologian, nor as one intervening in a theological dispute. The Pope is explicitly teaching a doctrine to which by divine patrimony he avers the Catholic Church is unalterably committed. He reaffirms the Church's certainty on the subject. He rejects the possibility of altering its substance.

In essence, Ford-Grisez say: If the Catholic tradition on contraception is not infallible teaching, what can be called infallible?

Even an affirmative answer to this question will not settle the argument for dissenters. But it does put the argument back in context. Michael Novak, for example, only recently has come to recognize (in the debate over the ordination of women) what he did not accept in the earlier argument over contraception:

> For centuries the Church has had an unbroken tradition, so unchallenged that reasons for it have not been articulated. Obscurely, many persons sense some weight in those reasons [*Commonweal*, September 2, 1977].

Christ did not win all his public debates over what he was *revealing.* The Church has also learned that the validity or certainty of a teaching does not depend for acceptance on its perusability or on the solemnity of the preaching. Faith in the *given* teacher usually settles the argument for the believer. This does not terminate intellectual discussion because the Church, with its intellectual tradition, encourages research and investigation. Eventually formal pronouncements by the Church's teaching authority set parameters for theological exploration. Ford-Grisez know that scholars are tempted to read history backward and find practices, attitudes, and institutions incompatible with the law of Christ that once were accepted or tolerated by Christians, and even by the Magisterium—for example, slavery. This becomes the basis of proposing contraception as a new Christian insight comparable to the Church's late acceptance of political equality. However, what the Church accepts and tolerates is quite distinct from what it teaches. Insight into the unstable mentality of modern culture enables the Church to realize why certain marriages today can be declared null and void that formerly would not have been so understood. It does not follow, however, that the Church's teaching on the indissolubility of a sacramental marriage itself changes.

The contraception teaching must be judged in this light. An infallibly taught doctrine continues to be taught without formal definition because factual questions keep recurring. For example, what is a contraceptive? When the Pope and the Council undertook a second study of the pill they were dealing with factual questions. If the pill could be judged noncontraceptive, at least under certain circumstances, it would not fall under the Church's general ban. The Magisterium, never in doubt about the immorality of contraception itself, was in momentary doubt about the absolute immorality of the pill. Since *Humanae Vitae* the Church is no longer uncertain even about that.

A major management problem remains, however. This is the dissonance between doctrine and practice. The issue is no longer contraception but the ability of the Church to make its doctrine live in the lives of the faithful.

## CHAPTER VII

The Battle for the Catholic Family, or the Siege of
Chicago

## I. The Cana Conference of Chicago

Until 1963 most substantial Catholic doctrines, including the one on contraception, were in the safe possession of the faithful. On September 5, 1963, the University of Notre Dame and the Cana Conference of Chicago cosponsored what would become three lengthy meetings over eighteen months on the moral and theological considerations of the population problem. The Ford Foundation provided the money, which was to be used to promote other regionals of this kind.

The first session resulted in a volume called *The Problem of Population,* called by the publisher "an authoritative study from the University of Notre Dame." Invitees were chosen by Dr. George Shuster of Notre Dame, and by Fr. Walter Imbiorski, and Fr. John L. Thomas, S.J., of Chicago's Cana Conference. The June 7 invitation to Msgr. John C. Knott advised the NCWC family-life director that this conference would not be "wide open" but would concentrate on formulating a Catholic position. Msgr. Knott replied to Dr. Shuster seven days later, remarking: "It is of vital importance that the Catholic position be clarified on the many and varied questions arising from the problem . . . to formulate as definitive a Catholic position as possible. It is, to my mind, equally important to select competent people from various disciplines with different, even divergent, points of view. . . . In view of the importance of the meeting itself and even more of what may come of it, I feel I must state frankly that the list [of invitees] shows a certain imbalance."

The results of that conference indicate that the participants were hand-picked with a particular view in mind. Most conferees later be-

came associated with procontraception views, including Fr. Andrew
Greeley, Fr. Walter Imbiorski, Fr. John A. O'Brien, and Fr. John L.
Thomas. One of those invited to formulate "a Catholic position" was
Dr. Dudley Kirk of the Population Council of New York, an organization dedicated to international population control through contraception, sterilizaton, and abortion. Dr. Shuster saw the anomaly when,
while explaining that *The Problem of Population* "is largely devoted to
clarifying the teaching of the Catholic Church," he realized: "It is of
course true that if the group had been differently constituted we might
well have obtained another product" (p. xiii). Advance criticism by
Msgr. Knott and postconference complaints by Fr. Thurston Davis,
S.J., of *America* and of theologian Fr. John Lynch, S.J., of Weston,
Massachusetts, did not change the orientation or results probably because the Notre Dame effort claimed the advance blessing of Albert
Cardinal Meyer of Chicago.

The imbalance was clearer when in 1965 "thirty-seven American
Catholic scholars"—after the Notre Dame meetings—issued a public
statement giving "qualified endorsement of contraception" and
suggested "a change in the Church's traditional position on birth con-
trol." This document was brought to Rome twice, the first time by Fr.
Theodore M. Hesburgh, president of Notre Dame and, when it seemed
lost in Vatican officialdom, once more by Joseph Cardinal Ritter. Later,
John Cogley made a front-page story of the dissent (New York *Times*
September 28, 1965), listing as signatories, among others: Fr. Gregory
Baum, Fr. Felix Cardegna, S.J., Fr. Walter Imbiorski, Fr. John A.
O'Brien, Fr. John L. Thomas, Fr. Robert O. Johann, Fr. Bernard
Cooke, Mr. Robert Hoyt, Mr. Philip Scharper, and Mr. Donald Thor-
man.

The Cana Conference of Chicago began in 1945 as an exciting family movement of the Catholic Church. It became in 1965 a focal point
of contraceptive infection for the American Church. The dynamism
that impelled Fr. John Egan and Fr. Walter Imbiorski into national
Catholic prominence ultimately served the cause of those who challenged the continued relevance of Catholic doctrine in the lives of
Catholic couples.

Factors in Chicago that made Cana a constructive movement for
Catholic family values later harmed the Church once its machinery was
directed to different purposes. These factors, present in varying degrees
in all Catholic dioceses, were uniquely packaged in the Chicago environs: charismatic and overpowering energy in the priest leadership;
educated and classy laity waiting to be motivated for a cause; a good
cause at the right time; a free-wheeling, independent style of behavior
typical of the Windy City itself; and relatively permissive bishops.

These latter qualities of Chicago Catholicism are not descriptions fabricated by jealous outsiders but descriptions provided by proud residents on the Midwest scene. Shortly after the doors of Vatican II closed, *America* magazine, prompted by the musings of Bishop James P. Shannon, sought to explain the "unique vitality" of "Catholicism, Midwest style" which had been evident in Rome from 1962 to 1965. Prominent Catholic writers and observers were asked on February 12, 1966, to define that uniqueness. Donald Thorman thought "its greatest blessing has been its permissive hierarchy." Andrew Greeley explained that unlike eastern Catholics, who are often a majority but think and act like a minority, Midwest Catholics "who are quite unaware that they are a minority often think and act like a majority." Justus George Lawler used the words "more open, more deviant, more free." Joel Wells of *The Critic* boasted that "most of the Catholics in the East make their living by writing and talking about what is being done in the Midwest." Msgr. John Tracy Ellis opined: "During the period since the red hat first came to Chicago in 1924, the ordinaries of that see have for the most part, it seems to me, allowed things to happen among their clergy and laity the while they have maintained a vigilant, masterly inactivity." Ellis complimented Chicago for extending its influence throughout the Church of the United States and even abroad.

A different assessment of Chicago Catholicism was given by the only two grass-roots Catholics invited by *America* to make comment. John and Eileen Farrell, then very active in Chicago's Cana Conference, were naturally proud of all their hometown's virtues. Adjectives used by Carl Sandburg in describing the Great Lakes' single most solitary boast were cited by the Farrells with relish—"proud to be alive," strong, laughing, husky, brawling, bragging, fierce, cunning. But then the Farrells, already ten years involved with Cana, delineate aspects of the local scene that have since 1966 become quite familiar to Catholics nationwide.

> The Chicago approach, as might be expected, has the defects of its virtues. Enthusiasm can and does become impetuosity; boldness often turns into arrogance; being "proud to be alive" can become pride of life; an inordinate taste for action, the toil of piling job on job, can abort the intellectual and especially the interior life. . . .

> We like to reform people and institutions, but without the burden of continuing self-reform. We like to originate all the worthwhile movements or at least be under the terrible burden of destiny to provide them with effective leadership. It seems

that we cannot start a project without deprecating every other past or present effort in the same field; as for the future, we are the wave of it. We are paternalistic. We make a fetish of the new and the big and the well-publicized, never suspecting that the real seeds of sanctity sown in our midst are growing very quietly. We are impervious to contrary points of view or fraternal correction. We have, you might say, a Messiah complex. You can see why there are those who talk about the Chicago syndrome.

We mocked the poor old Catholic and his ghetto mentality. But all the while, by means of our circumscribed acquaintance and the narrowness of our reading list, we have constructed an even higher ghetto wall of our own. We have talked about involving married people democratically in the work of the apostolate, but sometimes the loudest exponents of the will of the majority have been the most totalitarian of all. And it usually turns out that tight little hierarchies of laity, staff, or clergy, or all three of them, run most of our works. . . .

We have talked vigorously about renewal but neglected to evaluate the premises of the movements in which we were involved.

A dozen years later, in every part of the country, Catholics have become familiar with, if not accustomed to, the denigration of the Catholic past, brawling within the Church, ruthless disregard of sacred pieties, anticlericalism, anti-Romanism, monopoly power held by the few used against majorities, the lone pastor, or the bishop. But when these words were first drafted in 1965 the Farrells were writing out of long years of experience with Fr. John Egan's and Fr. Walter Imbiorski's Cana Conference of Chicago.

It was not that way back in 1945, when Msgr. Reynold Hillenbrand, Fr. Jules Marhoefer, and Fr. James Voss decided that "the field of marriage" offered the best opportunity for the kind of Catholic action in which the three of them had a consuming interest. While Cana in Chicago began with married couples and Jesuit John Delaney as Family Renewal Days, its organization as that of the Christian Family Movement came under the influence of a young priest trained by Msgr. Reynold Hillenbrand, once the rector of Mundelein Seminary. The dedicated Hillenbrand, who later would become distressed by the activity of some of his "creatures," continued year after year to define what the spirit and objectives of the family apostolates, the role of its priests, and the relationship of this apostolate to the Church should be. Hillenbrand called this family apostolate

> . . . a movement of the Church. As an organization, at every level, it falls under the bishop. Its purpose, under the bishop, is to train lifelong apostles so that they will be equipped for their task in the total apostolate of the Church [ACT, August 1965].

Both Cana and CFM, strictly speaking, were lay apostolates, but their priests had "all-important formative tasks." Without priests, according to the founding father, there were no formed apostles. Besides, priests are "the link with the bishop, who officially teaches and rules" and also "the main source of doctrine and of complete spiritual formation." So spoke Msgr. Hillenbrand at the very moment both Cana and CFM in Chicago were veering from the course he chartered for them.

However, driven by Hillenbrand's apostolic energy, Cana, for ten years after 1945, exercised a powerful influence on Catholic family life, not only in Chicago but also across the country. By 1956 almost 7,000 Chicago couples annually attended conferences on marriage and parenthood, with an equal number of engaged couples absorbing Pre-Cana teaching prior to their wedding. By 1956, at least 500 leader couples were already involved in promoting and staffing Chicago's Cana program, and according to Fr. Egan's 1956 report to Cardinal Stritch, they were also involved in similar programs for 13 other dioceses. Cana existed in other places, notably in St. Louis, Milwaukee, Buffalo, Newark, Brooklyn, Washington, D.C., and Hartford. But ten years after its creation Chicago still had the best and most dynamic program. By 1963—the year when the contraceptive movement began in earnest within the Church—the family-life apostolate had taken root within 133 dioceses of the United States.

Side by side with this marvelous energy, growth, and spiritual impact, certain other features of teaching and organization began to appear, which when permitted to run riot led Cana and CFM in directions hardly intended by the original founders. Only three need be mentioned here, which from 1952 onward were sources of ongoing controversy among the personnel of Chicago's Cana Conference.

1. The shift from stress on God's revelation concerning marriage to stress on human experience within marriage.
2. The change from a theologically determined activity to a sociological enterprise.
3. The rise of anticlericalism and anti-Magisterium.

1. *Revelation vs. Experience*

If ever a movement was organized to invite couples "to put on that mind which is Christ Jesus Our Lord," Cana was. *Cana was loving, emotional, liturgical, but most of all Cana provided intellectual and spiritual formation around the doctrines of the Catholic Church.* That was why it came into being. That was its particular genius. That was why priests, doctors, and leader couples entered the movement, and what they sought to accomplish.

The day-to-day problems of marriage, real or imagined, experienced or anticipated, were always treated within the context of formation. Participating couples were brought *up* to the norms of revelation not as dreamy ideals unattainable for the few but as the essential reality necessary for a healthy Catholic marriage. Cana never was allowed to go *down* to the couples' level save as a way to lifting their sights and intentions. The impact of the approach was immediate in most cases, delayed in some, and ineffective for those who found Cana doctrine too hard to follow.

But then in Chicago first, the content of the Cana Conference began to be determined by the subjective response of the audience, not by the objective nature of marriage as created by God, treated in Scripture, or defined by the Church.

This shift, hardly noticed at first, came about after the introduction of "buzz group" discussion. Fr. John Egan was a "buzz group" devotee. Break people into groups. Get them involved. The learning process went a long way with a little participatory democracy. John Dewey would have approved.

A "buzz group," if its purpose is to locate people's *feeling* about a problem or to reach a group decision has something going for it. But group discussion, at least in Catholic circles, was not intended to be a substitute for the teaching process. For one thing, group discussions do not allow for a teacher-pupil relationship, for a hierarchy of knowledge or truth, for a distinction between teacher or learner. The priest, who in a Cana Conference was ostensibly drawing on the wisdom of Christ, of Church Fathers and Church Doctors, of Catholic doctrine, in order to lead parishioners from error to truth, from imperfect to more perfect understanding or performance, had in a buzz group no greater qualifications than the most ignorant, heretical, or immoral of the participants. Buzz groups have been defended as more satisfactory teaching instruments when people do not like being talked at or down to. Factually, however, little teaching goes on in a buzz group, unless the group comes under the direction of a "leader" skilled in the art of manipulating group discussions and thereby indoctrinating, almost without anyone realizing what is happening. When group discussions are more than experiences in shared ignorance or emotional ventilation, there can be manipulated audiences. Once Cana leadership turned away from Catholic doctrine toward contraception, group dynamics proved an effective means of insinuating contraception without the leader having openly to appear to be violating Catholic norms.

Whether the "experience" of the informed group or that exercised by a dominating leader prevailed in a given situation, the shift in focus from doctrine to experience proved catastrophic for the Catholic family apostolates.

2. *Theology vs. Sociology*

In the early Cana conferences there was very little sociology and only a little psychology, hardly more than common sense. Men and women had different thought patterns and emotional responses. Marriage brought them together so that they could complement each other through the union of their differences, together do a better job of bearing and raising children, than they would individually, etc.

The only importance sociology had for the early movement was the rationale developed for Cana by John L. Thomas, S.J. The secular social situation justified Cana's goal to develop and support a "Catholic family subculture" safe from secularist contamination. Sociology entered the content of Cana Conferences in earnest only when the need arose to justify the small Catholic family and contraception. Sociology became important then because by definition it is the science that computerizes and rationalizes human experience. What Fr. Egan began with buzz groups, Fr. Imbiorski completed with sociology workshops.

In a report for a Chicago prelate, Dr. Herbert Ratner, one of Fr. Egan's Cana Conference medical pioneers, summarized the change as follows:

> Although seeds of what was to come were apparent much earlier in the Cana Movement, a sharp change of direction in Cana thinking occurred about three years ago (i.e. about 1962). At that time, under the influence of Fr. John L. Thomas, S.J., Fr. Imbiorski committed Chicago Cana to a sociologic rather than a theologically determined movement. The implicit assumptions, many of which became progressively explicit, were along these lines: (1) The small family was the family of the present and the future and was to be promoted; (2) sexual maturity and early marriage were *de facto* and the Church had to accommodate its position to satisfy the desires of young people; (3) sexual activity was to be

thought of as divorced from essential procreative ends and the sexual revolution must be made the occasion of a new development in the Church's theology; (4) the population explosion was a here-and-now reality that also demanded a radical change in the Church's concept of marriage; (5) the Church's position against contraception (and one may suspect against sterilization and abortion) was antiquated and pressures had to be exerted to force a change in the Church's position; (6) the rhythm method was to be promulgated as a way of life and as a means of introducing the contraceptive mentality among the faithful; (7) the promotion of the birth-control pill by Cana was undertaken as a further step on the road to the Church's revision of its position on contraception; (8) then an anti-baby point of view in harmony with secular society and personalist values was to be inculcated among the faithful.

The date of Dr. Ratner's report was October 4, 1965, during the final session of the Second Vatican Council and eight weeks away from the council fathers' ratification of the following sentence: "Sons of the Church may not undertake methods of birth control which are found blameworthy by the teaching authority of the Church in its unfolding of the Divine Law" (*Gaudium et Spes*, No. 51). Ratner was suggesting by then that Chicago's Cana Conference had gone beyond these norms.

The forewarning of Cana's directional change was probably evident only to a seer when, at the start of a new archdiocesan year (1961), Fr. Imbiorski invited Fr. William Gibbons, S.J., to inspire his Cana personnel with a talk entitled "To Breed or Not to Breed." This lecture was aimed at promoting the small family. Babies were discussed as arithmetical entities and discussed in the presence of Planned Parenthood representatives who were Fr. Imbiorski's guests. Fr. Gibbons was the first of a long line of speakers between 1961 and 1965 who were invited to "train" Cana leaders in the same vein: Fr. Gregory Baum, Archbishop Roberts, Michael Novak, Louis Dupre, Fr. Stanley Kutz, O.S.S., Fr. Kieran Conley, O.S.B., Fr. Bernard Cooke, S.J., Fr. Bernard Häring, C.S.R., Fr. Felix Cardegna, S.J., John and Mary Perkins Ryan, John Noonan, and Dr. Alan B. Guttmacher, president of the International Planned Parenthood Federation. With the exception of minor window dressing, the Cana personnel of Chicago were denied the opportunity of hearing contradictory—that is, orthodox—points of view. The ultimate impact of these repeated lectures with their recommended literature—Dupre's *Contraception and Catholicism*, Novak's *The Experience of Marriage*, Roberts' *Contraception and Holiness*, Noonan's *Contraception*—was the reorientation of Cana couples and Cana priests toward opinions contrary to Catholic teaching.

By 1965 Fr. Imbiorski had begun to veto speakers who were pro-orthodox. That year, at a July meeting of the program committee for the International Symposium on Rhythm to be held in Kansas City five months later, Fr. Imbiorski expressed opposition to the following recommended speakers: Fr. Stanislaus de Lestapis, S.J., who was proposed as the keynote speaker; Fr. Francis Canavan, S.J., of *America*, proposed as speaker for "Public Policy and Birth Control," and Fr. Richard McCormick, S.J., who was to be invited to discuss moral problems. All three at the time were considered anticontraceptionist. A month before, on June 15, 1965, Fr. Imbiorski took issue with Fr. McCormick at a meeting of the Chicago Catholic Physicians' Guild. McCormick had insisted with the doctors that they were obligated to follow Pope Paul's strictures (following Pope Pius XII) on the use of the pill. Imbiorski took the position that since several prelates in Europe and Archbishop Pocock of Toronto expressed different opinions, Catholics were free to make their own decisions in the matter.

By this time, of course, many observers were convinced that Imbiorski was already committed to contraception. He was a Catholic participant in the May 5, 1965, meeting of the American Association of Planned Parenthood Physicians in which he alleged that the Church's position on contraception was a historical accident. These were the opinions filtering through the Cana network forcing many Catholic Chicagoans to complain how Cana was now promoting birth control openly, how Cana priests and physicians were advocating the pill for contraceptive purposes.

A confrontation was held on June 15, 1965, between the Chicago Catholic Physicians' Guild and Fr. Richard McCormick with priests and physicians associated with Cana. The occasion was a symposium on the pill, and the arena of debate was the Little Company of Mary Hospital.

Dr. Ratner's subsequent report on the event for the archdiocese reads as follows:

For many it was the first time that the radical nature of Cana's position became evident. Some of the positions maintained by the Cana priests and physicians were as follows: (1) Priests and doctors are not obligated in their public role to inform consciences; (2) subjective conscience has priority and it is proper to prescribe the pill to those who request it; (3) Catholics have their choice of authority and are not bound by Pope Paul's directive of June 23, 1964.

At this meeting Fr. Imbiorski was invited to answer a direct question: "Suppose Pope Paul, contrary to your guess, reaffirms that contraception is wrong and that the pill is contraceptive, how will you be able to undo the damage caused by raising false expectations and promoting false teachings?"

Dr. Ratner reports Imbiorski as having no answer.

Imbiorski realized he was under fire. In March 1965 he wrote an article on birth control for his Cana personnel in which he suggested dialogue.

These reflections and discussions must not be adversary proceedings—conservatives against liberals; new breed against old guard. They must not be mere exercises for a position one has decided on beforehand. In dialogue we must be open to the other and his view of truth.

Factually, Imbiorski was already acting as if he had inside information that Rome was about to accept the pill. His predecessor, Msgr. John Egan, at this time director of Chicago's Archdiocesan Conservation Council, was also counseling Msgr. John C. Knott of NCWC's Family Life Bureau not to "stick his neck out" on birth control because he, too, sensed the imminent change in the Roman position.

To help nudge the change of Roman heart, Imbiorski enlisted the support of the Christian Family Movement. John Noonan wrote an article for CFM's official publication that raised questions about the irreformability of Catholic doctrine. In the same issue of ACT (July 1965), Imbiorski himself asked ten questions of CFM members about birth control. Some of the questions proposed for study and their phrasing insinuated their own answers: Would permission to use contraception in marriage undermine our traditional position on premarital chastity. If the Church makes no modification in its stand on contraception, is it in some sense turning its back on one of the key problems facing mankind today? Why is it that in Western society only Catholics by and large recognize and acknowledge this prohibition? Do you find your Catholic friends who practice contraception against the stated law of the Church in other respects exemplary people? One Chicago priest (Fr. Frank Tobin) immediately saw the significance of the Imbiorski article: "I can easily see people reading this article and justifying practicing contraception. This is a poor way to develop Christian families." By July 1965, however, the CFM leadership were already contraception supporters. A few months later *ACT* published (October 1965) an article against "the negative eleventh commandment: Thou shalt not commit contraception."

The word in the Chicago archdiocese was becoming clearer and clearer. Catholics had new options about contraception. Back in 1960 Cana's popular little booklet for engaged couples, *Beginning Your Marriage*, which was used by Family Life Bureaus everywhere, asked this question: "Precisely what types of family limitation are forbidden?" The answer given then (p. 110) was: "Every type of artificial contraception is forbidden." When the booklet was revised in 1966 family limitation is again discussed, but that question and answer are deleted. The 1975 edition of *Beginning Your Marriage* has much to say about togetherness, love, and sex but nothing at all about children, neither having or not having them!

Three years after this program was operative, Pope Paul issued *Humanae Vitae*. The day after the encyclical, a CFM leader from the East—far removed from Chicago—who from 1958 was a stanch teacher of lived Catholic doctrine at Pre-Cana conferences, reacted to the Pope's words as follows:

> Most couples who have been struggling with the problem have made up their minds and settled their consciences about what they consider right . . . and the encyclical is not going to change them [Washington *Post*, July 30, 1968].

### 3. *Anticlericalism and Anti-Magisterium*

When the new episcopal moderator of Catholic family life walked into a Chicago Hotel in 1959 to his first exposure to the Cana movement, he witnessed muscular Christianity in action. Bishop Christopher Weldon sat on the sidelines fascinated by laypeople complaining about their priests, and young priests carping about their reactionary pastors. The give and take, always humorless, was surprisingly bitter. Participants from the outside, who previously credited Chicago's Cana priests and couples with vitality and warmth, left such meetings later determined to shield their own family life personnel from the "bite" that seemed to characterize apostles who boasted of freedom and the permissiveness of Bishops. However, Chicagoans in those earlier days were people in a hurry to change the world. They used a bound copy of the latest papal encyclical to subdue anyone who stood in their way. Chicago's Cana movement had a large supply of charm in store, if it was likely to work. But it also had what the Farrells called "a Messiah complex," which impelled Cana people to make an end run, to climb over opposition, if this was necessary, in order to make the Church apostolic in the way the Popes were saying it should be. End runs and power politics were common in 1959, if the cause was the Pope's. Catholic actionists understood the Pope to recommend virtue more than power. They also were trained to lose to higher authority with grace. Pope John XXIII never sanctioned treatment of Church matters with the disrespect legitimately reserved for back-of-the-yards stench or Chicago habits of stealing ballot boxes.

The Catholic Church of 1959 was certainly dragging its feet in the United States on two major apostolates promoted by Pope Pius XI; one to the family (*Casti Conubii*, 1930) and another to the socioeconomic world (*Quadragesimo Anno*, 1931). These remained untended areas of Catholic concern ever to the end of World War II. It was to the credit of Chicago Catholic actionists that they moved into both fields with vigor, and sometimes with an end run.

The first end run was around the Family Life Bureau, NCWC. Established in 1931 by the American bishops as a national center for family-life education, the FLB lacked a mandate to organize grass-roots programs throughout the country. Fr. Edgar Schmiedeler, O.S.B., its director and a professor at the Catholic University of America, directed his energies toward professional family-life educators rather than to the rank-and-file Catholics. This approach was defensible, but NCWC's literature, conventions, and information services rarely touched the lives of the family people for whom they were intended. Msgr. Hillenbrand had a different approach. Begin with people and reach out to more people. Later when his student, Fr. John Egan, took over the primitive organization, Cana in Chicago and elsewhere would move in that direction. Fr. Egan ran into trouble with Fr. Schmiedeler almost immediately because of that "elsewhere." Egan, not satisfied with success in his own archdiocese, began to organize Cana anywhere people would have him—with or without the knowledge or consent of bishops, and sometimes without pastors. He developed his own literature and operated on the principle "Have Cana outlines, will travel." Study weeks and Cana institutes crossed diocesan lines. Before long a new national family-life organization was in the making without benefit of bishops. The conflict between NCWC's Family Life Bureau and Chicogo's Cana was evident in 1953 according to the agenda of the bishops' meeting. Several bishops had already condemned Cana for its interference in parishes of their dioceses. Cardinal Stritch kept the issue from reaching the bishops' agenda in 1952, but questions about the relationship of Cana (and CFM) to bishops and pastors continued to arise. At this point (1953) Bishop Peter Bartholome of St. Cloud, from 1944 onward episcopal FLB moderator, met with Fr. John C. Knott of Hartford, Fr. Harry Sherer of Newark, and Fr. Robert Ford of New York to discover how a peaceful settlement could be reached. Nothing substantial resulted from Bishop Bartholome's efforts until Fr. Schmiedeler retired in 1955, to be succeeded by Msgr. Irving A. De Blanc of Alexandria, Louisiana. De Blanc more than anyone else healed the breaches and within a few years led the way to a wide proliferation of Family Life bureaus throughout the United States. Fr. John Egan and the Cana Conference of Chicago had achieved a noticeable victory.

But Fr. Egan and the affiliated Chicago-based family apostolates did not rest on their laurels. They continued working across diocesan lines, independently of Msgr. De Blanc. The Christian Family Movement resisted every effort to place it under NCWC supervision. Objections to Chicago activity outside Chicago continued to be heard, first because others did not approve of its attitudes toward Church authority, and second because CFM seemed to insist on rigid control of its own affairs without suitable oversight by local bishops. From the viewpoint of diocesan authority, the Chicago influence was becoming disruptive. People were being encouraged to run around local pastors and bishops in the establishment of Cana programs; at the same time they were denied opportunity to shape effectively the national programs of CFM to meet local needs. CFM remained in the hands of Msgr. Hillenbrand. In either case, disrespect for or dissatisfaction with Church authority, however unintended, was the result that many FLB directors wished to avoid. In simple terms, restlessness with authority always seemed to follow whenever Chicago's Cana or CFM appeared on the local scene. One national FLB leader explained to Fr. Egan why Chicago's "super salesmen irritated and disappointed" him—one either bowed before their demands or suffered their disapproval, even though they lacked jurisdiction anywhere save in Chicago. Agitation and repeated agitation was Chicago's ongoing technique of winning battles. Many diocesan leaders remained as far away from Chicago as they could. On the other hand, dioceses with their own CFM units were pulled in the direction of Msgr. Hillenbrand's priorities. Cana conferences were training married couples to have babies, to tend to their domestic knitting, to provide support to other couples, while CFM told the same couples to get out on the street, reach out to the world's problems of poverty, bigotry, war, population, race—apostolates, once Cana did its work, for which they had little time. Pope Pius XI, who was the Church's father of Catholic action, in the last written message of his life made it quite clear that "the first duty of Catholic lay action is the restoration of the family to Christ." But if a local bishop decided this to be a goal for his CFM couples, he discovered them impelled in a different direction by the national office of CFM, located in Chicago.

Because of these contradictions and tensions, Cana and CFM never made their way, not even in Chicago, into everyday parish structures as Holy Name societies, sodalities, and Czanam guilds did in an earlier day. In a sense this was a loss to the Church. Bishops may partly be at fault because they did not appreciate the need for and the potential of both movements. On the other hand, Cana and CFM in Chicago as ongoing "separatist" activities, for their pride in being independent of supervision, for their inability to work patiently through the larger machinery of the Church in order to gain total episcopal approval (and, therefore, accept some control) share responsibility for their final collapse. Because they remained "separatist" they were vulnerable to neglect or "take-over." Today they no longer exist as positive forces for good in the Church.

Chicago's Catholic actionists had a penchant for an adversary relationship with Church authority. The mass of Chicago Catholics were no different than Catholics everywhere—they went to Mass, sent their children to Catholic school, and were happy to support their pastor. But anticlericalism among elites instigated by clerics seemed more noticeable in Chicago than in dioceses or archdioceses like Brooklyn, Boston, New York, Philadelphia, San Francisco, and Los Angeles. Indeed, it was clear during the contraception crisis that activism in Chicago was expected to pay dividends in obtaining a favorable papal decision. The Cana leadership took a certain pride in the confrontation. The June 1966 *Cana Newsletter* (when hopes for contraception were high) contained this enlightenment: "The Family Life Bureau (NCWC) leads off with a Theological Symposium on Marriage in Washington, D.C., July 1 through July 4. Chicago Cana personnel are being encouraged to attend to assure appropriate theological fireworks in keeping with the season." By this time Fr. Walter Imbiorski was involved with Dr. Mary Calderone in SIECUS—the Sex Information and Education Committee of the United States. Mary Calderone was a longtime aide to Dr. Alan B. Guttmacher of the Planned Parenthood Federation of America, whose philosophy is summed up in her own words on the tenth anniversary of SIECUS' founding: "Everybody must develop their own standards of sexual morality" (New York *Times*, June 28, 1974). The official "SIECUS position statements" endorse masturbation, homosexual activity, contraceptives for minors, and pornography.

Cana in Chicago, which began in such high hopes in 1945, reached its nadir in 1972 when a self-styled "Cana Symposium on Marriage" completed its deliberations recommending a change in Church teaching on divorce. According to the NCR account (February 4, 1972): "None of the speakers (who included Fr. Ramond Godert of Chicago's marriage tribunal and Fr. James Burtchaell of Notre Dame) and few of the participants stood by the traditional teaching of the Church." Chicago's Cana had come full circle—from stress on children to stress on no children to stress on no indissoluble marriage.

## II. And Then There Were More

A Chicago priest speaking a few years ago about conditions in his archdiocese said this: "People do more by going around the cardinal. What he doesn't know he can't stop" (NCR, August 27, 1976). A pugnacious attitude toward bishops' authority is now quite common in Catholic circles, especially among elites, but prior to Vatican II this was a rarity in American dioceses, save perhaps in Chicago. Even Chicago had established safety values for most priests in the persons of Vicar General George Casey and Chancellor Edward Burke—both appointees of Cardinal Stritch. Monsignors Casey and Burke allowed the "young Turks" to blow off steam, as they kept them in line.

This was not an uncommon phenomenon in most large American dioceses. Middlemen in chancery positions regularly stood between the bishop in his Cathedral and priests "out there" in parishes. The bishop, busy about large diocesan questions, often was not in close personal touch with the daily doings of his parish priests. Nonetheless, he was likely to have clear expectations about priestly behavior and, if taken by surprise by disclosure of unpleasant facts or complaints from the wrong quarter, a bishop could be a firm disciplinarian. To protect the bishop from errors in judging situations from which he was personally removed and as a humanizing feature to ecclesiastical bureaucracy, "chancery" in the United States became quite important. The bishop liked that. Chancery kept petty diocesan details off his back. Priests liked it too. It was easier to give straight talk to a monsignor. As a result, chancery monsignors, not the bishop, really ran many large dioceses.

There were obvious advantages to these relationships, and disadvantages, too. Since the bishop in those days was an impressive father figure, the monsignors became popular or unpopular depending on how the bishops used them. The popular figures with priests were usually those more permissive than the bishop. On the other hand, if the chancellor was the enforcer, the bishops gained popularity by overriding his chancellor's strictures. How effectively the informal power system worked—the shuttling of decision-making or counseling from one office to another—depended on the quality of the bishop and his chief Chancery officers. In Chicago—as in other places, New York, Boston, San Francisco—it worked quite well for many years.

Chicago's social actionists reveled in their "freedom," finding security in the early protection from their excesses afforded by Monsignors Casey and Burke. (By 1965 there is reason to believe that Cana's gloss in chancery quarters, and CFM's too, had worn down.) If Cardinal Cody later on became "the Chicago Fire Extinguisher," part of the explanation is found in the past, as given by Mark Winiarski:

> . . . Cody's predecessors had mildly encourage social action or allowed it to flourish through benign neglect. . . .

> Meyer, too often in Rome for the Vatican Council, had abdicated his role in archdiocesan affairs [NCR August 27, 1976].

The rise of confrontation tactics in the Church—as a method of determining Catholic truth or solving diocesan problems—cannot solely be attributed to the transfer of John Cody from New Orleans to Chicago. The seeds of confrontation were already planted there. Archbishop Cody's personality and leadership style may have brought matters to a head quicker. A bishop's judgment of principles or facts, his skill at getting followers, his timing, his suavity at human relationship, his measuring the strength of opposing forces, vary with the man. Exercising the complex art of ruling allows for the same man to be absolutely right and absolutely wrong at different times. Only history determines which.

One wonders, however, what archbishop could have headed off the Chicago confrontation building slowly in years prior to Vatican II. Even capitulation would have only whetted the appetites for further concessions, regardless of what has to be an archbishop's commitment to Catholic doctrine, to canon law, to the wishes of rank-and-file Chicago Catholics, to the Holy See, and to the National Conference of Catholic Bishops. Cody had hardly settled into his new archdiocese before two organizations grew up to keep the archdiocesan pot boiling—the Association of Chicago Priests (1966) and the New Federation of Priests' Councils (1969), each based in his see, both brought into being through the active assistance of Msgr. John Egan.

The NFPC, as it is usually known, under the initial leadership of Chicago's Fr. Patrick O'Malley, set the tone in many places for the new

federated priests' effort by interjecting itself into the dispute between
Cardinal O'Boyle and the Washington priests. As the request for intervention was spelled out, O'Boyle did not have a chance. The NFPC,
which was not a juridical Catholic body, sought to sit as judge over an
American bishop and the doctrinal issue too. Not succeeding in that,
O'Malley turned to the canon law meeting in Boston the same year,
where he received a favorable resolution requesting due process for the
Washington priests after "proper expression of dissent." The NFPC
then pushed on for optional celibacy for the clergy, favored anti-Viet-
nam protests, and opposed the B-1 bomber. A 1976 summary by NFPC
of its claimed leadership role looked more like a platform for a political
party than a list of priestly accomplishments. The dominant focus of
interest over seven years proved to be the economy, housing, oppression
in Latin America, colonialism, conscientious objection, and military ex-
penditures. There is no way that priests need avoid involvement in
these issues if they simultaneously demonstrate an interest first in the
conversion of their own local peoples, the spiritual life of their faithful,
sin and virtue, the vitality of parish life, Catholic unity with their
pastor and bishops, and the Catholic formation of the young, including
the frequent reception of the sacraments.

The NFPC, however, whose national preoccupations were fashioned
in Chicago, only symptomized the difficulties that would face any archbishop there.

The real nemesis for him would be the Association of Chicago
Priests. ACP was aimed directly at a new archbishop's ability to exercise
final authority in his archdiocese. The brainchild of Msgr. John Egan,
whom NCR's Winiarski calls "the Lyndon Johnson of archdiocesan
politics," ACP came into being shortly after Cody transferred Egan
from director of urban affairs for the archdiocese to the pastorate of
Presentation Parish. The creation has been described as follows:

> The Egan affair was the last straw for a handful of priests who
> had seen and endured enough: "What they did to Egan they
> can do to all of us," said one priest, summarizing the situa-
> tion. Priests began to organize what was to become the Associ-
> ation of Chicago Priests (ACP).
>
> Strategy was formulated: Organize the priests around their
> self-interests [NCR, August 27, 1976].

What was fairly routine in most organizations, religious and secular,
the shift of staff by a new bishop, became in Chicago the reason for
confrontation. Not only did Egan and his curate, Fr. John Hill (first

and second presidents of ACP, respectively), organize priests around self-interest, but they also set out to redirect the priestly mission away from "narrow self-interests"—that is, parish and ecclesial concerns—toward their own hidden social-action agenda. Later on Hill made clear what he thought about the parish priesthood. After reading Jacques Duquesne's *Church Without Priests* and John A. O'Brien's twelve stories of *Why Priests Leave*, Hill told the readers of *Worship* magazine (December 1969–January 1970): "Parish life is Dullsville." Why? Because priests have to visit the sick, bury the dead, go to cemeteries, counsel uptight people, and fill out marriage forms. Why Dullsville? Because there is little significant or exciting going on in parishes. He tells how he wanted to clap "hurrah" every time the page of O'Brien's book announced another decision to leave.

While Hill's personal views may explain why so many American parishes are dying and why Hill himself later took his departure from the priesthood, it is the underlying theology about priestly and Church affairs that reveals the real difficulty in the Church today. An ecclesiology that departs from the best religious traditions of Catholicism in favor of the transfer of Chicago's ward politics into Church business inevitably results in scandal to the faithful, in the censure of bishops by priests (as happened in Chicago in 1971), the picketing of bishops by nuns (as happened to Cody's train arriving for the first time in Chicago), in organized petitions and newspaper advertisements (as when Cody closed four schools), and in a ceaseless round of never-ending confrontations until the bishop concedes what he may not concede or until there is schism or disaffection.

The Association of Chicago Priests, which, unlike the Diocesan Priests' Senate, may not represent many of the 2,222 priests active in archdiocesan work, manages to become involved in most of the well-publicized controversies with the ordinary. ACP claims a membership of 577. Only a minority of these continue to make headlines. In 1977 140 ACP priests responded to a survey by its leadership, the results of which made national headlines. "Chicago Priests Report Divergence from Tradition" said the headline in the Brooklyn *Tablet* (September 8, 1977). Eighty-seven and 78 per cent, respectively, of the responding priests do not believe birth control or masturbation wrong; almost half do not support in private counseling the Church prohibition on premarital sex; nor do they take seriously Vatican decrees on matters such as the first confession of children. About 60 per cent report themselves as encouraging remarried Catholics to receive the Eucharist, even when the previous marriage is presumptively valid. A small minority of priests diverging from Church teaching is disconcerting enough, but not disruptive of Catholic tranquillity as their willingness to portray their "divergence" on the national Catholic scene as "significant."

That ACP press release also provides the rationale used by dissenting Chicago priests to justify confrontation not only with their own bishop but also with the Pope himself—that is, "differing concepts of the Church." Here is the key statement. Chicago's so-called *American Catechism* defines what their Church is: "[The Church] is not in the first instance an organization or a means of salvation. It is not the hierarchy or the clergy. The Church is a community" (Chicago *Studies*, Fall 1973, p. 242). What theologians like Richard McBrien offer in the classrooms of Catholic seminaries and universities as "new doctrine" the ACP seeks to "organize" and "institutionalize." The "institutional Church" has bishops for leaders. The "community Church" will have leaders too, and ACP seeks to establish the mechanisms by which the new "community leaders" will emerge. Since they will not be bishops appointed by Rome, they will come from the people. Since they are not now available, potential leaders must be identified, trained, and organized—trained to see the Church in new terms, given the will and the organizational skills necessary to guarantee the reshaping of the Church according to the proposed new "model." The new Church, the "community Church," will also have new priorities determined and enforced at the grass roots, not in Vatican palaces or cathedral offices. Bishops are needed as tie-ins to tradition and as symbols of unity in a new pluralist Catholic world, but they will rule by consensus with vocal grass-roots groups and will decide against that consensus only at their own peril.

Who is best qualified to organize this restructuring of the Catholic Church? Those fifty- and sixty-year-old priests trained in Jocist techniques. The techniques of Cardinal Cardijn developed to enable small Catholic cells to penetrate post-Christian secular institutions with Christian influence are now to be used to Christianize the Catholic Church itself.

Another recent program proposed (August 1977) for the archdiocese of Chicago by Msgr. John Egan and his associates has been called the Parish Corporate Renewal Network. The request for support of this experiment from Catholic foundations and the archbishop of Chicago made the following claims:

A. The Parish Corporate Renewal Network is to be incorporated and funded over a three-year period to the extent of $595,873 for the purpose "of dramatically changing the way Catholic parishes serve themselves and the secular community of which they are a part. *Heretofore, parishes have principally focused upon the salvation and grace of their members. The purpose of this project is to unleash the capacity of parishes to be apostolic organizations with a new vision, mission, and capability for developing the greatness and well-being of mankind* [italics added].

B. "Grass roots" teams will be organized and trained by a newly established Internal Corporate Renewal Institute to gain a new vision and mission, to acquire new skills of interpersonal relations and of organization, to rediscover the theology of shared communion and gospel living.

C. These "grass roots" teams "will assist the parish in developing corporate patterns and structures that facilitate an ongoing, open-ended rhythm of communal discernment and corporate theological reflection."

D. These "grass roots" teams will be sustained by the ongoing support from the professional staff of the institute that trained them.

E. These "grass roots" teams "will be Corporate Reflection Centers (small faith communities) engaged in the continuous identification of parish issues." They will be "apostolic sign communities."

The first draft of this proposal (January 1977) diagramed the "grass roots" teams working on the inside of each of eleven parishes, while the overall implementation of renewal and restructuring would rest in the hands of a supervising Board of Directors (or advisers), who would be the incorporated officers controlling policy, programs, and the dispensation of funds.

The proposal as described can be reconciled with the purpose and structures of the Catholic Church under the following conditions:

A. If the incorporated body *as Catholic* is responsible to the archbishop of Chicago and the local pastor appointed by him for the protection of Catholic doctrine and the observance of Church law.

B. If the incorporation provides some mechanism for the archbishop of Chicago and the local pastor, whereby social-action concerns of elite "grass roots" groups are balanced against the needs of the Catholic masses or the Catholic priorities determined by the Holy See and the National Conference of Catholic Bishops.

C. If the incorporation contains mechanisms that prevent either the "network" of the "institute" from becoming a rival body for Catholic loyalties to the archdiocese of Chicago itself.

D. If the appointments of members to the Board of Directors (or advisers) are made with the consent of, not ever against, the archbishop of Chicago.

As presently designed, none of these conditions are met: The men who propose this experiment are in many cases men known for their opposition to the archbishop of Chicago, to values and policies dictated by the Holy See, committed also to the primacy of social and political action and to confrontation procedures as effective means of obtaining objectives.

As a device for "flattening" the Church, for debilitating the authority of bishops further, for segmenting the Church into disparate doctrinal camps, and for launching a "runaway" Church, the Parish Corporate Renewal Network makes a good beginning.

### III. The Chicago Hurricane: Andrew M. Greeley

If Jimmy Carter awoke one morning to read a headline of the Washington *Post* that labeled the President of the United States "a madcap tyrant" because one of his own staff said so, the chances are that the headline grabber not only would lose his place on the White House mailing list but his job as well.

One morning Cardinal Cody learned that he really was "a madcap tyrant" because Fr. Greeley said so. When Greeley discovered he was dropped from a subsequent diocesan mailing, the sociologist opined that Cody wanted to get rid of him.

Fr. Greeley is a well-known figure in the Chicago complex that has contributed to the unsettlement of the Church.

Greeley is pure Chicago Catholic elite. He does not like elites but, as in so many other cases, he speaks for a specific population group—not for the hierarchy certainly, nor for the large Catholic group in Chicago who are distressed by what goes on there, not for Hispanic and black Catholics with whom he has no relationship, not for the priests who refuse to join the Association of Chicago Priests—but for the Chicago activists from which he came, with whom he is associated, even when he demonstrates his unpredictability by criticizing them too.

Greeley is furiously Catholic. He loves the Church even though he despises its hierarchy. Kenneth Briggs of the New York *Times* did him a disservice in his review of Greeley's *The American Catholic* by suggesting that the book might otherwise by entitled *Why I Stay in?* Greeley can be and has been a formidable witness for the Church, especially as antagonist of anti-Catholic and tepid Catholic establishments in the United States. Better than anyone else Greeley has demonstrated that Catholics are smart, ambitious, educated, successful, socially and politically progressive, and a force for good in American society. He may not have convinced the Catholic haters, but in the post-Greeley era it will be a little harder to insinuate that Catholics are dumb, lacking in ambition, undereducated, bigoted, anti-intellectual, or backward. His accumulated data indicating that Catholic schools simultaneously have served academic and religious purposes, enforced Catholic family values, and are related to upward mobility and Catholic adherence are by dint of his apostolic urge well known.

Greeley is also pure Chicago, where loyalties are fierce and hates are just as savage. He lights a Chicago fire as easy as John Wayne starts a fight. In Greeley's judgment Chicago is the best, and people who leave it, like John Cogley, pay a price. Richard Daley was Greeley's hero. Papal politics may strike him as corrupt, but not ward politics in Chicago.

For some of his positions and his language, Fr. Greeley has taken it on the chin. He has been called a "constipated twerp" by Chicago journalist Mike Royko and a "loudmouthed Irish priest" by Morris Janowitz of the University of Chicago, where he was denied tenure eight times. Since his academic qualifications were as good as many others there, denial of tenure may have come as much for being a priest as for being a gadfly. Liberal Catholics treated with disdain his early books *Religion and Career* and *The Education of Catholic Americans* simply because they had nice things to say about the Church and its school system.

In his turn, however, Greeley gives as much as he takes. David O'Brien, who is one of his sympathizers, admits that Greeley has dispensed "enough insults to anger bishops, the nations cultural elites, and the minions of both" (*NCR*, May 6, 1977). When he is not conferring the Lunacy Award on *Commonweal*, Greeley excommunicates his critics with such epithets as "demented drivelers" or "Mousketeers." An admirer of Fr. Hesburgh, he nonetheless is not above accusing Notre Dame of "Hosting a Wake for American Catholicism" (*Long Island Catholic*, January 8, 1976) or showing such little respect for sociologists that he is driven to resign from the Editorial Board of *Concilium*

(*NCR*, July 15, 1977). When rejected by a formidable opponent, the Greeley retort can become highly personal. Long before Greeley was important on the Chicago scene, sociologist John L. Thomas, S.J., was a key counselor for several important Chicago apostolates. However, when veteran sociologist Thomas doubted whether Greeley "proved" that *Humanae Vitae* caused the contemporary Catholic declines, the younger man called the old pro "a man whose published work does not reveal competency beyond the most simple cross-tabulations" (*Our Sunday Visitor*, May 2, 1976). Whereas the bishops' National Catholic Directory is for him a "failure," their Bicentennial booklet on social justice was a "disaster" (*NCR*, May 2, 1975).

The important thing here is not the good deeds or polemical lifestyle of Fr. Greeley. The Church will profit from the one and survive the other. But insofar as he represents a cluster of values about and techniques of administration for the Catholic Church—drawn from his learning in Chicago and widely dispensed through the nation by him— those values and techniques deserve a closer look. *Time* magazine (May 24, 1976) and the secular press in general look upon him as Catholicism's most influential spokesman. And even though he did not like being paired with Billy Graham and Rosemary Reuther, Greeley, taking note of his rating, quotes the remark a friend made to him: "Hell, you're even one of the eleven 'most influential' Christian thinkers in the world. You are the most successful priest of your generation" (Gregory Baum, *Journeys*, p. 203). It would be a mistake, therefore, to overlook the influence of Andrew Greeley's writings and lectures.

Fr. Greeley describes his introduction to the priesthood in *Journeys* (pp. 179–84). Writing about his first and only parish-priest assignment, he has this to say:

> Almost everybody in Christ the King parish in Beverly went to Church. I used to tell the young people that it was virtually impossible for them not to go to Church, so strong were the cultural pressures. Religious loyalty, paradoxically enough, seemed to be more important in Beverly than it was in St. Angela's [his boyhood parish]. Everyone went to Catholic schools, everyone went to Catholic high schools, almost everyone went to Catholic colleges. There were no fallen-aways to reclaim, no bad marriages, no public-school children to be instructed, and no alcoholics to be counseled at the rectory. There were few mixed marriages (years would go by without one), everyone went to Pre-Cana, almost no convert instruction took place, and there was no serious juvenile delinquency.

There seemed little for a parish priest to do but go to wakes
and weddings and funerals, count the Sunday collections, and
mimeograph the weekly parish bulletin.

His later journeys through the Church pay little notice to the patrimony bequeathed him, nor to the bishops, clerics, religious, and parents who gave him such an easy start. It is quite evident, however, that
his predecessors had powerful impact on the Catholic lifestyles of their
people. Unquestionably, too, their success derived from hard work on
behalf of the convictions of their Church. Greeley concludes his odys-
sey: "After ten years at Christ the King, I left the parish a failure. My
work with the adults and the young people of the parish had very little
impact." "What went wrong?" he asked. His answer to himself: "We
were terribly short of scholars." Fr. Greeley went off then to work for
the University of Chicago.

In this account Greeley does not seem to associate the "excitement,"
"challenge," and "risk-taking" then being encouraged in Chicago with
making him feel less effective as a parish priest than his predecessors.
One little-noticed comment on Greeley's 1976 study of Catholic
schools by John L. Thomas, S.J., questioned the study's favorable conclusions about Catholic schools: "The official doctrine of the Catholic
Church has changed very little. If the schools are teaching the official
doctrine, they are not getting through" (*Our Sunday Visitor*, April 11,
1976).

Perhaps here may be part of the problem now quite commonly noticed in parochial ministry: Are the doctrines of the Church and their
practical implications for Catholic life not getting through to the people
because priests, religious, and young parents trained by them have other
things on their mind than Catholic doctrine, or are they no longer good
at getting it through? Or have they alternatives to Catholic doctrine
that are getting through?

The possibilities in this line of thought are many. Many too are the
case histories that indicate how the pastoral ministry of the Church can
be made ineffective.

For example, a complaint went to the archbishop of Chicago on August 22, 1973, from an engaged couple with a professional background
who by parish requirement attended a Pre-Cana conference. The conference in question was led by a young childless married couple. The
complaint reads in part as follows:

The young man who (together with his wife) led the conference spoke out in favor of premarital intercourse, saying he

thought "it was a fine thing for some people." The wife for her part said that "nowadays there are many different styles of marriages. There are marriages with children. And there are other types of marriages. What's right is what works for you."

When the subject of "needs" was opened up for discussion, the complaining about-to-be group suggested the topic "children." The wife panelist at one point replied: "Well, having children seems to be *your* particular need. Let's hear about the needs of the other couples."

During the course of the Pre-Cana night the engaged couples were asked to evaluate the importance to their marriage of color television, pets, air conditioners, etc. In turn, the married panelists, asked why "children" were not mentioned in the survey, replied: "You can write in 'kids' at the bottom of the list if you want to."

The complaint to Cardinal Cody concluded with the comment:

No mention was made by the discussion leaders of God's values or providence or of any values or principles that would distinguish a Christian marriage from marriage in a purely secular society. The priest, we were told, would speak to those matters but not the Cana couples themselves.

In view of the fact that Catholic doctors in many parts of the country no longer participate in Pre-Cana because they refuse to answer questions priests evade, failure of official doctrine to get through to audiences may be the result of the ascendancy over doctrine given to social-science content and social-science techniques.

Fr. Greeley symbolizes this trend better than most. So three words in his lexicon are worth examining. They are *sociology, methodology,* and *authority.*

1. *Sociology*

Sociology is an effort to make some judgments about what is going on in an institution based on a disciplined study of the evidence. It is not a study of what should go on, nor of what people would like to go on, but a description of a factual situation as that can best be grasped. The sociologist relies for his data on what people say and what they do. When he is finished he is very certain, certain, or not too certain of the results, depending on how simple the problem was to study and how effective his methodology was in getting at the facts. A lot depends on how well his sample reflects the universe he wishes to describe. If in trying to trace behavioral patterns back to their causes he must deal with many variables that are not easily isolated from each other, the sociologist presents his results tentatively. Because he knows from experience how much data are around to support different explanations of the same phenomenon, he is doubly cautious. Furthermore, since there is no mechanism in sociology to measure the contribution of nature (biology, genes, etc.) or the nonempirical (nonmeasurable, spiritual, divine) to a given situation, the sociologist by professional option confines his explanations of human happenings to the social world itself, to the goings-on among human beings, to their circumstances, their clime, their culture. Nothing else is sacred. Nothing at all is absolute. He acts as if fully convinced that a social phenomenon can be explained when the given social situation is fully understood.

Turning to religion, the sociologist sees nothing more than what people do that is called religion, and hears nothing save what they say it all means. The sociologist as such does not know "God," "soul," "revelation," "moral law," or "heaven," nor does he see religion as a relationship between man and God. Sentences taken from the National Catechetical Directory have no meaning for a sociologist: "From the beginning he [God] has gradually made known the inexhaustible mystery of his love"; "God reveals himself through creation"; man is destined for "a life eternally with God." Whereas the religionist, certainly the Catholic religionist, deals with a substantive relationship between God and man and objective concepts about what that relationship should mean in the concrete, the sociologist of religion only knows what people tell him about that relationship. He can even be a total unbeliever in any objective religious reality and still describe "belief" as it is described for him. The sociology of religion will seek to find the common denominator in all religions because sociologically speaking all religion has a common denominator. Christianity, therefore, is no different from nationalism or socialism, if in a given society the latter take on "religious attributes." When all his studies are piled together he will have analyzed the two basic sociological aspects of the religious question—how religion *functions* in and what its *meaning* is to a given society.

While sociology is strictly considered a speculative science—that is, it develops theories about social institutions, how they originate, function, change, provide meaning, and die—it has some pragmatic uses. It is well to understand those uses.

• There are various schools of sociology—different theories—
that can be used either to bolster a given institution or to tear
it down. If the sociologist is an activist he can find suitable
data to promote either cause. And sociologists today tend to
operate out of a given ideology.

• Sociological data can be and are frequently used to manipulate public opinion. This is especially true when it is necessary
to mitigate the strictness of prevailing social standards.

• Absolute social or moral norms are particularly vulnerable to
this kind of manipulation because a significant proportion of
the population neither believes in nor adheres to the norm.

• If, for example, the norms are heterosexuality, differential
roles in marriage, large family, strict enforcement of law, and
capital punishment for murder, it is not difficult to find sociologists who can "prove" from data that the norms are neither
absolute nor effective.

• In society dominated by the empirical, social norms tend to
become moral norms.

When Fr. Greeley decided to apply his talents to the sociology of
religion he chose to become an expert not in functional sociology but
more in what may be called phenomenological sociology—the meaning
of religion to people. As he wrote in *Journeys*:

I am attempting to develop operational measures of a person's
ultimate values. If religion is a person's ultimate world view, his
answer to the most basic questions a human can ask about life
and death, then we should be able to find out what the world
view is and how it influences the rest of his behavior. This is
much more important than knowing what he thinks about
doctrinal propositions or what denomination he is affiliated
with or how often he goes to Church [p. 194].

For the sociologist who concerns himself with religions meaning as
*seen from man's perspective*, this is a fair statement of goal. But
religion as *seen from God's perspective*, from the functions God as-
cribes to it, to the meaning men should find in it, is what the Church
conceives as goal. Sociology and theology, therefore, begin with
different source material, have different methods and expectations,
reach different "truths," and make different demands on people. Each
discipline can serve the other's purpose, but they are independent—at

least for those who believe that religion is more than the sum of what people say about it. Consider the definition of religion given by Andrew Greeley's catechism *The Great Mysteries*, and Thomas O'Dea's definition in his textbook *The Sociology of Religion*.

| Greeley | O'Dea |
|---|---|
| Religion is grounded in human experience. In the midst of the frustrations, the ambiguities, the sorrows, the pleasures, the joys, the uncertainties of our lives, we occasionally sense that there may be something else going on. For some people, this "something else" is encountered in a dramatic, overpowering, ecstatic way. | The Central interest of religion appears to concern something comparatively vague and intangible, whose empirical reality is far from clear. It is concerned with a "beyond," with man's relation to and attitude toward that "beyond" for human life. It is concerned with something that, to use the phrase of the Italian sociologist Vilfredo Pareto, "transcends experience." |

In each case the definition, aimed at different audiences, is purely sociological.

Another example of how Fr. Greeley speaks more as sociologist than theologian is his endorsement of "communal Catholics" as acceptable models for tomorrow's Catholicism. Communal Catholics are sociological realities—from *man's perspective* they always have had a place in the Church and always will. But from the *Church's perspective* they are hardly "models," since they consciously reject the institutional Church and many of her doctrines. Catholicism may still have meaning for "communal Catholics" as do national origin or ethnic strain (a sociological phenomenon), but the objective meaning of that phrase is not *Catholic* (in the doctrinal definition of that term).

2. *Methodology*

Sociologists, if they are good at their science at all, are only as good as their methodology, the limited scope of their research, and their objective approach to data. The more they try to "prove," the more uncertainty there is about conclusions. Reporting opinions or "facts" is a reasonably safe enterprise because sampling procedures have been perfected sufficiently to make those reports reliable. When explanations of the "facts" are in order, difficulties arise because tracing the meaning of human responses is more complicated than following Pavlov's dog from bell to food to saliva. Things are more complicated still when the sociologist allows his emotions to become entwined in his research, his compilations, and his interpretations.

Fr. Greeley emotes whenever the suggestion is made that his methods are less than perfect, that his explanations are unsatisfactory, that he is too close to his subject matter. Yet pastors sometimes argue that way, much to Greeley's chagrin. Msgr. Charles Owen Rice, hardly a defender of reactionary causes, once made bold to say, "Father Greeley has no facts. His Opinion Research entity deals with opinions. Opinion is opinion no matter what you do with it. You may mill it, grind it, stuff it, polish it, even filter it, and it remains opinon, subjectively. After Father Greeley and his company examine an issue and take their polls and samples, they end up where they started, all previous opinions miraculously confirmed" (*Commonweal*, June 24, 1977).

Although Greeley later dismissed Rice as an "authoritarian churchman" (*Commonweal*, August 27, 1977), Greeley lends himself to this charge unfortunately because he readily confesses to wearing a "sociologist's cap" and a "social commentator's beret" too. At a press conference announcing *Catholic Schools in a Declining Church*, Greeley claimed a sociological hypothesis, to wit: *Humanae Vitae* caused the decline in Catholic adherence. Then announced Greeley: "We don't speculate that the cause of the Catholic decline was the birth-control issue, nor do we simply assert it. We prove it with the kind of certainty one rarely attains in historical analysis" (*Our Sunday Visitor*, April 18, 1976). Few sociologists would have spoken so dogmatically. Later, three Notre Dame professors, writing for *Contemporary Sociology* (November 1976), were not so sure either of his methodology or conclusions. The South Bend social scientists doubted the "encyclical explanation" of Catholic decline, reasoning that Greeley and company did not give proper credit to alternative explanations because "they conflict with the author's *a priori* assumptions."

Similar complaints have been made by sociologists about Greeley's other books. In a generally favorable review of *The American Catholic* (*Commonweal*, August 19, 1977), Sr. Marie Augusta Neal took note of Greeley's case against the stereotype that Catholics were poor achievers, as follows: "Greeley has been determined to expose what he knew from his own experience." Veteran sociologist Msgr. Paul Hanly Furfey, who was doing mathematical sociology before Fr. Greeley was born, wondered about the methodology in *The American Catholic*, thought Greeley's samples rather small, the psychological scales he used "to be quite poor," and finally concluded: "Unfortunately the reader with little experience in social research is not likely to realize how very, very shaky most of these figures are" (Washington *Post*, March 27, 1977).

J. Milton Yinger, hardly an unrecognized name in the upper echelons of professional sociology, criticizes *Ethnicity in the United States* (1974) for its methodological weaknesses, notably its definition of ethnicity, saying: "With only a weak measure of a major variable, only tentative statements are possible" (*American Journal of Sociology*, March 1977, pp. 116–18).

Sigmund Dragastin, a onetime researcher for the National Opinion Research Center, objected to Greeley's explanation of why priests under pressure to leave the priesthood still stay as "inadequate research" drawing "slender conclusions" and being an overstatement of the case (*NCR*, October 18, 1974). Protestant theologian Tom Driver, reading Greeley's *Sexual Intimacy*, asks: "Greeley writes as if he knew everything. Perhaps he does but on what authority?" Then Driver concludes: "Whatever scholarship may lie behind the book's judgments has been carefully (or do I mean carelessly?) hidden" (*America*, December 8, 1973).

Richard Robbins of the University of Massachusetts thinks *Unsecular Man* is "a vehicle for displaying Greeley's list of friends and enemies" (*Contemporary Sociology*, September 1973). William Silverman of New York University calls *The Denominational Society* a "musical and theological hodgepodge" (*Contemporary Sociology*, May 1973). Peter I. Rose of Smith College, another well-known name in the field, looked into *Why Can't They Be Like Us?* to find that Greeley "interjects his own views," and in his favor to the Irish provides "a wee bit of Gaelic one-upmanship in the midst of what the author contends is a scientific treatise" (*Contemporary Sociology*, January 1973).

3. *Authority*

Far more damaging to the Church than the demand that Popes and bishops worship at the altar of sociology before they preach its uncertainties is widespread defiance of legitimate Church authority. The proper word to describe the situation no longer is disobedience, not even disrespect. Defiance, rage, rebellion characterize many centers of Catholic activity, even at the parish level. What may be more significant is that ecclesiastical officers, in the face of such confrontation, seem to go out of their way to cajole the very people they are appointed to manage. Everyone takes for granted civil society's breakdown of law and order and political officeholders looking the other way. Sometimes mayors and governors even trot out sociological studies designed to show that what the man on the street sees really is not so. And as revelations continue to spill over front pages of more and more "white-collar crime" going on in high places, even within the sacred precincts of high office itself, the crimes of the streets receive official understanding, if not justification.

Very few people a decade ago would believe that "religious crime" could ever become widespread within the Catholic Church, religious crime being defined here as serious public offenses against the public law of the Church. Crime is not usually what is discussed in the confessional box or the room of reconciliation. Crime has to do with deeds that the high authorities of the Church interdict and penalize because they threaten the functioning and good order of the Church. The examples of these are legion: Public confrontations with Pope and bishops, misuse of the Eucharist, scandalous public misconduct by priests and nuns have been quite common. So forceful have the organizers of "religious crime" become that bishops and religious superiors, and the Holy See itself, have backed away from enforcing their own well-known and well-understood laws. Indeed, by devious political enterprises canon law, like so much civil law, has been rendered a dead letter, the issue of violations made moot by nonattention.

Widespread proliferation of unsanctioned behavior is not the end of the matter. The real evil lies in the hearts of men who instigate or tolerate crime. All lawful society, including that of the Church, and democracy especially, presumes virtue in most of its citizens. Society's well-being and development come to a halt when officeholders need turn away from those tasks to keep order among a large segment of their masses. Sanctions in law are only intended to be used against a few miscreants to protect the innocent to be sure, but also to teach everyone the rights and wrongs of living together.

Social life begins to fall apart when the conviction is aggressively proposed and without contradiction is allowed to grow that the country is corrupt, the Church is corrupt, the family is corrupt. Virtue then belongs to those who topple the cursed institution. Rage, defiance, rebellion take the place of serenity, respect, obedience. And this is the point at which the Catholic Church currently finds herself.

The data indicate unexpected deviance among the Catholic masses. But more hurtfully, defiance within the upper echelons of episcopal bureaus, theological societies, Catholic universities, and religious orders is the contagious canker sore on the Church body. In the Church as elsewhere somebody has to give orders and someone to take them. No one pretends that the givers are holier than the takers, but greater respect and reverence—and compliance—are due the former because a great deal rides on their successes or failures. No machinery will ever be perfect enough to soften the impact of bad decisions on human lives. On the other hand, some "takers" cannot really take it at all. However the process of decision-making is perfected, someone, be he Christ, a Roman centurion, a President, or a bishop must say "Go" or "Come," and that should end that. At least for a given moment. But this no longer happens.

While disrespect for authority in the Church is now a national phenomenon, it was more noticeable first among the Catholic literary elites
of the East and among the priest elites of the Midwest. Fr. Greeley is
merely the latest and more flamboyant example of the disdain of authority now ravaging the vital organs of the Church body. This is not a
new charge to be laid against him. He boasts of his scorn for bishops.
People who read his books or articles hear the message. Kenneth Briggs
was one who did. Reading *The American Catholic*, the religious editor
of the New York *Times* put it this way:

> He blasts away at incompetency and lackluster leadership of
> American bishops and paints a gloomy scenario for the
> Church's future. It is difficult to sort out the hard evidence for
> this prophesy, however, from Fr. Greeley's personal rage
> against the authorities and, perhaps, against authority itself
> [New York *Times*, May 28, 1977].

Occasionally, Greeley lashes out at scholars who "persist in flailing the
ecclesiastical institutions and indulging in ritualistic and empty left-
wing political posturing" (*Catholic News*, September 1, 1977). But he
is more consistent and public doing that than they are. The "corruption
and dishonesty of the Roman Curia [are] already an international scandal" (Brooklyn *Tablet*, September 12, 1976) according to Greeley,
hardly any different from what he thinks of the home-grown variety of
bishop. Even when he comes up against a bishop who could hardly be
called "incompetent" or lackluster," Greeley gives him the torch if the
bishop might be a boss Greeley could not cower. Referring to his work
for the Ford Foundation, the sociologist made this aside: "I'd hell of a
lot sooner work for them than for Cardinal Krol." (NCR, February 25,
1977).

But then Greeley has a strange idea of what authority is. He holds
the American bishops up to ridicule for not enforcing *Humanae Vitae*
"if (they think) the issue is the teaching of Jesus on a matter of faith"
but he is glad they did not (Brooklyn *Tablet*, August 5, 1966). Indeed,
he is a one-man crusader for the nonenforcement of the encyclical.
Then he turns and tells the bishops to fire summarily the staff of the
United States Catholic Conference responsible for the National Catechetical Directory. He calls the content "embarrassing drivel" and its
authors "incompetent fools." To the bishops he says:

> If the bishops approve the Directory, they will be guilty of
> grave failure of their magisterial responsibility. For all the talk

about the importance of "Magisterium" they are not willing to exercise it when it counts [Brooklyn *Tablet*, September 22, 1977].

When, however, that "magisterial authority" (in this case) turns its eyes on issues or people more dangerous to the Church (for example, Hans Küng) than USCC's views of Catholic social doctrine, then Greeley's words are "repression" and the "last gasp" of a dying body (Brooklyn *Tablet*, August 12, 1976). He may know what authority is supposed to do, but rages when he sees its restraining power directed at his causes. His folk heroes are those priests "who stay to fight," not those who leave, and he quotes two of his friends to back him up: "In the words of John L. McKenzie, 'Why quit? Stay and bother them.' And in the words of Hans Küng, 'Why should I quit? Let the Pope quit'" (*Priests in the United States*, p. 199).

This posture promulgated, propagated, and permitted to pervade an institution leads to general lawlessness. When the institution is a Church, the very nature of its mission is subverted. The justifying word for defiance may be "maturity," "fulfillment," "conscience," depending on age and state of life. The end result of encouraged disrespect for Church law is ecclesiastical chaos.

Fr. Greeley does not see it that way. When Bishop Charles Helmsing dropped his column from the Kansas City diocesan newspaper (*NCR*, August 31, 1973) for its "negativism," Greeley expressed "hurt," defending his conduct as part of "a long tradition of tough, independent journalistic criticism," yet seemingly unmindful that much of the tradition involved muckraking, which men like Westbrook Pegler and Drew Pearson turned into a fine art. In spite of the importuning of friends, Greeley still feels no compunction. His contribution to *Journeys* (p. 204) ends on this note:

> When it was a question of speaking out or holding my tongue, over the last ten years I have rarely done the latter. "Surely, Father," a pious clergyman once said to me, "you would say or write some things differently if you had it to do over again. Wouldn't you?" He continued, "On mature reflection I'm sure there's an awful lot you would want to change." My response was a mostly unconscious paraphrase of Frank Skeffington and James Michael Curley: "Not one damn thing!"

## CHAPTER VIII

The Battle for the Catholic Child, or Psychology vs. Parents

## I. The Religious Educators

It is not surprising that the first battles after Vatican II took place not in chancery offices, but in parish schools and catechism classes, where parents came face to face with the effect of the "new catechetics" on their children's lives. James Ebner characterizes the polarization as "a struggle between those who want to think in today's terms and those who understand loyalty as clinging to traditional ways" (NCR, January 9, 1976). But there is at least one other explanation. Before bishops and Roman officials took a close look at what was happening at the grass-root levels of the Church, parents, who by virtue of their Catholic schooling were highly sophisticated about Catholic doctrine, watched in wonderment. They saw the "new theology" at work and did not like what they saw. When they complained they found themselves overwhelmed by the claims of religious educators to superior knowledge. Catechetical renewal, pursued with single-minded fervor by teachers and publishers, led religious educator Gerald Sloyan to observe that opposition from Catholic laity reminded him of the Duke of Wellington's concern about his troops: "They may not scare the enemy, but by God they scare me" (Commonweal, March 27, 1970). Yet it was the parents who held an attentive ear to what Pope and bishops were saying. They had reason to be concerned about the things their children were hearing in the classroom.

In early post-Vatican II years, no novel theological concept escaped experimentation at the parish or diocesan level. First came salvation history, with stress on God's love of man manifested through historical circumstances. The meaning of Catholicism was to be grasped—not through abstract formulas or disciplinary procedures, but through participation in liturgical and social activity. The handbook of Christianity was Scripture, not catechism or canon law. This approach prepared the way for Gabriel Moran's "continuing-revelation theory," according to which God reveals himself continually in human affairs as once he did through prophets. The old concept of a deposit of faith (dubbed "static") to be guarded, handed down, reinterpreted, and binding on Catholics was not in favor. God's presence was to be searched for in the contemporary world. His meaning *now* and *for me* was the proper object of catechetics. Only one step remained to complete the move to the experiential approach to catechetics. Instead of adapting Christian life to textbook definitions, the child is to be taught to experience his faith. Catechetical experts alleged that this method of instruction was authorized by Vatican II. Textbooks about the Catholic faith were, henceforth, to reflect the ongoing believing experiences of the faithful. A Swiss Jesuit religious educator, Mario Von Galli, summed up the process in one line: "In ten years people will believe only what they experience; anything else they will not believe" (*U.S. Catholic*, June 1968). The real world where people live is the teacher. In this world there are no absolutes, no evil unless people see the evil.

The religious educators who adopted this methodology defined the "real world" without delay. When they decided that the real world demanded the restructuring of the Church, catechetics placed high priority on (and indoctrination in) social protest. Christian witness on a picket line may not have been the real world for many Catholics, but the young were made to feel that nonparticipation in social movements (especially the approved ones—peace, poverty, feminism, freedom) indicated less than a full Catholic faith.

Regardless of the particular point of departure used by this or that teacher or textbook, religious education began to assume the following characteristics:

1. *Search and inquiry, not the transmission of knowledge, became the dominant objective.* Gabriel Moran's 1971 book *Design for Religion: Toward Ecumenical Education* distinguishes the role of bishops as preservers of Jesus' gospel from the role of educators who lead students to explore the meaning of their own experience. "The supposition that the bishop is the teacher of the diocese and that religion teachers in the schools are an extension of the bishop is simply a fallacy that must be put to rest" (p. 149). Teaching Christian doctrine is not religious education. Bishops are propagandists for a particular religious tradition, but religious educators ought not be. While the Church

should continue its involvement in formal education, the Christian religion should not formally be taught to the young. Ideally, this is an adult enterprise.

2. *The stress on the authority and tradition of the Church was diminished.*

"Indoctrination" is undesirable. Open-ended education should lead learners wherever the search took them. Little place is assigned to authoritative answers or absolutes of any kind. Traditional answers and pieties, whatever their historical relevance to the particular cultures that spawned them, are esteemed as important relics but hardly useful to the contemporary Catholic scene. The experimental method represents a democratic approach to education, even if in practice it leads to indoctrination contrary to the mind of the Church as represented by the Magisterium. The freedom of the child (under the guise that Jesus came to set men free) can be set against the authority of the Church to interpret Jesus' meaning or prescribe disciplinary regulations for the common good of Christian life everywhere. The sudden drop in Mass attendance and confessional regularity were probably the first signs of the new indoctrination going on in Catholic circles.

3. *Subjective interpretations became more important than objective reality or the good of the Church.*

The stress on "experience" as the approved methodology for raising the religious consciousness of contemporary youth had led in some cases to a "smorgasbord Catholicism," which permits the student (or the believer) to decide for himself what Christ or Catholicism means. Subjective Catholicism has always been a factor in the daily lives of Catholics. Since religion is personal, the existential world of religion conveys wide behavioral and believing patterns. Many Catholics died in the odor of sanctity after a lifetime of appropriating Christianity to themselves, sometimes loosely, sometimes rigidly. In recent centuries, however, educated Catholics have been aware of Catholic definitions and requirements established by Church authority. Those trained under the "new catechetics" sometimes believe that the options are now in their hand.

Some theologians are content with this situation, since in their view the classic Catholic concepts of structure and discipline are in process of re-examination. Fr. Mario Galli thinks they are all highly uncertain: "I say welcome to the tensions and the turmoil and the divisions. At last the Church is showing her stuff. At last idealism, vitality, and life are bursting out all over. Now we shall see if there really is anything to her or not." (*U.S. Catholic*, June 1968).

Parents, however, take a dimmer view of an uncertain Catholic outcome for their children. They do not intend to raise an indeterminate child. If public-school parents are outraged by an educational process that turns out illiterate and undisciplined youngsters, Catholic parents oppose religious ambiguity that leaves their children after twelve years of Catholic training imprecise about Church doctrines and the requirements of Catholic belonging.

Religious educators, on their part, committed to the new methodology, are defensive in the face of complaints that question their professional effectiveness. The response of professionals is that their critics seek a return to the simple-minded *Baltimore Catechism*. The National Congress of Religious Education denounces criticism. Publishing houses such as Our Sunday Visitor or the Daughters of St. Paul, which publish (with an *imprimatur*) catechetical textbooks, find their books frozen out of parishes by edict of the school, or CCD office (sometimes by a bishop) or at times by innuendo. If pastors and parish school boards exercise their rightful role to decide what is best for religious education, as three in Chicago did six years ago, the result is nuns quitting or being fired, and explanations from diocesan headquarters (such as the following) that gloss over the real nature of the problem. In the Chicago case, Fr. Thomas Sullivan, then in the school office but now at Catholic University, explained the problem:

> Some pastors end up being threatened. They have been trained in different theological syntheses than have the sisters. Consequently, they quite often become defensive when confronted with the new understanding of theology that many of the sisters have [NCR, July 7, 1972].

Religious educators continue to resist bishops with the regularity that theologians oppose the Holy See. The religious educators seem to operate out of the disdain for bishops that Peter Hebblethwaite attributes to John Courtney Murray: "Some people say the American bishops should lead: "I'm not so sure—after all, who knows where they would lead?" (*The Runaway Church*, p. 13). The Holy See itself had a difficult time with American religious educators over its determination (1971) to publish the General Catechetical Directory. When the National Conference of Catholic Bishops published the *Fundamentals of Religious Education* (as a statement in 1972 of fundamental subject matter for inclusion in programs of religious education in schools and in the Confraternity of Christian Doctrine), the upcoming president of the Catholic Theological Society, Richard McBrien, called for the "document to be completely rewritten." In McBrien's view "the catechetical challenge is not so much the determination of *what* the Catholic Church has taught over the years, but rather the discovery of the *meaning, value,* and *relevance* of such teachings" (*NCR*, April 7, 1972; italics his). McBrien did not like the stress on baptism as the instrument of remission of sins, the Eucharist as real presence, the Church as a hierarchical society, and "the restrictive treatment of marriage," particularly its moral theology.

When the bishops began to work in 1971 on a National Catechetical Directory for the United States, ambiguities turned up in the first two drafts—concerning revelation as a deposit of faith, formulas of faith, original sin, the Church's hierarchical structure, the evils of contraception and sterilization, the binding authority of Magisterium—ambiguities that condoned considerable vagueness about Catholic doctrine. For example, marriage was defined as "a free union of two people joined in and by a loving covenant to which they give themselves to one another." The absence of any reference to children or the fact that marriage is a heterosexual union of man and woman did not go unnoticed. "Experience" continues to thrive in the religious education and to have impact on the parochial life of Catholics, especially in liturgical matters. Stress on "experience" is leading to the denigration of infant baptism, private confession, the Eucharist as Body of Christ, marriage as family, priesthood as sacramental ministry.

This confusion could have been averted had the Fathers of Vatican II published a *Catechism of the Second Vatican Council.* They did not because, after voting for collegiality and national conferences of bishops, they agreed that "catechisms," whatever else their nature, should reflect the needs of local Catholic population groups. They also bowed to arguments in favor of decentralizing and de-Romanizing the Church. The influence of the periti may also have been more dominant during the Council than bishops realized. Periti said then, and still say, that universal answers to Catholic or Christian questions no longer exist. Periti also wanted flexibility to develop their own answers. In practice, they became as committed to their answers as Roman curialists. Momentarily, periti supported dogmatic and moral pluralism as a means of preventing Rome or bishops from closing doors periti did not wish closed. These ambiguities have been used to the advantage of periti— and a variety of particular catechisms, the *Dutch Catechism,* the *American Catechism,* the *Catholic Catechism,* the *Catechism of Vatican II* —some of which have forced the Holy See to issue corrections, interpretations, even warnings. In the meantime, the particular catechisms dominated the local scene, permitting what was taught in one school or class to be denied in another.

The Fathers of the Council of Trent did not make that mistake. Almost as soon as Trent opened (December 13, 1545), the assembled bishops saw the need for an official book of instruction. Within four months (April 5, 1546), a catechism was programmed. Progress toward publication was slow until 1562, when St. Charles Borromeo took charge of the project, and by 1566 the catechism was completed. According to Dominicans John A. McHugh and Charles J. Callan, Borromeo saw that the scholarly draftsmen avoided in their composition "the particular opinions of individuals and schools" and expressed only "the doctrine of the universal Church, keeping in mind the decrees of the Council of Trent." The great master of the Latin tongue Charles Borromeo studied the text to guarantee the coherence of literary style and doctrinal meaning. And before publication Pope Pius V appointed expert theological revisers to examine each statement from the viewpoint of doctrine. As translations into the vernacular proliferated and as saintly scholars, from Francis De Sales to Cardinal Newman, sought doctrine for their sermons, the authoritativeness and stature of the Tridentine catechism as a source book of Catholic inspiration grew. As late as 1921 an archdiocese like New York developed A Parochial Course of Doctrinal Instructions based totally on Trent's catechism.

In the vacuum left by Council Fathers following Vatican II in some fundamental areas of Catholic doctrine, opinions contrary to Magisterium spread through the Catholic faithful. Corrections by bishops and Pope were always belated. The periti have been able to charge the hierarchy with reneging on Vatican II because the latter always seems lagging behind the interpretations put on Vatican II by theologians. Had the Council Fathers in 1965 exercised the foresight of their predecessors in 1565, this might not have occurred.

## II. Textbooks Tell the Story

Combined stress on personal creativity and hostility to authority have been insinuated into more than one religious textbook since Vatican II to the denigration of standard Catholic formation. The driving goal in Catholic education seemed to become personality formation above all else. This was a distinctly American objective in education since the days of John Dewey. Up until recent times Catholic educators stood fast against the temptation to conform, but the pressure became overbearing.

Empirical psychologists Jean Piaget and Lawrence Kohlberg appeared on the scene seemingly having proved by hard data that education must proceed not by imposition but by following natural laws of learning. According to Piaget children grow intellectually as they grow physically—in stages. They cannot be rushed. Harvard Professor Kohlberg goes Piaget one step farther. Not only does Kohlberg see cognitive reasoning developing in stages, but also moral reasoning developing in the same way. What counts is not what the outside world puts into the child, but what the child sees or does at different stages of his life. At *Stage One* the child seeks approval; at *Stage Six* the mature adult seeks fidelity to universal principles. Most people, however, arrive at *Stage Four*, respecting law and order, and a few in *Stage Five* show willingness to challenge the law in the interest of higher principles. Under their influence student-centered education dominated the schools and developmental psychology became its chief handmaid.

"Becoming a person" concepts in one form or another eventually worked their way into Catholic textbooks and into religious education programs. The clearest example, of course, is the "becoming a person" program pioneered by Walter Imbiorski for the archdiocese of Chicago and used in the school systems of many dioceses. BAPP, as it is sometimes called, is a program in moral guidance designed for Christians. The subject areas include the family, self-understanding, maturity and psychosexual development, the ability to relate to other people, and the intrinsic cogency of Christian principles values. It is to be used before or after a social-science or religion class, not as a substitute for either. More an exercise in social science than theology, BAPP accepts the premise that the best foundation for good behavior (or virtue) is a healthy personality. Personality development, therefore, is its dominant theme, as is clear in the treatment of subjects like sexuality, authority, and conscience.

The BAPP series has been accused of overstressing the individual. Parents have complained when their second-grade children in the program are encouraged to rehearse in the classroom family fights that went on at home. Some teachers have objected to the assertion made to fifth-grade children that "sex is the determining factor in our human relationships." When the subject of birth control is introduced to seventh-grade children, those familiar with Church documents have found this response inadequate: "For good reasons a couple can decide to control or limit the size of their families, but there are certain methods that are sinful." And although the student does not use the teacher's manual, the instructor receives there a short course in contraception methods for any practical discussion that follows the introduction of the subject. The topic "authority" is treated as if authority figures need not command obedience.

"Becoming a person" questions are ones that experimental researchers say engage children's attention at given ages. The methodology is designed to lead students from the *existential* world of their personal circumstances to an awareness of the *essential* principles of human and Christian life. Psychologists credit BAPP for the high value it places on independence and autonomy but, as is true of other contemporary course material, complaints have been registered that the students are left ignorant of basic information needed for life situations. The BAPP approach is faulted, also, for failing to demonstrate that it can produce a superior moral character. This was its chief selling point to educators, many of whom now join the list of those who bemoan the increasing lack of disciplined behavior in their graduates.

Although BAPP programs make no pretense of dealing with catechetics, it is inevitable that judgments will be made about its impact on the religious life of children. An *imprimatur* was not obtained for the series, because a general course of personality development does not need approval from Church authority. This does not, however, put an end to pastoral or parental concerns. There is a powerful educative force at work in any series that accentuates search for growth, personal understanding, and sexual development, while underplaying the supernatural, divine law, the Church as Christ's instrument, childbearing in marriage, and sin. Such a course teaches much more than merely how to become a person. BAPP programs, whether the editors disclaim catechetical intent or not, have been involved in controversy among Catholics for one of two reasons. One is the *factual* dispute, to which reference has already been made. Does this psychologically-oriented curriculum teach a useful body of knowledge? The second dispute is more substantive because it is *ideological*. Does this series tend to break the ties that bind students to their social worlds, especially the family? Does it tend to relativize moral and social norms?

The risk of substituting psychology for religious training is more perilous in textbooks that do carry an *imprimatur*, which reach the mass of Catholic children in Catholic schools and through them the rank and file of Catholic parents. What is that risk? That a generation of Catholics comes into being that lacks the firm answers to questions about their faith that have been raised in the Church's classrooms. In the quest of personality development students are encouraged to ask questions and to reach for their own answers. Teachers are cautioned to avoid "imposing" answers, or to suggest their answer as an option.

An example of the problems facing a given parent or pastor by the psychologizing of children in the classroom is the Benziger edition of an eighth-grade religion text, entitled *Seek*. The affected students will often never receive formal Catholic education again. The opening lines of *Seek* read as follows:

I sit at my desk, head cupped in my hands, staring into space.

What do I see? I see me.

I see myself as doing my own thing,
the master of my own destiny.

I see the child who loves home and parents,
who rebels against rules and yet wants them.

I see challenge and security all mixed up in me.

I sit staring into space. What do I see?

I see others. . . ."

These are the questions allegedly being asked in the eighth-grade class of a Catholic school.

For the rest of the course the book agonizes over the answers. Reaching answers becomes painful. "Decisions! Decisions!" "Should I get involved?" "The choice is not always simple." Even the "tried and true" gospels are called "unpredictable." The authors' positive effort to build the self-esteem in students, to indoctrinate them with ethical values about violence, honesty, and prejudice make it appear that the values proposed are always the student's values, never anyone else's. When the name Jesus is first introduced to the text, it is in connection with building self-esteem, self-image, personhood, and sexuality.

"Authority," a subject raised for discussion in the last part of the course, is given psychological treatment without raising the commitment aspects of the subject. God is acknowledged as the source of authority, but "the one in authority sees others as persons and tries to help them become the kind of persons that they can be." Pointing to the authority of the Apostles, the text reminds the young reader how Jesus said the one who ranks first must be the last one of all and a servant. Obeying law never enters the discussion.

The last two units of the eighth-grade course introduce the student to "the search," first for "the impossible dream," then for Christianity. Life is quest, a challenge for men seeking answers. Those who do not dare to quest or challenge lose their chance for greatness. The gospel itself is a challenge to search. The Church is a people who are searching. The sacraments are challenges.

At the end of the book appears "the final exam," which centers on the statement: "It is good to question." What is life all about? Where are we going? Why are we here? Do I believe in Jesus and his Church? How do the teachings of Jesus and his Church affect my life? "Search," the student is admonished. "Ask questions." The book is reassuring: "We will eventually find our answers." Where? The book suggests: "Ask the Holy Spirit."

The approach of *Seek* to the religious formation of the Catholic young must be evaluated against some of the things the Church historically has said about the human person and his Catholic education:

1. Each human being is created by God from the moment of his conception to be a unique person.

   In a real sense, therefore, there is no such thing as "becoming a person."

2. The uniqueness of the human person consists not only in his individuality and special intellect, but also in his ability to act on the social situation.

   The human being is not by nature a victim of circumstance. He can misuse opportunity but also can triumph over adversity.

3. The human person is weak in his capacity to recognize what is true and to do what is right.

   This weakness is the result of original sin.

   Education, therefore, must include training body, mind, and will. Knowledge alone is not power, not even virtue. Knowledge of the psychological processes does not guarantee learning or responsible behavior.

   The habits of intellect and will derive as much from repeated exercise—stimulated by custom, discipline, and law—as from understanding.

4. The baptized person is also graced. He is a temple of the Holy Spirit. Not only is he better than he looks, but also, under grace, he can do what no one thinks he can.

   Like John Vianney of Ars, Bernadette of Lourdes, Theresa of Lisieux.

   Since he is vulnerable he needs Mass, the sacraments, good example, moral support, and spiritual direction that is more than counseling.

   Lawrence Kohlberg's conclusion that the human person cannot

move to a higher stage of moral development without first experiencing a lower stage not only in an unprovable assertion but
also takes no account of what the Catholic educator must—
grace.

5. The Christian person has Christ.
But the Christ he must come to know is the Savior who came,
not to make him a personality pleasing to given secular cultures,
but to make him a son of God pleasing to the heavenly Father.
Christ came to save the person as much from himself as from
the world and Satan.
Students must learn to see the forgiving *Savior* in Christ but
also that he is *Lord*—he gives commandments—and *judge*—he
rewards and punishes.

6. The Christian person has the Church.
The Church is a way station for man's pilgrimage to God.
There comfort, consolation, reconciliation, and salvation may be
found.
But also Christ's authority to command and to judge.

Even though the National Catechetical Directory claims that "catechesis is not limited to one methodology," the fact is that contemporary religious education is more sensitive to the writings of the developmental school of experimental psychologists than to the official
documents of Church authorities. The net result is a heightened sense
of self-appreciation and autonomy in the student, without necessarily a
knowledge of Catholic doctrine or felt obligation to the Church and its
requirements.

## III. What Other Psychologists Say

Because developmental psychology at present saturates Catholic education, it is important to recognize what has been said about its validity
and pretensions. Sociologist Philip Rieff, surveying the moral education
that has gone on in recent years, states the common complaint: "Perhaps the greatest problem of moral education lies in the paradox that
the best sort of people it can produce lack all conviction (*NCR*, May
13, 1977). According to Rieff, they would rather switch moralities than
fight about any.

A recent effort by a psychology professor at Johns Hopkins University
offers evidence in support of the theory that learning does not come
through a natural developmental process at all, but through man-made
mechanisms. After surveying the literature and conducting his own

tests, Robert Hogan constructed a "theory of moral development" (expounded in *Psychological Bulletin*, April 1973, and popularized four years later in *National Observer*). Hogan began his career as a probation officer in California, where he puzzled over why youngsters go bad. He asked whether there was something wrong with their moral development. During his years as a doctoral candidate in psychology he came to the conclusion that Freud saw the world backward. You cannot study neurotics to learn about normals. You must study normals to understand delinquents. After examining tragic human situations like heroin addiction, Hogan concludes:

> The conventional wisdom is that heroin addicts are sick. Compared to neurotics, they are not sick at all. Rather, they are comparable to you and me. There is nothing wrong with their self-confidence and self-esteem. There is not one shred of evidence that they are sick, that they are living a dark night of the soul. They are just hedonists; they are just having a good time. Heroin addiction is not a medical problem. It's a moral problem.

In his judgment psychopaths are not defective because they are without norms. Psychopaths know all the rules. They just do not obey them.

Professor Hogan's developmental theory sees human morality unfolding in three progressive stages: (1) *socialization* during the preschool years; (2) *empathy* during elementary school; (3) *autonomy* during high-school and college years.

What is *socialization*? Learning the rules of society through parents. This stage of life teaches the young to live with authority, some becoming overrespectful, some becoming rebellious, most surviving relatively well. This should be a time of love and affection but not of permissiveness. Hogan thinks children come into the world preprogrammed to accept the rules of adults. At this stage the child learns to live with authority.

What is *empathy*? Learning to live with society by "feeling out" one's way with peers. At this stage the teen-ager, for example, learns what his equals expect of him. Because he wants approval of his peers, as he does of parents, he learns to play the game of accommodating himself to both. He begins to understand what is right and fair, what is wrong and unjust, in a way somewhat different from the lessons first taught him by parents. The waters of life are a little muddier now, but he still plays the game of rules, established now as much by peers as by parents. At this stage the young become concerned about other people.

What is *autonomy?* Learning to live with oneself. Learning to live one's own life. Some people make it. Some people do not. Here is the time of life when people make up their minds about what they believe in—that is, their ideology. Most people become independent and socialized at about the same time. They live their lives within the context of their loyalty to the particular society they prize. Following the *AA-Daytop* line, Hogan thinks you cannot change lives by abstract education. Attitudes toward authority and other people cannot be changed by a book. But people's beliefs or ideology can be changed by people. This is what is known as conversion. Once beliefs are changed, other changes follow. The Marine Corps does it. The Black Muslims do it. The Catholic Church has a long history of doing it. The Communists do it. The Nazis and the Fascists did it. So, too, do developmental psychologists.

Hogan confesses he does not have a prefectly drawn theory. He is not sure how people move from one stage or another, nor how to define "empathy" or measure "autonomy." He is sure of one thing: Without socialization there is no legitimate autonomy. High socialization can mean company men. High empathy can mean pleasant personalities. High autonomy can mean revolutionaries. What counts is the mixture, which begins with men knowing the rules, with input to the person from the outside, with a body of ideas and practices learned in the early years that are taken for granted as true and right.

What about Piaget's suggestion (*The Moral Judgment of the Child*) that autonomy develops "through the natural processes of cognitive development and peer interaction"? Hogan's 1973 article in *Psychological Bulletin* entitled "Moral Conduct and Moral Character," after comparing child-rearing practices, concludes that "on this point Piaget surely seems to be wrong." Exclusive peer interaction inhibits autonomy. So do permissive parents. Hogan's major point is that controls precede autonomy. When independence of external controls is achieved, it is not absolute. By a certain time of life, the subject has already internalized social norms and conforms effortlessly to these norms, but in his own way. Psychologist Hogan sums up his position:

> Most such [psychological] theories describe development as preceding through preset stages [that] can be achieved after all the preceding stages have been mastered. This paper suggests that socialization, empathy, and autonomy are major transition points in moral development.

Moral development come, but later stages do not depend on transition from earlier stages. Indeed, evidence of moral maturity may be conformity to social norms. Hogan's "theory" is far removed from the postulates of developmental psychology.

### IV. Experimental Psychology and the Catholic Church

The Church seeks answers to questions from many sources. A long history of doctrine, rules, ritual celebrations, experienced lifestyles, and laws contribute to the process of Christian education in every era. The opinions of experimental psychologists are new resources. The Church, also, balances two views of human nature—man is good, man is prone to evil, man can learn by reason and experience, man learns by revelation and faith. The Church, furthermore, knows that left to himself man tends to maximize his private satisfactions, so it stresses formation and the importance of society, including religious grouping. The Church, therefore, wishes people to develop on their own initiative but with one eye on the laws of God and man. It is not a devotee of a no-control environment. Frequent exercise frequently nudged by authority helps moral development. Virtue reinforced by common practice and supported by faith systems tends to remain virtue.

The capture of institutions, including churches, by developmental psychology calls for inquiry. Four questions in particular can be asked about the effect of these "psychologies" on the Catholic faithful.

1. Do they aggravate selfishness or stimulate skepticism in matters of faith?
2. Are they diminishing the importance of social rules in the lives of Catholics?
3. Are they making it difficult to teach doctrine or establish common discipline?
4. Do they create a false picture of the normal world and the normal Church?

William J. Bennett and Edwin J. DeLattre, writing in The Public Interest, a magazine edited by Irving Kristol and Nathan Glazer and devoted to intelligent and scholarly critiques of critical social issues, have raised similar questions (Winter 1978) about moral education in the public schools. They object specifically to the educational techniques of Sidney Simon of the University of Massachusetts and Lawrence Kohlberg of Harvard. Simon, for example, asserts, "None of us has the right set of values to pass on to other people's children." For Simon the content of people's values is not important, only the process of valuing. Whatever the student thinks is religious, is religious. Bennett and DeLattre conclude their critique of Simon: "Finally and ironically, Simon's approach emphatically indoctrinates by encouraging and even exhorting the student to narcissistic self-gratification." When parents in Great Neck objected to the methodology used in the schools, Simon is quoted as saying, "An Orthodox Jewish, right-wing group got hold of it and just raised hell."

*The Public Interest* critics seem more concerned, however, about the influence of Lawrence Kohlberg, because of his high standing in the university community, particularly in departments of psychology and philosophy, and in schools of education. Kohlberg, unlike Simon, proposes a search for objective moral truth through exercises in training children to solve moral dilemmas. He, too, is opposed to indoctrination as undemocratic and unconstitutional ("the child's right to freedom from indoctrination"), but hopes the teacher (beginning with the dilemmas proposed by Kohlberg) can help students determine the "stages" of their moral development and help them grow. The exercises are also intended to improve moral perceptions and behavior.

In *Hypothetical Dilemmas for Use in Moral Discussions,* prepared and distributed by the Moral Education and research Foundation at Harvard, the following is one of the proposed dilemmas:

> Sex as a need: The Johnson family (with four children) was a very happy and close one. Mr. and Mrs. Johnson were in their thirties. One day Mr. Johnson fell from a third-story building where he was working. He broke his back in this accident and was totally paralyzed from his waist down. The accident did not result in economic hardship because of workman's compensation. Three months after the accident, when Mr. Johnson came home, the problem began. Mrs. Johnson, who was a young person, realized that she would have to give up sexual intercourse with her husband. If she did not want to give up her sex life, she had the following choices: either get a divorce, or have extramarital affairs.
>
> 1. Is it possible to separate sex from affection? What do you think she should do? Give reasons.
> 2. Do you think this woman should remain married to the husband? Why or why not?
> 3. What do you think would happen to the family if she had an affair?
> 4. If she decides to have an affair, should she tell her husband or keep it a secret? Why?

The range of Kohlberg's choices for solving this particular dilemma is obviously limited, even from a secular humanist standpoint. The case itself is weighted in favor of the wife's predicament, not that of the husband's or the children's and the moral principles to be induced remain ambiguous.

Bennett and DeLattre, after reviewing this and other Kohlberg cases, make the following criticism:

1. They doubt that what Kohlberg describes in his case is morality at all.
2. They accuse both Simon and Kohlberg of indoctrinating—the celebration of wants and desires, for one thing—but indoctrinating, too, *against* traditional moral values.
3. Their view of the world—a place of coldness and conflict—is arbitrary and untrue.
4. They leave no room for passing on knowledge and experience.

Conclude the critics: "Children are invited to a world where it is a travesty and an imposition for anyone to tell them the truth."

More than public-school parents have a vested interest in the outcome of educational procedures now widely used in the United States.

CHAPTER IX

Embattled Nuns

## I. Where Did It All Begin?

One morning in March 1977 an older generation of Catholics opened their daily newspaper over the morning's orange juice to be startled by an advertisement for a movie revealing the shapely silk-stockinged leg of a Catholic nun enticing the reader to come see a movie entitled *Nasty Habits*. It is difficult to decide whether a nun's legs brazenly protruding above the knee from what looked like an old Ursuline habit shocked more than the story, which pitched a power-hungry Nixon-type religious superior running for office against a jazzy Sister Felicity, who in the movie was already carrying on a madcap affair with a Jesuit brother and soliciting votes with promises to turn the convent into a love-abbey.

The National Coalition of American Nuns cried "foul," but a movie critic, the New York *Daily News'* Rex Reed, countered with the remark: "In the light of the daily headlines, we know nuns are doing all sorts of unsavory things in real life, so the protest seems a bit unjustified" (March 18, 1977). Whether the viewer thought both ad and movie foul or funny, it was clear that Leo McCarey's days of *The Bells of St. Mary's* were over and both Loretta Young and Rosalind Russell—the prototypes of Hollywood nuns—interred in the film industry's library of tales of long ago.

Why this sudden disrespect? Within the Catholic Church and in worldly American society nuns were esteemed more highly than priests. Even Catholic reformers like Michael Novak looking backward thought nuns to be the most interesting women he ever encountered precisely because their lives were "richer and more disciplined" than their lay counterparts. Recently nuns seem to have fallen from grace.

We are still too close to the scene to evaluate why fifty thousand nuns left the convent between 1966 and 1976, or why so few seem interested in entering now. Marcelle Bernstein's *The Nuns* blames the chauvinist hierarchy of the Church, affluence, and increased opportunities for women in the modern world. A Chicago study in 1975 blames "the inability to be me" and "too much tension within the community" following Vatican II. Monica Balwin, the Englishwoman who thirty years ago wrote *I Leap over the Wall*, now in a penitential mood, blames the neglect of prayer and the interior life, not structural faults in the Church or oppressive authorities. John Cogley, prior to his conversion to Episcopalianism, thought the explanation was modernity. He took note of the fact that "those who got what they wanted in the way of reform head the list of departees" (NCR, December 4, 1968). It is unquestionably true that the greatest losses appear to have occurred in affluent countries and in orders of women making the greatest effort to modernize. The most "advanced" communities were attracting almost no one, and excuses that reforms were not yet radical enough seem inadequate. As well-known Sisters Jacqueline Grennan or Mary Corita Kent departed to scene, the symbols of religious reform looked tarnished.

There is, of course, another diagnosis of decline, one hardly more objective than those given above but frequently stated in private gatherings. An internationally known mother general who, when asked what happened to American nuns, said: "They were betrayed by their major superiors." Another explanation places the cause not in betrayal as in weakness in high office. A nationally known Jesuit, writing for his confreres several years ago about the problems of his own community, said openly what many unhappy sisters are saying delicately:

1. A *coup d'état* is occurring in religious society.
2. The dissolution of the established community has been accomplished with ease.
3. The majority have meekly suffered the wreck of the society in the face of a determined minority.
4. Nothing but a miracle can save us.
5. The Jesuits ought to be divided into two groups, independent of each other, each sharing the resources and the apostolates.

Explanations or excuses notwithstanding, the devastation of American convents has profound implications for the future of the American

Church. In recent history three times as many American women as men served Catholic institutions, and the losses among women have been staggering. Historians will sift the evidence objectively when all the results are compiled. But there are some events that can be reported as part of the unfolding story.

## II. The Conference of Major Superiors of Women (CMSW)

Before the Second Vatican Council, the Holy See on its own initiative decided to upgrade and revitalize religious life throughout the Catholic world. The 1952 World Congress of Mothers General in Rome had set the stage for an American meeting of major superiors in 1956. The thrust of this Chicago meeting of 235 major superiors, under the aegis of the Congregation for Religious in Rome, was to encourage and actively promote the internal renewal of individual communities and the creation of the Conference of Major Superiors of Women (CMSW) as an American body to deal with the Holy See on "the spiritual welfare of the women religious of the United States of America." By the time of Vatican II, CMSW had statutes approved by Rome that were conceived to promote "greater apostolic efficiency, closer fraternal co-operation, and representation with constituted authority."

In view of the fact that CMSW became a runaway organization, the Article IV, Section 1 statute approved in 1962 in Rome has only historical significance:

> The conference professes and declares to the Apostolic Delegate and to the hierarchy of the United States the profound respect which is due to those whom the Holy Spirit has appointed to govern the Church, and a perfect allegiance in full conformity with canonical legislation.

Under that inspiration CMSW continued to be a positive influence in improving not only the education of women religious and the quality of their community life (begun in the 1940s as the result of urgings from Rome) but also their relationships with each other and with the Church in general.

But in 1966—immediately after the Council's close—CMSW decided to do a massive sociopsychological survey of 139,000 women religious in the United States, and from then on nothing remained the same.

The *Sisters' Survey*, as it came to be called, was not simply a quest for information. It became an instrument of re-education. A total of

778 questions, some of which had 80 parts, were drawn up to elicit response from both major superiors and their subjects. The subject areas included belief, notions about religious life, obedience, reading habits, and so forth. Respondents were asked to mark off or check the statement that best reflected their personal views on the various topics. The proposed statements were extrapolated from secular studies of a similar nature and redesigned to cover Catholic Church matters.

Under *belief*, for example, the nun was asked to make selections among a variety of propositions, some of which read as follows:

> I think of God as unchanging essence and uncaused cause.

> I regard the Word of God as speaking always and in diverse ways through events, other persons, and my own conscience, as well as through the Bible and the Church's Magisterium.

> *Or*, I think the Church as the assembly of believers called together by God's word in Christ.

> A good way to explain what the Church is, is to describe the relationship of the Pope to the bishops, and of these to the priests, religious, and laity.

The statements about *religious life* included contrasts such as these:

> The traditional way of presenting chastity in religious life has allowed for the development of isolation and false mysticism among the sisters.

> *Or*, With the vow of poverty we must dare to live precariously, setting out like Abraham, who did not know where he was going.

Asked to speak about *obedience* as practiced in their religious houses, the sisters could indicate their experience with:

> I feel that any initiative on my part is stifled.

> I feel it has kept me immature and overdependent.

> I feel it has been an excuse for me to dodge real responsibility.

Questions about *reading habits* were phrased in such a way as to un-cover what the authors of the survey might decide were the "better-read theologically" and "better-informed politically."

The *Memo on Sisters' Survey*, submitted by Sr. Marie Augusta Neale in June 1969, drew conclusions not only insinuated by the ques-tionnaire itself, but also reported the results of the re-education of American nuns that had been going on in mother houses since the opening of Vatican II. Not since the seventeenth century, when French nuns were thoroughly infected with the rigorism of Jansenism, was religious life so thoroughly reordered against the express wishes of the Church's highest authorities. The *Sisters' Survey* demonstrated this to be true.

The notions of a finite God in process, of the Real Presence abiding in every person, of a Church of believers without a hierarchy, of Mass without a priesthood, of revelation equated with human experience, the caricature of the Church with Pope and bishops lording it over the rest of the faithful were proposed as answers to survey questions, but they were also the commonplace convictions of contemporary writers who had since the close of Vatican II been challenging the historic Catholic faith—in convents especially. In fact, Sr. Marie Augusta Neale's *Memo* (p. 2) suggests that the sister who preferred a pre-Vatican II belief ori-entation manifested "proneness to Fascism." Indeed, she found (p. 1) those sisters bound down by "traditionalist" forms of belief to be "more concerned with saving their own souls than in helping in the renewal of the world" (p. 1). Even though most of these nuns worked long hours for the educational and welfare agencies of the Church, their penchant for prayer and concern for celibacy were said to inhibit daring involve-ment in worldly pursuits and secular relationships. Sisters were called "up to date" who had difficulty with obedience and scored high for "post-Vatican thinking" if they read the "liberal" authors (p. 2), many of whom questioned the historicity of the Gospels, claimed that religious life was no longer possible, and denied the validity of ecclesi-astical law or the Church's moral prescriptions.

By the time the *Sisters' Survey* was completed, the religious com-munities of the United States were in disarray. A survey of 230 com-munities with a population of 114,000 members discloses the sudden shift in commitment.

| Year | New Members | Withdrawals | Net Change |
|------|-------------|-------------|------------|
| 1964 | 1,794 | 634 | +1,160 |
| 1965 | 1,196 | 957 | +239 |
| 1966 | 598 | 1,488 | −890 |

This net loss of almost 200 per cent in two years continued to increase year by year. By 1970 the net loss for that one year alone was 7,286.

Those who administered the survey placed the blame for the losses not on the reindoctrination of religious contrary to Vatican II going-on in convents, but on the convents themselves, on archaic rules, stress on spiritual rather than worldly life, discipline rather than freedom. Sr. Marie Augusta Neale concluded for the *Survey* (p. 3):

> Decline in religious vocations rather than being due to unrest in the religious orders is in fact related to the relevancy of the order in its form of life and service to the realization of the Gospel in our times.

As her questions indicated, religious life could prosper if nuns would work on local community boards, demonstrate on picket lines, or enjoy freedom from superior's or bishop's commands.

When the results of the *Sisters' Survey* began to filter into the leadership of the Conference of the Major Superiors of Women, an effort to review CMSW's statutes (which had been approved by Rome in 1962) began. The management-consultant firm of Booz, Allen & Hamilton was employed to restructure CMSW. This secular counseling agency, lacking knowledge of or experience in religious life, followed customary procedures by drafting a reorganization plan based on the answers given to its questions. When the management report was issued in 1969, it was clear that religious life in America was to be restructured around four key concepts:

1. Minimal stress upon the spiritual aspects of religious life.
2. Altered concepts of authority, to include collegiality and subsidiarity.
3. Autonomy from ecclesiastical authority, especially Rome's.
4. The creation of a national secretariat composed of professionals and managed by an executive secretary.

A revised CMSW obviously was intended to be autonomous not only from bishops and the Holy See but also was to be "managed" not by major superiors but by a core group of hired staff.

Little time was lost in putting the recommendations of Booz, Allen & Hamilton into effect. By 1970 new draft statutes for CMSW rejected in principle the basic law of 1962. A list of sample deletions from the

1962 statutes offers some idea of how complete the transformation was to be. The new statutes omitted:

1. Every reference to CMSW being governed "in conformity with the desire of the Sacred Congregation of Religious."
2. Every reference that the purpose of the Conference was "to promote spiritual welfare of the woman religious of the United States."
3. The explicit provision that the Conference is open to all major superiors and to these only.
4. The entire article "Subordination of Conference to Authorities" simply disappeared.

Although it came into existence as a creature of the Vatican, it was clear that CMSW was by September 1970 critical of Rome's "high-handed methods" of treating American religious and was prepared to resist expected Vatican regulations. At the CMSW National Assembly (September 9–13, 1970), John C. Haughey, S.J., gave an address to the nuns entitled "Where Has Our Search Led Us?" Haughey later capsulated his approval of the "sharp turn" CMSW was about to take. He looked upon its direction as a concrete expression of "women's lib" and suggested that anything coming from Rome on religious life would be of the same genre as *Humanae Vitae* and might be ignored or disregarded by the nuns (*America*, September 25, 1970).

Was CMSW ready for *Humanae Vitae* of the religious life? CMSW was not. By 1971 the statutes of the organization were changed to by-laws, which asserted complete independence of Rome and hierarchy. The section on "authority" was dropped and sentences like "with due regard for the authority of the Holy See and of the bishops" were eliminated.

The CMSW went out of existence in 1972 and the Leadership Conference of Women Religious took its place.

## III. The Immaculate Heart of Mary Community in California

The I.H.M.s were the group of nuns that Peter Hebblethwaite, in *The Runaway Church* (p. 12), once said were "hounded out" of Los Angeles by Cardinal McIntyre, an example also, to use words coined by Eugene Kennedy, of the "frustration and suffering that has been visited upon sisters who have done nothing more than change their habits" (*The People are the Church*, p. 20).

The "I.H.M. Affair," as it came to be called, is one case study for history books on the renewal of religious life as perceived by its advocates. In 1968 a petition reportedly signed by twenty-five thousand laymen and religious was sent to Pope Paul VI supporting I.H.M.-type renewal (*Catholic Mind*, June 1968), and for their efforts I.H.M. sisters gained a reputation in a popular Sunday supplement (*Pageant*, July 1970) as "the nuns who turned their backs on the Pope."

Perhaps the place to start the story is with what they turned their backs on.

This was contained in a letter to Sister Anita Caspary, I.H.M., dated February 29, 1968, and signed by Thomas R. Gallagher, O.P., apostolic visitor for the Holy See to the I.H.M. community. Because of its significance for the religious life of the Church everywhere, it is worth quoting in its entirety:

Dear Sister Anita:

As promised when I met with you and the General Council on January 31, I referred at once to the Holy See about the pressing problems which created a sense of urgency for you. I now have a letter of 21 February 1968 (n. 493/65) in which the Sacred Congregation for Religious directs me to make known to you the following decisions:

"1. The members of the Institute have to adopt a uniform habit, which will be in conformity with the prescriptions of paragraph 17 of the Decree 'Perfectae Caritatis.' The use of lay clothes is not only against the above-mentioned Decree, but violates Common Law and the prescriptions of the Motu Proprio 'Ecclesiae Sanctae II,' par. 6, which states that: 'The General Chapter is empowered to modify on an experimental basis certain prescriptions of the Constitutions . . . provided that the purpose, *nature and characteristics of the Institute are preserved intact.*' The habit pertains to the nature and characteristics of any Institute for which it has been approved, and the interpretations given to the Sisters in this regard by certain so-called 'competent Theologians' have absolutely no foundation, either doctrinal or juridical.

"2. Every community of the Sisters of the Immaculate Heart should meet daily for some religious exercises in common. They should at least attend the Holy Sacrifice of the Mass together every day.

"3. The Sisters should keep in mind their commitment to education as specified in their Constitutions: "The specific end is to labor for the salvation of souls through the work of Catholic education in schools and colleges . . ." (Art. 3). Here, too, the above quotation from the Motu Proprio 'Ecclesiae Sanctae II' is applicable, namely that the purpose (specific end) of the Institute must be kept intact.

"4. The Sisters must observe the prescriptions of the Conciliar Decree 'Christus Dominus' (NN. 33–35) and of the Motu Proprio "Ecclesiae Sanctae I" (NN. 22–40) in regard to collaboration with the Local Ordinaries in the works of the Apostolate in the various dioceses. These prescriptions hold for all Religious, especially for those of Pontifical Right."

While I convey to you these directives of the Holy See I encourage all the Sisters to give their generous cooperation to their implementation in a spirit humility, obedience and love of our Holy Mother the Church.

At the further behest of the Holy See I would also urge you to be keenly aware in this matter of the common good of the Church and to appreciate the concern she has for the religious education of the children who are so precious to her.

With sentiments of deep personal affection and esteem for the community, I remain

Confrontation, however, began in April 1964, when final approval was given to a five-year plan for the I.H.M. community. This revision of community objectives later inspired new rituals for the reception of postulants, experimentation in dress and community life, and a re-examination of I.H.M.'s commitment to the elementary schools of the Los Angeles archdiocese. In that year 637 I.H.M. sisters staffed more than sixty schools, two hospitals, a retreat house, and their own novitiate. Their most important asset was Immaculate Heart College.

The I.H.M.s arrived in Los Angeles in 1880, second in time only to the Sisters of Charity, who had opened an orphanage earlier. The I.H.M.s grew rapidly until at one point sixty postulants applied for membership annually. This flourishing condition enabled the community to staff parochial schools in the western dioceses from San Diego to British Columbia. The I.H.M.s came to be looked upon as the outstanding religious educators in the West, and their institutions as hostels for traveling missionaries, including St. Francis Cabrini and Fr. Patrick Peyton, C.S.C., who began his rosary campaign in their motherhouse.

I.H.M.s were also innovative. They were the first nuns to drive cars, the first nuns to receive permission from Rome to travel singly rather than in pairs, the first nuns to abolish the lay-sister status in their community. Apostolic works, including service to the poor, were integral parts of their apostolate. With the expansion of the Los Angeles archdiocesan school system, the I.H.M.s found themselves gradually betrayed by their own generosity. Overextending the sisters in the active apostolates led to a certain neglect of the life of prayer essential to the survival of religious life. The appeals of pastors were resisted. Overcrowded classrooms, extracurricular activities, making altar breads, washing linens, counting collections, directing choirs, even doing janitorial work resulted in dispensations first from the recitation of the office, then from periods of mental prayer.

Side by side with a generous faith and dedication to the works of the community, the I.H.M.s were less than adequately trained in Scripture and theology, and their convents often lacked suitable liturgy. Many chaplains and confessors (except those who themselves were members of religious communities) did not understand the religious life. And the minutiae of permission-seeking were frequently annoying distractions. In hindsight, some I.H.M.s thought that the community suffered from weak superiors or were discomforted by the politicking that went on in the community.

For the better part of three decades the I.H.M.s were ruled by what has been called a "dynasty"—a succession of major superiors, all friends and protégés of each other. Maternalism and laissez-faire alternated as ruling styles. As sisters grew in educational attainment, due to the general excellence of their own college and postgraduate training in centers far removed from Los Angeles, dissatisfaction began to manifest itself at various levels. Sisters were deeply affected by their new learning. Within the "dynasty" itself new leaders came to office and power who entertained new plans for both college and community. If the decade following 1960 was turbulent, so was the mood of the new I.H.M. leadership. The new leadership, without always informing or consulting the superiors of local communities, was in contact with a wide range of experts.

In April 1965 Fr. Bernard E. Ransing of the Sacred Congregation of Religious told the I.H.M.s: "A community is free to experiment with the habit as long as the experimentation does not include the entire community, and is limited to a definite period of time." I.H.M. officers had already gone beyond these guidelines. Because of Rome's concern, Cardinal McIntyre personally made the first of two canonical visitations in May of that year. (The second, in November, followed Sr.

Anita Caspary's trip to Rome, where she held discussions with some of the periti of Vatican II, then coming to a close.) In December 1965, Fr. Ransing himself came from Rome to discuss irregularities with the I.H.M. leadership. A conference at the chancery office between Cardinal McIntyre and the mother general followed. While the community *Chronology* of I.H.M. events between 1963 and 1969 began at this early date to speak of the cardinal, the real drama was the contest between I.H.M. and the Holy See. This was under way by January 1966, when the first sisters were permitted to work outside the community for pay, in a county hospital in secular dress, about the time they were appealing to Ildebrando Cardinal Antoniutti in Rome for greater latitude in experimentation. The objective was to gain self-government through the community chapter, rather than by directions from Rome. However, a request like the one made in January 1967 to change "the vow formula," with its radical implications for religious life, was rejected by Rome. The tug of war continued until July 1967, when the Ninth General Chapter of the I.H.M.s in Los Angeles convened to revise community decrees.

By "Chapter Day" (October 14, 1967), the new directions—with absolute stress on free choice in dress, prayer, conduct, and of apostolates, with rejection of hierarchy's right to approve apostolates—were ready for promulgation. The entire community, called to assembly in full habit for the last time, heard selections of these decrees, which equivalently abolished the constitutions approved by Rome in 1960. The Chapter effectively pointed to the I.H.M.s becoming a noncanonical community.

The insistence of the Chapter was "on the latitude to serve, to work, to decide according to their lights," "to abandon dying forms in order to pursue living reality," "to weigh the value of any change and to be ready to choose it without regard to the cost" (*Catholic Mind*, January 1968).

The decrees were brought to Cardinal McIntyre on October 16 by Mother Humiliata (Anita Caspary), president of the Ninth General Chapter. Cardinal McIntyre expressed himself as unwilling to have teachers in his schools who represented "a supposed religious community." The new education decrees of the community offended him, but perhaps more the mode of religious life described in the decrees. The I.H.M. leadership stayed with its position.

At this point, as frequently happens in confrontations, judgments were about to be made from which there would be no return. Although the I.H.M. leadership deplored limitations on the community's freedom, it began to consider some compromise over the parochial schools.

They thought McIntyre would back down. In turn, McIntyre approached confrontation day with confidence that the bishops of the western United States would stand together in demanding that the sisters abide by the decisions of the Holy See. Neither the cardinal nor the I.H.M. leadership calculated their support correctly. The cardinal, deciding that the community decrees were an unacceptable ultimatum, rejected them. When the I.H.M.s stood fast against any compromise with Rome, McIntyre found himself alone. The seven neighboring bishops permitted the I.H.M.s to remain in parochial schools without habit or community life. The I.H.M.s also miscalculated their support among rank-and-file Catholics. Although they made good use of the media—presenting their case as steps toward smaller classes in Catholic schools, relief for overworked principals, upgrading of sister education, and support for "the new mode of religious life," which they told the media "was authorized by Pope Paul," there was opposition from many priests and parents.

The cardinal became the object of an "I hate McIntyre campaign," but he was not without resourceful support of his own. Important lay members of the Board of Trustees of Immaculate Heart College resigned, giving detailed reasons for not continuing their association with a secularized community of ex-sisters. Major superiors from other communities—in self-defense against the possibility of similar secularization within their own households—began to offer nuns to McIntyre's schools should the I.H.M.s withdraw. (Not a single school staffed by I.H.M.s was closed by their withdrawal.) More significantly, the I.H.M. community, by defying the Holy See, lost its "privileged sanctuary." Criticism of the public and private conduct of I.H.M. nuns, hitherto reserved for chancery office files or in the living rooms of still-respectful laity, began to spill out into the public forum. Sr. Anita Caspary was also confronted by members of her own community.

When Cardinal McIntyre insisted (December 19, 1967) on the pertinence of "ecclesiastical jurisdiction" to religious life and the policies of a Catholic community of sisters, the die was cast. The day after Christmas, Sr. Anita Caspary told her nuns that they were bound exclusively by community decrees, which were irreversible. Any I.H.M. nun who wished to stay in Cardinal McIntyre's schools would have to leave the community. Just as immediate was the appeal made by sisters who knew the limitations of a superior general's authority. The apostolic visitor advised Sr. Anita to retract her ultimatum to the community.

Anita Caspary, operating under her original name, took her case to the parents of the children, defending I.H.M. conduct as "obedience" to Pope Paul. She did not succeed in getting endorsement from the

Conference of Major Superiors of Women, which (March 15, 1968) told I.H.M. defenders: "Means of achieving our ends may differ from one community to another, but we all know that religious life cannot be divorced from the authority of the Church." A year later, new CMSW leadership did not alter the situation. I.H.M. failed to gain necessary supporting votes again. The defeated caucus decided to take its case for support of I.H.M. through the CMSW mailing list, which was now in the hands of central-office staff.

The next stage in the drama came (April 1968) when a study commission of bishops was established to review the controversy and make recommendations. I.H.M. leadership, conscious of how decisions affecting their community would affect the direction of religious throughout the world, looked upon themselves as representatives of the Spirit in the Church. After a May 7 Chapter meeting, Sr. Anita Caspary requested the division of the community into two groups and that the sisters under her charge be allowed to continue their experimentation. On June 6, 1968, the "Bishops' Commission"—composed of Archbishops James Casey of Denver and Thomas Donnellan of Atlanta, Bishop Joseph Breitenbeck of Detroit, and Fr. Thomas Gallagher, O.P., of the apostolic delegation in Washington, decreed that: (1) the I.H.M.s be divided into two groups, each to act separately; (2) the majority group under Sr. Anita Caspary come to a decision about "canonical status"; (3) the minority group (54 nuns out of 400 under Sr. Eileen MacDonald) make its own arrangements to teach in the archdiocese of Los Angeles; (4) a postponement be made of a decision on the division of community property, which was to remain under the jurisdiction of the majority group. The community property at that time included Immaculate Heart High School and College, two hospitals, and a retreat house, whose total assessed valuation was listed as $17,451,000.

During the next twelve months each group set up its own housekeeping procedures. The "minority group," having no access to community finances, experienced difficulty. They were given two thousand dollars to take care of fifty-four nuns for three months. Their right of access to the motherhouse was severely restricted. Sr. Anita Caspary struggled with the management of community holdings and with public opinion. The first divestiture came with the transfer of one hospital to a community of brothers. In the meantime, Cardinal McIntyre continued to seek compliance from I.H.M. with Rome. On April 2, 1969, he asked Sr. Anita to revise her decrees and send them to Rome for approval. That argument was effectively terminated by July 2, 1969, when 354 I.H.M.s (all that remained of the pre-Vatican II 637) voted on the new religious lifestyles. Only six sisters agreed "We should make every effort to incorporate the four points and to abide by the intent of the directives from Rome"; 233 said, "We should respectfully reaffirm the general direction established in 1967, with the willingness of being judged noncanonical." (The remainder took middle positions.) For all practical purposes the I.H.M. community as a body of Catholic religious was abolished. The "Bishops' Commission" revisited them on May 29, 1969, asking for reconsideration of the "four points." There was no accommodation. The I.H.M. majority told their members (August 20) that the Roman requests conflicted with "the highest authority of the Church, the Vatican Council," expressing, also, a desire for an "equitable financial settlement" with the minority group. On December 25, 1970, the new archbishop of Los Angeles, Timothy Manning, announced in his diocesan newspaper, *The Tidings*, what the paper called "the conclusion of the Immaculate Heart situation." The group under Sr. Anita Caspary, though no longer "constitute[d] a religious community of the Church," received control of the community assets, including the high school, college, a hospital, and a retreat house. From the $17,451,000 in assets, the minority group received what was called "an equitable transfer of funds" in the amount of $225,000. A few months earlier (June 30), the archbishop, with faculties from Rome, dispensed approximately 270 of the majority group from their vows. The day after the financial settlement (December 26), Anita Caspary issued a press release announcing that the new Immaculate Heart Community "now admits men as well as women, and married as well as single persons, [and] continues to staff parochial schools in six dioceses."

While the minority group continued to receive benediction from the Holy See, identity confusion persisted when many of the laicized members continued to call themselves "sister" and use "I.H.M.," as if they were still a canonical establishment. The last public notice of Anita Caspary was the picture in *The Tidings* showing her in protest against her exclusion from the priesthood by conducting an "unfinished liturgy" (that is, without using the words of consecration) for the National Association of Women Religious.

Hardly anyone on either side of this controversy has taken any satisfaction in the outcome—the total disintegration of a once-vibrant religious community—but the issues in dispute need to be recapitulated. They seem to be the following:

1. The Second Vatican Council's decree (1965) on religious life entitled *Perfectae Caritatis* (No. 4) and Pope Paul's implementing *motu proprio* entitled *Ecclesiae Sanctae* (1966) gave both

the Holy See and local ordinaries a positive role in experiments by religious communities.

I.H.M. claimed a mandate for "wide-ranging experimentation" without regard to ecclesiastical supervision or approval.

2. Catholic teaching and policy place the apostolates of religious communities under the judgment of bishops and/or the Holy See.

I.H.M. insisted that they could no longer accept uncritically the judgment of ecclesiastical superiors.

3. *Lumen Gentium,* the Vatican Council's constitution on the Church, requires (No. 44) that each religious community be faithful to its approved works.

I.H.M. demanded the right to do what it called relevant works of the day on the basis of Vatican statements about apostolates proper for Catholic laity.

4. Vatican directives sought to reanimate religious communities according to the original charism of their founder.

I.H.M. claimed this to be unnecessary if contemporary discernment dictated otherwise.

5. The Holy See has always defined the necessary limits to the patterns of living by religious.

I.H.M. departed radically from approved lifestyles.

6. The Holy See required *some* religious habit.

I.H.M. approved any kind of dress.

7. Religious life traditionally came to mean community living.

I.H.M. left prayer and community styles up to individuals, even if these new activities precluded both.

8. Religious life always involved the right of a superior to make final decisions, a state not unknown in secular affairs.

I.H.M. placed decision-making power with the individual without regard to its effect on religion.

There were other disagreements—about the formation of novices, the use of money, and the alienation of property—but these eight areas of division delineate the distance between I.H.M. and Rome. While Sr. Anita Caspary insisted that I.H.M. stood for Vatican II renewal, Archbishop Luigi Raimondi, apostolic delegate to the United States (as of April 9, 1968), told Mother M. Omer, president of CMSC, that the complaints of I.H.M. are "really groundless." The Holy See, he said, has "no objections" to many innovations but on basic points of religious life—the four points—there would be no compromise.

Throughout the confrontations within the Church since 1965—on social involvement, contraception, the ordination of women, etc.—one consistent misjudgment keeps recurring—namely the point at which the Holy See draws a line against change in tradition. How did the I.H.M.s come to misread the Holy See? Their appeal to the Vatican Council over the Pope reflected the thinking of dissident male theologians more than female political power. How did the I.H.M.s from 1966 onward reach a point of major disagreement? If there is a single reason, it may be that they listened to men theologians and social commentators who themselves were unclear about the essential requirements of Vatican II. Few communities of women associate their breakup or breakdown with men of the Church, but from the midpoint of Vatican II onward male Catholic authors dominated the reorientation of religious women's thinking. In the I.H.M. case the men most frequently mentioned in their documents were prominent dissenters on the Catholic scene, vigorously used by leading religious women as their private counselors. In this role the male authors repeatedly pointed the finger at Church authority for being reactionary and oppressive of women. The "strike" of Charles Curran in 1967 against Catholic bishops was also decisive in molding the response of religious women seeking liberation.

Once the Ninth General Chapter of the I.H.M.s convened in July 1967, the male influence became clear. Two meetings of I.H.M. leadership (July 13 and 22, 1967) provided ample evidence of the prevalent attitude of I.H.M. leaders at the time they were negotiating with Vatican officials and their local ordinary. They repeatedly asserted *in camera* their desire to be obedient to Paul VI, even as they were arguing that it was not possible to preserve their individual dignity under the Pope's regulations. They seriously questioned whether it was possible to stay within the Church structures at all. It was clear that by now many I.H.M.s considered that more genuine community life could be realized outside of canon law. And so they proceeded to explore the concept of a lay community removed from Church strictures with few, if any, regulations. Even the idea of making vow commitments to bishops was considered impossible, and *a fortiori* the other impossible Roman demands. Since in their view Vatican II reordered the Church away from hierarchy and made the Church "ourselves," there was no longer any need to look toward hierarchy for legitimacy. No bishop is needed to give religious women approval. Modern women, including nuns, had advanced far enough in status to realize that cardinals in Italy are not the last word on religious life.

As the Chapter meetings progressed, it became clear that I.H.M.

leadership, looking upon traditional religious life as a dying structure in need of early burial, moved to terminate their structured relationship with the Church. One delegate did not even think that a Church connection was necessary for communicating the Gospel. The assembly expected ultimate rejection of their ideas by bishops and pastors, the loss of their convents, and the need for money-making jobs, but considered themselves courageous pioneers charting new courses for Catholicism. As for vows, kneeling down in a group to recite a formula really was a mistreatment of human dignity. A vow documented by a piece of paper was meaningless. A vow only had the meaning given to it by the heart. One major superior openly declared that she did not really care about the official Church. American religious were not the peasant girls of Rome. They were educated professional women, and Rome had to be taught to accept them as such, even if it took a break with Rome to gain that recognition.

The majority identified themselves with the People of God, where the real Church actually resides. The majority had been told that by the "best voices in the Church" (their men consultors) and felt the time had come for nuns to pass this word on to others. The propriety of this conduct was justified by the prior conviction that within fifty years bishops would come to recognize how right the I.H.M.s were in 1967. But that day of enlightenment would not come until the dying, dehumanizing structures that frustrated personal growth were eliminated. The other side of that confrontation would involve educating bishops to realize how they had misunderstood and misused the role assigned bishops by Christ. Leaving the present bishops' Church behind was only a step toward entering the Church more fully, and this only by seizing now the opportunity to become fully developed human persons.

During the post-Vatican II period the efforts of certain religious communities to liberate themselves from the overarching male domination of the Church received the headlines. The more significant development—one whose dysfunctions appeared only in stages—was the transposition of disrespect for authority from nuns to children. While hierarchy argued about habits and convent life, the Catholic children were infected with an anticlerical virus alien to the American Catholic tradition. Parents, the first to notice the changes in the lives of Catholic schoolchildren, were discredited. They may have observed, better than the hierarchy, that the critical issue was not religious lifestyle, nor a new catechetical methodology, but the attitude of professed religious toward the Church's authority.

## IV. The School Sisters of St. Francis in Milwaukee

The "Milwaukee Case" may describe what happened to religious women since 1965 better than the "I.H.M. Affair." If the I.H.M.s were a relatively small community confined to the West Coast, the School Sisters of St. Francis with the motherhouse in Milwaukee was a well-established German community of international proportions. Their American foundation alone had more than three thousand sisters blanketing the parochial-school systems of Wisconsin, Illinois, Nebraska, and Omaha, and represented in regions as far away as New York, Mississippi, and Costa Rica. This was an industrious and educated community of nuns. One of their New York parishes, for example, between 1944 and 1954 had eighteen of the thirty-six nuns with master's degrees. No young School Sister came to her classroom without a bachelor's degree. When a New York educator in 1956 told a Chicago educator, "Those School Sisters are the best nuns in New York," he received the reply, "Don't kid yourself. They're the best in Chicago, too."

The "enviable reputation" of the Milwaukee Franciscans was richly deserved. Testimonials to their long and productive service to American Catholicism were received from the lowest and the highest officers of the Church, even from Rome. This was no aging, hard-nosed, unsmiling group (the customary stereotype of nuns unkindly passed around by critics of little experience with them). This was a young and vibrant religious community. The School Sisters were loved everywhere by everyone.

No picture of the School Sisters can be painted so favorable that the shadows in their religious life can be neglected. If a family of three has problems, a family of three thousand had more than a few. Some nuns did not belong in religious life—scrupulous, overstrict, catty, or worldly. The screening process in Milwaukee, however, was sufficiently competent that the difficult cases could be endured in a convent luxuriating in nuns. In metropolitan centers at least, Franciscan convents were filled with active nuns. A German community, to be sure, possessed the virtues and vices attributable to refugees from the *Kulturkampf*. German pastors in the Midwest were dominating figures in parishes. A German-founded order of nuns was also pleasing to Irish pastors, whose experience with nuns of other traditions sometimes inclined to keep priests out of the parish school completely. Milwaukee nuns, including principals and superiors, could be counted on to be occasionally authoritarian, sticklers for the letter of the law, reporting to Milwaukee all suspected deviance, and parsimonious in the use of community money. But School Sisters were so lush in religious vocations that the major superior enjoyed ample flexibility in moving her subjects into more congenial surroundings. These difficulties never spilled over into the parish community.

The mother general of the School Sisters was an important figure in administration.

Until 1960 the matriarch of this community was Mother M. Corona, who saw that most nuns came home to Milwaukee at least once a year for retreat and a chat with "Mother." Mother Corona was genuinely loved. She was also a one-woman show. She ran the nationwide community with one assistant, a council of three, and no provincials.

When Archbishop William Cousins became archbishop of Milwaukee in 1959, Rome permitted him (since the Franciscans were a pontifical institute) to call for a new superior (Mother Corona had served for eighteen years), for a shuffling of local superiors, for new faces in positions of authority, for representative voting for delegates to the Chapter, and for four new self-sustaining provinces. (Rockford, Omaha, Wisconsin, and Chicago followed, and a new rule was approved June 4, 1969.) Mother General Clemens accomplished these reformations before she retired from office in 1966.

However, a new spirit of experimentation moved with those planning the 1966 chapter, which elected Sr. Francis Borgia Rothluebber. By September of that year the new mother general said to her School Sisters that there was a need for "a communitywide experiment in communal living." She was also ready to abandon the Constitution of 1964, then only two years old. A letter to the community, published in *Up to Now* the same month, said that Pope Paul's implementing decree *Ecclesiae Sanctae* (issued August 6, 1966) did not apply to the School Sisters.

Sr. Francis Borgia was not mother general long when she sponsored an institute (June 25–July 8, 1966) with a $20,000 grant from a New York foundation interested in liberating women. The theme was "Woman in the Modern World." Sidney Callahan told the nuns that Catholic thought placed women in a subservient position, that now they should develop meaningful relationships with other individuals who were not religious (Milwaukee *Journal*, July 3, 1966). Gregory Baum told them: "Change or die," become free of the institution, speak out against superiors. What the Church needs, he said, is not preaching and sacraments as much as dialogue (*Catholic Herald Citizen*, July 9, 1966).

The small-group discussion technique was introduced to the community as a means of developing a new kind of leader. Thirty participants were chosen in 1966 and thirty more in 1967; they received special training in the goals and methods of translating religious women into the changemakers for modern society. A document entitled *Response in Faith* replaced the 1964 Constitution as the Policymaker for Franciscan activity. In March 1967 the Franciscans were lectured on "The Heresy of the Split-Level Convent"—that is, the superior-subject relationship. The future of the Church, nuns were told, depended on rediscovery of Martin Luther's insight that Christ speaks only through the hearts of the faithful discerning the meaning of Scripture.

The Sisters' Survey of 1967, which had such an impact on the I.H.M.s, also affected the Franciscans. Although large numbers of School Sisters were still wearing the religious habit and were opposed to community life with lay members and to antiwar protests, 78 per cent already thought that house rules should be decided by vote, not by superior; 82 per cent thought that there should be more involvement in civic affairs; 54 per cent expected a radical change in theological expressions. The Franciscans sensed the tide of events, even though personally many were opposed. In spite of what they considered inevitable change, 61 per cent anticipated a drop in vocations—two years after Vatican II and three years after a large class of postulants.

If three times as many nuns by 1966 withdrew from all American communities as applied for admission, the story of the Milwaukee Franciscans is even more symptomatic of the decade. The formation program of postulancy, novitiate, and juniorate was abolished in that year and a new unstructured affiliate program was introduced. Following the *Sisters' Survey* a national convention of the School Sisters in August invited Daniel Berrigan as keynote speaker as part of a general theme entitled, "The World in Revolution." At this convention Franciscans for the first time appeared en masse in secular garb in the presence of Sr. Francis Borgia, who wore the habit. The caucus that planned this demonstration took little account of discussions about the use of the habit still being conducted at the Chapter level. Sr. Francis Borgia told the "1968 Perpetual-vow Class" that no essential difference exists between a vow and a promise, that they did not have to pronounce vows. Indeed, they did not have to express themselves in any set form or formula. "Each sister may use words that are meaningful to her" were the concluding words of Sr. Francis Borgia's instruction. The pressure to conform to the new order was strong. Doffing the habit was the least important manifestation of the new conformity. Exercising liberty, including not rising for morning Mass, was for many a new rule. No one was empowered to prevent scandalous behavior. "Where for thirty years I felt only love in my community, now I see naked hate," rued one Franciscan principal. Nuns once so overwhelmed with people that parish priests would request parishioners to leave convents at ten o'clock at night, so that the nuns could begin their day at 5:30 A.M. decently rested, now moved into guarded apartments ten stories above ground so that oddly the barrier between them and their people could be dissolved! Leaving behind convents that people had built out of meager earnings at the request of the Franciscan motherhouse became a matter of minor moment.

Few observers of the developing Franciscan scene were surprised that the Holy See moved to correct aberrations within one of its pontifical institutes. When Sr. Francis Borgia decided to inform the community members that an apostolic visitation was in the offing, she did not share Archbishop Raimondi's letter with them. Instead, on July 5, 1969, she made her own announcement, in a letter that alleged that the visitation at this time looked like an investigation and she wanted her nuns to know in advance that there was to be no return to institutional living with its depersonalization and inhumanness. The School Sisters were also reminded that the hierarchic Church was being transformed into the People of God Church. The day of huddling together to save our souls is gone. The purpose of religious life is no longer eternal salvation but the humanization of humanity (*Celebrate*, 1971).

The apostolic visitor turned out to be a Franciscan priest named Fr. Benjamin Roebel, who introduced himself to Sr. Francis Borgia by letter in July 1969. One year later (August 17, 1970), as a result of this visitation, the Congregation for Religious wrote to the mother general, saying in part:

> [After reminding Sr. Francis Borgia that many of her innovations had no basis in Vatican II or Catholic teaching, Cardinal Antoniutti said:] There seems to be an exaggerated cult of freedom in your Institute to the point where complete permissiveness on the part of those in authority holds sway. . . .
>
> There is a tendency to nullify authority on all levels, even the local. . . .
>
> The special end of your Congregation (i.e. schools) seems to have been relegated to a subordinate place. . . .
>
> All this leads to a neglect of Community Life, of Community Prayer, of regular observance, to a disregard for the obligation of the vow(s). . . .

Most regrettable and unedifying are the division and tension reflected within your community. . . .

[Cardinal Antoniutti then concluded with the admonition that if "uncontrolled experimentation" was leading to life-styles irreconcilable with religious life, then the nuns responsible should follow their convictions outside the religious state:] It is altogether unjust to remain nominally in this state, harming it from within for those who wish to preserve it and live it.

Sr. Francis Borgia took her case to the Conference of Major Superiors of Women, which convoked a special meeting on her behalf (September 3, 1970). The St. Louis Seminar of Major Superiors, as it was called, took issue with the right of the Holy See to interfere in the life-style of American religious institutes, saying: "We deem it destructive if a religious congregation is required to ask a brother or sister to depart, or the congregation itself is asked to abandon its public ecclesial character for the reason that a particular style of life is deemed, a priori, incompatible with religious life." Sr. Francis Borgia expressed resentment to Time magazine (February 23, 1970, p. 55) for hierarchy seeing "nuns as a convenient labor source." The CMSW backed the Milwaukee mother general in her conflict with Rome. With support from other major superiors, Sr. Francis Borgia proceeded to go her way, as if Rome had not spoken.

Among the sisterhoods of the American Church she was a pioneer of "open placement." Essentially, "open placement" gives initiative for employment within or without Church structures to the individual sister. She goes where "the Spirit" and her personal decision lead her: A sister, whose degree in education or the social sciences was earned in religious life, enjoyed the full option of where she wanted to exercise her talents without reference to those who made that possible. Women who chafed under the restraints of community life might opt for a secular environment while receiving a substantial salary. The special nature of the "School Sisters" did not impede the right of the individual Franciscan to choose an apostolate that had nothing to do with schools.

When Sr. Francis Borgia finally distributed the Holy See's letter to the School Sisters (September 8, 1970), her commentary was longer than the Vatican communiqué. She warned her nuns that new directions could not be reversed. In fact, the national press reported the Milwaukee "Sisters Won't Drop Renewal" (National Catholic Reporter, February 12, 1971). Furthermore, a new Constitution was ratified in

Chapter (January 30, 1971), in complete defiance of Rome's instruction that no new statutes could be promulgated by her until "they had been seen by this Sacred Congregation." Two sections of the new document were explosive for religious life: *Associate membership* for women who had no intention of living a celibate life; *community priorities*, to be four in number: the renovation of power structures, improvement of environment, alleviation of hunger and alienation, and elimination of prejudice. The original purpose of the School Sisters of St. Francis was not mentioned.

More than a year passed before Sister Francis Borgia received an appointment in Rome to report what she had done to implement Cardinal Antoniutti's directive (August 17, 1970). Explaining her anticipation at terminating the apostolic review once and for all, Sr. Francis Borgia explained to her nuns on September 20, 1971, that to her "obedience" means listening and offering our own reflections in the decision-making process. Everyone has the responsibility of evaluating decisions. That is what obedience means.

The Roman meeting came and went. Sr. Francis Borgia returned with her account of the event. But Vatican officials, now well experienced in the use of communications, circulated widely their own account of the meeting.

The final chapter in the history of the Franciscan School Sisters' alienation from hierarchy had really been written during the November 1970 session with the Congregation for Religious. The meeting was necessary because nothing had been done by Sr. Francis Borgia to meet the stated requirements of Rome.

Three versions of what transpired between Sr. Francis Borgia and the Roman officials have emerged—one is contained in documentary data (the account given by Sr. Francis Borgia), and the official Roman account (which emerged piecemeal).

The Congregation developed a memorial document, which concentrated on eight different areas of concern about the new Franciscan way of life.

1. *Overt Secularization.* The Holy See has been deluged with letters from within and without the community concerning the neglect of fundamental supernatural values: personal union with God, communal and private prayer, understanding of the vows.

2. *Existing Community Divisions.* What once had been a united community was now divided over the place of the supernatural in Franciscan life.

3. *Lay Lifestyle*. Not only was the religious habit discarded but also there was introduced a whole gamut of expensive accouterments beyond the capacity of the average layperson to afford.

A report entitled *Financial Need of Sisters, 1972–73 School Year* established a norm of payment: "A Sister's earnings must cover most of the expenses met by her lay counterparts." And then threatened: "If salaries are not increased to meet the Sisters' financial needs more adequately, some may find it necessary to seek employment outside the Wisconsin Catholic School System."

4. *Exodus from Catholic Schools*. From the ascendancy of Sr. Francis Borgia to the superior general's chair (1966) to the beginning of the final year of her first term (1971), the data for the Omaha province show that only 16 to 26 schools were still staffed by Franciscans. In 1966 there were 48 aspirants in Omaha; in 1971 there were none.

For the Milwaukee, Chicago, and Rockford provinces, where the Franciscans were concentrated, the number of schools staffed dropped from 96 (1966) to 73 (1971); the number of religious teachers fell from 1,021 (1960) to 548 (1971).

This community, which in the Milwaukee province had 384 aspirants, postulants, and novices in 1966, stopped publishing these data by 1971.

5. *Disobedience to the Holy See*. Directives from Rome were publicly ignored.

6. *Community Disregard for Religious Obedience*. Once the primacy of the individual was assumed over against the common good, superiors as representatives of communal unity become dispensable.

The strongest single word used by the Holy See to the Milwaukee Franciscans was its description that their so-called "Fellowship-authority is *detrimental* to true authority."

7. *Temporary Membership*. The canonical concept of postulant, novice, and religious under temporary vows disappeared. Instead, "affiliation" in the form of a legal contract, which spells out how her earned monies are to be shared with the community, became the common practice for aspirants. After this initial period, "temporary commitment" took the place of what once were known as "temporary vows." The difference between the two is not small. Historically, a young nun admitted to first vows intended to make a permanent commitment to the religious Life. The time period of one, two, or three years permit-

ted Church authorities or the novice to terminate the commitment if the young sister decided or proved she was incapable of living a religious life. The new Franciscan rule permitted admission to the Franciscan ranks those with no intention of giving themselves permanently to the religious life, yet possessing all voting rights in a community whose decisions were now made by ballot. In the same house, therefore, celibate-oriented persons coexisted side by side with "marriage-oriented persons."

8. *Neglect of the Elderly.* The Congregation for Religious had been avalanched with complaints on this score up to the eve of the Roman dialogue.

Some quotations from the complaints read as follows:

"Sisters who have given fifty or more years of service are forced to live in dependence upon the crumbs that fall from the table."

"Buildings intended for the use of retired sisters are offered for sale because it is more economical to put the sisters in the cramped quarters of a nursing home."

"All habits were taken away from the sisters on this floor. To some it's a heartbreak and tears were shed."

The School Sisters at the grass-roots level never saw the memorial document that was given to Sister Francis Borgia. Instead of seeing the Roman complaints, the community was assured that the Roman meeting exonerated the Milwaukee leadership of the charges brought against it. A *Report on Meeting with Sacred Congregation* (November 29, 1971) spoke of the Roman meeting's openness and its light moments, explained that the polarization that alarmed Rome was seen as resulting from the pre-Vatican II uniformity, that the sacramental nature of authority was now understood, not as decision-making but as a spiritual relationship of the leader with the group. The impression (from reading Sr. Francis Borgia's summary) is that Rome accepted the O.S.F.s as a vital community with only normal, healthy tensions.

To soothe her sisters further, the superior general explained how, when she told Roman officials it was their visitation that caused "a breakdown of trust within the community," the Congregation assured her that their "visitation was one of inquiry and report, not at all of censorship or condemnation." In the same irenic spirit, her press release assured the country how completely Rome changed its mind about her community. The headline read "Vatican Pleased with Zeal of Franciscan Nuns" (Milwaukee *Sentinel*, December 11, 1971).

Not all Franciscan nuns were pleased. Word reached a few that Sr. Francis Borgia was given a Roman document to be shared with the community. Ten days after she issued her press release, eighteen representatives from the four Franciscan provinces visited the motherhouse asking why the sisters had not been given Rome's list of complaints. Sr. Francis Borgia's answer was that it might be used against the Congregation. Finding this explanation unsatisfactory, five of the eighteen departed for Rome on Christmas Day (1971). They were encouraged to come to Rome by Cardinal Antoniutti. Not only was their "case" heard with sympathy, but also they were accepted as representatives of religious life. Sr. Joan Tabat, Sr. Bernadette Counihan, and three others flew home (New Year's Day 1972) assured that Cardinal Antoniutti would not be upset if they contributed to the exposure of "Sr. Francis Borgia's cover-up" of the true nature of Rome's complaints. For months thereafter a state of siege existed between Sr. Francis Borgia and her critics.

According to standard norms, Sr. Francis Borgia was secularizing the School Sisters without the blessing of Rome, which once gave this community pontifical status—that is, the right to function under the protection of the Pope rather than that of the local bishop. By the end of her first term Sr. Francis Borgia's critics were the outsiders. They might engage in a tug-of-war, but she controlled the power centers of the community—provincialates, training programs, and Alverno College in Milwaukee. She did not gain all the objectives announced in community meetings, but neither was she vanquished by Rome or her critics.

The School Sisters of St. Francis are more fragile today. They have lost heavily in numbers, perhaps a net loss of at least 1,000 nuns in ten years. Sr. Francis Borgia rejects this criticism because in her judgment too many women flocked to the convents during the rule of Mothers Alexis, Corona, and Clemens. Reliable data on losses are not readily available, but the 1,195 Franciscans claimed in the 1976 Catholic Directory represent at least a one-third shrinkage since 1966, when the tabulation at the Milwaukee motherhouse was approximately 3,000.

When Sr. Francis Borgia left office in 1977, her crusade had not ended. A clue to her ultimate goal is evident in an interview reported in the Milwaukee *Journal* (March 25, 1978) on the ordination of women. Women priests merely symbolize the need to change the entire centuries-old structure of the Roman Church. Says Sr. Francis Borgia of the hierarchical organization: "Nothing can happen as long as that kind of stratification exists. The pattern is hierarchical when it should be concentric. . . . The Church needs to change to come closer to the creation Jesus had in mind." The ordination of women would help this come about.

S.S.F. (rather than O.S.F.) has begun to appear after religious

names of her community. The Order of St. Francis, the title that was
the canonical basis of the popular name School sisters of St. Francis, no
longer was relevant to the projected reality. Alverno College is a center
for the popular secular movements. Late in 1977 Alverno College was
involved in controversy with some of its own faculty. Fr. Raymond Parr,
college chaplain for twenty-four years, was prohibited from officiating
at school liturgies. The college was accused of promoting "radical and
active feminism," failure to support prolife activity, the lack of Catholic
identity, and the failure to require courses in religion. Sr. Joel Read, the
president, responded that "religion is not simply an object of study; it is
a matter of the way one lives one's life" (Milwaukee *Journal*, November 21 and December 15, 1977, and January 8, 1978).

Younger nuns still follow Sr. Francis Borgia as if the traditional
religious life does not exist. One nun, who considers herself the bridge
between the worlds of Mother Corona and Sr. Francis Borgia, is Sr.
Joan Puls, who has been a co-ordinator of the Franciscan ministry for
religious women. Joan Puls in 1952 at age nineteen came to Milwaukee
from a small border town named Louisburg. She describes her life in
religion at each state (Milwaukee *Journal*, June 21, 1972):

> Through those first years I was happy, very happy. The
> prescribed lifestyle, the rigidity was appealing and comfort-
> able.

> [After she received her Ph.D. in philosophy, however, and en-
> tered the "real world," she found herself straining against re-
> strictions more and more.]

> Fortunately the doors opened just as the conflict became most
> troublesome to me. . . . Now I'm satisfied that the only re-
> striction for any of us is our own fear. . . .

> Vows are no longer a prerequisite for entry into an order. A
> girl is able to live with other sisters immediately. . . .

> They stay with us because they really want to—unlike the girls
> who were once pressured by social stigma into staying. . . .

> Choices are open, dress, vocation, lifestyle, and because they
> are, we feel we are moving toward a greater life, not only for
> us but for all society.

The results are not promising. In any given week the Milwaukee motherhouse may record the burial of one or two Franciscans, the departure from religious life of three others, while hardly more than three apply for admission to a province in a given year. The Franciscans are maintained by the large numbers of nuns who had entered thirty and forty years ago.

One of the main concerns of Rome has been the evident decline of the faith dimension of the School Sisters.

The response of Franciscan leadership to questions of the Holy See on this matter was given in February 1972 in a paper called *Continuing Dialogue: The Sacred Congregation for Religious and the School Sisters of St. Francis: First Area of Concern—Faith Dimension.* The thoughts expressed, while modern, were not likely to be endorsed by Church authority.

> Divine life is normally through the *natural-growth* process. . . . God has not chosen to bypass human development, especially interpersonal growth . . . as his ordinary way of self-gift." The suggestions that supernatural grace is normally communicated through natural means lessens the importance of the Church, the Mass, or the sacraments as divinely instituted channels of supernatural grace. Instead, social relations with one another become the instrument of sanctification. Says dialogue: "God does not need to step outside of what he created in order to share himself with us. It is not necessary for him to create another 'way of holiness' apart from man's social nature and his God-given vocation to become a person." God, therefore, communicated himself to man within a man's human growth as a person. . . . Grace, like faith, is not added to life but discovered within life. Another word for supernatural is humanization.
>
> Vatican II began a new movement in the Church, we are told, away from faith as a bag of beliefs toward faith as personal experience encountered in the marketplace—pursuing careers in administration, law, medicine, and as social activists in the vanguard of political protest.

These concepts undercut the *structures* of religious life as they are established by a Church that has different ideas about what faith, the supernatural, and Catholic social action mean. For Sr. Francis Borgia traditional structures do not have first priority. Speaking of what the Franciscan program of renewal was doing to the community, she remarked,

> In the past when women entered a convent it was a way toward status, toward security. Today the reasons have become more personal. We are going to have fewer people aligning themselves with us.

And as if to vindicate her evaluation of the quality of younger as against the older nuns, she says that St. Francis of Assisi defends such declines:

> It's obvious Francis didn't want a big group; he was anti-establishment. He wanted people specializing. But his dynamism attracted so many people that there must have been thousands in his group when he died. That must have bothered him. In the same way our group will be smaller, but more intense [Milwaukee *Journal*, March 26, 1972].

Whether St. Francis would agree cannot, of course, be known. But there are verifiable data that indicate that future trends among the Franciscans are radically downward. When the School Sisters celebrated their hundredth anniversary in 1974, the motherhouse published statistics showing that for this anniversary year the Omaha Province had 2 novices, the Rockford Province 1, the large Wisconsin Province 1, and the large Chicago Province none. Several decades ago this community regularly had between 50 and 100 nuns fully professed each year, and at the opening of the Vatican Council reported in the 1962 Catholic Directory 158 newly professed sisters, 171 novices, 90 Postulants, and 146 aspirants. The last-known Franciscan class with 1 novice was 1909, when the future Mother Corona was about to begin her professed life.

In any case, St. Francis of Assisi was hardly an apt paradigm for a twentieth-century religious daughter, since the first Friar, whatever his shortcoming as a theologian, recognized the hierarchy's right to govern the Church's religious life. Had not Francis obeyed Pope Innocent III and his College of Cardinals in 1210, an Order of St. Francis would not have come into being. The American foundress of the School Sisters herself, Mother Alexia, cast in the same mold, told her nuns on her deathbed, "Honor the priests." She meant the hierarchic Church. These norms have been challenged by Sr. Francis Borgia in the official response to the Congregation of Religious called dialogue. In her understanding dialogue does not mean input of data to the decision-making process. Dialogue means conversation among peers intended to develop a relationship that optimally would lead to a mutually acceptable decision that each party can accept voluntarily. In pure dialogue of this kind all issues are negotiable and there is no hierarchy—that is, no given decision-maker.

When conflict appears among dialoguing parties it is presumed that communication has broken down. Dialogue can have other implications. Wherever two or three are gathered together, someone dominates —perhaps an expert at dialogue who wears down opposition until he dominates or, as frequently occurs, paralyzes decision-making by legitimate authority. Furthermore, in every institutional arrangement there are issues in dialogue that are nonnegotiable. A husband does not negotiate with a rival about his wife. The very fact that he endures dialogue on that subject dooms him to defeat.

The case of the School Sisters, like the I.H.M. affair before, exemplifies why hierarchy frequently loses from too much dialogue accompanied by too little decision-making, by decisions made too late or too little enforced. The Holy See began the process of renewing religious life long before Vatican II and then found itself with a revolution of liberated American women on its hands. Its failure to manage the revolution along reasonable lines is partially due to the fact that its own bishops intervened. Although Rome is ever aware of the danger of Pelagianism (salvation through good works), American bishops, tending toward the practical, paid little attention to the ideas being disseminated through their religious communities. Bishops openly favored renewal. In fact, the archbishop of Milwaukee was the first force in Franciscan renewal from 1959 onward. Later he and the archbishop of Chicago, where most Franciscans taught, were disinclined to believe that Sr. Francis Borgia meant what she said, or that the practical results of those ideas would produce the effects Rome predicted. The American bishops wished to be co-operative with the nuns and, when the nuns became angry with Rome, the bishops cautioned the Holy See that the School Sisters would withdraw from their schools if the Congregation for Religious took decisive action. In the early days of the controversy, Sr. Francis Borgia repeatedly claimed the backing of the archbishops of Milwaukee and of Chicago. Partly because of these tactical differences, the Congregation for Religious retreated from decisive action. A "paper war" began. Press releases and memoranda on one side were countered by official declarations and regulations on the other, each of which were appropriately filed and ignored.

In the process supporters of Catholic tradition within religious life were left to shift for themselves. Disinclined by prior training to quarrel publicly with superiors, they permitted power to shift to revolutionary leaders. As the nuns who staffed the vast network of Church-sponsored welfare and educational agencies depart the scene, replaced by the few having what Sr. Francis Borgia calls the "new awareness of woman, of multinational corporations, of organizational power, fluidity of structures and relationships," the School Sisters seem to face bleak long-range prospects.

## V. *The Sisters of Charity in New York*

On May 8, 1972, the New York *Times* carried the following story:

> A caller telephoned the New York Roman Catholic Arch-diocese chancery last week and asked where to find the members of the Sisters of Charity of New York. An official replied, "Have you looked on the floor of St. Patrick's Cathedral?"

The previous Sunday five members of the Sisters of Charity had been arrested for prostrating themselves in the central aisle of the cathedral during Mass. They were protesting United States policies in Vietnam. Religion Editor Edward B. Fiske looked upon their conduct as "indicative of the changes that have overtaken an order that for most of its 163 years has been a symbol of tradition and orthodoxy in the Church."

While Sr. Elizabeth Ann Seton did not likely contemplate this role for her nuns, especially during Mass, protest in or out of Mass had become common among "Charities" in New York under the early presidency of Sr. Margaret Dowling, who assumed office in 1971. The author of the *Times* piece, though subsequently accused of bias for his reporting (and he certainly had made no contact with the "old guard"), did report accurately what the "new nuns" stood for.

A Sister of Charity in the new dispensation is free to choose her own job, select the sisters with whom she will live, and develop her own life-style. She can choose to wear a modified habit or no habit and can work where she wills. No longer is she to be "assigned." Even the living space became a matter of option—convents or apartments. In either situation the concept of a superior is no longer valid. The justification offered to Mr. Fiske for this freedom was that it is no longer possible for one person to keep in touch with all of the needs that the order should meet. Sr. Mary Alice (who later left religious life) summed up the new position: "I can do anything that any other adult Christian can." The line between nun and laity had been erased.

Even the "evangelical virtues" were redefined. Poverty was described not as deprivation but as "a willingness to live in a nonacquisitive manner." Chastity was not so much moderation of passion as "availability to others." Obedience was not surrender of one's will to a superior but "accepting responsibility to be obedient to the Spirit." In pursuing her view of religious life, Sister Eileen Storey said: "We're a lot freer than priests. We're not tied to the hierarchy." Sr. Mary Alice even resented the "idea of bringing in a figure from outside to celebrate the Eucharist just because he is a male."

The New York Sisters of Charity were a little slower reaching this point of "renewal" than the I.H.M.s of Los Angeles, and they have not attracted the same national attention as Milwaukee's School Sisters. But west side, midtown, or east side, "renewal" came to mean the same thing—individualism, secular involvement, divorce from hierarchy, and woman's liberation.

Freedom turned out to be a one-way street, however. The nuns on the floor of the cathedral presumed the quiet blessing of the new administration, but they misread the mind of the troops in the field. Sr. Marie Lenore Fell spoke for the majority of the order in saying that they chose the wrong method to emphasize the concept of peace. They disrupted the right of people to worship in peace. Mount St. Vincent was deluged with telephone calls and telegrams from Charity nuns all over the archdiocese of New York denouncing the behavior of the prostrating sisters and demanding sanctions.

The Sisters of Charity were in many ways a unique community of religious. Other nuns worked in dioceses and for a bishop. In a real sense the "Charities" were New York. At one point the archbishop was "the cardinal of charity" because of works of Catholic charity in which these nuns pioneered—three hospital establishments named after St. Vincent de Paul, one of the best-known foundling hospitals in the world, orphan asylums, a Catholic protectory, child-caring homes, schools for the deaf and dumb—in the city, out in the country—and prior to their decline, in charge of the largest number of parochial schools in New York. Once upon a time there was hardly a Catholic of any prominence in New York who had not been subject to a Sister of Charity's influence.

The "Charities" were New York for another reason. Bishop John Hughes made them so in 1846 when he separated *his* nuns from Elizabeth Seton's Emmitsburg foundation. The New York bishop did not want them under dictation from the outside, especially from French Vincentians. Hughes also was the kind of man who wished to rely, when he could, on his own resources. From that moment on, the Sisters of Charity were an archdiocesan community, whose superior general was the archbishop of New York. Approval of major community policies rested with him. By 1927 this fact was so well taken for granted that when Cardinal Hayes was handed the name of Sister Mary Josephine Taaffe as the newly elected mother general, the archbishop asked and got a new vote, which gave him Sister Marie Dionysia, who was more acceptable. (Sisters who believe God always prevails like to point out that three succeeding mothers general died in office, so that Mother Josephine could be elected finally to the post in 1941.)

These relationships would later be ridiculed as examples of garrison Catholicism, with its stress on discipline and obedience. But the family-type kinship of the archbishop of New York and the Sisters of Charity was more natural than this stereotype suggests. Man and woman in marriage more often than not have satisfying and free dealings when the roles and decision-making power are clearly defined. The Sisters of Charity were subject to the archbishop, but they enjoyed prestige far beyond that enjoyed by many communities of men. Cardinal Hayes died in one of their institutions. Cardinal Spellman's early moves helped them turn St. Vincent's Hospital into one of the country's finest medical centers. He frequently funded their foundling hospital. Toward the end of his life he gave the comanagement of Cardinal Spellman High School over to them and became an important promoter of Mother Seton's canonization.

A three-volume work entitled *The Sisters of Charity of New York*, written in 1959 by Sister Marie De Lourdes Walsh on the occasion of their 150th year in the archdiocese, documents the alliance of community and bishop. From the day of Mother Seton's deathbed charge to her nuns: "Be children of the Church, be children of the Church," they were far from being protected children. Imaginatively, they confronted the challenges of the eight generations without becoming case histories of traditionalism or future shock. Sr. De Lourdes' conclusion was: "Through the years [St. Vincent de Paul's] spiritual ideal has been adapted to changing needs by a succession of earnest, resourceful, prayerful woman whose American heritage gave flexibility to their interpretation of the ageless councils of perfection" [I, p. 336].

Sr. De Lourdes could not foresee, however, the drop in *enrollment* in her community from 1,482 at the time of Elizabeth Seton's beatification in 1962 to 900 fifteen years later. The Sisters of Charity had suffered losses before—notably during World War II—but the declines now were directly related to the type of renewal that was initiated earlier in the decade. The forces that worked to enervate I.H.M. and the School Sisters took their toll among the Sisters of Charity. Driven by a new spirit tolerated by administration, nuns were beginning to cause problems and dissension in parishes. Under the rising tide of "open placement" it became almost impossible to stabilize religious teachers in parochial schools. In spite of community statements, the Sisters of Charity were opting into more affluent schools at the expense of some poorer parishes. Polarization took place in convents: Younger sisters protected by administration made life difficult for older nuns and forced the latter to "opt" for places in the diocese where they could find relief but were not needed. The endorsement by their motherhouse of individual choice instead of corporate commitment was proving to be expensive. During President Johnson's last term in office, the cost of living was rising everywhere, especially for a religious community with an aging population and few stipend-earning newcomers. But expensive tastes among nuns and individual lifestyles were also costly. During 1970, when a porter at the New York Foundling Hospital and father of a family was only earning $7,800 (before taxes), a single sister cost a parish $5,442, including health and hospital benefits.

By 1970 renewalists were preparing to assume command of the community. Strategically placed in large institutions like St. Vincent's Hospital (which at one time had 60 nuns on staff), the New York Foundling Hospital, Cathedral and Cardinal Spellman high schools, Mt. St. Vincent's College, and the Motherhouse, they were able by ready access of assembly to plan and supervise the future direction of the "Charities." The vast majority of sisters clustered in groups of five or six scattered throughout parochial schools in a ten-county archdiocese were relatively voiceless. The takeover of the community, however, was not accomplished without a struggle. The "dissidents"—those who were for the standard religious commitment—were not well organized. The administration, which used the term "pluralism" to explain change, called the defense of tradition "divisive." Reading the correspondence of the period immediately preceding the 1971 Assembly, one is struck by the frequency of terms used by older sisters such as "fear of reprisal" and "wounds self-inflicted by ourselves," and by charges that they were "rigid, resistant to change in a harmful way." The terminology favoring change spoke of the "search for new avenues of ministry," "a person can be only by being wholly in relationship with others." When politicking for the 1970 Assembly of the Sisters of Charity was at its height, a leader of what was now a minority voice saw the majority leadership as "an entity operating solely on its own," "committed to work on problems of human misery in a human way," and if they see "the community as a part of 'Church' at all, they see it is a part of a national Church freed of necessity of affiliation with the Universal Church in Rome." The minority lost not only the following year's election, but also a significant place in the higher councils of the Sisters of Charity of New York ever since.

The shifting direction of the New York's Sisters of Charity is evident also in their various constitutional statements both government and vows. The three significant constitutions are those of 1948 (in whose drafting all professed sisters were invited to participate, at Cardinal Spellman's request), the interim document of 1967 (resulting from Rome's directive and with large in-put from the members), and the 1970 booklet *That We May Have Life*, which is the basic document by which the Sisters are presently regulated and that, without ecclesiastical approval, introduced an entirely new form of community government.

| 1948 | 1967 | 1970 |
|---|---|---|
| *Articles 248–49* | Section IX | [There is no mention at |
| Eminent authority in the | Authority in a religious | all of either Pope or |
| congregation and over all | congregation belongs pri- | bishop. Authority is said |
| its members belongs to | marily to our Holy Father, | to reside "in the believ- |
| the Roman Pontiff to | the Vicar of Christ, and | ing community" and "in |
| whom submission is due | to his legates; within the | each member of the |
| by virtue of the vow of | diocese, to the Ordinary | Church" as the Spirit |
| obedience. The Sisters | and to those who share his | speaks to her. The section |
| shall cherish a filial devo- | authority in accordance to | on government says: "This |
| tion for our Holy Father, | the law of the Church. | we consider to be the most |
| the Vicar of Christ, shall | | basic principle of author- |
| faithfully obey his every | | ity in the Church."] |
| mandate. | | |
| The Most Reverend ordi- | | |
| naries into whose dioceses | | |
| the Congregation has been | | |
| admitted, exercise author- | | |
| ity over the Institute. | | |

The 1970 document (as amended in 1974, still without reference to hierarchy) contained definitions of both poverty and obedience that stand sharp contrast to the ones used in 1967.

| 1967 | 1970 |
|---|---|
| By our profession of *poverty* we yield the exercise of the rights which the ownership of property ordinarily affords. | Poverty of spirit is rooted in a radical openness to an ever-deepening relation-ship with a loving God. |
| We obey our superiors whom faith pre-sents as God's representatives and through whom we are guided in the service of the Church. | *Obedience* in the widest sense is "the total openness of the whole man to the meaning of all events in his life situa-tion." . . . We believe that the proper balance between externally prescribed ac-tion and individual freedom is variable and therefore cannot be legislated." |

## VI. Where Will the Divisions End?

Two definitions of religious life are currently at war with each other within the Church and not infrequently within the same community.

The *traditional view* looks upon religious life as a vocation from God to a permanent and approved apostolate of the Church.

Good works are important but not so fundamental as holiness, which comes from living a common life of poverty, chastity, and obedience.

The functions of the religious community, therefore, is to witness holiness publicly, commonly, and *in the special way determined by its founder or foundress* and currently approved by the Church.

Vows commit members to these purposes, while providing the stability necessary for the Church's proper witness. Simple leeway must always be provided for the creative reinterpretation of mission in order to meet new needs. Because this apostolate is considered so central to the Universal Church's own mission, hierarchy reserves the right to approve or disapprove the constitutions of particular congregations. In turn, congregations ordinarily accept such limitations on their autonomy.

Those who subscribe to this view of religious life see the "renewal" of Vatican II as a call to perfect the holiness of institute members, to reinvigorate the special apostolates of the community in the charism of the founder, to update communal prayer and common life, to create a climate conducive to faithful religious life, including involvement of all members in the decision-making process. Renewal, therefore, does not mean abandonment of prayer for good works, blurring of the line between religious and lay life, the end of rule, religious garb, or superiors, including the denial of the authority of bishops and Pope.

The *recent view* understands religious life to consist almost exclusively in a celibate association living and doing something for the Kingdom of God. Since poverty and obedience to God will be required of all Christians, celibacy becomes the only requirement for contemporary religious life, somewhat in the manner of the early Church's virgins, widows, and deaconesses. Apostolates, therefore, are determined by the people themselves, and they will vary in style and content. Religious so defined need not live together in strict community nor demonstrate their witness publicly—for example, through a habit of some sort. Even the commitment can be temporary. The experience that goes with it counts most. The Spirit may lead a religious elsewhere later on in life.

"Renewal" for this latter group places heavy stress on flexibility and involvement in secular occupations. Outside persons, including bishops or Pope, may not interfere with them as they discern the Spirit in the events of a given day or culture.

As stated in these terms, the *recent view* hardly requires authorization from hierarchy at all. Any group of Catholics can assemble for the purposes outlined. Only the requirements of good conscience and prudence condition such activity for the Kingdom of God. Hierarchy under these circumstances, if they would not always approve, would hardly claim any right to intervene. Dorothy Day has founded "communities" of this kind through four decades without sensing the need of ecclesiastical approval or direction, although she always enjoyed good relationships with bishops, who sometimes were made uncomfortable by some of her causes and some of her allies. A special problem with the *recent view* arises in two circumstances: (1) when a new community of this kind alleges to be a *public witness or spokesman for the Church* or to be a society that "takes" vows. Religious vows are commitments made to God binding one to service to the Church. The bishop has the right to see and approve what people are vowing in the Church's name. (2) When a *community of this* kind "takes" autonomous control of a vast institutional network of services to the young, the sick, the aged, the deformed. This is a rich patrimony of service to which the Church is already heavily committed. Since valuable services can be threatened or destroyed by improper or inadequate administration of religious institutions and resources, bishops and Popes have an interest in the nature and practice of new definitions of religious life that jeopardize those services.

The shift of emphasis has been more radical than transition from *religious community life* to *secular institute*. Members of a secular institute also act under Church authority because they commit themselves by vow to the work that the Church has *approved for them*. Brother Gabriel Moran, on the other hand, places both religious order *and* secular institute outside ecclesiastical control. Rejecting the charge that he might be fusing the two, he writes:

> I am not changing the one into the other, I am erasing the line between them. A distinction between people who live in community and those who do not is no longer meaningful. Everyone needs to live in a community, but no one should live in *one* community. . . . The distinction between religious and secular institutes [is] obsolete. The real distinction will pertain to the forms of community that a person prefers [*The New Community*, p. 132].

Moran would also permit various relationships, such as celibates and potential marrieds to coexist within the same community (p. 128).

The recent view of religious life goes to the heart of what is at issue between conflicting forces: evangelical counsels and regular ritual prayer are relativized, community life is outmoded, interpersonal relationships are given highest priority; a corporate apostolate is rejected, and shared decision-making transcends authoritative decrees at every given moment of the enterprise.

The two points of view in conflict are irreconcilable. The Conference of Major Superiors of Men, for example, has come to discover that social-action efforts by religious have been found wanting, to recognize the meaning of the recent flowering of male contemplative communities, to see that communities based on compatibility rather than on specific religious values have been short-lived, to realize that the exercise of authority by superiors is a necessary component of leadership (*Origins*, September 5, 1974).

Women religious, on the other hand, are still being encouraged to continue their independent prophetic role. The *National Catholic Reporter*, for example, has decided that the future of its Church belongs to the nuns:

> Sisters across the land are generally more progressive than priests, bishops, or members of the laity. They are as a group better educated and better organized than other segments of the Church. Furthermore, on the whole their own organizations, their particular religious communities, are more responsive to the needs of its members than is the diocesan or hierarchical structure of the Church, which is more sensitive to the Vatican [than] to its own members. [January 18, 1974].

Many major superiors continue to think so too. Recognizing limitations on their power to effect change, they continue to avoid direct confrontation with authority, while keeping their policy statements sufficiently ambiguous so as to elude premature censure. In the meantime, however, they have eliminated from constitutions (sometimes from entire constitutions) phrases that restrain their use of community resources. Expressions like "only experimental" or "available options" enlarge their power to re-order community structures in whatever direction they and their councils decide. The machinery of educating and re-educating is used to effect. Meetings, workshops, seminars, letters, and releases reinforce the new directions, insinuating, when they do not aver, that the end result of renewal is inevitable.

However, this process type of renewal has its dysfunctional side.

1. Disrespect for authority continues to grow among religious.
2. The decline of respect for religious life itself.

Although the number of vocations is increasing rapidly in Africa and Asia and especially in most Catholic Iron Curtain countries, religious vocations among women in the United States are almost at point zero, except among communities that observe traditional standards. (See a report of Sr. Bernadette Counihan, O.S.F., in *HPR*, February 1978.) Secularized nuns once told they were the best hope for true Church renewal have, in many instances (after reorganizing communities), left their communities. Others have come to see their limitations as social reformers. Requests among young postulants and novices for a structured life are increasing. Younger nuns find little inspiration in a ongoing contest with local bishops or the Holy See, and in discovering belatedly that Vatican documents have been suppressed or reinterpreted in such a way as to obscure the meaning of religious life. Traditional-minded sisters are scandalized, too, when they find vicars for religious, sometimes bishops, showing favor to secularized nuns within a diocese while keeping garbed communities at arm's length. During early renewal days "coercion" of nuns by priests was a much-discussed matter in convents. "Coercion" now has often come to mean pressure on nuns from nuns to seek satisfaction, not in community life but in professional accomplishment, in economic emolument, or in nonreligious friendships.

Low morale and failure to attract candidates are only part of the problem of contemporary religious life. More ominous for the future well-being of the Church is the *de facto* schism existing within many communities. Communities continue to exist, but their day-to-day operation is often spiritless. Nuns with different ideologies, not necessarily old versus young, are content now to avoid open confrontation, each settling down to doing their own work, making the best of the opportunities for service to the Church and to people. However, a very serious question still remains to be answered: Is the Church's patrimony—its vast array of institutions—being used against the designs of Vatican II and the hierarchy?

In some cases this seems to be true. If it is so, what can be done to prevent this from continuing?

The easiest course is to permit the present cold war to continue within religious life. Passive response from the hierarchy certainly avoids heated controversy. But in the process bishops equivalently tell bystanders: The issues are not so important as to require further intervention. Some religious already have the impression that traditional community life is being phased out. Dedicated but older nuns are being told privately that their works are of no future account.

At the same time, many bishops believed that the drift from traditional structures has gone on for so long that precipitous action would now lead to scandalous public warfare.

Given the present polarization, some believe the prudent future course for Church authorities is to "create" new communities. Not only would this permit an appropriate division of labor, but it would also allow a sensible division of resources also. This was attempted in the I.H.M. case. The division of the I.H.M.s came too late and was inequitably made. The proper kind of division made amicably and fairly has several advantages. Experimenting nuns can be encouraged to develop their specialized apostolates without the burden of managing established institutions in which they no longer believe. Bishops, too, can begin to insist on the application of Church law to those who accept obedience as part of commitment.

In any event, some positive action by bishops seems necessary to protect the Church's committed apostolates and the religious who are needed for their functioning.

## VII. The National Assembly of Women Religious (NAWR)

NAWR was established in 1968 as a "grass roots" organization of Catholic sisters to distinguish it from organizations of religious superiors and leaders. It was intended to be "a cutting edge" for change in the Church. Unconnected with Church authority in any way, its officers exercised their freedom to espouse radical causes. Nonetheless, they are frequently invited by diocesan officials to contribute toward the formation of bishops' policies on ministry and personnel placement.

At the present moment NAWR is encountering difficulty. Its once-claimed membership of six thousand has dwindled to below half that size. In 1977 the organization did not find it easy to persuade members to volunteer for elected office.

NAWR bluntly says what many nuns believe. At the 1977 convention in New Orleans, when questions were raised whether it was straying from the Catholic mainstream, activist sisters proclaimed: "We are the Church." Sociologist Sr. Marie Augusta Neale encouraged these sentiments when she told her audience: "A mandate for the conversion of bishops is a task that some [sisters] should take as an apostolate." Many of the convention sisters agreed that their work placed them at odds with the Church, one confessing "sisters are beginning to adopt a feminist/socialist perspective." In these audiences both the nation and the Church are painted as monsters, and the primary mission of sisters is to battle against "the system." Sister Roseann Mazzeo of Newark said: "People never give you power. You have to take it" (NCR, August 26, 1977).

NAWR nuns seek to transform the Church into the most effective catalyst for radical reorganization of the world's socioeconomic structures. Says Sister Catherine Pinkerton, a founder and past president:

> I thought I was joining the convent (thirty-two years ago) for the glory of God. I had the romantic ideal of linking myself

up with Christ. But today women like that shouldn't join the Church because convents don't offer that kind of security.

[Her mission is to bring about corporate change in the Church], the multinational corporation that could make the difference in the world [New York *Times*, August 27, 1975].

Her nuns intend to challenge the hierarchy. Only last year NAWR drew the wrath of Archbishop Phillip Hannan of New Orleans for supporting a nun in Vermont who as head of the state's Human Resources office approved the use of state funds to pay for abortions for poor women. NAWR supported her (Sr. Elizabeth Candon's) "decision of conscience" and "the equal access of all women to legal rights." The archbishop called the stand "absolutely deplorable" (*NCR*, September 2, 1977).

But as nuns insist on holding political office, confrontation with hierarchy will increase. The Church—for at least several centuries and especially in the United States—has opposed clergy involvement in politics. Reform of social institutions is designated as "the apostolate of the laity." The Catholic divisions that resulted historically from the political involvement of priests plus the frequent compromise of Catholic doctrine by Royalist or revolutionary clerics made these strictures necessary for a more orderly Church. Nuns now are challenging the policy that most priests take for granted.

## VIII. *Leadership Conference of Women Religious* (LCWR)

LCWR is the official representative of American nuns in the Councils of the Church in the United States. Its role and legitimacy derive from Vatican II's declaration calling for "conferences or councils of major superiors, established by the Holy See" (*Perfectae Caritatis*, No. 23). This, therefore, is the Sisters' organization with which American bishops and Rome's Congregation for Religious deal on a day-to-day basis. From its inception as successor to the Vatican-established Congregation of Major Superiors of Women, LCWR has declared its independence of Rome and the American hierarchy.

When CMSW's provisional career was coming to an end in 1970, draft statutes of a new permanent organization of major superiors were already designed to depart from CMSW's original constitutional purposes as they were approved by Rome. The section dealing with "authority" was dropped, the reference to Rome deleted, the phrase "with due regard for the authority of the Holy See and of the bishops" eliminated. Beyond the general statement that the new conference was "established within the Church," nothing in the bylaws suggested that LCWR was an organ under the guidance of the Roman Catholic hierarchy. The entity once acknowledged in writing by major superiors as established "by the decree of the Sacred Congregation for Religious" became instead the creature of a consciously autonomous group of activist nuns. Even the Holy See's objection to the new name—Leadership Conference of Women Religious—as unsuitable for a nun's organization made no difference. The name remained.

LCWR from the beginning wasted no time laying down the law to the Vatican. Its first president, Mercy Sr. Thomas Aquinas Carroll, greeted the 1972 Vatican statement on religious habits with the accusation that the Holy See was seeking to restore a pre-Vatican II understanding of authority and obedience. In the face of the Vatican order that religious communities "may not abolish [the religious habit] altogether or leave it to the judgment of individual sisters," Sr. Carroll issued her own critical memorandum:

> If such a woman is not to be trusted with a decision as to how, when, and where she is to wear a particular form of dress, she can hardly be entrusted with the really serious matters of conscience which absorption in today's apostolate requires.

But that was not even the core of Sr. Carroll's complaint. Her anger came to surface not so much over (she said) the regulation of religious habit ("everybody can live with this letter") but because the Holy See sent the directive to her and other major superiors *through* the apostolic delegate. (Rome normally deals with bishops and archbishops through the office of the apostolic delegation in Washington.) She wanted her organization to be dealt with directly.

> The staff of the Congregation for Religious welcomes major superiors, tries honestly to listen and dialogue with them. Then documents appear which give little evidence of such openness [NCR, April 21, 1972].

Another nun, from Sister Carroll's home state of Pennsylvania, saw the matter differently: The real issue was "habit": "Who is there [she wanted to know] who believes that [LCWR] would take any interest in promulgating such a directive? As for sending the statement directly to religious communities, would anyone believe that those who ignore the authority of the Holy Father would more easily submit to their major superior?" And then Sister Mary Jeanne Steinacker concludes: "The authority which gave religious the impetus to renew during Vatican II apparently no longer has this authority" [NCR, May 26, 1972].

By the time the 1972 convention of LCWR met in Seattle, where Sr. Francis Borgia Rothleubber of the School Sisters was groomed for national presidency, the program of the sisters' organization was becoming clearer. Fifty nuns left their hotel to carry placards in a street rally for presidential candidate George McGovern. The nuns supported Sr. Elizabeth McAllister, the antiwar nun sentenced to prison in Harrisburg, and listened to a woman canon lawyer's fulminations over the Church's treatment of women. The newly elected president, Sr. Margaret Brennan, expressing gratitude for important ecclesiastical presences, said, "It is important that the Sacred Congregation for Religious understand the movements in religious communities today." The correspondent for the *National Catholic Reporter* (September 29, 1972) sensed the significance of the Seattle meeting in this way:

> Even the Apostolic Delegate, Archbishop Luigi Raimondi, and the Secretary of the Vatican Congregation for Religious, Archbishop Augustin Mayer, were there by sufferance; it was a conclave of women and religious.

Five years later a new president of LCWR, Sister Joan Doyle, B.V.M., on assuming office in Chicago, predicted that by the 1990s structures will free sisters who will no longer be "docile and dependent" but will instead become more involved in decision-making on all levels of the Church and society. Sisters, she continued, will no longer "fill slots in the Catholic Church but will be involved in a variety of emerging ministries such as drug and alcohol rehabilitation, theological professorships in Catholic and state colleges and seminaries and elective public offices."

Speaking of her past, Sr. Doyle told the LCWR assembly, "Apostolic communities of women seldom were allowed the freedom to become what they were meant to be. . . . Vatican II gave women religious the theological principles needed to effect deep and radical structural changes for renewal. . . . But of equal importance is the women's movement."

Sr. Doyle's address was complimented by the counsel given by the outgoing president, Sr. Joan Chichester, O.S.B. who caricatured the old ways as follows: "The old vision of religious life says that the purpose of religious life is to be a labor force—that religious take vows to keep laws—that religious life is a state of perfection—that the purpose of religious is to transcend the world." Then fearful that LCWR leadership may be losing following, asserting that future survival of congregations depend on her vision, she concluded: "Like the Israelites under siege, we cannot afford now to succumb to pressures, to succumb faithlessly in fear. We cannot succumb to the inwardness of our communities. We cannot become reluctant leaders. Reluctant leadership is worse than no leadership at all. Do not state something and then wring your hands in fear it will happen. Of all the religious in this country we are the ones who must go into the wilderness" (*Origins*, September 22, 1977).

Part of LCWR's ongoing mood is represented by a booklet issued from its headquarters in 1977 entitled *Choose Life*. The document was authorized by the LCWR Board in "support of the bishops' plan (*NCCB Pastoral Plan for Pro-Life Activities*) and suggesting ways in which women religious should actively promote pro-life activities within the context of a deep concern for the quality of life." Hardly days went by after its publication than Msgr. James McHugh, speaking for the same American bishops, termed the document "a missed opportunity to provide a better understanding of the abortion issue while sensitizing sisters to the unique roles they can play in helping women meet their responsibilities to their unborn children, their families, and themselves." According to McHugh, "Nowhere in the statement is there a direct affirmation of the Church's teaching that abortion is morally wrong, nor an explanation of the moral tradition for that teaching." He went further and called the LCWR's "opposition to elective abortion" a very weak position because within the context of medical practice the word "elective" is meaningless. McHugh then concluded: "Implicit throughout [*Choose Life*] is the supposition that abortion is the result of other problems, which, if solved, would do away with the problem of abortion. This is not accurate. Even if all social problems were solved, many people would defend abortion as a way to avoid inconvenience or as a private decision of a woman" (*Origins*, November 3, 1977).

Whether, therefore, LCWR is leading religious life to survival or to destruction remains to be seen. Leadership there, however, is leading where it wants to go, while the Holy See objects and the bishops watch. Recently, Rome has informed religious superiors that LCWR is *not* an official organization for American nuns.

## IX. Other Responses—The Consortium Perfectae Caritatis

A book would be required to report adequately the activities of all the organizations of women religious now functioning in the United

States. The number of these groups—official, semi-official, diocesan, regional, and ad hoc—are legion. Most of them like, the National Coalition of American Nuns, the National Sisters' Vocation Council, and the Woman's Ordination Conference, generally have been created in the mold—or have helped create the mold—of the previously mentioned major superiors' conferences. Even in the case of ad hoc groups, the tendency seems to be the same. A half dozen years ago, for example, the "Easter Group" of thirty-five influential sisters popped up in Chicago's Cenacle—later to die—but the counsel and direction they sought was familiar. Msgr. John Egan, then that archdiocese's director of urban ministry, told the thirty-five that Gospel theology "wasn't meant to have us be stopped in fulfilling our ministry by structures. The focus now should be on what we can do individually as ministers. We're asking for radical change—and to do that we need to bring about human growth within and outside the [Church] structure." [NCR, April 21, 1972].

But this was not what another group of ninety major superiors saw as the meaning of renewal. Calling themselves Consortium Perfectae Caritatis (after Vatican II's document on religious life), they rejected the ideology of LCWR and struck out on their own.

From its inception Consortium considered LCWR's primary interest in technological progress and the secular order a distortion of Vatican II. Instead Consortium listed what its charter members called the "seven essentials of religious life" contained in the Vatican II documents:

1. Pursuit of holiness through the practice of the evangelical counsels.
2. Support of the Holy See and its right to interpret the norms of religious life.
3. A permanent ecclesial commitment by vow to a corporate apostolate under the guidance of the hierarchy.
4. Response to the Roman Pontiff and his authority as exercised through the Sacred Congregation for Religious.
5. Life in a Eucharistic community under duly chosen superiors.
6. Witnessing of commitment by wearing a distinctive religious habit.
7. Daily community life within a program of communal prayer.

These "seven essentials of religious life" were the elements LCWR challenged as necessary in their entirety to religious life. Consortium, following the great founders and counselors of religious communities, including Benedict, Francis of Assisi, Ignatius, Theresa of Avila,

Frances de Chantal, Frances Cabrini, and Elizabeth Seton—sought to demonstrate that the evangelical counsels of poverty, chastity, and obedience were essential prerequisites of an enduring Catholic religious life. For these reasons Consortium looked upon many recent events in convents as betrayals of "the renewal" intended by the Council.

The polarity of LCWR and Consortium is evident in two documents—*Widening the Dialogue* and *"Widening the Dialogue"*—two different responses by each group to the *Apostolic Exhortation on the Renewal of Religious Life (Evangelica Testificatio)* issued by the Congregation for Religious (June 29, 1971). LCWR saw the Vatican letter as merely another step in "dialogue" with the Holy See, not at all a definitive word on the subject of religious life. This view is consistent with other declared opinions that all decisions are basically personal, that nothing is final, even when an explicit document is issued by the Holy See.

Consortium placed its booklet *"Widening the Dialogue"* in quotation marks because its membership did not believe that in this case dialogue was what the Holy See intended. To Consortium a serious Vatican document was not another stage in an ongoing debate about the nature of religious life. The primary object of discussion concerning conciliar and papal documents was (1) to determine how to implement its spirit or letter and (2) to seek exceptions if circumstances made clear that exceptions were necessary. Consortium took umbrage at LCWR's effort to downgrade *Evangelica Testificatio* as the work of a "Frenchman" (not of Pope Paul VI) and the LCWR attitude that was revealed in the sentence: "The day when the documents of the Church and translations of them were received in unquestioning, uncriticizing, and unresponding awe is past."

Consortium came down hard on Sr. Marie Augusta Neale's LCWR treatise on obedience, which claimed in part: "The task of religious obedience does not become the following of anyone else but God, who alone is Father. There is no Gospel basis for assuming that leaders are more his representatives on earth than are followers. . . . The authority system of work teams requires some to command and some to obey, but the choice of who does one or who does the other is functionally specific to election, competency, skill, or rotating office. It needs no supernatural claim to be accepted but simply adequate performance and credibility to the membership." Consortium sees that statement as opposed absolutely to Vatican II's *Lumen Gentium* (Nos. 43–47) and *Perfectae Caritatis* (Nos. 12–14). Consortium repeatedly accuses LCWR of distorting both Gospel and Catholic theology concerning nuns' roles in the reconstruction of social institutions. In the first place, says Consortium, this secular mission belongs primarily to the laity, not to religious. In the second place, poverty means first on identification with the poor Christ, not pursuit of social justice. In the third place, renewal really consists primarily in developing a perfect love relationship with Christ, not in pursuing sociological goods.

By these stances Consortium placed itself on a collision course with everything LCWR claimed "renewal" was to be.

The price paid by Consortium (even if its founders made no tactical errors of their own) for resisting the post-Vatican II tide among religious toward secular involvement was to be labeled "divisive, exclusive, and self-serving" by the National Association of Women Religious (NCR, January 18, 1974). Later on Consortium was dismissed as "a reactionary group of religious" (New York Times Magazine, November 28, 1976). Adherence to rule, common prayer, religious habit, and hierarchy—Consortium staples—projected a bad image among those who deprecated all four aspects of religious life.

Consortium, however, gave critics a handle to use against it. The traditional major superiors did not help their public-relations cause by choosing a Latin name for their organization. This only helped confirm in many sisters' minds that Consortium was static in a living Church that had abandoned popular use of the ancient tongue. Its programs and leadership have also been criticized by ideological friends for lackluster performance and overdefensiveness.

If Consortium expects to capture for the Holy See the attention of American nuns, it will have to resolve several internal difficulties. Individual sisters may apply for membership in Consortium only with permission of the mother general. This deprives Consortium of strength and support from supporting nuns at a time when Consortium needs all the help it can organize. Furthermore, some religious communities have interest in but keep their distance from Consortium because they fear it may be too traditional and unhelpful to their own efforts at renewal. Finally, Consortium spokeswomen spend too much time at local levels arguing about the religious habit.

A more puzzling mystery surrounds Consortium in its attempt to give leadership and status to American nuns within the ecclesiastical structure. Consortium Perfectae Caritatis did not come into being without encouragement from the Holy See, which clearly was not happy with the possibility of having more than one hundred thousand American nuns represented by LCWR. Whatever its tactical errors in projecting an image or "taking to the platform," Consortium does represent the values Rome wants kept alive among religious. On a per-capita basis Consortium communities have been more successful in attracting new postulants than LCWR. Consortium explicitly encourages a strong hierarchical relationship among nuns, bishops, and Pope. Strangely, however, official episcopal bodies keep Consortium at a distance. The bishop's approval of Consortium is private and verbal, while LCWR's acceptance (if not approval) is public and official. Consortium stands with the hierarchy without the bishops as a group being willing to help it or individual major bishops willing to support its cause. The bishops identifying with Consortium usually come from small dioceses.

Just as significant, perhaps, is the distance some "conservative" communities keep between themselves and Consortium. They may see LCWR as a contemporary disaster for nuns. Many do not wish to follow LCWR. But they find it embarrassing—at this moment—to follow Consortium. Membership in NCWR is justified as a means of reforming that organization. Membership in Consortium is often forsworn by its secret friends because the position of the bishops seems unclear.

There are some signs of a totally unexpected "religious renewal" taking place in the United States. Not only is the Consortium Perfectae Caritatis holding its own in attracting members, but its 1978 annual March meeting brought five hundred women religious to St. Louis in defense of structured religious life. A month later in the same city, the Institute on Religious Life convoked two thousand priests and religious for the same purpose. IRL, founded in 1975, is not so much an association of religious as a think tank for religious seeking to deepen theological understanding of their special commitment. The establishment of IRL was inspired by Roman authorities and is gaining an increased following, especially among nuns disaffected by the radical organizations.

On November 16, 1978, John Paul II met with the International Union of Mothers General, and he reminded religious women throughout the world (1) of their commitment to the evangelical councils (i.e. "the sacrifice of conjugal love, of material possessions, of the completely autonomous exercise of freedom"); (2) of the importance of daily prayer ("a sufficiently long period of time every day to stand before the Lord"); (3) of the sign of their consecration which is their religious habit ("a sign that our secularized world needs"); (4) trustful relations with local pastors, local churches, and the Congregation for Religious and for the Secular Institutes in Rome. The new pope said the same things, almost in the same words, in an audience eight days later with the major superiors of men's religious institutes (English *L'Osservatore Romano*, November 30, 1978).

## CHAPTER X

Embattled Priests, or the Disorder of Melchisedech

## I. A Most Respected Breed of Priests

The Catholic priesthood once was one of America's most respected institutions. Hats were doffed at the coming of the priests. Ladies rose in their presence. Doors were opened to their influence. In many a Jewish community "the monsignor" was more important than the rabbi. Esteem did not come to priests because the Roman pontifical called them "consecrated and sanctified." They earned it by hard work. Priest-historian Joseph Moody recounts a typical story of the midnineteenth century when a Maryland congressman found a single workman at the construction site of a church. He asked: "Who is the architect of this church?" "I, sir." "Who is the mason?" "I, sir." "Who is the pastor?" "I, sir." Phrases like "zealous clergy," "apostolic superiority of the American clergy," and "quality of the clergy" fill the manuscripts of olden commentators. The most peevish and unreasonable critics of the priesthood then as now were priests themselves, but to the outside world priesthood meant excellence.

Critics of priests were guarded in their language. If writers jibed at them it was within a redeeming context. A worldly-wise pastor could be called "Dollar-bill Monaghan" as long as *The Cardinal* was treated with due respect. Frank Skeffington during *The Last Hurrah* was permitted to put a Roman collar on a postal clerk but only to steal votes from Boston's Protestant wards. A stuffy bishop, Anselm Mealey, was sufferable because the Keys of the Kingdom of China were properly in Fr. Frank Chisholm's hands. And if Graham Greene exploited a "whiskey priest" for literary gain it was only fitting that the priest die a martyr to the power and the glory of his priesthood.

Respect came to American priests slowly, mostly as a result of their careful selection and improved education. By Civil War's end fifty seminaries were educating nearly a thousand future priests to care for four million Catholics. At the turn of the century a hundred seminaries educated almost five thousand candidates for ministry to twelve million Catholics. During the Second Vatican Council a thousand seminaries and scholasticates were the houses of formation for almost fifty thousand seminarians volunteering to meet the challenges offered by a Catholic population now well beyond forty million. By 1960 the great majority of priests enjoyed their priesthood, and the great majority of satisfied seminarians yearned for the strains of Cardinal O'Connell's ordination hymn: *Juravit Dominus et non poenetebit: Tu Es Sacerdos in Eternum Secundum Ordinem Melchisedech.*

## II. Whence the Decline?

Decline here means more than lowered numbers. It means saddened priests too, men with empty lives and disrespect. One best seller of 1977—already serialized in pulp newspapers and on its way to international circulation through motion pictures and television—tells the difference. Colleen McCullough's *The Thorn Birds* is the story of a priest who impregnated a young girl of his parish and used her aunt's thirteen million dollars to buy his way into a Roman bishopric. This disrespect, which may in the long run injure the priesthood more than anything else, is a disrespect due in great part to the sayings and doings of priests themselves. Pope Paul VI, who called defecting priests his "crown of thorns," once said that the priestly mission is being undermined by harsh critics in its midst (New York *Times*, November 12, 1975).

The official figures in the Catholic Directory do not tell the whole story. If one takes the summary data at face value, there has been no alarming net leakage of priests at all. No growth, but no leakage of priests comparable to that of religious women. The 58,301 priests listed for 1977 and the 58,632 reported in the 1965 Directory indicate that the statistical situation is stable. If during this period, as is commonly reported, approximately 10,000 American priests departed the ministry, the loss at worst represents a 17 per cent decline, somewhat below the 27 per cent leakage rate for nuns. There seems to be proportionately more departures from religious communities of men than from diocesan clergy, but comparisons cannot readily be made because the Catholic

Directory does not distinguish the "active" from the "inactive" religious priests, as it does from diocesan clergy.

The data on active diocesan priests, however, have distinct patterns. The South Atlantic section of the country, for example—from Wilmington to Miami—shows a 12 per cent *increase* in active priests. In all other sections, with some exceptions, the *net loss* in active diocesan priests is consistently under 10 per cent. Some dioceses, like Boston, Hartford, Worcester, and Camden, show no losses at all. A few, like Trenton, Washington, Atlanta, Miami, Columbus, Joliet, New Orleans, Denver, and San Diego, show modest increases in active diocesan priest workers between 1967 and 1976. Dioceses like Chicago, Detroit, Milwaukee, New York, Philadelphia, St. Paul, Dubuque, and San Francisco have proportionately less active priests than ten years ago, in part because of the large number of overaged pastors who were required to retire in the iterim. Coastal dioceses make up for this lack by large numbers of extern priests, usually from foreign countries. It is also clear, however, that in priest power, the Church no longer shows the native growth to which bishops and laity are accustomed.

The parish system is currently supported by the large ordination classes from 1955 back through 1935—men nearing fifty years of age and men coming to retirement at seventy. More ominous is the decimation of ordination classes following 1960, which in some dioceses has been high, and the flight of priests from parish work, where the basic work of the Church requires daily doing. It is this trend that prompted Jesuit Robert E. McNally almost immediately after Vatican II to predict that "in the course of the next century the Catholic priesthood might almost disappear" (*America*, June 25, 1966). Since that prediction the leakage has stabilized somewhat, but the ratio of priests to Catholics continues to rise alarmingly: 1 for 850 Catholics in 1975 compared to 1 for 600 in 1945. The ratio has not been so high since the turn of the century.

The declines, though worldwide, do not coincide in every instance with Vatican II. Pius XII during his lifetime began to relax (without abandoning control) procedures by which priests could leave the ministry. European priests more than Americans were the early beneficiaries of these dispensations. But forces of secularization had begun to set in before Vatican II in places where decline was least expected. Holland is the notable case in point. Data in the *Annuario Pontificio* indicate that declines in priest numbers began there in 1960 (when the Council was first announced), especially among religious orders, but in seminary enrollment as early as 1955. Ten years later, all worldwide religious communities were declining rapidly, although contemplative communities showed attrition in 1960. Loss of numbers is not always associated with attempts at renewal. The Jesuits—who experimented sooner and more thoroughly than most—had a stable seminary population from 1955 onward but gave evidence of the steep decline only while the Council was in session. During this period religious orders suffered more losses than dioceses. In the United States, for example, the number of seminary institutions conducted by bishops remained around 100 between 1960 and 1975, while religious institutions dropped in number from 440 to fewer than 300 beginning in 1960.

The telltale figure for the future Church, therefore, may be the number of seminarians and the curve of decline in priest numbers. At Council time almost 50,000 Americans were enrolled in seminaries—almost equally divided between dioceses and religious orders. By 1974 the diocesan enrollment had fallen to 11,000, the orders down to 6,500. The curve of enrollment for the country shows no sign of reaching a stable plateau, although individual seminaries report an upswing in the making. In dioceses like New York there are now more pastors than curates, and as of 1977 more priests functioning at ages 70–74 (39 priests) than at ages 25–29 (28 priests). At one time the number of priests in the young age bracket was 200.

These statistics have been seen and analyzed by bishops, scholars, and parents without a clear idea of what they mean for the long run of American Catholicism. At the moment they mean the priesthood is in trouble. But the reason for the trouble cannot be traced to a single factor. Almost ten years ago American bishops hired experts to provide them answers, but the expert opinion was controverted by those who felt that the multifootnoted volumes merely vindicated the preconceptions of the scholars.

The final data on decline remain to be evaluated. One can legitimately exclude, however, any interpretation that blames renewal. Vatican II was intended to renovate the priesthood, not lead to a denial of the nature of the priesthood or the denigration of the priestly role or status.

The strengths of the American priesthood—which were developed through the years bounded by the founding of St. Mary's Seminary in Baltimore (1805) to the beginning of America's participation in World War I—include the following:

• A clearly defined doctrinal role
• Increasingly careful selection and training of candidates
• A priestly fraternity fostered by bishops but prized by priests themselves

• Challenging Church conditions
• Authoritative leadership and precise roles
• High expectations for output and results
• General following from the faithful Catholics
• Personal esteem and status

Not everyone functioned in that system with identical expectations, performance, or satisfaction. But individual preference and effectiveness were less important than total Church accomplishments. However much individual priests fell short of realizing their own ideals or the expectations of their superiors, as a group their productivity was noticeable. Most priests ordained before World War II were adequately prepared for their role, if the ever-expanding Church body is the norm of judgment. Later, critics using more subjective norms complain about both the training and the role. Onetime seminary rector Louis Putz thought the seminary education of his period was "putrid" (NCR, February 4, 1972). Eugene Kennedy felt the mistake was in ordaining men to be "separate and better." The "De Gaulle-like mystique" imposed on priests was an "immense burden," which (according to Kennedy) denied priestly life "a private dimension" (NCR, March 23, 1973).

These different reactions to seminary training and role expectations are the results of different institutional views as well as of personal feelings. The ideological disagreement is the more important. An officer in every social system has a state of mind and lifestyle conducive to the well-being of the group. Once on the staff of a successful institution—be it the Editorial Board of the New York Times or the New York Yankees, the individual begins to think and act as a Times man or as a Yankee—or he moves elsewhere. The Catholic priesthood was no different. It was an elite group that called for special initiation and clearly defined behavior.

While the number of "characters" in the priesthood was always large ("characters" defined here as those whose feats of nonconformity to general rules were legendary and oft-recounted), all priests were bound together by the Church, by shared mutual respect, and by common agreement on faith, morals, and ideals. Men of different ages argued in the same rectory within a framework of accepted definitions. If the arguments called for answers (and most at midnight did not), priests knew where to find them—in approved theological texts or in official decrees of Pope, bishop, or pastor. Some priests more than others chafed under this "communality," but "the system" rarely was credited for their happiness or made the scapegoat for their failures.

Demurrers have been entered against this view of the pre-1960 priest-hood. Jesuit Robert McNally has written: "The past five or more years have witnessed a most thorough criticism (mostly justified and badly needed) of the sacerdotal way of life" (*America*, June 25, 1966). Daniel Callahan, touched by the plight of the priest who could not "make his own decisions about the best ways to use his prestigious sta-tus," once recommended: "Until the priest learns some of the survival skills of the layman—scrounging for jobs, a tolerance for insecurity, knowing how to do without status—authority will continue to get the better of him. There's a lot of freedom down here in the ecclesiastical gutter—nothing to lose and everything to gain" (*NCR*, December 11, 1968). Complaints from ex-priests also create an "either-or" impression or give credence to the surmise that "the best priests are those quitting" an oppressive system (*NCR*, June 11, 1971).

It should surprise few, therefore, that the priesthood, like every sys-tem, is afflicted with its own unique *dysfunctions*. These are the "weaknesses" that Vatican II was intended to correct, and they affect individual priests differently. They include:

- The routinization of sacred things
- Ascendancy of administration
- Saving the saved
- Laissez-faire in the apostolate
- Rise of special apostolates and professionalization
- The pastoral power of nuns
- Affluence and social acceptance
- Breakdown of religious and social supports

Priests of recent vintage in prosperous parishes or depressed ghetto areas faced different circumstances than their predecessors, who dealt with successive waves of Catholic immigrants in their neighborhoods through World War I. The people were poor but aspiring Catholics. Creating households of the faith were challenging experiences for priests but rewarding. The priest was an all-important figure, and his service to the flock was demonstrably appreciated. Whereas old-time priests created legends for themselves by "making the rounds," often on a parish census, later ordination classes worked out of fine churches and with grand outings, swelling parish missions, and having long confes-sional lines. Those priests no longer needed to—and often could not—"make the rounds." The rectory, the church, and the school were hubs of intense parish activity. That pattern of Catholic life had very definite consequences for ministry. Pastors became building-conscious.

Work with people was given over to curates. A large segment of pastoral work passed from the men to the women, when nuns became available. In time there were enough hands available to make it possible for some priests to be cut off from elemental aspects of parish life. At times, curates were excluded from parish schools by the pastor's wish or nuns' demand. In these circumstances industrious priests were forced to create work.

Among the welter of recent complaints about priests, few have centered on the lack of creative initiative among those priests who, far from being forced into a mold of pastoral endeavor, needed to create a mold of their own if their lives were to be meaningful. Many did not or could not. One nun, speaking to a symposium several years ago of her forty years in parish work, summed up her experience in this wise:

> The pastoral work of the Church has been carried on by a handful of extraordinary parish priests and a large number of hard-working nuns. By and large the parish priests of my lifetime, though good men, did not work hard. They enjoyed their priesthood but no one seemed able to get most of them to do a good creative week's work.

As a generalization this statement needs qualification by area or diocese and by the nature of particular situations. Finances and personality often determined the workload of priests. But if variability of circumstance is conceded, it remains a fact that by the midtwentieth century, the parish priesthood functioned through routine procedures. Many of the things a priest was called upon to do daily did not require much time. Routine is the characteristic of well-organized institutions. Scheduling, discipline, and established procedures represent good order and efficiency. Set daily Mass, set rounds of Communion calls in the morning, set prayers for wakes in the evening, regular rides to cemeteries, altar-boy rehearsals on rubrics and genuflections—these became effortless, and often unthinking, chores of the priest.

The other side of routine is monotony. During the first days of priestly ministry routine simplifies apprenticeship. However, doing the same thing can lead, after ten years, to formulas recited by rote, to magical incantations, not meaningful invocations to God. Routine also makes for leisure. This was not an important psychological factor during the immigrant Catholic era when everyone's life was filled with routine ten hours a day, six and seven days a week. If pastors did not mandate multiple chores for priests, concentrated Catholic crowds did. With the rise of eight-hour days, five-day weeks, and the dispersal of successful Catholics to suburbs, many priests in city and suburbs found themselves regularly with time on their hands for a variety of reasons. Going out of the parish for involvement was standard practice. Out-of-parish activity only moved the affected priests farther from the lives of parishioners and afforded the priests more free time. As professional study for priests became popular (encouraged first by religious orders for their special apostolates), parish priests in large numbers went back to school—some for the wrong reason. Continuing education gave the industrious priests also new interests outside their primary area of responsibility. Bishops unwittingly helped this process of alienating priests from their parish work. Priest specialists in spreading chancery bureaus, many of whom were monsignors at an early age (when parish priests comparatively were not), diminished the esteem for parish ministry further. The selectivity process in seminaries was not adjusted to the new need for self-starters in the priesthood—those with ability to make the most of every human situation. Some priests could turn the ride to the cemetery into an invitation to renewed Christian life. Others merely read the paper.

The institutional strictures were hardly oppressive for most priests, at least in large dioceses. The Church imposed some limitations on priests everywhere, both socially and psychologically. But in comparison with the paternal power exercised by pastors of the pre-World War I era, the general parish rule in later years was *laissez-faire*. As long as routine chores were maintained, freedom of initiative and freedom from supervision belonged to the individual priest. The system remained cohesive because canon law or synodal statutes required priests to sleep in rectories every night, wear a common clerical garb in public, and attend diocesanwide retreats and clergy conferences, and because of a public opinion among the laity that enforced the approved priestly lifestyle. In the post-Vatican II equation of renewal with freedom from restraint, these protective barriers were disestablished, sometimes with the help of bishops. Once they came down the priestly body began to bleed somewhat.

### III. The Continuing Morale Problem

If the priestly body in 1978 no longer bleeds profusely, there are discernible aches and pains still seeking relief. Low morale is one continuing symptom of a serious problem. When *esprit de corps* is low in an elite fraternity, the institution is in trouble. Pride of membership is the hallmark of confident groups.

Once upon a time it was easy to rally priestly troops by the hundreds for the simplest of Church reasons, like a forty-hours' devotion. At these events all kinds of priests rubbed shoulders—chancery officials and curates, spiritual directors and social actionists, the old and the young. And they enjoyed the company.

This *joie de vivre* no longer exists to the same degree. In 1977 a young priest wrote this letter to his diocesan newspaper (the diocese is large, its name unimportant) stating part of the problem:

> What I say as a priest for five years is my opinion, but it may well reflect the thoughts of other priests. I believe that one of the most pressing issues facing the diocese today is the morale of its priests. That's a hard thing to gauge, but I would venture to say that the morale of the priests right now is rather low. In speaking with priests I detect a certain pessimism, a sense of uncertainty as to the future of the diocese. What we need is a new sense of ourselves and our purpose. . . .

> We priests have been floundering as a group unable to reach a level of united purpose and vision and unable to acquire enough power to safeguard that purpose and vision.

The young priest mentions the demands and burdens imposed on him.

Older priests experience a different pressure. Although age has always had a debilitating effect on apostolic energy, compensating factors worked to keep their spirits on an even keel, perhaps a new parish with young curates, the monsignorship, or a grandfather status in the neighborhood. These bonuses have almost gone. Terms of office, the general lack of young curates, or testy curates, the end of monsignorships, factions in the parish, the flight of nuns or disagreeable nuns, and financial burdens make pastorates—the key office in the local Church—less desirable. Senior priests now tend to shy away from increased responsibility, to a parish without a school, perhaps without a curate, sometimes back to curacy, chaplaincy, or early retirement. Older priests also bemoan, as the bane of their aging years, the breakdown of discipline in rectories.

High morale will not likely nor easily return to the priesthood. Too many centrifugal forces are at work that neither Pope nor bishops can at this time easily control. The trend in dioceses or communities is to divide unity into little bands or permit special interests to pursue private objectives. A grand design that would rally priests around their bishop seems to be missing. Another aspect of contemporary Catholicism that depresses the morale of priests is the force of repeated attacks on the Church's parish structures. Initiated by intellectuals in France, where parish life has not been vigorous since the French Revolution, persistent downgrading of the parish ministry denigrates the role of priests who commit themselves to this work. No large institution has been so closely situated where the masses of people live as the Church. Parishes to this day remain the instrumentality by which the Church remains as small as a family, even though it is simultaneously national and universal.

Territorial parishes are not outmoded. Secular megalopolies wish they had so many local administrative units. They are merely not exploited the way they once were. When, for example, was there last a parish census of the faithful? Or a diocesan census? In many places not for three or four decades. The failure to Catholicize blacks or Hispanics is attributed to the territorial parish. That failure, however, is more human than institutional. Modern American priests have not been trained, organized, or supervised with a highly efficient territorial parish in mind. The territorial parishes house all kinds of people living at different social levels but worshiping on terms of equality, one of the few meeting places of its kind. Academicians like Jay Dolan tend to belittle the importance of the parish to the contemporary scene with statements like the following:

> The Church existed for many centuries without the parish being the sole center of religious life and the shift that is taking place is not as critical as it might seem. For those Catholics who cannot see beyond the twentieth century it might appear as a catastrophe, but it is no more a catastrophe than the demise of the Latin Mass.

In addition to the fact that the universal spread of Mass in the vernacular was accomplished rapidly only because Pope and bishops had parishes, there is Archbishop Lefebvre failing in his effort to keep the Church Latin, because he has no parishes. Notre Dame Professor Dolan, after relegating parishes to a decreased role and lauding the rise of new groups "with considerable freedom from episcopal control," makes a gratuitous prediction: "This does not necessarily mean that religion will be any less fervent or that Catholicism will be any weaker as a religious institution" (NCR, May 31, 1974).

A case can be made, to the contrary, that fragmented institutions are weak, that "sects," underground churches, or "communal Catholicism" offer only momentary satisfaction to elites but are not objects of universal pride because their accomplishments are modest in scope. There is no evidence that sects represent extraordinary piety. Even if they did they need priests less than the masses of faithful in a Church fragmented by sects.

More critical perhaps for clergy morale than the life or death of the territorial parish is the public attention given in recent years to priestly misconduct. Clerical behavior in the United States was so consistently good that the Roman collar was the occasion of deferential treatment. These favors were bestowed not by demand but as the result of generations of earned respect. Reverence for the priesthood was such that occasional public misconduct by an individual was glossed over as exceptional or unmentioned—often by a non-Catholic—lest suspicion be cast on the lives of exemplary priests. Being a priest under those circumstances was heady responsibility, but it also meant pride of office. Pope Paul more than once noted the anti-Catholicism that inspires efforts to topple priests from this pedestal.

The problem today is twofold—the press and priests themselves. It was not long ago that the press would file the story of a bishop arrested for drunken driving. But lately news for news' sake is the compelling moral norm for revelations regardless of the consequences, even by NC News. Magazines like Newsweek have a penchant for shocking audiences with stories about irregular priests. Several years ago Eugene Kennedy was forced to challenge the authenticity of Newsweek's story (December 3, 1973) on priests dating, a report that implied that dating was becoming the "third way" for priests, between celibacy and marriage. Unnecessary exposure of human foibles was once the mark of "yellow journalism." Responsible reporters and editors operated out of other moral norms than "news for news' sake." One other norm was "all the news that's fit to print." The sanctity of marriage, of religion, of reputation were respected values then. In a secularized culture, however, nothing is sacred, especially the sacred. Deflating or dethroning authority figures is fashionable.

Departing priests have found fortune in the media. Where once they left quietly, they now mount pulpits, leave by the middle aisle, issue press releases, and take to the airwaves. The media give their complaints a value that they may not have and perpetuate the myth that the best really leave. Investigative reporting fairly done would deflate the prominence of these stories, but investigative reporting is done usually on bishops and religious superiors, who are compelled by office to silence about subjects and former subjects. This is a source of backlash on the lives of young priests, whose roots in fraternity are still at surface level, whose supports are not yet firmly set. But even the misadventures of Richard Ginders, James Kavanaughs, James Groppis, William Dubays, and Anthony Girandolas paraded before public audiences are not the core of the morale problem. As featured in media these ex-priests upset the Catholic laity more than priests. Few priests identify with them. On the other hand, when a bishop or the provincial of a large community leaves to marry a divorcee, or a prominent pastor walks out after his silver jubilee with a blast at the Church, "surprise" and "shock" are mild descriptions for the impact (*NCR*, July 24, 1968). *Avant-gardists* who fight structured priestly life in principle are not the only offenders. Jesuits Daniel Lyons and John McLoughlin of Nixon White House prominence raised more than a few eyebrows in the wake of their going after badgering "liberals" for years. There is no case on record of public confession of personal fault, except in the example of Monica Baldwin, who lived long enough to make her *mea culpa*. When Charles Davis abandoned the priesthood in 1966, stating that the "Roman claims" of the Pope filled him with "revulsion," not only was no apology forthcoming, but also Fr. Herbert McCabe, Dominican editor of London's *New Blackfriars*, rushed into print to express his sympathy, editorializing: "The Church is quite plainly corrupt" (*Commonweal*, March 3, 1967). A Church declared corrupt by one of its prominent spokesmen is not very attractive.

Fr. Philip Berrigan and Sister Elizabeth McAlister, folk heroes to priests and nuns during the Vietnam War, went one step farther. Not only did they end up marrying each other, but also they confessed in 1973 that they were married four years before, even as each continued to live a religious life with the Josephites and Sacred Heart Sisters, respectively. Their particular apologia concluded: "We hope that our ministry will serve the Gospels" (*NCR*, June 8, 1973). The "horror stories" of departed and departing priests continue unabated. The Episcopal Church announces that Catholic priests are increasingly becoming Episcopal priests (*NCR*, March 22, 1974). A group of one hundred ex-Maryknollers establish an association called Maryknoll in Diaspora committed to the continued celebration of Mass and marriage ceremonies (New York *Times*, August 10, 1977). The Chicago Association of Priests convenes a meeting at which resigned priests are urged to continue public pressure to force their return on Church leadership (Brooklyn *Tablet*, March 14, 1976).

Young clergy may be more thin-skinned than their elders, but widespread bad example never boosts morale. One priest admitted that in thirteen years of service he found among priests "as much real goodness as I think you will ever find in this world," but also complained:

> Many priests I know are really horrible. Their zeal seems to
> have been very quickly blunted by the yawn of habit around

them, by the timidity, cowardice, and sloth of their fellow priests. I dread becoming like many older priests—potbellied with hair growing out of their ears and noses, dolloping out sacraments, continually running after worldly gewgaws [NCR, August 3, 1973].

Priests who remain sometimes do not help the clerical image. Paul Wilkes authored a book entitled *Why These Priests Stay*, which contains a bizarre view of the priesthood. His "Father Bill" was as weird as the family from which he came. Among his "confessions" to a tape recorder were the following: He did not discover his sexuality until he was thirty-two years of age, was almost thrown out of the seminary because he played baseball on a field while girls watched on the sidelines, he could not have special seminarian friends, he found himself after ordination oppressed by his pastors and the chancery office because he was popular, he rediscovered energy for the priesthood after a clandestine week with a nun in Canada, etc. The story, which sounds like it was written for a soap opera, has the hero sighing in the Third Act: "I don't think any bishop, Pope, or pastor could drive me out of the Church" (New York *Times Magazine*, October 3, 1973). Priests generally look upon the "Father Bill" type as an ecclesiastical oddity, who once in a while slips through all the screening processes set up to keep his kind out of the priesthood.

Patrick Sanford, a diocesan priest writing under a pen name, capsulated in five points the major cause of bad morale among the clergy (*America*, June 24, 1967):

1. The position of priests in the Church is not as fully developed in Vatican II documents as that of bishops and laity.

2. Christian service of man to God—at which the priests formally are expected to excel—is giving way to a contemporary eminence for man-to-man relationships, at which priests may not excel.

3. Priestly confidence is undermined by the downgrading of their special expertise, by their own inability to see results from their work, by anticlericalism, and by the scandalous behavior of departing priests.

4. Parish priests observe theologians snatching ecclesiastical leadership from bishops, even from the Pope. The growing emphasis

on personal conscience cuts the ground from under the priests' preaching authority.

5. Priests worry about the absence of uniformity in the Church's doctrine and law. A priest can now be found anywhere to bless what another priest has refused to bless. Uncertainty is the name of the clerical game, a condition not conducive to commitment or enterprise.

## IV. The Problems of the New Structures

The illusion of contemporary politics is that the answer to yesterday's problem is a new structure. The illusion of contemporary psychology is that the answer to yesterday's unhappiness is looser structure.

In response to both politics and psychology, the Church in recent years has created three new structures: Priests' Senates, personnel boards, and team ministries. These were developed from the thinking contained in the Vatican II decree on the pastoral, *Office of Bishops in the Church* (*Christus Dominus*). This document is traditional in its treatment of priesthood, including a section on the diocesan clergy that reads: "The bishop must have requisite liberty in making appointments to ministries and benefices. All rights and privileges which in any way restrict that liberty should accordingly be abrogated" (No. 28). However, the Council did propose the creation of a Priests' Senate (No. 27) with a consultative vote with the bishop in managing diocesan affairs. Neither personnel boards nor team ministries are mentioned by the Council Fathers. These two agencies became developments, not creations, of the Second Vatican Council.

The Priests' Senate was singled out by the Council—along with cathedral chapters, boards of consultors, and ad hoc committees—as a desirable collaborator with the bishop in the pastoral work of the diocese. Personnel boards and team ministries became later extensions of the concept of shared responsibility. In each case the object of the new agency is improved performance in pastoral activity. It was reasoned that better input from the priests themselves would facilitate constructive episcopal decisions and more general compliance. Neither the Council nor the Holy See saw in these structures the dilution of the bishop's authority to make decisions or obtain obedience from his priests. The personal satisfaction of individual priests, though enhanced by improved consultation, was not intended to transcend more important values. Rockeville Centre's former priests' personnel director, Fr. John E. Murray, learned from his own recent experience: "The shortage

of priests has built an inflexibility into the systems so that options are severely limited. Jobs must be filled; therefore personal hopes and wishes
cannot always be filled" [*Long Island Catholic*, October 20, 1977].

If there is a certain disillusionment throughout the country with each
of these new structures, part of the reason may be that the original
promoters, including some bishops, oversold their purposes and nature.
The impression given by some Priests' Senates is that they were intended to be coequals with bishops in managing the diocese. Some
priests, too, came to look upon personnel boards and team ministries as
instruments of their personal fulfillment over all other considerations.
When practice did not follow expectation, disenchantment was an inevitable result.

It is also important to view these new diocesan structures within the
context of what they were intended to supplement or replace. Prior to
the creation of the Priests' Senate the only consultative body in a diocese was the Board of Consultors, whose members were all appointees
of the bishop, most of them pastors of mature age. Occasionally, younger
diocesan officials were also consultors. As a general rule the items
discussed monthly were matters the bishop wanted discussed. Consultors meetings, of their nature, were usually tame affairs. Free-wheeling
exchanges between exponents of rival viewpoints occasionally took
place, with the bishop an amused or highly observant bystander. As dioceses were unfolding in the past century the range of issues reserved for
consultors included public deportment of priests and their ministry, the
appointment of vicars or the nomination of bishops, faculty for the
local seminary, appointment of permanent rectors, local politics, anti-
Catholicism, or the establishment of a Catholic college. More recently
the temporalities of older dioceses preoccupied consultors more than
pastoral concerns. Boards of Consultors at their best had several serious
limitations—the various populations of the diocese were under-
represented (for example, the young priests and priests themselves had
nothing to say about membership on the Board). From another van-
tage point, that of diocesan collaboration and harmony, priest consultors had a virtue that priest senators sometimes do not consider necessary for office-holding: The priest consultors were totally loyal to the
bishop. Even if they disagreed or were overruled by him, no consultor
would consider public confrontation with his bishop a proper form of
priestly behavior. This occurred at various times in local histories, but
by way of exception. Leaking information to the press or public statements chastising their bishop for not going beyond or not enforcing
decrees of the Holy See—both of which happened in the case of two
Priests' Senates in 1977—simply was not done.

The different and conflicting concepts of what a Priests' Senate should be may explain why the majority of priests do not actively participate in Senate affairs, and why the National Federation of Priest Councils has experienced most resistance not from bishops (who ignore it) but from priests who do not subscribe to its policies, priorities, or methods. Immediately upon the Council's close, social activists seized control of the elective process in many prominent sees to ensconce like-minded confreres in Senate seats. A tone for Priests' Senates was established thereby that turned off many of the people they were representing. Smaller diocesan Senates—Hartford is a good example—enjoyed a better image, partly because the priests knew each other, partly because ordinaries like Archbishop Henry O'Brien were beloved figures whom potential senators wanted to help, not fight. More frequently, however, the press featured senators who were fighting the war in Vietnam, for amnesty to military deserters, and against discrimination in athletic clubs. At the same time they were fighting their bishops for higher pay, over accountability in the use of diocesan monies, and over due process other grievances.

So much coverage was given to this side of Priests' Senate activity that a new voice of the American priesthood seemed to be clamoring for attention. Though most priests were speechless on the Catholic issues that fascinated reporters, John Deedy, managing editor of *Commonweal*, was sufficiently impressed to announce that the laity—not the priests—were the real "barriers to liberal trends" in the Church. Said Deedy:

> In parish after parish, many observers of the Catholic scene contend, one can find almost the precise reverse of ten or more years ago, when the clergy was predominantly conservative and the laity mixed—but including a strong liberal element. Today there is not a radicalized clergy, to be sure, but a clergy which shows new signs of being committed and involved; and a laity whose ideological cast seems to become more and more conservative . . . which through parish councils and the pocketbook has a leverage that the American laity has not known [New York *Times*, March 19, 1972].

A good summary of experience with Priests' Senates was made two years ago by Archbishop Jean Jadot, apostolic delegate to the United States:

> The record of Priests' Senates in their first ten years has been a mixed one. While most began their work with a sense of

hope and a vision of renewal, they all encountered and still encounter factors which are disturbing and often disrupting—individuals endeavored to manipulate Senates for selfish designs and purposes—excessive confrontation, pressure, misunderstanding and disagreement were too often prevalent [*Origins,* April 1, 1976].

Jadot expressed pleasure at what he considered mature development in priest-bishop collaboration on issues of pastoral concern. Jadot was right. Things are quieter now. As Senates reflect better the wishes and needs of the priest majority, a different kind of Senate leadership is coming to the fore. Even the National Federation of Priest Councils—threatened by loss of dues and secession by diocesan bodies—is responding to local opinion. The problems of ministry at the level where most priests are—evangelization, catechesis, reconciliation, spirituality—are being given high priority.

A different problem has begun to arise lately in the councils of priests. This one was not foreseen. What happens when the Priests' Senate begins to enquire of the bishop: "Why are not the decrees of the Holy See being enforced in this diocese?" "Why is there teaching in our seminary contrary to the documents of the Council and the declarations of the Pope and Roman Congregations?" Ten years ago bishops often ignored or rejected the demands of Priests' Senates for action that transcended the limits of Church law or doctrine. Today some senators believe that some bishops have acted outside and against the law. Archbishop William Borders only last year was forced to respond in his arch-diocesan newspaper to senators' complaints about the low quality of priests' morale in Baltimore. Borders himself articulated what he understood the charge against him to be: "[His] tendency to cover over real differences in theology by calling each of them instances of plurality when they may be a collection of contradictories" (*The Catholic Review,* October 21, 1977). Throughout the Church different doctrines—not different theologies—are often dispensed in high diocesan places, and possibly provide a surprisingly new area of conflict between some priests and their bishop.

If this kind of conflict develops the issues will be doctrinal, not structural. Shared responsibility in the Vatican II Church comes to an end with a bishop's decision. Consultation is ongoing and provides new input into a bishop's decision. Consultation does not mean the power to decide. Whether a bishop enforces or does not enforce Vatican decrees, whether priests have senators with good or bad judgment, whether the input is adequate or inadequate, a diocese can have only one lawmaker. If the bishop is not doing his work, Rome has the power to remove him. Rome assumes blame for failure at that level. If the Priests' Senate is obstructing pastoral work, the bishop has the power to disband it, as readily as he can disband the Board of Consultors. But the work of any institution comes to a halt if there is warfare between bishop and senate or if the unending process of consultation inhibits decisions.

The "Chicago Case" is, as one might expect, a clearer example of the first tragedy. Cody closes four schools, his Senate does not like the decision, and they fight in public. Cody says the Senate is a consultative body without authority to force a decision on him or to sit in judgment on his administrative decision. In the cardinal's view consultation and decision-making are "two separate processes." The Senate puts together a six-page statement of its own challenging the cardinal's "understanding of the process of consultation" (Origins, August 14, 1975). The press is entertained but not the Catholic priests and people of Chicago.

The plague of unending consultation was aptly described by Bishop Francis Shea of Evansville when he suspended his Pastoral Council. It just was not working, Shea claimed. Not only were the "authentic voices of the people of God" not being heard because input came only from "a faithful few," but also due process became the instrument of flooding his diocese with "oceans of undue process" for the majority (Origins, September 30, 1976).

A somewhat different problem faces the bishop once he establishes the Priests' Personnel Board. Whereas no bishop permits the Priests' Senate to run his diocese, there is evidence that many bishops turn over to the Personnel Board total responsibility for assigning priests. This is a more or less situation, to be sure, and a bishop's ruling style may make it unclear who actually makes appointments. In many cases, however, the bishop's appointed personnel director and the Board elected by the priests sometimes convey the impression that all appointments of the clergy rest with them. Occasionally, the bishop himself, who knows where the decision-making power really lies, will threaten an unco-operative priest with the Personnel Board.

Granted the variety of practice, there is one common principle that underlies the creation of both Senate and Personnel Board agencies: Each body is to be a source of input for the bishop, but the decision-making power remains with him. This is a very important principle in priest assignments because on ordination day the new priest places his recently anointed hands into the hands of the bishop. There is promise of lifelong "reverence and obedience" to the bishop—not to a Personnel Board. The documents of Vatican II in the decree on bishops enjoin bishops (No. 16) to make priests "objects of particular affection" and to regard them "as sons and friends."

The Personnel Board came into being as a reaction to what many considered the cold-blooded manner of dealing with priests in the pre-Vatican II Church. In former days, some ordinaries were close to priests, others were not. Some had a buddy system and took care of their own; a few acted as if they were placing square pegs in round holes. Assistant priests complained that in the eyes of the bishop pastors could do no wrong. Later, as permissiveness began to pervade the ranks of the clergy, pastors began to grumble about the amount of nonsense the chancery office tolerated from the "new breed" who in their eyes obtained reassignment almost for the asking. In larger dioceses, where the relationships between priests and ordinary were more distant, either a vicar general or a chancellor was the *de facto* manager of priestly assignments, and the locus among priests of complaint and expressed preference. The filing cabinet for both was the mind of the chancery official, who was good or bad depending on how long he held office and how well he "commanded" priests. How bad was the pre-Vatican II assignment of priests? Better than some say and never as good as its defenders. The "boardless" system meant frequent personal contact with a man of actual and patent decision-making power in the diocese. Everyone knew who made or denied appointments and where the buck stopped. On the other side, the "one-man show" meant a limited range of input. Decisions were sometimes made without all the "facts" or on the basis of judgment by a limited number of people. Since busy chancellors or vicars general could ill afford the luxury of unending consultation, their discussions were held within the framework of close associates. In these circumstances many priests did not get what they wanted and were forced to accept what they did not like or what made them unhappy. In other cases good fortune and happy lives fell on those who did what they were told rather than have their own way, which sometimes would have led them to disaster.

Several aspects of the priestly personnel problem do not change regardless of structures. Large dioceses or religious orders with plentiful priests have great flexibility in pleasing constituents while seeing that the appropriate works of the Church are done. Smaller dioceses and smaller communities—through no fault of their own—do not have this luxury. An alcoholic, distempered, misfit, antisocial, or nonproductive priest in confined situations cannot readily be placed so that the harm he inflicts is minimal. Sometimes it is the bishop who does not get his way. In particular cases he may have to respect the wishes of a priest, even at the price of not putting a talented man in the spot that calls for special ability. When in 1940, for example, the new archbishop of New

York, Francis J. Spellman, was opening new high schools, he could only persuade a few young priests to leave parish work for teaching. His alternative was to turn to the newly ordained, who lacked some of the experience Spellman considered important to high-school teachers. However, Cardinal Spellman had one advantage that post-Vatican II bishops seem not to have: the authority and power to assign priests where he thought they were needed, and the understanding on everyone's part that if he insisted, they went. Like all bishops then he was not a helpless persuader. In an emergency he could rely on the respect priests paid his office, even when he made no demands. Once a pastor responded to Spellman's offer of a larger parish with the quip: "I'm happy here. I don't want to go." Spellman's reply was equally direct: "I was happy in Boston, too." That ended the discussion.

Partly because this method of dealing with priests has been called paternalism, Personnel Boards came into existence. Formalizing input, collecting data on priests from a wide range of sources, negotiating transfers through dialogue are now standard procedures. Is the new system better than the old? Is priestly morale better? Are the faithful served or apostolic works done better? Answers concerning any large system—new or old—vary. The advantage of a Personnel Board is everyone's right to a day in court and a hearing. And—because the personnel director usually is not the chancellor or vicar general—the priest need not fear disapproval or reprisal. To the extent, therefore, that the personal grievances or desires are now creditably heard, priests have little about which to complain.

But as one listens to priests in various parts of the country discuss the new situation, certain dissatisfactions are beginning to surface that have implications for institutional health.

1. *The appointment system has become a shadowy operation.*

Priests—especially pastors—as the upper echelon in Church management expect to deal directly with the "top" man. Unless the personnel director is a bishop, this is not likely to happen. Their requests instead go into "the hopper," with no certainty as to how they will come out. If they are pleased with the result they do not know who to credit. More importantly, if things go bad, they do not know how to seek adequate redress—certainly not by going back to "the hopper." The frustrating aspects of this kind of situation were demonstrated for the nation in the Nixon White House where the "top man" was isolated from the most important officials of his own government. When the appropriate moment came these officials, kept at bay by a palace guard, vented full fury on him.

Administratively, it may prove unsatisfactory to place a bureau between a bishop and his priests. A bishop or vicar general can meet priests' needs better than a personnel director who cannot speak in his own name or make firm promises. Priests have left the office of the bishop disappointed but with the satisfaction of knowing that nothing more could be done for the moment. In dealing with a "Board" there is no sense of equal directness. If the status of the priest is higher than that of Board members, the psychological difficulties are compounded.

In the normal course of events, the bishop does not wish to have a Board between him and his priests. He can hide behind a Board if he chooses, at the price of gaining disrespect. But the bishop's power to appoint priests is his most precious asset. Since the conduct of ordinary diocesan affairs depends on priests, the bishop recognizes the importance of using priests well. Appointment power is patronage. By rewarding the faithful, hard-working priests with compatible assignments, the bishop binds priests to him by friendship and respect. The appointment power is also a vital experimental tool. The bishop can use it to try daring things and to test the caliber of young men. It is an instrument too of order and discipline. Manifest displeasure by the bishop for misconduct or bad performance is necessary to good management. The diocese in which anything goes does not function well when the appointment power is exercised too far beneath the bishop; there are new problems for priests, who will accept from a bishop with grace what they deny to lesser figures.

The way in which priests are allocated reveals the goals and priorities of a bishop. The reason why Vatican II insisted he have "requisite liberty in making appointments to ministries and benefices" was the need of the Catholic community's shepherd to have such flexibility. If the appointment process gets away from or overwhelms him, the bishop is no longer the leader of his priests. Decisions are usually compromise judgments by every executive. But decisions made by a committee of part-time officers with incomplete information and limited responsibility involve more than compromise. They often mean indecision, delay, uncertainty, and a preoccupation with satisfying the appointee, rather than getting a job done. Furthermore, when the decision-making process from request to assignment appears to be endless, some priests lose confidence in the ability of a Board to satisfy their need or handle their grievance. The new expectations place greater burdens on personnel officers.

All of these difficulties are surmountable, however, if the input role of a Personnel Board, a necessary and valuable improvement, is not fused or allowed to seem fused with the appointment power of the bishop, which always stands alone.

2. *Priority given to personal preference undermines the religious commitment.*

The "open placement" policy, which has fragmented religious communities, is now at work within dioceses. The principle is not officially recognized, but the practice tends in the direction of people choosing more or less where they will work. As a result, the will of the bishop to fill a role in a certain way no longer dominates the assignment process —if the unhappiness of the affected priest becomes an issue. Bishops still have leverage, but they no longer can rely on "obedience" to tip the balance in their favor.

The Catholic system relies on commitment signified by words such as "vow." To dismiss the evangelical counsels as inherited forms of servitude in favor of negotiated agreement is to misread the nature of Church society. Civil society obtains stability and performance by powerful economic rewards and socioeconomic sanctions. If one wants to earn a living, the stern rules of the marketplace must be obeyed. For government jobs, oaths of office, loyalty oaths, blacklists, and prison for malfeasance are controlling strictures. The Church can offer prestige and power to a few, but most priests are tied to a bishop by the sense of religious vocation, which includes doing the bishop's will when demanded. Free-wheeling in the priesthood not only undercuts the notion of "vocation" but also debilitates the Church's function. This is clear at the parish level. If "open placement" is the common option, it is difficult for a pastor to have a curate do anything he really does not want to do. Parish life has certain basics—regular Mass schedules, house calls, instruction classes, parish organizations, wakes, funerals, weddings, and other demands, which require planning, punctuality, and solid performance. If, for example, the pastor sets a goal of ten home visits a week for his priests, there must be a recognized penalty for the man who shirks his duty. At the present time there is no such penalty. Today the one likely to give up insisting on norms is the pastor, who may be forced, if he is able, to do the work himself. Conversely, a curate may enter a rectory where the pastor is a regular absentee. The curate, then, finds himself carrying the parish all alone without authority. This may please him for a shorter or longer period of time, but the lesson of the absentee pastorhood (usually known to the bishop) is not lost on the young man.

3. *A devalued pastorate becomes a burden.*

The pastorate is the most important post in the Church. The local pastor is a "little bishop" or a "little Pope." If the pastorate is in trouble, the Church is in trouble. The pastor is to the Church what a line officer is to the Army, the principal to a school, the store manager to a department-store chain. If those officials are incompetent, lazy, ineffective, or disenchanted, the entire system grinds more slowly. Everyone who works under the leader is affected by his élan or its lack.

Today pastors complain about the personnel policies of the bishop more than the curates do. Inability to obtain adequate "assistants" is only one of a pastor's difficulties. A pastor may have to wait months, perhaps a year, before his request is heard. He may discover that it does not have high priority with the Personnel Board. A potential curate may be offered the opportunity to look over or veto a proposed assignment, but the pastor generally is forced to take what he gets or else go without assistance. The personnel director, when contemplating a transfer, may be sufficiently solicitous about visiting a young man in his rectory without the pastor knowing that he is about to lose a curate.

Pastors cope with these imbalances in different ways. Those properly situated and well endowed find their own clerical help, independent of the bishop. This explains the presence of foreign priests and religious-order priests in many diocesan parishes. Ghetto and rural pastors have no such options. In either case the conscientious pastor finds himself heavily burdened. Other management problems of the Church—financial problems and the frequent violations of doctrine, liturgy, or canon law—are his to control, at the time when his authority is downgraded. What once was the most desirable post in a diocese no longer is attractive.

There is a third and entirely new structural component to the contemporary priesthood, which may create difficulty in the long run. This is team ministry. The only approximations to this concept of parochial management were the copastorships of the early American Church, which were outlawed by the 1829 Council of Baltimore. Present canon law calls for permanent parishes under the jurisdiction of permanent pastors. The Second Vatican Council spoke of "collaboration" and "cooperation," but the phrase "team ministry" does not appear.

What, therefore, does "team ministry" mean? In what does its significance consist? In the popular understanding it refers to "group management" as distinguished from one-man rule symbolized by the pastor, chancery official, or bishop. The term implies compatibility of goals and personalities, collaborative skills, and consensual decision-making. "Team ministry" began as an effort to upgrade the status of nonoffice-holders, of curates, brothers, and sisters by making them coequal partners in the operation of a parish or special apostolate.

As popularly defined, "team ministry" is contrary to canon law. For the same reason, the official definitions are always couched in terms compatible with the law. The guidelines for team ministry in the diocese of Cleveland, for example, use the terms in this way:

> Parish team ministry—as envisioned by these guidelines—is an association of a number of designated pastoral ministers who jointly share the responsibility for the pastoral ministry of a parish. Following consultation with the team members, one of these pastoral ministers, who must be an ordained priest, is also to be appointed by the bishop, to serve as administrator, having the administrative rights and responsibilities as established by canon law [*Origins*, October 27, 1977].

This definition protects not only the parish role of priests but also the hierarchical nature of the Church. The Cleveland guidelines call the chief team minister "administrator," but strictly speaking he is the canonical pastor. The pastor in law has prescribed rights and responsibilities. Within his territory or apostolate his authority is similar to that of the bishop. Unlike an "administrator," a pastor is not subject to the arbitrary whims of parishioners or bishop. A pastor may not be removed save as a "promotion," with his consent, or after a canonical trial. The Holy See has long recognized the need to protect a pastor against arbitrary action. The stability of the Church made this a requirement. Onetime Pittsburgh Bishop Hugh Boyle made a habit of appointing "parish administrators" instead of "pastors" because the former were removable at will. Rome made him terminate the evasion.

In the process of encouraging "team effort" the Cleveland guidelines are careful to protect both the role of the priest and the hierarchical structure of the Church. Other users of the term are not so careful. The Center for Applied Research in the Apostolate (CARA), reporting on team ministry in the archdiocese of Hartford, said this: "A pastoral team in which two or three priests are equal in authority is something difficult to understand" [*Origins*, September 18, 1975]. The words of significance are "equal in authority." Team ministry, if seen as a device for flattening authority structures or a prototype of a bishopless Church, may encounter resistance. There are indications that team ministry is insinuated as an experimental model of future ecclesial development. In CARA's study of the Hartford experiment, use was made of a "dogmatism scale"—a measure drafted by secular psychologists of people's alleged concern for power, for belief in absolute authority, for inflexibility in attitudes and judgments. Though the measure is a dubious tool, CARA was able to say, however slight the statistical difference, that "team priests are less authoritarian than other priests." This judgment has implications for bishops who prefer pastors.

The important question may be: Does team ministry work? CARA concludes: "It cannot be said from available data that team ministries are more effective than other ministries as they exist in the archdiocese [of Hartford] today. But it can be said that they are effective." While the scholarly conclusion is hedged, the report contains favorable reactions—"team work like a family"—and suspicions also that underlying team ministry is a *de facto* man in charge, who "from behind the scene runs the parish." Competent priest-observers in Hartford and elsewhere maintain that "team ministries" are neither effective nor suitable alternatives to the pastor-led parish. Team ministry is favored by priests who are dissatisfied with the mode of parish life they know. They look favorably on any experiment that seeks improvement on what they consider a worn-out mechanism. Yet the terminology itself is confusing. Most successful parochial enterprises are the result of team effort by priests, nuns, and lay leaders—occasionally motivated by a go-getting pastor or curate. "Team ministries," in spite of the terminology, surprisingly has meant three men working in separate directions and disparate parochial factions. Evaluations based on "tests for dogmatism" may report "psychological success" but say little about whether the team ministers do productive work. Conversions, improved Mass attendance, rates of growth or decline in school/CCD classes, and the well-being of social influence or temporalities are measurable indices of effectiveness that have little to do with personal-satisfaction tests. A bishop knows how a traditional parish functions, if he wishes to know. "Team ministry" is not easy to evaluate because its constituents are more difficult to rate.

The ideal-type situation for team ministry is missionary, where ministers begin their work almost with nothing. Whenever traditions, institutions, and inherited obligations loom large in daily operations, then hierarchical authority becomes important—to protect the patrimony. On the other hand, dire need and critical challenges equalize symbols of authority, even though someone is always a decision-maker when two or three gather together. Someone is always responsible for the authenticity of the Church's message in the Catholic situation. The Cleveland diocesan guidelines note what happens when "the team becomes deadlocked concerning an issue." The four-tiered process in Cleveland of mediation and arbitration up to the bishop may be realistic, but it adds tiers of bureaucracy at the bishop's level while paralyzing the local administrator.

Team ministry—if that means the absence of someone empowered to make a decision apart from agreement—has built-in difficulties when there are traditions and obligations. Movement from a subsidized parish to a self-sustaining parish, for example, requires a leader who thinks parochial independence to be an important value. Leaderless teams have demonstrated little interest in fund-raising—or in keeping operational costs at reasonable levels. A certain scorn is heaped sometimes upon "brick-and-mortar priests," who were men who paid their own bills.

4. *The problem is really doctrinal.*

Nothing will undermine the Catholic priesthood except perhaps the growing belief that Jesus Christ never established the priestly order in the first place.

The doctrine of the Church on this point is clear. The Council of Trent anathematized everyone "who says that there is no priesthood in the New Testament, or that there is no power of consecrating and of retaining sins, but only the office and sheer ministry of preaching the Gospel." Holy Orders, according to Trent, is "a true and proper Sacrament instituted by Christ" not merely "a rite of sorts for choosing ministers of the word of God and of the sacrament" (Denziger, Nos. 1771–73).

Four hundred years later, the Second Vatican Council says priests were "consecrated in order to preach the Gospel and shepherd the faithful, as well as to celebrate divine worship as true priests of the New Testament. On the level of their own ministry sharing in the unique office of Christ, the mediator, they announce to all the word of God. However, it is in the Eucharistic cult or in the Eucharistic assembly of the faithful that they exercise in a supreme degree their sacred functions, their acting in the person of Christ" (*Lumen Gentium*, No. 28).

These firm statements of Magisterium have in various ways been minimized since 1965. The undercutting of priestly status may not have been the intention, and frequently resulted merely from sincere attempts to build bridges to Protestant ministry. The Dutch Pastoral Council, for example, in one such effort made priestly ministry the result not of episcopal ordination but from a commission by the Christian community. This theological opinion, which holds that the clerical office-holder represents the faith of the believing community in Christ, not Christ himself, though designed to open doors for the validation of Protestant "orders," equivalently lowers present Catholic priestly status. The Catholic priest unquestionably is a congregational minister of his people, but fundamentally, according to Vatican II, he "acts in the person of Christ." Role-playing of the latter kind distinguishes the Catholic priest from other Christian ministers.

When experimental thinking of this kind filters down to the popular level, certain other developments follow. Newspaper headlines that read "Married Deacons Viewed as Replacing Priests" (New York *Times*, December 4, 1972) or "Abolish Clergy, Continue Priesthood" (NCR, November 2, 1973) are samples. Older priests, secure in the tradition, may find these predictions silly. Some younger priests are inclined to give serious thought to the possibility, and occasionally one of them acts out his uncertainty by debunking his role, like the reported account of the celebrant who refused to elevate at consecration time—pushing the host out at the people and shouting: "Christ came to be with men, not to be adored." Then there are the delegates of the 1976 convention of the National Federation of Priest Councils who confessed to not knowing how to describe adequately their role as ordained priests (*America,* May 21, 1977).

There are other serious reasons for priestly discouragement. In the past decade there has been a negative tendency to seek Church renewal by turning the clock back to the simplicity of primitive Christianity. Lecturers or authors following this line do not deny outright the clear teaching of the Church on priesthood, but they insinuate doubts about its roots in Christ. The question is raised whether the priesthood after all may be a human invention, the result not of Christ's mandate but of man's craving for power over other men. Hans Küng's *Why Priests?* clearly moves in this direction. He would uproot the official priesthood. Starting with the premise of Church as community of believers, Küng ends up promoting liberty, equality, and fraternity of all Christians— with no sacrificing priest. Ministry, according to Küng, really did not become sacred until the sixth century. Trent's decrees on Holy Orders are nothing more than historically conditioned and provisional statements designed to fight off Protestant concepts. Küng does not deny the need of Church functionaries, but he does not think they need be full-time, or commissioned for life, have any social or sacred status, or even be specially trained.

These and similar views were unwittingly disseminated further when the American bishops contracted first with Bernard Cooke, then with Carl Armbruster—at that time both Jesuits—to do a theological study of the priesthood. When completed in 1971 the bishops refused to publish what the Cooke-Armbruster team produced. The report eventually was leaked to the press, including those sections that maintained there were no theological barriers to the ordination of women, and sections that questioned both the permanency of priestly orders and the right of apostolic succession. The study said in part: "Theological reflection suggests that in a sense it is the entire Church which succeeds the apostolic college, a succession realized in a dramatic but by no means exclusive way by the episcopal college of the Catholic Church." The biblical part of the study concluded: "We can go on to say that there is no evidence in the New Testament that any one individual exercised all these (priestly) functions in the first century of the Christian era." On this basis neither the episcopal nor the priestly office can claim definitive formulation (NCR, May 12, 1972). Bernard Cooke later wrote his own book, *Ministry to Word and Sacraments*, which likewise denies that priests "stand between Christ and community." They derive their role "from the more basic priesthood of the community," "function for the sake of the community priesthood," and "in a sense (their priesthood) is a specialized or intensified expression of that common priesthood" (pp. 641, 648).

At the very time that Küng, Cooke, and Armbruster were publishing the results of their private research, the Third Synod of Bishops was meeting in Rome on ministerial priesthood. The bishops' document, issued on November 5, 1971, took a stand against these theological opinions. Priesthood is defined in terms of "orders," not solely in terms of other things he may do, such as preaching or directing souls: "By their vocation and ordination priests of the New Testament are indeed set apart in a certain sense within the midst of God's people. But this is so that they may be totally dedicated to the work for which the Lord has raised them up" (No. 3-1). The priesthood, therefore, exists in and for the Church, to be sure, but in the concrete this means permanency of commitment, oneness with their bishop, and distinctiveness from lay ministers.

Neither the Vatican Council nor the bishops' synod seemed to have reassured priests at the local level, especially those who have chosen to abandon the priesthood. Voices continue to speak differently. Lawrence Cardinal Shehan—a priest's bishop with intellectualistic credentials—took note of this confusion on the occasion of his retirement as archbishop of Baltimore, after fifty years as a priest in three American dioceses. The crucial question for Shehan was this:

> In the atmosphere of today's Church, with so many priests confused about the true nature of their priesthood and the permanence of their priestly obligations, I consider it not only significant but extremely important to know that Christ Himself did institute the office of Christian priesthood and did personally initiate the Christian priestly ministry.

Cardinal Shehan was particularly disturbed by the way in which Raymond Brown's book *Priest and Bishops: Biblical Reflections* was being used. Early in this book is the heading: "The Absence of Christian Priests in the New Testament." On the same page 13, lines such as "no individual Christian is ever specifically identified as a priest" and "the author of Hebrews does not associate the priesthood of Jesus with the Eucharist or the Last Supper" arise as questions, to which the answers are negative. There is another Brown observation, which Shehan ignores but which is even more radical, namely that New Testament silence about priesthood derives from the fact that early Christians acknowledged the Jewish priesthood as valid and therefore never thought of a priesthood of their own. Says Brown (p. 17):

> Many of our assumptions about the early Christian community flow from the erroneous supposition that Christianity was thought of as a new religion with its own religious institutions. But our best evidence is exactly to the contrary; at the beginning Christians constituted a movement within Judaism, differing only in some features.

Brown's views have been widely circulated among priests far more than Cardinal Shehan's correction, and far more than the views of other scriptural scholars. Franciscan Scripturist Manuel Miguens, for example, in his book *Church Ministries in New Testament Times*, acknowledges some of the difficulties of "proving" doctrines from Scripture, but is also in obvious disagreement with Brown. Concerning the probative value of Scripture, Miguens opens his study with the warning:

> Sometimes it will not be easy to find in the New Testament a direct answer to some questions. The main reason for this is that the New Testament does not offer sufficient elements of information for such an answer. It is my conviction that the only honorable and scholarly way to deal with this problem is to admit the fact as it is; namely, to admit the lack of information, instead of trying to supplement the New Testament with subjective and one-sided hypotheses, probabilities, likelihoods, etc., just to make the New Testament say what a particular scholar or a denominational group of scholars want [p. xvi].

Miguens goes on to assert what Christ did to establish a "new" following (p. 5), that he did select officers as rulers with some degree of authority (p. 109), and that "today's Church is the same Church of the New Testament, with the same authority, the same powers and the same vital drive" (p. 131). Concerning the controverted ministries and the terminology used in the New Testament to describe those ministries, Miguens has this to say:

> No single writing offers a complete picture that could be compared, for instance, with our present situation. This, of course, can be explained on the grounds that the writers of the New

Testament were not facing our modern problems and questions, and as a result, they do not intend to collect information to solve our uncertainties. In fact, all pieces of information about our subject are given rather by chance than deliberately or on purpose.

On the other hand, it is also true that in the New Testament we do not find any definite information about the modern notion of priest, the man who celebrates the Eucharist.

The question that, in this regard, the New Testament leaves open is whether in fact those officers referred to in the New Testament discharged all or most of the duties that the ministers discharged after the New Testament—already in Clement and Ignatius (late first, early second century).

Or whether the post-New Testament ministers are the sum total of the various ministries which appear here and there in the New Testament, in the various communities, an alternative this second one, which is not likely at all because the New Testament itself distinguishes already between bishops and deacons, and this also is the case of Clement and, particularly, of Ignatius, who makes another clear distinction between bishops and presbyters.

And so Miguens' final conclusion as a Scripturist reads:

There is not true and undebatable evidence that the monarchic bishops is represented in the New Testament, not even in the Pastorals. The evidence available rather points in the direction that "presbyter" and "bishop" are the same thing and that bishops/presbyters were (perhaps) several in every community—whereas an outstanding Apostle (Paul or John) retained the true leadership of the communities (particularly those founded by the Apostle; this is the case of Paul). It is likely that the monarchic bishop emerges as a factual event or necessity when the "apostolic authority" (the last of the outstanding Apostles) in a given area comes to an end; Peter in Rome, Paul for Phillipi and other Pauline churches, John for the community of 3 Jn. and in some of the communities of Apocalypse. As for the New Testament, this is mere speculation [pp. 97–98].

Where speculation begins or ends depends on those who speculate against the constant Church reading of its own foundations, and others, who accept Church teaching on the subject as legitimate and authentic. The Church has been given "all power," including the authority to refashion or reordain the priesthood to meet new or critical old situations. By now it is clear that the Church continues to look upon the priest as *alter Christus*. The ordinatus may not be worthy of this status, but this is what the Catholic Church says he is and what he was intended to be by Christ himself. This traditional doctrine may preclude the ordination of women and does not simplify ecumenical dialogue, but continues to be put forth as the given for future development concerning ministry shared with laity, including women and other Christians. (One other Catholic value is involved in this controversy: If the priesthood is the human invention of the Christian community, it would seem that the episcopacy and papacy may well be also.)

A separate clerical state placing priests *above* others in the Catholic community, by office if by no other title, is not a preferred value in a secularized world or Church. There are no intrinsic statuses in either place—none certainly given by God. Status goes instead to those who serve a useful purpose. Function, practical use, democratic selection, and temporary commitment are the new criteria of secular society. Even the purely spiritual aspects of ministry are not accentuated. These are recent difficulties for the Church, which never had an easy time recruiting and keeping the kind of priests it wanted. For more centuries than Ludwig Von Pastor has researched their history, priests did not say Mass often, if at all, spent more time eking out existence or making a fortune than in shepherding the Christian community, and were at times known more for lechery than for holiness. Religious orders arose in the Church generally because parish priests were corrupt, ignorant, irresponsible, at times hardly Christian. The Council of Trent was a marvel because it reversed fifteen hundred years of shabby priestly performance. The American priest became one of Trent's best products. It is, therefore, a surprising turn of events to see a movement develop that would undo Trent's progress. Even Fr. Charles Meyer, who writes fine things on priesthood, has felt it necessary to belittle self-disciplined and self-assured priests of an earlier time, the kind that saints and scholars of ancient days hoped for. One of Meyer's analyses to attempt to help priests cope with the post-Vatican II problems in their life began as follows:

The priests of yesterday were confident that no one could deviate in the slightest way from the pronunciamentos of magisterial authority without being squelched by it. They were thoroughly indoctrinated with a philosophy of absolutes. They were largely committed to completely other-worldly ideals. They were imbued with an appreciation of hardships and sacrifice as stepping-stones to sanctity. They were trained to accept opposition and adversity with stoic equanimity. They were expected to rally together under the aegis of faith to ward off attacks by atheist, agnostic, Protestant, and Jew. They were taught to soothe the gnawing irritations of anomaly and doubt in the balm of a spirituality heavily larded with what would be regarded today as "eschatological will-o'-the-wisps." They were supplied with an arsenal of prefabricated solutions to problems. Like all well-equipped soldiers, they were men inculcated with an indomitable *esprit de corps*. They were men who radiated self-reliance. They were men sure of themselves, their mission and their loyalties [*Homiletic and Pastoral Review*, August 1967].

These qualities ordinarily would be praised in secular societies, instead of being faintly damned for the Church institution. However, the sentiments represent a trend. The uncertainty, doubt, and loose discipline of secular society now became starting points for Catholic consideration. Meyer sees the problem as a question: "Do they really have identity as priests?"

There are other forces at work in the declericalization of the Church besides uncertainty. The campaign for the ordination of women to the priesthood is one. If the priest does not represent Christ, and so is not really "another Christ," there would seem to be no reason why women should not be ordained priests. As delegates of the believing community, not Christ himself, they would qualify. But the very argument that justifies women's ordination also lowers the status of the priesthood, whether it is staffed by men or women.

The move to develop a distinct catechetical class in the United States is also an effort to seize power and status from priests. The Albany Forum, held in the New York capital in January 1977 (whose reports have been published in a pamphlet entitled *Theologians and Catechists in Dialogue*), did not conceal its mind on this subject. Under the general heading "Ministry of the Catechist," three major conclusions emerged from the Albany dialogue: *Ministry is function and service; the need for declericalization in the Church; and the practical problems of self-image for the catechist*. Fr. George MacRae, S.J., of Harvard Divinity School, opened the session with an opinion that ministry as a distinct class in the Church ought to disappear. MacRae is quoted as saying:

> We have to recognize one another's ministerial functions without imposing on them a hierarchy of values which says it is more important to be a priest than to be a religious educator. It simply is *not*. There is no scale of values in the life of the Church or the service of God which makes it a higher dignity to be an ordained person than to be a teacher of children or adults [p. 23].

Fr. MacRae would not dispense with the priest, but "ministry can no longer be localized in specific, ordained individuals."

Brother Gabriel Moran expressed a political view. Fearing that all clericalized statuses—even permanent deacons—become powerless in the Church, Moran called for counterforces to fight the clerical structures. Catechists are one such group. Unpaid, unordained volunteer catechists can change the Church because they are beholden to no one—not even pastors. Catechists are financially independent and, unlike diocesan religious educators, are not beholden to the Church.

Fr. Bernard Marthaler, executive editor of *The Living Light,* official publication of the United States Catholic Conference, talking to the low-self image of catechists, quoted the on-the-job experience of one religious educator: "Don't let anyone take one of these jobs unless they have read Saul Alinsky's little book on rules for radicals." One of the featured participants in *The Albany Forum* was Bishop Raymond Lucker, former education chief at USCC and presently bishop of New Ulm.

Meetings with similar results going on regularly throughout the Church have more impact on catechetical thinking than official statements of bishops themselves. If these meetings reveal at times ambition for power or radical difference with Church doctrine—an aspect of dialogue rarely reported for formal assemblies—it is for the reason stated by one Albany participant: The documents of Vatican II "Have launched a revolution in Catholicism that is only beginning to be felt." This may explain why the fights over the General Catechetical Directory issued in Rome (1971) and the National Catechetical Directory approved by the American bishops in 1977 have been so fierce.

## V. *Whither Goes the American Priesthood?*

It is possible that priesthood may become for Catholics what ministry is frequently called by Protestants—"the uncertain calling." At this moment the diocesan clergy are sufficient in numbers to keep Church doors open. Quality of service may be suffering, but the Church's institutions and apostolates are more than amply staffed by fifty-nine thousand priests. What happens twenty-five years from now when most of the active priests forty-five years old and more are dead or retired is a matter of conjecture. With ordination classes of twelve priests where once thirty-six new priests yearly were standard, the prospects are not bright. The statistics are not the only aspect. The Catholic Church in the United States has not had to face such a low morale both of laity and clergy since its earliest days.

Crisis, however, does not necessarily mean defeat for the Church's priesthood, let alone its extinction. Pope John XXIII's renewal of priests—including greater sanctity and commitment—at the moment is a cropper but, properly managed, can become an opportunity for new evangelization efforts. The Church has often been subdued by secular culture, only to rise to later power and influence. The Gregorian reforms of the eleventh and twelfth centuries literally tore clergy from the bedrooms of mistresses, and sacraments from the hands of money-grabbing princes. When the clergy returned to the business of *cura animarum*, the thirteenth—"the greatest of centuries"—followed. The Tridentine Reforms of the sixteenth century dealt with a similar moral, fiscal, and doctrinal corruption, but succeeded in structuring a Church in which the crimes against religion were never fewer. The Pope, the bishop, and the pastor had their rights recognized but their responsibilities too were spelled out in detail by Trent. Priests serving their own cause, living separate ways, preaching their own doctrine often without training, responsible to no one, using the priesthood for gain or fame were made objects of command performance and accountability. Three centuries were still needed—well after the devastating effects of the French Revolution on clerical life had receded—before priestly life was deepened and regulated. Not until the twentieth century did priests acquire the role and status designed for them at Trent three centuries before! A new design, currently in the making, may begin to be productive only in the twenty-second century.

From the evidence of things as they are, it is apparent that a new design or plan of future clerical life will depend on how three questions are answered: What does Church authority see as the pressing needs of the modern world that the Church alone can or should satisfy? The Second Vatican Council was convoked precisely to offer some direction, but the documents of Vatican II have been so variously interpreted, at times in contradiction by bishops themselves, that the present efforts to develop a new, attractive, and stable priesthood seem jejune.

However, even if Church authority decides—as Trent decided—what its response to the world of the next century should be, a second dubium must be resolved with some precision before practical programs for priests can be formulated. It is this: What "Church" is to engage the presumably understood world? As long as the Church is made to appear uncertain about its nature and function, the priesthood will be uncertain. If doubt lingers about what the Church is, the status, role, and desirability of the priesthood will also be doubtful. The attractiveness of the priesthood depends on the attractiveness of the Church. *Deus providet* is a tried and true axiom of faith. But God provides through the humanities. Young men—unsettled almost from birth by the instruments of a dying culture—are not likely to find goals and meaning for their own lives or the wish to offer themselves to a religious institution that flounders like everything around them.

Finally, there is the matter of institutional follow-through. A Church certain about its chosen priorities also needs determination and structures that channel the new energy and the new programs, and a system of accountability and enforcement. Blueprints do not make a house, nor papal declarations a Church. Trent was successful because it produced the kind of Church—and priesthood—the Council Fathers designed. Going beyond Trent, without dismantling the machinery and discipline it took three hundred years to make its decrees work, the Vatican II Church needs better seminary training, better priestly spirituality, better priestly life and supervision.

The first Catholic priority is to determine the needs of the modern world. Here a clear distinction must be made between the world's needs and its wants. The Church is called to satisfy one, not the other. The last, longest, and most contested document of Vatican II, entitled *The Church and the Modern World*, opens auspiciously by expressing "the solidarity of the Church with the whole human family." Immediately before approving this document, the Council Fathers ratified another, *The Ministry and Life of Priests* to the Church and to the world, as if the two documents were called upon to go hand in hand.

What is this "world" of which the Council speaks? The world has many peoples. The voice heard is not always the *vox populi*. When, therefore, the Church is told to express its solidarity with the human family, it must listen first to the voices of selected spokesman, usually intellectuals or politically active groups. What do *they* say to the Church? One message is that the Church must accept certain facts of life about the modern world. This is a world of people on the move, searching for fulfillment in life, with a need to control the shape of that life. People today seek personally satisfying styles of living without long-range commitment. The Church that does not accept these phenomena has no chance of receiving a hearing. The social situation is fluid. Temporary society will no longer accept a monarchical church, imposed forms of worship or behavior, or traditions that are not meaningful to this culture.

The prescribed response of the Church to these conditions, as the message continues, is flexibility in the administration of Church law, membership through personal choice, small group arrangements instead of large, and participation by all in decision-making. These mechanisms will make the Church more dynamic and more adaptive to rapid change, which is one absolute characteristic of secularized society.

The further suggestion is made, said to be a mandate of *Gaudium et Spes*, that to serve man's this-world needs, the Church can no longer remain an enclave, a spiritual or religious subculture detached from secular civilization. Instead, the Church should move to help solve human problems and to discover new ways of molding public opinion to the values it represents. Since it is competing on unequal terms for men's minds and hearts, the Church must accustom itself to apostasy. Sociologists and theologians already speak of Catholics—like Jews before them —being in Diaspora. Jacques Maritain first spoke of "spiritual catacombs" for Catholics. Hilaire Belloc predicted that the paganized West would eventually be re-Christianized by missionaries from the Orient. Karl Rahner uses the term "pious remnant" for what Peter Berger says are actually "cognitive minorities"—people who think alike but do not count in culture. During this siege the Church will survive, as it did in Japan for centuries, in little groups—waiting for the day of restoration.

In the "little Church" of the future, the priest obviously will be a less effective institutional leader because his voice is crying in a wilderness. The world of "religion" is not important. A priest achieves importance, however, by what he does *through* laymen. They are the Catholics who represent the modern world. By going *into* the world himself a priest can enhance his influence. Together these local Christian assemblies of involved priests and lay apostles will provide a new leadership for the Church that is tested and tried in the cauldron of ongoing experimentation. What can possibly follow is impenetration of the world, not engineered this time from the top—that is, hierarchy—but by grass-roots armies of dedicated Christians. There are dangers for the Church's future in this approach—following fads that do harm being only one—but these risks must be taken. Secularized mankind will only accept a Church that proceeds about its business in this fashion.

In the present detraditionalized society, where spirits are low and institutions corrupt, the Church must seek to elevate man's inner life, to lift his sights through worship, to be present in his hour of need, to give him hope, and to be a symbol of what lies ahead. The big Church once did all these things well. That approach now is obsolete. It is the local Church that can best handle this world's fights, while preparing its members for the next life.

A variety of contemporary psychosocial scientists, and some theologians, have given one or the other parts of this counsel to bishop and religious leaders. Prominent Americans, however—Andrew Greeley, Thomas O'Dea, Eugene Kennedy, Augusta Marie Neale, Harvey Cox, and Gibson Winter—are merely echoing earlier European intellectuals who, among other things, conceptualized the "worker-priest movement" for the French bishops. As a proposed perfect tool for winning back the mass of Catholic workingmen lost to the Church in the nineteenth century, that movement, among others, was a disappointment.

There is plausibility in the preceding description of contemporary man's mental states, and accuracy in the Council's wish that the Church be involved in human problems and their solution. The recommendation that the Church become a mass-media phenomenon also is sensible, since the media constitute the marketplace of modernity.

In the last analysis, however, it will be the Church's convictions about itself that will be as important as its convictions about the world. The Catholic Church defines itself as the Church of Christ, as his representative to the world. If, as is currently alleged, such a declaration is true only in the broad or highly nuanced sense, then the priesthood itself and the catechesis for which priests are responsible are ambiguous entities. However, the official Church gives no evidence that it accepts many of these scholarly analyses or recommendations. Should hierarchy weigh the possibility of becoming ambiguous about the Church's nature or direction, there is evidence from the Protestant community about where the new directions would lead.

Working papers, prepared by a group of scholars for the Rockefeller Foundation, capture the problems of contemporary Protestantism. Several years ago the Rockefeller Foundation commissioned George Lindbeck, a distinguished professor of theology at Yale, to head a scholarly team that would evaluate the contemporary situation in divinity schools that the foundation subsidized. Harvard social scientists Nathan Glazer and Karl Deutsch were part of the investigative team. The working paper, entitled *University Divinity Schools*, published later in 1976, tells as much about sponsoring churches as it does about schools. In fact, the volume clearly defines the "ideal type" American Church.

It is obvious that any ecclesiastical operation that seeks approval from secular society must do away with particularism. "Heritage" is still valued as religion's contribution to "wisdom," but particularism (dogma, credal standards, denominational loyalty) is divisive. Even when particularism appears in less objectional forms, such as ethnicity, it is still divisive.

The approach of the Lindbeck study to definitions of Church and ministry has distinct characteristics: (1) It brooks no dogmatic interference, (2) has no credal standards, and (3) incorporates many traditions—that is, is pluralist (p. 6). Ecumenical study—not particularistic or denominational theology—dominates the formation of faculty and students. Denominational seminaries and Church administration offices are likewise fashioned through the influence of the "doctors" that university divinity schools produce.

The Lindbeck Report summarizes the effect of university involvement:

1. *On theology itself.* Theological education cannot easily be defined. Says the report: "In most Church colleges the teaching of religion has become very nearly as nonsectarian as in secular institutions" (p. 36); further, "The growth of religious studies is a major force in making theological studies less theological" (p. 38).

2. *On theological knowledge.* "Learning to think critically and independently in terms of a particular religious heritage has become increasingly difficult. The students know no single tradition well enough to display it with some consistency" (p. 61).

3. *On Protestantism.* "Of all the changes, the most important for the older nondenominational university seminaries is what has been called 'the eclipse of the Protestant establishment.' Not only has the WASP elite lost much of its former importance, but it has also lost its religion. The number and social, cultural and economic status of those interested in mainline Protestant churches and seminaries have fallen" (p. 46).

4. *On Catholicism.* "The upheavals following Vatican II have led to constant experimentation and often radical changes of content [in Roman Catholic seminaries]. Candidates for the priesthood in any given class are likely to have had much the same education, but not those in successive classes. Courses with such traditional labels as 'Fundamental Theology' or even 'Doctrine of the Trinity' sometimes change *toto caelo* from year to year. Thus it is sometimes even more difficult to predict of a recently ordained Catholic priest than of a Protestant clergyman what

he has learned in the course of his theological training" (pp. 29–30).

5. *On Recruitment of Ministers.* "Less than 5 per cent of [Protestant] clergy with full seminary training come from the universities." (But the seminary professors usually do.) (p. 10). The university-related theological centers are weaker than they once were except in the production of seminary professors. "Their graduates are less likely to become leaders within the institutional Church and indeed the majority do not enter Church occupations at all (in this contrasting sharply with the graduates of denominational schools of theology" (p. 23).

6. *On ecumenism.* In nondenominational university theological centers "ecumenism is now rather boring; it is no longer a new frontier" (p. 44). The gap between the new ecumenical churches and the university seminaries that are *prima facie* the most ecumenical is widening.

A Pennsylvania State University sociologist has placed his finger on why in Protestantism the full effects of "enlightened" concepts of Church have led to what his book calls *The Ministry in Transition*. Says Yoshio Fukuyama (p. 129):

Respondents attending university-related schools are indeed freer of institutional commitment, tend to be more critical of the profession and its institutional framework, and more often to alternative styles of work and education.

University-based professional education is dysfunctional for the denomination in the sense that the Church exercises little or no control over the students' technical training and has little opportunity to elicit students' loyalty or commitment to the organization.

The ascendancy of the university in the American power structure and theologian aspirants to hierarchical status in the Church have profound implications for Catholic definitions and priest-training programs. The Lindbeck Report is only one of many (Claude Welch of Berkeley did another study earlier in 1971) that indicate how far churches have come under university influence, whether they like it or not. It is the "university think tanks" whose papers filter through the churches' communication system to priests in the parishes and sisters in the schools. Unless properly channeled, the university norms become the rules by which Church policy is evaluated. If Church authorities are bold enough to make independent judgments the chances are that unconsulted university power centers will mock the proposals.

A mood spawned first in secular universities hovers now over Catholic campuses. Religion has come to mean group experience rather than doctrinal content, ecumenism rather than particularism, policy statements by ecclesiastics only with the consent of the scholarly establishment, clergy training with an intense intellectual component judged by secular standards. Princeton's John F. Wilson, writing for the Council on the Study of Religion, finds no difficulty with religious scholarship that "seems less constrained by definitions of material and approach bearing the stamp of ecclesiastical traditions or particular religious communities" (*Bulletin*, December 1976).

If these are the postulates, the problems for both Catholic Church and its seminaries are likely to increase. Whenever the claim by a religious body to have truth is looked upon as specious, or fixed beliefs are said to stand in the way of learning, faculty so trained cannot help but be torn between their religious commitment and a self-induced intellectual need to be independent. Doubt in the name of academic integrity becomes contagious. The effects on the Catholic Church can hardly be different than what is already evident in mainline Protestant denominations. (Evangelical sects, on the other hand, founded on a clear understanding of divine revelation, which commit their ministers and apostolates to this understanding seem to be flourishing.) In 1974 Protestant seminary enrollment grew to thirty-two thousand from twenty-three thousand in 1968, mostly because of evangelical expansion.

The Catholic trend since 1965 in definitions and policies has been in the direction of those once enthusiastically celebrated by mainline Protestant bodies. Theological giants of that tradition, such as Paul Tillich and Reinhold Neibuhr, were able to keep their churches and scholarship in close relationship so as to earn for themselves a reputation as fathers of neo-orthodoxy. Neo-orthodoxy is no longer alive. Mainline Protestantism and Catholic theologians like David Tracy are beginning to say that neo-orthodoxy is not viable for futuristic Catholicism either.

Part of the motivation for following secularistic leadership in scholarship is to put the ghetto church and ghetto priests behind Catholics forever. Fear of return to "siege Catholicism" is strong among American Catholic intellectuals and their ecclesiastical spokesmen. When Rome, for example, launched a study in 1971 of priestly formation programs with the idea of keying future priests to the "real world," *Commonweal* editors applauded for this urgent reason: "One of the reasons the Catholic ministry became mired in trouble is traceable to the detached, incubator-like atmosphere in which the clergy was shaped; the world seldom conforms totally to its classroom and textbook description" (April 16, 1971). There is truth in this analysis, as every good heart surgeon and bridge-building engineer knows. It is just as true that experience without solid textbook and apprenticeship training leads to corpses and fallen bridges. Differing opinions about the quality of early Catholic forms does not invalidate the need of definitions and policies for Church and priests that are framed within the Catholic context and institutionalized.

The rush to "ecumenical clusters" of theologates with nondenominational university centers can produce scholars of first rank but whose ties with the Church are tenuous. The trend has been justified because an ecumenical dimension is needed in priestly preparation. Faculty, course work in "clusters," and library holdings are of high quality. But "clusters" also enhance individualism in priestly life-style and formation, and an open posture toward free association with nonseminarians and women during the early period of formation. CARA, the Washington research group (*Origins*, May 24, 1973), has observed that "if the trend to enroll laymen and women in Catholic seminary theologates continues and increases at a significant pace, this will definitely have an impact on the entire 'personality' of the Catholic seminary."

Here once more, definitions and policies become important. If women are to be ordained, priests to be specialized, part-time, or married, laymen raised to coequal status in Church offices, the described trend has its justification. However, if ultimate definitions and policies are in the opposite direction, the present trend is certain to cause difficulty. Practice cannot outrun theory endlessly without undermining an institution. Examples are many in recent years of priests ordained who consistently missed daily Mass or dated women regularly during their seminary years, of seminary faculties split between alleged "modernists" and "fundamentalists," of bishops' seminaries testing "maturity" through a wide array of permissive practices, including homosexuality. This situation reflects confusion of goals as much as weak administration. Bishops or seminary rectors uncertain about what the Church is or is to be, are in an undesirable position for developing future staff. Goals and methods for priests cannot be any less vague than those for other important public leaders. Young surgeons are not imprecise about what they should do once they cut open the chest to operate on a human heart. The Church may speak of ideal conduct but it also works on behavior modification. An important objective for the Church is to turn out certain kinds of people doing or not doing certain kinds of things, and priests who can get this task done.

At the present time the Church seems to be engaged in a management by trial balloon rather than management by objective. Official statements and practice do not always coincide. Programs cannot favor simultaneously freedom and structure, social action and personal piety, communal living and personal option. Given the pervasive influence of modern psychological priorities, the quest for personal religious experience will transcend all concern for institution. There is evidence that a new tide is rising against the phenomenon of the past decade, but it is too early to tell whether the Church will lead or follow the mood that secular cultural leaders initiate.

Rome is not unaware of these difficulties nor of the tendencies within the Church. Efforts are being made to repossess control of both definitions and training. One recent example was the February 22, 1976, document of the Congregation for Catholic Education titled *The Theological Formation of Future Priests*. Rome recognizes that "tomorrow's priests will be exposed to greater dangers to the faith than in the past" (No. 7) due to the unbelief and skepticism all around them and expects bishops and seminary rectors to consider priestly formation their "most important and most demanding ministry" (No. 119). The entire document takes up the pitfalls that Catholic theologians must avoid, especially the temptation to translate the methods and findings of secular sciences, which would mean a theology "which has no basis in faith" (No. 43). However, the insistence that bishops and Pope have "the power to pass judgment" on theological writing (No. 47) is only as good as the practice. At the present time the tension between Rome and theologians remains. Arguments about whether Rome or bishops should have final say over who teaches "Catholic theology," whether pontifical seminary classrooms should be led by priests with pontifical degrees, and whether ex-priests should be teaching theology at all are minor skirmishes compared to the larger battle. Some of Rome's problems are created by ex-priests and theologians with little Catholic identity in training or teaching. It is valid enough to insist on the principle that theological degrees from secular universities and ex-priest theologians pose special problems. Catholic university and seminary rectors, including not a few bishops, have treated these concerns of Rome too lightly. On the other hand, some of those who fight hierarchy and Catholic formulations do have pontifical decrees. Toward the end of his life Cardinal Spellman was questioned by the then apostolic delegate, Aegidio Vagnozzi, about the heterodoxy of a New York priest. Spellman's reply was in character: "I know that allegation. That man teaches just what he was taught at a Roman university." The implication was that Spellman could take care of New York's problems if Rome took care of its own.

CHAPTER XI

The Defeat of the Bishops

## I. Background of the Problem

Would-be bishops may have their mind set on a noble task, or so thought St. Paul, but the Apostle to the Gentiles must have had the contemporary situation in mind when he warned his appointees to be "of even temper, self-controlled, modest, and hospitable" (1 Tm. 3, 1). Today's bishops need these virtues probably more than those who came after Paul. Bishops still know they are bishops, but a lot of other people no longer seem to care. Catholics were instructed by the NCCB in 1967 that "without the episcopacy there is no Eucharist, no priesthood, no historic continuity with the apostolic age," but there are not wanting theologians who would modify these affirmations to be less absolute. Even among those to whom the office is still a divine institution there is a tendency to show mounting disrespect. This was first noticed in scholarly circles during and after Vatican II, when the intelligence and competence of Catholic bishops were often questioned. "Real-estate managers," "bureaucratic pragmatists," and "Cadillac owners" were among the milder epithets used to dismiss them. It took an Andrew Greeley, however, to inform the secular world through his syndicated column that the American episcopacy included office-holders who were "just stupid," "dunderheads," and "mitered birdbrains."

Should a bishop be "a charming gentleman, a loyal churchman, a delightful raconteur, master of the *bon mot*, and a sophisticated citizen of the world," he still might be faulted for being "a Roman Catholic." Such is how an editorial in *The National Catholic Reporter* (August 4,

1972) put down John Wright, Boston priest, Pittsburgh bishop, and presently cardinal prefect of the Congregation of the Clergy in Rome.

It no longer seems likely for a bishop to receive thunderous applause from all sides.

Some bishops take all of this in stride. They develop thick skins against diatribe, dismiss the bitter comments as the ravings of a lunatic fringe, or find their consolation in the crowds waiting for them outside of church or in the lines for ashes on the first day of Lent. Some bishops, too, are better leaders than others, commanding respect even from those who want the Church run otherwise, and enjoying the challenge. A long, hard look at the positives in Catholicism prompted the American bishops in 1974 to declare that "American Catholicism is changing, not collapsing."

The Catholic Church is not likely to collapse, but it is in for some difficult days ahead, and the bishops know it. The final NCCB presidential address in 1977 of Archbishop Bernardin to his colleagues was a rallying call for conversion and evangelization—but this time to fallen-away Catholics as much as to any other group of Americans.

Even if the American hierarchy satisfied every standard of sanctity, scholarship, and administrative genius, their problems would not likely go away. The causes of disturbance far transcend the Church's present ability to cope with their effect, not the least being the widening belief among educated masses of Americans that secularity—this world—is what counts, not the supernatural and the search for eternal life. The call for new bishops to reinterpret the Gospel in secular terms could be "a recipe for the self-liquidation of the Christian community" (Peter Berger's phrase); nonetheless many people down the line of Catholicism are looking for new bishops to go secular. Those who devote a great deal of time proposing new procedures for electing bishops expect the priests or laity to hurry along this accommodation with the world. Elected bishops, however, may be no more disposed to do this than the present group of appointed bishops. In either case, Rome ultimately does the choosing, and the Pope—any Pope—valuing the integrity of the Church, would endorse such bishops only by accident. The new president of NCCB, Archbishop John Quinn, at the moment of election in 1977, listed the papacy as Catholicism's first and foremost resource "in saving the faith and the Church."

Whether elected bishops could be better, smarter, holier, or more relevant is a matter of judgment. The chances of the expected priest becoming a bishop is 200–1, whose popular selection would be as much the result of happenstance and timing as anything else. The best bishops—like the best Presidents or the best generals—are not always

the top men in their ordination class or the most popular. Some outstanding graduates turn out to be poor performers. The right bishop is
no more a matter of programming than the selection of Gerald Ford
and Harry Truman as Presidents of the United States, while the respected Thomas E. Dewey and Adlai E. Stevenson were passed over.
Ford may have been fate's answer to the needs of the nation more than
the talented but erratic Nixon. However, when the choices are made,
politics are involved, and democratic procedures may or may not help.
If municipal politics are any guide, the end result may be worse. Consultation is only one element, since the final decisions on important executives in any institution—even a community-based agency—are always the prerogatives of those in power.

There is one special element peculiar to the bishop-naming process,
however. Politics in civil government can lead in any direction—
wherever people can be led, or where 50 per cent can be persuaded to
go. There is no reason why civil governments cannot be liberal
democracies, welfare-state oligarchies, radical or conservative dicta-
torships—if the voters so choose. What they stand for is unimportant if
they are winners. But Catholic bishops are pledged to certain *givens*
over which Church membership or bishops have no authority. Secular
theologians dispute this, of course, but the Catholic tradition and the
Second Vatican Council are reasonably firm about the deposit of faith,
which is nonnegotiable.

What is more discussable, however, is the pace at which high Church
authority changes its ideas of the bishop type best suited to meet new
circumstances that have nothing to do with faith. Bishops named to
missionary dioceses are usually different than those chosen to oversee
affluent populated Catholic metropolitan sees. In one case, evangelizing
skills have priority. In the latter situation, it may be more important for
a future bishop to have talent at managing a vast network of functions
and keeping their demands in balance. The Stepinacs, Mindszentys,
Berans, and Wyszynskis came to ecclesiastical power in Eastern Europe
because they had the requisite toughness to confront the Soviets. It is
not surprising that Cardinal Wysyznski stays on in Warsaw beyond retirement age, because Rome does not have at hand a man of his stature
and strength to take his place.

Similarly in the United States, the qualities that made for a good pioneer bishop carving his way through the wilderness are not necessarily
those that make for the highly successful manager of an organized
Catholic community. Pastor types also, effective at the parish level,
have brought large dioceses to the point of bankruptcy. Conversely, successful administrators are not likely to be remembered as missionaries

or defenders of the faith. Those who are perfectly suited as leaders of the healthy Church may be the last ones qualified to oversee the Church in turmoil. The problem per se is not with the type of leader but with the time lag that normally transpires between new needs and the rise of new leader types. During this transition period a business-as-usual approach can be the source of additional difficulty for the Church.

The American Church is under unusual stress at this time. Some of these arise from the general cultural situation, some from the result of the Church's own shift of direction, some from the customary management style of bishops themselves. There is a tendency to believe that bishops can do little about the cultural patterns and that they must accept stoically the competition of civil religionists in the knowledge that the odds are stacked against the bishops. These very assumptions preordain expectations of what bishops ought to be or do. If, for example, the new communications media system is contemporary society's second government, with as much power over people as the first, what ought bishops be doing about it? The burdens of tomorrow's bishops might be eased if effective long-range planning by bishops was now at work to redesign the Church's public evangelization procedures. The same can be said of the need for leaders who can bridge tradition and the changes proposed in Vatican II. Bishops who see no need for change, or who have no understanding of the traditions are not helpful. During these difficult days special bishop types are needed, and until they emerge or until Rome finds them there will be confusion and disorganization.

Other problems of the Church are typical of modern times. Pope Paul hardly let an opportunity pass without reminding hierarchies one by one to stop passing their problems on to him. The French and Dutch bishops were sternly warned of this in separate visits to Rome. Rome is also sensitive about the charge that "an emerging American Church" is in the making. Two successive NCCB presidents have spoken of bishops' responsibilities for the Church's internal peace. The former president of the Canadian hierarchy, Bishop G. Emmet Carter, has gone so far as to call his fellow bishops "a bunch of pussyfooters." During the 1977 Roman synod Carter told a press conference that in his view "the bishops were somewhat responsible for the kind of confusion which came about" (OSV, November 13, 1977). Doctrines that were "not only pernicious but false" filtered through the Church while bishops stood aside terrorized into silence by journalists and theologians. Scholars have come to recognize that the condition cannot continue indefinitely. James V. Schall, S.J., for one, takes note of the fact that hierarchies may have betrayed their pastoral duty by following rather than leading the flock. For the Jesuit: "I still prefer the miter to the survey, and the local synod to the association of professors." (*America*, January 15, 1972).

Recognizing the problem, however, does not solve it. If the new mood, as expressed by one French bishop—*Maintenant, cela suffit* (Now, that's enough)—is becoming universal, there are still obstacles to the restoration of Catholic order. While there is no single pattern in these difficulties, there are five factors that complicate the ruling role of bishops:

1. The powerful attraction that secularity has come to have for Catholic intellectuals.
2. The contemporary disdain of authority at all levels of the Church.
3. Confusing signals from Catholic chanceries almost everywhere.
4. Respectability given to dissent under the nomenclature "pluralism."
5. Conflict of bishops with each other and with Rome.

A few of these difficulties are more apparent than real. Some are blown out of proportion by the media. Some are part of an overall strategy to bypass bishops without confronting them. Others still are created by men on their own staffs or by those who work not far from bishops' unwatchful eyes. In all of the recent controversies within the Church over research, catechetics, birth control, religious life, liturgy, and social action—even on such minor matters as communion in the hand—one or the other of the above factors have exacerbated bishops' relationships with priests and laity.

Consider the *secularity* question as a case in point. For a Church that for so long resisted the worldly tide, Catholicism today is awash with secularity. Not only has the Church jumped into that stream with both feet, but it has also been carried over the waterfall. Protestant Langdon Gilkey thinks the collapse of Catholic battlements is due to modernity's triumph over its onetime sturdy foe. Jewish Leo Pfeffer, rugged antagonist of Catholic interests, is of the opinion that the Church after years of fighting has succumbed to secular humanism. The bishops' fight over abortion, he thinks, is the last hurrah of ecclesiastics whose people have gone secular.

Triumphal secularity stamps its own identifying marks on the Church: for example, top priority to human values, primacy of the individual, centrality of sex to human fulfillment, social betterment through evolutionary social mechanisms, strong government for social improvement, and *laissez-faire* and conscience in all other matters. Reduced to everyday language this means public control of politico-economic life, and no public control of personal life. In order to be relevant participants of modernity, religious leaders are expected to endorse social-action programs, even to the point of telling people what they should or should not eat. If they value status among seculars, however, they may not tell single or married people what to do in the bedroom, nor tell doctors what to do in operating rooms.

Unlike some of their religious peers, Catholic bishops are not entirely comfortable as social reformers, if that means binding the faithful on boycotts as they bind them in marriage. Yet, when secularity rises to overwhelm the supernatural component of Catholicism, the bishops' directions seem to lack consistency. Their statements on sexuality, especially abortion, are relatively clear. But their timidity about contraception—a family bomb of nuclear proportions—is read as acquiescence to the times. The national body of bishops has backed the Humphrey-Hawkins full-employment bill, national health insurance, amnesty for war resisters, federal firearms control, the end of capital punishment, food stamps, majority black rule in Africa, and strictures on multinational corporations. But on the Equal Rights Amendment, about which Catholic bishops might be expected to have some balancing insights—primarily because of the Church's long exaltation of motherhood, child education, and the homemaking role of women—there is literally no guidance at all. All social issues must be judged in terms of some perceived Gospel principle. Yet the social causes promoted or ignored by bishops in recent years tend to follow instead the preferred agenda of the Washington political establishment. If Catholic bishops want the Panama Canal to be given back to the Panamanians as a moral must, they can properly support this action because the Catholic bishops in Panama consider native ownership of native resources to be a matter of justice. But by expressing unwillingness to communicate their resolution to American Catholics in any dramatic way, the hierarchy give evidence of uneasiness with their own secular authority.

Bishop Joseph McNicholas of Springfield, Illinois, after persuading his fellow bishops to endorse the withdrawal of American presence from the Panama Canal, told a press conference: "The bishops don't like to get involved in this sort of thing. I don't especially like it either. The staff people [at the United States Catholic Conference] want us to take positions on everything under the sun. Some people think that when they say 'Jump' we go so high. That just isn't true. Neither I nor anyone else is going to go out on that floor and get clobbered for them" (New York *Times Magazine*, January 16, 1977).

The management problem of bishops, however, goes beyond the secularity pressure. The *contemporary disdain for all authority* has made bishops nervous about the use of authority in the Church. The big word is "leadership," which has a more mellifluous ring and sounds less threatening than "authority." Yet the concepts are totally distinct. Authority means the power of decision-making with the understanding that compliance follows. Leadership means the charism or power of persuasion that begets disciples and adherents. Leadership is a desirable attribute for every authority figure. But it is not a substitute for authority. There may be charismatic figures better qualified at manipulating people than authority figures. But it is to offset this possibility and to ensure the stability of society that authority is reposed in office-holders. The office-holder need not be a great leader, but he must command policy and compliance. Franklin Roosevelt, for example, was both a great authority figure (he closed banks and sold destroyers) and a great leader, leading Americans into war because that was where he thought they belonged. Harry Truman exercised greatness in his presidency without notable leadership qualities. Margaret Truman's reminiscence about her father's first Cabinet meeting with Roosevelt holdovers provides insight into the difference. After explaining how important Cabinet advice was to him, whether he liked it or not, the new President made it clear that, once made, presidential decisions were to be implemented without deviance. The President's diary read as follows: "I told the Cabinet members the story about President Lincoln—when he was discussing the [Emancipation] Proclamation—he put the question up to the whole Cabinet and they voted no. That is the way I [Truman] intend to run this [Cabinet]." That is authority in action, but not charism.

Catholic bishops once would have been voted the most likely to succeed against the trend to flatten authority figures. Many bishops looked ten feet tall even while they maintained large measures of grass-roots support in their own dioceses. These men have been called authoritarian by those who do not want authority (that is, the enforcement of law or policy) to come down against their favorite causes. Yet most of them were decisive and enjoyed large measures of popular support. Elites and journalists were sometimes annoyed that men of this stature did not sanction lawlessness. Bishops always knew that canon law or Church documents, like social encyclicals, were ignored or violated, but they rarely created a public uproar about it. Either the issues were of

minor moment or they involved areas of judgment or legitimate freedom. When the matter was important, bishops rarely hesitated to enforce the law or sanction violations. Removing a seminary professor for
conducting underground liturgies for future priests was standard operating procedure. Before his death Cardinal Spellman threatened to close
his major seminary if Dunwoodians went on strike, as their counterparts in Boston had done earlier against Cardinal Cushing. In many situations bishops were men conscious of their role and accustomed to
make decisions.

The recent story of commanding respect or enforcing Church law is a
different tale. Some bishops make a practice of confessing their un-
worthiness or faults in public. One young bishop, declaring his intent
to be a "street priest," said: "I hope that if I'm not that kind of bishop,
somebody kicks me in the pants" (New York *Times*, March 27, 1976).
The fashionable thesis says that genuine authority is not held or given
but earned. In practice this means that officials should act as if they
were running for office, not holding it with a view of making hard decisions. The popular manuals project authority figures as counselors
skilled in the arts of persuasion (which many are), not management
officers elected or appointed to get something done. New bishops, and
some older ones, have followed this recipe for leadership uncritically.

Once the debasement of their position is institutionalized, confusing
signals begin to go out from Catholic headquarters. Infractions of liturgical norms, for example, can be notorious—Mass without vestments,
without chalice, without Scripture readings, without bread and wine,
sometimes without the words of consecration—and little strong effort
made to see that these aberrations do not occur again. This is a critical
aspect of contemporary Catholicism: *the unusual toleration by bishops
of public dissent or disobedience against post-Vatican II policies of the
Church.* A certain amount of disobedience is normal in every society,
even when it is not recommended. In spite of allegations to the contrary, there was a large amount of dissent in the pre-Vatican II Church,
particularly over the social encyclicals and certain biblical interpretations. But by and large there was also self-discipline among independent functionaries and a common understanding that change occurred within the framework of established rules. Only the most
obstreperous felt they could go their own way, and few wished to topple or supplant bishops. Lately, a new twist has been given to the
phrase "bishops are not the Church." Intellectuals and activists, claiming an independent spirit, began to act as if the bishops did not count
at all, especially the ones in Rome. It was on this basis that Donald
Thorman singled out for praise "the sisters who hold off the curial di-

nosaurs in Rome" (NCR, December 24, 1973). Sometimes a bishop would stand up to confrontation and the headlines would read "Cardinal [Medeiros] Admonishes Priest for Unauthorized Latin Mass," or "Bishop Elwell Walks Out of Unauthorized Mass" (NCR, February 22, 1974, and February 25, 1972). But as a general rule, bishops suffered greater indignities than these with remarkable aplomb.

At times they were dissuaded from the enforcement of Canon law because of *conflicts among themselves and with Rome that were public knowledge.* No bishop cares to clamp down on "abuses" in his diocese when across the river the same things might be looked upon as "new discernment of the Spirit." But even here the variations were not the cause of serious Catholic confusion. Variations always existed to a greater or less extent—for example, in matters of fast and abstinence. But when the issues in conflict among bishops became substantive, this was a different matter. Bishops are entitled to have their own views about how much latitude local ordinaries have in making certain decisions governing the welfare of their diocesans—for example, on the rules concerning marriage tribunals, age for first confession, and age for the diaconate. When they process their requests for wider latitude through ordinary channels, they do not deserve headlines such as "American Bishops Showing a New Readiness to Take Issue with the Vatican" (New York *Times,* November 19, 1973), or "Two U.S. Bishops' Votes Go Against Vatican Decisions" (NCR, November 23, 1973).

On the other hand, it is common knowledge that certain bishops' names or opinions do manage to surface in news stories that pit some bishops against other bishops on substantive issues and about which Catholics expect agreement. One of the notable cases occurred during the annual bishops' meeting in 1976. For two years Bishop John McDowell had been trying, with the help of a national committee and wide consultation, to produce a document on Catholic moral values. The proposal itself was evidence of bishops' concern that the faithful were being led into lives of sin by wrong direction from dissenting theologians and religious educators. The finished product, entitled *To Live in Christ Jesus,* was presented in November 1976 to the national body of bishops. A minority of bishops, with some university and press backing, moved to table the McDowell draft. "It lacks compassion," said one bishop, the grist for the media mill, which made the majority appear hardhearted traditionalists in a world of groping sinners seeking mercy.

The diversionary move of the minority was brought to a halt when McDowell arose to tell his fellow bishops that if after two years more time was needed to instruct the faithful about what Catholic moral values were they could get another chairman. *To Live in Christ Jesus* passed overwhelmingly. But the damage was done. The specter of bishops wavering uncertainly over Catholic moral values, of bishops meeting in caucus to obstruct a carefully prepared document of the National Conference, was not an image conducive to engendering confidence among those asked to live with Jesus in the manner prescribed by bishops.

The same game played with serious consequences goes on locally: catechetical textbooks saying different things, sterilizations in Catholic hospitals, contraception openly promoted in diocesan Pre-Cana conferences, and divorced Catholics remarried without benefit of Church annulment. These practices frequently go on below the bishop's level but in some cases not without his toleration. In other cases the bishop may be embarrassed by his own subalternates, as when the Brooklyn *Tablet* editorialized (January 22, 1976) against the Vatican declaration on sexual ethics. Rome had given answers a month earlier to some serious questions that the editor wanted to remain open in the Church— premarital sex, homosexual acts, and masturbation in particular. With the disclaimer that "no disrespect is intended," the Brooklyn diocesan paper went on to reject "the presumption that ecclesiastical authority can create the truth."

But then, some American bishops, egged on by local scholars, have decided that the time has come to clip Rome's wings. When Bishop James Shannon was about to depart the episcopate for marriage, he sounded more like Hans Küng than a Catholic bishop (*The Priest*, June 1969). A recent example was Rochester Bishop Joseph Hogan's advisory to his diocesan Sisters' Council that Rome's statement on the ordination of women was a "theologically horrible document" and "subject to correction." He also had published in his diocesan newspaper, the *Courier-Journal*, the remark, "If the Magisterium closes off investigation, it deserves the response I give to it" (February 16, 1977).

This gap between bishops and Rome may widen if more and more bishops begin to reflect not Roman doctrine but contemporary theology as articulated by dissenting scholars. While Andrew Greeley is afraid of a "new repression on the way" (Brooklyn *Tablet*, August 12, 1976), American bishops give no evidence that they have any clear idea how to present a united front on doctrine. Neither has that prototype of ecclesiastical domination—the German hierarchy—either. In December 1977 the German bishops published ten more pages of complaint against Hans Küng, who remained unimpressed. Far from correcting errors, Küng felt "imposed upon" and promised still another book. Even when bishops do agree with each other, they continue to live by scholars' rules, which permit only verbal remonstrance. In the meantime, the scholars continue to evangelize priests and bishops to their new way of thinking.

If one scans the list of regular lecturers at "theological seminars" for bishops sponsored in Rome and the United States, the faculty imbalance in favor of controversial scholars is quite noticeable. Immediately after the 1976 Eucharistic Congress, for example, a bishops' study week featured three lecturers: Raymond Brown, Avery Dulles, and Richard McCormick. Bishops are told in lectures sometimes delicately, sometimes bluntly, that the historical roots of episcopacy are shadowy, that the Pope was wrong on contraception, that their ethical directives for Catholic hospitals are quaint but outmoded, that there is a second Magisterium. At home local ordinaries and state conferences of bishops subsidize continuing education of priests that seethe with dissenting indoctrination. One priest lecturer at such a series in New York State would not stand by the proposition "Jesus is God" unless it was properly nuanced. Fr. Charles Curran drops in on these courses as an invited guest, even in seminaries where the bishop would not have him as a faculty member. Jesuit James Schall recounts hearing a priest lecture on worship, telling his audience that the Mass was a celebration of brotherhood, of "our openness to one another," with no hint that Christ's divinity had anything to do with the liturgy. The speaker received a standing ovation. Said Schall: "On leaving the hall, I chanced to bump into the chancellor of the local diocese, a man I did not know. 'What did you think of the talk?' I asked, trying to check my impressions. 'The man does not believe in God,' he replied without hesitation" (*Clergy Review*, July 1977). But that was the end of the matter for the diocese.

A clear example of confused leadership was given by the auxiliary bishop of Los Angeles, Juan Arzube, who in a homily given during the April 25–28, 1978, convention of the Catholic Press Association told editors that "dissent from the ordinary teaching of the Church" was legitimate providing the dissenters were competent and sincere. Not only was his theologizing inexact (for example, ordinary teaching, though undefined, can also be infallibly taught without formal definition), but also it represented the views of well-known theological dissenters, not those of the Congregation for the Doctrine of the Faith. Where did Arzube get his views? The Los Angeles auxiliary tells his listeners:

A couple of years ago I took theology courses in Rome with other bishops from the United States, and as a result of them

I became more aware, for instance, of the different way in which we are to accept infallible and noninfallible teaching.

Some of the faculty giving those courses were well-known dissenters. Advocates of greater pluralism in the Church have no difficulty with this state of affairs, but serious pastors are at times demoralized. Fr. J. Sweeney of Pueblo, for example, retired from diocesan service because these questions were unanswered.

> What are the obligations in obedience of a priest and what re-course does he have when he finds that his own ordinary is, in the words of Pope Paul, "not preaching the Gospel in its integrity and purity"? What are the obligations of a priest to his ordinary, and what recourse does he have when he finds that the policies and attitudes of his ordinary are not in consonance with the long-accepted and even defined teachings of the Church? [*Homiletic and Pastoral Review*, February 1977].

## II. The National Catechetical Directory

How American bishops manage to deal with the centrifugal forces pulling the Church in disparate directions was evident during their annual meeting November 14–17, 1977. It was here that they gave final approval to a revised National Catechetical Directory, under which the next two or three generations of Catholic Americans will be formed and fashioned. The process by which NCD came into being and finally received official endorsement from the hierarchy is itself the story of the contemporary Church.

Prior to the vote of the bishops there was a great deal of public and private debate about what should or should not go into a catechetical directory designed for American parishes. Contributors or readers approved or disapproved depending on how much method dominated content, on whether secular ideology too much or too little rearranged the traditional supernatural orientation of catechetics. Exchanges of viewpoints on catechetics during the four years of consultation were not always polite because those in charge of the production wanted the stress in the final document to be positive and pastoral. Their critics, however, were determined that the final document would also be precise in its doctrinal content. Neither side prevailed, because during the transition from draft to approved text the bishops themselves intervened. What was given to the bishops as the product of one hundred thousand consultations underwent substantial revision on the floor of the Statler-Hilton Hotel in Washington, D.C. More than one hundred amendments were voted, adding, deleting, or amending paragraphs and sections until the bishops got the document they wanted. Some revisions were merely stylistic, but a few altered the directory substantively.

The approved directory has been called a bishops' document. This is not certainly accurate, because not all bishops were happy with every part. In fact, some bishops manifested little knowledge of or interest in the contents at all. Still, though NCD does not satisfy everyone, the bishops have expressed general satisfaction with their handiwork. John Cardinal Krol called the amended document "great" because of the bishops' role in its finalization. Archbishop Joseph Bernardin, outgoing NCCB president, told his confreres: "I believe we will be very proud of it." More surprising, Dale Francis, the editor of the *National Catholic Register*, endorsed the document with high praise:

"We have a National Catechetical Directory. It will serve the Church for decades to come. It is an excellent directory and it will accomplish the 'sharing the light of faith' that it proposed in its title to do."

This encomium was penned by a man who a short time before called the final draft weak on such important subject areas as creation, original sin, the sacrifice of the Mass, the Ten Commandments, the first confession of children, and Magisterium. Dale Francis made this startling statement about the bishops' text: "What probably can be said accurately concerning those amendments that passed was that they stressed orthodoxy even more strongly than the original text—although there was nothing in the original text that was called unorthodox" (OSV, December 11, 1977).

The ones unhappy with the product seem to be some members of the NCD committee. Their complaints took various forms. Sister Anne Marie Mongovan said the bishops "almost ravaged" the document. Revealing a special view of the episcopal role, the nun objected that bishops could change parts of a document "that we spent hours and sometimes years developing in a matter of minutes." As she saw it, NCD "survived" but "it's been patched up so that there are some really jarring notes" (NCR, November 25, 1977). Bishop William McManus of Fort Wayne used similar language when he said that one of Cardinal Cooke's amendments "would introduce a jarring note into what is a warm pastoral document." McManus, a Chicago priest, at one time headed up the bishops' education department in Washington, D.C. and was himself a member of the NCD committee. Dissatisfaction was also expressed by the committee member who said: "The bishops turned the catechetical movement back 150 degrees by their amendments."

The reactions to the approved NCD text represented a reversal of opinion, even by bishops, some of whom would have scuttled the entire document if they thought they could justify four years of work without fruit. Why the sudden shift? Because the bishops' amendments—without touching the major portion of the presentation—inserted language that staff assiduously had rejected. The final NCD document still is handicapped by its uncritical acceptance of developmental psychology, already under fire in secular circles. The stress on the social obligations of Christians, though reaffirmed by bishops, will be resisted by affluent American Catholics. Even so, a key sentence in the text—"The development of the concept of 'social sin' is another example of how the Church seeks to highlight the social dimension of Christian morality"—stood against an effort to strike it.

Many bishops during the deliberations came to understand the lacunae or the ambiguous language that had developed in the text in the course of the consultation process. The amendments reflected their concerns and their sense of the Church's need.

A poignant moment came to the bishops' meeting as the final votes of approval were being counted. Bishop McManus, who had been staff spokesman throughout the sessions, rose to a point of order and politely requested some other bishop to move the withdrawal of Cardinal Cooke's amendment on memorization. He could not do this himself according to the rules. McManus made this request because three committee members told him they could not live with the amendment. Not one bishop rose to support their request. There was nothing left for McManus to do but sit down. What was the "jarring note" in the Cooke amendment that the three committee members wished to eliminate? The requirement that children be taught to memorize prayers, parts of the Mass, the list of the sacraments, and the commandments of God and the Church. Not only was the amendment intended to correct a draft that read "Formulation and memorization should be used with discretion so as not to overburden or confuse," but also to correct the observable condition of young Catholics after twelve years of Catholic schooling graduating without precise knowledge of the basic elements of their faith. Upon his return home, Bishop McManus still continued to doubt the value of memorization. In an interview (December 18, 1977) in his diocesan newspaper *The Harmonizer*, McManus said: "Frankly, I doubt there was any bishop there voting in favor of Cardinal Cooke's amendment who knew from memory all the things that ought to be required in the catechetical program. I doubt that many bishops could recite all the beatitudes."

A comparison of the changes from NCD draft to text indicates the areas of catechetics that the bishops felt necessary to strengthen.

1. *Articles 47 and 58 on Magisterium in Catechesis*

|  *NCD Draft*  |  *Bishop's Version*  |
|---|---|
| All truths taught by the Magisterium pertain to faith. But some, central to the Gospel message and necessary for salvation, enjoy a higher priority. | [Adds two significant paragraphs.] This task of catechesis, not an easy one, must be carried out under the guidance of the Magisterium. . . . |
|  | The primary position of authority over programs of catechesis is held by the bishop. Under him the pastor holds the office of direct responsibility in the local Church. The teaching of what is opposed to the faith of the Roman Catholic Church, its doctrinal and moral positions, its laws, discipline, and practice should in no way be allowed or countenanced in catechetical programs on any level. |

This language was particularly offensive to Bishop McManus because "it casts a very unhappy image of bishop as kind of policeman ready to pounce down on any catechist who steps on the flag" (*NCR*, November 25, 1977). But the amendment passed overwhelmingly not only because Pope Paul twice had requested American bishops to guard the integrity of the faith, but also to put an end to the abuses in teaching that were common at all levels of Catholic education.

2. *Article 49 on Revelation*

|  *NCD Draft*  |  *Bishop's Version*  |
|---|---|
| [Speaks of revelation without defining it.] | [Adds a paragraph that distinguishes between "Revelation in |

general and in the strict sense."]
[In the strict sense Revelation is]
a gift of God upon which no one
has a claim. Because it goes beyond anything which we can dare
imagine, the proper response to
this Revelation is that self-sur-
render known as the obedience
of faith.

While the NCD staff opposed this amendment, the bishops, conscious
that some theologians were denying "a once and for all" revelation
from God, insisted that catechists make clear the difference between
"Revelation" with the capital "R" from "revelation" with the lower-case
"r." The amendment was also a reproof to those who spoke only of
God's ongoing Revelation through human events. The practical effects
of this misplaced emphasis was the denial of moral absolutes. If man's
understanding of God was evolving, so were God's laws.

This corrective was an important bishops' statement to theologians as
well as to catechists. Section 59 was later amended over the opposition
of staff to make clear that Revelation was "given to the Church and
guarded by the Magisterium."

### 3. Articles 96–97 on Mortal Sin

|  NCD Draft  |  Bishop's Version  |
| --- | --- |
| [Introduces the notion of "funda-mental option" in a footnote without defining it.] | [In footnote 40 the bishops cite in exact language the Holy See's reprobation of the idea that mortal sin occurs only when there is a deliberate, formal turning away from God. The catechist is reminded that every serious transgression of God's law is a mortal sin.] |

This amendment was intended to put an end to the growing practice of
teaching three kinds of sin—venial, serious, or mortal. Sins such as masturbation or fornication were being called serious—but not so mortal as
to deny access to the Eucharist.

## 4. Article 101 on Conscience

| NCD Draft | Bishop's Version |
|---|---|
| [The draft version spoke of "a rightly informed conscience . . . in accord with the moral order."] | [The bishops made this specific addition:] "Conscience is inviolable but it is not a law unto itself; it is a practical dictate, not a teacher of doctrine. Doctrine is taught by the Church whose members have a serious obligation to know what it teaches and adhere loyally to it. In performing their task catechists should present the authentic teaching of the Church. |

The import of this amendment is its rebuke to those religious educators following theologians who make conscience the arbiter of God's will.

## 5. Article 131 on Ordination of the Priesthood
The bishops added to the draft Pope Paul's teaching that only men may be ordained to the priesthood.

## 6. Article 133 on the Celebration of the Mass
The bishops added that no one, not even a priest, may change the liturgy on his own authority.

## 7. Article 188 on Conscience Formation

| NCD Draft | Bishops' Version |
|---|---|
| When faced with questions which pertain to dissent from noninfallible teachings of the Church, it is helpful for catechists to keep in mind that the presumption is always in favor of the Magisterium, and that expressions of theological dissent do not question or attack the teaching authority of the Church, and scandal is not given. | [The transverse paragraph was dropped because it seemed as written to be an invitation to dissent. The following clarification was added:]<br><br>It is the task of catechesis to elicit assent to all teaching of the Church. The Church in fact is the indispensable guide to the complete richness of what Jesus teaches. When faced with ques- |

tions which pertain to dissent
from noninfallible teaching, it
is important for catechists to
keep in mind that the presumption always favors Magisterium.

The complete excision of the paragraph on dissent is a measure of the
marked concern of bishops on this subject. The "theology of dissent,"
itself a dubious concept as used in the workaday Church, has relevance,
if at all, only to research theologians. That it should be part of a document intended for catechists of eighth- or ninth-grade children is a co-
nundrum that puzzled many readers of every NCD draft. Yet each new
draft, including the one presented to the bishops on November 14,
1977, contained a sentence on dissent by catechists. It seems that someone was determined to steer this concept through the bishops. Bishops
took quick note that the phraseology justifying dissent was a cover
under which authentic teaching of the Church could be subverted on
the parish level. There were multitudinous examples of this in their
own dioceses. Permitting catechists to dissent if their reasons were serious and "well founded," if they did not "attack the teaching authority
of the Church" nor cause "scandal" was an invitation to turmoil. The
bishops' version starts with a different premise—namely, that the catechist himself is an assenter, working to develop other assenters to the
demands of the faith. The bishops then proceed to tell the catechist
that when "questions that pertain to dissent" are raised, presumably by
students, the catechist always favors Magisterium. This directive may
become the bishops' most important NCD victory if the future practice
can be made to follow the Directory theory.

The Holy See did lose one skirmish during those Washington
debates. The NCD staff consistently opposed the Roman requirement
of first confession for children prior to first Communion. On several
previous occasions one or the other NCD staffer had publicly stated
that Roman documents did not close this issue. As a matter of fact, since
many of the bishops in attendance were themselves in violation of Vatican directives, the episcopal body was reluctant to accept amendments
designed to insist that children be led to confession before admission to
the Eucharist as a general rule. They did insist, however, that catechesis for confession precede a child's first Communion and that the
norms set down by Rome be respected. But this was as far as they would
go at this time.

Not all bishops were actively involved in the amendment process.
When modifications of the NCD draft were made the interventions of

Cardinal Baum of Washington, Cardinal Medeiros of Boston, Cardinal Cooke and Bishop Mahoney of New York, and Bishop Welsh of Arlington, Virginia, were decisive. Archbishop Peter Gerety of Newark, on the other hand, had two of his amendments rejected (Nos. 128 and 147), that would have eliminated from NCD those sections that spoke of religious submission of will and mind to the Pope and immoral methods of family limitation.

In the aftermath of the bishops' meeting, the most important question to be asked is this: How did bishops permit a document to develop over four years in ways so alien to bishops' thinking that last-minute surgery was required? The woman religious who complained about bishops undoing quickly what a committee labored hours and sometimes years to compose seems legitimate. The NCD committee did eliminate some dubious presentations one at a time. But how did a definition survive almost until the very end that called matrimony "a free union of two people joined in and by a loving covenant through which they give themselves to one another"? The homosexual implications of the definition are too clear. The fact, also, that no one at the bishops' meeting rose to question the overdependence of NCD on the psychological theories of Lawrence-Kohlberg indicates how far the bishops as a body trusted staff to make some hard decisions on their behalf. With some nudging from Rome, the bishops reclaimed control of the theological questions, but if the pedagogical presuppositions are questionable, this theological victory may be pyrrhic.

The difficulty bishops had with the National Catechetical Directory is only one side of their larger problem. As the NCCB itself reported to the Roman Synod on Catechetics: "Religious education became [after Vatican II] one of the major battlegrounds for those who had opposing views on the Church and the world." This fight will not end with a document. Some bishops, leaving Washington after approving the revised NCD, feared that staff would manage to devise a commentary that explained away the true significance of the bishops' own amendment. Religious educators—now a special elite in the Church distinct from Catholic schoolmen—are happy with the new catechetics and its emphasis on liturgy and the Word of God. They tend to take for granted that human experience and social science will bring desired results, because each will make textbooks and classroom discussions more meaningful. They also approve the movements toward greater parent involvement, the emphasis on love rather than fear, as motive, the new ecumenical awareness, and their own improved professional status. When criticized they place blame for poor results not on their methodology, but on general breakdown of cultural order or on the rift between theologians and Magisterium, which was not of their making.

Parents, pastors, and bishop generally—certainly the major congregations in Rome dealing with doctrine, sacraments, and clergy—have not been uncritical observers of the contemporary catechetical scene. Parents were the first witnesses to the breakdown in their young of "thinking with the Church." When the son or daughter after Vatican II came home saying "Sister says," the cited opinion often was not thinking with the Church at all. Pastors and bishops came to know that new-style presentations were frequently limited in cognitive content, when they did not omit, downgrade, or distort some vital tenets of Catholicity. Teachers trying to prove that Christ was no legalist frequently provided the young with an abundance of legal loopholes to escape their moral or canonical responsibilities.

Rome from the beginning saw that religious educators and dissenting theologians frequently were partners in evading official documents, that some important spokesmen for their ideas neither wanted a General Catechetical Directory from Rome nor a national directory approved by Washington. Indeed, some catechetical leaders had reached the point in their lives of feeling that since teaching religion might lead someone out of the Catholic Church, teachers should live with this as "useful tension." Fr. George MacRae had something like this in mind when he told the Albany Forum that catechists "find themselves caught in the crossfire between theology and the official Church. They are expected to have a certain loyalty to official positions and at the same time are required to be acquainted with contemporary theological positions. When discussing religion with young people, such a posture can put great demands on teachers' integrity. They do not wish to dismiss the institutions as irrelevant. Nor do they wish to accept theological positions without criticism . . . It is unfair to indoctrinate them or to give them a false sense of uniformity in the Church" (pp. 22–23). There are others still who go further and deny that catechesis should be restricted to the Catholic view of Christianity, or even to the Christian view of the human race.

These challenges from uncertainty have prompted local bishops and Rome itself to set up their own catechetical centers and diocesan guidelines. The larger difficulty, however, still remains, compounded in part by the lethargy of bishops. When the NCCB in preparing a report for the 1977 Roman synod on the subject solicited views from bishops, less than 30 per cent responded.

The final authoritative word from Rome on the NCD was conveyed to the president of the NCCB, Archbishop John R. Quinn, on October 30, 1978, by the Congregation for the Clergy. Calling the American directory "outstanding for its ecclesial spirit, its clarity of expression, its emphasis on memorization of basic prayers and doctrinal formulations, its solid argument and flexibility," the Congregation nonetheless added that "there are certain points of importance that should be reworked before the publication of the first edition." These are: First, the word "revelation" is to "signify public, divine revelation in the strict sense"; some other expression must be chosen to indicate other forms of God's manifestation to men. Secondly, not only "should the *catechesis* for the Sacrament of Reconciliation precede First Holy Communion, but youngsters should normally *receive* the Sacrament of Penance before their First Communion." Also, general absolution is to be administered rarely and only in serious circumstances. Thirdly, "the specific nature of the priesthood should be more exactly expressed." The priest "acts not only in the *name* of Christ but 'in the person of Christ'" and his priesthood differs from that of deacon and unfaithful "essentially and not only in degree." These subject areas—revelation, first confession, priesthood—have in recent years been broadly interpreted by certain theologians and religious educators who opt for a more contemporary understanding of these terms. The broad interpretations permit an ecumenical reading of scripture and tradition against hitherto official Catholic positions, the downgrading of private penance as a necessary instrument for the forgiveness of sin, and a more horizontal, rather than a hierarchical, priesthood. All of the stricter views are imbedded deep in the Catholic tradition and pose difficulty for those seeking the reunion of Christian bodies.

Rome to the contrary notwithstanding the long-range interpretation of what NCD will mean at the parish level may be written in Washington, D.C. As of this writing the USSC has decided on an official *Commentary* on the NCD text. The dominant influence on the composition of this *Commentary* will be Fr. Bernard I. Marthaler, chairman of the Department of Religion and Religious Education at the Catholic University of America. Fr. Marthaler's thinking is somewhat at odds with Roman understandings. Immediately prior to the NCD corrections imposed on the American bishops by the Congregation of the Clergy, Fr. Marthaler declared himself in favor of the concept of "ongoing" or "continuing" revelation as against the traditional opinion that revelation strictly speaking "closed at the end of the Apostolic age." Writing in the *Military Chaplain's Review* (Fall 1978, p. 83), Marthaler considers the traditional view (which Rome has upheld) to be represented by "a hard-core and articulate minority of Catholics." He called the three-year fight over the meaning of revelation "a struggle which has extensive ramifications for the ministry of the Church in general and for the catechetical ministry in particular." This priest who has been called upon by the USCC to be the architect of the final meaning of NCD considers himself a "revisionist" in theological and catechetical matters. Speaking of the rise of neo-orthodoxy, even among Protestant religious educators, Fr. Marthaler wrote the following: "I appreciate the supportive atmosphere of the neo-orthodox context. It is a shelter in which I often take refuge to find respite and rest from the struggle to design a revisionist catechesis" (*Religious Education*, January–February 1977, p. 37).

### III. Catholic Agencies in Washington, D.C.

The chief executive of any organization rarely has trouble with his own staff. Hand-picked to serve his general purposes, the staff does research, provides input, gives counsel, does legwork, and represents "the chief" whenever that role is needed. The term "White House," for example, may mean the President or his staff. Ordinarily it makes no difference. They are presumed to be one.

The staff of the local bishop is called "the chancery office." The staff of the national body of bishops is the United States Catholic Conference.

A contemporary problem for the American bishops is that the USCC at times seems to be running the Church on a different track than the National Conference of Catholic Bishops, who are the employers. The composition of NCD was merely one example of what many bishops consider is a common occurrence—namely, USCC represents a constituency other than bishops.

Prior to Vatican II this could not be said. The Catholic Conference from World War I, staffed by some of the Church's great names—Fr. John Burke, C.S.P., Msgr. George Johnson, and Msgr. John A. Ryan—was totally subordinate to bishops on two counts: control of individual staff by a watchful executive secretary, who himself answered to a Board tightly managed; and ready resistance from individual bishops whenever a Washington priest seemed to interject policies at variance with those of the local diocese. Even a Conference aide with the stature of Msgr. Ryan—who was on the safe ground of promoting papal policy on social matters—treaded lightly on local bishops' toes. The Church was no different than the political order of the time. Anything coming out of Washington was looked upon with suspicion. In fact, bishops often paid their tax to the national office in the quiet hope that their fealty ended with the mailing of a check. Important metropolitan archbishops or cardinals had such a modest opinion of the Washington operation that they rarely permitted their priests to work there. Some refused for another reason—namely, that priests who went to the capital city to represent the Church became priests who represented instead the mind of Washington to the Church.

With the changes in federal government since World War II have come changes also in the United States Catholic Conference. The opening of Vatican II marked the second shift. Both bureaucracies have grown in numbers and power. Bishops, like elected officials, come and go, but the bureaus remain with staff. Staff unsupervised but well subsidized can develop organizational muscle. When that happens bishops, like Presidents, can be intimidated, especially if they go to Washington hardly more than one week out of the year.

The difference between the present USCC and its predecessor is simply stated. Hitherto, if tension existed between the National Conference and its bishops it was for the reason that conference staffers were promoting policies of the Holy See to which individual American bishops assigned a lower priority. American bishops felt more comfortable in those days working for Catholic education than involving themselves in sociopolitical questions, although Rome was clearly in favor of one almost as much as the other. Many bishops would not publish statements of the National Catholic Welfare Conference (as it was known then) on economic questions, and diocesan newspaper editors like Patrick Scanlon of the Brooklyn *Tablet* regularly attacked NCWC's Social Action Department.

In recent years, however, the disagreements of bishops with USCC staff cover a wider range. Some of the bishops still deny that the Washington office represents their viewpoint, but the complaints cover a wider spectrum of issues. Some of the differences are a matter of public record—on the National Catechetical Directory, "Call to Action," on the politics of "right to life." Some of the differences have not surfaced or are covered over by the administrative board of bishops. While many staff positions, to the annoyance of some bishops, are one-sided presentations of complicated issues, it is in the area of religious education that the serious grumbling has gone on. When one USCC staffer, for example, tells religious educators in Virginia that the new rite of baptism intends to make the baptism of infants the exception, not the rule, or another after reviewing a catechetical text informs the publisher that "Scripture scholars tell us that this [original sin] was most probably a commentary on the sin of David, which was later adapted to the first book of the Bible," bishops most sympathetic to staff work have reason to question the reliability of the counsel given in their name.

There are also published clues to directions of several USCC and other Washington-based agencies that have been a source of wonder and anxiety to some bishops.

1. Fr. Thomas Kramer, when executive secretary of the National Conference of Diocesan Directors at the USCC, reviewing four new catechisms for the *New Catholic World* (July–August 1976), found much to praise in the two that lacked an *imprimatur* and much to criticize in the two that had an *imprimatur*. He found *The Common Catechism*, a scholarly and ecumenical effort, to be "the most interesting and stimulating of all," even though in its effort to be ecumenical this catechism treats many points of Catholic doctrine unsatisfactorily. To cite one example, *The Common Catechism* reads: "The resurrection of Jesus means, therefore, that God identifies himself with Jesus and his cause in a way appropriate to the God of the Living." (p. 183). At no time does the book say that Jesus actually rose or was raised from the dead. *An American Catholic Catechism*, which originally appeared in two issues of *Chicago Studies*, is also praised for its chapters on moral law and personal conscience, according to Kramer "among the best in the book." In Part II of the Chicago catechism (p. 233), author John Dedek, asking whether there are any absolute precepts, says: "The prohibition of adultery, abortion, premarital sex, contraception, sterilization, masturbation, etc., are concrete moral norms. In the past Catholic moral theologians described these actions as intrinsically evil, immoral in themselves, and therefore always forbidden under any circumstances. Today, however, many Catholic moralists argue that concrete moral norms are not absolutely binding." Richard McCormick in the same section (p. 251), asking whether an individual act can be a mortal sin, responds: "A significant number of authors have begun to deny this. They argue that human freedom (core or fundamental freedom) is such that it can be realized only in a series or pattern of acts. Thus they see mortal sin as a process no single act of which need be or even can be a mortal sin. Rather mortal sin is committed over a period of time."

When Kramer came to judge John Hardon's *The Catholic Catechism*—a best seller among Catholics—he finds "he would not recommend this book for individual reading, nor for group instruction at any level." Hardon, according to Kramer, is preoccupied with law, ritual, and Scholastic theology, not with mystery, symbol, and the human dimension. Kramer seems most annoyed, however, with *The Teaching of Christ: A Catholic Catechism for Adults*, not the least reason being its sexist language. Cardinal Wright's Introduction irks him also because of the prelate's assertion that parents in some places have had to pull "as if from the burning, their children from the hands of mere professional religious education." Kramer expresses his greatest uneasiness with the title, as if the teaching of the Catholic Church as presented is identifiable with the teachings of Christ. He objects specifically when "the authors attribute to Jesus clear intentions for the formation of the Church," when "the Genesis account of creation and the fall, the infancy narratives of Matthew and Luke . . . are discussed almost as being literally true," when they speak of "the seven sacraments instituted by Christ without any qualification." In summary Kramer says, "This book is a clear, smooth exposition of traditional Catholic theology," but hardly the best kind of religious instruction.

2. On November 17, 1977, as the National Catechetical Directory was receiving amendment and final approval from the bishops, Fr. Robert P. Stamschor, who succeeded Fr. Kramer as executive secretary of the National Conference of Diocesan Directors of Religious Education, wrote to diocesan directors concerning the future implementation of the new NCD text, which was to involve activity by his office. A commentary on the NCD itself and compatible teaching tools were items high on his agenda. Then speaking of the forthcoming national convention of directors in Milwaukee (1978), Stamschor proposed one area of major study for the convention: "Pastoral and philosophical reflections on some of the principal challenges to clear vision and effective change: *Specifically institutionalism and the alienated and a positive response to conservatism*" (italics added). Since the bishops' final amendments to NCD were considered "conservative" of Catholic doctrines and procedures that the staff glossed over, "positive response to conservatism" by CCD directors would of its nature be directed in part against bishops.

3. Msgr. W. Paradis, the most recently appointed chief officer of USCC's Department of Education, reported on the 1977 Roman synod dealing with catechetics in *The Living Light* (Spring 1978), a USCC publication. Paradis was one of three advisers to the six American bishops attending as delegates. His report, called "Excerpts from a Personal Journal" is interesting for what it insinuates more than for what it clearly articulates, but it is nonetheless typical of how contemporary staff men approach their work for bishops. Take the question of "dissent." Although this subject was rejected by the American bishops for the NCD (on the grounds that dissent had no place in catechesis), Paradis reports an effort in Rome during the synod to have the delegates of the NCCB intervene to have the subject matter treated by the synod as a whole! This proposal was rejected again by the bishop delegates. Toward the synod's end Paradis finds the proposed synodal state-

ment defective for many reasons, one of which was its failure to "inform people on the various levels of assent that can be given to noninfallible teaching." This is merely the other side of the dissent question. By downgrading noninfallible teaching catechists legitimate dissent on many levels. The bishops rejected the ploy, but Paradis is disappointed. He also is distressed that the bishops too frequently describe catechesis as education or formation. In Paradis' judgment this leaves little room for "the God we experience now." It also leaves less room for tampering with doctrine.

At the end of this "Personal Journal" of the Roman synod, the chief officer of USCC's Department of Education muses about the experience: "Was it all worth the time invested and the money?" His answer: "Only the quality of the papal statement on catechetics that will very likely appear in some twelve to eighteen months will answer that question."

4. Even though the book *Human Sexuality* had been criticized by the bishops themselves on doctrinal counts, *The Living Light*, a publication of the United States Catholic Conference, published a review of the book (Winter 1977) that called it "a welcome and valuable contribution to the continuing dialogue that goes on in the Church community" for the reason that "few have complete and untroubled certainty about the rights and wrongs of sexual behavior." The reviewer adds: "*Human Sexuality* helps us to take positions with coherence and consistency and with an assurance that leaves room for flexibility."

5. Confusion over how best to implement basic Catholic goals continued to pervade the USCC operation as late as November 1978, when immediately prior to the bishops' meeting, the creation of a permanent episcopal Commission on Marriage and Family Life was announced. The USCC-appointed committee membership failed to include any notable supporters of *Humanae Vitae*. In fact several appointees are considered ambivalent on the papal encyclical which shook the Catholic upper intellectual world in 1968. Since any future Catholic commission on marriage (presuming the Church's continued belief in its own doctrine) would be entrusted in part with turning Catholic public opinion around on such subjects as contraception, sterilization, and abortion, the appointments were hard to explain. Even more surprising was the nomination of Dr. William McCready as the only nationally known commission member. McCready is a well-known dissenter from *Humanae Vitae*, co-author of the volume *Catholic Schools in a Declining Church*, which called the encyclical "an organizational and religious disaster." He is also on record with a definition of religion (*NC News*, May 28, 1974) which is far removed

from Catholic understanding and is highly critical of the Catholic hierarchy (*NC News*, April 9, 1976). Questions about the propriety of such an appointment have been raised with the highest officers of the American Church. Of special concern is the effect of a dissenter's presence in a bishops' commission on Catholic leaders who have sacrificed personal gain to defend the doctrine which the American bishops with the pope have taught as binding on the faithful.

6. Other groups not directly under the control of the bishop and that may have greater influence than the USCC on the thinking of diocesan catechetical leaders include the National Catholic Education Association and the Federation of Diocesan Liturgical Commissions. The NCEA's National Conference of Directors of Religious Education published a *Curriculum Guide* for religious education programs that is defective from a doctrinal point of view. Its treatment of the Eucharistic celebration (pp. 14–15) offers eight recommended concepts to be developed by teachers: Eucharist as a meal, "Jesus is with us," "We come to listen to God's word," "We thank God," "We tell God how much we love him," "We show love for each other," "Jesus gives himself in the Eucharistic bread," and "The Eucharist is the Bread of Life." One need not be a doctrinal purist to ask: Where is the treatment of the Eucharist as the body of Christ? To say that "Jesus gives himself in the Eucharistic bread" does not seem to express adequately what the Church teaches.

On April 12, 1977, at NCEA's national convention in San Francisco, religious educator Fr. James Schaefer of Baltimore gave an address on the question: "Can the Roman Catholic Church tolerate the emergence of mature believers?" He was critical of *Humanae Vitae*, the Vatican Declaration on Sexual Ethics, and the bishops' pastoral on moral values, *To Teach as Jesus Did*. He saw the Church's problem as preoccupation with orthodoxy and behavioral choices at variance with authoritative moral teachings.

In NCEA's official bulletin, *Momentum*, which is published quarterly for the Catholic educators of the United States, an article appeared (December 1977) by Samuel M. Natale, S.J., entitled "The Quest for a Humanized Sexuality." The author, beyond analyzing without serious criticism CTSA's *Human Sexuality* and drawing on Planned Parenthood (notably on SIECUS and Lester Kirkendall, one of its veteran spokesman from the academe), writes this paragraph:

Who is the final arbiter when social science and the tradition of the Church clash head on? This is the overwhelming task of the classroom teacher who seeks to educate rather than propagandize. Anyone could indoctrinate a child with dogma or, on the other hand, advocate a current psychological position regardless of its long-term implications. The courage to teach must involve the ability to present both points of view with respect for both, and then back off.

Fr. Natale, a university professor of psychology, turns a suitable technique for counseling agitated clients into a teaching tool of Catholic teachers in classrooms of the young. Through the medium of NCEA his viewpoints are carried to teachers throughout the country, including one that considers *Human Sexuality* a step backward in forward thinking because it presumes that such an independent reality as sexual ethics exists at all.

7. Liturgical commissions are also important because liturgical practices are based upon dogmatic concepts. Underground liturgies are underground because they reflect doctrines that the Church does not accept. An example of the interrelationship is contained in a paper given in 1976 by Fr. Tad Guzie, S.J., at the IX Regional Meeting of the Federation of Diocesan Liturgical Commissions. His topic was "The Rite of Christian Initiation of Adults: A Rite for Adults Only?" Guzie's introduction of his thesis begins with the sentence: "Although infant baptism is an ancient practice which can be theologically justified, the adult rite implicitly cancels the theology of original sin which, for well over a millennium, has provided the main reason for baptizing infants." By reason of the accident of history baptism became "your ticket into the Church" and "the credit card which you simply had to have in your purse or wallet if you were to get anywhere in Christendom." Guzie alleges that the new rite makes adult baptisms "normative," the baptisms of children "derivative" because the new rite prescinds "from the idea that there is anything like an original stain, which needs to be washed away as soon as possible." Baptism does not even constitute our entrance into the Church. So maintains Fr. Guzie.

These are a few examples where bishops and priests connected directly or indirectly to the Washington scene, where national Catholic organizations, including USCC, flourish, are not always one on substantial Catholic matters. How these differences will be resolved is by no means certain. James Rausch, general secretary of the USCC before becoming bishop of Phoenix, tended to be protective of the national Catholic agencies. At a dinner on March 5, 1974, in his honor at Catholic University, Rausch took note of the hostility "regarding the manner in which I execute my responsibilities." He lashed out at critics of the new theology, especially those third parties "who are taking it upon themselves to exegete and theologize and engage in analysis without possessing the required tools of scholarship" and who "are assuming a role reserved to the official Magisterium by passing judgments on the orthodoxy of scholars." These critics, he thought, deserved public rebuke for pretending to possess a competency for which they are not qualified. It was generally presumed by observers that Rausch was echoing an earlier complaint of Raymond Brown (*NCR*, March 22, 1974), who became enraged at the free-wheeling, brutal, and at times savage attacks on new scholarship by *The Wanderer* and by featured columnists of the *National Catholic Register*. Frenetic expressions such as "heretic" and "apostatizing priest" were rashly used (*Origin*, October 11, 1973). That acrimonious controversy has receded in memory even as scholars such as Brown are coming under fire from scholars for different reasons. Last year, Fr. John McKenzie leveled stern criticism at Brown's hedging his convictions about the infancy narratives in Matthew and Luke. Says McKenzie: Brown "manages to avoid saying there is no historical evidence for the Davidic descent of Jesus, for the birth in Bethlehem or for the virginal conception, at the same time affording ample evidence for the perceptive reader to draw this conclusion" (*NCR*, December 2, 1977).

But in 1973 Brown was considered beyond criticism save by the "strident voices" of papers like *The Wanderer*. Rausch clearly came down on Brown's side without giving any notice to some things going on within the USCC itself. The secular press took notice of the one-sided rebuke. *Time*, for example, viewing the Rausch blast (July 8, 1974), astutely observed how bishops lately have begun to wield the hierarchical clout against "the right," once used exclusively against "the left." The excesses of "the right," which were many, occurred most often outside the bishops' own machinery, while those of "the left," the ones most freely criticized by the Holy See, frequently were occurring within the households of bishops themselves.

The tensions can be crippling for the Church because clearly defined Catholic doctrines are involved. The position of the Church on abortion, for example, is clear, precise, and absolute. Bishops assign a higher priority and value to the morality of killing an unborn fetus than they do to the social doctrines that are clear but whose implementations vary with circumstance and private judgment. Not every Catholic theologian agrees with this distinction. In articulate Catholic circles the bishops' preoccupation with abortion is considered obsession. At the very moment when ecumenical relations are mellowing, the charge is made, bishops raise a divisive issue, which exacerbates those relationships. Disagreement on this issue broke out within USCC itself during the 1976 presidential campaign between Gerald Ford and Jimmy Carter. The NCCB's executive committee of bishops met with both candidates. Press reports made it appear that Ford was more acceptable to Catholic bishops than Carter. USCC staff members were incensed. They wanted it made perfectly clear to the Catholic voter that the Church was not a "one issue" institution. Under pressure from staff, the NCCB bishops called a press conference (September 16) to deny "preference for either candidate or party." While making this disavowal, they issued at the same time a staff position paper providing evidence that the Democratic Party platform was more consistent with USCC positions than the Republican platform. The USCC paper treated customary interests of the Church such as right to life, poverty, health care, and education, but also offered counsel on South Africa, the Panama Canal, arms sales, handgun control, red-lining, and monetary credit. Staff supported more of these positions than bishops (*Origins*, September 30, 1976).

Bishop Rausch admitted that the public clarification was needed because "many staff members would have concluded they could no longer effectively do their work." At least four of the staff, perhaps more, were prepared to resign. Kenneth Briggs considered the reversal an indication of collegiality at work. Said Briggs: "What might have passed unchallenged in past years was directly confronted" (New York *Times*, September 26, 1976).

It has been several years since anyone was publicly fired from the USCC staff. Fr. Louis Colonnese was in 1971 for radical activity in South America (*Origins*, September 16, 1971). A few others have been recalled by their bishops. But differences, while sometimes ideological, occasionally indicate the bishops' failure to control their own bureaucracy. The bishops sometimes respond negatively to staff only indirectly by cutting or denying funds. One of the reasons for killing a national collection for communications media was some important bishops' displeasure with NC News, their own information agency. An examination of *Origins*, NC's documentary service (for the years 1971–72, 1975–77) discloses that, apart from official statements of Pope and bishops and their agencies, the individuals likely to grace the weekly pages are preferably those who are frequently critical of the Church establishment. The names of Theodore Hesburgh, Andrew Greeley, Avery Dulles, Richard McCormick, and Hans Küng have appeared with some regularity. Other Catholic spokesmen of reputation, supportive of Church policies, would never be well known in Catholic circles if their public fame depended on *Origins*. In the normal course of the year, one could expect that Jesuits John Hardon, Kenneth Baker, John

Sheets, Sister M. Claudia, Mrs. Phyllis Schlafly, Professor Germain Grisez, and Dr. Herbert Ratner—all of whom lecture widely—would have said something that deserved reporting by a bishop's documentary service. But their viewpoints are not documented in *Origins*.

## IV. The "Call to Action" Program

Less was said in 1978 than in 1977 of the "Call to Action" convention held in Detroit October 20–23, 1976 to celebrate the Bicentennial of the United States and the Catholic Church's involvement in that history. Two similar conventions were held—in 1893 to mark the four-hundredth year of Columbus' coming, and in 1899 to celebrate the Centennial of the American hierarchy. But no convocation in American Catholic history was quite like this. Initiated as a celebration of the nation and the Church, it may have passed into history without profoundly affecting either society.

The theme—"Liberty and Justice for All"—was a good one. Early complainers were pained that the bishops did not borrow the other theme in the country's pledge of allegiance—"One Nation, Under God." Nonetheless, as Bishop Rausch explained to the Catholic University audience in 1974: "Because of my personal orientation and because of what I believe is an objective assessment of the realities in our society, I see this as an extremely important event in the history of the Church in our country. Too many years have passed by since *Pacem in Terris* and *Gaudium et Spes*. Too little has resulted on the grass-roots level of the Church." Rausch anticipated no social progress "until our people, informed in Christ, have developed sensitive consciences to the issues involved." He looked upon the contemplated Detroit meeting as an opportunity to develop "a truly Catholic conscience on peace and social justice," one that would inspire the entire American community.

When the consultation process began in February 1975, Cardinal Dearden, who was to be host and chairman, established the goal as the involvement of the American Catholic Community in "the economic, political, and cultural benefit of all persons." His successor as chairman of NCCB, Archbishop Bernardin, later specified the criteria by which the Detroit assembly could be judged successful: evaluation of recommendations concerning sociopolitical issues, programs possible within the limited resources of the Church, and "the teaching of the Church, its laws and discipline."

The organization of "Call to Action" was placed in hands of the

United States Catholic Conference, under the leadership of Bishop Rausch.

Almost from the beginning the preparations ran into the kind of trouble that would plague the consultation process and the Bicentennial convention itself. Complaints began to be heard that "the hearings" were slanted and that the seminars conducted by the USCC were unrepresentative (*NCR*, February 25, 1975). When the final booklet, *Liberty and Justice for All*, appeared, the charges began to fly. Loudest of the critics was Fr. Greeley, who called it "a bitter and sometimes violent attack on American society," "a shabby, shameful, and disgraceful attack on the American people," "a product of the liberal wing of the American hierarchy" (*NCR*, February 8, 1975). "From support for Vietnam to America hating is a path the hierarchy has traveled with astonishing speed," concluded Greeley.

Almost at the same time as one booklet was out for evaluation, USCC published another volume—more scholarly in tone, but unflattering in its presentation of the economic accomplishments of American society. *Poverty in American Democracy* lays heavy stress on the abuse of the poor in the United States, the maldistribution of wealth, and the identification of the Church with power to the poor. Nothing at all is said about American economic progress or the accomplishments of American labor, nor did offer any criticism of the present welfare system, which at the time was widely criticized in secular forums.

From the other side of the political spectrum came the charge that the Bicentennial operation was on its way to becoming a defense of "bourgeois capitalism and pre-Vatican II Catholicism." Gary MacEoin, writing in *America* early during the consultation process (April 19, 1975), wanted a radical "Call to Action" convention, not a "balancing act" between conservatives and liberals. MacEoin called for raising the hard questions to Catholic consciousness like "the Church's continuing complicity with oppressive structures," for doing "to Karl Marx what Thomas Aquinas did for Aristotle," for understanding "the role of violence in the process of creation." He had little confidence in ecclesiastics having this kind of boldness, but he thought Catholic women might, especially nuns, because they had firsthand experience with society's oppressive structures, including those of the Church.

For the remainder of 1975 Greeley-MacEoin types exchanged views in a series of hearings held in Washington, San Antonio, Minneapolis, Atlanta, Sacramento, and Newark. The theory underlying the hearings was that grass-roots meetings with experts by a USCC-appointed panel would develop a good synthesis of Catholic views on how best to energize Catholic conscience on social-justice matters. The resulting "working papers" could then be used by diocesan delegates to the Detroit convention from which would derive recommendations to the bishops and to the general Catholic body.

The final recommendations of "Call to Action," formally published in January 1977 by the U. S. Bishops' Conference on Liberty and Justice for All, may be summarized as follows:

1. *On the Church*
   • Church accountability through parish and diocesan councils.
   • Due process, more consistent administration of the annulment process, voice in the selection of pastors and bishops, end to discrimination, evaluation of clergy, theological pluralism, fostering of vocations, return of laicized priests to ministry, ordination of married men, ordination of women.
   • Women involvement in ministry. Church decision-making, removal of sexist language from documents, girl altar servers.
   • Adult education programs, education boards, Catholic schools, nonpublic school aid (especially for poor), racial integration of public schools, involvement in public education, better homilies, scholarships, stress on social justice in NCD.
2. *On Personhood*
   • Develop parish community, small worshiping communities, women and youth in ministry, lay preachers, communion in hand.
   • Concern for the aging, support of prolife activities, justice for women, youth ministers, role and office for the handicapped, rehabilitation and government assistance also, end of institutional racism, support rights of prisoners, no new prisons, end to capital punishment, apostolate to ex-offenders.
   • Assistance in forming conscience on moral dimensions of human sexuality, freedom of conscience on contraception, sex education, pastoral care of homosexuals, and end to civil discrimination, care for rape victims.
   • A "Catholic Bill of Rights," including procedural rights to be included in the Revised Code of Canon Law.
3. *On Family*
   • Combat forces that threaten family, family life programs, family-centered worship, family social service, family ministry.
   • Family-action programs, public-policy legislation, political action, media input and evaluation.
   • Pastoral care of separated, divorced, divorced/remarried, end to discrimination. Reception of Communion under certain

conditions, study of breakdowns, repeal of the penalty of automatic excommunication.

4. *On Neighborhood*

• Renewed parish leadership, strong but small Eucharistic communities, ordination of leaders from the community, sacramental preparation, neighborhood community groups, interfaith coalitions, care in selecting pastors.

• Person-to-person assistance, budgeted training programs for leaders, community organization, local support services, political-action programs subsidized, welfare programs, special apostolate to inner city and to collegiate neighborhoods.

• Church support for the powerless, including their use of Church property and resources, parish accountability for its priorities and financing, programs of sharing funds between parishes, social-justice courses, neighborhood involvement in school closings, advocacy for poor through Catholic agencies.

• Rural life offices and ministry, farmland preservation, protection of farm workers, new ministries to rural people, better allocation of funds to rural dioceses to alleviate rural poverty, especially in Appalachia, support of rural wage earners, including migrants and small-businessmen.

5. *On Humankind*

• Diocesan office of peace and justice, national office with staff, related educational programs even at parish level (especially workshops), invite Third World speakers, organize grass-roots groups.

• Defend human rights internationally, no support for offenders, special attention to multinational corporations, investments made with justice in mind, end to malnutrition, more generous Catholic support, more simple lifestyle, protection of undocumented immigrants and political prisoners everywhere.

• Condemn nuclear weapons and their production, emphasize at parish level evils of arms race, support conscientious objectors, amnesty for Vietnam resisters, disclosure concerning war prisoners, another ministry to soldiers besides chaplaincy, identify with suffering people in South Africa, Chile, Iron or Bamboo Curtain countries, Korea, the Philippines, Northern Ireland.

6. *On Nationhood*

• Political responsibility to participate in decision-making, parish committees.

• Programs for peace and disarmament, protection of human

life from the beginning, the elimination of poverty, racism, crime, insecurity of employment, reform of tax laws, public-health plan for all, limit land speculation, decent housing, students' rights, endorsement of ERA, amnesty for un-documented aliens, unconditional amnesty for all draft, military, and civilian resisters to the Vietnam war, better public assistance.

• Criticize national policy on abortion, peace, hunger, discrimination, research exploring alternative economic structures, raise awareness of manipulation of public opinion by media.

• Ongoing consultation in Catholic life structured into Church, dialogue with bishops through special task force.

7. *On Ethnicity and Race*

• Distinguish problems of ethnicity from those of race, proportional representation in forming and implementing Church policy, affirmative-action programs within diocese, budgetary commitment to combating discrimination.

• Cultural diversity, positive response to cultural demands, multilingual education programs, correction of media stereotyping, scholarly research on diversity, cultural forms in worship, ethnic representation in hierarchy.

• Honor treaties with American Indians, Indian secretariat, quality education, leadership training, increase awareness of Indian contribution, special ministry.

• Office for black Catholics and Spanish-speaking, USCC office to implement policy, research on needs of poor whites, education programs, legislative and social action to eliminate racism (influence media to this end), diocesan task force.

8. *On Work*

• Equal employment opportunity in dioceses and USCC, pastoral letter on subject, use investment leverage (especially in Third World countries).

• Full employment, education on practical programs, teach social doctrine in schools, endorse ERA.

• Social doctrine taught in seminaries, promote unions actively, fight right-to-work laws, participation by workers in management, aid farm workers, support amnesty for undocumented immigrants, end of human-rights abuse. Expose multinational corporations that force emigration, affirmative action for Vietnam era veterans.

• Pastors should be trained in Catholic social teaching, pastoral centers to support working people, vocational counseling, ongoing dialogue with economic leaders.

Reaction to the "Call to Action" convention, which attracted 1,340 delegates, depended on how the bystander viewed the final product—that is, the recommendations—and how one judged the value of the consultation process organized by the USCC. A majority of Catholics, if polled, probably would endorse a majority of the recommendations because they met Archbishop Bernardin's criteria for a successful meeting. Not only were the majority of items proposed relevant to social justice and compatible with "the teaching of the Church, its laws and discipline," but also they demanded merely the outpouring of fresh determination and organized effort by Catholics. Only a quarter of them needed formal approval from bishops. The body of the document needed only encouragement and support from bishops.

Why then did "Call to Action" not have greater impact than it did?

There are no easy answers to this question, but three things are part of any answer:

1. Many recommendations had little to do with Catholicism as such.
2. Many recommendations derived from other than Catholic doctrine.
3. The consultation process was faulty.

### 1. Remote "Catholic Concerns"

Whenever social doctrine is an issue there are at least two expected Catholic responses—from those who know what it is, and from those who do not. Catholics familiar with the thought imbedded in modern papal encyclicals expect the Church to sponsor a host of recommendations on sociopolitical problems and on matters of war and peace. This group would accept such preachments even though in practice their own vested interest might have them wish for something else. Informed Catholics, too, understand that it is the responsibility of the Church to enlighten unenlightened Catholic social consciences through programs and task forces at every level possible. Furthermore, recommended political-action programs for parishes, as potential channels to political power centers, can give Catholics a voice they never had before. Finally, since social-justice issues tend to be complicated, Catholics, generally, though not universally, might appreciate factual descriptions on specific controversies. Informed Catholic opinion on the plight of agricultural or garment workers cannot be left to the secular media alone. Since Catholic bishops have access to special data, they legitimately can pass these on to their own constituency in the interest of even-handed justice, as long, of course, as the bishops' treatment of such subject areas is itself even-handed.

On the other hand, most Catholics are likely to raise their eyebrows at the suggestion of "Call to Action" that there is a necessary or inevitable link between "liberty and justice" and the removal of sexist language from Church documents, gay rights bills, inviting Third World speakers to parish halls, unconditional amnesty for draft dodgers, ERA, racial-ethnic ratios for Catholic hierarchy, and some other specific demands presented in such a way as to suggest these are Catholic issues.

If Detroit was a "Catholic milestone," as the Jesuit *Center of Concern* said (January 1977) because it involved "listening to the rank and file at parish and diocesan levels," then something went wrong in Detroit. Parishioners would consider many recommendations the warp and woof of what separates Democrats from Republicans, not Catholics from each other. More than one reporter on the scene looked upon the final product as a political platform about which conscientious religious thinkers would be on both sides of many issues.

Those recommendations, however, were the direct product of working papers with a predetermined viewpoint. More than Fr. Greeley has made this observation. One respected Catholic editor said Detroit represented mainly a segment of lower-echelon Church bureaucrats and a host of special-interest groups, where emphasis seemed to be on the reformation of Church and social structures that they did not like. Corruption in labor unions and poverty programs, the widening stranglehold of government bureaucracy on human rights and freedom received no attention at all. Indeed, the solution offered for problems of liberty and justice was a demand for more bureaucracy both in the Church and in government. What USCC hearings disposed for the content, the writing teams composed. According to the official booklet: "The writing committees have addressed their recommendations to different levels of Church authority and Church membership." The writers were the ones who framed the wording of the resolutions and the recommendations. While the delegates were chosen by the individual bishops, the writers were selected by the USCC staff. The eleven writers from the archdiocese of New York, if they were representative of USCC selections across the country, could easily have been made by the editors of *Commonweal* or the *National Catholic Reporter*. Joseph and Sally Cunneen, Sidney Callahan, Philip Scharper, and Dorothy Dohen are well-known people of talent, but they represent only one segment of thought in the Catholic community. As a final touch and to guarantee that the written resolutions were processed correctly through the delegates, the USCC chose Msgr. John Egan of Chicago and Notre Dame to be the chairman with the gavel. Egan was committed in advance to the final recommendations.

2. *Other than Catholic Doctrine*

Most conventions have specific directions to ban certain items from discussion. Convention managers see to that. George Meany hardly permits a serious effort to abolish wage rates, no more than Franklin Roosevelt in the 1940 Democratic convention permitted resolutions to favor Adolf Hitler. The Catholic bishops in their first experience of this kind allowed "Call to Action" to get away from them on doctrinal matters. This occurred in the advocacy of freedom of conscience in using contraceptives, in recommending the ordination of women, and in the frequent references to homosexuality without necessary distinctions.

These confrontations with Church doctrines may have been given undue notice by the media. Yet USCC organizers knew in advance the attention these resolutions would receive. Bishops stood aside seemingly unaware that the "consultation process" itself is now an important instrument on the American scene in opinion-molding for change. The hierarchy, which once wrote a pastoral letter (1961) entitled "Unchanging Duty in a Changed World," were made to appear parties to a process of change where change is not coming. Though the doctrine may not change, Catholic opinion and practice does change, especially if abetted by bishops themselves.

The question involved is not one of political strategy or its lack. A precise theology was at work. Richard McBrien saw "Call to Action" as an instrument of breaking new ground as to what the future Church will be about with the remark: "The Detroit conference uniformly adopted the 'People of God' image of the Church as the primary focus of self-understanding." Future policy decisions, he indicates, are "to be formulated in and through a collaborative process involving all whom the decision affects" (*NCR*, November 12, 1977). Monarchy is out, said the theologian. Since actual decision-making at end point always involve a monarch ("Do this, not that"), the question for the bishops is: On doctrinal matters, who is to be the decision-maker?

Another puzzlement concerning Detroit centers on the unaccented aspects of Catholic doctrine. If, for example, a clear doctrine is involved (for example, on contraception), and in the ideal order sound Catholic thinking should begin from that point, why was more attention not paid to natural family planning? One line introduced as a afterthought from the floor rounded out what this bishop-sponsored convention had to say on the subject: "Each diocese should have established effective means of making natural family planning training available to all couples, including non-Catholics" (Call to Action Report). Since Detroit expected Catholics to begin their political thinking on disarmament with the many practical suggestions made on that subject, which is less directly involved with doctrine, one might properly expect more on natural family planning where Catholic doctrine is clearly involved.

3. *Faulty Consultation Process*

Those who endorse the recommendations, though embarrassed by the tone or rashness of some, turn criticism of Detroit aside with the affirmation: "It was the consultation that counted." They deny that the representativeness of the assembly was important. What if Everyman in the pew was not represented? What if the largest Catholic organization—the Knights of Columbus—was not invited, while the homosexual group Dignity was actively involved? The people who came represented, it is argued, an authentic voice of Christ living in his Church today.

If Detroit was Christ's voice, there was a tone that the mass of bishops had not planned on. Some bishops complained that the convention was not representative but, if so, as one lady from Fairfax, Virginia, reminded them later, it was their own fault (*America*, December 11, 1976). Bishops chose the delegates or had someone else do the choosing for them. Sometimes USCC's regional meetings ran with the opinions of their own appointees. At a meeting in Chicago on May 2, 1976, for a multistate region, the diocesan delegates were given a preset list of topics for buzz-group discussions. The main topics were to be ordination of women, use of contraceptives, role of the hierarchy, amnesty, disarmament, and criticism of the capitalistic system. These were alleged to be the major questions gleaned from parish consultations over two years. While some knowledgeable delegates never heard these items discussed anywhere in their diocese, the prescribed agenda could not be broken. In addition, the personal reflections of the buzz groups were passed on to the national office through previously chosen discussion leaders.

More than disagreeing or disagreeable social reactionaries or doctrinal purists are of the opinion that "'Call to Action' was captured by liberal extremists." This is the judgment of novelist Thomas Fleming, writing for the New York *Times* (January 16, 1977). He likened Detroit to George McGovern's zealots routing Mayor Daley's helots during the 1972 Democratic convention. A Catholic convention intent on adding a religious dimension to social life was expected to be something else. The issues were important and the process too. But the bishops let it get away from them. When will there be another? Snapped one bishop: "Maybe we'll try it again for the Tricentennial."

## V. *First Confession for Eight-year-olds*

Rarely has a conflict in the American Church been so trifling yet divisive as the one over making children go to confession before they make their first Holy Communion. Family spats over eight-year-olds seems inanity for a Church in turmoil on more serious counts, yet if anger is a measure of seriousness, then this battle between Rome and professional catechists in the United States is not a small skirmish. The involvement of parents and children makes this conflict doubly different. Unlike theological disputes that affect the faithful only indirectly, the first-confession fight is carried on in school halls with principals, in rectories with the parish priests. Feelings on all sides have acquired surprising depth, fanned by the intuitive sense of the combatants that the stakes are high. Sometimes the issues are phrased as if victory by Rome or the catechists means only the triumph of one legalism over another. The dispute, to be sure, involves law, someone's law, but much more is involved. How certain questions are answered on this single issue may depend the future of the Church as a saving institution. What should the Church say about sacraments and those who receive them? Who has the last word?

Rome is saying that pastors and parents must see that eight-year-olds go to confession before first Communion.

Catechists want pastors and parents—and catechists—to prefer the postponement of first confession by several years at least.

The underlying reasons for each position may not be so important as the reactions of religious educators to three important Roman statements on the subject. The educators have become increasingly irate.

When the General Catechetical Directory in 1971 sought an end to experimentation with the order of the first sacraments without explicit permission from the Holy See, the tendency to ignore the demand was justified on the pretext that the request was made in an Appendix, not in GCD itself. The National Conference of Catholic Bishops later requested (1972) permission to continue experimentation with the sacramental order for two more years. But when on May 24, 1973, two Roman congregations (on clergy and sacraments) summarily demanded that the postponement of first confession cease, reactions came on strong. Donald Thorman called the order "the *Humanae Vitae* of religious education." Parents and religious educators were not about to let "an arbitrary decision from Rome" take away their rights (NCR, September 14, 1973). Fr. Howard Basler of the Brooklyn CCD office explained it away and encouraged the contrary practice at the local level (*BT*, August 21, 1973). Peter Riga thought the American bishops are obligated to "blow the whistle on this abuse of authority. If they don't, then the American bishops will set back the cause of religious education in this country by a decade" (*NCR*, August 31, 1973). Attleboro Sr. Marie Forcier wanted to know how "men such as Cardinal John Wright and company can mislead the Pope in imposing on the universal Roman Catholic Church a reverse direction. Have they not yet awakened to the fact that we live in a pluralistic society where imposed uniformity does not hold anymore?" (*NCR*, May 17, 1973).

Four years more went by before Rome returned to the fray (March 31, 1977) by formally answering for the American bishops a direct question:

> "In the light of the Declaration of May 24, 1973, is it still to be permitted, as a general rule, to have first Communion precede the reception of the Sacrament of Penance in those parishes in which such a practice has been followed in recent years?"

"[Answer] The Sacred Congregation for the Sacraments and Divine Worship and for the Clergy have, with the approval of the Supreme Pontiff, given a negative answer.

"All experiments in reversing the order of the First Sacraments are expected to cease."

The NC report of reactions to this latest order followed customary patterns, reflecting the situation in a given diocese or the ideology of a journalist. The Catholic diocesan newspaper of Richmond thought the requirement to "be contrary to fundamental Church teaching"; in Worcester a "cause of some confusion"; in Davenport "an assertion of naked power" (*OSV*, June 19, 1977); in Newark the editor thought it "out of touch with the actual healthy development" (*Advocate*, June 9, 1977); in Brooklyn the editor saw the pastoral question "not how to deal with children but how to deal with cardinals" (*Tablet*, May 26, 1977). A religious educator from Rockford, Illinois, decided that Wright and Knox "will certainly not be faulted for sensitivity to psychological and pedagogical data" (*NCR*, June 17, 1977). Fr. Thomas F. Sullivan, who left the Chicago archdiocesan school system to take a post at Catholic University teaching religion, summed up his sentiments:

> Children have the same right as other Catholics to receive the Eucharist and so have no obligation to go to confession if they

are not in the state of mortal sin. Diocesan or parish regulations that demand that children go to confession first as a condition for being admitted to the Eucharist patently disobey
the law of the Church and violate the rights of its seven-year-
old members [*America*, September 10, 1977).

Dioceses already in conformity with the Vatican rules generally endorsed the reaffirmation as "laudable and necessary."

The arguments against Rome are contained in those newspaper comments—child's rights, parents' rights, local authority, better psychology,
better catechesis, expert opinion, and contemporary practice. Some
bishops also became dissenters to the mandated practice, notably
Bishops Joseph Hogan of Rochester and Charles Buswell of Pueblo,
Colorado. As early as 1973 Hogan thought the decree was "a personal
disappointment" (*NCR*, August 3, 1973). The national hierarchy itself
was ambivalent on the matter, first seeking delay in the implementation of the Roman directive, then releasing a study that was used
to postpone implementation. The thirty-five-page document prepared
by the USCC-CCD office, while proposed as a compromise position,
did not require compliance with the Vatican director. The one concession made to Rome was that catechesis for penance should precede catechesis for communion. Prior catechesis was the real intent of Rome,
not uniformity of sacramental order, the USCC report suggested. The
authors acknowledge that Rome had more in mind than this, but since
the Vatican directive did not have the force of law, return to the older
practices was in their judgment "neither possible nor desirable" (*Orgins*,
September 27, 1973).

Very little about first penance changed on the American scene after
that. Most dioceses conformed more or less, but at least fifty continued
to proceed as if Rome had not spoken. As the only major body of
bishops who sought exception to the general rule, the hierarchy's example by itself was sufficient justification at the local level to follow any
order that pleased. But Rome, including Pope Paul himself, returned to
the subject once more on April 30, 1976, in an unpublished letter to
Archbishop Bernardin. Cardinals Knox and Wright informed the president of NCCB that the Redemptorist Fathers in the United States had
asked what they should do about the "unduly elastic interpretation"
given in the United States to Rome's first-confession decrees. Bernardin
was advised further that Rome shortly intended to make formal response to the Redemptorists, but wished the American hierarchy to
have advance warning that the requirement of confession first "except
in cases clearly called for exception, is binding on the universal
Church."

Almost one entire year went by before public Roman response was issued (March 31, 1977). The delay was unquestionably the result of behind-the-scenes politicking by bishops who wanted no reaffirmation of the ruling at all. More than once Cardinal Wright had insisted that there was no tension between the Vatican and the United States Church (NCR, August 3, 1973). That statement can be accepted at face value because most American bishops were in accord with Rome on the discipline. The major difficulty seemed to be the management power of religious educators who had led large members of priests and nuns down a forbidden path with the passive acquiescence of many bishops. These educators were in a position to make a fuss within some dioceses, not unlike the stir theologians made over *Humanae Vitae*. Enforcement of the Roman decree would be castigated as "retreat," when it merely was calling troops back from fields where they did not belong in the first place.

The issue, simple in the beginning—an eight-year-old child and his *one-time* first confession had become imbedded in a hornet's nest where complicated issues did repose. No divine law tells Catholics when they should go to penance, let alone at eight years of age. Church law bound under pain of additional sin for members beyond the age of reason to receive Holy Communion during the Easter season. This required annual confession only for those conscious of mortal sin. In actual fact, therefore, there is not now an obligation on any Catholic to confess his sins at any time in the course of his life, unless he does become a mortal sinner.

What, therefore, is all the commotion about? Certainly not the obligations of eight-year-olds to confess. No one alleges today, nor did they in predevelopment psychology days, that tots can commit mortal sin.

The controversy is reducible to two propositions: (1) the right of the Church to set up a discipline that encourages frequent confession, devotional confession, the importance of seeing the relationship of a pure heart and the reception of the Eucharist; and (2) the correctness of the Church's judgment that this discipline should begin with children prior to their first Communion. Unlike other sacraments, the commonest reference historically to the Church's system of dealing with the forgiveness of sin is "penitential discipline." That discipline has varied at times allowing for Communion before penance. In recent centuries, because Communion was unduly delayed, penance tended to precede by several years. Pope Pius X put an end to this in 1910 by demanding in *Quam Singulari* that both penance and first Communion be available to children. And because at that time penance customarily preceded Communion for adults, the practice was made operative for children too. For five decades after 1910 young children trotted into confessional boxes a few days before they walked up the church aisle with their white armbands or white veils to "receive Jesus."

The one thing in favor of the post-1910 discipline, especially as it was made to function in the United States, is that it worked. Whatever Pope Pius X really intended for the details of administration, the discipline proved effective—if its purpose was to develop from an early age awareness of sin, the importance of the state of grace, and the habit of frequent confessions and Communions. The confessional lines on any Saturday afternoon or night prior to Vatican II—of young and old alike —are *prima facie* evidence of that fact.

In the burst of activity on behalf of renewal following Vatican II liturgists first, then sacramental theologians and religious educators, sought to improve on this performance—enriching the understanding of penance as distinct from Eucharist, striving to make the reception more personal, less routine, restoring the communal aspects of penance —that is, reconciliation with the Church body as with God himself. There was also an ecumenical dimension to be considered—new forms of reconcilation that might be acceptable to those Protestants who generally deny that Christ instituted such a sacrament at all.

During the process of making these improvements and adjustments, another successful discipline broke down. If the drop in Mass attendance has been large, the decline in the use of penance and reconciliation by Catholics, especially the young, has been precipitous. If older people, trained in that discipline, now go irregularly, if at all, the young, who do not know discipline in this area of Catholic life, have less impulse to "confess" their sins. The argument that those who do seek reconciliation experience Christ's redeeming favor with better meaning is valid only for a small minority. The older discipline, as part of the Church's socialization of members, never operated perfectly. Those who spent many years hearing confessions of children can testify to that, but confessors who remained in parishes saw those same children grow into pious Catholic adults.

Religious educators who determined that this sacrament, since it worked best on serious sinners, need be imposed least of all on children, took little account of how the Church's use of penance as a pious exercise and an opportunity for spiritual direction and growth had developed in this century. Concentrating on the sin element and using Piagetan psychology, which questioned whether anyone is responsible for wrongdoing until after age ten, educators pushed for the reversal of the customary order. They advocated the "love sacrament" (Eucharist), not the "guilt machine" (Penance) as the preferable way to initiate the young into the Christian mysteries. In order to make their case look

stronger, horror stories were circulated that seemed to justify penitential postponement. The religious editor of *Time* did not conjure this
following description by himself (September 3, 1973):

> The results (of first confession for half a century), many
> Catholic educators agree, were often disastrous. Some young
> penitents became haunted by the fear or mortal sin and going
> to hell. Others developed false consciences, accusing them-
> selves of sins that were only the harmless exuberances of a
> child. Still others dreaded the whole experience so fiercely that
> they gave it up for good as soon as they were able to. Those
> who continued to receive the sacrament were sometimes spirit-
> ually stunted, unable to go beyond the role formulation; vet-
> eran confessors recall adults as old as sixty-five who still
> confessed to disobeying their parents, even after the parents
> were dead. Even those who grew into a healthier under-
> standing of the sacrament often unconsciously tied it to the
> sacrament of the Eucharist, feeling unworthy to receive com-
> munion without confession, etc., etc.

The "etc., etc." sums up how hopeless the case for first penance was
made to seem in order for the new order of things to be initiated. Few
Catholics who experienced any of these horrors recognized this as reality in their week-by-week experience in the "black box." Overlooked,
too, were the great novelists who made first confession—even the pulling of a cat's tail—a matter of literary legend.

Throughout all of this byplay another message was going to Rome.
The "experiment" was no experiment at all. Unlike approved experimental liturgies that were carried on under controlled circumstances—
for example, on university or seminary campuses—the first-confession
trials were being carried on in parishes without any controls. Wherever
nuns or pastors could be persuaded to accept the new order as the wave
of the future, it was initiated. No laboratory tests determined whether
performance in confessional matters improved, what the ill effects of
"voluntarism" might be. Within a relatively short time Communion
was received by eight-year-olds who had no idea of what penance or
confession meant. In the absence of controls and successive testings,
there was no experiment.

Rome discovered that, contrary to the nature of true experimentation, pressure was being brought to bear on parents and children
to bypass first confession. Pressure became a weapon of unauthorized
change. Delegates of NCCB who attended the 1977 Roman synod on

catechesis—Archbishop Bernardin, Cardinal Manning, Archbishop Whealon, Bishop Lucker—were to endorse the Roman view that it is "an absurd and unjust discrimination and a violation of his conscience if he (the child) were prepared for and admitted only to Holy Communion. It is not enough to say that children have the right to go to confession if this right remains practically ignored." Reports were coming to Rome of parents who wished confession for their child first being intimidated to accept the new order. Those who resisted "impositions" from Rome were setting conditions of their own.

In 1973 the Canadian bishops asked Cardinals Knox and Wright to specify what they had in mind in seeking the enforcement of *Quam Singulari*. The clarifications turned out to be four: (1) No one child should be regimented; (2) no child should be prevented from first confession; (3) moral constraints (under penalty of sin) are not intended; (4) but the two sacraments should be prepared for in sequence. Rome is conscious of the child's rights but realizes too that parents, confessors, and pastors are trustees of those rights. Eight-year-old children, who are not ordinarily permitted to decide whether they can cross a city street, are not likely candidates to have final say over their spiritual direction or their sacramental preference. Recently religious educators had intervened to make choices for both parent and children. The Holy See disagreed with their choice. Rome wanted pastors to "gently lead" young children to first confession before Communion. In effect Rome has rejected the contrary discipline and the reasons that underlay the proposal of catechists. The practical questions remain about the implementation of that decision.

And as if to make sure that everyone understands the message, Paul VI used the *ad limina* visit of New York bishops to make a personal point: First confessions should precede First Communion. Said the Pope: "The norms of the Apostolic See [ought] not be emptied of their meaning by contrary practice" (*Origins*, May 4, 1978).

## VI. *The General-absolution Controversy*

The general-absolution controversy is more serious than the conflict over first confession, because this time Catholic doctrine is involved and it is bishops who are eluding, when not confronting, papal definitions.

What the Catholic Church thinks about the need for absolution from sins says a great deal about what the Church thinks about itself. The Church teaches that its priests have power from Christ to forgive man's sins. The Church does not usurp God's power to forgive sins directly, but asserts that for believing Christians the normal way of forgiveness is through the Church and the sacrament of penance. If believing Catholics willfully or maliciously refuse to submit to this discipline, they would be on the face of it in trouble with Christ himself and in effect unforgiven. Since the Church's basic purpose is like Christ's "to save people from their sins," this area of Catholic belief is not a matter of little importance.

Essentially, Protestants do not accept this understanding at all. In their view the Church can dispose, but forgiveness is directly a personal matter between God and the sinner. Rituals may be helpful and confession to a third party also, but these are matters of personal taste that should not interfere with the essential task of reconciliation.

One other difference between Catholics and Protestants is the stress among Catholics on the need for a visible sign that the sinful deeds or lifestyles are being left behind. This may mean only a firm expression to the priest that the sin will not be repeated. The priest may require more of penitents who are habituated to sin. This may be a request of a policeman that he seek a transfer from a station where corruption, in which he participates, is rife, or that a man give up a lady friend not his wife. Protestant theology does not call for such "invasions of privacy." The Catholic priest might even be obliged to refuse absolution and declare indisposed for communion a Catholic who did not give some evidence of "a firm purpose of amendment." The sacrament of penance and reconciliation calls for integrity on both sides. Absolution given to a mortal sinner with no serious intention of altering his lifestyle would be, in the Catholic view, invalid and collusion in additional sinfulness.

Certain concessions are made by the Church to human frailty and unexpected emergencies—without denigrating the essentials for forgiveness: sorrow for sin, confession of sin, willingness to atone through private or public acts of penance. The ritual for forgiveness is not objectified so absolutely that impossible demands are made on the weak, the sick, the old, or the dying. Priests freely dispense absolution *sub condicion*—that is, on condition that the basic intention of the Church is being served. Public emergencies—war, sudden calamity, great congresses of people in real need—have prompted the Church to recommend general absolution to those who, without a specific confession of sin, express only general sorrow. By so doing the Church continues to assert the centrality of the sacrament for forgiveness. When and if normality recurs, the "forgiven" Catholics in their turn are expected to follow the ordinary discipline of private confession for the serious "forgiven" sins. There are no exceptions to this prescription—unless death intervenes.

The exceptions to law and the accommodations to human need are in no way intended to undermine what is understood as Christ's general requirement—namely, forgiveness of sins for Catholics through the sacrament. The danger with ritual, of course, is that it can become a cover for insincerity or lawlessness on the part of priest or penitent. It is impossible to exclude fraudulent use, since penance is a sacrament of the "internal forum." At best Church authority issues guidelines and penalizes flagrant abuses, instruments that of themselves serve to keep a proper balance between the objective and the subjective elements in the sacrament.

The Congregation for the Doctrine of the Faith did issue guidelines for the administration of general sacramental absolution on June 16, 1972. As translated by one American bishop, the Vatican regulations read for the archdiocese of New York as follows:

> The new rite of penance permits general absolution in cases of serious necessity. It indicates that serious necessity involves the fulfillment of three conditions:
> • When in view of the number of penitents there are insufficient confessors at hand to hear properly the confession of each,
> • With the result that the penitents through no fault of their own would be forced to do without sacramental grace or Holy Communion,
> • For a long time.

Cardinal Cooke has decided in most areas of his archdiocese that "the necessary conditions are not presumed to exist." New York has many priests and few people would be denied access to confession or communion *for a long time.* But since the possibility always remains, especially in rural counties, general absolution services in New York—following the letter and spirit of the Roman decree—are permissible under the following additional conditions:

> • With the actual or presumed permission (later reported) of the chancellor or episcopal vicar.
> • The penitents intend to follow the usual confessional requirements later. (They may not participate in a second general-absolution service if they failed to honor the earlier commitment.)
> • The penitential service is not part of the celebration of Mass.
> • The penitential service was demanded by a factual emergency not the result of "public scheduling or announcement."

Why all those cautionary procedures? To prevent "general-absolution services" from becoming a substitute for private confession.

The "renewal" of the penitential discipline following Vatican II of its nature does present a few practical problems for pastors and bishops. Three forms of penance have been approved formally by the Holy See: private penance, public penitential service with private confessions, and communal penitential service with general confession and general absolution. Difficulty can arise when a pastor-bishop announces the second rite but is overwhelmed with people expecting absolution. In those circumstances bishops can permit and, where allowed, pastors may move to the third rite, which excludes private confession for the time being.

This three-stage ritual makes it possible for a bishop or priest to manipulate general-absolution services by staging a communal service with an offer of private penance which he knows will not work. He knows in advance, for example, he has not secured enough confessors or cannot use them. Some Catholic scholars accept this as development. If general absolution becomes frequent, the doctrinal differences with Protestants over penance may come to be less insurmountable. Workshops in Catholic circles already accentuate positively the widened use of general absolutions. Stress on private confession, except perhaps in the face-to-face situation, receives little emphasis. The forward movement is toward the use of communal services with general-absolution days during Lent and Advent, when the priest is fatigued and when confessions cannot be heard properly, as, for example, when the hour or the penitents are late. The trend is enhanced with the growth of feeling that communal penance with general absolution is really the superior form of reconciliation. Ottawa Archbishop J. A. Plourde, though cautious, leaned in this direction when he said: "Even today's penance services, this joy of having found reconciliation in common is lessened, almost disappears, when each one goes his separate way to receive individually forgiveness for the failings for which we are collectively responsible. A communal celebration on occasion would break the individualistic yoke of our self-examen, which too often fails to focus on our participation in the 'sins of the world'" (*Crux*, April 25, 1977).

Liturgists are inclined to favor frequent use of the communal practice. When Rome was being restrictive, the Liturgical Conference in Washington objected. In its view the central pastoral issue is not "Under what circumstances may general absolution be given?" but "How can people and ministers responsibly seek reconciliation and healing in their daily lives?" The liturgists wanted the individual local bishop to set the standards. *America* editorialized (December 25, 1976) toward the "unchallengeable conclusion" that "there are simply not enough priests to reach a growing number of alienated Catholics personally and in situations that really foster reconciliation. In addition, the gulf between the thousands of alienated Catholics and the institutional Church is, in a real sense, an 'emergency.' The risk of misunderstanding, especially on the question of marriage, is not insignificant and cannot be ignored, but far more important is the effort of one bishop and one diocese to extend the healing power of the sacrament to those who might otherwise have simply been untouched and thus forgotten."

But the "insignificant" aspects to general absolution are germane to the present controversy. Extending "the healing power of the sacrament" must be balanced by recognition of those audiences unprepared for reconciliation on Catholic Church terms. Though participants in what looks like a sacramental ritual, they remain untouched. The first public responses to the Memphis reconciliation came from the North American Conference of Separated and Divorced Catholics, which claims a membership of ten million. General absolution is seen by them as part of a struggle to persuade bishops to take a more permissive attitude toward Catholics who break Church law on a variety of moral issues. Not only remarried divorcés are interested in such a development but also homosexuals, those who practice contraception, and those who engage in premarital or extramarital sex. Priests commonly disregard these offenses on the parish level, or urge parishioners to settle the issue themselves in the privacy of their consciences. But a "fresh crop of bishops" are looked to for a more sympathetic approach to people that transcends regard for the strictures of law. General-absolution services become the signals of the new Catholic direction (New York *Times*, December 8, 1976).

*The Alaska Case.* Challenges to the use of general absolution in missionary dioceses are almost nonexistent. One of the first bishops to take advantage of the new rite of penance was Bishop Francis T. Hurley, then of Juneau, Alaska. In 1972 he initiated these services where the "emergency" he described resulted from an unusual mixture of a badly trained Catholic population living in isolated areas of America's forty-ninth state, frequently fearful for their lives, served by sixteen priests scattered over a dispersed coastline (*America*, September 23, 1972). Later, when he moved on to Anchorage as archbishop, the former USCC official, writing in his new diocesan newspaper (*The Inside Passage*), extended his justifying reasons somewhat:

Less obvious but no less real are other obstacles: fear of the "box," a bad experience with a particular priest, a long time away from the sacraments, a hangup on private confession, a lack of humility to admit one's sins to another, a lack of anonymity, inability to confess to the only priest available, inadequate religious training. . . . Many Catholics have been disenchanted with the Church and feel alienated by the authorities in the Church or by the institutional Church. Yet they love the Church and yearn for the sacraments. For many of them private confession poses a major obstacle until the alienation has been dissipated.

Archbishop Hurley has shifted his justifying reasons for general absolution from objective conditions (crowds, no freedom of choice of confessor, lack of anonymity) to include subjective states (that is, alienation). Though sacramental rites are not intended as psychological devices for motivating conversion, the inevitable question must be answered: Why should anyone choose the more difficult private confession, if serious subjective difficulties (for example, shyness) stand in the way? Under broad interpretation of the law, the erosion of the private penitential discipline is possible.

*The Memphis Case.* Rome objected strenuously to the use of the general-absolution rite by Bishop Carroll Dozier of Memphis, December 5, 1976. The reasons why Rome objected are contained in a letter sent to Archbishop Bernardin for all American bishops shortly after the event (*Origins,* March 3, 1977).

1. General absolution is not to be a focal point either of spreading the Gospel or reconciling sinners.
2. Large gatherings of the faithful are not to be convoked with general absolution in mind.
3. When large crowds can be anticipated—as during festivals or pilgrimages—arrangements for confessors should be made.
4. When held, communal celebration must be distinct from the celebration of Mass.
5. Invalidly married Catholics must intend to remove the scandal *before* general absolution and must remove the scandal *before* the reception of Communion.

According to Rome, anything less than the observance of these norms is "a serious abuse": "Let all pastors carefully prevent such abuses out of awareness of the moral duty enjoined upon them for the welfare of souls and for the protection of the dignity of the sacrament of penance. . . . New pastoral initiatives that go beyond the directives of the norms must not be introduced without prior consultation of and approval by the appropriate offices of the Holy See."

What did Bishop Dozier do to bring such a stern warning to all American bishops from the Holy See?

• He held a penance service with general absolution for 11,500 people in the Memphis Coliseum.

• In conjunction with the celebration of Mass.

• As a result of a well-planned and well-organized education campaign toward reconciliation in the diocese after what Dozier called "three months of total indoctrination." This effort included use of the media, pulpit, and classroom teaching aids.

According to the bishop, "the Memphis rites" were intended to be a reaching out to inactive Catholics and, after the fact, one young priest's remark to his bishop, "It was beautiful, wasn't it?" reflected the warm response of many participants. Few institutions are better at moving masses of people through public celebrations than the Catholic Church when effectively led by a determined and energetic bishop. Public rites are part of a Catholic tradition which, for example, brought hundreds of thousands of Catholics to Philadelphia in 1976 for one of the most moving Eucharistic Congresses ever held. Subsequent to the December 5 event a survey of Memphis priests, released by Dozier himself to indicate how right he was and how wrong his critics were, reported a rise in private confessions in parishes and marriage cases in the Memphis tribunal.

Apart from the positive results, the question raised with Dozier by his fellow bishops prior to December 5 is the one still to be answered: "Does general absolution under those circumstances weaken the penitential discipline of the Church?" (NCR, December 17, 1976). Many of Dozier's peers thought so and disassociated themselves from the action. Rome tried to head Dozier away from the rite almost as soon as he made the first announcement.

Rome has several sensitivities about this subject, not the least being penance services in conjunction with Mass. There are not wanting those in the Church who now think Mass itself is service enough for the forgiveness of sin. Rome also has strong views on "simulated sacraments"—that is, rites performed that have no meaning. In that category would be a ritual that would seem to absolve those who cannot be absolved or that would distribute unconsecrated hosts at Mass to those who may not properly receive Holy Communion. Furthermore, there is the question of "manufacturing" an emergency in order to take advantage of a legitimate accommodation that the Church has already made to meet peoples' needs. One such simulated emergency is the convocation of large crowds for the purpose of general absolution, knowing in advance that private confession is impossible. Rome sees no long-range pastoral advantage to rituals that lower the standards required for true reconciliation with God and the Church. In telling Dozier that "general absolution is not to be the focal point either of spreading the Gospel or reconciling sinners," Rome was saying: "You went too far."

Bishop Dozier does not agree. He knew he was stretching "the rules" to the breaking point but proceeded with his program in the face of Vatican displeasure. This was in character. At the 1973 convention of the National Association of Laity, now defunct, he virtually pleaded with NAL delegates to come back to parishes to help progressive bishops like himself implement reforms over the objections of conservatives. In his defense of his December 5 ritual he took a similar stand. Three months later he still made no apology for his motives or conduct. Interviewed by Kenley Jones on the nationally telecast morning show "Today" (March 10, 1977), Dozier spoke about the large number of alienated Catholics and the responsibility of the Church to take the first step to bring them back. General absolution was his personal choice as that first step. When he related that "the cardinals in Rome in charge of the sacraments were unenthusiastic about our absolution program" and added "but there is nothing they can do about it," the religious sisters sitting with him laughed along with the bishop. NBC opened this segment of its morning show with a narration that suggested that the general-absolution rites held by Bishop Dozier afforded an opportunity for Catholics who had stopped going to church to come back with no questions asked.

These ongoing public statements were serious enough to prompt James Cardinal Knox, prefect of the Congregation for the Sacraments in Rome, to level public criticism at Dozier for violating the Church's pastoral norms. Dozier was criticized on March 25, 1977, for:

• Considerable advance publicity on general absolution in circumstances not covered by the Vatican norms.

• Celebrating it in conjunction with the Eucharistic liturgy in explicit violation of those norms.

• Ignoring a personal letter of September 17, 1976 (when the Memphis preparation had just begun).

• Not consulting the members of the episcopal conference.

• Conveying the impression afterward that Pope Paul VI approved what was done when in fact the Holy Father had in private audience (March 23, 1977) referred him to the norms.

Dozier was reminded henceforth to observe those norms "thus contributing to that unity of mind and heart which should prevail in the Church."

The Memphis bishop did not take this rebuke lying down. In his own response to fellow bishops, released publicly on April 26, 1977, he denies all of Knox's allegations and asserts his "union with the Holy Father." There the matter presently rests.

*The Newark Case.* A headline in the New York *Times* on December 12, 1977, read as follows: "Catholics Get General Absolution in Newark Area for First Time." The archdiocesan services, held in four different deanery churches, were entitled "A Father's Embrace" and conducted by Archbishop Gerety himself with four auxiliary bishops. The plans for the four services were announced on September 10 and held over a two-week period during Advent 1977. Approximately five thousand received general absolution, all of whom were notified of the need for private absolution later if in mortal sin. Confrontation with Rome was avoided because the advance publicity did not accentuate general absolution. However, in the literature distributed to priests, acknowledgement was made of its possibility, and priests understood that general absolution would be the route finally taken at each of these services. While it was announced that numerous priests, as many as fifty, were reported in attendance at each Church, no serious arrangements were made at any center for private confessions. As a matter of fact, none were heard. But the sense of the proceedings has been understood by many priests precisely as the New York *Times* captured its newsworthy component. In effect "pastoral necessity" came to be what the bishop wished to make of it. General absolution became a facile means of reconciliation. The following item appeared in the Jersey *Journal* (Jersey City) on January 17, 1978: "During the last week of school prior to the Christmas vacation, Hudson Catholic students participated in a new form of confession. Through the permission of Archbishop Peter Gerety, Fr. Leo Grazzi of Hudson Catholic (H.S.) was able to administer group confessions. Students were asked to close their eyes and confess their sins directly to God without having to talk to a priest."

Donald Thorman objects to an American bishop having to think first what Rome says "before considering the needs of his people." (*NCR*, May 20, 1977). The implication is that Rome does not think of people. Beyond people, however, there is an additional element—namely, Christ's will. Bishops and Rome must consider the divine law first. If for people's sake a bishop can violate the law, directly or indirectly, so may pastors, and so may curates against a pastor. The effect on sacramental discipline is clear.

The Pope knows this and has intervened personally with the bishops who have stretched the rules and has publicly warned bishops, "General absolution is not to be used as a normal pastoral option, or as a means of confronting any difficult pastoral situation. It is permitted only for the extraordinary situations of grave necessity" (*Origins*, May 4, 1978).

## VII. *Bishops—Lambs Among Lions?*

An Italian sociologist named Vilfredo Pareto may have some unprovable ideas on institutional leadership but they have a ring of plausibility if applied to particular situations such as the contemporary Catholic crisis. It may be true that there is no sure recipe for turning declining institutions around, but Pareto's general sociology thinks it is all a matter of "the circulation of elites."

According to Pareto every society is governed by elites of one kind or another. Elites tend to rotate their hold on political power much the same as Democrats and Republicans switch chairs in the American presidency. Pareto's elites are of two kinds—Lions and Foxes. The Lions are the builders—bold, forceful, daring, resolute, strong, men of character. But their virtues have a seamy side. In time Lions become overbearing, hidebound, bureaucratic, unadaptable, and remote. Their society becomes stagnant because the Lions fail to develop the new skills demanded by progress. It is at this point that Foxes take command of the public stage. Foxes are smart, shrewd, inventive, flexible. They favor progress and prosperity. Not only are they adept at undermining a corrupt establishment but they are also good at manipulating popular opinion. Their victory over the once-invincible Lions makes them attractive rulers.

Once in power, however, Foxes, like Lions, reproduce their own kind and simultaneously reveal their great weakness in ruling. Foxes tend to forget that essential to good government is a certain amount of force. Social-minded citizens are ruled by good sense and law, but the weak and the recalcitrant, says Pareto, conform to neither. Having come to power by cunning, Foxes live under the illusion that guile can overcome all obstacles. Faced by enemies they turn aside—rather than openly resist—hoping to undermine the opposition by rewards or blackmail, if need be. Foxes, because they are not long-range planners, will pay any price to keep the peace.

It comes as no surprise, therefore, that society managed by Foxes ultimately is reduced to shambles. To restore order a new revolution is needed, led this time by a new breed of Lions. The "circulation of elites" begins another turn.

Pareto sums up in one paragraph how revolution and counterrevolution occur:

A small group of citizens, if prepared to use violence, can impose its will on governing circles which are unwilling to meet violence with equal violence. If humanitarian sentiments are mainly at the root of governing authorities' abstention from force, the violent minority easily achieves success [*Sociological Writings*, p. 257].

Although the Lions and the Foxes in the Church are not absolutely distinguishable, it is clear that power shifts have already occurred through force rather than by planning or rational discussion. Bishops and Rome occasionally use force—an editor dropped from this paper or that, a priest suspended, or a professor fired. There is no instance of sanction against rebellious nuns. These most timid stabs at enforcing Church law bring cries of "purge" from those accustomed to post-Vatican II bishops playing the role of lambs.

Orchestrated cries of outrage are merely another form of force used against hierarchy. Ridicule, threats, pressure applied to a vulnerable area of episcopal jurisdiction in the form of picket lines and collection boycotts are ways in which bishops have come to be intimidated. The tactics have been so successful that the rules of role-playing in the Church have changed and new definitions of normal Catholic behavior are in the making. Once upon a time the priest worried about a remonstrance from his bishop. Now the bishop frets for months about how best to handle a recalcitrant priest. Priests sometimes refuse to see a bishop without a lawyer-type witness in the room and have told stories of chastising the bishop and stomping out of his presence in high dudgeon. These role-reversal responses are leading to a new order of definitions. The bishop is the man who now must justify himself to one about to leave the priesthood. Defending the teaching office itself, obeying law or superior, wearing religious garb, saying the rosary are no longer considered representative Catholic responses.

When Archbishop John Quinn keynoted a symposium at the University of San Francisco—calling Magisterium "essential to the very being of the Church"—a Religious News Service reporter, not meaning to be unfriendly, looked upon the event as an abnormality. The opening lines of his news story were: "It was as if fifteen years of Church history had been erased and all the words of change never spoken. The symposium on Magisterium and the teaching authority of the Catholic Church was

an opportunity for Catholics with conservative views to be heard"
(Oakland *Catholic Voice*, November 14, 1977).

The Church has fallen victim to the same domination by adversary
forces that has brought civil government to its knees. One bishop, unwilling to take abuse, no longer speaks of "conserving the faith." In the
cultural mood of the moment, establishment is bad, change is good. Institutions are bad because they represent the past, experiment is good
because it is not final. Morality changes, too, because it means greater
freedom—to have a six-inch décolletage today when three was once a
moral limit, to abort if need be so as to avoid the encumbrances of dangerous contraceptives. Campaigning for public office—even the presidency—means running against the office itself. The successful candidate
may be the one who is more persuasive about his ability to dismantle
the office. Little attention is paid to the social costs of eternal change.
The only institutions prospering under these circumstances are governments, which become the instrument of enforced change at any price,
and academe, which offers research data in place of the wisdom of the
ages.

Riding under their own designed banner representing Vatican II, a
small band of Catholic changemakers have succeeded in imposing their
will on governing circles within the Church. Even when they lose (as
they have on the ordination of women, to cite only a single example),
they maintain the initiative against those who stand in the way of their
proposed changes. They do not hesitate to punish "conservatives," if
only by ridicule or boycott. Rome—sometimes the Pope himself—is the
favorite whipping boy. Bishops are unwilling at this moment to meet
this force with equal force. Indeed, some bishops now can be counted
on the side of "reformers." Doctrinal differences among bishops have
not yet fully surfaced, in part because Rome is keeping a more watchful
eye here than elsewhere. But even if bishops choose not to notice, there
are some doctrinal differences in their disagreements over the major
Catholic policies contained in disciplinary decrees of the Church.

Some of these are subtle actions or omissions that suggest that
bishops are accepting, if not abetting, directions contrary to those
defined in the documents of their own conference or by Rome.

> • There is not record of a bishop scrutinizing religious com-
> munities to discover to what degree the common requirements
> of the religious life are being observed.
> • The *imprimatur* has been permitted to become an uncertain
> guide for Catholic readers. Some bishops have given the
> *imprimatur* to books whose contents are at variance with

Catholic doctrine. Some books like Hans Küng's *On Being a Christian* or Anthony Kosnik's *Human Sexuality*, lacking an *imprimatur*, are used uncritically in Catholic classrooms, even of seminaries. Some Catholic scholars publish works of theology or Scripture without receiving or requesting the *imprimatur*. Some Catholic publishing houses regularly publish books opposed to Magisterium without protest from bishops.

The more serious threat to the bishop's role is the rising respectability in the United States of a theological view that there is a second and competing teaching authority in the Church that is the property of theologians independent of bishops. The president of NCCB, Archbishop John Quinn, has rejected this view on the ground that without the Magisterium of bishops "the apostolic heritage of the faith" cannot be preserved. Whereas the theory would make the bishop ruler, not teacher, Quinn insists that bishops are both by divine law. Said Quinn: "I do not see how there could be any point of real certitude for the faithful if the Magisterium is conceived as a fugue of frequently dissonant voices forming a choir with no director" (*Origins*, November 17, 1977).

But if the Church is a choir, the soprano section, which reaches for the highest notes—in this case bishops—follows a director, too. If their voices lag behind the basses, they will likely not get a hearing. This is what happened when the American bishops delayed six months before they responded publicly to CTSA's *Human Sexuality* in a statement softened by a preamble that "recognize[d] the importance of theological discussion and research without which the Church could hardly fulfill its teaching mission." Insofar as the bishops had a year earlier condemned the very opinions that *Human Sexuality* thought tolerable, the subsequent mild censure will not inhibit the Paulist Press from reprinting the disapproved text for ongoing use in Catholic classrooms.

Cacophony sounds forth in the episcopal choir when one least expects it. In spite of Rome's score on priestly celibacy, the newly elected vice president of NCCB, Archbishop John Roach of St. Paul, allowed himself to be quoted as saying: "I would not be disturbed in that instance if the Church were to, in a sense, run a two-track system of celibate and noncelibate clergy. I would not have any problem with that" (Minneapolis *Tribune*, November 15, 1977). His confrere Archbishop Peter Gerety is quoted at length on the sorry state of the priesthood in NCCB's *Origins* (December 22, 1977). The Newark archbishop looks upon the decline in priestly numbers as one of the "signs of the times . . . inviting us, indeed directing us toward the goal of the realization of the Vatican II vision of the Church of God." All of what is occurring, he says, "is happening under the impulse of the Holy Spirit," and this includes fewer priests and "a very different Church from what we knew who were trained before Vatican II." When Gerety finishes his pessimistic picture of the present and rosy prediction of the future priesthood and Church, it is clear that he speaks more out of the writings of radical theologians than from Vatican II documents. His insistence that "the exercise of authority has been less and less seen in the context of a Church as a pyramid and more and more in the context of a Church structured in the horizontal dimension" cannot be found in any official document of bishops, Council, or Pope since 1962. Statements of that kind, however, are being used to level episcopacy and priesthood, so that as used by a bishop it leaves the reader wondering why anyone should aspire to be a priest or a bishop if he could do as well for the Church as a social worker or a community organizer.

These may not be the central issues to be faced by bishops who are well aware that their own seminarians are dating, that sermons on the "myths of Christmas" have been given at Midnight Mass, that priests are already multiplying general absolutions without announcing the need of private penance. These are incidental problems compared to the need of defining and enforcing at all levels of their jurisdiction the authentic definitions of what Vatican II Catholicism means in the concrete. The key words are "defining" *and* "enforcing." If this issue remains unsettled, definitions and rules become the private business of everyone, reducing the bishop to the role of conciliator of warring factions. There are not wanting those in the Church who accept this condition as the by-product, if not the specified goal, of the Second Vatican Council.

Dissenting theologians are already articulating and enforcing their own definitions above and around bishops. These theologians have succeeded, even at the popular level, in putting bishops in their place. Bishops in their stead have not yet responded effectively to this new reality, which Richard McBrien spells out for them in a few declarative sentences:

• Bishops and theologians are prone to natural enmity;
• Bishops are concerned with order; theologians are concerned with truth;
• Older theologians were wrong in acting as explainers and defenders of doctrine;
• The newer theologians see their ministry as an exploration, investigation, criticism, and communication;

• If theologians are more concerned about Church order than truth they would be unfaithful [Brooklyn *Tablet*, March 14, 1974].

Why are bishops timid about face-to-face confrontation with this obvious challenge? To that question everyone has his own answer. Hard-pressed bishops, who do not like to play lambs in dens of lions, sometimes blame themselves. They sometimes point the finger of their difficulty in the direction of Rome itself. Pope Paul understandably reminded them of their responsibilities more than once. One of his most forceful exhortations was given to bishops on December 8, 1978, marking the fifth anniversary of the close of Vatican II. (The document is called *Five Years After the Council*.) Paul said that some one of them might be surprised at his raising this issue ("Someone may even protest"), but he wanted them to know that bishops were chiefly responsible for clearing up "the accumulation of ambiguities, uncertainties, and doubts" about the essentials of the faith. And the essentials he talked about were dogmas concerning Christ and the Trinity, the Real Presence of Christ in the Eucharist, the Church as the institution of salvation, the priestly ministry, moral requirements, indissolubility of marriage, and respect for life. He took note of the fact that even the divine authority of Scripture had not escaped demythologization. He wanted each bishop to take care that he "did not betray the truth and continuity of the doctrine of the faith." He did not want surveys to "constitute a determining criterion of truth," nor the learned to be looked upon as authentic interpreters of the Church's faith. This was the bishop's "personal and absolutely inalienable responsibility." He returned to this requirement again at the canonization of American Bishop John Neuman. "Venerable brothers, we beseech you to guard the content of the Catholic and apostolic faith" (*Origins*, June 30, 1977). But then, say beleaguered bishops, he was not too successful at this in Rome itself.

## CHAPTER XII

The Sack of Rome, or Rome Has Spoken, the Case Is
Still Open

## I. The Strange Case of Archbishop Lefebvre

Pope Paul said it as well as anybody.

> Our predecessors [as Pope] to whose discipline he [Lefebvre]
> presumes to appeal would not have tolerated a disobedience as
> obstinate as it is pernicious for so long a period as we have so
> patiently done [Associated Press, June 28, 1977].

These remarks were made the day the Pope made his friend Giovanni Benelli a cardinal and on the eve of Lefebvre's ordaining of
priests in defiance of the Pope's explicit command to the contrary. On
that day, June 28, 1977, the Pope's remarks were construed as an implied threat of excommunication, but if the papal warning was intended to be a deterrent, it failed. The following day Lefebvre ordained
fourteen priests and twelve deacons in his seminary at Econe, Switzerland.

The Lefebvre case is strange on several counts, not the least of which
is Paul VI's seeming preoccupation with an archbishop who has no following to speak of anywhere in the world—and none at all among
bishops. Yet Paul VI seemed more upset by this old man's failure to
comply with a "cease and desist" order than with the many refusals of
Hans Küng, who continues to exercise worldwide influence.

Why this special concern about Lefebvre?

A papal letter to Lefebvre issued one month to the day after Pope
and archbishop met face to face at Castelgandolfo (September 11,

1976) offers clues to the deep Roman anxieties without fully explaining them. This is the letter in which the Pope accused Lefebvre of "scandalous words and gestures against ecclesial communion," not the least of which is his continuing to function as a bishop, even after being suspended by the Pope for refusing to close the Econe seminary.

The Pope's charges against the retired archbishop were spelled out in some detail:

1.  Lefebvre has no special charism or authority as a bishop, lacking a canonical mission to correct Catholic abuses. This is the Pope's job for the universal Church, made more difficult by Lefebvre's disrespect for authority and his accusations that the Pope is a neo-modernist and a neo-Protestant.
2.  Lefebvre's theology of the Church is warped. He refuses to recognize that the Catholic tradition is a living tradition. Nothing done by Vatican II or Pope Paul violated that tradition. Lefebvre, on the other hand, subverts it. Said the Pope: "There is room in the Church for a certain pluralism, but in licit matters and in obedience."
3.  For restoration to good standing in the Church, Paul VI demanded of Lefebvre the following things:
    • That he "sincerely adhere to the Second Vatican Council and to all its documents—in their obvious sense" and to the canon law of the Church;
    • that he cease leveling public charges and abuse against the Pope.
    • that he abstain from preaching, administering sacraments, holding conferences, writing;
    • that he accept the suppression of the Priestly Fraternity of St. Pius X and its seminary;
    • that he turn over to the Pope all his houses of formation and institutions [*Origins*, December 16, 1976].

Perhaps in this last demand of the Pope is the key to his extraordinary anxiety about Lefebvre's activities. At the end of this letter Paul made passing mention of "the psychological state in which you find yourself," but what seemed to trouble him more was the specter of this agitated man—apparently stocked with unlimited resources and the power to ordain—running around the world setting up the beginnings of "little Catholic Churches." Those who were close to the Pope made frequent reference to his fear since 1965 of the kind of schism that followed Vatican I in 1870. The "leakage" going on, especially in the United States, also distressed him, but a juridical break led by an archbishop seemed to him a greater long-range threat to Catholic unity. Many far removed from the Roman scene think Paul's fears were farfetched because the "infinitesimal Lefebvre sect" has little drawing power, especially among American Catholics. But the Pope may have known more than he revealed and for reasons never fully clear he stepped out of character to do battle with a seemingly inept archbishop.

The real questions, therefore, may be: Is Lefebvre really inept? Can he be brought to heel without great damage?

Lefebvre was an unlikely candidate for the role of Pope fighter. A priest since 1929, he has spent most of his life as an African missionary where he served as archbishop of Dakar, Senegal, from 1954, and later as the Pope's apostolic delegate in French West Africa. Prominent enough to be made a member of Pope John's preparatory commission for Vatican II, Lefebvre ultimately approved and signed fourteen of the sixteen documents of the Council, including the Constitution on the Liturgy, which he now rejects. Later, when he was disturbed by excesses in the Church and virtually retired after being named an assistant at the papal throne, Lefebvre was permitted to set up an "experimental" community of priests, called the Priestly Fraternity of St. Pius X. Then in the fashion of the dissidents he castigates, the French prelate used the cover of his experiment to establish a seminary at Econe, this time without permission either from the Vatican or the local Swiss bishop. Once Lefebvre's ulterior purposes attracted Vatican attention, he agreed to close Econe. He later reneged on this promise and was suspended from priestly duties. From this base in Econe, he established centers in England, France, and South America. He operates a seminary for twenty future priests in Armada, Michigan, and with an expenditure of one million dollars he intends to build a new American seminary to rival Econe.

While the issue between Lefebvre and the Pope is often reduced to one—the alleged ban on the Latin or Tridentine Mass—the Frenchman actually is the enemy of collegiality, of dialogue with the modern world, of ecumenism and religious freedom as defined by Vatican II. The Pope has rejected all his allegations on these matters.

The Latin Mass is largely a nonissue. Latin is still the official language of the Church. Masses can still be said in Latin, the official missals contain the Latin readings, the Gregorian Chant is used at will. If the vernacular is now the popular form, it is as a result of national hierarchies' sense of the people's preference. The popularity of the vernacular liturgy does not preclude Latin Masses where people want them. Lefebvre objects to certain new formulas and procedures that

have been introduced into the Mass since Vatican II, including participation by the faithful and wider flexibility to priests in their choice of
prayers. These additions have been well received and Pope Paul refuses
to return to the old formulas or to let Lefebvre use them, because he
wishes to use them against the Church. Popes have been changing liturgical formulas from the beginning, including Pius V, who made improvements in 1570 as a result of the Council of Trent. Leo XIII, Pius
X, and Pius XII did the same thing in modern times. While the
Roman liturgy is only one of nine used in the Church (many Eastern
Churches have their own), its formulas are identical in all vernacular
translations. Since formulas reflect doctrinal beliefs, Rome does not permit anyone, including an archbishop, to tamper with them, except on
Rome's terms. The issue, therefore, is not Latin, but the worldwide
unity in liturgical forms from which no worshiping priest or community
is exempt.

The bitterness of the Lefebvre activity is also not easy to comprehend. A young priest follower, only twenty-six years of age, in a sermon
to a Virginia audience, told his congregation that pastors and bishops
"have turned into wolves instead of shepherds. Now that you have
come home to the true Catholic Mass, don't go back. Don't return to
those services, which have been taken over by Christ's enemy" (*Catholic News*, August 18, 1977). Lefebvre himself is responsible for some of
this. In his March 1976 letter to the Pope, he called upon Rome "to
abandon this baneful enterprise of compromise with the ideas of modern man" and suggested the reason why Paul undertook this sorry mission: "[It is] an enterprise that takes its origin from *a secret understanding between high dignitaries of the Church and of Masonic
lodges, dating from before the Council*" (*Origins*, December 16, 1976;
italics added).

This political remark in a doctrinal complaint to the Pope reveals another significant dimension to the controversy—its political aspect.
While the archbishop himself capitalizes on his clerical state, his followers and defenders level acerbic criticism of the Pope's sociopolitical
postures and involvements. The Church is the professed body of Christ
preaching salvation and a moral code, including social responsibility.
But it is also a political institution conducting its mission within vastly
different cultural and governmental arrangements. Its religiopolitical
entanglements with African Bushmen, Soviet Politburo members, or
Baptist Presidents are commonplace and frequently advertised. Popes
have political policies and make deals. To this end modern Popes have
developed their well-known "social doctrine," which provides theological and philosophical underpinning to social-welfare programs—now

inaugurated mostly by governments in all three worlds. While insisting on man's basic rights to family, property, and religion, and opposing contraception as an answer to people's poverty, the Church is highly visible in national capitals and at the United Nations supporting human rights, the Third World, self-determination, opportunity for emigration, and sharing of wealth. The Church is also willing now to make accommodation with the Soviet Union and its satellites, whose rise to dominance it so long fought.

These are dangerous political waters for the Barque of Peter to sail. Powerful establishment figures on every continent—especially in one-time colonial lands with vested gentry—resent Church participation in their disestablishment. Socialist or Marxist-minded priests, on the other hand, have translated the pacific papal documents into violently revolutionary and antireligious terms. Politically right-wing Catholics are outraged on both counts, even when they have no great wealth to safeguard. The Lefebvre movement has taken on some of these political overtones, and it may be that the well-informed Vatican senses this as the great danger in Lefebvre—his manipulation as a political foil by economic royalists or by their well-intentioned but misinformed partisans.

There are examples of Lefebvre supporters arguing loudly against Pope Paul VI's social policies. One of the most articulate is ex-Communist Hamish Fraser of Scotland who, in conjunction with associations of laymen and priests in France, Australia, Britain, and America, have engaged in a running battle with Rome and its supporting bishops. The chief instrument of the ever-widening controversy is a private publication called *Approaches*. Interspersed with defenses of Lefebvre and attacks on Protestants and communion in the hand, the articles comprise a mixture of scorn and arguments worthy of the radical Catholics that Fraser followers consider the real enemy of the Church.

The July 17, 1977, issue of *Approaches*, for example, speaks of "popolatry" as a recent development in the Church. The Pope's limitations as an infallible figure are set out in no uncertain terms, with readers told the precise criterion for deciding which noninfallible statements to follow. This debunking of the papacy antecedes a caustic review of the Marxist takeover of the Church, giving specific references to the "folly" attributed to the bishops of Latin America. Names and deeds of bishop felons in Chile, Brazil, Mexico, Ecuador, and Argentina responsible for the extension of Marxism in otherwise Catholic countries are laid out in systematic fashion, as if to constitute public exposure. After deploring the return of St. Stephen's Crown to Hungary "as

an insult to the memory of Cardinal Mindszenty," *Approaches* concludes with a warning from an anonymous Roman theologian about
Freemasonry and "high ecclesiastical dignitaries" who "embrace the
principal Masonic ideals" (p. 103).

What is to be made of all this? This scatter-gun criticism has proved
ineffective, if its object is to bring down alleged Modernists or Marxists
in the Church. A. J. Matt, editor of *The Wanderer* and a caustic critic
of Catholic "liberal" causes, looks upon Lefebvrites as "desperate and
confused." Fr. Gommar De Pauw, founder of the Catholic Traditionalist Movement, who had trouble with his own ordinary over the
Latin Mass, is on record as calling Lefebvre a "hypocrite" who, he
claims, has reached out for the support of right-wing fanatics and neo-
Fascists in Europe and John Birchers in the United States. De Pauw
apparently wanted Lefebvre to head up a traditionalist movement ten
years ago, but the French prelate at that time was uninterested.

Whether it is a "psychological state" or powerfully placed political
solons who make an old man move the Church to the point of schism,
reactions to the strange case of Archbishop Lefebvre make interesting
reading in themselves. Holy Cross Father John Reedy raises the most
frequently asked question: "Why are the heavy guns of Church authority trained on him [Lefebvre], while progressives say and do all kinds of
strange things without drawing similar fire?" Reedy thinks that the answer is that the Frenchman has done something, not merely theorized.
Rome with the same vigor would go after a progressive bishop if he ordained women (*Catholic News*, September 22, 1977). A Passionist
priest, writing in *Sign* (October 1977), equivalently says the same
thing. He thinks that only time will tell whether the Küngs, Currans,
and Berrigans are prophets, whereas Lefebvre has defied "the legitimate demands of authority." The *Sign* correspondent concludes: "My
own feeling is that Pope Paul has acted with heroic restraint in han-
dling the archbishop." Fr. Richard McBrien faults Lefebvrites for
rejecting the social teachings of the Church and for preserving "an
orthodoxy of their own making, not the Catholic Church's" (Brooklyn
*Tablet*, September 22, 1977).

These explanations do not entirely satisfy. The moral demands on
Catholics of *Humanae Vitae* (which rejects use of contraceptives by
Catholics) are somewhat stricter than those imposed by a social encyclical. Affirmative obligations (honor mother and father) admit of exceptions, while the negative commandments do not (thou shalt not
commit adultery). Lefebvre's actions in operating a seminary or in ordaining priests are in defiance of law. As a social progressive Pope Paul
may have seen great danger to the future of the Church in a political

right-wing movement among Catholics led by an archbishop, but as a dogmatic conservative he uttered more warnings against theological radicals than he did against Lefebvre.

Lefebvre tries to minimize the dispute by saying: "[Though] the Pope is angry with us . . . [he] is not very strongly against us because if he were he would excommunicate us" (*Register*, November 20, 1977). But this may be only one part of the problem. No one is certain what good excommunication would do, since his suspension did not work. Yet Pope Paul's inability to make an archbishop obey the law was a running sore on his pontificate. A bishop of Rome trained in the diplomatic arts under Pius XII, Paul probably was more alarmed by the possibility of a small formal schism with political overtones than an informal schism, which can be healed through improved pastoral ministry. Choosing one priority over the other is a matter of judgment. But terminating schism of any kind involves the high exercise of the ruling arts, and it was here that Lefebvre posed a particular challenge to the effectiveness of Pope Paul's pontificate.

Pope John Paul II met with Archbishop Lefebvre on November 19, 1978, a month after the new pope took office (N.Y. *Times*, November 20, 1978). The audience was requested by the Archbishop. Subsequent conversations were held with Yugoslav Cardinal Franjo Seper, prefect of the Congregation for the Doctrine of the Faith, dealing not only with the discipline of the Church but with its doctrine. It does not seem likely, however, that Lefebvre is willing to bend. Quoted in the Milan weekly magazine *Domenica Della Correre*, the French Archbishop insists that he has no intention of retreating from his opposition to the reforms introduced by Vatican II. "Why should I give up the truth? It is Rome that is wrong, not I" (Brooklyn *Tablet*, January 25, 1979).

## II. The "De facto Schism" in Holland

From the attention given Dutch Catholicism in recent years, one could gather the impression that Holland represents a large segment of the Church. The fact is that there are only seven bishops in the Netherlands and only 5.5 million Catholics, of whom slightly more than a third are active churchgoers. These figures are substantially below the size of the Catholic Church in the New York City metropolitan area. The Dutch Church has, however, fascinated the secular press and been held up as a paradigm of the renewal intended by the Second Vatican Council. Rarely mentioned is the fact that prior to the Council Mass attendance in Holland was as regular as in Ireland, that the Dutch Church there was lush in priests and religious missionaries and remarkable for its close ties with Rome.

The post-Vatican II decline in Dutch Catholicism is explained differently by different people. One thing is clear: In Holland the bishops actively collaborated with intellectuals to create the situation that led to internal dissension and to direct conflict with Rome. Programs of renewal in Holland did not get away from bishops. Bishops themselves eluded Rome. No one can determine with accuracy the extent to which bishops or intellectuals in so doing represented the Dutch Catholic people. Estimates made in 1976 that 20 per cent of Dutch Catholics were "progressive," in the sense that this word is used by the press (New York *Times*, February 8, 1976), were not the ones used by Jesuit W. Peters writing from Nimmejen, when he chided *America* (March 28, 1968) for reporting popular support for the Dutch Pastoral Council. Fr. Peters maintained: "Don't think that a clique of about 10 per cent of the lay people (certainly not more) and let us say 25 per cent of the clergy (certainly not more) equal 'Dutch Catholics' or 'the Catholic Church in Holland.'" Peters insisted that most Dutch Catholics were fathers and mothers and people with jobs who do not have the problems intellectuals and bishops seem to think they have.

But the Dutch bishops seemingly followed a path predestined by their own intellectuals. If the 1968 Dutch Pastoral Council was less noticed in Holland than in the United States by those who considered it a milestone in ecclesiastical development, the initiative was only one of many to lead Holland's bishops into difficulty. Their first sortie was the *Dutch Catechism*, which lacked precision in doctrinal matters such as original sin, the Eucharistic sacrifice, the creation of the soul, miracles, and contraception. Dialogue on the *Catechism* between representatives of the Dutch hierarchy and Rome went nowhere. The futile discussions held during 1967 at Gazzada (Italy) were later fully published in a 319-page paperback named *Il Dossier Del Catechismo Olandese*. The inability of Rome to make changes in the Dutch position or control publication of a religious document merely indicated the diminishing power of the Holy See over a national hierarchy. More significant may have been the scornful attitudes on both sides. Though the six discussants were either Dutch or Belgian, Desmond O'Grady reported the Dutch side as believing that one Roman made a reactionary, two a Curia, and three a Mafia, whereas the Romans felt that one Dutchman made a theologian, two a discussion group, and three a schism (*NCR* August 24, 1968). The Italian paperback suggested that Rome publish a better catechism than the Dutch. This would have been no solution if the catechisms taught contradictory doctrines.

The first Plenary Assembly of the Dutch Pastoral Council held January 3–5, 1968, in an obscure village of the Netherlands became the second *cause célèbre* for the media, and an object of concern in Rome. The 109 delegates were called together by the Dutch bishops to produce documents that would "reflect the faith experience of the believing community" and "the more refined reflection of experts" on the subject of authority. The position papers—the "Loeff Report"—predisposed both deliberations and the final resolutions. Bernard Cardinal Alfrink also set a tone with his public statement that the Dutch Pastoral Council does not necessarily conform to Church law and added rhetorically: "Is this indeed the most important factor?" (*America*, March 23, 1968). The Loeff Report distinguished the Church as a functional community with a job to do, and a community of persons who are "brothers and sisters in the Lord." One community has hierarchy, the other has none, but the latter is the more important of the two communities. Any community outside and beyond the believers themselves, it was argued, is unacceptable to modern man. Ministers of the Church must imitate the powerless Christ. The resolutions from the Dutch Synod called for structures and procedures that curtailed the exercise of priestly power, including that of Rome, and made it subject to consensual approval by believers.

Only one bishop—P. Moors of Roermond—rose to object to the one-sidedness of the Loeff Report, which concentrated on office-holders only, not on those who live under authority also, which said nothing of the more fundamental crisis of faith, which was aimed to please intellectuals more than the faithful. Moors stood alone. No other bishop defended his views, although later Pope Paul himself conveyed similar criticisms and ordered the Dutch hierarchy to discontinue discussions on the 1968 model.

The third area of friction between Holland's hierarchy and the Holy See was the appointment of bishops. The Dutch Bishops' Conference, flexing its autonomy muscle, expected Rome to rubber-stamp nominations to open sees. The Vatican, on the other hand, after centuries of entrapment in Spain and South America, was less likely than ever to permit national hierarchies final say in this vital ecclesial area. Seeing what was happening in Holland, Pope Paul decided he would make his own appointments to that Church. Once the sees of Rotterdam and Roermond opened, Paul VI filled them with two forty-year-olds of his own choice. Not only were bishops Ad Simmonis and Jo Gijsen papal loyalists, but also they had been publicly critical of the hierarchy they were now to join. The appointment of Gijsen to Roermond and his ordination on February 13, 1972, were particularly galling to the five remaining bishops. Gijsen, in a 1971 booklet called *The Priest and the Crisis*, criticized the post-Vatican II management of the Dutch

Church. As Alfrink was preparing to ordain him a bishop in Holland, Paul VI decided to transfer the ordination to St. Peter's Basilica with the Pope as the consecrating prelate. In one of Paul VI's resolute decisions, he also bade Alfrink to attend the ceremony in Rome. The Dutch leader at first demurred but finally participated, not without saying later that the nomination of Bishop Gijsen had harmed the authority of the Dutch bishops. A theologian adviser to Alfrink speculated publicly that the time may have come for the Dutch (responding to a Gospel demand) to disobey the Pope (NCR, February 25, 1972).

When Alfrink retired on his seventy-fifth birthday, Dutch-born Jan Cardinal Willebrands was chosen to succeed. The appointment of the president of the Vatican Secretariat for Promoting Christian Unity to the See of Utrecht was greeted with approval by all. Not only was he respected in Holland, but also he obviously had the confidence of the Pope. Willebrands walked into difficult responsibilities, into a seriously divided Dutch Church, Mass attendance at new lows, almost no priest vocations, discussions already under way about permitting laymen to take up parish duties, with liturgies frequently violating all guidelines and marriage tribunals known to sanction loose annulment procedures, while bishops looked the other way at well-advertised ecclesiastical abuses.

The fact that Willebrands still has work to do was evident when Pope Paul VI (November 17, 1977), receiving the Dutch hierarchy for their *ad limina* visit, gave the seven bishops a stern lecture. His remarks covered all areas of papal concern. At the outset he expressed satisfaction that they had "come to see Peter," a testimony to the "fact that the Church of the Netherlands wishes to remain and will remain founded on the solidity of the apostolic rock," but Paul stated the problem:

> The life of the Church in your country has undergone deep perturbations—in spite of the teachings and repeated reminders of the Holy See—in the field of faith and morality, and also of liturgical and ecclesiastical discipline, all that being accompanied by many defections of priests who have not succeeded in remaining faithful to their commitments [English *L'Osservatore Romano*, December 1, 1977].

The Pope from that point began to lay out the specific areas for attention by the Dutch bishops:

1. Denials of revealed truths or interpretations that suborn the meaning of the Catholic faith. He called upon theologians to be

the first to gather around the bishops in supporting and promoting the faith.

2. Catechesis that does not always proclaim Catholic truth faithfully. Then in precise Latin, as if not to trust the vernacular, the Pope reminded bishops that there are catechists and catechetical authors today who do not teach Christian truths of faith and morals in silence. The Pope wanted catechesis to be Catholic.

3. Bad liturgies and misadministration of the sacraments. He stressed observance of the rules of the new missal for Mass and private confession, with general absolution "limited to exceptional cases."

4. Re-establishment of seminary life according to the prescriptions of the Second Vatican Council, with particular stress on the spiritual life of priests, including the use of the divine office.

At the very end the Pope Paul, now in a hurry, indicated that time did not permit him to discuss in detail other matters. But he listed the additional subject areas of Dutch Catholicism that concerned him: necessity of ecclesiastical discipline, the lifestyle of religious men and women, mixed marriages, and social action for justice and peace.

### III. The Roman Synods

Roman synods are gatherings of bishops with the Pope to discuss the Church's business. Representatives of every national conference in the world come to these meetings not merely to give the Pope advice but also to share with him the governing of the Catholic body. The synod concept is collegiality and is the result of the Pope's decision in 1965 to implement Section 5 of the Council's Decree on the Pastoral Office of Bishops. Though originally expected to meet irregularly—whenever the Pope felt it necessary—the synods soon developed a pattern, meeting first biennially in 1967, 1969, and 1971, and afterward every three years, in 1974 and 1977, in order to give busy diocesan bishops more time to prepare and less time away from their sees. The early synods had crowded agendas that proved unworkable. Lately, the two hundred bishops, meeting for a month at a time, have concentrated on single themes—evangelization in 1974, catechesis in 1977. Upon completion of the synod, the Pope usually issues an official document based on resolutions or recommendations of the bishops, which is the basis in subsequent years of policies and practical programs at diocesan and parish levels.

If there is a simple statement that can be made about the five synods thus far held it is that they have remained under the firm control of the Pope. Paul VI may have looked in vain as runaway theologians and occasional bishops took segments of Catholicism down disapproved paths. Perhaps because of this, the Pope decided to exercise firm control over the Roman synods. Paul VI made the final decision on recent themes (in 1974 the bishops wanted "the family" discussed, but instead discussed "evangelization"), and he endorsed or rejected recommendations as he pleased.

If the purpose of the synod of bishops, according to its founding document (*Apostolica Sollicitudo*), is "to encourage close union and valued assistance between the Sovereign Pontiff and the bishops of the entire world," then the bishops seem satisfied with the results. Columnists conjure catch-phrases like "the angry bishops"—to suggest that bishops and Pope are not collaborating willingly—but these are the inventions of those who wish results different from what the bishops are providing. Archbishop Bernardin probably reflected the sentiment of most bishops when, prior to the 1977 meeting, he said: "The deliberations of the four synodal assemblies since 1967, as well as the evolution of synodal structures and processes during this time, reflect a continuing effort— still in progress—to achieve fuller understanding of these purposes and realize them more perfectly" (*English L'Osservatore Romano*, August 11, 1977). Bishops and pressmen differ in their ratings because the former meet to plot the long-range benefit of the Church, the latter to provide news and headlines for readership. Captions such as "The Synod of Small Expectations" (*Commonweal*, March 19, 1971) or "The Slumbering Synod" (*America*, November 12, 1977) will be well filed in library catalogues as the results of each synod continue to make their way gradually out of Rome down through chanceries and parishes and into the lives of the local faithful.

Critics of slow movement in post-Vatican II Catholicism sometimes express anger because the successive synods have not so far lived up to the press's expectations, nor developed as intellectual elites wish. Those who want the Church to reverse itself on contraception, do away with celibacy for priests, limit the Pope's supremacy, permit divorced Catholics to remarry, hasten union with Protestants and orthodox or endorse violent revolutions in South America expect the bishops in synod to do what they have not succeeded in getting the Pope to do. Though critics have developed a significant following for these "Catholic" priorities, they have failed almost completely to alter basic Catholic policy on any of these points. In frustration, they lash out at bishops for their unwillingness to turn the Church into a parliamentary or congressional democracy, whereby their favored policies have a better chance of becoming law—if not all at once, then bit by bit. Demands, protest, media exposure, concessions, more demands, more protests, more concessions—these are methods of the new agenda men that never seem to get them what they want.

The treatment of the 1971 Roman synod by Redemptorist Francis X. Murphy and Chicago's Andrew Greeley is an example of how bishops are alleged to deny effective hearing to the "voice of the faithful." (This synod discussed "priesthood" and "justice in the world.") Murphy was annoyed that it retained celibacy for priests. His article in the *National Catholic Reporter* (January 21, 1972) was given the title: "The Last Word on a Sad Event: Despite Synod, Reform Will Happen." Though the synod document treated the Church's doctrine on the priesthood, in Murphy's view "true reform" is not holier priests, nor harder-working priests, nor better preachers and evangelizers. True reform means married priests. Says Murphy: "In the judgment of many journalists and observers, the synod was a retrenchment, if not an outright failure." Murphy accused the Pope of "failing to appreciate the awful actualities of numerous situations." A married clergy, according to him, is a sign of the times that the synod ignored.

Andrew Greeley is also negative about the 1971 Synod, but happy that the real issue in the Church at last is forced into the open. The real issue for Greeley is not celibacy but bishop power. Declaring himself incompetent as a theorist of ecclesiastical authority, he calls upon competent friends to tell him that bishops function out of the wrong theory. Speaking of the continued rejection of a married clergy, Greeley says:

It has been said that the American bishops in their meeting last April and the bishops of the world at the synod did not care about the opinions of their priests or indeed about the opinions of the non-Catholic world. But this is completely false. Bishops read the newspapers. Indeed, according to NORC research findings, they read far more than priests do, and they worry very much about what their priests and the rest of the world think. They would desperately like to be able to respond, *but the theory of their own positions makes it impossible to do so*; they have the awesome responsibility of protecting the Church in troubled times. As humble as they may be about their personal inadequacies, *they are confident that the charism of their office provides them with special inspiration from the Holy Spirit*. The policies that they are convinced are right are those dictated by the Spirit [*America*, November 20, 1971; italics added].

The crux of the issue may not be Spirit or bishops, but Greeley's concept of authority, about which he has declared incompetence to speak. Greeley leaves the 1971 synod dismayed that the bishops seem more determined to follow Rome's directions in synod than they might if he could reach each of them individually. The tendency of the Roman synod to reinforce the Pope is a source of annoyance. Greeley concludes: "The problem is rooted in a theory of ecclesiastical authority that forbids those who have authority to share effective decision-making power with anyone else." This is why (he thinks) bishops are beyond the pressures that normally humble other political leaders.

The Greeley criticism, commonly made by political leaders who seek institutional power, fails to acknowledge certain facts and essential Church principles.

1. Bishops have always shared decision-making power and been subject to pressure.

   Vatican II has only legitimized the principle of consultation and widened its use. No leader, except a megalomaniac, decides alone. Neither is he free from the pressure of competing interests.

2. Sharing decision-making is distinct from decision-making itself.

   The sharing comes with consultation while decision is in the making. The decision is made only by the person empowered to make it. The office-holder must select one course of action while rejecting alternative courses. The decision may prove to be right or wrong, but in either case it cannot be faulted by those whose views are rejected. These rarely admit how wrong they are when events prove the leader right.

   A shift in policy toward greater sharing in decision-making does not shift the center of right and power for decision-making itself. Resisting the 1971 synodal judgment on priestly celibacy, Greeley seems to imply that "sharing" did not take place because his preferred pressure group failed to change Church policy. Greeley's theory of shared decision-making—government by pressure group—has had negative effects on basic social institutions (in public education, for example), which when transferred to the Church can destroy its hierarchical nature. Under the Greeley theory disobedience to law is as normal as obedience, since those failing to gain their way are impelled by the dynamism of the theory to continue battering decision-makers until they do.

3. Bishops are more lonely decision-makers than most institutional officers, because they alone determine the content of the Catholic faith.

Although the statement is offensive to scientific ears, Catholic bishops together with the Pope determine the content of the Catholic faith. In a real sense they define "Catholic truth."

The celibacy issue, on the other hand, involves no Catholic truth. The bishops with the Pope could allow a married clergy in the West, as they have for the East. What is involved here is a practical judgment whether the extraordinary accomplishments of celibate priests in the past four centuries are no longer possible, because celibacy itself is unacceptable. For the moment, the Catholic bishops, measuring the accomplishments of married clergy elsewhere, remain unconvinced. While a certain amount of pressure is legitimate on the celibacy issue, the decision ought not be coerced by means of the warfare characteristic of urban American politics.

Pressure tactics have no place in definitions of Catholic doctrine or moral pronouncements. Vigorous debate between theological schools is an accepted part of Catholic life, and strong representations of differing points of view reach the highest authorities of the Church. But recent forays against the teaching authority of bishops and Pope—especially the tactic designed to give theologians coequal status—have more in common with city politics than with scholarly investigation.

Paul VI was aware of the situation. During Mass in the Sistine Chapel at the opening of the 1971 synod, he went out of his way to warn the assembled bishops of overt pressures that, he said, were dangerous and of doubtful conformity with the teachings of the faith. He placed the contemporary pressures on synod delegates in the following categories:

- Against authentic traditions
- Toward worldly ways of thinking
- For enticing or troublesome publicity
- Accusations of anachronism or legalism

The secular press, fed by Catholic critics, has been an instrument of pressure on bishops. In 1974, at the conclusion of the synod on evangelization, a lead story in the New York *Times* by Israel Shenker (October 28, 1974) was captioned: "The Bishops Rebuffed." The substance of the report was that Paul VI called upon his supreme authority to reject the synod's advice. Shenker's view of the nature of a synod coincides with that of Catholic critics. Viewing the synodal body as an independent parliament or congress, Shenker wrote:

> The agenda was set up by the Pope, bishops were given no right to decide anything on their own, and conclusions were regarded as only advice to the Pope. This was less than collegiality and the 208 bishops and other Church notables— most of them elected by their colleagues—had found that out quickly. . . .

> Bishops from Africa pleaded for "indigenization," adapting Roman Catholic worship to local culture. Latin American bishops spoke up for "conscientization," participating in the struggle for social, economic, and political liberation. Asian bishops insisted on the importance of understanding the great religions of their continent, where Christianity is a minority faith.

It is doubtful if anyone but a reporter would have used words like "insisted" or "pleaded" in speaking of a report of bishops to the Pope on spreading the gospel. The Pope did not rebuff the bishops at all. In acknowledging what he called "a fruitful exchange between those in charge of the local churches," he listed seventeen positive accomplishments of the synod, not the least of which was his opportunity "to hear the voice of the local churches" in "a fraternal, simple, and genuine atmosphere." On three subject areas, especially the suggestions "to come out of the *circuli minores*" (little buzz groups of bishops, not the entire body), the Pope thought there was need of further refining and more exact statements. First, preaching the Christian Gospel is not the same as sociological or political action on behalf of human betterment. Second, however adapted to local scenery, "the content of the faith is either Catholic or it is not." Third, small communities of Catholics (charismatic groups) are fine but they are not exempt from legitimate ecclesiastical authority or to be left to the arbitrary impulse of individuals (*Origins*, November 7, 1974).

Hardly any bishop quarrels with these refinements. As a reciprocal process, the Synod enables the Pope to give Catholic counsel to bishops on the local scene who might be tempted to endorse popular activities without considering their effect on the Church's mission to spread Christ's gospel.

The 1977 Roman synod seemed to please everyone. Perhaps the subject matter—catechesis—made the difference. Bishops know something about this, and once discussion transcends the United States, the areas of controversy are few. Perhaps Pope Paul, being eighty years, in a sentimental mood, and bishops accustomed to synodal procedures helped add to the collaborative mood. Things were so irenic that Sebastian Cardinal Baggio, who helps make bishops, was forced to complain: "It is grotesque to have to defend an ecclesial assembly against the charge of having finished its work in harmony."

Even so, there were vested interests in synodal activity and differing reactions to the synodal process that reflect the ongoing problems of the bishops every time they meet together. The synod stressed a number of things. Among the more noteworthy of the thirty-nine propositions are the following:

- Catechesis is to proclaim Jesus Christ and his word; the baptismal catechumenate is a model form; and the faith must be handed down authentically.
- Catechesis celebrates the memory of Christ, and certain formulas, texts, and creeds should be memorized.
- Catechesis involves living witness. Law and moral principles must be taught.
- Families, parishes, and schools are normal places for catechesis.
- The bishop is the primary catechist.

These affirmations were a worldwide response by bishops against criticized trends in catechetical programs. The emphases, for example, on memory, on moral law, and on the discouragement of theological speculation at the catechetical level were not inserted by accident. The suggestion that everyone is a catechist, not merely the professionals, has already been taken by some as a criticism of those who have made catechetics appear to be an elite enterprise.

The different views of what was or was not intended by the synod's final paper is evident in two reports made for the *National Catholic Reporter* by correspondent Mark Winiarski (November 11, 1977) and by Msgr. Wilfrid H. Paradis, adviser to the American bishops at the synod and NCD project director (November 18, 1977). Winiarski reported that U.S. participants considered the document defective because of its "soft approach to social justice," "the failure to discuss catechesis' experiential dimension," and "lack of mention of catechesis for the handicapped." While Paradis clearly was not enthusiastic about the synod's "worth in terms of the time involved and the considerable expenditure of money," he thought the synod made a strong affirmation of the new catechetics because it led off with approval of learning through experience. Paradis thought the synod sidestepped many burning issues of the day, especially the world of youth, and ventured the guess that "most people today are repelled by attempts to cast their ecclesial lives in terms of obligation."

Although there is no indication of what John Paul II will do with the synod's request that the Pope prepare a formal statement on catechesis, fidelity to Church doctrine was on Paul VI's mind. During the synod an appeal was made by over one hundred well-known French theologians and lay figures complaining against their own National Catechetical Directory, which they claim resulted in ignorance of the faith. Led by men of the caliber of Henri De Lubac, the French petitioners asked Paul to put an end to the "serious weakness" of the present French system of religious instruction, accusing "the new *French Catechism* of betraying the faith." Whether the bishops will follow this initiative remains to be seen.

Pope Paul capitalized on the synod's regular presence in Rome to recapture control of essential Church functions for bishops, some of whom have been seeing the Catholic picture from a new perspective. Archbishop Dermond Ryan of Dublin told a press conference there that overlong "priests and bishops too were frightened of catechetical experts." The American delegates, too, took a stronger stand for the first confession of children than the American hierarchy did a month later in its own NCD, telling the synod that "preparation for the reception of the sacrament of reconciliation should precede preparation for first Communion" and "it is not enough to say that children have the right to go to confession if this right remains practically ignored."

The bishops obviously are coming face to face with some of the ambiguities of Vatican II and, prodded by Rome, are moving to provide clearer guidelines for their daily operations. But there is also some unhappiness with any movement to satisfy Rome's desire for tightened procedures. Jesuit Donald Campion, writing in *America* (November 19, 1977), recently made this observation:

> As an exercise in collegiality the synod seems to be in the process of growth and evolution. It is unlikely that it will move quickly to even an occasional exercise of that formal deliberative function also provided for in the statutes originally laid down for it by Pope Paul. Still "it moves" and that is perhaps enough for now.

It is not likely that the Roman synod can move by itself without the Pope. Not even Vatican II did that.

## IV. What Is Happening to Canon Law?

The canon law of the Church in force since 1917 has recently been lightly regarded by bishops, priests, and religious. There are few references to its statutes anymore at the parish level. Although "the Code," as it is called, has not been superseded, "guidelines," "provisional norms," and "experimental procedures" now rule many segments of Church affairs as part of the renewal initiated by Pope John XXIII. Yet it must be recalled that the first stated objective of the old Pope, when he announced an ecumenical council on January 25, 1959, was "the desired and awaited bringing up to date of the Code of Canon Law." Two months before his death in 1963 John XXIII created a Pontifical Commission to do just that.

Fifteen years have passed and "the Code" has still not been revised. There are those who think another decade or more may pass before the new body of Church law will be promulgated. Why the delay? Why with modern methods of communication and reproduction does this revision require twice the span of years Cardinal Gasparri spent structuring the 1917 Code?

There are many understandable and some conflicting reasons. The consultation process is wider and deeper today than it was sixty-odd years ago. Then, some of the concepts of Vatican II need precise canonical formulation, and this requires many interchanges. Finally, there are disagreements over terminology, such as the definitions of "interdict" and "excommunication," and the more serious conflicts between the Commission of Cardinals, led by Pericle Felici, and a body of canonists and theologians, including Americans, over what should or should not be enacted by the new Code. One body of opinion prefers to see no new Code for the time being, complaining that the drafts so far have no pastoral significance for the modern Church, being nothing more than warmed-over versions of Cardinal Gasparri's creation. Another school of thought interprets the dispute as a tug-of-war between those who want enacted into law the principles of Vatican II documents as understood by the Pope, the synods of bishops, and the Roman Curia, on the one hand, and those who in recent years have resisted papal pronouncements on theology, on university and religious life, and on Catholic discipline, on the other. As in the case of all drawn battle lines, the real contest over the new canon law is conducted somewhere in between.

Few argue the need for public law in a body as large as the Catholic Church. Pope Paul reminded the Pontifical Commission on May 28, 1977: "Ecclesial life cannot exist without a juridical structure." The forces at odds with each other disagree, however, on what laws are appropriate for the Church after Vatican II. The disputants may or may not represent the same factions that engaged in bitter controversies during the Council. The results at that time were ambiguous documents and unresolved conflicts. The Pontifical Commission, unquestionably at Pope Paul's behest, seemed determined to restrict the range of future interpretation. The present draft of the new Code contains a constitution for the Church, sections dealing with the administration and judicial procedures for future Church operations, canons regarding religious life, and a section on penal law dealing with sanctions against those who break Church law.

The Canon Law Society of America, at its annual convention in Houston on October 12, 1977, with three hundred of its twelve hundred members voting, formally declared that all present drafts of the proposed new legislation examined so far by its members, except one, were "unacceptable in their very substance." The exception to this general disapproval of the canonical work going on in Rome was the draft on religious life.

What has made the American canon lawyers so thoroughly unhappy? Canonist Richard A. Hill of the Jesuit School of Theology at Berkeley succinctly states their case: "Canon lawyers around the world, at first suspicious, are now alarmed by what they see, not as crowning to Vatican II, but as its requiem" (America, November 5, 1977). This is not dissimilar from the judgment made by a Commonweal correspondent seven years ago (July 9, 1971) when the first drafts appeared. "Trying to undo the Council" was his view of the situation then.

The canon lawyers made their first formal protest as early as 1971, when Cardinal Felici asked bishops to tell him whether the time was opportune for a new fundamental law of the Church and, if so, asked what observations they would care to make. The Canon Law Society of America said at that time (NCR, July 2, 1971): The time is not opportune and we have many objections.

The case they made can be reduced to the following propositions [NCR, July 2, 1971]:

• The Church is evolving to be something different than it has been. This development will be frustrated by premature juridical formulations of the Church's nature and mission.
• There are not yet enough consultative bodies in the

Church for adequate deliberation. In their absence, a premature law would diminish still further respect for Church authority. Some theologians, like Karl Rahner, even think a constitution for the Church is not possible at all.

• There is too much stress in the present proposals on the Church as an organized society, less on it as believing people with a mission to the world. Overemphasis on the Church's internal life, rather than as a pilgrim people reaching out to the world, represents a limited view of the Church.

• The treatment of the relationship of Pope and bishops is one-sided and narrow. The synod of bishops, for example, is pictured only as a consultative body.

• Pastoral councils and Priests' Senates are not mentioned.

• While the rights of the faithful are treated, there are too many limitations on these rights and not enough stress on due process.

• There is too much emphasis on the prerogatives of the hierarchy and the pyramidal pattern of the Church. This perspective "could have disastrous and shattering effects." The treatment of Church offices should begin instead with the functions of all the faithful. Only then will the Church be seen as a servant of the world.

• The style of the documents is paternalizing and triumphalistic. The Pope, for example, should not be called *Summus Pontifex* but *Romanus Pontifex*.

• Instead of a new fundamental law it seems advisable during a time of transition to prepare instead of a declaration of essential rights and governmental principles for all Church people, accompanied by a strong articulation of the need to protect and defend these rights.

Contained in these criticisms by canonists is an intellectual posture toward the Church. But a contemporary American cultural mood is also at work. The mood may be more important than—indeed, may determine—the posture. Public law is the device by which society works out its objectives. Law conditions the behavior of citizens, no matter what their private beliefs happen to be. Law controls the outrageous conduct of those who jeopardize society's goals or society itself. Usually intellectuals and lawmakers agree on the importance of law and the necessity of its enforcement. The "revolution of the sixties," however, made law-making, law-abiding, and law enforcement less than absolute requirements for social well-being. For almost two decades the general political trend in the United States has been antilaw in matters of private morals, and strict regulation of citizens' behavior that conflicts with government social policy.

The Catholic establishment, however, employs a system of law that owes very little to recent political experience in the secular order. Canon law has really been Roman law modified through two millennia of the Church's own experience. Modern canonists sometimes poke fun at it. It is commonly said, for example, that Romans make Church laws that are to be observed by all other Catholics. Latins seem to have developed the facility of violating law while leaving it intact. *Marriage Italian Style*, starring Sophia Loren, was no fiction of an Italian movie producer's mind. Roman selectivity also went beyond closing eyes to public aberrations. Since law was enacted to control sinners, not saints, Church enforcement differed with time and place. When Catholics were a disciplined body, Church leaders tended to enforce law strictly, with some gentility when the faithful seemed undisciplined. Early Church discipline was stern. It is still more strict in Ireland and Poland than in certain other parts of Europe. A third form of Catholic selectivity grew out of the hierarchy of values represented by the laws. Some laws were enforced strictly because they represented values closely connected with what the Church understood to be the "mind and will" of God and Christ. A Pope might give up the Church in England rather than allow Henry VIII a second legitimate wife, and yet look the other way at the King's mistress. At times Catholics were forbidden to follow the opinions of theologians. Strict interpretation of law, for example, has been required by the Church in the administration of sacraments and in matters as serious as life-taking. A priest may not marry someone once married, even though doubts are raised whether the first marriage was valid. A Catholic doctor is expected to act differently with his surgical knife in the likely presence of a fetus in a sick mother's womb.

All these variations in practical responses tended to make the sacredness of law a fundamental Catholic principle. Presumption always favored law, and lawbreakers knew it. Even if the offender was later called innocent by a confessor, the penitent was not a judge in his own case. A great deal of casuistry built up in Catholic circles, much of it the butt of jokes and derision. Yet, with the exception of the few absolute commands, Church laws did not cover individual cases. A certain amount of human judgment—and hair-splitting—frequently separated right from wrong, whose line of demarcation was at times thin. Law— the protector of the common good—also laid its burdens on citizens unequally. But within the Catholic context and for the protection of everyone's well-being, it was understood that only a competent legislator can make laws, say what they mean, set up machinery for their enforcement, and judge the "exceptions," which proved that a general law did exist. Some laws are more readily enforceable than others. In situations where the law was not easily enforceable, the Church had more options than a secular state. The Church, like the state, enforces its marriage laws in the public forum because marriage is a public act and needs public endorsement. But unlike the state, the Church can reach into conscience to deal effectively with "marriages" that lack the benefit of clergy. Denial of sacraments is an important sanction for the believer, whose faults may not be public or publicly known.

A number of contemporary American canonists would have the Church depart from some of these strictures. Their sentiment seems to favor experimentation and freedom in wide areas. Berkeley Jesuit Hill says: "There is no inherent need for a comprehensive new Church order. It was entirely logical for Pope John to plan the future as he did in 1959. But his Council itself turned out so different from what he expected. What we need now is a long period of maturation, of growth" (*America*, November 5, 1977). If Rome insists on new laws, then efforts must be made to build into its statutes canons that restrict authority's enforcement power, especially that of Rome. In Hill's discussion it is clear that collegiality, due process, statements of rights, provisional norms, and democratic choice of bishops are the proposed means to this desired end. This end also includes forcing shared power over determinations of Catholic doctrine and the administration of sacraments, especially marriage.

Each of the cited articles in *Commonweal* and *America* reinforce the growing tendency to evade canonical procedures (1) by petitioners creating false residences in dioceses that have acquired a reputation for speedy adjudication and (2) by making certain concessions that are not in conformity with right doctrine (*English L'Osservatore Romano*, February 1978). The Romans are aware that "annulment mills," like divorce mills, can develop with little encouragement. How this struggle over the final shape of the Church's marriage courts finally ends is at this moment anyone's guess.

Another source of tension is the proposed schema on religious life. The *Canons on Institutes of Life Consecrated by Profession of the Evangelical Counsels*, the one document to pass muster with American canonists, has disturbed some leaders of religious communities. The canonists are pleased with it because the schema leaves room for a great deal of liberty and local determinations. On the other hand, the authors of the schema hoped to create legislation on religious life broad enough to encompass all its varieties.

Some of the difficulties being articulated are traceable to the paragraph on page nine of the schema, that reads: "Without a doubt, in the conciliar documents, the term 'religious' must be understood to include not only the members of religious institutes as defined by can. 487, but also the members of 'societies' of men or of women living in common without vows, and the members of secular institutes." This statement, using Vatican II as justification, is being interpreted as saying that the term "religious," a term hitherto reserved to those who live in convents, wear habits, and follow a common rule, now applies to members of "secular institutes" who live in the world, without habit, and without common life—although vowed to poverty, chastity, and obedience, and as well to "the members of 'societies' of men or of women living in common without vows."

Vatican II's *Constitution on the Church* (Nos. 43–47), in the section on religious, speaks specifically of "profession in the Church of the evangelical counsels," which create a distinct "religious state of life," one bound to "show respect and obedience toward the bishops in accordance with canon law." The present Code of Canon Law specifies the unique characteristics of religious: convent life; privacy from the world; common use of goods, clothing, and furniture; religious habit; and special spirituality.

The schema for the new Code attempts to define broadly enough members of religious orders, but to include not only secular-institute members with vows, but also members of apostolic associations who have no vows at all. Some major superiors are questioning the wisdom of this effort. If approved religious lifestyles are to be so varied, they argue, what special status is there for the traditional religious community, which has been so highly praised by Council and Popes? What urgency will there be to maintain strict community life or vows?

There are other questions also raised about the schema on religious life. The distinction between "vow" and "other sacred bond" is not clear-cut. What is the difference in the religious commitment of each? Why is "obedience" given so little attention in the schema? Is it because the community "superior," according to the draft, is no longer superior but "moderator"? A moderator, however, is not a person of authority. He or she is at best a facilitator or chief counselor with no power to command obedience. What does this institutional shift in terminology mean for the office of pastor, bishop, or Pope? A major thrust of modernity has been the flattening of Church authority. The schema on religious life leans in that direction. The ambiguities of these canons and the voluntarism they encourage—daily Mass, for example, is merely "commended" to religious—if they are advanced as representing "the new mind of the legislator," can lead to Rome permitting through one door access to options and understandings that are denied at other doors.

The test of the new Code will be its penal section. Law without teeth is advice, not law. Without the obligation to obey and the penalty for noncompliance clearly stated, the unity of the Church cannot be guaranteed. This is precisely what law is intended to provide— security for society and its members. If exhortation replaces juridical demand, the individual and his private interpretation of "law" takes precedence over the commonweal as determined by the Church's law-makers. The Church has always claimed as innate and proper the right to discipline violators of its law (Can. 2214). While the Church generally prefers sentences to be passed in each case after a particular crime is committed, canon law has also provided for automatic penalties when the issue was sufficiently grave. The person who had an abortion, for example, was automatically excommunicated, as was the Catholic doctor who performed it. There were also special penalties (Can. 2317) for those "who obstinately teach or defend either publicly or privately a doctrine which has been condemned, thought not as formally heretical, by the Holy See are to be excluded from the ministry of preaching the Word of God or of hearing sacramental confessions, and from teaching in any capacity."

While there is no guarantee at this time that the final product will follow the drafts, the penal section has been reduced to eighty canons, practically all automatic penalties have been eliminated, and the penalty for abortion has been changed from *excommunication* to *interdiction*. The legal significance of the latter change is small—since both exclude offenders from the sacraments—but the world's media are certain to seize on the replacement as another sign of the Church edging more and more in pursuit of the times. Excommunication in the popular mind is an understood term. The end of automatic penalties—for example, on a priest who married or a Catholic divorcé who remarried— places all the burden on local bishops. Bishops frequently were relieved that some penalties were automatic, because they were absolved from entanglement in sticky cases and in public controversy. With the onus of judgment and penalty passed on to bishops, conflicting decisions from bishops will multiply and geographical Catholicism as well, the Church approving in one place what it denies elsewhere.

How long will Rome wait to promulgate its new law? What will it contain? Will it re-establish order within the Church? These questions are still unanswerable. Drafts on several books of the new Code have not been seen by anyone as yet. The "new Code" may be issued in

436 THE BATTLE FOR THE AMERICAN CHURCH

parts. The key problem—over and above definitions—will be how to deal with dissidents in the Church. Speaking of the offender who remains contumacious after being warned, Christ said: "If he ignores them, refer it to the Church. If he ignores even the Church, then treat him as you would a Gentile or a tax collector" (Mt. 18:17). This text became the basis for excommunication in the early Church. St. Paul, who had his difficulties with doctrinal dissidents, once told the Galatians (1:8): "Even if we or an angel from Heaven should preach a gospel not in accord with the one we delivered to you, let a curse be put upon him." And he repeated the sentence in case his audience misunderstood his meaning. Two thousand years later the same problem exists in the Church, although anathemas and curses are out of style. What substitutes the Church can find to sanction contumacious misbehavior, if negative sanctions are not proposed, will determine the immediate future of Catholic stability.

## V. *Apostolic Delegate Jean Jadot*

Eugene Kennedy once said: "One thing is clear: What Jadot does is precisely what Paul VI wants done in the American Church."

Msgr. John Egan said: "The Pope [Paul VI] wanted to know the truth about the United States and felt he wasn't getting it. He is now."

Fr. Andrew Greeley, who makes casual references to his invitation to dine at the apostolic delegation, makes this judgment: "The work of Archbishop Jadot in reforming the American hierarchy has been rapid and dramatic, at times almost breathtaking. If his enemies do not succeed in removing Jadot and if his health continues to be good, I would suspect that in five years from now, the American hierarchy will be one of the best in the World. . . . The reform of the hierarchy depends almost entirely on one witty, brilliant, ingenious, and thoroughly remarkable man" (*NCR*, September 6, 1974).

Speaking of Jadot's episcopal appointments, one midwestern bishop remarked: "They're not the kind of bishops who'll get their pictures on the front page of *The Wanderer*" (*NCR*, September 6, 1974).

The religion editor of the New York *Times*, Kenneth Briggs, who usually has open lines of communication to the Catholic intellectual community, reviewed Jadot's four years as delegate (February 27, 1977) with the following observations: Jadot has "power and influence"; he has made a deep mark on "the selection of progressive bishops"; he "clearly sympathizes with those who are willing to risk unorthodoxy in reaching out to non-Churchgoers"; he is known "to criticize bishops' actions in private"; the fight on the hierarchy's 1976 statement on moral values "was led by some of the bishops whose appointments he has facilitated."

While these opinions about Archbishop Jadot are one-sided evaluations of the apostolic delegate, they are repeated often enough to create an impression that may not be true. They may be figments of imagination among Catholic writers who enjoy influence in the media. This apostolic delegate, like others before him, plays a role in the Church which is private and diplomatic. Jadot creates impressions, but the fundamental quality of his mission can be discovered only if one has access to his diplomatic pouches or to his private conversations with high Vatican officials. Jadot, like the late Pope Paul VI, is a quiet personality given to gentility and openness. But whether Jadot thinks or moves in the direction of the image created for him is another question.

Apostolic delegates have never had an easy time in the United States. Rome made an initial effort in 1853 to have an Italian representative check on American Catholic doings, only to have the chosen candidate, Gaetano Bedini, almost returned to Rome in a pine box, so violent was the reaction. Forty years later, the American hierarchy, led by Cardinal Gibbons, fought the appointment of a permanent apostolic delegate, right up to the day of his appointment by Pope Leo XIII in 1893. American bishops, therefore, have become accustomed to delegates only since 1895, when Leo XIII insisted on naming Archbishop Francesco Satolli. Prelates like Amleto Cicognani gained eventual acceptance, partly through graciousness and partly for surviving in the post for twenty-five years, from 1933 onward. But even then, powerful prelates like Cardinal Spellman took a certain pleasure in going directly to Rome over the head of or around the Pope's representative in Washington.

An Apostolic delegate walks a tightrope in Church affairs. He does represent the Holy See's universal interests and in that sense is a "watchdog." He siphons to Rome data that in his judgment interest the Curia or the Pope himself. He carries Roman letters and documents to American bishops, and Rome's complaints too. In this role he is a policy shaper who must not appear to be a meddler in internal American Catholic matters. While he walks carefully wherever cardinals are on the scene, his influence in smaller or less prestigious sees is powerful. The role of bishopmaker gives Jean Jadot his most potent influence.

Rome sometimes is faulted for sending out contradictory signals through influential middlemen. Cynics attribute this double-talk to the Latinity of Vatican bureaucrats. Yet curial officers, including apostolic delegates, are usually careful to be ambiguous on the right issues, and to be misunderstood as the normal risk of diplomacy. Given the nature of the huge Church bureaucracy and the political personalities involved, multiple voices seem at times to be calling the institutional Catholic tune, when that may not be the case at all. Or if a particular Church policy is clear but controversial, a subaltern may leave the impression that the position he is articulating or quietly passes over need not be taken at face value. Sometimes he does this by an inflection of the voice or a shrug of a shoulder.

Archbishop Jadot is a Vatican official whose role is doubly difficult. Beyond the normal risks of office he encounters the efforts of those anxious to give him an image as a Church reformer in the American mold. Jadot's concerns for the pastoral care of the nonchurched and for social justice to the poor are given appropriate media approval. But then, by permitting himself to be drawn into a lengthy interview with the *National Catholic Reporter* (March 25, 1977), Jadot exposed himself to the risk of being misused. When asked two questions that touched Catholic doctrine—one about the ordination of women, and a series of inquiries about contraception, including a suggestion to Jadot that *Humanae Vitae* was "an insensitive document"—the Belgian prelate was reported as offering neither defense of the Roman position nor an exposition of the doctrines involved. He is presented to the American public as not challenging Arthur Jones' pejorative description of *Humanae Vitae*, a theme that Paul VI reaffirmed time after time through ten years. (A year later—March 10, 1978—Jadot told *NC News* in Portland, Oregon, that a majority vote favoring contraception "will have no impact on Church doctrine.")

In November 1975 Jadot asked for "a few minutes" of the NCCB's executive session to speak on two items—Priests' Senates and "our role as authentic teachers of the faith." He read a statement reminding bishops of their responsibilities according to Canon 1381 to follow theological teaching in Catholic universities and suggested that if they were too busy to play this role personally, they might appoint an episcopal vicar for doctrine. After the meeting word was passed around that the Jadot reading on this subject was somewhat perfunctory and exercised without enthusiasm.

Whether he realizes it or not, the apostolic delegate's name is constantly associated in the media with certain bishops more than with others. Archbishops William Borders of Baltimore and Peter Gerety of Newark are two ordinaries commonly assigned to "the Jadot faction." Borders led the opposition in 1973 to the Vatican directive on the first confession of children. In 1976, after Cardinal Garrone had publicly rebuked NCEA for misreading the Roman document on Catholic higher education, Borders arranged for Fr. Theodore Hesburgh to lecture

NCCB's executive committee on the problems Catholic universities historically have had with Church authority. Peter Gerety managed four general absolutions in spite of Rome's clear displeasure with the procedure. Jadot had ample advance notice in 1976 that Rome was displeased at the general absolutions planned by Bishop Dozier in Memphis. In the public forum at least the apostolic delegate did not appear as an inhibiting influence, and his follow-up explanation that he had no authority to intervene was mild compared to the reproval given Dozier by Cardinal Knox in Rome.

Archbishop Jadot has at times appeared ambivalent about some of Rome's concerns. One example is his letter dated February 28, 1976, to Archbishop Joseph L. Bernardin, then president of NCCB. The subject matter was the "proper attire for priests and religious." The Holy See wanted Jadot to remind American bishops about the need of clerical and religious dress, however simple, in order to signify "the consecration" of the wearers. Jadot opened by reminding Bernardin that these values have been widely neglected with the consequent bewilderment of the faithful. He also cited Cardinal Baggio as connecting the arbitrary rejection of appropriate attire for priests and religious and certain bishops who have tolerated abuses or who have not given the proper example by their own choice of clothing. Some bishops are blamed for advising religious communities of women in their dioceses to abandon the religious habit.

Then after instructing Bernardin to tell priests and religious "to observe the rules," Jadot concluded by saying that in his experience the Roman directives were not aimed particularly at the United States! In view of the fact that Rome over many years had specifically engaged several American communities on the issue of religious habit and the fact too that "renewed" communities have in practice all but abandoned the "habit" completely, Jadot's disclaimer seemed to be neither a statement of principle nor of fact.

## VI. What's Going on in Rome?

Romans know better than anyone what is going wrong in the Church, even about the failures of bishops. Francis Cardinal Seper, prefect of the Congregation for the Doctrine of the Faith, once blamed bishops for some of the Church's troubles. In speaking of contemporary difficulties in defending the faith, Seper said:

The bishops, who obtained many powers for themselves at the Council, are often to blame because in this crisis they are not exercising their powers as they should. Rome is too far away to

cope with every scandal—and Rome is not well obeyed. If all
the bishops would deal decisively with these aberrations as
they occur, the situation would be different. It is very difficult
for us in Rome if we get no co-operation from the bishops
[*Origins*, May 4, 1972].

Local bishops in far-flung dioceses may be part of the problem, but
many of them say that Rome itself is another part.

A walk during the spring of 1977 down the broad Via Della
Conciliazione, which leads from the Tiber directly into the doors of St.
Peter's itself, offers a clue. This avenue, which Pius XII brought to
completion, is flanked on both sides by one splendid Catholic bookstore
after another, each owned and operated by a religious community,
Salesian, Society of St. Paul, Coletti, and on to Ancora, which is at the
mouth of the piazza, itself immediately across from the Pope's top-floor
window. The displays in the windows of these bookstores are designed
to catch the eyes of pilgrims from all over the world and are a study of
the Roman situation by themselves. Rome, already enduring a new
Communist mayor, also functioned under the sign of Antonio Gramsci,
a Communist "martyred" by Benito Mussolini forty years earlier.
Gramsci's months in prison were spent writing a treatise on how to capture the intellectual and academic life of Catholic Italy. His *Quaderni
Dei Carcere* (Milano: Einaudi), in four volumes is one of Italy's best
sellers and is featured in every Catholic window of Vatican City. One
salesman in Ancora told an observer: "Gramsci is in the greatest
demand. We can't keep him in supply."

Other items given prominent display on the Via were the following:

• Bayle's *Dizionario Storico-Critico* (Roma: Edition Laterza) now in
an expensive reprint. The treatise "The Good Atheist" goes back to the
seventeenth century.

• Solignac's *La Nevrosi Christiani* is promoted everywhere. Its thesis:
Christianity is a massive neurosis owing its origins to special historical
circumstances.

• Delumeau's *Le Christianisme Va-t-Il Mourir?*, which leaves Christianity's death an open question.

• Pancera's *I Nuovi Preti*, about the new priests who are upsetting
the Church. This raging 1977 best seller reached its second edition in
eight days, concluding with a piece on Giulio Girard, an avowed
"Christian Marxist."

• Girardi's own *Fede Christiana et Materialismo Storico*. This Salesian priest, a follower of Don Bosco, is a self-proclaimed atheist.

The Vatican's lack of control of its own bookstores is merely symbolic of the larger problem. The press sometimes reports Rome's seem-

ing losing battle to tidy up its own household. Occasionally a headline reads "Progressives in Rome Are Under Pressure" or "Pope Orders Investigation of the Lateran University." When Scripture scholar Fr. David Stanley is dropped from Gregorian University for leaking the report on women's ordination (NCR, April 1, 1977), or Benedictine Abbot Giovanni Franzoni is suspended for urging Catholics to vote against repeal of Italy's divorce law, that is news and receives international attention (New York Times, April 6, 1975), because such sanctions rarely occur against dissenters.

On the other hand, rarely was publicity more thorough than when the Pope made an intense effort to return the Society of Jesus to obedience. Once a Pope's most competent and trusted allies, whose famous fourth vow of special loyalty to the Pope made them an elite order of the Church, the Jesuits had split among themselves and in many parts of the world became leaders of causes highly offensive to Paul VI. Doctrinal dissenters counted many well-known Jesuits among their numbers. Fr. Pedro Arrupe, superior of the world's Society of Jesus, was forced at one point to remind his subjects that the fourth vow still held, that they were to stop criticizing Pope Paul. Arrupe accused his Jesuits of criticizing the Pope not as a means of helping him but because they are "seeking out popularity" (NCR February 1, 1972). Three years later, during the General Congregation in Rome of 235 Jesuits from 80 countries, Pope Paul took strong stands against his favorite order. Jesuits were not allowed to water down their fourth vow, he told them, demanding that they reintroduce discipline into their community and that they temper their worldly involvements. Pope and Jesuits then proceeded to struggle over the documents the Congregation was to publish. For all the press attention paid to this family fight and the feelings that were exchanged on both sides, nothing about contemporary Jesuit life seems to have changed, either in their training, schools, or publications. The contest of Jesuits with Rome seems to be ongoing, capsulated in the comment of one Jesuit who departed the Roman meeting somewhat unsettled: "Pope Paul is afraid that the order will disappear by becoming too secularized. But there's a danger that he might annihilate it by taking it over and turning us into dusty little papal valets" (Time, March 17, 1975).

Another Roman case in point is Redemptorist Bernard Häring. In recent years public criticism of the German theologian by Vatican organs has not been uncommon. But for fifteen years during and after the Council, Häring has used his close ties with the Holy Father and his position at the Alphonsianum, the Redemptorist university in Rome, to carry around the world his dissent with the Holy See on marriage, contraception, abortion, and moral law generally. In his Roman lectures

Häring has caricaturized past performance of the Church, reducing traditional conscience formation to telling people what to do if they did not want to go to hell. While not an original thinker, Häring has popularized moral positions condemned by Rome but still taught in Roman seminaries and universities. Häring is not the only offender, however. It is possible for future priests to return home after four years studying Scripture in Rome with little confidence in the Bible as "the word of God."

Rome's treatment of Hans Küng has also been two-sided, leaving bishops elsewhere with no clear example of how to deal with dissenting theologians at home. Küng himself naturally is convinced of his own righteousness: "I will not tolerate being prevented from pursuing my theological services to my fellow man" (*Time*, March 3, 1975). His friends, like Andrew Greeley, castigate Rome, who condemns Küng "for the pure hell of it" (Brooklyn *Tablet*, February 27, 1975). But Küng has neither been condemned by Rome nor inhibited in his personal conduct by its disapproval. Hans Küng also may not be one of the Church's foremost scientific theologians, but he is clearly its most successful political dissenter. He challenges the Catholic Church's most central doctrines on revelation, on Christ, and on the nature of the Church. He speaks as if he is only presenting abstract ideas to theologian peers but actually has a highly developed knack of "selling" his ideas to the Catholic world. One of his favorite objectives is to lower the Pope's status. Küng's book *Infallible? An Inquiry* illustrates both his content and his technique. Under the guise of a scholarly inquiry, Küng proceeds to raise doubts not only about infallibility but also about the teaching office of the Pope himself. Rome saw the problem Küng was creating for the Church immediately. The book was taken for review by the Congregation for the Doctrine of the Faith on June 25, 1971. Though allegedly committed to dialogue, Küng refused to collaborate, alleging the hearings were rigged and a form of Inquisition (*Origins*, March 16, 1972), in spite of the fact that the new Roman procedures were sufficiently flexible even for Küng.

It took the Vatican four years to issue its verdict on Küng, and then it made only a complaint. The issues Küng raises are not small Catholic matters. He equivalently rejects the doctrine that the Pope cannot make mistakes when speaking *ex cathedra* on faith and morals, and suggests that baptized Catholics can celebrate the Eucharist. A warning that he was teaching serious error and must not write or say anything that undermined the defined teachings of the Church was not a strong response to his challenge. Although it was the first *monitum* issued against a theologian since 1962, when the Vatican posthumously admonished the use of certain works of Pierre Teilhard de Chardin because they abounded with ambiguous statements and some errors, the warning had no effect on Küng. Since then he has repeated his allegations on the proscribed subject matter. The "Küng case" has been called a "no-win situation." Rome is caught in a need to disassociate itself from Küng's views without appearing intolerant or oppressive. If German bishops talked Rome out of sterner action on the grounds that they could handle him better, they have not succeeded either, because Küng still pays less attention to them than to Rome.

Once upon a time no-win situations were about all the Church had. An early Church heresy, which fascinated John Henry Newman, was typical of the young Christian era. Arius, a priest of Alexandria, taught that Jesus was God's most sublime creature but was not his Son. For this Arius was condemned by the Council of Nicea in 325. In spite of that condemnation Arius' followers for the better part of several centuries continued to control important episcopal sees, including the most ancient dioceses of Antioch, Jerusalem, Constantinople, Lisbon, and Arles, while Rome looked on helplessly. Rome's staying power and ultimate victory in that controversy is proposed as a lesson for contemporary critics of the papacy to remember.

As a result of heretical efforts and schismatic forays on Church unity, Popes have developed a battery of internal defenses. Some of them were crude at times. Because of excessive abuses during the Inquisition, which sought to punish alleged offenders directly, sometimes violently, the Church, without abdicating its power of excommunicating recalcitrant members, forestalled future difficulties through censorship, which was a more indirect form of control. The familiar *imprimatur* (let it be printed), *nihil obstat* (nothing interferes), and *imprimi potest* (it can be printed) were not seals of approval on content but simply signs for the unwary that the content of a book was not opposed to Catholic doctrine. Catholic authors usually had no problems with censors, who rarely tried to rewrite an author's point of view.

The service of prior censorship to Catholic truth—because it corrected doctrinal error in advance—has been unappreciated by most Catholics. The *imprimatur* even had a certain money value for publisher and author because potential readership received instant assurance. Catholic authors sought this stamp of clearance as readily as readers. Few books were refused the *imprimatur* because after errors were brought to the author's attention corrections were usually made. Denial of the *imprimatur* or even the threat of denial was sufficient notice that neither publisher nor author could profit at the expense of the Church's truth.

When Catholic scholars took on the ideological stance of their secular counterparts—asserting that few, if any, absolute truths needed such blanket protection—they took a strong position also against prior censorship unless it was a purely voluntary act by the author.

Church authority after Vatican II bowed to this pressure and relaxed its censorship regulations. On March 7, 1975, the Congregation for the Doctrine of the Faith issued new rules that shifted the control point from author to user. Henceforth, books dealing with faith and morals that lack ecclesiastical approval may not be used as teaching texts in Catholic schools nor sold in churches; priests and religious are "earnestly recommended" to seek permission from their superior to publish; the faithful "may not write" for papers that are manifestly anti-Catholic; the censor must give his evaluation in writing, especially if the *imprimatur* is refused.

Under these new guidelines from Rome the following things have occurred:

- Priests publish books on doctrine and dogma without an *imprimatur*, even without asking for it.
- Churches, even in Rome, and schools are no longer solicitous about the *imprimatur* on books they display or the texts they use. Nor is there any episcopal overview of abuses.
- Catholic religious institutes publish books that clearly offend faith and morals without interference from bishops or Rome.
- A new technique of evasion—omitting key points of Catholic doctrine—is used to gain the *imprimatur*, which is then used in classrooms to further causes disapproved by Rome.

Catholic scholars have also argued that in place of prior censorship the Church can legitimately provide pastoral warning against damaging books, much after the fashion of an X rating. Practically speaking, however, warnings are hardly ever given, and when given they are tepid in tone or issued too late to inhibit the dissemination of error. Were they unduly strong the academic community would express vigorous resentment or accuse bishops of harassment.

The power to control dissent and deviance has moved out of the hands of bishops with the blessing of Rome. The Holy See in its effort to conform to leadership patterns demanded by critics proposes directives nervously hoping for compliance but expecting and tolerating disagreement and disobedience within the ranks from clerics who normally would be the enforcement channels. Earlier Popes had little difficulty issuing directives that were clear and ready for enforcement. When

Pius X, for example, on August 7, 1910, issued his directives on first sacraments for young children, the key sentences were terse and determined:

> The custom of not admitting to their first confession children who have come to their use of reason, or at least of not giving them absolution, must be completely given up. The local ordinary must see that it absolutely ceases; he should, if necessary, even take proceedings against those who resist [*Quam Singulari*, No. 8].

Nothing of comparable determination emanates from Church authorities at this time.

## VII. *What About Pope Paul's Pontificate?*

The day before his coronation as Pope, Giovanni Cardinal Montini went to the church of San Carlo in Milan to say farewell to his diocese. It is said that he shed tears and at one point asked the people: "*Che cosa sara di me?*" (What will become of me?) Fifteen years later he was still wondering what more could happen to him. Giving evidence of the same sadness he had the day he ascended to sit in the Chair of Peter, he spoke late in his life of weariness. Paul acted as if he came to Rome, like Peter, only to be crucified.

In many different ways he was crucified, if abuse and defections are the external signs. Because he seemed so hesitant and worrisome he was called a Hamlet, and because he reserved so many decisions to himself personally scoffers would make him like Pius XII, "the last Pope." Sympathizers referred to him as a progressive with a conservative style, the Pope who did the modern thing in an old-fashioned manner. Well aware of what was said about him, Pope Paul once approached a group of pilgrims and asked: "Do I look like a reactionary? A Pope must be neither a reactionary nor a progressive. He must be a Pope—that's all."

Perhaps the key to Paul was Montini. Speaking to the bishops of eastern France prior to Christmas 1977, Pope Paul went out of his way to relate personality with episcopacy: "Above all the bishop must keep his personality as a guide, taking care not to let himself be conditioned by the interlocutors of today to yield before the impressions of the moment" (*English L'Osservatore Romano*, December 22, 1977). Why? Because, Paul added, "He is in a special way the witness to faithfulness in the Church . . . the pastor charged with seeing where, in the long run, he must lead his sheep." To Paul personality by divine will was a part of apostleship.

Paul VI—a deeply spiritual man—saw himself and his special style as the instrument chosen by Christ to lead the Church during these times. British correspondent John Organ quotes an embittered curial Cardinal dismissing Paul's tenure with the remark, "It has become a pontificate of gestures" (London, *Sunday Telegraph*, January 4, 1976). Both sides of the extreme political spectrum would agree with this judgment. But since the final verdict of history cannot yet be made, Paul was entitled to look upon himself as the special person chosen for the particular purpose of keeping the Church together at the time forces worked to break it apart. Paul VI inherited a difficult situation. The highly centralized Church was being moved to decentralize, to break long-established ties within its own community, to re-establish ties with strangers. He may, therefore, be remembered precisely as the Pope who preserved Catholic unity when it did not seem possible. Local churches have a freedom today they did not have before. But had Paul VI not acted as a brake on the Dutch hierarchy (without appearing to trample on their autonomy), collegiality in the Church might have led to chaos. Similarly, in places like South America the Pope encouraged liberation theologians and political activists—but only up to a point. They pursued their causes aware that the Pope in blessing the objectives was not about to endorse, even by indirection, either violent revolution or communism.

Scholars and the press—both his most articulate critics—have given Pope Paul's pontificate a few passing grades.

• His journeys to the United States, South America, and India brought the papacy to the world's youngest people. These trips were no mere gestures. They symbolized an interest, which will not be lost on his successors, in the emerging continents, where the Church perhaps has just begun to flower. His statements both on social reform and evangelization point the way for future Catholic direction, the fruits of which may not be seen until the twenty-first century.

• Pope Paul's ecumenical contacts were outstanding, from receiving the archbishop of Canterbury to a journey to Istanbul to embrace Patriarch Athenagoras. No longer is the Church defensive or shy about dialogue with other Christian and non-Christian religions. Christian unity cannot be expected as an early by-product of Vatican II, but Paul took one giant step toward the final union, without making the doctrinal concessions some theologians would freely make. He lifted the excommunication of the Orthodox Church of Constantinople and established concrete relationships with the World Council of Churches in Geneva without blurring their understanding that Paul considered himself to be Peter.

• His *Ost-Politik*, which annoyed many rabid anticommunist Catholics, improved the religious conditions of several hundred million Christians living behind the Iron Curtain—not a great deal, but somewhat. Hard-liners willl not forgive him for the forced retirement of Cardinal Mindszenty as the primate of Hungary, nor for the return of St. Stephen's Crown by the United States to Communist leaders there. But given the *de facto* and juridical control by the Communists in East Germany, Czechoslovakia, Hungary, Romania, Bulgaria, and Poland, it was important in his eyes that the rights of Catholics in those lands be broadened. Paul VI seemed to sense that long after Communists in Eastern Europe have passed from the scene, his successors will be happy to know that the Church in those countries is still alive.

• His internal reforms loosened the rigidities present in pre-Vatican II practice: Bishops retire at seventy-five; curial officials have five-year renewable terms rather than lifetime sinecures; cardinals over eighty no longer elect Popes; national bishops' conferences, the synod of bishops; new consultative procedures for the nomination of bishops bring a measure of shared responsibility that did not exist before.

• Under Paul, more than fifty papal documents implemented the sixteen decrees and constitutions of Vatican II. Almost all of these have dealt with liturgical matters, a dozen concern ecumenical relations, a half dozen refer to renewed religious life. Surprisingly, the longest document of Vatican II—*The Church in the Modern World*—has only one implementing document dealing with dialogue with unbelievers.

Paul VI was considered ahead of Catholics on social issues, even though he failed to bring many priests and a few bishops, to say nothing of the laity, back to Catholic doctrine on contraception. In each case he may have been a prophet without honor in his own Church. However one views particular papal declarations, Paul on balance presided over all the decisive actions of the Council and their follow-up. The mind of the Council in liturgical, disciplinary, administrative, and doctrinal matters was largely spelled out in detail by Pope Paul. Swiss Reformed Presbyterian theologian Oscar Cullman gives good reading to these accomplishments:

> We must reject at once any one-sided comparison of John XXIII and Paul VI, as if all the light was on the side of John XXIII, who certainly was possessed of great qualities, and all the shade on the side of Paul VI; as though the primer's prophetic was destroyed in a moment by the reactionary attitudes on the part of the latter. Journalists have done much to establish this simplistic cliché. History will bring a very different

judgment to bear on the pontificate of Paul VI. It is the merit of John XXIII that he summoned the Council; it was Paul VI who brought it to a satisfactory conclusion in spite of extraordinary difficulties that his predecessor never foresaw [*English L'Osservatore Romano*, December 22, 1977].

This encomium is echoed differently by a Roman cardinal: "In the long term, people will see that Paul VI was right; he broke no bridges and he excommunicated no one." The fact that the papacy has never been so widely discussed outside, as well as in the Church, may be a sign of Catholic vitality. Those who see Paul VI as "the last Pope" in the sense of monarch making final decisions for the Church or who foresee his successors as great chairmen of a board presiding over far-flung churches may be disappointed. *Commonweal* editor John Deedy thinks the Reformation stresses on conscience, freedom, and personhood after four centuries have finally found their way into Catholicism thanks to Vatican II (New York *Times*, October 12, 1972). Pope Paul did not agree. New York *Times* editor Edward B. Fiske's estimate of the Pope's problems may be the truer insight (October 1, 1972).

Pope Paul faces two major difficulties. One is his personal style. Partly because he suffers by comparison with the joyful Pope John, he tends to convey a sense of sadness and lack of confidence. Second, he has not been able to generate creative leadership at the second and third levels of the Church.

Pope Paul scolded a lot, especially those whom he thought were naughty, and late in his life he began to direct his fire at bishops. But those now in high positions of dioceses or Curia were his appointments. If they do not provide the inspiration or leadership he deemed necessary, there is little other explanation than the failure of the Vatican machinery to provide its own inspiration, or its inability to place forceful leaders who will implement policies the reigning Pope established.

This is the aspect of Paul's pontificate which encouraged dissenters of one extreme or another. Archbishop Lefevbre stretched Paul's patience to the limit by counting on his reluctance to use force against anyone. Although dissenters of the opposite persuasion decry legalism in the Church, they too took notice of Pope Paul's unwillingness to take legal action. Gregory Baum, for example, has argued that Rome's grip on the Church can be loosened by careful violations of law. In Baum's view freedom from Rome's law can be obtained by seizing it in the knowledge that violations will go unpunished. Baum points to the success of religious orders and Catholic universities standing up to Rome without suffering any sanction. The Dutch hierarchy's introduction of married priests into Holland's pastoral ministry, excluding the celebration of the Eucharist, is also cited as a case of Roman disapproval but also a Dutch effort "modest enough not to provoke legal action." The procedure of several American dioceses admitting Catholics in second marriages to Holy Communion receives Baum's approval because no harm comes thereby to Church unity with Rome only "mildly disapproving."

> [Rome's grip on ecclesial life can be loosened] not through the rewriting of the legal code but through astute action on the part of local churches, which courageously serve the religious needs of their people with some independence, while preserving the unity of the universal church. . . . With courage and the right kind of discretion, bishops and local churches could deal with their problems even without total approval from the papal offices without risking the slightest rupture with the Pope [NCR, November 10, 1972].

This was the Achilles' heel of Pope Paul's pontificate. What will the unity of the Church be if the Gregory Baums continue successfully to have unlimited confidence in their power to restructure the Church without a care for the Pope? Is this perhaps what Malachi Martin had in mind when in his *Three Popes and the Cardinal* he made a prediction?

> There will be, instead of the Church we know, a series of independent "churches," in addition to one hard-core group clustered around the bishop of Rome, the traditional claimant to be the successor of St. Peter and sole head of the Church which Jesus of Nazareth founded in the first century of this era. But we cannot really call them churches. There will be no central authority for teaching and jurisdiction. There will be a general—but virtually nominal—similarity among all groups. But there will be no centralized control, no uniformity in teaching. No universality in practice of worship, prayer, sacrifice, and priesthood [p viii].

However, this will not occur if the new pope has his way. On the morning of Tuesday, October 17, 1978, the day after his election, John Paul II spoke to Cardinals:

"Fidelity implies not a wavering obedience to the Magisterium of Peter especially in what pertains to doctrine. The 'objective' importance of this Magisterium must always be kept in mind and even safeguarded because of the attacks which in our time are being leveled here and there against certain truths of the Catholic faith. Fidelity too implies the observance of the liturgical norms laid down by ecclesiastical Authority and therefore has nothing to do with the practice either of introducing innovations of one's own accord and without approval or of obstinately refusing to carry out what has been lawfully laid down and introduced into the sacred rites. Fidelity also concerns the great discipline of the Church of which our immediate predecessor spoke.

"This discipline is not of such a kind that it depresses or, as they say, degrades. It seeks to safeguard the right ordering of the mystical body of Christ with the result that all the members of which it is composed united together perform their duties in a normal and natural way. Moreover, fidelity signifies the fulfillment of the priestly and religious vocation in such a way that what has freely been promised to God will always be carried out insofar as life is understood in a stable supernatural way." [*English L'Osservatore Romano*, October 26, 1978]

# WHITHER GOES THE FUTURE OF THE CATHOLIC CHURCH?

## I. All Is Not Lost

Gerald Shaughnessy opened his classic study *Has the Immigrant Kept the Faith?* with these lines

> Dedicated to the American hierarchy, the American priests and the American people who under the guidance of the Holy See built the Church in the United States better than they knew.

Few people today have particular reason to appreciate how glorious are the pages of Catholic history in the United States, how entrancing is the romantic record of its pioneer priests. The accomplishments were unique because the beginnings were so inauspicious and the populations they dealt with were so difficult. Peter Guilday, in his *History of the Councils of Baltimore,* described the loose discipline facing pioneer American bishops as follows:

> The Church here during this period of its infancy was sadly hampered by priests who know not how to obey and of laity who were interpreting their share in Catholic life by non-Catholic Church systems [p. 85].

As for people, the numbers were staggering. Immigrants numbered 20,000 in 1827. By 1850 they added up to 1,071,000. By 1830 the

Church was called to care for nearly twice the numbers it had in 1820. By 1840 the immigrant population doubled again, practically tripled by 1850, doubled again by 1860. Within a 40-year period the Catholic population multiplied 16 times so that by Civil War time it stood around 3,000,000. In city centers, where most of these immigrants huddled, the faithful relied on the Church and on the ability of priests to build the churches, the schools, the hospitals, and the asylums they desperately needed. Almost miraculously the Church rose to the occasion. Priests multiplied more than 14 times in the same period—from 150 in 1820 to 2,200 in 1860. (There was 1 priest to every 940 Catholics in 1920 compared to 1 to every 1,300 Catholics 100 years earlier.) The immigrants they were servicing were frequently bad Catholics to begin with. Historian Emmet Larkin estimates that "most of the 2,000,000 Irish who emigrated between 1847 and 1860 were part of the prefamine generation of nonpracticing Catholics, if indeed they were Catholics at all" (*American Historical Review*, June 1972).

The buildup of the Catholic community was not in any way dramatic but the result of single-minded, plodding effort. By the end of the Civil War there were records

• of priests crossing rivers by ferry, driving twenty, thirty, forty miles with horse and buckboard to bring Mass and instruction to rural farmers and tradesmen.
• of laymen walking twenty miles to attend Mass and to receive the sacraments.
• of pastors rising before dawn and traveling twenty-five miles to visit a parishioner or to say Mass at a mission.
• of an incessant round of house-to-house visitations in every parish.

By the First World War the American Church was a rallying place for Catholic loyalties. Sheer size also made the Church an important part of the nation itself. Catholics were not yet socially suitable for White House occupancy (indeed, the Church's German, Italian, and Slav members would in 1924 face further restrictions on their immigration). But the Irish and the Germans were saying a great deal about how key American cities should be run. Unnoticed at the time too—though fairly clear in hindsight—those immigrants, especially the Irish, were making the social ladder a stepping-stone to fame and fortune, moving slowly into prestige positions in industry, labor, and banking. Their children were entering college, the priesthood, and religious life in large numbers. The Roaring Twenties became the era when Catholics came not from a neighborhood or town, but from a parish. By this time, however, the new piety of Catholics now owed much more to the industry of religious brothers and sisters rather than of parish priests. In 1950 the Catholic Church boasted

- 60,000 priests (with 25,000 seminarians in training) and 150,000 religious educating.
- 5,000,000 youth in Catholic schools from kindergarten to university, with 5,000,000 more young people under catechetical instruction.

What kind of Catholics were they? The first large census study in Florida of 50,000 American Catholics (completed in 1944) indicates that the Catholicization process that had begun one century earlier was complete. The religious behavior of Catholics matched the Church's highest expectations:

- 75 per cent of the married Catholics attended Mass every Sunday.
- 50 per cent received Communion at least monthly.
- 85 per cent made their Easter duty.
- 85 per cent of the single people went to Mass every Sunday, regardless of whether they were 19, 29, 39, 49, or over.
- 50 per cent and more of the single people received Communion monthly regardless of age.
- The college-educated Catholics were more regular in Mass attendance than anyone else, went to Communion more often, and had the largest families.

The growth of the Catholic School system and the importance of religious brothers and sisters are reflected in the following diocesan figures of school enrollment, from the *Catholic Directory*:

|              | Year |      |
|--------------|------|------|
|              | 1913 | 1960 |
| Chicago      | 120,000 | 427,000 |
| Milwaukee    | 39,000 | 159,000 |
| New York     | 111,000 | 352,000 |
| Philadelphia | 70,000 | 330,000 |
| St. Louis    | 35,000 | 114,000 |

These data, corroborated by later studies, suggest a number of things:

• The overwhelming majority of the Catholic people had been effectively reached by the Church's manifold structures. They were practicing Catholics.
• The Church through its supported family life and school systems became the instrument of Americanization and upward social mobility.
• The leaders of the Church—bishops, priests, religious, lay apostles—won the loyalty of the vast numbers of Catholics in major matters involving Catholic doctrine and Church policy.
• Catholic parishes for the most part were important local communities. Sometimes they were solely ethnic, most often neighborhood centers for Catholics, and occasionally social communities that related successfully to indigenous non-Catholics and to custodians of muncipal affairs.
• The institutional Church also presided over the emergence of a Catholic elite—mainly through its colleges, seminaries, and lay apostolic movements for social justice, international peace, family life, and spiritual perfection. These movements owed their existence to the impetus given them by the Holy See from Leo XIII onward. Even the loyal opposition (typified by John Courtney Murray and Dorothy Day) proposed new approaches and new accommodations within the framework of the Church structure.

As a *tour de force* by a religious group, the institutional and community accomplishments of the American Church are unsurpassed in Catholic history. Though the tendency today is to accentuate the deficiencies of the American Church, there are those who think that its equal cannot be found anywhere.

The problems facing the American Church of the future, on the other hand, are those rising from affluence and education rather than poverty and illiteracy. Some of the recent data reflect what those problems are since the close of Vatican II.

• Perhaps as many as 10,000,000 Catholics stopped regular attendance at Sunday Mass—a 30 per cent decline. (In some metropolitan archdioceses only 30 per cent of the Catholic population goes to Mass every Sunday.)
• The declines are more severe among the young, including those receiving a complete Catholic education, and surprisingly among middle-class women in the middle years of life, who hitherto were exemplars of Catholic piety.
• A once-proud Catholic school system is down almost 2,000,000 in enrollment.

• The number of babies baptized has dropped by almost 500,000.
• There are almost 50,000 fewer converts.
• Catholic attitudes toward the Church and its teaching have radically changed. From remarkable conformity in belief and practice, researchers have found among 1976 Catholics that:
  • 3 out of 4 approve sexual intercourse for engaged couples.
  • 8 out of 10 approve of contraception.
  • 7 out of 10 approve of legalized abortion.
  • 4 out of 10 do not think the pope is infallible.

In spite of these discouraging estimates, the Catholic Church of 1979 has more going for it than the infant, depressed, isolated Catholic body of 1789. There is little reason, therefore, to believe that Catholic genius and faith are now so debilitated that chroniclers of the next century will be unable to record additional Catholic gains once the precise goals of Vatican II are institutionalized as effectively as those of Trent. These are the pages still to be written.

## II. *The Forecasts*

The numbers of people forecasting the future of the Catholic Church are already legion. Entire volumes have been given over to the subject, mostly of the downbeat variety. Even books that predict a prosperous twenty-first century for the Church may not be speaking of the Catholicism everyone knows. Henri Fesquet of *Le Monde* adopts Montesquieu's famous quip: "The Protestants will disappear, but by the time they do Catholicism will have become Protestant." For Fesquet the Church body has "the stomach of an ostrich," an elasticity that German theologian Karl Rahner would deny. Rahner instead sees the future Church scattered in "tiny flocks" (in Diaspora) distinguishable from the secular environment yet offering worldliness only a dream of better things to come. Bernard Alfrink, the retired Dutch cardinal, speaks of the new Catholicism as "the Church nobody knows"— in Diaspora to be sure, pluriform, ecumenical, helping the world solve mundane problems.

Paul VI, who sighed (September 11, 1974) that the Church appears "destined to burn itself out," in an earlier optimistic mood told the College of Cardinals (June 22, 1973) that the Church might be a tiny flock at the moment, but the Catholic objective was still making disciples of all nations. Here the Pope was reasserting the traditional Catholic institutional goals.

Clearly, expectations for the Church follow preconceived understandings of what Catholicism is in the first place. The Second Vatican
Council's effort to fuse Catholic tradition with the intellectual demands of modernity has been interpreted differently by various leadership segments of the Church.

In all probability the Catholic extremists worth mentioning are those
who would follow the example of liberal Protestantism, which for more
than a century attempted to consummate the same marriage with
indifferent results. Novelist Irving Wallace in *The Word* has a Dutchman describe what the sense of this new Christianity might be (pp.
349–54):

> "What I believe in, what millions in every land who believe as
> I do stand for, demand, insist upon, is a new church, one
> meaningful for and relevant to today's society and its
> needs. . . .

> ". . . As the heirs of all the investigators from Galileo and
> Newton to Mendel and Darwin, we find it implausible to ac-
> cept, 'the inheritance of Original Sin from Adam, the Immac-
> ulate Conception of Mary, the Virgin Birth of Jesus, the
> Atonement for sin by his Crucifixion, his physical Resurrec-
> tion from his death, his corporeal Ascension into Heaven, and
> the resurrection of our bodies from death on the morning of
> the Last Judgment, which will consign us both physically and
> spiritually to everlasting bliss or everlasting torture.' . . .

> ". . . Belief in Jesus Christ as a Messiah or as a historical being
> is of no importance to religion today. What is of importance
> is rereading, in a new depth, the social message of the early
> Christians. . . .

> ". . . The new church I advocate will be one church, Protes-
> tant and Catholic as one. It will have Christian unity. An ecu-
> menical spirit—one world in one church—will prevail. This
> church will not promote a blind faith, miracles, celibacy and
> irrefutable authority for its clergy. This church will reject
> riches, will spend its money on its people and not on massive
> cathedrals like the Westerker, Westminster Abbey, Notre
> Dame, St. Patrick's in New York. It will work in the commu-
> nity, through small groups which will not suffer sermonizing
> but will enjoy spiritual celebrations. It will integrate minori-

ties, it will acknowledge the equality of women, it will promote social action. It will support birth control, abortion,
artificial insemination, psychiatric help, sex education. . . .

". . . Ask your associates whether they are prepared to give up
dogmatic church teachings for free discussions. Ask them what
they are doing—now—about race relations, poverty, the unequal distribution of wealth. Ask them whether they are
prepared to surrender their fat institutions for a universal
Christian community, where the minister or priest is not a
special person, not a dignitary, but simply a servant who can
bring to those who employ him spiritual life. . . ."

Most Catholic renewalists would reject this vision of the Church to
come because they reject Wallace's *Word* for its lack of faith in the supernatural. However, they might accept a broader-based Church and a
more flexible Gospel. Marcel Legaut spoke for many French Catholic
intellectuals when writing first for *Lumen Vitae* (1972) he gave his
"Glimpse of Tomorrow's Church":

The Church of Christendom, which was essentially a governing Church, whose ideal was to organize society, to build "a
City of God" and hence to reach individuals from without
and in a global fashion in order to Christianize them, must be
succeeded by a new Church witnessing to Jesus Christ and capable of being present everywhere and to all men. Without
constituting a society similar to that of other religions, she will
radiate her light thanks to her members and to the spiritual
influence they will exercise both as individuals and as community. Taking men as they are, she will help them to set out on
their specific path so that, individually and collectively, they
may become capable in turn of acceding to the faith [*Cross
Currents*, Spring 1973].

The mission of the Church to the world in this view will be more
personal than institutional, an invitation to faith in the person of Jesus
Christ more than faith in propositions or human structures, the personal experience of believers more than a group membership or a group
phenomenon.

This approach to the future Church, alleged to be the one mandated
by Vatican II, tends to accentuate certain elements rather than others.

Because it is popular with featured Catholic writers, the substance of its proposals merits attention.

### III. The Modern View of Futuristic Catholicism

There is no single satisfactory catalogue proposed for the new Catholicism. Certain elements, however, are widely endorsed by many intellectuals and by those in the popular media who find their presentations persuasive. Some of these are the following:

1. *The Rise of the Charismatic or Pentecostal Movement*

Charism—over and above office-holding—was a featured characteristic of the primitive Church, where the emphasis was on personal commitment to Christ and enthusiasm for his Gospel. "Living faith" describes the early Christians, not the external religion that grew up long after Christ.

A return to personal Gospel living is of special significance in modern times. Contemporary man has become weary of formalism, legalism, and traditionalism. He seeks fulfillment and self-actualization. If the Church is to satisfy the needs of modernity, it must return to its beginnings, even though many historic accumulations must be divested.

The return of Pentecostal forms is also demanded on the grounds that most Catholics are not living the Gospel life. Quite the contrary, many are a scandal to unbelievers, who factually may be better witnesses of God's love than Christians.

The evil in pre-Vatican II Catholicism that must be eradicated is institutionalization, with its tendency to have believers look for Christ in external things, not within themselves. Even reception of the sacraments or heeding the voice of the bishops are not substitutes for genuine personal commitment to Christ.

2. *Small Companies of Jesus*

The first stated constituent of a renewed Catholicism makes the second a necessity. Personal religion can best be realized in small group communities that meet for worship, for discussion, and for the performance of good works.

Bigness is bad, even in the Church, because it depersonalizes. Big parishes and big dioceses become ends in themselves rather than way stations to faith. They become arbitrary and rigid, if not oppressive. The primitive Church was local and autonomous; so must the future Church be.

3. *Communal Decision-making*

Not only did early Christians hold property in common, they also made critical decisions for the Church together. The lord of the community was first its servant.

Dominating authority figures, as necessary as they are with growth, came later in the Church, justifying their role as spokesmen for Christ and as knowledge bearers to later population groups, who were at that time underdeveloped intellectually and socially. Modern man, on the other hand, knows a great deal and sees too many sides to human problems to believe that authority figures by themselves have the answers. Furthermore, historical research has indicated that Christ promised the Spirit to the whole Christian community, not simply to an elite.

The Second Vatican Council recognized the importance of participation by all in the decisions of the Catholic community. Words and phrases like "collegiality," "shared responsibility," and "consensus-building" reflect the desired future direction of authority in the Church.

4. *New Forms of Speaking and Acting*

Since the future of the universe itself is unknown, traditional insights, even in religious matters, have little relevance. For one thing, believers must relate the Gospel to their particular life situations. The mind and will of God cannot be predetermined for them in abstractions. The Church can inspire men to examine the Gospel before making personal judgments, but different communities will find different imperatives applying to their particular situations. Even the word "God" has different meanings for modern man. Consequently, old orthodox formulas, even those about Christ, must be reinterpreted so as to become meaningful to an age that has little confidence in the supernatural or the miraculous.

This demand of modernity will force the Church to re-examine its accumulated corpus of ancient doctrinal propositions, to hold up the living Christ as the reason for having faith.

5. *A House of Many Mansions*

Dominican Cletus Wessel made a succinct prognosis: "Unity of Spirit, yes; unity of faith, yes, but there is no demand for uniformity in terms of structure, government, worship, and doctrine." (NCR, January 19, 1973).

Pluralism and diversity, which characterized the Church in the early centuries, are the qualities most suited to post-Vatican II Catholicism. The word "Catholic" will be restored to its original meaning—"universal"—an all-embracing Church reaching out to all nations, freed of enslavement to historic forms and concepts, many of which no longer make sense to or have value for modern man.

6. *Salvation of the World*

Faith thinking for the next century will be man-centered. The emphasis will be on Christ's humanity, on finding Christ in other men, on liberating men from poverty and oppression so that they can find

Christ. The Church will work to make "justice and peace" the operative virtues in national and international affairs. Without abandoning its traditional charitable services to the poor and the beleaguered, the future Church will actively engage in political action on behalf of social causes. To do this well the Church must learn to appreciate the religious values inherent in the secular world, values at times first discovered by unbelievers. Once involved in the causes that interest modern man—his temporal well-being—the Church will have an opportunity to witness Christ in the world in a way it has not in centuries.

7. *One Law of Love*

The renewed Church will encourage Christians to live more by the Sermon on Mount Thabor—the beatitudes or counsels of perfection—than by the commandments of Mount Sinai. All men—even unbelievers—are called upon to live according to the minimal principle of doing good and avoiding evil. The Christian is called to a higher lifestyle. The Gospel call and Christ's personal example require that his followers be poor, compassionate, forgiving, forbearing, and critics of those who would oppress other men. The "casuist's conscience" ("How little do I need do to be Catholic?") must be uprooted from the Church to be replaced by the general acceptance of the evangelical counsels. The beatitudes are the normal way of Christian life, not the special calling of the few, be they "saints," "monks," or "nuns."

These seven concepts, each of which find real or apparent justification in Scripture and Catholic tradition, are said to have been restated anew in particular Vatican II documents. There is considerable variance, of course, between the official interpretation of what those concepts mean and the developments that certain Catholic scholars would like to see occur that would enlarge their meaning. There are other concepts, however, also with a scriptural base, that are imbedded in Catholic tradition and in the documents of Vatican II. These are integral, if not essential, parts of any definition or description of the future Catholic Church.

1. The Church is the Body of Christ. If men are called to Christ, they are also called to his Church. The Catholic Church is uniquely this Church, although other churches also claim origin in Christ. For those who profess faith in Christ as revealed through the Catholic Church, the group experience and the group membership, originating in Christ's own revelation, transcend the experiences or private revelations of any given individual.

2. The authetic Catholic experience, therefore, and the living witness of Christ's revelation, are to be found in the worship, in the doctrinal teaching, and in the disciplinary traditions that have been handed

on to the successive generations and through various cultures and that the Church considers essential to the faith and binding on Catholic believers.

3. The teaching and pastoral life of the Church, whether in passing on traditions (especially revealed doctrines) or accommodating its style or institutions to various cultures and ages, must always be conducted so as to intensify, if possible, the commitment of Catholics to the Church and to the Church's view of what Christ requires or asks of believers.

4. The supreme judge of the value or correctness of new forms, new laws, new teachings, or personal religious experience is the Pope in union with the body of bishops, and by the bishops in union with the Pope.

5. Small companies of Catholics, like larger entities, various modes of decision-making, are useful or not depending on their conformity to Catholic doctrine, their approval or acceptance by legitimate authority, and how they build or damage the universal Body of Christ.

6. The many mansions of the Church or the diverse forms of Catholic expression find unity not only around Christ, but also after the Ascension around the Pope and the bishops.

7. The object of Catholic involvement in secular problems is to enhance mankind's religious and spiritual life, to lead mankind thereby to Christ's promised eternal salvation.

8. The celebration of the evangelical counsels or the pursuit of Christian perfection presumes that the fundamental moral laws of God and the Church are observed and respected.

## IV. What the Teaching Church Says About Its Future

The Church, even while experiencing the institutional crisis of its life, is very much moving in new directions. What Catholicism ultimately will look like when Vatican II principles penetrate the Church as completely as Trent's did is anyone's hazardous guess. Yet an examination of official documents indicates that five signs of what that Church might be are already present in the contemporary Church:

1. The Catholic Church remaining the one true and unique Church of Christ.
2. The Church actively engaged in ecumenical efforts to reunite all Christians.
3. The Church encouraging continued dialogue with intellectuals as it has rarely done in modern times.

4. The Church pursuing the causes of justice and peace and the liberation of oppressed peoples everywhere.

5. The Church setting an intellectual and moral tone consistent with its authentic understanding of God's law and Christ's revelation.

These propositions are understood and interpreted by the Pope and the bishops with a certain consistency and in such wise that the growth and development of the Vatican II Church is likely to follow their definitions, and few others.

1. *The Church of Christ*

The final declaration of the 1974 synod of bishops, which was devoted to evangelization, ended with this reaffirmation:

> We want to confirm anew that the mandate to evangelize all men constitutes the Church's essential mission.

One year later (December 8, 1975), marking the tenth anniversary of the close of the Second Vatican Council, Pope Paul VI issued a twenty-one-thousand-word statement entitled "Evangelization in the Modern World," in which he forthrightly said that the deepest inspiration of the Church was Christ's command "To the whole world! To every creature! To the ends of the earth!"

During the following year Pope Paul devoted nine general-audience addresses to the theme "Building the Church." In these addresses he identified the Church with the Kingdom of God that Christ preached (July 7, 1976), whose ancient structure must be renovated "in a spirit of fidelity to tradition" (July 21, 1976), under the direction of hierarchy "whose power is from Christ" (August 4, 1976) and whose identity is discovered in the line of St. Ambrose: "Where Peter is, there is the Church" (September 1, 1976).

Throughout these documents the Pope and the bishops are speaking obviously of the Catholic Church.

What is the relation of the Catholic Church and other Christian bodies? Pope Paul's 1975 exhortation on evangelization gave this delicate answer:

> The Catholic Church also is zealously concerned for those Christians who are not in full communion with her. While together with them she prepares for the unity Christ willed and has unity based on truth as her aim, she is fully conscious that she would fail seriously in her duty if she did not bear witness

before them to the fullness of revelation which has been entrusted to her. . . .

We make our own the wish of the fathers of the Third General Assembly of the Synod of Bishops: that we might collaborate ever more fervently with those of our Christian brothers
to whom we are not yet united in perfect community.

These statements contain several clear future directions:

A. The Catholic Church, while working toward Christian unity,
   continues to insist that she is the Church of Christ to which
   "the fullness of revelation has been entrusted."
B. The Catholic Church's renewal, whatever else it signifies and
   whatever else contemporary Catholic problems may be, does
   not mean retreat into "tiny flocks."

The first direction is important to understand because there are not
wanting theologians who have interpreted the documents of Vatican II
to suggest that the Church no longer lays claim to the unique title "the
Church of Christ."

The second direction is intended to counteract those who in rethinking the nature of the Church are tempted to reduce it to a loose network of local believing congregations with very little universal or institutional shape, one highly declericalized, ambiguous in its doctrine,
committed to secular pursuits, unified only in their commitment to
Christ, and with a Pope with limited jurisdiction.

What Rome is rejecting are the sentiments expressed in paragraphs
such as the following:

To be an open Church means much more than to be a
Church with open doors. It means thoroughly to embrace all
of contemporary life, finally to break with the nostalgia and
isolation characteristic of the Church under the four recent
Piuses. Openness also means facing the deep religious problems of contemporary life—acknowledging, for example, that
it is not easy to say exactly what "God" means today. To say
whether the orthodox formulas are not mainly empty and to
say precisely when love of neighbor is not sufficient religion.
Similarly we have not adequate ecclesiology for the increasing number who are "selective" in their faith, who cling to
some doctrines and reject others. We are already an ecumeni-

cal Church, in the sense that we are solidly pluralistic. If we are courageous enough to accept organizational and doctrinal pluralism more forthrightly, letting more ways of following Christ just be and interact, we could really start to think of ourselves as united [*America*, February 16, 1974, p. 111].

### 2. *The Church of Reconciliation*

The most important long-range effect of the Second Vatican Council may be the ultimate reunification of many Christian bodies into the One Church of Christ. There may never be perfect unity this side of the New Jerusalem, but Vatican II has already given enlarged impetus to the ecumenical movement among Christians, whose ultimate fruition can be optimistically speculated. A dozen years of new conversations has accomplished significant agreement among Catholic theologians and their peers in important segments of the Anglican, Lutheran, and Orthodox churches.

This process began with the decree of Vatican II on ecumenism (ratified November 21, 1964), which expressed the hope that "little by little, as the obstacles to perfect ecclesiastical communion are overcome, all Christians will be gathered in a common celebration of the Eucharist, into the unity of the one and only Church, which Christ bestowed on his Church from the beginning. This unity, we believe, subsists in the Catholic Church as something she can never lose" (No. 4).

Paul VI took personal pride especially in what he called "the new era of brotherhood" between the Catholic Church and the Orthodox Church. His meeting with Patriarch Athenagoras of Constantinople, whom he referred to as "Brother Athenagoras," was so deeply moving that when Paul met with Metropolitan Meliton of Chalcedon, head of the delegation of the Patriarchate of Constantinople on December 14, 1975, the Pope felt constrained to tell the Orthodox:

> The Catholic Church and the Orthodox are united by such a deep communion that very little is lacking to teach the fullness authorizing a common celebration of the Lord's Eucharist.

A Pan-Orthodox Commission is already engaged in theological dialogue with the Catholic Church. Unity with the Orthodox churches is seen by Rome as a first ecumenical possibility because liturgical, spiritual, disciplinary, and theological diversity between West and East can legitimately coexist here with relative ease.

The ecumenical problems of Catholic-Protestant relations are more complicated, but even in this area Paul VI was able to tell the College of Cardinals on December 22, 1975, that reconciliation "is becoming more and more a subject of growing care and attention on the part of the Catholic Church and the other Christian communions" (*English L'Osservatore Romano*). He takes satisfaction in Vatican participation in the World Council of Churches, not only in its general assemblies but also in its committee work. The Secretariat for the Union of Christians, under the presidency of Cardinal Willebrands, has become the instrument through which various Protestant denominations have acquired uninterrupted contact with the headquarters of the Roman Catholic Church.

Consultation between theologians of the Anglican communion and the Roman Catholic Church already seems to have reached substantial agreement on certain key elements of faith matters. Statements of the Anglican-Roman Catholic International Commission have been widely acclaimed ecumenical formulations. The Windsor Statement reflected substantial agreement among the cosigners on the Eucharist, the Canterbury Statement on the priesthood, the Venice Statement on authority in the Church. Certainly these statements are a far cry from agreement between Rome and Canterbury. Nevertheless, the Venice Statement, for example, considers itself to be "a significant convergence with far-reaching consequences. For a considerable period theologians in our two traditions, without compromising their respective allegiances, have worked on common problems with the same methods. In the process they have come to see old problems in new horizons and have experienced a theological convergence which has often taken them by surprise" (*Origins*, January 12, 1978). In 1896 Pope Leo XIII's *Apostolicae Curae* equivalently declared that the Church of England had neither valid priesthood nor valid Eucharist, since the time of the Edwardine Ordinal (1559). What has happened since then is that an important segment of Anglicanism has become deeply concerned about a valid priesthood and Eucharist, and Roman Catholicism is willing to encourage this return to pre-Reformation Christianity among many Anglicans.

The Lutheran-Catholic dialogue has been similarly propitious. Some Lutheran scholars are prepared to accept the primacy of Peter and a Petrine function for the Pope, who not only symbolizes the Church's unity but also fosters communication and collaboration among local churches. Lutherans have their own ideas about what the papacy should be in the concrete, and many see it serving a leadership role. They have not advanced substantially on Reformation positions, but recently hoped that the Pope could see himself not simply as the chief bishop of Catholics but also as pastor of all Christians (*Origins*, May 2, 1973).

The Catholic Commission for Religious Relations with Judaism issued guidelines on December 15, 1974, that called for increased education, joint prayer, dialogue, and co-operation in social-action programs with Jews. In the area of Jewish-Christian relations, the Vatican commission, deploring the climate of suspicion, called upon Christians "to acknowledge their share of responsibility for this situation." Dr. Eugene Fisher, executive director of the U. S. Bishops' Secretariat for Catholic-Jewish Relations, summarized the progress: "At first, the dialogue between us, to be frank, consisted of good-will gestures, of appearing together in public and in homes, and saying nice things about one another. More recently, however, a change has occurred which I think is most significant. We are now showing the ability to get down to concrete situations, in both theological and pragmatic areas. We are analyzing and changing textbooks, creating educational curricula, facing issues such as education and proselytism—in short, working together on a day-to-day basis" (*Origins*, January 5, 1978).

The Church has actually gone beyond dialogue among professionals. From the day before the council's closing (December 7, 1965), when Paul VI and Partriarch Athenagoras withdrew the excommunications in force between Rome and Constantinople since 1054, practical gestures have been made to ease tension between Catholics and other religionists. Mixed marriages involving Catholics can be witnessed by other than priests; non-Catholics no longer are required to agree in writing that the children must be educated as Catholics, and the couple may be married within Mass; Catholics marrying before non-Catholic ministers are no longer excommunicated; dioceses have been instructed to establish ecumenical commissions; indiscriminate conditional baptism of converts from Protestantism is discouraged; days of prayer in common with Orthodox and Protestants are encouraged; Catholic sacraments may be administered to separate brethren in danger of death or in urgent need if they have faith in these sacraments and have no access to their own minister for a prolonged period of time; Catholics may on occasion attend non-Catholic liturgical services for good reason.

This growth in intercredal co-operation has generally been irenic. The Secretariat for the Union of Christians (August 15, 1970, No. 10), in specifying that from the Catholic side "the participants [in theological dialogue] are appointed by the hierarchy to attend not in a personal capacity but as delegated representatives of their Church" and "the Catholic participants have a special responsibility toward the authority that has sent them," has contributed to the responsibility of these discussions. Although institutions and large social groups rarely entrust critical discussions to scholars or intellectuals alone (although they may provide input), the high authorities of the Church at both Roman and diocesan levels have entrusted a large part of the initial breakthroughs to members of the Catholic university community. As a result the ecumenical discussions have tended to concentrate on concessions that the Catholic Church might find compatible and the requirements non-Catholic churches consider necessary before Christian unity is possible.

The Anglicans, for example, think the bishop of Rome is too authoritarian, and wish in an ecumenical church a great degree of local self-government, individual expression, and a plurality of theological affirmations from region to region. The Venice Statement still looks upon the claim of the Pope to "universal immediate jurisdiction" as a source of anxiety because it is open to illegitimate use. There are also contradictory (and irreconcilable) differences between the two churches on the moral principles governing marriage, family life, and sexuality. The Lutherans do not consider that the primacy of the Pope is due to any divine law but is the result of purely human circumstance. Some of their leaders would wish the Pope to give up the practice of naming bishops. There also remain important doctrinal differences on the ordained ministry, the sacramentality and indissolubility of marriage and the Eucharist.

The recent ordination of women in the several churches of the Anglican communion has created an additional obstacle to unity both with Catholic and Orthodox churches. The leaders of the Russian Orthodox Church have told Anglican Archbishop of Canterbury Donald Coggan that it is an "insurmountable obstacle." Abortion is another issue about which there is likely to be no agreement.

The Jewish groups are more direct in their statements of disappointment. Not only were Jews unhappy with the 1974 Vatican "Guidelines for Catholic-Jewish Relations" because they did not make express contrition for persecution of Jews by Christians, nor recognize the link between Judaism and Israel, but, according to Dr. Eugene Fisher, Jews are still not happy with the treatment in Catholic classrooms of Pharisees (usually vilified as legalists and hypocrites) and Christ's passion, nor with the idea that Christianity has supplanted Judaism in God's plan for the world.

Some of these controverted issues will not be resolved in every case and some of them are not resolvable because, on Catholic principles, they are not negotiable. On the other hand, a dozen or so years are little

time to judge progress in reuniting religious groups who have been separated at times for five centuries, some for an entire millennium or more.
The difficulties are not small but the forward movement is sufficiently
strong to have the Catholic Church pursue unity over the opposition of
some of its own members with the same determination it has always
promoted institutional identity.

Paul VI himself took an optimistic view. In a general audience (January 18, 1978), and after admitting that "the problem" seems insoluble
because the unresolved issue is "real unity" ("It is impossible to admit
any unathorized pluralistic interpretation of this sacred word 'unity'"),
Paul was content with the progress in communion already evident, with
the bonds that demand from the Mother Church "immense patience
and exemplary humility." And he concluded: "We must pray." Paul
VI knew that the re-establishment of unity among Christians finally
depends on prayer and the providence of God.

3. *The Recovery of Catholic Intelligence*

The second obvious positive result of Vatican II (after ecumenism) is
the movement within the Church to assign status and role to intellectuals and scholars. Unquestionably the period since 1962 has been
one of intellectual ferment, Catholics seeking to gain academic respectability, Church authorities hoping for creative development and more
effective evangelization of the modern world thereby. The accusation
that the Church prior to Vatican II refused to enter honest dialogue
with the secular mind apparently has stung Catholic thinkers to independent initiative and Church authority to permit intense questioning
of all religious suppositions in the interest of enriched understanding or
legitimate accommodation with the world's intellectuals. The Church
seems determined to continue this process until by trial and error it
sifts those strands of modern thought that can be baptized Catholic,
confirmed with a Christian meaning, and utilized in the conduct of
Catholic affairs.

Latter-day Catholic academicians have been embarrassed by their
lack of new Christopher Dawsons or Jacques Maritains, of men in the
Church capable of virtuoso performances at things intellectual, of
Catholics recognized by peers for their deserved influence on social
thought. As a result there has been a rush among Catholics to become
scholarly and intellectual. However, apart from the question of whether
Dawson or Maritain would fit today into the contemporary intellectual
scene as comfortably as they once did, there is another difficulty peculiar to these times.

Modern intellectualism is disrespectful of ties that bind men permanently to institutions and to dogmas that rationalize these loyalties.

Rooted adoringly in the scientific method, modern intellectualism lacks reverence for God in heaven, for Jesus Christ born before all ages as Son of the Father or in time as the son of a Virgin, for *priori* knowledge called revelation, for an immortal soul that defies empirical scrutiny, for a beatitude beyond the grave.

The contemporary intellectual world, therefore, makes little allowance for serious entertainment of Catholic faith or doctrine. Its criteria for judging what is worthwhile in religion are not faith criteria. Instead, practical contributions to society or personal meaning are considered the primary justifications for modern man having religious faith at all. This ethos is so powerful that even "religious" intellectuals are tempted to strip faith concepts to their bare bone, to make doctrine compatible with what scientists and philosophers say (on the evidence they appreciate) is at least credible or a good working hypothesis.

The intellectual counterrevolution being promoted by the Catholic Church, however, is expected to move in a different direction. Fr. James Schall, S.J., states the objective simply: "Catholicism needs to regain its own intelligence." If Catholic intellectuals are vital to the process of post-Vatican II renewal (and the Church thinks they are), they ordinarily will follow the tradition of John Henry Newman, Charles Peguy, François Mauriac, Edward I. Watkin, and Étienne Gilson, or so the Church expects.

Newman, for example, thought the true intellectual was a man not only of ability and talent but also a man of virtue. He thought that the great misfortune of his times was the separation of intellect from virtue, and virtue from intellect. In a sermon at Dublin's University Church, Newman rued:

> It will not satisfy me, what satisfies so many, to have two independent systems, intellectual and religious going at once side by side, by a sort of a division of labour, and only accidentally brought together. It will not satisfy me if religion is here and science there.

Étienne Gilson in *Spirit of Medieval Philosophy* hardly sees the Christian thinker thinking except within the world of revelation. What Gilson says unashamedly of Christian philosophy applies to all intellectual effort by believers:

> Christian revelation has intervened and has profoundly modified the conditions under which reason has to work. Once you are in possession of that revelation how can you pos-

sibly philosophize as though you had never heard of it? The
errors of Plato and Aristotle are precisely the errors into which
pure reason falls, and every philosophy which sets out to be
self-sufficing will fall into them again, or perhaps into others
still worse; so that henceforth the only safe plan is to take revelation for our guide and make an effort to understand its contents—and this understanding of the contents of revelation
will be philosophy itself [p. 5].

The Vatican is hopeful that aspiring Catholic intellectuals will become steeped in their own tradition, especially in its recognition of spiritual reality. They must also accept the Church as the world's unique
representative of that spiritual order. A thinker who captures the world
while losing the Church or who gives the highest priority to the compatibility of doctrine with modern thinking is not likely to take his
place in the forefront of leading Catholic luminaries. Fr. Schall believes
that the primary intellectual task of Catholicism is to recover its own
doctrines. The great Catholic minds of history assumed almost without
argument that Catholicism had its own content whose meaning is
amplified by its own rigorous intelligence. Traditionally this has meant
"thinking with the Church" (*sentire cum Ecclesia*). The outstanding
Catholic figures in literature, history, drama, theology, and philosophy
usually did. John Henry Newman was willing to root his thinking in
the Magisterium of the Church.

The most obvious answer to the question, why we yield to the
authority of the Church in the questions and developments of
faith, is that some authority there must be if there is a revelation given and other authority there is none but she. A revelation is not given, if there be no authority to decide what it is
that is given. In the words of St. Peter to his Divine Lord,
"To whom shall we go?" [*Development of Doctrine* (1906),
pp. 88–90].

James Weisheipl, in *Friar Thomas D'Aquino: His Life, Thought, and
Work*, records a similar sentiment from the "Dumb Ox," who as he received Viaticum said to the abbot:

I have taught and written much on the most holy Body and
on the other sacraments, according to my faith in Christ and
in the Holy Roman Church, to whose judgment I submit all
my teaching [p. 326].

The newly created Fellowship of Catholic Scholars had this understanding when in its founding statement of purpose it said:

> We wish to form a fellowship that is gladly obedient to the Word of God spoken in His Catholic Church. We accept willingly in faith the defined teachings of the Church's ordinary and universal Magisterium. We acknowledge also our duty to adhere with religious assent to those teachings which are authoritatively, even though not infallibly, proposed by the Church, as for example, in the papal encyclicals [*Lumen Gentium*, 25].

> Aware of the duty scholars have to serve the whole community of faith, we wish to give whatever assistance we can to the Church in answering contemporary questions. We will seek to do this, faithful to the truth guarded in the Church by the Holy Spirit, and sensitive to the needs of the family of faith.

Christopher Dawson, who was at home with Catholic intelligence and culture, looked upon religion, particularly Catholicism, as central to human society's development:

> At every step the religion of society expresses its dominant attitude to life and its ultimate conception of reality. Religion is the great dynamic force in social life, and the vital changes in civilization are always linked with changes in religious beliefs and ideals [*Progress and Religion*, p. 234].

The Catholic Church is not likely to make too many radical concessions to contemporary secular intelligence primarily because Catholicism by the nature of its own being manages to remain other-worldly and supracultural. It holds on to the substance of what it says, whenever the saying is important. Catholicism does not always dominate a particular civilization, time period, or place but manages to maintain its own view of the promised land. In those circumstances it becomes a subculture imposing its views on believers and working to penetrate its hostile environs. As a living religion with roots outside and beyond human societies, the Catholic Church is a center around which the thinking of its faithful and potential believers revolve and to which the secular life of Catholics usually relates. As an effective society in its own right, especially when the number of Catholic adherents is large, the Church develops support systems for the faithful and defenses against forces that threaten spiritual life or the external destiny of mankind. This is the essential social role the Catholic Church assigns itself: to speak for the eternal and universal in man's common being and to lead him to a spiritual life. The Church does not organize the general culture of a given society (any more than the free state does), but through the propagation of its particular ideology, the Church exercises influence.

This is the world to which the intellectual must adjust if he would also be Catholic. The Church is his primary reference group.

Consequently, the Catholic Church will resist a culture or an ideology or a method that puts man in first place rather than God, that stresses worldly happiness to the exclusion of the eternal, that considers private opinion on religion the equal of its own Magisterium, or reduces the Church to a body of people rather than the Body of Christ. Part of the reason the Church has in recent centuries lost influence is that the modern intellectual tends to be antireligious and anti-authority. Aspiring Catholic intellectuals in this environment are easily influenced in the same direction. The Church's renewed task is to win intellectual converts all over again. Peter in Rome, Paul in Athens, and John in Ephesus faced similar and overwhelming odds preaching to unbelievers of the highly sophisticated Greco-Roman civilization. The modern Peters, Pauls, and Johns—especially as bishops—run more dangerous risks in the enterprise of evangelization. The early Church had little to lose institutionally by dialogue with intellectuals. The number of early Christians were counted in the few thousands. The contemporary Church represents 750 million Catholics whose faith must be safeguarded as its evangelizers seek ways to preach effectively to several billion people who do not believe in Christ or the Church.

A Catholic intellectual revival in the Church's understanding of that reality is what is contemplated in the broad sweep of post-Vatican II academic ferment. How is this revival to be accomplished? Christopher Dawson once expressed the following confidence:

> It must be activated from above by being once more brought into relation with the forces of Divine Power and wisdom and love. The Faith in the possibility of this divine action on the world is the foundation of Christian thought [*The Judgment of Nations*, p. 125].

### 4. *Champion of Justice and Peace*
It should be clear that the Catholic Church at official levels and at the grass roots is involved in a host of social issues that formerly were considered none of its business of saving souls. Bishops make so many

recommendations about war, the death penalty, labor unions, strikes, boycotts, school desegregation, level of welfare payments and eligibility, food stamps, and national health insurance that their involvement in these matters by now is a commonplace fact of Catholic life. Parish groups and diocesan committees confront local politicians, help run public-school and community boards, and collect petitions for or against proposed laws to such an extent that the traditional image of the Church as the neighborhood center of prayer and worship tends to be blurred in the public eye.

What many people tend to forget, however, especially critics of Catholic political involvement, is that the Church has been nagging its faithful on these issues for a long time, without many of them, including priests, taking the social message seriously. Popes especially—from Leo XIII onward to the present—have developed a body of Catholic social doctrine that places the Church in the middle of all human problems connected with justice and peace. The social encyclicals are impressive: *Rerum Novarum* (1891), *Quadragesimo Anno* (1931), *Divini Redemptoris* (1937), *Summi Pontificatus* (1939), *Mater et Magistra* (1961), *Pacem in Terris* (1963), and *Progressio Populorum* (1968). This magisterial teaching of the Church on social matters was proclaimed because Leo XIII, Pius XI, Pius XII, John XXIII, and Paul VI each felt compelled to place the power of the Church behind movements for social justice and international peace. What Leo XIII said in *Rerum Novarum* (1891) was "so utterly new to worldly ears" that forty years later Pius XI confessed that the Church "was held suspect by some, even among Catholics, and to certain ones he [Leo] gave offense." By the time of the Second Vatican Council the Church was on surer ground with its own. *The Pastoral Constitution on the Church in the Modern World* (*Gaudium et Spes*, 1965) made the salvation of the world, especially the well-being of the poor, an essential part of the Church's mission. The synod of bishops in their 1971 document *Justice in the World*, which they submitted to Pope Paul, spelled out the new mandate:

> Action on behalf of justice and participation in the transformation of the world fully appears to us as a constitutive dimension of the preaching of the Gospel, or, in other words, of the Church's mission for the redemption of the human race and its liberation from every oppressive situation.

The post-Vatican II Church remains faithful to this definition and to the commitments it involves. Assemblies of Catholics, sometimes with priests, sometimes without them, are so involved in both foreign and domestic affairs that at the parochial-diocesan level the social apostolate and all that it implies takes its place alongside liturgy, catechetics, education, family life, and spiritual formation as a regular part of the Church's daily business.

Few would gainsay that this is risky business, not because there are two right sides to every social question, but because equally informed and properly motivated Christians in demanding action may begin with a different set of facts or draw on different principles—for example, freedom from government or governmental responsibility. Foreign affairs—peace in the Middle East, race relations in Africa, SALT talks —are even more complicated, since they involve conflicting claims far away and national or racial self-interest.

The Church pursues these risks with two important provisos:

A. *The social apostolate is better carried on by lay apostles than by clergy.*

Paul VI reaffirmed a policy as old as the papal encyclicals when in *Progressio Populorum* he said:

> While the hierarchy has the role of teaching and authoritatively interpreting the moral laws that apply in this matter, the laity have the duty of using their own initiative and taking action in this area without waiting passively for directions and precepts.

This freedom permits properly motivated Catholics to be on several sides or in the middle of social issues, while preserving the priests (who should be forming consciences) from a political factionalism that divides the faithful unnecessarily.

B. *The Catholic social apostolate is designed to advance the Kingdom of God, not purely secular ends.*

Pope Paul in his exhortation on evangelization (December 8, 1975) raised this thought to Catholic consciousness.

> It cannot be denied that many Christians, generous people who are concerned about the serious questions liberation raises and who want to involve the Church in the liberation, think of the Church's mission and try to limit it accordingly—would have her restrict herself to political or social action without any concern for the spiritual or the religious.

> But if this were a true picture of the Church, she would have lost her meaning.

Two years later the International Theological Commission, an advisory body serving the Pope, examined this question. While calling efforts "to change inhuman conditions . . . a divine command . . . God's will," the practice of the faith "is not reducible to changing the conditions of society"; "politics (for the Christian) is not the final ground that gives absolute meaning to all in life"; "in many individual circumstances it is possible for Christians to opt freely among different paths." The Theological Commission was gravely concerned about the perils to the Church's unity, not only from violent class struggles but also from Catholics refusing to celebrate the Eucharist with confreres of different political persuasions (*Origins*, November 3, 1977).

The tensions over social issues are built into the nature of the Church: a body that says the Kingdom of God is here and is yet to come, is not of this world but is very much in the world, whose Christ was condemned for calling himself the Son of God and as a political zealot plotting Rome's overthrow.

Political activists today, as always, tend to accentuate the here-and-now conditions of men and aggressively pursue the Church's role in their amelioration. The Church of the future is more than ever prepared to engage in this balancing act of promoting the values of both worlds, is prepared to confront inhuman situations with courageous protest, but reminds its following that silent suffering, even martyrdom, is sometimes the price of being Christian.

5. *A Unique Catholic Content to the Church's Message*

One of the surprising things about the post-Vatican II Church is that Pope John XXIII's early hope ("the growth of the Catholic faith and the renewal along right lines of the habits of Christian people") is not mentioned more often when "renewal" is discussed. To deepen and spread faith and to bring mankind *up* to Christian norms of thinking and acting are still the oft-stated goals of the papacy and of Catholic bishops whenever they talk about the evangelization necessary for modern times.

However much else the Church has changed its direction or policies (in the interest of greater attractiveness), Catholicism through the centuries has preached a message about man's purpose, life, and end that has remained consistent and constant. The Catholic message is based on the Church's understanding of God's revelation in nature, and especially through Christ. This message has substance and content, and its core is the center around which all other Catholic activity is organized. However else the Church renews, her fundamental statements of faith and morals are certain to be ancient.

First of all, the Catholic message proclaims prophetically that man has another life ahead of him. This life transcends time and history, the world and its experience. What is not realized in this life will be manifested in the life to come. Jesus Christ not only is the symbol of God's love for men, he also brings God's love and promises God's love, which in the end comes through dying. The cross is not, therefore, an incidental symbol of the revelation Christ came to convey. It is the revelation that by dying (to self, to the world, to sin) man rises to new life here (through grace) on his way to consummate union with God forever.

Preaching this message is the first role of the Church—including the reminders to men of their sinfulness, of their need to do what is right, of the importance of the Church and its sacraments.

Second, the message is explicit about what is needed in concrete in life for the functioning Christian person:

- Strong and deep faith.
- Union with God through prayer and meditation.
- Compatible witness to the faith in personal life and social relations.
- Bearing of the cross.
- Confidence in Christ's presence here and now.
- Hope in the ultimate triumph of Christ.

There are additional and unambiguous demands on the practicing Catholic:

- Obedience to the Ten Commandments and the Precepts of the Catholic Church.
- The Decalogue teaches the absolute priority of serving God first, respect for neighbor, and the incompatibility of certain acts or dispositions (adultery and lust are both condemned) with the love of God.
- The Precepts of the Church cover the obligations of Catholic to attend mass on Sundays and holy days of obligation, to lead a sacramental life in accordance with Church requirements to observe Church marriage laws, to support the Church, and to do penance at appointed times. Catholics are also called upon to practice the virtues.

There is no dispensation from these fundamentals in the Gospels or Epistles, by the Fathers and Doctors of the Church, nor in the two-score ecumenical councils, including the documents of Vatican II. Neither Christ nor the Church has ever told Christians: "Do as you think best." Contrariwise, Christ urged his followers to go beyond the law, to do more than was demanded of them by God or religion's law. "It is not those who say to me, 'Lord, Lord,' who will enter the Kingdom of heaven, but the person who does the will of my Father in heaven" (Mt. 7:21). St. Paul considered himself "not free from God's law, but under the law of Christ" (1 Cor. 9:21). Christ's law was more demanding than, not a dispensation from moral law.

Paul VI told the International Theological Commission (December 16, 1973) that the Christian moral law relates directly to salvation, a matter about which the Church cannot remain silent if men are to act correctly. He was thinking of "moral questions of the highest gravity" (contraception, abortion, sterilization, euthanasia, divorce, homosexuality, and premarital sex). Nothing said by the Pope suggests that the post-Vatican II Church is less strict in its moral demands, even though some priests are telling Catholics that they may accept and follow views contrary to authentic Catholic teaching. Paul VI quoted Peter: "We have left everything and followed you" (Mt. 19:27). And St. Paul: "Do not be conformed to this world" (Rom. 12:2)—in answer to those who make the mistake "of allowing the easygoing ways of the world to creep into their lives" (*The Pope Speaks*, Winter 1974, pp. 315–16).

Although "renewal" is frequently associated with the relaxation of Catholic standards of sexual behavior, the traditional norms are reasserted regularly by bishops and Popes. It is wrong today as always for Catholics to engage in deliberate solitary sexual activity, in the unmarried state, with someone besides a spouse, with members of the same sex, or with animals. With little difference, save perhaps in the tone of the preaching, Church authorities still call sexual impurities evil deeds and, when deliberate, serious sins subject to the penitential discipline of the Church. The teaching is the same even though the discipline of dealing with sexual sinfulness tends to be more gentle than before Vatican II. The *Declaration on Sexual Ethics* issued by the Congregation for the Doctrine of the Faith (December 29, 1975) reaffirmed the standard Catholic norms and placed them within the context in which "God has revealed his plan of salvation," maintaining that the principles of Christian morality are perennial and warning that the Church "keeps a sleepless watch over the truths of morality and transmits them without falsification."

The Catholic Church may be redesigning its goals in accordance with Vatican II and developing machinery to institutionalize the new objectives. In many respects it will be a new Church. In other respects there will be no change at all. Nothing that the church does in this area will satisfy everyone, neither those who want it to fulfill spiritual needs only, nor those who think the material needs of the poor are the first demand of Christian witness from the institutional Church. The Church is on sure grounds in specifying the needs of man's spirit, because revelation has much to say on this subject, and the Catholic tradition here is secure. Even the poor are called to salvation. Those who wish the Church to attend to social needs more than private needs may be asking more than the Church can or ought to give. It took many centuries for the Church to extricate itself from the worst features of the secular world, and there is good reason to believe that the corruption of modernity is no less than before. The arguments made that the Catholic Church is too introverted, is the keeper of exclusive European and Catholic traditions, is too concerned with believers and the affluent are charges that beget soul-searching but are little likely to affect Catholic policy substantially. The Church will pursue its social mission in the future with a more effective program of consciousness-raising on the problems of peace and justice, will make its voice heard more strongly on specific public issues, will encourage self-help efforts by those subject to oppression, but will not permit itself to become an arm of the secular state in the Third World, nor the spokesmen of radical activists in the First.

## V. *What Does the Catholic Future Hold?*

The leadership of the Church is optimistic about the future. Recent efforts—to reduce distance between Christianity and the world, to build bridges among religious bodies that never should have been severed, to penetrate contemporary intellectual and moral life—have received plaudits as much within the Catholic community as without. Even the reformulation of fundamental Christian truths and the rediscovery of forgotten traditions have been endorsed by the highest authorities, although some constituents are not happy with the results. But the future of the Church does not depend on widespread popular acceptance of all its features, nor on the wisdom of every ecclesiastical decision. Two millennia of experience help, as does the divine promise of Christ to be "with you always, until the end of the world" (Mt. 28:20). Favorable outcome to present difficulties can be anticipated because the Catholic Church works securely out of its conviction of a divine mandate. Outsiders and some insiders are annoyed with this claim, as the Elders of the Jews were with Christ for making a similar claim (Mt. 11:27-33), yet the sacredness and seriousness with which this role assertion is made partially explains the longevity of faith in and commitment to the Catholic Church.

Repeated role assertions by themselves, however, will not eliminate all difficulties, but they do remind critics and dissenters that the Church, whether preaching something new or old, speaks for Christ and teaches with his authority. The special problem of modern times is that hardly anyone else claims to teach with authority. This may make the Church unique but it also creates particular tensions in these times.

The Church speaks of itself as a teacher with special qualifications, one that has received a message from God, with the right and responsibility to protect and defend the integrity of the revelation. In the Catholic view all other teachers must refer their private insights on Christ's teaching back to the source from which they received it. These may be literati, savants, research scientists, bishops, retreat masters, or plain farmgirls with visions of the Virgin. When it comes to the soundness of doctrine the savant is no more an autonomous Christian than the unlettered farmgirl.

At various times in history teaching with authority is easy or troublesome. Occasionally society gave "teachers of authority"—including the clergy—special status and power. The very presentation of Church teaching brought reasonable compliance. If dissent or disturbance became a social nuisance, the authoritative teachers were encouraged to protect themselves and the common good by penalizing the troublemakers. The consistent enforcement of public norms with an assist from educational institutions, beginning with the family, usually resulted in a high degree of agreement on belief and on the ideals of behavior. Church controls not only kept serious malefactors in check, but also taught the faithful what the expected conduct of Catholics ought to be.

This situation no longer obtains by virtue of the radical change in society itself. A Gresham's law operates today for ideas as it does in economics. Under this economic law bad money drives out good money or in the present religious case, bad values drive out good values. The leaping growth of crime rates, pornography, abortion, and teen-age pregnancy are only the obvious examples.

Standards of belief and behavior are no longer taught with authority. Values untaught, not internalized, nor legitimized in custom or law tend to decline in importance. Conformity to norm is cheapened, while deviance becomes an acceptable alternate lifestyle for large numbers. Some respond to these difficulties with the indiscriminate use of sanctions, failing to understand that undue reliance on sanctions turns society into a quasiprison. A society held together by sanctions is a society in which authority figures have failed in their more fundamental teaching role—that is, to have its beliefs and code properly internalized.

There is still another dimension to society's modern dilemma. The problem is not merely the absence of "teachers with authority" or the nonenforcement or bad enforcement of its value system. The more critical question may be: Is there a consensus on any value system about which society's leadership can agree? It is doubtful. A great deal is made of the word "consensus" among American elites, but at levels where decisions must be made, authority figures are paralyzed because there is no consensus. Nowhere is this more evident than in the management of public education. The U. S. Supreme Court has ruled the constitutionality of discipline in public schools (including corporal punishment) and at the same time decrees that disciplined students have the constitutional right to due process. The result of this ambiguity is that decisions are not made at all. Uncertainty and indecision in high places take command.

The political ethos of contemporary secular society is now considered an appropriate norm for managing Church structures. This cultural accommodation is justified because of the alleged overassociation of Church teaching with the stick that St. Paul threatened to use on Corinthian converts who were causing him trouble. A more plausible reason is the stress in Vatican II's *Constitution on the Church* that pastors should recognize the "contribution and charisms" of their coworkers and call them to responsible service in Church affairs. While sanctions in the Church, at least in modern times, were not used routinely, serving only as extraordinary teaching devices, input by subalterns in the Catholic system was less than adequate, and one-man rule without informed input was more common than necessary.

The modern problem for the Church, as for the state, is not more input, shared responsibility, participation in decision-making, and consultation with those to be affected by official decisions. These are legitimate contemporary counterbalances to the sometime arbitrary, thoughtless, or uninformed decisions of office-holders.

The problem has become decision-making itself. Those constitutionally empowered to act in the name of society or the Church frequently do not act, and those citizens or religionists bound to compliance frequently do not comply, with no suitable remedy for the vacuum created. Both authority figures and subjects lose in the process, because society, if its necessary works are to be done or if it is to keep its unity, needs decisions and compliance. In Catholic affairs there is also the question of Christ's authority given to men to preach, to make disciples, and to govern the Church. Without authority, human or divine, there is political or ecclesiastical confusion. This becomes a highly desirable condition only for those who value confusion as a condition of liberty.

In the United States and in many parts of the Western world authoritative decision-making power has moved away from authority figures to
those normally the subjects of authority—from parents to children,
from teachers to students, from corporate managers to shop stewards,
from elected officials to various "veto groups" within their jurisdiction
who threaten chaos if certain decisions are or are not made. The common tendency in contemporary society is for "subjects" to make
demands on civic rulers and to threaten disobedience or violence to get
their way. Constituted officials are now accustomed instead to make
requests, may even apologize for seeming to demand, or seek mediation
in cases where law has been violated or violence has already occurred.
An office-holder who threatens sanctions receives a bad press, and this
must be avoided at all cost, even though the historical personages were
often prophets without honor in their own time. The result of this
reversal of roles is that law is not taken as seriously as it once was. If
law is not explained away or is unenforced, officials are sometimes made
to appear unworthy to enforce the law.

How far this confusion of fact and social principle has permeated the
Church cannot be determined with finality. But the penetration is considerable. Speaking up to pastors, bishops, and Pope is commonplace,
as is defiance. Church officials rarely call in a recalcitrant priest or head
of a dissenting Catholic organization for a stern warning or reprimand.
Dissent from Catholic teaching, from liturgical or disciplinary norms by
those who hold positions of trust, is publicly tolerated by high officials.
For this reason alone, Catholic dissenters have acquired a role and
power that normally would not be theirs. In adopting a social-science
model of rulership, rather than maintaining the balanced wisdom of
the Catholic tradition, bishops tend to institutionalize in the Church
the present weaknesses of fragmented secular society. A recent USCC
statement, for example (*Origins,* March 9, 1978), gave over eleven
thousand words to the causes and prevention of crime, with almost no
meaningful statement (hardly fifty words) on the importance of law
and its enforcement, or on the role and dignity of society's officers.

Even when the organic relationship of priests and bishops within the
Church is the question, the USCC statements leave the issue of authority imprecise and inexact. A booklet entitled *As One Who Serves*
(1977), an effort to assist priests in their ministry and the result of
nineteen months' consultation carried on in thirty-five dioceses, makes
the priest's relationship with his bishop (pp. 39–40) equivalent to
psychological growth, maturation, respect, and dialogue. No mention is
made of the bishops' right to command or the priests' obligation to
obey. In fact, at one point, the booklet says: "The personal respect and
love on the part of the priest is expected to be strong enough to

confront at times in order to help to grow, and to be capable of expressing indignation in the light of any injustice which limits the life
of the Church." (p. 40). Not a single word is said about the bishop's
right and duty to confront or express indignation at wrongdoing on the
part of priests, especially since in the management of the Church
bishops and priests are not on equal footing, or equally responsible for
the Church's common good.

Law enforcement by itself does not, of course, fully explain the presence of virtue and peace in society. On the other hand, social unrest is
related to the low status of society's officials and the lack of law enforcement. If the secular confusion on this subject becomes a staple of
Church management—or a commonplace among the faithful—the
decrees of the Second Vatican Council can never be enforced with any
regularity. Partisans of one interpretation or the other will do as they
will. Parishes next to other parishes will follow opposite courses—not in
the incidental aspects of Catholicism but on substantial matters, such
as doctrine and the reception of the sacraments.

The toleration of serious public acts against public law or doctrine is
frequently justified in Christ's name. Yet Christ, when the issues were
important, faced the adversaries of his day with determination. He
upbraided some scribes and Pharisees of his time because "they put
aside the Commandment of God to cling to human tradition" (Mk.
7:6-13); for being faithless (Mk. 9:19); for their pursuit of money and
false positions (Mk. 11:15-18: 12:40); for their abuse of women, hy-
pocrisy, blind leadership, grafting, extortion, murder (Mk. 14:6, Mt.
23:13ff). He accused the Sadducees of understanding neither the
power of God (Resurrection) nor the Scriptures (Mk. 12:27). He asserted his own authority without shame (Mt. 11:27-33) and promised
severe sentences to his adversaries (Mk. 12:40). Christ constantly re-
monstrated with his disciples as well:

For their *failure* to understand the truth of what he says (Mk. 4:13):

> Do you not yet understand? Have you no perception? Are
> your minds closed? Have you eyes that do not see, ears that do
> not hear? Or, do you not remember? [Mk. 8:17].

For arguing with each other (Mk. 9:33; Mk. 10:35-45).

For *overstepping* their authority in rejecting children (Mk.
10:14) and for rebuking Samaritans (Mk. 9:15).

More than once Christ challenged Peter to confess personal faith (Jn.
6:67), to be single-minded ("you are to follow me" Jn. 21-22), rebuk-

ing Peter at one point: "Get behind me, Satan. . . . You are an obstacle (*skandalon*) in my path because the way you think is not God's way
but man's" (Mt. 16:23).

St. Paul offers another example of how the teaching office was exercised in the early Church. Since he was responsible personally for more
new churches than any other Apostle, Paul's founding and teaching
role prompted him to oppose in principle the circumcision of Gentile
converts (Ga. 2:4ff) and Peter's compromising conduct on this issue
(Ga. 4:11ff) (not Peter's belief). Paul anathematized Galatians—who
"want to change the gospel of Christ" (Ga. 1:7ff), demanded an end
to public squabbling (over women's behavior in the churches), saying:
"To anyone who might still want to argue: It is not the custom with us,
nor in the churches of God" (1 Cor. 11:16). To accusations that he
was a weak leader, Paul replies:

> Once you have given your complete obedience we are pre-
> pared to punish any disobedience. . . . Maybe I do boast too
> much about our authority, but the Lord gave it to me for
> building you up and not for pulling you down and I shall not
> be ashamed of it" [2 Co. 10:2–12].

Impurities, fornication, and debauchery among his converts called for
patience, but repeated offenses prompted him to hold Corinthians to
account: "When I come again, I shall have no mercy" (2 Co. 12:20;
13:3). Some converts, now "self-important," were men whose words
outran their deeds. Against these Paul warned: "Do I come with a stick
in my hand or in a spirit of love and good will?" (1 Co. 4:19–21). Even
the author of the Book of Revelation, discovering the sinfulness in
Pergamum, threatened: "You must repent or I shall come to you and
attack these people with the sword out of my mouth" (Rv. 2:16).

Whether the future Church can institutionalize the policies of Vatican II—and the traditions that it maintains—depends on its ability to
receive general compliance, especially from priests and religious, who
are the ones in charge of implementing policy at the local level. Consensus-building, pluralism, and shared responsibility do not stand in the
way. Good teachers of the Church usually are good consensus builders,
do a great deal of listening, and appreciate the wide variety of thought
patterns and lifestyles available to Catholic believers. There are times,
however, when pastors must make decisions in the name of Christ and
the Church without necessarily having the approval of their constituencies. When the decisions are doctrinal this is an exercise in Magisterium, about which the vote of the faithful (if that is to imply its
truth) is not a primary consideration.

Catholic Church leaders at present are trying to use consensus techniques that are working no more successfully for bishops than they are for politicans—if unity or community is the desired end result. Consensus of the people never results from these procedures. What results is agreement only among the leaders of veto groups who accept, tolerate, or defy a particular decision. Whatever other role consensus plays in the management of the institutional Church, it does not create or maintain people's adherence to Catholicism. Only faith does that. Rarely has hierarchy dialogued so much with such unsatisfactory compliance. Until the Church works out an enforceable policy for dealing with dissidence, internal turbulence is sure to continue.

Even if the principles of consensus-building could be more sharply delineated and the technique more widely used, there is no reason to expect compliance for those dissatisfied with the results, regardless of the side of the political spectrum from which the dissenters operate. Sister Margaret A. Farley, R.S.M., in an unpublished presentation to the annual assembly of the Leadership Conference of Women Religious (September 1, 1977), made this quite clear. She has a problem with the "generally promulgated Church teaching" whenever it conflicts, for example, with the corporate conscience of a religious community. The issues might be sociopolitical, liturgical restrictions on women, or doctrines (on contraception or sterilization) that limit what a Catholic hospital or what Catholics can do. Which takes precedence, she asks: integrity of the religious community's ministry or loyalty to the institutional Church? She wishes that nuns' dilemmas did not exist, but after assuring her listeners "that Jesus Christ did not leave a complete blueprint for the institutional Church" and "there are no specific moral teachings that are infallibly defined," "corporate public dissent" may be the only thing for nuns to do. As an example she points to the recent adoption by the General Chapter of the Religious Sisters of Mercy of the Union of criteria for public dissent. Sisters of Mercy, originally a Irish-based community, operate schools, colleges, and hospitals.

There is another danger—namely, that the emerging Church of Elites uncontrolled will undermine the Church of the Masses. The Church of the Masses has not been shattered by the present crisis, only slightly bruised. Most of its numbers still adhere to their accustomed practices. However, if age is a factor, the signs of severe leakage are acute. Some speak of the "lost Catholic generation" whose total recovery for the Church is said to be unlikely. If this becomes an absolute fact, and the evidence points in that direction, then more attention must be paid to the continuing effect on the masses of the latter-day Church of Elites. In contradistinction to an older generation of elites, recent Catholic spokesmen are less conventional, selective in their doctrines and moral imperatives, increasing likely to reject Church teachings publicly, and organize opposition to Pope or bishops. There is a contagious element in the present situation that did not exist before.

This is a new kind of pluralism within the Church—self-created coteries of Catholics who have little intention of following Magisterium except selectively and on their own terms. Older forms of common-law Catholics who lived within but on the fringes of the Church have now been called "communal Catholics" or "community Catholics," who claim to speak out of the Catholic tradition without necessary regard for the authentic teaching and disciplinary decrees of Vatican II. While the Church has never endorsed selective Catholicism, regardless of the nomenclature, the new communal Catholicism justifies itself in the American experience. Since Judaism is not identified with the rabbinate nor Protestantism with ministerial associations, there is no longer any reason why Catholics need defer to the teaching and pastoral government of their bishops, so the argument is made. In this sense communal groups of Catholics have more in common with cultural Protestantism than with their historic faith.

If the "communal Catholics" functioned within the Church as their antecedents did—individually or dormantly—the threat to Catholic solidarity would be small. But if these self-styled *ex lex* "ecclesial communities" see themselves as adversary to bishops or independent forces within the Church for molding Catholic opinion, then the "House of God" is certain to be divided against itself. A splintering of the Church into elite, special-interest, or atomized communities presents problems for American Catholicism, whose masses in the immediate future will be Spanish and poor. The institutional Church has permitted elitist concepts and ministries to function before without allowing either to dominate. Since the Church's pastoral ministry essentially consists in the approved liturgies, the general and particular laws, the universal educational and welfare services and parishes for everyone, it can accept and encourage diverse co-operators but is not likely to tolerate within the body active rivals or opponents. Furthermore, since the universal Church led by bishops and Pope is the fundamental Catholic community, splinter groups are little likely to contribute to the renewal contemplated by Vatican II.

At some point—if the divided Catholic community is to receive new solidarity and reinvigorated purpose—the bishops and the Pope will have to lay out the rules for the new Church once and for all and make them distinguishing marks of a bona fide Catholicism mandated by the Second Vatican Council to which a certain compliance is necessary. Not only will bishops be required to say clearly and with authority where the renewed Church is going, but they will also need to delineate what they will not accept. They will also have to appear to mean what they say. They will have to swim against the strong currents in the cultural tide of the United States. Where civic leaders are weak, they will have to personify strength, using their pulpits and the media once more personally, reclaiming supervisory power over their own agencies and schools, competing with rivals for public influence, rewarding and punishing, making certain that the bishop's office is not belittled, that a second Church does not develop in their jurisdictions.

The contemporary secular world makes it difficult for forceful office-holders. Unless they are able to develop a posture compatible with the television media, which favors bland personalities, authoritative leaders can be made to appear as undemocratic types. Weak political personalities have been common on the American scene for several decades, the stronger highly vulnerable to criticism and negative analysis. Hardly any strong Catholic religious leader enjoys a good press. The fact that bland types have no social or ecclesial influence seems less important than their avoiding controversy in which media forces are arrayed against them. The truth of genuine democracy and its present need, on the other hand, lie in another direction. More than any other form of government, people's rule needs virtue and strength at all levels of its citizenry, notably in its public officials. The Catholic Church has a rare opportunity to help American society rectify its most recent political errors and set a standard of purposeful leadership conducive to public well-being.

Bishops and Pope may assimilate all the modern forms of leadership without ceasing to be bishops and Pope. Bishop James Hickey of Cleveland is one diocesan ordinary who has provided a good model. While demanding that "each member of the Church by reason of baptism has the right and duty to participate in the Church's mission," that parishes in Cleveland must open up to shared responsibility and parish councils, Hickey made clear also that his directives did not mean:

> That every member of the Church has the same responsibilities or is equally empowered to exercise the responsibilities of another.
>
> Nor does shared responsibility mean the organization of the Church according to any form of secular government, democratic or otherwise.
>
> [That shared responsibility disrespects the hierarchical order:] Deacons, priests, and bishops joined with the bishop of Rome

as successor of St. Peter have the specific responsibilities of
their office.

Nor does shared responsibility mean that the clergy or laity of
a given parish or diocese may establish statements of belief or
rules of government at variance with the faith and law of the
Catholic Church in this country or throughout the world [Or-
igins, March 2, 1978].

The American Church has new challenges ahead, perhaps as serious
as anything it has faced since the founding here of the Catholic hierarchy by Pius VI on November 6, 1789. Within 190 days after George
Washington was inaugurated as the first President of his country, the
Catholic Church of the United States was born with the appointment
of John Carroll as the first bishop of Baltimore. It was the weakened
condition of the Church at that time—its declining membership, the
shortage of priests, unruly priests, and the lack of money—that
prompted faithful pastors to ask the Holy See for a resident bishop.
After much delay Pius VI issued the founding brief *Ex Hoc Apostolicae*, in which he told the pastors of the young Church he was founding:

• To promote their own and their neighbors' spiritual advan-
tage.
• To adhere to the heavenly doctrine delivered by Christ to
the Catholic Church.
• Not to be carried away by every wind of doctrine.
• To reject the new and varying doctrines of men, which en-
danger the tranquillity of government.
• To rest in the unchangeable faith of the Catholic Church.
• To learn from the Church's voice not only the objects of
faith but also the rules of conduct.
• Not only to obtain eternal salvation, but also to regulate this
life and to maintain concord in this earthly city.
• To learn from the apostles, and especially from St. Peter, the
Prince of the Apostles, on whom alone the Church is built.
• To be assured that neither the depravity of morals nor the
fluctuation of novel opinions will ever cause the episcopal suc-
cession to fail or the bark of Peter to be sunk.

Almost two hundred years later, Paul VI hardly wrote any differently
than Pius VI. Indeed, on the occasion of this country's Bicentennial,
Paul told the American bishops attending the canonization of St. John

Newman that their Church needed a "second spring." No one can be sure that in making this remark Paul read in advance the classic sermon with the same title, preached in July 1852 before the first synod of the restored English hierarchy. Certainly the condition of the English Church then and the American Church now were substantially different. Newman takes note of three hundred years of suppression ("the old Church in its day became a corpse"), the utter contempt into which Catholicism had fallen, whose churches were defamed or destroyed, left with a mere handful of faithful. Catholicism in the United States, regardless of its problems, is hardly any of these things. Yet Paul VI was aware that for all the situations recounted in this book there has been a fall from grace, and lest the decline become more serious a "second spring" for American Catholicism is in order. Perhaps in this sense certain words of Newman spoken in 1852, at the beginning of a new chapter of English Catholic history, do have relevance to Catholic Americans of 1979.

One thing alone I know—that according to our need, so will be our strength. One thing I am sure of, that the more the enemy rages against us, so much the more will the Saints in Heaven plead for us; the more fearful are our trials from the world, the more present to us will be our Mother Mary, and our good Patrons and Angel Guardians; the more malicious are the devices of men against us, the louder the cry of supplication will ascend from the bosom of the whole Church to God for us. We shall not be left orphans; we shall have within us the strength of the Paraclete, promised to the Church and every member of it. My Fathers, my Brothers in the Priesthood, I speak from my heart when I declare my conviction, there is no one among you here present but, if God so willed, would not readily become a martyr for His sake.

Amen.

Abbott, Walter M., S.J., and Joseph Gallagher, ed. *The Documents of Vatican II.* New York: America Press, 1966.

*American Journal of Sociology,* July 1974; March 1977; September 1977.

*American Sociologist, The,* August 1977.

Auricchio, John. *The Future of Theology.* New York: Alba House, 1970.

Baum, Gregory, ed. *Journeys.* New York: Paulist Press, 1975.

———. *Religion and Alienation.* New York: Paulist Press, 1975.

———, and Andrew Greeley, eds. *The Church As Institution.* New York: Herder and Herder, 1974.

Bellah, Robert. *The Broken Covenant.* New York: The Seabury Press, 1975.

Berger, Peter. *The Sacred Canopy.* Garden City, N.Y.: Doubleday & Co., 1967.

Bouyer, Louis. *The Decomposition of Catholicism.* Chicago: Franciscan Herald Press, 1969.

Brown, Raymond E. S.S. *Priest and Bishop.* New York: Paulist Press, 1970.

———, S.S. *Crises Facing the Church.* New York: Paulist Press, 1975.

Brown, Robert McAfee. *Observer in Rome.* Garden City, N.Y.: Doubleday & Co., 1964.

Buhlmann, Walbert. *The Coming of the Third Church.* Maryknoll: Orbis Books, 1977.

Butler, Cuthbert. *The Vatican Council 1869–1870.* London: The Fontana Library, 1962.

Chadwick, Owen. *The Secularization of the European Mind in the Nineteenth Century.* London: Cambridge University Press, 1975.

*Chicago Studies,* 1973–77.

Cogley, John. *Catholic America.* New York: The Dial Press, 1973.

*Communio,* Fall 1977.

Conger, Yves, O.P. *Blessed Is the Peace of My Church.* Denville, Dimension Books, 1973.

Connolly, Francis X. *A Newman Reader.* New York: Image Books, 1964.

*Contemporary Sociology.* November 1976; January 1973; May 1973; September 1973.

Cooke, Bernard. *Ministry to Word and Sacraments.* Philadelphia: Fortress Press, 1976.

Coriden, James A., ed. *The Case For Freedom.* Washington: Corpus Books, 1969.

*Council Daybook:* Sessions 1, 2, 3, 4. National Catholic Welfare Conference, 1965–66.

Cross, Robert D. *The Emergence of Liberal Catholicism in America.* Cambridge: Harvard University Press, 1967.

Curran, Charles, et. al. *Dissent in and for the Church.* New York: Sheed & Ward, 1969.

Davis, Charles. *Temptations of Religion.* New York: Harper & Row, 1973.

*Declaration on Certain Questions Concerning Sexual Ethics: Commentaries.* United States Catholic Conference, 1977.

Decter, Midge. *Liberal Parents, Radical Children.* New York: Coward, McCann, and Geoghegan, 1975.

DeLubac, Henri. *Teilhard Explained.* New York: Paulist Press, 1968.

Devine, George. *American Catholicism.* Englewood Cliffs: Prentice Hall Inc., 1975.

Duggan, G. H. *Hans Küng and Reunion.* Cork: The Mercier Press, 1964.

Dulles, Avery, S.J. *Models of the Church.* Garden City, N.Y.: Doubleday & Co., 1974.

———. *The Resilient Church.* Garden City, N.Y.: Doubleday & Co., 1977.

Ellis, John Tracy. *American Catholics and the Intellectual Life.* Chicago: The Heritage Foundation, 1956.

———. ed. *The Catholic Priest in the United States.* Collegeville: St. John's University Press, 1971.

———. *A Commitment to Truth.* Latrobe: Archabbey Press, 1966.

———. *Documents of American Catholic History.* Milwaukee: Bruce Publishing Co., 1950.

Eppstein, John. *Has the Catholic Church Gone Mad?.* New Rochelle: Arlington House, 1971.

Falconi, Carlo. *The Popes in the Twentieth Century.* Boston: Little, Brown & Co., 1967.

Fesquet, Henri. *Catholicism; Religion of Tomorrow?.* New York: Holt, Rinehart & Winston, 1964.

Flannery, Austin, O.P. *Vatican Council II: The Conciliar and Post-Conciliar Documents.* Northport, New York: Costello Publishing Co., 1975.

Freire, Paulo. *Pedagogy of the Oppressed.* New York: Herder & Herder, 1971.

*General Catechetical Directory.* London: Catholic Truth Society, 1973.

Gleason, Robert W. *The Restless Religious.* Dayton: Pflaum Press, 1968.

Greeley, Andrew. *The Great Mysteries.* New York: The Seabury Press, 1976.

———. *Priests in the United States.* Garden City, N.Y.: Doubleday & Co., 1972.

———, William C. McReady, Kathleen McCourt. *Catholic Schools in a Declining Church.* Kansas City: Sheed & Ward, 1976.

———, and Peter H. Rossi, *The Education of Catholic Americans.* Garden City, N.Y.: Doubleday & Co., 1968.

Hardon, John A. *Christianity in the Twentieth Century.* Garden City, N.Y.: Doubleday & Co., 1971.

Häring, Bernard. *Christian Renewal in a Changing World*. New York: Desclee Company, 1964.

Hebblethwaite, Peter. *The Runaway Church*. New York: The Seabury Press, 1975.

Heenan, John Cardinal. *Council and Clergy*. New York: Herder Book Center, 1966.

Hildebrand, Dietrich. *The Trojan Horse in the City of God*. Chicago: Franciscan Herald Press, 1967.

Hill, Brennan, and Mary Reed Newland, eds. *Theologians and Catechists in Dialogue: The Albany Forum*. Dubuque: Wm. C. Brown Co., 1977.

Hollis, Christopher. *The Achievements of Vatican II*. New York: Hawthorn Books, 1967.

Hook, Sidney. *Education and the Taming of Power*. LaSalle, Illinois: Open Court Publishing Co., 1973.

*Human Sexuality* (A Study Commissioned by the Catholic Theological Society of America). Catholic Theological Society of America, 1977.

Hunt, John F., et. al. *The Responsibility of Dissent*. New York: Sheed & Ward, 1969.

Jedin, Herbert. *Ecumenical Councils in the Catholic Church*. New York: Herder & Herder, 1960.

Kaiser, Robert Blair. *Pope, Council, and World*. New York: The Macmillan Co., 1963.

Kelley, Dean M., *Why Conservative Churches Are Growing*. New York: Harper & Row, 1972.

Kelly, George A., *Catholics and the Practice of the Faith*. Washington, D.C.: Catholic University of America Press, 1946.

———. *Catholics and the Practice of the Faith: 1967 and 1971*. New York: St. John's University Press, 1972.

———. *The Catholic Church and the American Poor*. New York: Alba House, 1975.

———. ed., *The Teaching Church in Our Time*. Boston: St. Paul Edition, 1978.

———. *Who Should Run the Catholic Church?* Huntington, Indiana: Our Sunday Visitor Press, 1976.

———. ed., *Why Should the Catholic University Survive?* New York: St. John's University Press, 1973.

Kennedy, Eugene C. *The People Are the Church*. Garden City, N.Y.: Doubleday & Co., 1969.

Kirk, Russell. *Academic Freedom*. Chicago: Henry Regnery Company, 1955.

Küng, Hans. *The Council in Action*. New York: Sheed & Ward, 1963.

———. *On Being a Christian*, tr. Edward Quinn from German *Christ Sein*. Garden City, N.Y.: Doubleday & Co., 1976.

———, and Walter Kasper, eds., *Polarization in the Church*. New York: Herder and Herder, 1973.

———. *Why Priests?* New York: Doubleday & Co., 1972.

Martin, Malachi. *Three Popes and the Cardinal.* New York: Farrar, Strauss & Giroux, 1972.

McBrien, Richard. *Who Is Catholic?.* Denville, New Jersey: Dimension Books, 1971.

McCluskey, Neil, S.J. *The Catholic University: A Modern Appraisal.* Notre Dame: University of Notre Dame Press, 1970.

McCord, Peter, ed. *A Pope for All Christians?.* New York: Paulist Press, 1976.

McHugh, John A., and Charles J. Callan (translators). *Catechism of the Council of Trent.* Westminster: Christian Classics, 1974.

McNamara, Patrick H., ed. *Religion American Style.* New York: Harper & Row, 1974.

Menninger, Karl. *Whatever Became of Sin?* New York: Hawthorn Books, 1973.

Merwick, Donna. *Boston Priests 1848–1910.* Cambridge, Massachusetts: Harvard University Press, 1973.

Meyer, Charles R. *Man of God: A Study of the Priesthood.* Garden City, N.Y.: Doubleday & Co., 1974.

Miguens, Manuel, O.F.M. *Church Ministries in New Testament Times.* Westminster, Maryland: Christian Classics, 1976.

———, O.F.M. *The Virgin Birth.* Westminster, Maryland: Christian Classics, 1975.

Molnar, Thomas Steven. *The Counter-revolution.* New York: Funk & Wagnalls, 1969.

Nash, George. *The Conservative Intellectual Movement in America Since 1945.* New York: Basic Books, 1976.

Newman, Jeremiah. *Change and the Catholic Church.* Baltimore, Helicon Press, 1965.

Newman, John Henry. *On Consulting the Faithful in Matters of Doctrine.* New York: Sheed & Ward, 1961.

O'Brien, David J. *The Renewal of American Catholicism.* New York: Oxford University Press, 1972.

O'Brien, John A. *Family Planning in an Exploding Population.* New York: Hawthorn Books, 1968.

O'Collins, Gerald, S.J. *The Case Against Dogma.* New York: Paulist Press, 1975.

O'Dea, Thomas F. *The Sociology of Religion.* Englewood Cliffs, New Jersey: Prentice Hall, Inc., 1966.

O'Hanlon, Daniel, S.J., *What's Happening to the Church?* Cincinnati: St. Anthony Messenger Press, 1974.

Ohlig, Karl-Heinz, *Why We Need the Pope.* St. Meinrad, Indiana: Abbey Press, 1975.

Paolucci, Henry, *St. Augustine.* Chicago: Henry Regnery Co., 1961.

Pareto, Vilfredo. *Sociological Writings,* tr. Derick Mirfin. New York: Frederick A. Praeger, Inc., 1966.

Pelotte, Donald E., S.S.S. *John Courtney Murray: Theologian in Conflict.* New York: Paulist Press, 1976.

*The Pope Speaks,* 1971–77.

*Problems of the Church Today.* United States Catholic Conference, 1976.

*Proceedings of the Catholic Theological Society of America* 1973–77 (Published by Manhattan College).

*The Public Interest.* Winter, 1978.

Rahner, Karl. *The Shape of the Church to Come.* New York: The Seabury Press, 1974.

Reardon, Bernard M. G. *Roman Catholic Modernism.* Stanford: Stanford University Press, 1970.

*Religion and the Intellectuals.* New York: Partisan Review, 1950.

Rieff, Phillip. *The Triumph of the Therapeutic.* New York: Harper Torchbooks, 1968.

Robinson, John A. T. *Can We Trust the New Testament.* Grand Rapids: Wm. B. Eerdmans Publishing, 1977.

Rock, John. *The Time Has Come.* New York: Alfred A. Knopf, 1963.

Rynne, Xavier. *Letters from Vatican City.* New York: Farrar, Strauss & Co. 1963.

———. *The Third Session.* New York: Farrar, Strauss & Giroux, 1965.

———. *The Fourth Session.* New York: Farrar, Strauss & Giroux, 1966.

Salm, Luke. *The Problem of Positive Theology: An Abstract.* Washington: Catholic University of America Press, 1955.

Schroeder, H. J., O.P. *Canons and Decrees of the Council of Trent.* St. Louis: B. Herder Books, 1941.

Sheed, Frank. *The Church and I.* Garden City, N.Y.: Doubleday & Co., 1974.

Spaeth, Joseph L., and Andrew Greeley. *Recent Alumni and Higher Education.* New York: McGraw Hill, 1970.

Suenens, Leon Joseph. *Love and Control.* Westminster: The Newman Press, 1961.

Tavard, George. *The Pilgrim Church.* New York: Herder & Herder, 1967.

*Teachings of Pope Paul VI 1975.* Vatican Edition.

Teilhard de Chardin. *How I Believe.* New York: Harper & Row, 1969.

*Theological Studies.* 1963–68, 1974–77.

*Theses on the Relationship Between the Ecclesiastical Magisterium and Theology.* International Theological Commission—United States Catholic Conference, 1977.

*This Beats Working for a Living: The Dark Secrets of a College Professor.* New Rochelle: Arlington House, 1973.

Thomas, John L., S.J. *The Catholic Viewpoint on Marriage and the Family.* New York: Hanover House, 1958.

*To Live in Christ Jesus.* United States Catholic Conference, 1976.

Tracy, David. *Blessed Rage for Order.* New York: The Seabury Press, 1975.

————, et. al., eds. *Toward Vatican III*. New York: The Seabury Press, 1978.

Trisco, Robert, ed. *Catholics in America: 1776–1976*. National Conference of Catholic Bishops, 1976.

Valsecchi, Ambrogio. *The Birth Control Debate 1958–1968*. Washington: Corpus Books, 1968.

Van Allen, Rodger. *The Commonweal and American Catholicism*. Philadelphia: Fortress Press, 1974.

Van De Pol, W. H. *The End of Conventional Christianity*. New York: Newman Press, 1968.

Von Hildebrand, Dietrich. *Trojan Horse in the City of God*. Chicago: Franciscan Herald Press, 1967.

Wakin, Edward, and Joseph F. Scheuer. *The De-Romanization of the American Catholic Church*. New York: The Macmillan Co., 1966.

Wallace, Irving. *The Word*. New York: Pocket Book, 1976.

Walsh, Sister Marie De Lourdes. *The Sisters of Charity of New York 1809–1959*. (Three Volumes) New York: Fordham University Press, 1960.

Weisheipl, James A. *Friar Thomas D'Aquino, His Life, Thought, and Work*. Garden City, N.Y.: Doubleday & Co., 1974.

Wills, Gary. *Bare Ruined Choirs*. Garden City, N.Y.: Doubleday & Co., 1972.

————. *Politics and Catholic Freedom*. Chicago: Henry Regnery Co., 1964.

# INDEX